Find a Way or Make One

FIND A WAY OR MAKE ONE

A Documentary History of Clark Atlanta University Whitney M. Young Jr. School of Social Work (1920–2020)

Alma J. Carten

OXFORD
UNIVERSITY PRESS

OXFORD
UNIVERSITY PRESS

Oxford University Press is a department of the University of Oxford. It furthers the University's objective of excellence in research, scholarship, and education by publishing worldwide. Oxford is a registered trade mark of Oxford University Press in the UK and certain other countries.

Published in the United States of America by Oxford University Press
198 Madison Avenue, New York, NY 10016, United States of America.

© Oxford University Press 2021

Library of Congress Cataloging-in-Publication Data
Names: Carten, Alma J., author.
Title: Find a way or make one : a documentary history of Clark Atlanta
University Whitney M. Young Jr. School of Social Work (1920–2020)
Description: New York, NY : Oxford University Press, [2021] |
Includes bibliographical references and index.
Identifiers: LCCN 2020015774 (print) | LCCN 2020015775 (ebook) |
ISBN 9780197518465 (hardback) | ISBN 9780197518489 (epub) |
ISBN 9780197518472
Subjects: LCSH: Whitney M. Young Jr. School of Social Work. |
Social work education—Georgia—Atlanta—History.
Classification: LCC HV11.7 .C37 2021 (print) | LCC HV11.7 (ebook) |
DDC 361.3071/1758—dc23
LC record available at https://lccn.loc.gov/2020015774
LC ebook record available at https://lccn.loc.gov/2020015775

9 8 7 6 5 4 3 2 1

Printed by Integrated Books International, United States of America

In honor of my maternal great-grandfather James Isaac Miller, who was one of the former enslaved men who were a part of an interracial group of men who founded in 1895 Fort Valley High and Industrial School, giving birth to what is now Fort Valley State University—one of Georgia's ten historically black colleges and universities.

In memory of my parents, Connie Lee and Clara Mae (nee Carson) Jackson; they were a part of the Great Migration of blacks that changed American Society.

CONTENTS

FOREWORD

As a new assistant professor at Adelphi University in Long Island, New York, I was hired by Carl Scott, Associate Executive Director at the Council on Social Work (CSWE), as a project associate to the Black Task Force (BTF). The establishment of the BTF was in response to the work of the CSWE Commission on Minority Groups and their concerns that were problems and concerns unique to black social work educators. During the 1971–1972 program year, the BTF was initiated by the CSWE with financial support from the National Institute of Mental Health (NIMH), the Health Services and Mental Health Administration (HSMHA), and the Department of Health, Education, and Welfare (HEW). The task force, chaired by Dean Genevieve T. Hill of the Atlanta University (now known as Clark Atlanta University Whitney M. Young Jr. [CAUWMYJ] School of Social Work), was charged with developing guidelines for the inclusion of black content in the social work curriculum. Fifteen social work educators from across the United States were selected as members, and two meetings were held at the schools of social work at two of the historically black colleges and universities (HBCUs): Atlanta University and Howard University. It should also be noted that six of the fifteen-member BTF were from these two HBCUs. The BTF provided its members with the opportunity to meet and discuss the programs under way in various schools, share ideas, and assess strategies for achieving the goal of integrating black content into the social work curriculum. Faculty from the HBCUs also provided the members with information on their core curriculums, which reflected their unique mission of meeting the needs of the black communities that were served by their faculty, students, and graduates. Prior to the Civil Rights era most of the black social workers were graduates of either Howard University or Atlanta University. Much has changed since that initial report by the BTF, but the HBCUS continue to educate generation after generation of black students to meet the needs of black communities.

The BTF recognized that their efforts were just a start and that much more needed to be accomplished to achieve the inclusion of black content in the social work curriculum.

Among the effort to address issues raised by the BTF was the development in 1974 of the CSWE Doctoral Minority Fellowship Programs for Ethnic Minority Students, which was designed to (1) equip ethnic minority individuals for leadership, teaching, consultations, training, policy development, and administration in mental health and/or substance abuse programs and (2) enhance the development and dissemination of knowledge requisite for relevant clinical and social services to ethnic, racial, social, and/or cultural minority individuals and communities.

Dr. Alma J. Carten, who is writing this history of the Atlanta University School of Social Work, is a recipient of this Fellowship award and has achieved the goals of the program in scholarship, teaching, consultation, training, and policy development. She has now undertaken the development of this history of the CAUWMYJ School of Social Work, her alma mater. I met Dr. Carten already knowing she had been a recipient of the minority fellowship award under the leadership of CSWE Associate Executive Director Carl Scott and a co-editor with the former Dean of Fordham University Graduate School of Social Service, James Dumpson, on the book *Removing Risk from Children: Shifting the Paradigm* (Beckham Publishing, 1997) and the author of *Reflections on the American Social Welfare State: the Collected Papers of James R. Dumpson* (NASW Press, 2015).

Dr. Carten undertook this task as a member of the Committee to plan the celebration of the 100th anniversary of the School of Social work and on the recommendation of Dean Emerita Dorcas Bowles. She hopes that her colleagues in academia will find the book a useful teaching tool to counter the waning interest of students in social welfare history and that it will help faculty overcome the discomfort of examining America's original sin in explaining the persistence of the racial divide in the United States. The story of the historical development of social work education for and by blacks told from a black perspective is central to an accurate understanding and comprehensive documentation of the history of the profession of social work and social work education in the United States. *Find a Way or Make One* is organized into three parts: Part I, "Beginnings," which presents a broad overview of the history and origins of Atlanta University; Part II, "Moving the Legacy into the 20th Century," which examines events occurring during that tumultuous century; and Part III, "At the Midpoint and Beyond," which reports the history of the School from the mid-centennial and the decade of the 1990s. The final chapter brings the reader full circle and acknowledges the achievements over this 100-year history.

Integration has provided many challenges to HBCUs as they have had to compete with the Predominately White Institutions (PWI) for students, faculty, and government funding. Despite having fewer resources for educational programming, and as the title indicates, they have found a way or made a way to reach this milestone and provide social work education at the undergraduate, graduate, and doctoral program levels.

This history of the CAUWMYJ School of Social Work adds to the knowledge base and history of the first school of social work developed for and by blacks and highlights the ongoing contributions of this school and its role in the history of social work education and the social work profession.

During my almost fifty-year involvement with CSWE and the initial work of the BTF, we struggled to find content on the black experience. Current and future generations of scholars can now use this text as they research and teach about the struggles and contributions of these unique institutions and the forefathers and -mothers who found a way or made a way to provide quality services to black individuals and communities right into the 21st century.

—E. Aracelis Francis, ACSW, PhD
Director Emerita, Minority Fellowship Programs
Director, Office of Social Work Education and Research (Retired)
Council on Social Work Education

PREFACE

History, despite its wrenching pain, cannot be unlived but, if faced with courage, need not be lived again.

—Maya Angelou

My interest in writing this book was sparked in part by the invitation from Dean Emerita Dorcas Bowles to join the committee convened to plan the School's 2020 centennial celebration. As an alumnus of the School, I was grateful for the dean's invitation and the opportunity to give back to the School that had been my pathway into a profession that has given so much to me. The assignment was also an opportunity for me to revisit my Southern roots and my family heritage that is connected to those schools that emerged in the United States to educate blacks soon after the end of the Civil War and Emancipation.

I was born in Fort Valley, Georgia, which at the time of my birth was considered the deep, segregated South. And I am the great-granddaughter of a former slave. My maternal great-grandfather, James Isaac Miller, was one of the freedmen who were part of an interracial group of men who founded Fort Valley High and Industrial School in 1895, which was the seed for Fort Valley State University. Today, Fort Valley State University is one of Georgia's ten historically black colleges and universities (HBCUs) and is accredited by the Council on Social Work Education (CSWE) to award the baccalaureate degree in social work.

My family was among the Great Migration of blacks leaving the South to take advantage of the rapid industrialization that was creating new employment opportunities in urban areas in the North and Midwest. This unprecedented migration occurring within the nation was also the catalyst for the emergence of organized social welfare for blacks in the United States. In Georgia, blacks were migrating from the rural regions to Atlanta to find employment in a city that was fast becoming a thriving industrial center, but they were barred from receiving help from the racially segregated white agencies despite the enormity of their need. It was this presence of unmet need and social injustice that brought together an interracial mix of progressive-minded scholars and social activists in the city of Atlanta to plan for the founding of the School of Social Work that is the subject of this book.

Thanks to their hard work, sacrifice, and my father's obtaining employment (secured by union benefits and wage protection) with Warner & Swasey, a now long-closed major manufacturing company in Cleveland, Ohio, where my family resettled—likely a combination of all of the above as well as luck—my parents raised children who lived productive lives. As a kind of metaphor for "paying it both forward and backward," it was in part the country's effort to redress the legacy of its original sin that made it possible for me, through fellowship awards funded by the National Institutes of Health (NIH), to earn master's and doctoral degrees in social work at virtually no personal financial cost, but with the promise in a payback agreement to devote an expected portion of my professional career to practice or research that improved the mental health outcomes of historically underserved populations. Bringing to light the contributions of the School and the scholars and social activists connected with its founding is a part of what has been my ongoing effort to fulfill that obligation.

The School of Social Work was founded in 1920 as an independent institution of higher learning for blacks in Atlanta, Georgia. This was at a time when blacks were denied all rights of citizenship, including the power of the vote, and when Atlanta was described as the most segregated city in the South. Blacks migrating from the rural regions of the state to the city of Atlanta were forced to live under deplorable conditions of urban decay in neighborhoods that were virtually without services because of the neglect of city officials and blatant racism. Children were most vulnerable to these conditions and, as a result, were of major concern to the founders of the School. It was concern for children that led to the founding, in 1908, of the Neighborhood Union, the brainchild of Lugenia Burns Hope, who was among the founders of the Atlanta School of Social Work.

A full century later, on the occasion of the School's centennial year, 33% of children in rural regions of Georgia and 21% of those in urban areas live in poverty. According to the findings of a study published by the Annie E. Casey Foundation, black children in the city of Atlanta are poorer than black children in any other American city. An analysis of US Census data conducted by Bloomberg News ranked Atlanta worst in income inequality in the United States. And, despite a well-established black middle class, a segment of the black community in the city continues to face considerable barriers to opportunity. Moreover, Dr. Maurice Hobson, Associate Professor of African American Studies and Historian at Georgia State University and author of *The Legend of the Black Mecca: Politics and Class in the Making of Modern Atlanta* (Hobson, 2017), argues that the gains secured by an elite class of blacks have been made to the detriment of ordinary black Atlantans, who are persistently disproportionately represented among Atlanta's poor. Today, Georgia is staunchly Red and Republican. It is a frontrunner among states accused of voter suppression and of purging voters from the rolls who are largely the young and people of color. And, at the national level, the divisiveness and racial polarization in the United States that began soon after the Great Society and peaked in the aftermath of the Obama administration has reached an all-time high.

These occurrences, combined with an incumbent US president who remains for the most part unchallenged in his attack on American institutions and his disregard of the rule of law as established under the US Constitution, have raised increasing concerns about the decline of American democracy.

This current state of affairs mirrors those of the past that justified the need for a school for "colored" social workers. Thus, there could be no better time to bring into public view the story of a school that was founded by men and women who saw an opportunity for service, as expressed in the lexicon of the period in the interest of "the betterment of the black community," and courageously stepped in to claim it. Following the tradition established by W. E. B. DuBois and the Atlanta University Studies, they set about the work believing that the objective findings from empirical research could improve both the conditions under which blacks were living as well as race relationships between blacks and whites by dispelling flawed, empirically untested assumptions of scientific racism. Their pioneering work successfully laid the foundation that allowed the School to survive and excel within the context of the pervasive inequalities and racial injustice of the segregated Deep South and that it continued to overcome in the face of the less visible forms of structural and institutional racism following desegregation.

Recounting the history of the School in its various reiterations as it unfolded over a full century of the country's history of grappling with its troublesome track record on matters of race affirms the truism of Dr. King's inspirational words that "the arc of the moral universe is long, but it bends towards justice." The willingness of the individuals associated with the early history of the School to persevere in the face of the predictable backlash following gains in securing Constitutional rights for blacks illustrates that democracy is a continuing work in progress. Lessons learned from the history of the School impress us with the knowledge that African Americans' pursuit of full citizenship and the promises of democracy has been, and likely will be, a continuing struggle and must never be taken for granted. Despite the importance of history in understanding our present conundrum on matters of race relations in the United States, a recent survey conducted by the Pew Research Center found that Millennials, who are the future of the country, have little knowledge of history—66% of those surveyed had no knowledge of the Holocaust. I hope this book will be a useful teaching tool for faculty across academic and professional disciplines in illustrating the irreplaceable role of history in explaining the persistence of the racial divide in the United States and the irrationality of the US policy-making process on matters of race; yet despite its confounding nature, the policy-making process remains the best path for creating an inclusive, just, and civil society.

COMMITMENT TO SERVICE IN THE INTEREST OF THE BLACK COMMUNITY

Much of the conundrums of social welfare as it has developed in the United States is directly or indirectly related to what has come to be America's original sin. America's history is one grounded in race. And no story is more central to American history than the story of African Americans' long and continuing struggle for equal rights and full citizenship. Furthermore, race is central to the socioeconomic political forces shaping social welfare policy in the United States that, in turn, inform the knowledge and value base for the teaching and practice of social work. The story of the historical development of social work education for and by blacks and the telling of that story from a black perspective therefore is central to an accurate understanding and comprehensive documentation of the histories of the profession of social work and social work education in the United States.

Social work programs in the HBCUs are distinguished by a historic commitment to preparing graduates who are dedicated to using their education in service to the black community and in the pursuit of social justice for blacks in a country that has yet to solve its perennial problems on matters of race. Moreover, influenced by the scholarship and intellectual activism of DuBois, both the University and the School of Social Work have deep roots in the tradition of using objective research as a tool for documenting and seeking solutions to the problems impacting the black community. This is reflected in the Schools founder's replicating DuBois's *The Philadelphia Negro* in conducting the study process undertaken to justify the need for the School and to generate information for shaping the content of the inaugural curriculum.

THE USE OF RESEARCH AS THE TOOL FOR CHANGE AND REFORM

Today, with the growing emphasis on outcome-based practice, social work practitioners and educators are being held to a higher level of accountability in demonstrating the effectiveness and relevancy of practice interventions. This is reflected in the Grand Challenges set forth by the American Academy of Social Work and Social Welfare (AASWSW) that uses the tag line "social progress powered by science." Owing to the influence of DuBois, who launched the Atlanta University Studies as a vehicle for conducting systematic research on the black community, the School's use of research as a tool for systemic reforms has been a priority since its founding.

Over his tenure as director of the School, from 1924 to 1954, Forester B. Washington established a research department that undertook studies in partnership with city agencies for the documentation of inequities and for planning social programs for the black community (Barrow, 2002, 2007a). Washington's commitment to research as a tool for advancing the rights of blacks had been initiated at the School by E. Franklin Frazier, who had preceded Washington as the director of the School. The emphasis on research initiated by Frazier is but one of the many underreported contributions brought to light by this book of the men and women whose scholarship and activism filled the gap in the race-conscious content that was absent from the curricula of predominately white schools of social work. Their work brought to light the flaws of the scientific racism that justified the unequal treatment of blacks and from which the nascent profession of social work as it emerged during the Progressive era was not immune.

Furthermore, the use of research findings to shed light on racial inequities and to promote systemic reforms is also reflected in the choice of study questions that were topics of the master's thesis research interests of students in the early years of the School's history. Florence Victoria Adams, for instance, who authored a history of the School from its founding to its fiftieth year, identified study topics of required MSW master's theses in the early decades of the School's history: *Police Brutality*, *Negro Families in Need*, and *The Negro Boy in Atlanta* (Adams, 1981, p. 29). These topics are not only striking in their similarity to areas of research inquiry for social work scholars today, but also illuminate the stubborn persistence of racial inequities that contribute to disparate economic and social outcomes that have remained virtually unchanged for a segment of the black population over the full history of the School.

CONTRIBUTIONS TO THE LITERATURE

There is considerable added valued accrued from the examination and dissemination of information about the history and contributions of social work education as it developed in institutions of higher learning for blacks. Yet few of the scholarly books on the history of professional training schools that emerged in the United States in the mid-19th century provide a full and accurate examination of the rich histories of social work programs in the HBCUs. Neither do these publications give a thorough accounting of their unique contributions to providing the race-conscious content that was absent from the curricula of predominately white schools of social work.

Equally absent from these publications is a full reporting of the substantial contributions of those African American scholars who successfully shepherded these institutions through periods in the nation's history that were fraught with considerable environmental and systemic barriers rooted in race-based discrimination. And although recent years have seen more articles in the professional journals authored by African American social scientists and social work scholars—a welcomed beginning to closing this significant gap in the social work historical literature—the contributions of black scholars to the early development of the profession and social work education continues to be an underreported area in the literature.

This book adds to the extant social work historical literature by reporting the experiences of the first school of social work established in an HBCU, one that unfolded over a full century of American history. It does this against the ever-changing backdrop of socioeconomic, political, and cultural context in which the School was developing. The one constant in this evolving socioeconomic and cultural landscape has been the lingering effects of race-based inequalities that are rooted in doctrines of white supremacy and that have persisted into the present. Paradoxically, as this narrative endeavors to illustrate, these inequities have persisted even during periods of progressive policy development. For example, the enactment of progressive legislation to redress the inequalities that were the by-product of failed policies of "separate but equal" can and did have a differential impact on HBCUs and produced both welcomed and unintended consequences. The introduction illuminates some of these historical barriers following Supreme Court rulings and the enactment of civil rights legislation in the 1960s that outlawed legal segregation but were replaced with structural and institutional barriers that resulted in both costs and benefits to the School.

LESSONS LEARNED FROM THE PAST

The historical/qualitative research approach that shaped the design of the study approach used in preparing this book's narrative is found by scholars to be useful for shedding light on those confounding contemporary issues of US social welfare policy that constrain effective practice—and that, more often than not, are traced back to the nation's poor law heritage, a residual approach to social welfare policy development, and the persistent reluctance to deal fairly with blacks. This research methodology can be especially useful in explaining the social, economic, and political influences that shaped American social welfare policy, clarifying patterns in its treatment of ethnic and racial minorities and illuminating residual effects of the past on contemporary policies and practices.

This book adds to the recent growth in the literature examining historical developments in social welfare from an Afrocentric perspective. Due to these past oversights in including scholarly works undertaken from an Afrocentric perspective, the historical literature has been largely informed by a Eurocentric worldview. This one-dimensional view, as argued by Schiele (1997), constrains the conceptual base needed for the advancement of a more inclusive social welfare philosophy and accounts for the persistence of social problems among certain groups of African Americans.

Recognizing that perspective is central to the interpretation and analysis of the meaning of that history, the literature review for the book was mindful of the significance of the Afrocentric prospective in explaining the historical development of the School. Emphasis was given to identifying and mining historical documents authored by black social work scholars whose scholarship is virtually invisible in the social work historical literature. The intent was to illuminate their thinking on those matters of race that influenced their conceptualization of curricula to support best-practice approaches with black communities. Examples of these are *My Story in Black and White: The Autobiography of Jesse O. Thomas* (1967), *The Legacy of Forrester B. Washington: Black Social Work Educator and Nation Builder* (Sanders, 1970), *The Reflections of Florence Victoria Adams* (Adams, 1981), and *Social Welfare in the Black Community 1860–1930* (Ross, 1978).

Similarly, bibliographic references include the publications of individuals who have held leadership positions in conceptualizing the School's academic course of study and who themselves have published on the topic of professional education in the black community but are of low visibility in the historical social work literature. Foremost among these are E. Franklin Frazier's (1928) *Professional Education for Negro Social Workers* and Forrester B. Washington's (1935) *The Need and Education of Negro Social Workers,* and Ross (1976b). *Black heritage in social welfare: A case study of Atlanta. Phylon (1960–), 37*(4), 297–307.

This narrative brings to the forefront the notable contributions of the School's 19th-century founders and the subsequent leadership of its 20th- and 21st-century directors, deans, and other men and women associated with the School who endeavored to impact the broader field of social welfare. Among these are DuBois, who from his university post was among the leaders of the Niagara movement that led to the founding of the NAACP; John Hope, educator, administrator, and academic activist and the first African American president of Morehouse College and later Atlanta University; Lugenia Burns

Hope, a community organizer whose credits include the founding of the Neighborhood Union that is replicated as today's community-based neighborhood approach to service delivery; and E. Franklin Frazier, a sociologist and second director of the school, who was the first black elected president of the American Sociological Society. Along with Inabel Burns Lindsay, the first dean of the Howard University School of Social Work, Frazier was instrumental in the founding of the social work program, in the 1930s, at Howard that became the second school of social work established in an HBCU.

The activities of Forrester B. Washington outside of his directorship of the School included membership on President Franklin D. Roosevelt's Black Cabinet and his position as Director of the Negro Division in the Federal Emergency Relief Administration (FERA) (Barrow, 2007a; 2007b). Interestingly, he offered prophetic words of caution that policies that encouraged the long-term dependency of blacks on relief were as equally harmful as the exploitation and discrimination they faced in everyday life. Washington participated in the 1930 White House Conference on Children that convened a subcommittee on Minority Children that brought to light the plight of black, Puerto Rican, and Mexican children and reported that, in most communities, their needs were either poorly understood or wholly ignored. Both Dr. Ira Reid, a prominent sociologist and scholar of the period who held a faculty appointment with Atlanta University, and Dr. Eugene Kinckle Jones, Executive Secretary of the National Urban League, played a prominent role in producing the findings of this subcommittee (Billingsley & Giovannoni, 1972).

SOURCES OF DATA COLLECTION

The narrative for the book drew on the wealth of archival holdings stored in various locations of relevance to the examination of the history of the School. The papers of Dean Whitney M. Young Jr. are housed at the Columbia University archives, and some of his public speeches made over his term as president are in the archives of the National Association of Social Workers (NASW). Columbia University library also has in its archives the historical records of the New York School of Philanthropy, the first training school for social workers that evolved to become the Columbia University School of Social Work in 1963 and is a rich source of primary data for historical research. Florence Victoria Adams, who played a key role in the Atlanta University School of Social Work, and George Edmond Hayes, founder of the National Urban League and the social work program at Fisk University, are both graduates of the New York School of Philanthropy.

Documents in the archives of the Rockefeller Foundation provide records of the funding support for the launching of the School and the subsequent development of educational programs. Documents in the archives of the National Urban League and the NAACP, retrieved from the Smithsonian National Archives, were also used. The papers of W. E. B. DuBois were retrieved from the Special Collections and University Archives, University of Massachusetts Amherst Libraries.

Although many documents from these various archives were used in the preparation of this book, the historical documents mined were obtained largely from the archival holdings of the Atlanta University Center Richard W. Woodruff Library Archive Research Center and those located in the on-site archives of the School of Social Work.

PRESERVING THE BLACK PAST

The Richard W. Woodruff Library was constructed in 1982 and is named for philanthropist and former CEO of the Coca-Cola Company. The Center holds the archives of member institutions of the Atlanta University Center Consortium that includes Clark Atlanta University, Spelman College, Morehouse College, and Morehouse School of Medicine. Included among its extensive holdings of materials on the African American experience are the John Henrik Clarke Africana and African American Collection, the Henry P. Slaughter and Countee Cullen Memorial Collection, and the Tupac Amaru Shakur Collection, and it is the custodian of the Morehouse College Martin Luther King Jr. Collection.

The Atlanta University Center Robert W. Woodruff Library holds a formidable and imposing presence on the Clark Atlanta University (CAU) campus. Its modern exterior façade is encircled by African American sculpture, and its entrance faces the Brawley Greenspace Pedestrian Parkway that looks out over an expansive landscape of greenery along the full walk of the Promenade. Once entering the building, a modern glass interior showcases the works of African American artists and historical events of the African American experience that silently co-exist with open classroom space and secluded corner booths for study and research. Taken together, this presentation stands as a testament to the great significance of preserving the history of the African American experience for future generations for all of the University Consortium schools.

In addition to documents specific to the history of the School housed in the Woodruff archives, when available, other documents were found on-site in the School and included CSWE self-study reports that contain course syllabi, faculty credentials, and statistical data (such as the demographic profiles of students and faculty) and other documents that were pertinent to the purpose of the book. Tragically, many of the archival holdings of the School were destroyed in fires set over a five-day period during the University's 1995 spring break. Some of these irreplaceable documents could be salvaged and some could not. To deal with missing data that were critical to understanding events occurring at the School over the study period, efforts were made to obtain information in oral interviews with faculty who were present at the time of the fires or who were familiar with the history of the School.

Information of a qualitative nature was obtained from focus groups conducted with alumni who attended the School between 1970 and 2000 and with current full-time and retired faculty. The structured focus group questions with alumni obtained information about the extent to which graduates were carrying forth the mission of the School in postgraduate professional experiences and their perception of the educational philosophy of the School during the years of their enrollment and included an open-ended question allowing them to share personal narratives about the existential benefits of attending a HBCU social work program. The purpose of the faculty focus groups was to fill the gap in information with the loss of historical documents in the fire that destroyed the Quarles Washington Building and to collect their views about the challenges and opportunities the School would encounter in the coming years.

The historical narrative describing the context in which the University and School evolved drew generously from the documentary history of Atlanta University authored by Dr. Clarence Bacote (1969) who joined of faculty of the university in 1930 and was the first professor appointed to the graduate faculty. Dr. Bacote quotes extensively from Myron W. Adams' *The History of Atlanta University*, published by the Atlanta University Press in 1930. The primary sources for the discussion of the historical context of policy development in each chapter are from *Black Heritage in Social Welfare: 1860–1930* (Ross, 1978), *From Poor Law to Social Welfare State: A History of Social Welfare in America and Social Welfare* (Trattner, 1999), *Social Welfare: A History of the American Response to Need* (Stern & Axinn, 2017), *In the Shadow of the Poorhouse: A Social History of Welfare in America* (Katz, 1996), *The Undeserving Poor: From the War on Poverty to the War on Welfare* (Katz, 1989), and Carten (2015) *Reflections on the American Social Welfare State: The Collected Papers of James R. Dumpson, PhD, 1930–1990*.

ORGANIZATION

Find a Way or Make One is organized into three parts. The chapters in each of the three parts examine critical events occurring concurrent with the School's history during various eras of the nation's history. Chapters highlight trends in the profession of social work, social work education as reflected in changes in the NASW Code of Ethics, accreditation policies of the CSWE, and the changing thrusts in American social welfare policy and their implementation in Georgia and in the city of Atlanta. The ongoing struggle for black civil rights in the segregated south is an integrating theme of each chapter. Mega events such as the Great Migration, two world wars, the depression years, the introduction of the safety net programs enacted under the 1935 Social Security Act and their dismantlement under the conservative policies of New Federalism of the 1980s, and the civil rights movement are among the back stories of the environmental context in which the history of the School unfolded.

The chapters in Part I, "Beginnings," present a broad overview that includes the indelible influence of W. E. B. DuBois, whose thinking continues to influence contemporary thought leaders in the academy, and explicates the conceptual underpinnings of the book. The overview of the study approach leads into the historical context of the founding of the University by the American Mission Association soon after the end of the Civil War. Chapters discuss black enslavement in Georgia during the colonial period and federal Indian Removal policies that enriched the economies of what became the state of Georgia and the city of Atlanta and laid the foundations for white supremacy that shaped the institutional and cultural landscape of the state and city well into the 20th century. Subsequent chapters highlight the work of the pioneering founders of the American Missionary Association that sustained the growth of the University despite conventional wisdom born from scientific racism about the intellectual inferiority of African Americans. Part I ends with a discussion of the confluence of trends that led to the School's launching in 1920 as an independent institution of higher learning for blacks in Atlanta under the visionary leadership of black and white scholars, social activists, and social reformers during a time when Atlanta was described as the most racially segregated city in the south.

Part II, "Moving the Legacy into the 20th Century," continues the chronology to examine events occurring in the early years following the launching of the School. E. Franklin Frazier and Forrester B. Washington both trained as Urban League Fellows at what was to become the Columbia University School of Social Work. Their combined leadership was instrumental in the institutionalization of the Afrocentric perspective that subsequent leadership of the School has endeavored to preserve with varying degrees of success. The tenure of Whitney M. Young Jr., the first to hold the title of dean and for whom the School was renamed in 2000, began what would become a career as an international civil rights leader over his term as dean of the School. Under his mentorship, social work students joined with other students in the Atlanta University Center to spearhead the use of sit-ins in Atlanta. Despite being discouraged by the conservative university administrators and the city's black elite, their commitment to the cause of black equality catapulted Atlanta into being the epicenter of the Civil Rights movement under the iconic and charismatic leadership of Morehouse College alumni Dr. Martin Luther King

Jr. and is one of the most transcendent events of the 20th century. Chapter discussions overview the influence of the Civil Rights movement on the emergence of the National Association of Black Social Workers and on the reshaping of the Code of Ethics of the NASW and the Educational Policy Accreditation Standards of the Council on Social Work Education.

Part III, "At the Midpoint and Beyond," reports the history of the School from the time of its mid-centennial through the decade of the 1990s. The mid-centennial year of the School, occurring at about the same time as the accidental drowning death of Whitney M. Young Jr. in Lagos, Nigeria, became a landmark transition in the School's history. Under the deanship of Genevieve Hill, the School recommitted itself to the legacy of Forrester B. Washington on the occasion of the School's 50th anniversary under the banner of "The Legacy of Forrester B. Washington, Black Social Work Educator and Nation Builder." The School moved forward led by a new professoriate comprised of a younger generation of black scholars who introduced and refined the autonomous social work practice model. The model remains the anchor of the School's educational philosophy. The last chapters address the decades of a rising conservative ideology in US social welfare policy under New Federalism policies of the Nixon and Regan administrations and subsequent abandonment of the safety net philosophy introduced by the 1935 Social Security Act, the cornerstone of American social welfare policy; the hope that America had moved into a post-racial society with the election of the first African American president. The last chapter brings the reader full circle, to the current environment in which the divisiveness of political discourse in the country resembles that seen when the seed for what would become the University and academic home of the School was planted following the devastation of the Civil War. The challenges posed by the unfolding of these events concurrently create opportunities for the School to reclaim the position established by its founders as the leading voice on social work practice in the black community.

REFERENCES

Adams, F. V. (1981). *The reflections of Florence Victoria Adams*. Atlanta, GA: Shannon Press, Ltd.

Bacote, C. A. (1969). *The story of Atlanta University: A century of service, 1865–1965*. Atlanta University, Atlanta, Georgia.

Barrow, F. H. (2002). The social welfare career and contributions of Forrester Blanchard Washington: A life course analysis. https://elibrary.ru/item.asp?id=5255497

Barrow, F. H. (2007a). More than a school: A promotional agency for social welfare: Forrester Blanchard Washington's leadership of the Atlanta University School of Social Work, 1927–1954. *Arete, 31*.

Barrow, F. H. (2007b). Forrester Blanchard Washington and his advocacy for African Americans in the new deal. *Social Work, 52*(3), 201–208.

Billingsley, A., & Giovannoni, J. M. (1972). *Children of the storm: Black children and American child welfare.* New York: Harcourt Brace.

Carten, A. J. (2015). *Reflections on the American Social Welfare State: The collected papers of James R. Dumpson, PhD, 1930–1990.* Washington, DC: NASW Press.

Frazier, E. F. (1928). Professional education for Negro social workers. *Hospital Social Service, 17,* 167–176.

Katz, M. B. (1989). *The undeserving poor: From the war on poverty to the war on welfare, Volume 60* (pp. 173–187). New York: Pantheon Books.

Katz, M. B. (1996). *In the shadow of the poorhouse: A social history of welfare in America.* New York: Basic Books.

Hobson, M. J. (2017). *The legend of the black Mecca: Politics and class in the making of modern Atlanta.* Chapel Hill: University of North Carolina Press.

Ross, E. (1976a). Black heritage in social welfare: A case study of Atlanta. *Phylon (1960), 37*(4), 297–307. doi:10.2307/274495

Ross, E. L. (1978). *Black heritage in social welfare, 1860–1930.* Scarecrow Press, Inc. Metuchen, N.J. and London.

Sanders, C. L., & Atlanta University. School of Social Work. (1970). *Crossing over: Proceedings of 50th Anniversary at Atlanta University School of Social Work.* November 12–14, 1970. Atlanta, Georgia: University.

Schiele, J. H. (1997). An Afrocentric perspective on social welfare philosophy and policy. *Journal of Sociology & Social Welfare, 24*(2), article 3. https://scholarworks Hospital.wmich.edu/jssw/vol24/iss2/3

Stern, M. J., & Axinn, J. (2017). *Social welfare: A history of the American response to need.* London: Pearson.

Thomas, J. O. (1967). *My story in black and white.* New York: Exposition Press.

Trattner, W. I. (1999). *From poor law to welfare state* (6th ed.). New York: The Free Press.

Washington, F. B. (1935). The need and education of Negro social workers. *Journal of Negro Education, 4,* 76–93.

ACKNOWLEDGMENTS

This book may be more accurately described as an abbreviated documentary history of Clark Atlanta University Whitney M. Young Jr. School of Social Work. I say that because University policy only allowed for full-time faculty to serve as PI for grants overseen by the University and for which it serves as grantee. Not being a member of the full-time faculty and not wishing to abandon what I believed would make an important contribution to the literature, the work of preparing the book was undertaken without grant support that would have made for a more comprehensive study process by bringing more individuals on board. As the sole author of the book, it is also important to acknowledge, with humility, that the views expressed may not be shared by others who are knowledgeable about the School's history. This being said, there are a number of individuals whose support and assistance contributed to the successful completion of the book.

The idea for the project came about in conversation with my long-time colleague Professor Emerita Naomi Ward who, until her retirement, was a member of the full-time faculty of the School over many periods of curriculum renewal. Dean Jenny Jones graciously stepped in to lend the support of the dean's office when personal concerns prevented Professor Ward from continuing to collaborate with me on the project. Dionna Dallas, former executive assistant to the office of the dean, provided administrative supports needed for data collection, which included setting up and recording focus groups, liaising with the archival library staff, and much more. Retired faculty and members of the current full-time faculty of the School and Atlanta-based alumni were most generous in setting aside time to share information either in group or individually at the time of my visits to the campus to conduct research for the project.

Colleagues external to the School offering assistance included Dr. E. Aracelis Francis. With the exception of Carl Scott, the program's founder, she is the longest serving director of the Council on Social Work Education (CSWE) Minority Fellowship Program, and, characteristic of her commitment to the cause of diversity and inclusion in social work education, she immediately agreed to write the Foreword for the book. She also shared historical documents of the federally funded CSWE Black Task Force, comprised of the social work faculties of Atlanta and Howard Universities who pioneered the conceptualization of the Afrocentric and black perspectives, and of the early years of the National Association of Black Social Workers (NABSW) as it was becoming the premier professional organization for black social workers. Dr. Jerome Schiele, chair of the doctoral social work program at Morgan State University, is perhaps the most prolific of contemporary scholars publishing on the Afrocentric perspective, and he was among my go-to faculty for consultation on the evolution of thinking in the academy on the Afrocentric perspective. I am very much indebted to my colleague Dr. Jeanne Bertrand Finch, former Assistant Dean and Graduate Program Director at Stony Brook University School of Social Welfare, for voluntarily taking on the tedious task of reviewing the first draft of all of the chapters and for preparing the appendix describing the historical context within which the School evolved.

The granddaughters of Jesse O. Thomas, Nell Gibson and Rosemary Braxton, shared information about their grandparents and their personal experiences in growing up in a home where, owing to the legacy of their grandfather, the pursuit of social justice had become what they referred to as "the family business." Dr. Marcia Cantrarella, the daughter of Whitney M. Young Jr., shared the poignancy of her experience of accompanying her father's remains home from Lagos, Nigeria, and her firsthand knowledge of her father's work.

New York University (NYU) colleague Allen McFarlane, who is Assistant Vice President for Outreach and Engagement and Adjunct Professor at Africana Studies, was also generous in sharing time and his own expertise as a historical scholar on the African American experience. He provided information from his files about James Weldon Johnson, Atlanta University's most acclaimed alumni and the first African American to teach at NYU. Alumni colleagues who provided assistance included Dr. Ruby Gourdine, Richard Morton, Velma Banks, and Johnny Parham. They were enrolled at the School during or immediately following the civil rights years, and they shared their retrospective insights on their experiences as students during an era with significant implications for social work education. As always, Oxford University Press Executive Editor Dana Bliss and his assistants Stefano Imbert and Andrew Dominello provided expert consultation and guidance in seeing the book through the publication process, in time to be in print for the School's October 2020 Centennial Celebration.

There were a number of individuals that I was encouraged to interview who were described as reservoirs of information about the School. The most often mentioned was Mrs. Claudette Rivers-King who, along with Madeline White, the now deceased sister of Walter White, were the two longest serving executive assistants to the office of the dean. Study limitations prevented arranging interviews with these individuals that indeed would have brought a greater richness to the narrative. The book, however, is only one effort and hopefully will stimulate others who will engage a broader circle of individuals as the history of the School continues to unfold beyond the centennial.

Finally, the book moved into the production stage before the breaking news of the Covid-19 health crisis, and, at the time of writing these acknowledgments, the United States had become the global epicenter of the disease. Accompanying this was an abundance of reporting on the internet that historically black colleges and universities, already underresourced, would be especially hard hit by the effects of Covid-19, including dire predictions that some would shut down. Unsurprisingly, the crisis illuminated the racial inequalities and disparities in the United States that have implications for schools of social work that play a major role in the education and training of professionals for the behavioral health workforce. If history is a reliable informant, as described in the book, the School of Social Work will hopefully carry on the tradition of overcoming what have always seemed to be insurmountable obstacles and continue to prepare graduates committed to a career in service to the black community.

—Alma J. Carten, PhD
March 30, 2020

CHAPTER 1

Introduction

There is in this world no such force as the force of a person determined to rise. The human soul cannot be permanently chained.
                                        —W. E. B. DuBois (1910)

The preceding quote is taken from an essay written by William Edward Burghardt DuBois when he was a young sociology professor at Atlanta University. The seed for the founding of Atlanta University was planted soon after the Civil War, in 1865, with the beginning of a school founded in a discarded box car for the children of a race of people that had endured centuries of enslavement. Through a transformational process and against what by any measure should have been insurmountable odds, this little classroom evolved to become Atlanta University. And, over the course of this process, the University became the academic home of what is today the Whitney M. Young Jr. School of Social Work.

DuBois left an indelible imprint on the School of Social Work and on the academic culture of the colleges and schools that comprise what is now the Atlanta University Center Consortium. Reaching beyond the University Center, his legacy of intellectual activism continues to influence the thinking of generations of scholars in the academy on matters of race, both nationally and internationally. The force to which DuBois referred captures what has been an enduring theme of the African American experience in the United States since the forced arrival in colonial America of their enslaved African ancestors—the nation's original sin, one that has cast a long shadow and a legacy that has extended into the 21st century.

DuBois's concept of "double consciousness . . . an American, a Negro; two souls, two thoughts, two unreconciled strivings; two warring ideals in one dark body, whose strength alone keeps it from being torn asunder" (DuBois,

Find a Way or Make One. Alma J. Carten, Oxford University Press (2021). © Oxford University Press.
DOI: 10.1093/oso/9780197518465.001.0001.

1903) has also been an enduring if paradoxical theme of being black in America. Throughout the history of the country, despite the systematic denial of their own constitutional rights, blacks as a population have remained faithful stewards of the concept of American democracy not only for themselves but for other marginalized populations.

Themes of achieving in the face of seemingly insurmountable odds while remaining loyal custodians of democratic principles are also woven throughout the history of the Clark Atlanta University Whitney M. Young Jr. School of Social Work. This theme is captured in the title of this book, *Find a Way or Make One*, which has been the motto of the University since its beginnings. The book chronicles the rich heritage of the school of social work that was developed by blacks for blacks in cooperation with the progressive white leadership of social agencies and philanthropic organizations of the period. The School is celebrating its centennial year in 2020, and it is distinguished for being the nation's first school of social work established in a historically black college or university (HBCU).

AUDIENCES AND RELEVANCE

The book will be of special interest to the academic social work professional and social work education communities, and it is a worthwhile addition to course readings for students across a number of disciplines. Because it brings together in one volume the 100-year history of a school that was the academic home of notable African American scholars and activists and draws on the expansive archival holdings of the Atlanta University Center Robert W. Woodruff Library Archive Research Center, this book is a useful resource for scholars conducting research on institutions of higher learning in the United States. It will also be informative to a general readership since most Americans know little about the history of social work and social work education in the United States and even less about the contributions of black intellectuals and scholars to this history.

This book is also published at a time when questions are being raised about whether the HBCUs have outlived their usefulness. In light of the ideological divisions and highly polarized political climate troubling the country at the time of this writing, for social work educators who are deeply committed to an agenda of inclusion and are members of a profession referred to as the "moral compass" of society, these institutions are as relevant today as they were during the period when many were established, as the country attempted to redefine itself as a democratic republic in the aftermath of the Civil War and the period of Reconstruction.

Specific to the profession of social work, the findings of the 2018 CSWE National Social Work Workforce Study of 2017 graduates (Salsberg, Quigley,

Acquaviva, Wyche, & Sliwa, 2018) indicated that respondents who identified as members of historically underrepresented groups from all ethnicities and races combined represented a scant 11% of the 2017 sample of new social workers participating in the study. The modified methodology of the 2019 Study conducted of 2018 graduates yielded a larger percentage of respondents representing historically underrepresented ethnic and racial groups (Salsberg, Quigley, Acquaviva, Wyche, & Sliwa, 2019a, 2019b). Taken together, the findings of both studies provide empirical evidence that the social work programs housed in these institutions have a critical role to play in ensuring the presence of a diverse health and human service workforce that matches the increasing ethnic and racial diversity of the American population.

An added value that the social work programs housed in these institutions bring to the predominately white social work education programs is well documented in the literature (Ross, 1976; Gary & Gary, 1994; Schiele & Francis, 1996; Bent-Goodley, 2001; Carlton-LaNey, 2001; House, Fowler, Thornton, & Francis, 2007; Bowles, Hopps, & Clayton, 2016; Hopps, Lowe & Clayton, 2019). Moreover, social work programs in predominately white universities have only recently committed to the integration of antiracism models into their curriculum. Being their raison d'être, and borrowing President Obama's use of metaphor, these approaches are a part of the DNA and histories of the social work programs in HBCUs.

Finally, and far from being the least of the added value of these institutions to higher education in the United States, are the existential benefits they offer to the young adults of color who are counted among Generation X and Millennials and representative of a future generation that is finding it necessary to redefine the meaning of success and their place in a society in which racial inequalities are far from being a thing of the past. These benefits are illuminated in student narratives in the HBCU documentary *Tell Them We Are Rising* (Smith & Lomas, 2019).

HOW FAR HAVE WE COME

Now spanning a full century of the country's history, the School approaches this landmark year at a time when the nation continues to confront challenges of achieving the aspirational goals of a more perfect union. At the time of the founding of the School in 1920, tenets of white supremacy governed all aspects of black–white relationships in the South and in the city of Atlanta. It was these conditions that made it necessary to establish a training school for "colored" social workers to prepare a cadre of professionals capable of serving the black community whose members were barred from seeking help from racially segregated white agencies.

This was not only the situation prevalent in the South. The social work schools in place in predominately white universities in the North in the early decades of the 20th century were silently complicit in their failure to challenge de facto or de jure practices that effectively barred blacks from enrollment in these schools. At the same time that the doors to social work education were all but closed to blacks, and despite the extensiveness of unmet social need in their communities, blacks could not look to the racially segregated white agencies for help. These were conditions that provided more than ample justification for the need for a training school for "Negro" social workers.

The book's narrative takes the reader over the School's 100-year history as it evolved from its beginnings as the Atlanta School of Social Work, a free-standing institution of higher learning in the city of Atlanta established to provide professional training for "Negro" social workers at a time when social agencies and institutions of higher learning in the South were racially segregated, to its 2020 centennial year, with a significantly expanded mission to "prepare social work professionals, practitioners, and leaders with the knowledge, skills and abilities to address culturally diverse human and social issues locally, nationally and globally" (Clark Atlanta University School of Social Work, Our Mission). Ironically, and disturbingly, the School is celebrating its centennial at a time when the country is experiencing a resurgence of various forms of intolerance rooted in what are enduring notions of white supremacy that created the need for a school of social work for "colored" social workers a full century ago.

KEEPING PACE IN A CHANGING ENVIRONMENT

The School has undergone a number of transformations over the years in managing the effects of environmental changes that have implications for its sustainability and relevancy in American society's dynamic and ever-changing sociocultural and political landscape. The changing environmental context has created both challenges and opportunities as the School has endeavored to maintain institutional viability, its unique identity as an institution of higher learning for blacks, and the vision of its founders. It celebrates the centennial as one of the professional schools of Clark Atlanta University (CAU), with its renewed institutional identity brought about through the 1988 consolidation of Atlanta University, which offers graduate education, and Clark, a liberal arts undergraduate college.

The 1988 union was effectuated by the Boards of Trustees of the two institutions following a study process examining the possible advantages of a closer working relationship between the two institutions. Subsequent to the study process, the boards of both institutions ratified the recommendation of the report submitted by the joint committee for their consolidation

(Cole, 2013; Clowney, 2018). With the consolidation both remain anchored in their African American heritage as their coming together as one institution combines Atlanta University's motto of "I will find a way or make one" with Clark College's motto of a "Culture of Service."

This book overviews the history of Atlanta University from its beginnings at the end of the Civil War as the parent institution of the School of Social Work. The history of Clark College is detailed in a volume authored by James P. Brawley, who served as dean of the college from 1926 to 1941 and President from 1941 to 1965 (Brawley, 1977). Dr. Thomas W. Cole, Jr., President Emeritus of Atlanta University and Clark Atlanta University, is the author of *Clark Atlanta University, Charting a bold new future* (Coles, 2013) that is a record of the process that led to the 1988 consolidation of the two institutions.

Influenced by the scholarship and intellectual activism of DuBois, both Atlanta University and the School of Social Work have deep roots in maintaining an Afrocentric perspective in their educational programs and the tradition of using objective research as a tool for documenting and seeking solutions to the problems affecting the black community. This is reflected in the School's founder's replication of DuBois's Philadelphia study in conducting the study process undertaken to justify the need for the School as well as to generate information for shaping the content of the inaugural curriculum. Today, the tradition of conducting research is carried forward in the objective of the School's doctoral program, a primary objective of which is to increase the number of African American and other historically underrepresented groups preparing for careers in teaching, research, social policy analysis, human service management, and organizational development. According to information published in the program's Student Handbook, since being introduced in 1983 as one of the School's degree-bearing programs, more than 100 graduates are in positions of leadership in academia, policy-making governmental agencies, and private-sector social work agencies. Based on information obtained from alumni participants in focus groups, a growing number of the School's doctoral graduates are engaged in entrepreneurial private practices providing services to underserved populations in the city of Atlanta under contractual agreements with city and state governmental agencies.

CONTINUING CHALLENGES IN THE ERA OF DESEGREGATION

The School was successful in maintaining institutional viability over the decades of racial segregation sanctioned in both law and custom until the enactment of civil rights legislation that struck down racial segregation in US public schools with the Supreme Court ruling in the 1954 *Brown v. Board* decision and the 1965 Civil Rights law outlawing the racial segregation in all public spaces. Although much welcomed and long overdue, desegregation had both intended and unintended consequences for the viability of the School and brought a new set of challenges.

Desegregation made it possible for schools to recruit from a larger pool of students, now including both blacks and whites. At the same time, desegregation decreased the pool of black students for recruitment because they now had the choice of seeking admission to well-resourced predominately white schools. Moreover, with desegregation, the predominately white universities also had access to this larger pool of potential students, combined with the added benefit of being able to offer generous scholarships made possible by the new availability of government funds to support integration. On the other hand, access to government funds was limited for the cohort of HBCU schools because of the more invisible forms of structural and institutional discrimination that persisted with the ending of legal segregation.

During this same period, the Council on Social Work Education (CSWE) instituted reforms to push for great inclusiveness in the curriculum of predominately white schools of social work. Hence, the cohort of HBCU schools of social work are no longer unique in their recognition that content on racial oppression is essential to the social work curriculum.

Since the 1960s, a decade that saw increasing demands for more inclusive approaches to the integration of diversity content into the social work curriculum, the CSWE Educational Policy and Accreditation Standards (EPAS) has made the strengthening and integration of diversity content in the social work curriculum a priority for all accredited schools of social work.

Furthermore, these much-welcomed progressive policy advancements that intended to create more inclusiveness in diversity content and to include a wider variety of attributes of human diversity raised new questions around the "equality of oppression paradigm." As argued by Schiele (2007), the constantly increasing number of attributes of human diversity and marginalized populations that the CSWE Commission on Accreditation (COA) requires, when included in an already overcrowded curriculum, can have the unintended consequence of diminishing content devoted to discrimination based on skin color, which remains the most prevalent form of discrimination in the United States.

Moreover, for the HBCUs, democratization of the social work curriculum has the potential to diminish their continuing refinement through research of much needed diversity content on matters of race, in which this cohort of schools have a far greater degree of proficiency—if for no other reason than this has been the central focus of their educational programs since they came into existence. The cultural and race-critical perspective is therefore deeply embedded in all aspects of their explicit and implicit educational programming as well as in institutional memory, and this should not be eroded.

It is well worth mentioning that the ability of these programs to provide race critical education is further strengthened by virtue of their being the beneficiaries over the decades of the expertise of a distinguished roster of scholars committed to doing "race work," in the tradition established by pioneering scholars, through relying on findings of objective research as a tool for advancing the cause of social justice for blacks and challenging flawed assumptions of white hegemony.

Dr. Jerome Schiele has an extensive publications portfolio on social work education and race-conscious curriculum development. His research focuses on social policy analysis, racial oppression, and cultural diversity, and he is the current professor and chair of the doctoral department of the School of Social Work at Morgan State University. As a former chair of the doctoral program at the School of Social Work that is the subject of this book, Dr. Schiele was a participant in the faculty focus group conducted for the purposes of this volume. He summarized the unanimously expressed view among other faculty focus group participants in explaining the added value and unique contributions of the social work programs in the HBCUs in the conceptualization and teaching of race critical content.

> The statement essentially was that HBCUs apply and integrate a race-centered approach to social work education that places the lives and experiences of African Americans at the center, rather than the periphery, of their analysis and curricula. In fact, I would say that predominately white universities (PWUs) are race-centered also, but their focus tends to be on European Americans. So, I guess we can say that race/ethnicity is always at the center of any school of social work's focus and curriculum. What makes HBCUs special, however, is that they are institutional responses to the racial marginalization by PWUs of the content and emphasis on African Americans. Indeed, addressing this marginalization was a major theme of Forrester B. Washington and other pioneers of Black social work.

THE ONGOING QUEST FOR A MORE PERFECT UNION

The history of the School of Social work is also a story of the evolving definitions of concepts of social, economic, and racial justice and the long-standing challenges the United States has faced on achieving a more perfect union on matters of race. It is recognized that these are aspirational goals not easily implemented in practice, nor are these concepts easily quantified and measured. They nevertheless are the moral pillars of the country and serve as anchoring principles for the core values of the profession of social work and social work education. Indeed, these were the core values that undergirded the vision of those individuals who were key players in the School's founding. The men and women who founded the School understood that innovative approaches were needed to prepare graduates to carry out their work with blacks who interacted within socially and economically unjust systems in which they would not receive fair and equitable treatment. This recognition of the injustices and inequities that are embedded in American institutions is the rationale for the infusion and integration of the Afrocentric perspective throughout all aspects of the School's curriculum and educational programs.

EXPLORING THE AFROCENTRIC AND
EUROCENTRIC PERSPECTIVES

The Afrocentric and Eurocentric perspectives both make claims to be an embodiment of the concept of social justice. Broadly stated, the terms "Afrocentric perspective" and "Eurocentric perspective" refer to worldviews and ideologies that are linked to African and European culture and values, respectively. As discussed by Schiele (1997), unlike the Eurocentric worldview of individualism, self-reliance, and personal responsibility as the core values underlying American social welfare policy development, an Afrocentric world-view emphasizes an African heritage of collectivism, mutuality, and interdependence as the conceptual foundation for the organizing principles shaping responses to unmet social need. These values in turn are the underpinnings of the implicit and explicit curriculum of the School. This approach illuminates the challenges faced by the School in its efforts to remain faithful to the vision of its founders in an educational and cultural environment that mirrored dominant cultural norms that embraced a Eurocentric worldview.

The tensions in these opposing worldviews is illustrated by events during the years of growing activism in the profession following the social movements of the 1950s and 1960s. This growing activism within the profession began questioning existing social arrangements anchored in the Eurocentric world-view that was the standard for informing social work curriculum and criteria for accreditation and reaffirmation. Some academics argued that social work programs in the HBCUs were disadvantaged by CSWE requirements to meet standards of accreditation rooted in European worldviews in the development of the knowledge, values, and skill base for the teaching and learning of social work for practice with blacks.

For example, Lloyd Yabura, an associate dean at a time when the Atlanta University School of Social Work was preparing for CSWE reaccreditation in the 1970s, argued that the CSWE accreditation standards pressured predominately black schools to conform to European standards and eliminate content related to the African American experience from the curriculum: "thus began the genocidal process of whitewashing of the curriculum of black schools that had been specifically designed to meet the unique needs of black people" (Sanders, 1970, p. 31). Claims such as these are examined in the following chapters, primarily in the mining of reports prepared during the process of reaccreditation—self-study reports, site team visits, and summary recommendations from the CSWE—when these documents were available. The analysis of these documents endeavored to shed light on the extent to which the School was able to remain true to its founding mission as stated by Forrester B. Washington, the School's third director, who played a central role in the design of the inaugural curriculum.

> In order to provide its students with an equipment to meet the specific problems that face them when doing social work in black communities, the Atlanta University School of Social Work has just introduced a group of courses in social work, which as far as known, are not offered elsewhere in the country. These courses are given in addition to the full amount of technical experience in black neighborhoods in Atlanta, and it is felt that the students are better equipped than graduates of white schools to handle the complex problems of social work in black communities. (Sanders, 1970, pp. 30–31)

INTEGRATIVE THEMES AND CONCEPTUAL UNDERPINNINGS OF THIS BOOK

Several themes are integrated throughout the narrative and form the conceptual underpinnings of this book. Central to this is the integration of an Afrocentric and black perspective with social work's ecological theoretical perspective—the "person in the social environment" approach. Together, these perspectives were the lens for the interpretation and analysis of information yielded from the review of archival and other documents relevant to the School's history.

As discussed by African American social work scholars Bent-Goodley and her colleagues, the Afrocentric perspective is rooted in the concept of Afrocentricity that existed long before the concept was introduced to the contemporary social work literature (Bent-Goodley, Fairfax, & Carlton-LaNey, 2017). In a special edition of the *Journal of Human Behavior in the Social Environment* that examined both the philosophical and conceptual underpinnings of African-centered social work as essential for responding to the current challenges facing communities in the Diaspora, these scholars described the Afrocentric perspective.

> As a viable theory for social workers to use in practice, Afrocentricity utilizes African philosophies, history, and culture as a starting place of interpreting social and psychological phenomena to create relevant approaches of personal, family, and community healing and societal change. Theory development and application is the foundation of clinical and policy practice. Theory development is a necessary scientific process for scholars to engage in, so that best practices

may be developed and applied for discernible and life-altering outcomes. In order to respond to concomitant factors that impact members of the extensive African Diasporic community (African Americans, continental Africans, Caribbean Americans, African Latinos, African Canadians), this theory warrants elevation in the social work literature and scientific inquiry. More importantly, in order for the profession to remain relevant to this large global community in America, African-centered theory should be placed alongside long-standing theories that are taught in social work education. (p. 1)

These underlying assumptions align the Afrocentric perspective with the intent of social work's ecological, person in the environment, strengths-based approach. This distinguishing feature of the profession acknowledges the interdependence of people with larger networks of social, economic, and political systems. In doing so, recognition is given to the barriers in larger institutional structures that serve as obstacles to the full societal participation of certain groups of historic concern to the profession, who are disadvantaged by the socially constructed stigmatizing devaluations of their personal identities. Concepts drawn from the ecological theoretical framework serve as long established guiding principles for curriculum development in all schools of social work, and these concepts have guided the approach taken by the School's founders as they engaged in a study process to establish the need for such a School and for the design of the curriculum. In this regard, the School's founders may well be viewed as pioneering the Afrocentric perspective, a concept that is now extensively used and widely accepted in the lexicon of the social work literature. The following chapters examine this as an evolving theme guiding academic programs throughout the 100-year history of the School and over periods of curriculum renewal.

The following chapters are guided by social work's systems approach and the Afrocentric perspective. Relative to social work's systems perspective, the evolution of the School is examined within the larger sociopolitical economic and cultural context in which it is both changing and being changed by the larger systems and social forces that constantly influence the cultural landscape of American society. In regards to the Afrocentric perspective, the narrative assumes a tone that communicates the view that characteristic attributes that embrace the importance of interpersonal relationships and collectivism associated with the black community are virtues and highly valued. It advances a positive worldview of the African American experience as being different from, but not less than. This perspective validates the adaptive coping abilities that have developed in response to barriers imposed by the discrimination against and exclusion of blacks in the larger society and sees them as indicators of strengths and resilience—not as deficits and liabilities. This perspective is echoed in the mottoes "Lift every voice," "Lifting as we climb," "I will find a way or make one," and "Culture of service"—all easily recognized as maxims of a shared branding of the HBCUs as they emerged that continue to be expressed in the mission statement of the School of Social Work. Taken together, these phrases have come to symbolize the aspirational, collectivist, and self-help strivings of the black community that are enduring themes of the African American experience, and they stand as the hallmark of the educational philosophy of the School of Social Work.

REFERENCES

Bent-Goodley, T. (2001). Ida B. Wells-Barnett: An uncompromising style. In I. Carlton-LaNey (Ed.), *African American leadership: An empowerment tradition in social welfare* (pp. 87–98). Washington, DC: NASW Press.

Bent-Goodley, T., Fairfax, C. N., & Carlton-LaNey, I. (2017). The significance of African-centered social work for social work practice. *Journal of Human Behavior in the Social Environment*, 27(1-2), 1–6. doi:10.1080/10911359.2016.1273682

Brawley, J. P. (1977). *The Clark College legacy: An interpretive history of relevant education 1869–1975*. Atlanta: Clark College.

Bowles, D., Hopps, J. G., & Clayton, O. (2016). The influence of historically black colleges on the social work profession. *Journal of Social Work Education*, 52(1/Spring 2014), 118–132.

Carlton-LaNey, I. (1999). African American pioneers' response to need. *Journal of Social Work*, 44(4), 311–321.

Carlton-LaNey, I. B. (2001). *African American Leadership*. Washington, DC: NASW Press.

Carlton-LaNey, I. B. (Ed.). (2001). *African American leadership: An empowerment tradition in social welfare history* (pp. 99–110). Washington, DC: NASW Press.

Clark Atlanta University Whitney M. Young, Jr. School of Social Work. Our Mission. http://www.cau.edu/school-of-social-work/index.html

Clowney, E. D. (2018, July 10). Clark Atlanta University. *New Georgia Encyclopedia*. http://crdl.usg.edu/collections/ngen/

Cole, R. T. (2013). *Clark Atlanta University: Charting a bold new future*. Author House LLC, Bloomington, IN.

Council on Social Work Education (CSWE). (2008). 2008 Statistics on Social Work Education in the United States. https://www.cswe.org/Research-Statistics/Research-Briefs-and-Publications/2008-Statistics-on-Social-Work-Education-in-the-Un

Council on Social Work Education (CSWE). (2019). *2018 annual survey of social work programs*. Alexandria, VA: Author.

DuBois, W. E. B. (1903). *The souls of Black folk*. Chicago: A. C. McClurg.

DuBois, W. E. B. (1910). The economic aspects of race prejudice. *The Editorial Review*, 2, 488–493.

Gary, R. B, & Gary, L. E. (1994). The history of social work education for black people 1900–1930. *The Journal of Sociology & Social Welfare*, 21(1), article 7.

George Washington University Health Workforce Institute. (2018). Survey of 2017 Social Work Graduates.

Hopps, J. G., Lowe, T. B., & Clayton, O. (2019). "I'll Find a Way or Make One": Atlanta University and the Emergence of Professional Social Work Education in the Deep South. *Journal of Social Work Education*. doi:10.1080/10437797.2019.1671255

House, L. E., Fowler, D. N., Thornton, P. L., & Francis, E. A. (2007). A survey of African American deans and directors of US schools of social work. *Journal of Social Work Education, 43*(1), 67–82.

Ross, E. (1976). Black heritage in social welfare: A case study of Atlanta. *Phylon (1960), 37*(4), 297–307. doi:10.2307/274495

Salsberg, E., Quigley, L., Acquaviva, K., Wyche, K., & Sliwa, S. (2018). Results of the nationwide survey of 2017 social work graduates: The national social work workforce study. https://cswe.org/Centers-Initiatives/Initiatives/National-Workforce-Initiative/Survey-of-2017-SW-Grads-Report-FINAL.aspx#:~:text=Based%20 on%20the%20Survey%20of,license%20(see%20Figure%201).

Sanders, C. L. (1970). Atlanta University School of Social Work. (November, 12, 14, 1970). Proceedings of the 50th Anniversary. The Legacy of Forrester B. Washington, Black Social Work Educator and Nation Builder.

Schiele, J., & Francis, E. A. (1996). The status of former CSWE ethnic minority doctoral fellows in social work academia. *Journal of Social Work Education, 32*, 31–44.

Schiele, J. H. (1997). An Afrocentric perspective on social welfare philosophy and policy. *Journal of Sociology & Social Welfare, 24*(2), article 3. https://scholarworks Hospital.wmich.edu/jssw/vol24/iss2/3

Schiele, J. H. (2007). Implications of the equality-of-oppressions paradigm for curriculum content on people of color. *Journal of Social Work Education, 43*(1), 83–100.

Smith, N. L., & Lomas, Z. M. (2019). Tell them we are rising. *Journal of Student Affairs Research and Practice, 56*(3), 361–363. doi:10.1080/19496591.2018.1524769

PART I

Beginnings

CHAPTER 2
The Historical Context

The greatest success of the Freedmen's Bureau lay in the planting of the free school among Negroes, and the idea of free elementary education among all classes in the South.
—W. E. B. DuBois, 1903

The Historically Black Colleges and Universities (HBCUs) are defined by Congress as institutions of higher learning within the United States and established before 1964, with a primary purpose to serve African Americans in response to practices of legal segregation by the largest share of predominately white colleges and universities that barred the enrollment of blacks (US Department of Education, 2018). Some of these Schools were established well before the end of the Civil War by churches, missionary groups, free blacks, and philanthropists. Others were established at the end of the Civil War with the support of the Freedmen's Bureau, formally named the US Bureau of Refugees, Freedmen, and Abandoned Lands.

The Freedmen's Bureau was established by Congress in the US War Department in 1865 to help former enslaved blacks and poor whites in the South in the aftermath of the devastation created by the Civil War. Operating as the first federally funded and administered relief agency during Reconstruction, the Bureau offered a comprehensive mix of services to assist displaced whites—who for all intents and purposes were domestic refugees— regain stability and to help the more than 4 million former enslaved blacks make the transition from enslavement to freedom. In addition to providing aid in the form of "indoor" and "outdoor relief" of food, housing, clothing, medical and legal services, and land reallocation to both blacks and whites, by the time the Bureau had closed its doors in 1872, during Reconstruction, it had also participated in the launching of some 3,000 free schools for blacks and whites (Bacote, 1969). The prohibition against the education of

Find a Way or Make One. Alma J. Carten, Oxford University Press (2021). © Oxford University Press.
DOI: 10.1093/oso/9780197518465.001.0001.

an enslaved people was intended to ensure that blacks lived in perpetual ignorance. Despite this restrictive legislation and owing to the humanitarian efforts of some whites and free blacks prior to emancipation, as observed by historian Carter Woodson "as a result of these efforts, it is estimated that approximately five thousand of the 462,000 slaves in Georgia could read and write in 1860" (Bacote,1969, p. vii). These findings are an illumination of the enduring spirit and resilience that has shaped what is a historic characteristic of the black experience in the United States.

The free schools established by the Freedmen's Bureau and missionary groups were the first institutions of higher education in the South that provided formal education for blacks. These institutions later became known collectively as the HBCUs. Some of the schools benefitted from the 1862 Morrill Act enacted by Congress to grant land to states to establish colleges specializing in agriculture and the mechanical arts, schools known as *A&M colleges*. Today the HBCUs are an integral part of the network of institutions of higher learning in the United States. All of the schools currently receive the support of the federal government to ensure their continuing viability under provisions of the White House Initiative on Historically Black Colleges and Universities.

THE WHITE HOUSE INITIATIVE ON HBCUS

The first presidential action providing federal support to HBCUs was under the administration of Jimmy Carter. A Democrat with moderate views on matters of race, Carter was the 39th President of the United States. He also served one term as the Governor of Georgia, from 1971 to 1975, which makes him the only Georgian to be elected to the US presidency. An outspoken opponent of segregation when governor and as president, in his inaugural address when sworn in as governor of Georgia, Carter asserted that "No poor, rural, weak, or black person should ever have to bear the additional burden of being deprived of the opportunity of an education, a job, or simple justice" (Bourne, 1997).

President Carter gave meaning to these words when he assumed the office of the US presidency with the signing of Executive Order 12232, in 1980, establishing a federal program to support the HBCUs. At the time of Carter's signing, legal segregation and racial discrimination against blacks had been prohibited by previous civil rights legislation. The program of federal support was intended to address the lingering and less visible forms of institutional and structural racism and better ensure that these institutions had equity and parity with predominately white institutions of higher learning in access to federal funds. Federal support to the HBCUs was expanded under the Reagan administration with Reagan's signing of Executive Order 12320. The Reagan

1981 Executive Order established the White House Initiative on Historically Black Colleges and Universities (US Department of Education, 2018). Since this time the Initiative has been renewed by every presidential administration, symbolizing the nation's commitment to the right of every American to higher education.

When signing the Executive Order in 2010, President Barack Obama, a strong supporter of the HBCUs, acknowledged their rich heritage while reminding his audience that they had come about amid competing views about what would be their educational mission. One view favored an emphasis on industrial education offering training for the skilled trades and vocations. This was the view advanced by Booker T. Washington, who was among the first generation of blacks emancipated from enslavement and first principal of Tuskegee Normal and Industrial Institute, now Tuskegee University and a US Historical Landmark. The opposing view saw the schools offering education in the classics and sciences to prepare the next generation of leaders of a "talented tenth." This was the vision of W. E. B. DuBois, who was the first black to earn a PhD at Harvard. Speaking to the duality of the mission of these institutions today, President Obama observed,

> Today, at America's 105 Historically Black Colleges and Universities, our young men and women prepare to do both. They're the campuses where a people were educated, where a middle class was built, where a dream took hold. They're places where generations of African Americans have gained a sense of their heritage, their history, and their place in the American story. (Obama, February 6, 2010)

The HBCU White House Initiative is currently under the oversight of an Advisory Committee chaired by a presidential appointee who has an affiliation with the HBCUs. The initiative is staffed by an executive director and associates who are responsible for the day-to-day operation and implementation of the various activities of the Initiative. Included among the activities of the program are the publication of an annual report that provides statistical measures of the achievement of the established goals of the Initiative and other reports. A variety of other activities undertaken by the staff include the convening of an annual conference in Washington, DC, that brings together various stakeholders from across the country to share information about programs that, if replicated, could result in the improvement of the established goals of the Initiative relative to instruction, degree completion, and the impact of federal policies on influencing higher education. The Initiative also offers internships to undergraduate and graduate students that provide rich learning experiences and opportunities carried out under the guidance of staff on a range of policy issues of relevance to the goals and priorities of the Initiative (US Department of Education, 2018).

The National Center for Education Statistics (NCES) is the primary federal entity for collecting and analyzing data related to education in the United States. These data indicate that the HBCUs present considerable within-group diversity. Most HBCUs are four-year institutions and are located in the Southern United States. They represent a diverse set of institutions geographically, with locations in nine states, the District of Columbia, and the Virgin Islands. They are both public and private, single-sex and coeducational, predominantly black and predominantly white, two-year and four-year colleges, research universities, professional schools, community colleges, and small liberal arts colleges (Provasnik & Shafer, 2004). A number of these colleges and universities offer social work programs accredited by the Council on Social Work Education (CSWE).

HBCUS OFFERING CSWE ACCREDITED SOCIAL WORK PROGRAMS

Replacing earlier standard-setting entities that had been established with the growth of training schools for social work, the CSWE was founded in 1952, and today is the national accrediting body for baccalaureate and graduate social work programs. The membership of the organization includes more than 800 accredited baccalaureate and master's degree social work programs, as well as individual social work educators, practitioners, and social agencies. In addition to providing a forum for social work educators to disseminate information about the state of the art of knowledge in the field, the Council also serves a gatekeeping role in its responsibility for establishing standards and monitoring the performance of schools of social work in adhering to the Educational Performance and Accreditation Standards (EPAS) established by the Council's Commission on Accreditation (COA). The Commission is recognized by the Council for Higher Education Accreditation (CHEA), which oversees the quality of all higher education institutions and programs in the United States, as the sole accrediting organization for social work education in the United States (www.CSWE.org).

Each year, the CSWE compiles and reports statistical data on social work education on a number of variables. These data describe the profile of students pursuing social work degrees and the characteristics of social work degree-bearing programs. According to the CSWE 2018 Statistics on Social Work Education, there are currently 529 accredited programs conferring the bachelor of social work (BSW) degree, which is considered the entry level for professional practice, and 271 CSWE-accredited programs conferring the master of social work (MSW) degree, which is considered the terminal degree in social work. US Department of Education-recognized HBCUs (or minority serving institutions [MSI]) enroll 24.5% of all students, whereas 26.2% of all degrees are conferred at MSI (CSWE, 2018).

Enrollment in HBCU Social Work Programs

Of the total number of BSW graduates (N = 20,133), 9.5% were enrolled in an HBCU, and these institutions awarded 6.1% of the BSW degrees conferred. Of the total number of students enrolled in an MSW program (N = 67,084), 2.9% were enrolled in the HBCUs, and these institutions conferred 3.4% of the MSW degrees awarded. At the doctoral level, of the total number of students enrolled in PhD programs (N = 1,198), 9.5% were enrolled in an HBCU, and these institutions conferred 5.3% of the total number (N = 303) of degrees conferred at the doctoral level (CSWE, 2018).

LOCATIONS AND DEGREES CONFERRED BY CSWE-ACCREDITED PROGRAMS IN THE SOUTH

Social work programs in the South are well represented in the states of North Carolina, the home of nine HBCUs; Alabama, with seven schools; and Georgia, with five schools. Georgia schools conferring the social work degree accredited by the CSWE are Albany State University, located in Albany and awarding the BSW and MSW degree; Fort Valley State University, located in Fort Valley and offering an accredited BSW program; Savannah State University, located in Savannah and awarding the BSW and MSW degrees; and Clark Atlanta University, located in Atlanta, conferring both the BSW and MSW degrees; it is the only social work program in the HBCUs in the state of Georgia conferring the doctoral degree in social work.

CSWE COMMISSION ON ACCREDITATION

The CSWE's COA is responsible for overseeing the accreditation process of BSW and MSW programs. The process includes multiple steps of self-study, site-visits, and COA review and reporting of findings to the dean and faculty of the school and to the university president and provost. The Commission is invested with the authority to make decisions to fully accredit, impose conditional accreditation, deny, or withdraw accreditation of master's and baccalaureate social work programs. The Commission is also responsible for both formulating accreditation standards and policies and determining the criteria and process for evaluating these standards (www.CSWE.org).

Currently there is no recognized professional organization invested with the authority to rank CSWE-accredited social work programs on the quality of their academic programs. Nor does CSWE publish or lists rankings of social work programs. However, *US News and World Report* began publishing a ranking of the Best Colleges in 1983. In the past decades, this list has been expanded to rank several professional disciplines. CSWE-accredited graduate schools of social work are included in the *Report*'s rankings of graduate health programs.

The 2019 list included a ranking of HBCUs in which these colleges and universities were compared only to one another. To be on the list, the school had to be currently designated by the US Department of Education as an HBCU. To qualify for the *US News* rankings, a HBCU also must be an undergraduate baccalaureate-granting institution that enrolls primarily first-year, first-time students, and it must be a school that is part of the 2020 Best Colleges rankings.

The 2019 ranking of graduate schools of social work was based on a review of 262 MSW programs accredited by the CSWE's COA. The rankings were prepared from a peer review process, and analysis of the information was obtained from a survey sent by *US News and World Report* to the National Association of Deans and Directors of Schools of Social Work. The *US News and World Report* ranking system has not been without a degree of criticism and controversy within the social work academic community. Much of that controversy has abated since the journal first began publishing these rankings. Social work programs use their discretion in publicizing their place in the *US News and Work Report* rankings of Best Social Work programs.

THE CARNEGIE CLASSIFICATION SYSTEM

The Carnegie Classification of Institutions of Higher Education was created in 1970 by the Carnegie Foundation for the advancement of teaching. The system includes all accredited, degree-granting colleges and universities in the United States that are represented in the National Center for Education Statistics System. Institutions are grouped by type, and the basic classifications include doctorate-granting universities, master's colleges and universities, baccalaureate colleges, and associate colleges. The level of classification is based on the number of degrees conferred at the masters, baccalaureate, or doctorate level. Doctorate-granting universities, depending on their level of research activity relative to expenditures, doctoral degrees awarded, and number of research-focused faculty, are classified as R1 doctoral universities (with very high research activity) or R2 doctoral research universities (with high research activity).

HBCU OVERVIEW

The largest share of the HBCUs were established in former slave-holding states in the Deep South, where there were the largest populations of emancipated enslaved blacks at the end of the Civil War. Georgia is currently home to ten HBCUs: Albany State University, Clark Atlanta University, Fort Valley State University, Interdenominational Theological Center, Morehouse College, Morehouse School of Medicine, Morris Brown College, Paine College, Savannah State University, and Spelman College. Six of these, Clark Atlanta University, Interdenominational Theological Center, Morehouse College, Morehouse School of Medicine, Morris Brown College, and Spelman College are located in the city of Atlanta. These six schools are among the country's oldest HBCUs. Recent media reporting indicate that Morris Brown College is endeavoring to re-established its accreditation status loss nearly a decade ago because of financial difficulties (Stirgus, 2019).

Some of the HBCUs have histories dating back to before the abolition of enslavement at the end of the Civil War (Hornsby, 1991; Lovett, 2011). Three colleges for blacks were established before 1862: Cheyney University of Pennsylvania was established in the 1830s; Lincoln University in Pennsylvania and Wilberforce College in Ohio were established in the 1850s. Although these schools and colleges are dispersed throughout the United States, Georgia, along with other Southern states with histories of enslavement and subsequent policies of school segregation, have the highest concentration of these institutions of higher learning.

AMERICA'S ORIGINAL SIN

To understand the reasons for the continuing need for the School of Social Work and the underlying rationale for its curriculum design and thrust of its educational programs from the time of its founding to the current day requires looking back into the historical context in which the School evolved. To do this requires a consideration of the implications of black enslavement and the displacement of Native Americans, both of which were central in shaping the economic and political histories of Georgia and the city of Atlanta. Together, these events are considered to be America's "original sin" because of their significant departure from the democratic principles on which the nation was founded. Moreover, these transgressions of bedrock principles have created a "conspiracy of silence" and a revisionist tradition in recording this period of American history. Consequently, only recently has the country been able to engage in a nascent conversation about the inherent contradictions of a nation founded on democratic principles having its beginning in the forcible kidnapping and enslavement of Africans and the dislocation of Native Americans in the interests of economic gain.

UPENDING THE CONSPIRACY OF SILENCE

The rise in neo-Nazi white supremacy groups, as reported by the Southern Poverty Law Center (King, 2019) and the murder of nine parishioners of the Emmanuel Episcopal African American Church by a self-professed white supremacist are among the events of growing extremism occurring in the United States today. The rise in such events and hate groups is contributing to a growing willingness among Americans to engage in conversations about white supremacy and the reasons for its rise and strong staying power in the United States. Moreover, having had an African American first family in the White House has made it more challenging to ignore the significance of race in American history and the enslavement of blacks as central to that history.

Neither former President Barack Obama or First Lady Michelle Obama have shied away from the topic of black enslavement. As first family, they infused their personal sense of racial pride in the culture of the White House. Both have referred to the nation's history of enslavement in their public addresses; for example, then-Senator Obama chose Springfield, Illinois, as the site for announcing his historic candidacy for the American presidency, referring to the challenges President Lincoln faced in uniting a divided country. "Lincoln had his doubts. He had his defeats. He had his setbacks. But through his will and his words, he moved a nation and helped free a people. It is because of the millions who rallied to his cause that we are no longer divided, North and South, slave and free" (Morgan, 2007).

Mrs. Obama, who is a descendent of slaves and has extended family members who were among the blacks comprising the Great Migration, poignantly reflected on the paradoxical nature of the black experience in her own personal narrative. In her address given at the 2016 Democratic National Convention, the former First Lady said,

> That is the story of this country, the story that has this stage tonight, the story of generations of people who felt the lash of bondage, the shame of servitude, the sting of segregation, but who kept on striving and hoping and doing what needed to be done so that today I wake up every morning in a house that was built by slaves. And I watch my daughters, two beautiful, intelligent, black young women playing with their dogs on the White House lawn. (Bouie, 2016)

The raising of Americans' consciousness about black enslavement, brought about by the resurfacing of violence accompanying a rise in white supremacy hate groups and the new awareness brought to the White House by the Obama family, is a welcome development. The enslavement of blacks, however, throughout the history of the nation has been a topic cloaked in silence and stigma, or one about which a false narrative has been created—a myth of enslavement being a benevolent system that was in the best interest of blacks. Furthermore, for African Americans who trace their ancestry back to enslavement, authentic discussion can engender a range of feelings that may include shame, anger, and embarrassment. For whites whose ancestry makes them complicit, talking about slavery can engender feelings of guilt about a system that is incongruent with the democratic ideals on which this country was founded.

Conversations about enslavement have been muted by the media images to which the vast majority of Americans are accustomed that portray it as a benevolent system in which blacks were far better off for having been rescued from the barbarism of Africa. It was not until the work of the preeminent scholar on Africa and African American history, Dr. Henry Louis Gates Jr., the Alphonse Fletcher University Professor and Director of the Hutchins Center for African and African American Research at Harvard University, that the historical record was corrected by an objective scholarly examination. Dr. Gate's scholarship presents an authentic depiction of the facts of black enslavement as it developed in the United States and of the great civilizations present on the continent of Africa. This history has also been brought into wider public view among Americans by Dr. Gate's association with Public Broadcasting Television (PBS).

In popular culture, the film *Twelve Years a Slave* was directed by Steve McQueen (McQueen et al., 2014) and adapted from the autobiography of Solomon Northup (1853). Northrop was a free black man living in the North who was kidnapped and sold by enslavers. Unlike its predecessors, the most popular being *Gone with the Wind*, *Twelve Years a Slave* set forth an authentic depiction of the system of enslavement. Northup's first-hand reporting revealed the brutality and inhumanity of the physical and psychological social controls needed to sustain a system reliant on a docile and compliant enslaved labor force and the tenets of white supremacy.

In academia, Dr. Michael Simanga, adjunct professor with the Department of African American Studies at Georgia State University asserts that the enslavement of blacks remains an open wound that has yet to heal. The enslavement of blacks remains an uncomfortable subject because it forces the nation to confront the incongruence of the ideals of a democratic republic conceived in the proposition that all men are created equal owing its beginnings to the exploitation of a race of people for economic gain. Dr. Simanga argues that to address this contradiction would require fundamental reforms in all American institutional structures, which most Americans are not yet willing to do (Simanga, 2015).

Out of sight does not mean out of mind. Recent years have seen new theoretical paradigms that take a fresh look at possible causal linkages between the injustices perpetrated against masses of people that are passed on from generation to generation in the form of historical trauma.

Sigmund Freud, the acknowledged founder of modern psychoanalytic thought, initially defined trauma as those events that make excessive demands on the personality and the exposure to quantities of excitation greater than the capacity with which the personality can cope (Bowlby, 1969/1982, p. 10). More complex definitions are offered in the psychoanalytical literature today that build on Freud's original assumptions about the causes and potential effects of trauma on the subsequent mental health of the individual.

Contemporary scholars and mental health professionals view the historical perspective as a useful lens for examining possible causal linkages or associative relationships between the incidence and prevalence of social and behavioral problems endemic to populations who share a common heritage of horrific life experiences. These experiences may include such events as genocide, dislocation, mass violence, and living under the constant and unrelenting hardships of extreme poverty. Even though unrecognized, these events can lay the groundwork for psychological and behavioral maladaptations that are passed on from generation to generation.

The concept of historical trauma was initially introduced in the mental health literature by social work researcher and mental health expert Dr. Maria Yellow Horse Brave Heart in the 1980s. In an effort to explain the pervasiveness of social problems among the Lakota, Dr. Brave Heart employed a mixed qualitative and quantitative research method to lend new insights for establishing an associative relationship between the historical experiences of the Lakota of dislocation, colonization, the placement of children in federally run boarding schools, and other governmental policies aimed at their cultural extinction. The implications of her findings have been generalized to other First Nation people who suffered the effects of the federal government's Indian Removal policies. Her hypothesis has also been applied to other populations who share in common a heritage of mass group trauma (Braveheart, 1998, 1999).

African American scholars and mental health practitioners, for example, have applied underlying assumptions of historical trauma as a conceptual model for understanding the implications of the experience of enslavement and its legacy to explain the reasons for the stubborn persistence of poverty and its related problems in black communities (Carten, 2015; DeGruy, 2017; Poussaint & Alexander, 2000). There is also some scholarly speculation that historical trauma may account for the disproportionate representation of African Americans in populations impacted by substance abuse and the recent rise in suicide rates among African American youth (Poussaint & Alexander, 2000).

Arguably, more research may be needed to obtain a desirable level of scientific rigor to establish definitive associative relationships between the legacy of enslavement and social problems endemic to the black community. In light of the findings of the Adverse Childhood Experiences Study (ACES), this is a credible area for further empirical inquiry by social work educators and researchers.

IMPLICATIONS FOR SOCIAL WORK PRACTICE

The ACES was conducted in partnership with the Centers for Disease Control and Prevention and Kaiser Permanente. The study findings documented the extensiveness of untreated trauma among the general population of Americans, which has negative impacts on later health and mental health outcomes in adulthood. Moreover, based on these findings, the National Council for Behavioral Health encourages the use of evidence-based models found effective in the treatment of trauma and that trauma-informed care be integrated into all mental health and assessment and treatment procedures (Felita et al., 1998).

The MSW program of the Whitney M. Young Jr. School of Social Work prepares graduates for advanced clinical social work practice. The faculty is, therefore, especially open to the potential insights gleaned from innovative conceptual models that expand the theoretical knowledge base on the implications of historical trauma to mental health outcomes and that integrate an Afrocentric perspective. The two areas of concentration of the School are in mental health and children and families. Both concentrations are undergirded by the Afrocentric perspective and give special attention to the infusion and integration of content into the curriculum that is essential for understanding the black experience in the United States and that is embraced in the School's model of autonomous social work practice.

As described by the full-time faculty participating in focus groups held to gather information for this book, an Afrocentric perspective is infused throughout the curriculum and is reflected in the implicit and explicit academic programs of the School. The Practice and Human Behavior in the Social Environment curriculum areas devote substantive space to explicating the autonomous social work practice model. The course syllabus of the social welfare program and policy curriculum, the curriculum sequence in which the history and value orientation of American social welfare policy is taught, includes content on the history of enslavement as it evolved in the United States and as it was integral to the economic development of Georgia and the city of Atlanta and for shaping social welfare policy development for blacks in the city and state, both past and present.

HISTORICAL ANTECEDENTS IN GEORGIA

History does matter. And the first chapter of black history in the United States began with the arrival of their African ancestors in the British Colonies in the 1600s. Their arrival also marks the beginning of the historical context that created the need for a school for training "Negro" social workers that led to the launching of the Atlanta School of Social Work.

Since its beginnings as a British colony, Georgia has been influenced by a history of black enslavement and its legacy that intertwined issues of economic development and partisan sectional politics. Georgia was among the original colonies to sign the Articles of Confederation in 1781 creating a loose confederation of sovereign states that operated with little accountability to a weak central government.

With the recognition that, if the Union were to survive, it would require a central government with greater authority, Georgia was also counted among those signing the US Constitution on September 17, 1787. And it was the intertwined and highly charged emotional issues related to black enslavement, economic development, and sectional political interests that led Georgia to be among the first states to secede from the Union.

BLACK ENSLAVEMENT IN GEORGIA

Georgia's history began with its founding in 1733, by British aristocrat James Oglethorpe. Named for King George II, Georgia was the last of the original thirteen colonies to join what would become the United States and embark upon the American Experiment. Oglethorpe envisioned that the colony would be a pipeline for emptying out overcrowded British debtors' prisons and offer former inmates an opportunity for a new start in life. The colony was also envisioned as an asylum for the poor and a respite from religious persecution for Protestants.

Initially, enslavement was prohibited by the Board of Trustees, the governing body of the colony that was then under British rule. Slavery was not only prohibited by British law but was also believed to be immoral. This prohibition gave way under the lure of the profitability of an agricultural economy supported by a servile enslaved labor force and land that was most favorable for the cultivation of cotton. Indeed, "King Cotton" became the main staple of the state's income. The lucrativeness of King Cotton, along with black enslavement, fueled a thriving agricultural economy. In the end, Oglethorpe's altruistic idealism did not prevail. The colony was not settled by individuals rescued from England's debtor prisons, and the Board of Trustees lifted the ban against slavery in 1751. By the time of the colonial revolt against British rule, enslaved blacks comprised more than half of the colony of Georgia's population (Wood, 2014).

Moreover, despite framing the founding documents in the aspirational ideals of liberty, freedom, and equality, the pillars of the American Experiment, these documents made no mention of slavery. At the time of the signing of the Declaration of Independence in 1776, the enslavement of blacks was legal in all of the thirteen colonies. Depending on who is counted among the group as being the Founding Fathers, most owned slaves.

THE DISPLACEMENT OF FIRST AMERICANS

The city of Atlanta's origins and settlement are traced back to 1837 and the forcible removal of Native Americans of the Creek and Cherokee Nations from lands in Georgia, Tennessee, Alabama, North Carolina, and Florida. The forcible removal of First Americans from their ancestral lands was motivated by the economic interests of white settlers to gain possession of land on which to grow cotton. The white settlers were further emboldened by beliefs such as the *white man's burden* and *manifest destiny* embraced by some of the nation's founding fathers. These beliefs justified imperialism as a noble undertaking in the interest of advancing civilization. With this as a mindset and justification, the federal government enacted policies for the forcible removal of First Americans and the transfer of lands their ancestors had occupied and cultivated for generations to white farmers for the cultivation of cotton.

The Supreme Court ruling in *Worcester v. Georgia*, 31 US 515 (1832), stipulated that the Cherokee was a sovereign nation. As a sovereign nation with its own government and control over the geographical territory that the Nation occupied, white settlers had no legitimate claim to the Cherokee lands they coveted for economic gain. Despite its sovereignty, the language of the decision rendered by Justice John Marshall defined the relationship between the US government and the Cherokee as similar to that of ward to guardian. This ambiguity in the language of the ruling gave President Andrew Jackson the thumbs up he needed to negotiate several treaties for the removal of Indians from their ancestral lands. This action on the part of Jackson is counted among the most tragic and infamous policies undertaken by the federal government in American history. The forcible removal of Native Americans in the interest of the westward expansion of national interests is documented in the book *Bury My Heart at Wounded Knee* (Brown & Brown, 2007). The book chronicles one of the most ignominious eras of American history, rivaling only that of the nearly four-century enslavement of blacks.

The phrase "Trail of Tears" symbolizes the egregious treatment of First Americans by European settlers who justified their actions through empirically flawed assumptions bound together in the notion of white supremacy, a notion further imbued by the belief that it was God's will and the destiny of Anglo Saxons to develop the North American continent as a laboratory to demonstrate that Americans could build a utopian society, or "city on a hill," to advance the global flourishing of capitalism, democracy, and the Protestant religion. The noble vision captured by the phrase "city on a hill" and the less than noble events undertaken in the development of the New World are the roots of the ambiguous concept of American Exceptionalism.

AMERICAN EXCEPTIONALISM

Despite these less than morally admirable origins, the phrase "city on a hill" has come to symbolize the historic narrative of what was advanced as the noble mission of Europeans in the New World, symbolized by the concept of American Exceptionalism. The notion of the "city on a hill" has remained a part of the American cultural and political lexicon since it was initially used by Puritan Minister John Winthrop as he escorted Pilgrims to the New World to create a "New England." The arrival of Winthrop and other early settlers in the New World was the beginning of the American Experiment in democracy, which was embodied in the Declaration of Independence's proclamation of the self-evident truth that "all men are created equal; endowed by their creator with the right to life, liberty and the pursuit of happiness."

Ever since the phrase "city on a hill" was first used by Winthrop—more likely at that time as a social construction of a white hegemony envisioned for the New World—it has been invoked by several US presidents in the 20th and 21st centuries to communicate an inclusive interpretation of the phrase. Irrespective of political party affiliation or partisan concerns, the use of the term by modern US presidents reflected the growing democratization of the nation and a willingness to share the promises of the American Dream with new demographics previously perceived as "the other" at various times in the nation's history.

For example, facing growing Cold War tensions abroad and growing militancy in the struggle for civil rights at home, and having established a vision for his administration as the "New Frontier," President-elect John F. Kennedy, the first Catholic elected to the office asserted that

> I have been guided by the standard John Winthrop set before his shipmates on the flagship Arabella three hundred and thirty-one years ago, as they, too, faced the task of building a new government on a perilous frontier. We must always consider that we shall be as a city upon a hill—the eyes of all people are upon us. For we are setting out upon a voyage in 1961 no less hazardous

than that undertaken by the Arabella in 1630 . . . beset as it was then by terror without and disorder within. History will not judge our endeavors—and a government cannot be selected—merely on the basis of color or creed or even party affiliation.

Kennedy ended his remarks with the oft-quoted phrase. "For those to whom much is given, much is required" (Time, 1961).

Adding the word "shining," President Ronald Reagan used the phrase in his election-eve address, "A Vision for America," given on November 3, 1980.

> I have quoted John Winthrop's words more than once on the campaign trail this year—for I believe that Americans in 1980 are every bit as committed to that vision of a shining "city on a hill," as were those long ago settlers. . . . These visitors to that city on the Potomac do not come as white or black, red or yellow; they are not Jews or Christians; conservatives or liberals; or Democrats or Republicans. They are Americans awed by what has gone before, proud of what for them is still . . . a shining city on a hill. (Reagan, 1980)

Reagan used the phrase again in his January 11, 1989, farewell address to the nation saying,

> I've spoken of the shining city all my political life . . . in my mind it was a tall, proud city built on rocks stronger than oceans, wind-swept, God-blessed, and teeming with people of all kinds living in harmony and peace; a city with free ports that hummed with commerce and creativity. And if there had to be city walls, the walls had doors and the doors were open to anyone with the will and the heart to get here. That's how I saw it, and see it still. (Reagan, 1989)

US Senator Barack Obama, who in 2009 became the 44th President and the first African American elected to the office of the United States presidency, used the phrase in his 2006 commencement address at the University of Massachusetts in Boston. "I see students that have come here from over 100 different countries, believing like those first settlers that they too could find a home in this City on a Hill—that they too could find success in this unlikeliest of places" (Obama, 2006).

In speaking about the ambiguous interpretations that can be given to the concept of American Exceptionalism, and as illustrated in the divisive political climate of the country soon after he left the office of the presidency in 2016, Obama said "We have a core set of values that are enshrined in our Constitution, in our body of law, in our democratic practices, in our belief in free speech and equality, that, though imperfect, are exceptional" (Brooks, Koopman & Wilson, 2013).

COGNITIVE DISSONANCE THEORY

Cognitive dissonance theory (CDT) is popular among faculty teaching from a race-critical and antiracist framework to encourage critical thinking among students in an examination of the inconsistencies between policy intent and practice outcomes as social welfare policy has developed in the United States. Concepts drawn from CDT can also offer insights into why the white settlers were blinded to the incongruence of their noble ideals, which were to be the moral pillars of the American Experiment, with the exploitation of the labor and bodies of black men and women in a system of involuntary servitude and government policies that sanctioned the illegal dispossession of their land and the near extinction of First Americans.

Introduced by American social psychologist Leon Festinger (1962), CDT provides a theoretical framework for understanding the psychological dynamics that make it possible for people to maintain an internal feeling of homeostasis, or sense of a "steady state," when their behaviors are inconsistent with deeply held beliefs and values. The concept has been applied by Larry Davis, former dean of the school of social work at the University of Pittsburgh, in his book *Why Are They Angry with Us* (Davis, 2016) to lend insights into understanding Americans' complex conundrums in thinking and attitudes on matters of race. CDT is now widely used by social work educators to engage students in a critical examination of the historical roots of "white privilege" and its more nuanced presentations in society today. This theoretical framework also lends insights for understanding the sense of righteous indignation engendered in the Confederate states when the abolitionist movement threatened the Southern way of life and led to the secession of Georgia from the Union and ultimately ignited the Civil War.

THE ABOLITIONIST THREAT AND GEORGIA SECESSION

Concurrent with the entrenchment of the enslavement of blacks as a way of life in the South was the growth of a national abolitionist movement. Questioning the morality of the system of enslavement, the movement threatened the loss of what, for white plantation owners, had become a highly profitable and idyllic way of life on plantations in the Deep South. Secession had long been on the agenda of the Southern states whose economic well-being depended on a controlled and compliant free labor force. As abolition became more of a looming reality, Georgia was among the first states to secede from the Union. With an agricultural economy dependent on an enslaved labor force and as the southern state with the largest share of plantations among the slave-holding states, Georgia was an exemplar of plantation life and culture in the Deep South. Soon after the election of President Lincoln, as sectional tensions over the question of slavery escalated, abolition became an increasingly looming threat to disrupting a long-established way of life in the South. This provided the context for grievances laid out in the Georgia Declaration of Secession.

> The people of Georgia having dissolved their political connection with the Government of the US of America, present to their confederates and the world the causes which have led to the separation. For the last ten years we have had numerous and serious causes of complaint against our non-slaveholding confederate States with reference to the subject of African slavery. They have endeavored to weaken our security, to disturb our domestic peace and tranquility, and persistently refused to comply with their express constitutional obligations to us in reference to that property, and by the use of their power in the Federal Government have striven to deprive us of an equal enjoyment of the common Territories of the Republic. This hostile policy of our confederates has been pursued with every circumstance of aggravation which could arouse the passions and excite the hatred of our people, and has placed the two sections of the Union for many years past in the condition of virtual civil war. Our people, still attached to the Union from habit and national traditions, and averse to change, hoped that time, reason, and argument would bring, if not redress, at least exemption from further insults, injuries, and dangers. Recent events have fully dissipated all such hopes and demonstrated the necessity of separation. (Justice, 2017)

The secession document was approved on January 29, 1861, by the delegates to the Georgia Secession Convention.

THE CITY OF ATLANTA AND THE CIVIL WAR

The enslavement of blacks and forcible removal of Native Americans from the region as planned had proved to be most lucrative in building Georgia's economy. For the city of Atlanta, these developments, along with the extension of railroads that connected it to other parts of the region, were equally profitable as the city soon became a center of commerce and manufacturing. Atlanta was incorporated in 1848, and, by the time of the Civil War, it was the hub to a prosperous commercial region. As a thriving manufacturing center, Atlanta was soon vital to the South's entry into the Civil War.

The writing of the Constitution of the Confederate States and the election of Jefferson Davis as President of the Confederacy began what for some was an act of treason and for others an expression of liberty and freedom.

The city of Atlanta became of strategic military importance to the Confederate war effort. The city's well-developed manufacturing sector and railroad linkages made it a strategic location for the manufacture and distribution of wartime supplies and also made it a target for the Union Army and General Sherman's infamous "March to the Sea."

The destruction of Atlanta was memorialized in a scene from the film version of Margaret Mitchell's idealized portrayal of plantation life in the novel *Gone with the Wind*. As reported in the black media, the film was met with much angst in the black community for its stereotypical portrayal of blacks (Stevens, 1973). And when the movie premiered on December 15, 1939, at Atlanta's segregated Lowes Grand Theater, Hattie McDaniel and Butterfly McQueen, award-winning African American actors, were barred from the celebration because of their race and were not among the roster of white stars present for the opening ceremonies.

As the film portrayed, the city of Atlanta was all but destroyed. Sherman's military strike ended with a fiery onslaught that devastated the city and crippled the Confederate military effort with the burning of key railroads and manufacturing sites. The fall of Atlanta signaled the beginning of the end of the war—a war that ended with the abolition of slavery, initiated the period of Reconstruction, and ushered in what was to be the birth of a New South where it was claimed blacks would have equal rights with whites.

LINCOLN'S VISION OF A MORE PERFECT UNION

The meeting of Confederate General Robert E. Lee and Union General Ulysses S. Grant at Appomattox Court House and the signing of the Surrender on April 9, 1865, marked the official end of the Civil War. Less than a week later, the relief that had come with the end of a long and brutal war, one that pitted relatives against one another and caused the disruption of families based on their geographic location in the warring country, the nation was abruptly thrown into a deep period of mourning with President Lincoln's assassination on April 14, 1865.

Before his assassination, and three years into the Civil War, Lincoln had signed the Emancipation Proclamation as a presidential executive order on January 1, 1863, declaring that "that all persons held as slaves" within the rebellious states "are, and henceforward shall be free" (National Archives, The Emancipation Proclamation, p. 1). The document may well be considered a political statement of good intentions since it was concerned only with slaves in the rebellious states that had seceded from the Union, and it depended on the Union Army winning battles fought in those states. It had no impact on blacks still in bondage in the border states that had remained loyal to the Union cause.

Furthermore, the untimely death of President Lincoln meant that he was not present to guide a plan intended for undertaking Reconstruction. Lincoln's message of intended good will is captured in his second inaugural address as president given on March 4, 1865. Appealing to the nation's "better angels" Lincoln spoke of his vision of a path forward in uniting the country.

> With malice toward none, with charity for all, with firmness in the right as God gives us to see the right, let us strive on to finish the work we are in, to bind up the nation's wounds, to care for him who shall have borne the battle and for his widow and his orphan, to do all which may achieve and cherish a just and lasting peace among ourselves and with all nations. (National Archives)

This was not to be the case. The country has been crippled by the failures of Reconstruction. Moreover, these failures have resulted in a seeming refighting of the Civil War again and again.

THE FAILURES OF RECONSTRUCTION

Eric Foner, Pulitzer Prize-winning historian and DeWitt Clinton Professor of History at Columbia University has written extensively on the shortfalls of Reconstruction and the continuing influence of these on race relations in the United States (Foner, 1988). Foner traces Abraham Lincoln's changing views on black enslavement that evolved from his initial support of the colonization of blacks in Africa to his unequivocal position that the abolishment of slavery was required to save the Union. Lincoln's ability to evolve and change over his political career is seen as an indication of his capacity for growth, a trait that accounts for his uncontested greatness as a US president. Indeed, had he lived to oversee the process of Reconstruction, the country may have avoided what has become a recurring struggle to redress its "original sin" and redefine itself as an authentic democratic republic when the opportunity presented itself at the end of the Civil War. Foner addresses this lost opportunity in *The Fiery Trial: Abraham Lincoln and American Slavery* (2010). The book examines the flaws of Reconstruction that have had a rippling effect on race relations over the full course of the nation's history.

The title of the book is taken from the content of President Lincoln's December 1, 1862, Annual Address to Congress (Lincoln, 2002). While the Lincoln speech covered a range of topics of concern to the nation, much of the text dealt with the difficult questions related to emancipation. The president set forth a number of options that endeavored to set a path palatable to all parties and that would allow the country to be unified in the purpose of moving forth to form a "more perfect union." With financing as a central concern, including the costs of rebuilding the South, among the options set forth by the president was a plan to financially compensate white slave owners for the costs associated with the loss of a free labor force that was of immeasurable monetary benefit to them. Foreseeing the consequential and historical impact of decisions made by the Congress, in the concluding paragraph of the address Lincoln stated,

> Fellow-citizens, we cannot escape history. We of this Congress and this Administration will be remembered in spite of ourselves. No personal significance or insignificance can spare one or another of us. The fiery trial through which we pass will light us down in honor or dishonor to the latest generation. We say we are for the Union. The world will not forget that we say this. We know how to save the Union. The world knows we do know how to save it. We, even we here, hold the power and bear the responsibility. In giving freedom to the slave we assure freedom to the free—honorable alike in what we give and what we preserve. We shall nobly save or meanly lose the last best hope of earth. Other means may succeed; this could not fail. The way is plain, peaceful, generous, just—a way which if followed the world will forever applaud and God must forever bless.

Reconstruction, the period of 1865–1877, defines the years immediately after the end of the Civil War. During this period the country, still in recovery from the traumas associated with the war and assassination of the president, faced the daunting task of not only rebuilding the South but reuniting the nation after a bitterly fought war that failed to absolve for either side the highly emotional feelings around the "Negro Problem." The "Negro Problem" was, for politicians charting a path for what was claimed to be the "New South, " a redefinition of what had been the "Slave Issue" in the years leading up to the Civil War. Concurrent with this work would be the formidable task of integrating four million formerly enslaved blacks into American society. To accomplish this would call for a redefinition of the nation as a democratic republic.

Contrary to Lincoln's optimistic view of binding up the wounds and traumas of war, Reconstruction was one of the most turbulent periods in US history. Moreover, having never been fully resolved, the themes of Reconstruction continue to resonate in ideological differences between what political pundits categorize today as the Blue and Red states, with the Red states leaning toward more conservative views on political and cultural issues, including those on matters of race, and the Blue states embracing liberal views. These differences between the Blue and Red states reflect the geographical division on matters of race that intensified during the period of Reconstruction. Furthermore, because issues surrounding Reconstruction have yet to be resolved, they have flared up again and again over the country's history. Most notably, these flare-ups predictably occur when efforts are made to advance the civil rights of African Americans, repeatedly sparking a white backlash and the emergence of an ideological replay of the Civil War.

With Lincoln's death, oversight of the Reconstruction fell to President Andrew Johnson, who had served as Vice President for a scant forty-two days. Described as a man of limited formal education but of well-honed oratory and persuasive political skills, upon assuming the office of the presidency, Johnson was in frequent opposition to legislation that Congress passed to protect the rights of the freed slaves. Were it not for the Congressional override, his veto of the bill to establish the Freedmen's Bureau would have denied essential services provided by the Bureau that included protection of the legal rights of freed slaves, negotiation of labor contracts, and the setting up of free schools for blacks and whites.

Johnson's contentious relationship with Congress over the development of a plan for integrating the Southern states back into the Union while preserving a sense of dignity for the defeated Confederacy was among the reasons for his subsequently being distinguished—at least up to that time—as the worst president in the nation's history by some historians. And, although acquitted, Johnson was the first US president to be impeached for high crimes and misdemeanors.

THE RECONSTRUCTION AMENDMENTS TO THE CONSTITUTION

The Thirteenth, Fourteenth, and Fifteenth Amendments to the US Constitution, referred to as the Reconstruction Amendments, are intended to give full rights of citizenship to blacks (Foner, 1988, 2012). The Thirteenth Amendment, ratified in 1865, abolished slavery and involuntary servitude except for those duly convicted of a crime. The Fourteenth Amendment, ratified by Congress in 1868, addresses citizenship rights and equal protection of the laws for all persons. The Fifteenth Amendment, ratified in 1870, prohibits discrimination in voting rights of citizens on the basis of "race, color, or previous condition of servitude."

There is a wealth of evidence of the inherent contradictions in the promise of these basic rights for all as guaranteed under the US Constitution when examining the persistence of racial disparities across virtually all sectors of American society. These include the arena of health and human services where social work has the highest visibility (Carten, Siskind, & Pender Green, 2016). These inequities were present in the safety net program legislated by the 1935 Social Security Act and have been passed on in subsequent reforms of government safety net programs. Advocacy efforts aimed to reduce these disparities and to promote social justice for African Americans are a concern for social work programs in the predominately white schools of social work and of historic concern for those housed in the HBCUs.

The statistical evidence of racial disparities is glaring and unquestionable. For example, African Americans are more likely to be the victims of de facto and de jure forms of racial segregation that have persisted in housing, employment, and public education despite the enactment of the Civil Rights Act of 1964 (Wilson, 1996). Blacks are disproportionately affected by recent state legislation following the 2013 Supreme Court ruling striking down some aspects of the 1964 Voter Rights Act. The decision of the Court allows states to change their election laws without advance federal approval. Having its greatest impact on Southern states, the Court's 4–5 ruling makes it harder for Americans who are otherwise qualified to exercise their right to vote (Newkirk, 2018). The unequal treatment of blacks in the criminal justice system is especially glaring, as manifested in the disproportionate incarceration and execution rates of blacks (Alexander, 2020; Stevenson, 2014).

Relative to the criminal justice system, advocates for US prison reform have endeavored to bring to light the shortfalls of the Thirteenth Amendment, which abolished slavery and involuntary servitude with the exception of *those duly convicted of a crime*. The 2016 Netflix documentary *13th*, directed by award-winning filmmaker and producer Ava DuVernay, is a provocative examination of the implications of this wording and sheds light on the roots of the massive incarceration of people of color in the American prison system. The documentary also presents a compelling argument that this exception has allowed for practices that, by finding legal justification in the nation's judicial system, has perpetuated a system of slavery that reaches far beyond the end of the Civil War. The documentary's examination of the historical development of the US prison system brings to light themes reminiscent of convict leasing policies and peonage, both of which were extensively practiced in Georgia and other Southern states as a means of replenishing the free labor force that had been depleted with emancipation and in the aftermath of the period of Reconstruction.

Reconstruction, by any measure, was a monumental task as both the South and the North began efforts to reunite the country and redress the extensive and devastatingly profound destructive impact of centuries of enslavement on an entire race of people. Moreover, the pursuit of equality for blacks was a task that would be carried out within the context of contradictions from Supreme Court rulings. For example, the Supreme Court's ruling in the 1857 Dred Scott case (60 US [19 How.] 393 [1857]) stipulated that no black, free or slave, could claim US citizenship. The spirit of the 1857 ruling assigned blacks to a status of non-citizenship. This status of non- citizenship is embedded in the "separate but equal doctrine" established under the 1896 *Plessey v. Ferguson* (163 US 537, 1896) Supreme Court decision that covered virtually all areas of public life in the United States.

The early phase of the Reconstruction period is referred to as Radical Reconstruction. It was a time when Republicans and Democrats were, at best, operating from partisan, even disingenuous, motivations. The Southern Democrats were by no means prepared to relinquish the privileges of white supremacy and accept blacks as their social equals. And the Republicans were intent on punishing the South for its insurgency and lack of loyalty to the Union.

With enfranchisement, blacks were given the vote and subsequently held elective offices at the state and at some federal government levels during this early period of Reconstruction. These advances in black rights were short-lived. The ending of Reconstruction also ended black participation in the political life of the nation. In 1868, the Georgia House of Representatives expelled twenty-five black members, and the Senate removed two black members (Dittmer, 1980, p. 5). Soon after Union soldiers withdrew from the South and were no longer overseeing Reconstruction, the tenets of white supremacy were resurrected in the form of Jim Crow Laws and the Black Codes. These laws essentially replaced those of the years of Radical Reconstruction, which saw beginning legislation for black rights, with those that legalized racial segregation, placed severe restrictions on the freedom of blacks, and began a reign of terror for blacks with the emergence of the Ku Klux Klan in the late 1860s.

JIM CROW LAWS AND THE BLACK CODES

Jim Crow laws began soon after the end of the Civil War and the ratification of the 13th Amendment that ended enslavement for more than four million blacks. The Black Codes were a companion to Jim Crow Laws that prescribed the conditions under which blacks could live, work and how much they could be paid. These laws became commonplace throughout the South, effectively replacing enslavement with a form of indentured servitude. Together these laws took away the right of blacks to the vote and sought to control all aspects of the lives of blacks in freedom. The Ku Klux Klan became the official terrorist organization to enforce these laws by meting out inhumane acts of punishment on those who dared to defy them.

Jim Crow laws and the Black Codes were not only as equally oppressive as the system of enslavement, but they also promoted a view that, in the absence of strictly enforced controls, blacks would be a menace to white society and a threat to the social order of the South. These racist claims had the effect of advancing a widely held view of blacks as subhuman, corrupt, violent, and of inferior intelligence and of black males as lustful of white women. These beliefs were supported by empirically untested theories advanced by the pseudoscience of scientific racism held in common by whites since the 1600s. Moreover, these stereotypical depictions of blacks became a truism of conventional wisdom deeply embedded in American culture. These stereotypical beliefs about blacks were graphically portrayed and reinforced in D. W. Griffith's silent film *Birth of a Nation*, released in 1915.

Jim Crowism and the Black Codes played a central role in laying groundwork for the institutionalization of white supremacy in the United States. D. W. Griffith's film, *The Birth of a Nation*, was a powerful instrument reinforcing this pejorative narrative about blacks that has persisted over the decades. Originally titled *The Clansmen*, the NAACP was unsuccessful in its attempts to have the film censored for its vilification of the black race. And the thousands of blacks, organized by Monroe Trotter, founder of the *Guardian*, marching in protest in the city of Boston were equally unsuccessful in getting the blatantly racist film banned.

The last segment of the more than 3-hour film deals with the chaos of Reconstruction and ends with a blatant appeal to white racism and a glorification of white supremacy. In the closing scenes, the Klan rides in as an avenging posse cloaked in white sheets. The closing images portrayed the Klan as defenders of the South from Northern interference in deeply held beliefs and customs about black–white relationships, protectors of white women from rape by black men, and guardians to prevent the takeover of power by a savage race of people.

The film was previewed at the White House, at the invitation of President Woodrow Wilson upon the request of his friend, Thomas Dixon, author of the book *The Clansman* from which the film had been adapted. The historical literature does not definitively affirm the often quoted statement attributed to President Wilson: "it's like writing history with lightning, and my only regret is that it is all so terribly true," in reaction to the film (Benbow, 2010). But the film clearly promoted a narrative that glorified the traditions of the Old South, legitimated the honor of the Southern cause in the Civil War, and reinforced white supremacy and a false narrative about blacks that continues to influence black–white relations in the United States.

THE RESURGENCE OF THE KU KLUX KLAN

Emboldened by the enthusiastic public response to *The Birth of a Nation*, soon after the film was released a group of whites met at Stone Mountain near Atlanta to resurrect the Klan with a renewed commitment to the preservation of white supremacy. With its resurgence, the Klan was not only a vigilante group organized to terrorize blacks, but a terrorist organization that carried out violent attacks against other groups who were not Protestant, white, and Anglo Saxons; its reach soon extended to include Jews and Catholics.

Today's resurrection of US white nationalist groups chanting "Jews will not replace us" has fueled a climate of anti-Semitism that led to the Pittsburgh Synagogue shooting on October 27, 2018, during Shabbat morning services, an act that killed eleven people and injured seven more. This tragic event is similar to one in Atlanta's history that occurred in 1913. Similar to the synagogue massacre in Pittsburgh, the Atlanta tragedy of 1913 was influenced by the growth of a climate of anti-Semitism that reached a boiling point in events revolving around the murder and rape of thirteen-year-old Mary Phagan. The thirteen-year-old was an employee in the factory where she was killed, which was managed by Leo Frank, a Jew. Frank was accused of the murder, found guilty, and sentenced to death after a sensational and controversial trial that received national media coverage. Frank was unsuccessful in his legal appeals, but his death sentence was commuted to life in prison. While in prison Frank was kidnapped and lynched by a group of prominent white men whose identities were well known but who were never brought to trial (Carter, 2005).

THE TENACITY OF WHITE SUPREMACY

Since its resurrection during the mid-1900s and its flagrant flaunting of the rule of law, various forms of terrorism have become the calling card of the Klan, undertaken primarily to ensure the purity of the white race and the persistence of notions of white supremacy. Supporting this, a historic purpose of Klan activities has been to prevent the mixing of the races that would create what the Klan refers to as a "mongrel race of people" that, in their view, threatens the "purity" of the white race.

Concerns about preserving the purity of the white race, preventing the mixing of the races and laws prohibiting marriage and sexual relations between the races have been in existence since the Colonial period and were enforced in most states until 1967. These century-old laws barring interracial marriages, known as "anti-miscegenation laws," were found to be unconstitutional by the landmark Supreme Court decision in *Loving v. Virginia* (388 US 1 [1967], [1]) that struck down the decision of a lower state court ruling that "Almighty God created the races white, black, yellow, and red, and he placed them on separate continents. And but for the interference with his arrangement there would be no cause for such marriages. The fact that he separated the races shows that he did not intend for the races to mix."

After unsuccessful appeals at the state judiciary level, the case made its way to the US Supreme Court. Overruling the decision of the lower courts, Chief Justice Earl Warren, in rendering the unanimous decision of the higher court, wrote

> Marriage is one of the "basic civil rights of man," fundamental to our very existence and survival. . . . To deny this fundamental freedom on so unsupportable a basis as the racial classifications embodied in these statutes, classifications so directly subversive of the principle of equality at the heart of the Fourteenth

Amendment. . . . Under our Constitution, the freedom to marry, or not marry, a person of another race resides with the individual and cannot be infringed by the State. (Loving v. Virginia, 1967)

Nonetheless, despite the Supreme Court decision, the matter of intermarriage or sexual relations between the races was far from solved. States across the nation have been slow in removing miscegenation laws from their statutes. Alabama, the last state to officially accept the Supreme Court decision, did not remove its anti-miscegenation statute from the state constitution until 2000 (Novkov, 2008).

Furthermore, the new nativism that is dominating current US political discourse has been accelerated by shifting population and demographic trends that have exacerbated concerns about whites losing their place as the dominant racial group. The current political climate in the United States, although not a black–white binary, in many aspects mirrors the fears that dominated black–white relations during the years of Reconstruction.

REVISITING LOST OPPORTUNITIES OF RECONSTRUCTION

Few subjects of US history have been more thoroughly examined and reexamined by scholars and historians than the period of Reconstruction. The narrative of *Birth of a Nation* promoted the generally accepted belief that the failures of Reconstruction largely fell on the shoulders of blacks, a race of people thought to be inherently unfit for full citizenship. Unsurprisingly, this narrative transformed from conventional wisdom into historical facts that have had great staying power in American culture and further explain the tenacity of white supremacy in the United States.

DuBois in his 1935 publication *Black Reconstruction in America: 1860–1880* (DuBois, 1935) endeavored to correct the historical record that attributes the failures of Reconstruction to blacks. David Levering Lewis, in the introduction of the DuBois' 1935 manuscript, wrote that DuBois's planned entry in the 1929 *Encyclopedia Britannica*, "The Negro in the United States," was not included because the editors declined to include the following lines of text as DuBois had requested: "White historians have ascribed the faults and failures of reconstruction to Negro ignorance and corruption. But the Negro insist that it was Negro loyalty and the Negro vote alone that restored the South to the Union; established the new democracy, both for white and black, and instituted the public schools" (DuBois, 1935, p. ix).

DuBois's book on Reconstruction was written from his post at Atlanta University. He undertook the work with a grant award from the Trustees of the Rosenwald Fund and the Carnegie Foundation. John Hope, Atlanta

University president, relieved DuBois of faculty responsibilities to allow him to have the time to work on the manuscript. Challenging interpretations of mainstream historians of Reconstruction, DuBois speaks "To the Reader" in the language of the Afrocentric perspective, writing

> The story of transplanting millions of Africans to the New World and of the bondage for centuries, is a fascinating one. Particularly interesting for students of human culture is the sudden freeing of these black folk in the 19th century, and the attempt, through them, to reconstruct the basis of American democracy from 1862 to 1880. This book seeks to tell and interpret these 20 years of faithful history with a special reference to the effort and experiences of the Negroes themselves.

In speaking to the predisposition of the reader, he wrote

> It would be only fair to the reader to say frankly in advance that the attitude of any person toward this story will be distinctly influenced by his theories of the Negro race. If he believes that the Negro in America and in general is an average and ordinary human being, who under a given environment develops like other human beings, then he will read the story and judge it by the facts adduced. If, however, he regards the Negro as a distinctly inferior creation, who can never successfully take part in modern civilization and whose emancipation and enfranchisement were gestures against nature, then he will need something more than the sort of facts that I had set down. But this latter person, I am not trying to convince. I am going to tell the story as though Negroes were ordinary human beings, realizing that this attitude will from the first seriously curtail my audience. (DuBois, 1935)

By this time DuBois had become a controversial figure in academic and literary circles. Unsurprisingly, his interpretation and telling of the story of Reconstruction was met with much criticism among mainstream historians of the period. Some claimed that his objectivity was impaired because of his over identification with the plight of his people. More recently, a new generation of scholars writing in the early decades of the 20th century suggest that DuBois may have been well in advance of the times in his thinking about the era (Foner, 1982; Manning, 1977; Parfait, 2009; Robinson, 1977). This cohort of scholars brings a more race-conscious approach to the critique of DuBois's thinking and analyzes the themes set forth in the manuscript in consideration of the historical context in which he was writing. More recently Dr. Henry Louis Gates Jr. has continued in his efforts to correct the historical revisions in his most recent publication on the period of Reconstruction, *Stony the Road* (Gates, 2019).

Thus, was the beginning historical context for the school of social work. It is a historical narrative that extends back to the colonial period and black enslavement, and unfolded in the aftermath of the Civil War when blacks were determined to use education as a tool for redressing the egregiousness of four centuries of black enslavement; a failed period of Reconstruction, followed by a white backlash and institutionalization of tenants of white supremacy in American culture that justified the unequal treatment of blacks, that was especially pervasive in the southern region of the nation.

The Progressive Era in the following decades saw a push for social justice and systemic reforms in which the nascent social work profession would participate. These reforms, however, were intended to improve the living conditions of whites only, the effects of which gave rise to a more concentrated effort on the part of the race men and women and progressive social reformers in the city of Atlanta and paved the way for the launching of a school of social work for the training of "colored" social workers. The events and their residual effects described in this chapter have had a continuing influence on shaping the black experience in America and for curriculum development in social work programs in the HBCUs.

REFERENCES

Alexander, M. (2020). *The new Jim Crow: Mass incarceration in the age of colorblindness.* The New Press.

Bacote, C. A. (1969). *The story of Atlanta University: A century of service, 1865–1965.* Atlanta: Atlanta University Press.

Benbow, M. (2010). Birth of a quotation: Woodrow Wilson and like writing history with lightning. *Journal of the Gilded Age and Progressive Era, 9*(4), 509–533. http://www.jstor.org/stable/20799409

Bent-Goodley, T. (2001). Ida B. Wells-Barnett: An uncompromising style. In I. Carlton-LaNey (Ed.), *African American leadership: An empowerment tradition in social welfare* (pp. 87–98). Washington, DC: NASW Press.

Blackmon, D. A. (2008). *Slavery by another name: The re-enslavement of black people in America from the Civil War to World War II.* New York: Doubleday.

Boney, F. N. (2017). Joseph E. Brown (1821–1894). New Georgia Encyclopedia. http://georgiaencyclopedia.org

Bouie, J. (2016). The radical message of Michelle Obama's speech: America's story is a black woman's story. July, 26, 2016. https://slate.com/news-and-politics/2016/07/the-radical-message-of-michelle-obamas-speech.html

Bourne, P. G. (1997). *Jimmy Carter: a comprehensive biography from plains to post-presidency.* Scribner Book Company.

Bowlby, J. (1969/1982). *Attachment and loss, Vol. 1* (2nd ed.). New York: Basic Books, Tavistock Institute of Human Relations.

Brooks, S., Koopman, D., & Wilson, J. M. (2013). *Understanding American Politics.* University of Toronto Press. "Obama on AmericanExcelptionalism" pg. 8.

Brave Heart, M. Y. H. (1998). The return to the sacred path: Healing the historical trauma and historical unresolved grief response among the Lakota. *Smith College Studies in Social Work, 68*(3), 287–305.

Brave Heart, M. Y. H. (1999). Oyate Ptayela: Rebuilding the Lakota Nation through addressing historical trauma among Lakota parents. *Journal of Human Behavior in the Social Environment, 2*(1/2), 109–126.

Brown, D. A., & Brown, D. (2007). *Bury my heart at Wounded Knee: An Indian history of the American West.* New York: Macmillan.

Carten, A., Siskind, A., & Pender Greene, M. (Eds.). (2016). *Strategies for deconstructing racism in the health and human services.* New York: Oxford University Press.

Carten, A. J. (2015). How the legacy of slavery affects the mental health of blacks. *The Conversation,* July, 17, 2015. https://theconversation.com/how-the-legacy-of-slavery-affects-the-mental-health-of-black-americans-today-44642

Carter, D. (2005). And the dead shall rise: The murder of Mary Phagan and the lynching of Leo Frank. *Journal of Southern History, 71*(2), 491. doi:10.2307/27648797

Centers for Disease Control and Prevention. (2016). About the CDC-Kaiser ACE study: Major findings. https://www.cdc.gov/violenceprevention/acestudy/about.html

Council on Social Work Education (CSWE). (2008). 2008 Statistics on social work education in the United States. https://www.cswe.org/Research-Statistics/Research-Briefs-and-Publications/2008-Statistics-on-Social-Work-Education-in-the-Un

Council on Social Work Education (CSWE). (2018). Statistics on social work education in the United States. Summary of the CSWE Annual Survey of Social Work Programs. https://www.cswe.org/getattachment/Research-Statistics/Annual-Program-Study/2018-Statistics-on-Social-Work-Education-in-the-United-States.pdf.aspx

Davis, L. E. (2016). *Why are they angry with us? Essays on Race.* Chicago: Lyceum Books.

DeGruy, J. (2017). Post Traumatic Slave Syndrome: America's Legacy of Enduring Injury and Healing. 2005.

Dittmer, J. (1980). *Black Georgia in the Progressive Era, 1900–1920.* Champaign: University of Illinois Press.

DuBois, W. E. B. (1910 May). The economic aspects of race prejudice. *The Editorial Review, 2,* 488.

DuBois, W. E. B. (1935). *Black Reconstruction in America, 1860–1818.* New York. Harcourt, Brace.

DuBois, W. E. B. (2017). *Black Reconstruction in America: Toward a history of the part which black folk played in the attempt to reconstruct democracy in America, 1860–1880.* New York: Routledge.

Dred Scott case (60 US (19 How.) 393 (1857).

Felitti, V. J., Anda, R. F., Nordenberg, D., Williamson, D. F., Spitz, A. M., Edwards, V., . . . Marks, J. S. (1998). Relationship of childhood abuse and household dysfunction to many of the leading causes of death in adults. *American Journal of Preventive Medicine, 14*(4), 245–258.

Festinger, L. (1962). *A theory of cognitive dissonance Vol. 2.* Stanford, CA: Stanford University Press.

Foner, E. (1982). Reconstruction revisited. *Reviews in American History, 10*(4), 82–100.

Foner, E. (1988). *Reconstruction: America's unfinished revolution, 1863–1877.* New York: Harper and Row.

Foner, E. (2010). *The fiery trial: Abraham Lincoln and American slavery.* New York: W.W. Norton.

Foner, E. (2012). Panel II: Reconstruction revisited. *Columbia Law Review, 112*(7).

Gates, H. L., Jr. (2019). *Stony the road: Reconstruction, white supremacy, and the rise of Jim Crow*. New York: Penguin Press.

Hammond, S. J., Roberts, R. N., & Sulfaro, V. A. (2016). *Campaigning for President in America, 1788–2016*. ABC-CLIO.

Hornsby Jr, A. (1991). Black public education in Atlanta, Georgia, 1954–1973: From segregation to segregation. *The Journal of Negro History, 76*(1–4), 21–47.

House, L. E., Fowler, D. N., Thornton, P. L., & Francis, E. A. (2007). A survey of African American deans and directors of US schools of social work. *Journal of Social Work Education, 43*(1), 67–82.

Justice, G. (2017). Georgia Secession Convention of 1861. http://georgiaencyclopedia.org

King, R. D. (2019). Hate crimes: Perspectives on offending and the law. In *Handbook on crime and deviance* (pp. 437–458). Springer, Cham.

Leary, J. D. (2005/2017). *Post traumatic slave syndrome: America's legacy of enduring injury and healing*. Milwaukie, OR: Uptone Press.

Leary, J. D. (2017). *Post traumatic slave syndrome: America's legacy of enduring injury and healing*. Joy DeGruy Publications Incorporated.

Lewis, D. L. (1935). *W. E. B. DuBois: Biography of a race, 1868–1919*. New York: Henry Holt.

Lincoln, A. (n.d.). Second annual message online, by Gerhard Peters and John T. Woolley. The American Presidency Project. https://www.presidency.ucsb.edu/node/202180

Lincoln, A. (2002). *This fiery trial: The speeches and writings of Abraham Lincoln*. New York: Oxford University Press. http://www.civil-war.net/pages/georgia_declaration.asp

Lovett, B. L. (2011). *America's historically Black colleges & universities: a narrative history from the nineteenth century into the twenty-first century*. Mercer University Press.

Loving v. Virginia, 388 US 1 (1967), [1].

Mancini, M. (1978). Race, economics, and the abandonment of convict leasing. *Journal of Negro History, 63*(4), 339–340.

McQueen, S., Ridley, J., Pitt, B., Gardner, D., Kleiner, J., Pohlad, W., & Northup, S. (2014). *12 years a slave*. Film. Entertainment One.

Morgan, D. (2007). Transcript of Barack Obama's speech, February 19, 2007. https://www.cbsnews.com/news/transcript-of-barack-obamas-speech/

National Archives. The Emancipation Proclamation (page 1) Record Group 11 General Records of the United States. https://www.archives.gov/exhibits/featured-documents/emancipation-proclamation

National Archives transcript of Lincoln's Second inaugural speech https://www.ourdocuments.gov/doc.php?flash=false&doc=38&page=transcript

Obama, B. (2006). University of Massachusetts at Boston commencement address. *Best Speeches of Barack Obama through his 2009 Inauguration*.

Newkirk. V. R. (2018). *Voter suppression is warping democracy*. The Atlantic. https://www.theatlantic.com/politics/archive/2018/07/poll-prri-voter-suppression/565355/

Northup, S. (1853). *Twelve years a slave: narrative of Solomon Northup* (Vol. 1). Library of Alexandria.

Novkov, J. (2008). Racial union: Law, intimacy, and the white state in Alabama, 1865–1954. Ann Arbor: University of Michigan Press

Obama, B. H. (2010). Remarks on signing an executive order concerning historically black colleges and universities. February 26, 2010.

Parfait, C. (2009). Rewriting history: The Publication of WEB DuBois's Black Reconstruction in America (1935). *Book History, 12*(1), 266–294.

Plessy v. Ferguson, 163 US 537 (1896).

Poussaint, A. F., & Alexander, A. (2000). Lay my burden down: Suicide and the mental health crisis among African-Americans. Boston: Beacon Press.

Provasnik, S., & Shafer, L. L. (September, 2004). *Historically black colleges and universities 1979–2001*. Washington, DC: National Center for Education Statistics. US Department of Education. Institute of Education Sciences.

Reagan, R. (1989). Farewell Address to the nation. Gerhard Peters and John T. Woolley, The American Presidency Project. https://www.presidency.ucsb.edu/node/251303

Reagan, R. (1980). Election eve address: A vision for America. *The American Presidency Project*.

Reagan, R. (1989). Farewell Address to the Nation, January 11, 1989. *The Public Papers of President Ronald W. Reagan*.

Robinson, C. (1977). A critique of WEB DuBois' Black Reconstruction. *The Black Scholar, 8*(7), 44–50.

Rudwick, E. (1957). W. E. B. DuBois and the Atlanta University Studies on the Negro. *The Journal of Negro Education, 26*(4), 466–476. doi:10.2307/2293494

Simanga, M. (2015). *Amiri Baraka and the Congress of African People: History and memory*. New York: Palgrave Macmillan.

Stevenson, B. (2014). *Just mercy: A story of justice and redemption*. New York: Spiegel & Grau.

Stevens, J. D. (1973). The black reaction to *Gone With the Wind*. *Journal of Popular Film, 2*(4), 366–371. doi:10.1080/00472719.1973.10661707

Stirgus, E. (March 19, 2019). Morris Brown continues to seek reaccreditation. *The Atlanta Journal-Constitution*. https://www.ajc.com/news/local-education/morris-brown-college-seek-accreditation/mHUWzdYJ0r2nAOA7BeXWuM/

Serisier, T. (2017). Sex crimes and the media. Oxford Research Encyclopedia of Criminology and Criminal Justice. https://dx.doi.org/10.1093/acrefore/9780190264079.013.118.

Time Magazine. (1961). The president-elect: City upon a hill. January 1, 1961. https://millercenter.org/the-presidency/presidential-speeches/january-9-1961-cit

Todd, W. A. (2018). Convict lease system. http://georgiaencyclopedia.org

Towns, G. (1948). Phylon Profile, XVI: Horace Bumstead, Atlanta University President (1888–1907). *Phylon (1940-1956), 9*(2), 109–114. doi:10.2307/272179

US Department of Education. (2018). White House initiative on historically black colleges and universities. https://sites.ed.gov/whhbcu/about-us

Wilson William, J. (1996). *When work disappears: The world of the new urban poor*. Vintage Books: New York.

Wood, B. (2014). Slavery in Colonial Georgia. New Georgia Encyclopedia. http://georgiaencyclopedia.org

CHAPTER 3

The Emergence of Atlanta University

Tell them, General, we are Rising.

—Bacote, 1969

The above were the words of a youth spoken in response to General Howard's asking his class what they would like him to share with their peers in the North about their School. Indeed, the early years marking the beginning of Atlanta University occurred within the context of the process of rebuilding of the South in the aftermath of the extreme physical devastation and human costs of a war that had taken the lives of nearly as many as the combined number of Americans killed in all other wars waged by the United States in the 19th century (Catton, 2004). Moreover, this was a nation that was not only affected by deeply held divisions around what historian Kenneth Stampp (1835), in his examination of slavery in the antebellum South referred to as the "peculiar institution of slavery," but also by a seething anger over the loss of a war that cut deeply into the Southern sense of justice. Moreover, the South was still harboring feelings of righteous indignation over the interference of Northern "carpetbaggers" converging on the South during Reconstruction and their intent on dismantling the social contract established between blacks and whites that had been enforced since the Colonial period.

The beginnings of the university emerged from the work of the American Missionary Association, a protestant missionary group dedicated to the abolition of slavery. The work of the Association was joined by the Georgia office of the Freedmen's Bureau soon after it was established in 1865. With the Association taking the lead, the two organizations assumed the gargantuan task of integrating former slaves into what was to be the New South. Education was to be the primary tool for accomplishing this task.

Find a Way or Make One. Alma J. Carten, Oxford University Press (2021). © Oxford University Press.
DOI: 10.1093/oso/9780197518465.001.0001.

Believing that the gospel was a powerful weapon against slavery, the American Missionary Association had been active in the abolitionist movement long before the beginning of the Civil War (DeBoer, 2016; Richardson, 2009). According to the descriptive summary of the Atlanta University Collection housed in the archival holdings of the Auburn Avenue Research Library on African American Culture and History, the story of the University began immediately after the end of the Civil War. The seeds were planted when the American Missionary Association held its first classes for the children of freed men and women in a church and a discarded railroad boxcar. According to archival documents, these were children whose,

> . . . humanity had been acknowledged by the winning of that terrible war. These classes said, in effect, that there had been a purpose to all the war's suffering, that the situation of the children of the slaves was not hopeless, that they would be led to the highest expression of their humanity. (Atlanta University Collection, American Missionary Association, Auburn Avenue Research Library)

These first classes, known as the Storrs School, sowed the seeds for what would become Atlanta University and the academic home of the School of Social Work.

Bacote (1969), in his detailed account of the early days and weeks of the beginning of the School, described Atlanta as a city in chaos, endeavoring to rebuild itself in the ruins left by Sherman's Army. Frederick Ayer, who had a long history of missionary work with the Association and prior experience in setting up schools for Native Americans following their resettlement on reservations, was the first to be sent to Atlanta by the Association. When he arrived in the city accompanied by his wife to begin the work of setting up the school, he found a city overflowing with destitute and homeless blacks who had left rural areas seeking refuge in what they believed would be the "Promised Land."

Along with the federal government that was providing temporary shelters and distributing food to the estimated 35,000 Atlanta residents and the destitute from the surrounding areas who were in need of some form of relief, Ayer found two former slaves, James Tate and Grandson B. Daniels, who were conducting classes for other newly freed slaves in an old church building. This church was the original home of the Big Bethel African American Methodist Episcopal Church (Bacote, 1969, p. 4). These activities were not only the beginning of the first school for "Negro" children, but were also poignant representations of the resilience of blacks in this singular effort of two newly freed men. Functioning in the role of what is known today as first responders they established education as a priority in what was in essence a triaging of the needs of formerly enslaved blacks. In the years of disillusionment following the failures of Reconstruction, their efforts were an illustration of the continuing determination and commitment of blacks to work in their own behalf to secure the collective betterment of their race.

A further illustration of this self-help tradition as a historic feature of the black experience, the financial records of first efforts in establishing these schools indicate that blacks themselves made generous financial contributions to support the schools. In 1869, for instance, some of the schools in the state were supported exclusively by blacks. Others received substantial financial contributions from blacks in additional to large sums for the repair of churches and the erection to new schools (Bacote, 1969, pp. 14–15).

Lugenia Burns Hope, who pioneered the community-based model, along with her husband John Hope, who was the first African American president of Atlanta University and the Atlanta Baptist College (later renamed Morehouse College), played a major role in the founding of the Atlanta School of Social Work. She spoke to this self-help characteristic of blacks in her memoirs, observing that "the desire of colored boys and girls for an education and the desire of Negro parents that their children become educated furnish almost an epic story of the Negro in the United States." She went on to write that this attribute was misunderstood because blacks were not prone to flaunting their wealth or poverty. It was therefore not well known that Negroes

> are paying annually out of their own pocket hundreds of thousands of dollars for their education . . . much of the money given by church boards for the education of Negros goes to the payment of teachers' salaries and takes the place of what would ordinarily be covered by endowments, so Negro girls and boys pay about as much as high of a percentage of the entire cost of the education as the white boys and girls. (Trevor Arnett Library, John and Lugenia Burns Hope Collection)

The early years of the school were a time of rapid expansion and growth devoted to finding space for the construction of a new building to accommodate the need for classrooms, student dormitories, and faculty housing to support the growing student enrollment. The early years also saw continual renewal and revision of the curriculum and educational programs. The growth of and demand for these schools in Georgia and indeed throughout the South belied one of the most destructive myths of Southern efforts to justify the slave system: that blacks were content in the segregationist's definition of slavery as a benevolent institution (Stampp, 1835).

In illustration of the force of the desire for education as a means to a better life and as a denouncement of slavery, Bacote (1969) wrote about an incident that occurred at an exercise held at the School in the fall of 1868, when General Oliver Otis Howard, the first Commissioner of the Freedmen's Bureau, visited the School. When the General asked the students what they would like for him to tell the children in the North about their school, a twelve-year-old boy responded, "Tell them, General, we are rising." The same twelve-year-old was later said to have written a letter to the American poet John Greenleaf Whittier, a Quaker and abolitionist, correcting Whittier's use of the word "massa" in a poem he had authored about the incident, telling the poet he had mistakenly attributed the word to him "for I have given up that word" (pp. 10–12).

Born in Slavery: Slave Narratives from the Federal Writers' Project, 1936 to 1938 poignantly illustrates that, as was the case for this youth, enslavement was far from being a system in which people found contentment (Library of Congress Digital Collection, n.d.). Even though cloaked in the innocence of childhood, this youth understood the existential meaning of freedom as inherent to the souls of all living creatures—a force that could not be chained even under the oppressive conditions of enslavement.

As the school continued to grow concurrent with increased demand from a former enslaved people's eagerness to have access to education, the American Missionary Association appointed Asa Edmond Ware to come to Atlanta to aid Ayer as the work load became far too heavy for one individual to handle. For Ware, who was also a graduate of Yale, his work on the project was more of a calling than a vocation. For example, when asked the reason for his devotion to the black cause, he responded that this could simply be explained by his being "color-blind" (Towns, 1942). As the first president of the University, Asa Edmond Ware's steadfast commitment to the cause of educating a formerly enslaved people unquestionably accounts in large measure for the survival of the School through the fledging years of its beginning to its flourishing and emergence as a university known for the excellence of its educational programs. These successes were achieved despite considerable environmental obstacles that were the legacy of enslavement and Jim Crowism prevalent in the city of Atlanta and throughout the South.

The advances made in the School during Ware's tenure as president were significant. Commissioner General Howard appointed Ware superintendent of schools for the Freedmen's Bureau for Georgia. Under Ware's stewardship as superintendent of schools from 1865 to 1868, the Freedmen's Bureau spent approximately $100,000 for the development of public schools in Georgia. The American Missionary Association contributed approximately an additional $148,000 for the acquisition of land and buildings for school purposes, along with the distribution of in excess of $50,000 for clothing and other provisions for students. From these efforts, an estimated 30,000 freedmen gained basic education in reading, math, geography, grammar, and US history, and some received training in Latin and algebra (Bacote, 1969, p. 14).

After laying the foundation for a public school system in Georgia, Ware began to move forward in promoting his vision of a university for blacks. He had successfully shepherded the institution through its transformation from providing basic education to an ever-growing student enrollment that initially relied almost exclusively on the *McGuffey Reader* to teach the basics of reading, writing, and arithmetic, and he oversaw the beginnings of an evolutionary process that spawned a normal school for the education of teachers who would staff the fast-growing schools for blacks in the South and the North, a primary school, grammar school, high school, and a college. Ware's vision was to provide progressive levels of education with the overarching goals of training talented Negro youth, educating teachers, and disseminating civilization among the untaught masses. Ware's long-term vision was that, together, these progressive levels of education would be offered under the umbrella of a university (Bacote, 1969, p. 16).

The designation "Atlanta University" was initially used in 1867. Ware, however, recognized that at that time the use of the term "university" was aspirational since the curriculum offerings did not as yet merit the official use of this title. He moved his vision forward based on his conviction that blacks had demonstrated, as evidenced by the performance of his students in the early years of the school, the ability to master the demands of a rigorous course of academic study beyond the basic rudiments and industrial education. For Ware, the path for blacks to reach their full potential and citizenship was exposure to the best education, one that included both industrial and liberal education. An important step in achieving university status was realized when a petition, prepared by a small group of individuals who shared Ware's vision, was submitted to the Georgia legislature and approved on October 16, 1867. A charter was granted for a life of twenty years under the title of *The Trustees of the Atlanta University* (Bacote, 1969, pp. 16–17).

Bacote's historical account (1969) also states that when Ware was a student, he and his fellow Yale classmates were interested coming up with a motto that reflected the inspirational education they had received from Yale. When his vision of a university was realized with the granting of a state charter, the motto chosen for the seal was "I will find a way or make one" (p. 23), thus translating the spirit of Yale to what was to become the beacon for guiding the growth of Atlanta University over the following decades.

The spirit embraced in the University's founding mission and the achievement of students at all levels of academic programs offered dispelled yet another myth: that is, that blacks were not intellectually equipped to pursue a liberal education. Moreover, the charter made no reference to race or color, and the Board of Trustees made clear its race policy in a December 26, 1867, resolution "that the university of Atlanta never exclude loyal refugees and Freedman as such from the full participation in the educational benefits of the said institution or from any other class" (Bacote, 1969, p. 18).

The event celebrating the University charter was conducted with much fanfare. The theme of the keynote address given by an outstanding graduate was "Educate, Educate, Educate" and contained the statement "that white and black be educated together to accustom themselves in childhood to their new relations" (Bacote, p. 21).

Among the documents included in the cornerstone of the first University building were the Charter, the Bible, copies of the Constitution, the Declaration of Independence, the Emancipation Proclamation, the constitution of the state of Georgia, a report of the American Missionary Association, copies of the daily papers, and the names of all the teachers and other university workers (Bacote, 1969).

A reporter of the *Cincinnati Gazette* enthusiastically observed that the event marked a significant departure from the culture of the state and noted that, had anyone proposed seven years earlier to establish an institution embracing all sexes, all creeds, and all colors, "he would have suffered the death penalty but through God's will and the federal armies it has become a reality" (DeBoer, 2016). As significant as they were, these accomplishments had not been achieved in the absence of obstacles and barriers in the context of the hostile larger environment.

NAVIGATING THE POLITICAL TERRAIN

Despite the outstanding careers of the alumni and the progressive successes enjoyed by the School, skepticism continued among whites that blacks were capable of advancing beyond the rudiments of basic primary education. While there was compelling evidence to the contrary, popular opinion anchored in the pseudo-science of scientific racism and conventional wisdom held that the black race was of inferior intelligence. This was yet another myth posing as fact that would be dispelled as the founders of the University moved their work forward. This would not be a path without obstacles. The pioneering founders had to manage a prudent and astute political navigation of the system. This included balancing the inclinations of whites to willingly provide basic education that would allow blacks to take, at best, servile positions in American society and allowing limited access to advanced education to a select few, provided that no efforts were directed towards achieving the social equality of blacks with whites.

When, in 1785, Georgia established the University of Georgia, it became the first state to charter a state-supported institution of higher learning. And, as the credibility of the Atlanta University grew, the Georgia legislature made its first allocation of $8,000 to the University in October 1870. Reflecting both costs and benefits, the state allocation brought the School under the same policies as those governing the University of Georgia. The appropriation brought with it the requirement of a higher level of scrutiny from state officials. The School was now subject to state regulations requiring that a Board of Visitors conduct an onsite examination at the end of each academic year (Adams, 1930; Bacote, 1969; Towns, 1948).

Aware of the skepticism on the part of both the North and South about the intellectual capacity of blacks to progress beyond the rudiments of basic education, President Ware insisted that the site team include members who had been in strong opposition to higher education for blacks. One of these was the state's former governor Joseph E. Brown, who had served as governor of Georgia during the Civil War. Brown was described as highly influential in state politics, an ardent supporter of secession, and he had warned about the dangers of abolition, which he believed would lead to miscegenation and racial equality (Boney, 2002). Brown chaired the Board of Visitors, whose members were openly biased against higher education for blacks based on the belief of the inferiority of the black race. He exclaimed before undertaking the examination,

> I know these Negroes. Some of these pupils were probably my slaves. I know that they can acquire the rudiments of an education, but they cannot go beyond. They are an inferior race, and for that reason we had a right to hold them as slaves, and I mean to attend these examinations to prove that we are right. (Strieby, 1886, p. 363)

The site team conducted an extensive examination. Over three days from June 26 to June 28, 1871 all areas of operation from management to academics and the academic performance of pupils including the basics with the primary students, and for the advanced students in Latin, Greek Geometry and Algebra were reviewed. At the end of the visit, speaking on behalf of the members of the Board of Visitors, Brown reported that the performance of the students over the period of the examination had reversed his earlier thinking about the intellectual potential of blacks exclaiming that he was "*all wrong. I am converted.*" The final report prepared for the state legislature indicated that at

> every step of the examination we were impressed with the fallacy of the popular idea that the members of the African race are not capable of a high-grade of intellectual culture. This rigid test to which the classes in algebra and geometry and of Latin and Greek, were subjected, on equivocally demonstrated that under judicious training, and with persevering study, there are many members of the African race who can obtain a higher grade of intellectual culture. They prove that they can master and solve problems in mathematics, and fully comprehend the construction of difficult passages in the classics. (Bacote, 1969, pp. 46–48)

The report also commended the missionary zeal of the teachers despite receiving what was described as meager salaries hardly sufficient for sustaining the basics of a reasonable standard of living. Commenting on the motivation of this cohort of pioneering faculty in these first schools for freed blacks, DuBois wrote in *Souls of Black Folk* "they came not to keep the Negroes in their places, but to raise them out of their places where the filth of slavery had wallowed them" (DuBois, 1903, p. 75).

DuBois's observations were not shared by all. These pioneering teachers, who were largely whites educated in the North at some of the nation's most outstanding educational institutions, were disparaged for treating their students as if they were social equals, and referred to by some whites in derogatory racial terms for sharing meals and living quarters with their black students. Nonetheless, the faculty carried out their responsibility with courage and resolve in a hostile environment. They did so even though they were not adequately compensated in salary or gratitude for the quality of their work.

Despite the concerns about a program of academic study that prepared backs for more than the rudiments of basic education and the treatment of blacks by President Ware and his staff as social equals, media reporting on the outcome of the examinations not only boosted the standing of the School in Atlanta and the South, but also brought a level of national celebrity to the School. Media reporting helped to assuage concerns among Southern whites about an educational experiment that had the potential for advancing the cause of social equality for blacks since it was reported that the teachers were motivated by educational interests—not political interests.

Concurrent with these positive reviews, by 1887, under the presidency of Horace Bumstead who had assumed the presidency of the University after Ware's death, a perceived increased level of threat posed by the School emerged. This suspicion arose following a closer examination of operations and the increasingly positive public feedback received. With the School's growing credibility, concerns emerged about the possible upending of the black–white social contract. The University's growing prestige led the Georgia State Assembly to worry about the school's considerable influence in shaping public opinions around the intellectual capabilities of blacks. This was combined with unease over the level of trust established between pupils and teachers, which was felt could potentially nurture students' prejudices and negative feelings against their native state (Bacote, 1969, p. 50).

In an effort to mitigate these ever-present white fears, President Ware had earlier accommodated to the requirement that certain books found to be objectionable by the Board of Visitors would be removed from the course of study. He also endeavored to increase the sensitivity of the Northern-trained teachers who were native to the Southern way of life about the use of activities that could potentially alienate students from whites. Despite Ware's concessions, control of the budgetary decision-making process proved to be a powerful tool used by the state legislature to dictate the content of the educational programs and restrict the academic freedom of the faculty.

The use of the $8,000 annual budgetary appropriation from the state was modified in March 1874, at the time of Ware's presidency. A new act, "An Act to Equitably Adjust the Claims of the Colored Race for a Portion of the Proceeds of the Agricultural Land Script," was enacted under provisions of the Morrill Act that called for the establishment of agricultural colleges (Bacote, 1969, p. 49). The appropriation was made with the requirement that board members of the University of Georgia visit Atlanta University to inspect its academic programs and management. Despite President Ware's earlier concessions, concerns among whites had far from abated about the promotion of social equality among students studying at Atlanta University, given its experimental mission. As a preventive measure, these perceived threats were memorialized in the 1875 report of the Board of Visitors that the state budget appropriation would continue "so long as no improper or sinister attempt is made to foster jealousies, and hatred against the whites among the pupils of the School" (Bacote, 1969, pp. 49–50).

Atlanta University received the state appropriation from 1870 to 1873. Over these years, the Board of Visitors' reports were for the most part positive. However, in Bacote's historical accounting of the process, the University continued to be in jeopardy because of the bias among the Board of Visitors whose members were exclusively white men who had not fully bought into the goals of a liberal education for blacks. Consequently, the state legislature continued to use control of the purse strings as a powerful means for controlling the content of the educational programs in an effort to "keep blacks in their place" and prevent what, for whites, would be the creation of an "uppity class of blacks." Concerns for the intermingling of the races was also a concern to the state Board of Trustees.

According to the May 17, 1998, "Statement on Race" adopted by the Executive Board of the American Anthropological Association (1998), there is no scientific basis for assigning people to racial categories based on their physical features, including skin color. Today, the concept of race is typically taught in schools of social work as a political and social construct that assigns privilege and disadvantage on the basis of skin color. Not having benefit of the scientific clarity offered by the American Anthropological Association, prevailing views on the definition and meaning of race, for both the general population and social scientists of the period surrounding the early founding of the School, were informed by empirically untested assumptions of scientific racism that served as the justification for white supremacy.

Skin color was hardly an accurate determinate for separating the white student enrollees from their fair-skinned black student peers since the these black students were very likely to be the offspring of former slave owners.

The practice of white slaveholders siring children with their female slaves as both sexual perversion and for economic gain was a commonly accepted practice in the slaveholding South. The co-habitation or rape of enslaved women was another accepted practice of the "peculiar" institution of slavery, one that added yet other dimensions to the conundrum of complexities and myths surrounding race in the United States. For example, the practice made it possible for individuals of mixed racial heritage who chose to do so to slip easily from being black to white, beginning a practice of what is referred to as "passing." The practice of passing on the part of blacks choosing this option to free themselves from race-based discrimination or to intermarry with whites where their racial heritage may or may not have been disclosed created what historical scholar Daniel J. Sharfstein (2011) refers to as an "invisible line." This invisible line called into question conventional wisdom about the purity of the white race.

Considering the demographics of the school's population at the time, it also seemed obvious that white students would be enrolled since the largely white faculty preferred to enroll their own children in the School. Nonetheless, based on observations of the students' skin color, the Board of Visitors concluded that since both blacks and whites were among student enrollees, this co-education of the races was both a violation of state law and assault against a deeply felt taboo in the Deep South. When the Board of Visitors made its usual visit in May 1887, although the report filed with the Governor characteristically gave the academic and management high marks, it also raised concerns that "we find in attendance a number of white students . . . most of them having some connection to the faculty and other officers and one at least has no connection with the officials." The report went on to assert that the issue had been discussed with the faculty and that they had expressed their "avowed intentions to receive all white students who apply for admission into the school," a policy that the Board of Visitors interpreted to be "a desire to break down the existing barriers against the co-education of the races." In light of this transgression, the report concluded that "the admission of white children to a benefit of this appropriation for students" was both a violation of state policy and a misuse of public funds. The claims were in reference to the Morrill Act, charging that funds earmarked for use exclusively for black students were being redirected to the education of white students (Bacote, 1969, pp. 86–88).

The Georgia State Legislature acted swiftly to enact the *Glenn Bill* to stop the practice of the co-education of black and white children. The Bill made it illegal for any educational institution in the state established to train Negro children to admit any white person, for any educational institution for whites to receive any Negro pupil, or for any educational institution to accept both white and Negro children. Moreover, the punishment was harsh for transgressors of the legislation. The dictates of the Bill required that any teacher, manager, or controller of such institutions who violated the mandates of the Bill was subject to a fine not exceeding $1,000, imprisonment of not more than six months, or work on the chain gang or the public works for not more than twelve months. Judges were allowed to use their discretion in ordering additional punishments. The Bill also decreed that, for institutions chartered by the state, such as Atlanta University, not only the teachers but also the "president, secretary and members of the board of trustees or other persons holding offices on the Board" who disregarded the mandates of the Bill were subject to the same level of punishment outlined for all other offenders (Bacote, 1969, p. 90).

After a series of unsuccessful attempts to negotiate a plan that would be acceptable to the state legislature and the University Board of Trustees, the $8,000 state appropriation was withdrawn from the University in 1887. For the Atlanta University Board of Trustees, the founding principles of the University as outlined in the Charter for the equal treatment of the races were non-negotiable. Therefore, under no circumstance was the Board of Trustees willing to yield to the state requirement for the segregation of the races.

The stalemate meant that the $8,000 appropriation was left to accumulate in the state treasury. At least that was the case until the federal government stepped in and threatened to cut off funding since the funds were not being used, an action which in turn motivated the Georgia State Assembly to approve an Act in 1890 to establish the State Industrial College for Colored Youth. The College temporarily opened in Athens and later moved to a permanent location in Savannah. The new School met the state requirement for the exclusive enrollment of black students. And, in consideration of the shared goal—a priority among black educators—of increasing access to education for blacks, the new School became operative with a generous amount of technical assistance from the faculty and staff of Atlanta University. The name of the College was later changed to Savannah State College, then to Savannah State University in 1996.

As reported in the archives of the University of Georgia System, Dr. Cheryl Davenport Dozier, an alumnus of the Atlanta University School of Social Work, was appointed permanent president of the Savannah State University on May 9, 2011. On the occasion of her retirement in June 2019, she remarked, in the spirit of the founders of her alma mater, that "I've always been a leader. I will continue to be an educator and an advocate for student success" (University System of Georgia, n.d.a,b).

Savannah State University is now counted among Georgia's ten HBCUs. The negotiated compromise the Board of Trustees secured with the state board of governors at the time made it possible for Atlanta University to participate in expanding the number of institutions of higher learning for blacks, at the same time maintaining fidelity to the founder's vision of a program of excellence and of the highest quality of education open to all races. Despite formidable environmental threats imposed by the Georgia state legislature and the general population of whites, in keeping with the motto established at the laying of the cornerstone for the first building to "find a way or make one," the University made notable accomplishments over President Ware's administration.

Ware's vision of a University for blacks had taken root in the experiences of teaching the children of newly freed blacks in classes held in a discarded box car in the ruins of the city of Atlanta. At the time of his death, he had successfully garnered the support of individuals and philanthropic organizations in both the North and the South and gained financial independence from the American Mission Association. Enrollment more than tripled over his administration. Alumni were holding prestigious positions in the professions throughout the nation, with the largest share employed as teachers in schools for blacks. The University gained a unique reputation for its adoption of educational programs of both liberal arts and vocational training. Both specializations were carried out to ensure the highest standard of academic excellence, and this became a distinguishing feature of the University.

Towns (1948), writing on the contributions of Horace Bumstead who was appointed to the presidency after the untimely death of President Ware, suggested that Bumstead as the incoming president faced two challenges in moving the University forward over his tenure. One was continuing President's Ware's commitment to higher education for blacks beyond rudimentary levels in the face of considerable opposition from whites committed to the status quo, the other was maintaining the economic solvency of the University after withdrawal of the $8,000 appropriation from the State in 1887. The School continued to make considerable progress during the tenure of the second president. In response to the more blatant forms of white racism that accompanied white backlash as blacks crept closer to securing a reasonable quality of life, President Bumstead encouraged his students to "show courtesy without servility: conciliation without humiliation, manhood without defiance" (Towns, 1942).

The withdrawal of state appropriation called for Bumstead to increase the level of financial support obtained from individuals and philanthropic organizations. This required a good deal of travel around the state and the North. Initially, because of outrage from Northern progressives about the Georgia State Assembly's position on the segregation of the races, donations from the North increased, but soon dried up. In addition, individual donors and philanthropic organizations raised concerns about the duplication of services provided by the cluster of schools in Atlanta, and they encouraged the consolidation of educational programs in the interest of avoiding duplication and conserving costs.

Advances in the University throughout Bumstead's presidency continued to support its long-term sustainability, and the increase in the level of fundraising activities soon made it possible to establish an endowment. Moreover, Dr. Bumstead's decision to recruit the young and gifted scholar W. E. B. DuBois to join the faculty would ultimately bring a level of scholarly innovation and intellectualism about the black experience that would have a lasting impact on the academic culture of the Atlanta University Consortium. DuBois scholarship went beyond the University and influenced innovations in theory building that promoted an accurate understanding of the black experience that future generations of African American academics and social scientists would continue to build on.

THE ATLANTA UNIVERSITY STUDIES

Sharing DuBois's concept of the "talented tenth" in the belief that the progress of the black race would be advanced by "exceptional individuals," Bumstead brought DuBois to the University in 1897 to teach history and economics and establish a sociology department. This would be but one of the significant contributions DuBois would make over his tenure at the University.

While at the University, DuBois wrote some of his best-known works, including *The Souls of Black Folk*, *Dusk of Dawn*, and *Black Reconstruction*. He also established *Phylon,* a journal for the dissemination of scholarly works on the African American experience. Yet again ahead of his time, DuBois promoted science as the engine for driving social change and progress for the black community. Building on his ethnographic study of black life published in *The Philadelphia Negro* (1899), DuBois envisioned a central location at the University, a center that would bring together an interdisciplinary mix of African American scholars to conduct and publish findings from empirical research on virtually all aspects of the "Negro Problem."

The Atlanta University Studies were designed to examine the social, economic, and physical conditions of black Americans making the transition from enslavement to freedom and their migration from the rural South to metropolitan urban cities. In carrying out this work, DuBois established an annual conference to study a single aspect of Negro problems. The findings of each year's studies were published in the *Atlanta University Publications*. His plan was to replicate the study of each topic at regular intervals as a means of measuring changes in outcomes and examining causal relationships. Although the quality of the studies is said to have varied from year to year and was hampered by insufficient funding, taken together, they represent a major resource for understanding various aspects of the African American experience in the decades following emancipation. In spite of their limitations, except for this project, a continuous social survey had been almost totally lacking in North American sociology. Thus, Atlanta University was the only institution in the world that was conducting a systematic scientific study about

African Americans between 1910 and 1925. Moreover, nearly every study on Negro life during the period cited a publication from the *Atlanta University Publications* (Rudwick, 1957).

Phylon, currently published as a quarterly journal, was initially established by DuBois in 1940, as a means for bringing together scholars and researchers to examine and distribute findings of research conducted on problems and the solutions to these problems impacting African Americans. For example, in a letter dated April 4, 1941, to Alvin Jones at Xavier University in New Orleans DuBois wrote

> The dean of your university has indicated that you would be interested in the first Phylon Institute and 25th Atlanta University conference which we are holding Atlanta University April 17 and 18th and 19th Some 40 legal institutions of the South are going to be present and we are going to begin a systematic study of the economic conditions and trends of the American Negro. We are hoping to lay out a long-term plan of cooperation both for information and for remedies. We would be glad to have knowledge of any studies you have made touching the economic condition of Negroes in your state or elsewhere, board and lodging for the duration of the conference will be furnished free. (DuBois, 1941)

Jones enthusiastically accepted DuBois's invitation. His letter confirming his attendance indicated that he had far too many studies to list in the letter, and he directed DuBois to a study he had conducted with Carnegie Corporation support on labor and gambling in the New Orleans region (Jones, 1941).

COMPETING IDEOLOGIES OF THE "TALENTED TENTH" AND THE ATLANTA COMPROMISE

Booker T. Washington, along with DuBois, had considerable influence on thinking about how to educate blacks to bring the race into full citizenship. The two men were, however, of decidedly different minds on the best approach for accomplishing this goal. Unlike DuBois, who championed the concept of the "talented tenth," Washington, deferring to white fears, advocated a philosophical approach favoring industrial education for blacks. Washington's incrementalistic approach trumped DuBois's more urgent stance for securing the full political and social equality for blacks because it was more appealing to whites.

Washington, born into enslavement, was the founder, in 1881, and first principal of Tuskegee Normal School for Colored Teachers in Tuskegee, Alabama. Now named Tuskegee University, it is designated a historic US landmark. His autobiography *Up from Slavery* (Washington, 1901) is a composite of his many speeches and lectures that give insights into his thinking on matters of national concern about what by now was defined as the "Black Problem." The book begins with a narrative that provides a window into the system of enslavement around the years 1858 and 1859, which Washington believed were the likely years of his birth.

> I was born a slave on a plantation in Franklin County, Virginia. I am not quite sure of the exact place or exact date of my birth, but at any rate I suspect I must have been born somewhere and at some time. The earliest impressions I can now recall are of the plantation and the slave quarters—the latter being the part of the plantation where . . . the slaves had their cabins. My life had its beginning in the midst of the most miserable, desolate, and discouraging surroundings. This was so, however, not because my owners were especially cruel, for they were not, as compared with many others.
>
> Of my ancestry I know almost nothing. In the slave quarters, and even later, I heard whispered conversations among the colored people of the tortures which the slaves, including, no doubt, my ancestors on my mother's side, suffered in the middle passage of the slave ship while being conveyed from Africa to America. (Washington, 1901, pp. 1–2)

When the Proclamation of Emancipation was issued by President Abraham Lincoln on January 1, 1863, declaring "that all persons held as slaves within the rebellious states are, and henceforward shall be free," Washington was nine years of age. In an address given at the Republican Club in 1909, on the centennial of the birthday of Abraham Lincoln, and reflecting on his first recollection of Lincoln, Washington remarked being

> awakened early one morning before the dawn of day, as I lay wrapped in a bundle of rags on the dirt floor of our slave cabin, by the prayers of my mother, just before leaving for her day's work, as she was kneeling over my body earnestly praying that Abraham Lincoln might succeed, and that one day she and her boy might be free. You give me the opportunity here this evening to celebrate with you and the nation the answer to that prayer. (https://www.whatsoproudlywehail.org/curriculum/the-american-calendar/address-on-abraham-lincoln)

By any measure, Washington's rise from enslavement to educator, orator, author, and consultant to US presidents was far beyond extraordinary. While his accomplishments are formidable to say the least, and despite the wide breadth of his public talks, much attention has focused on his speech that has become known as the "Atlanta Compromise." This highly controversial speech was given in 1895, at the Cotton States and International Exposition in Atlanta. Washington's speech, "Cast down your buckets where you are"

(Washington, 1895), became one of the most important as well as infamous speeches of the period on black–white relations. Washington's position, as expressed in the speech, continues to be eschewed for the highly controversial phrase on what has become known as the "five fingers on the hand" portion of his remarks, a phrase that is widely interpreted as an expression of a willingness to accept second-class citizenship for blacks as a tradeoff for economic security through vocational training.

> As we have proved our loyalty to you in the past, in nursing your children, watching by the sick-bed of your mothers and fathers, and often following them with tear-dimmed eyes to their graves, so in the future, in our humble way, we shall stand by you with a devotion that no foreigner can approach, ready to lay down our lives, if need be, in defense of yours, interlacing our industrial, commercial, civil, and religious life with yours in a way that shall make the interests of both races one. In all things that are purely social we can be as separate as the fingers, yet one as the hand in all things essential to mutual progress. (Harlan, 1974)

In his autobiography, Washington wrote of how well his remarks were received by Southern whites who had feared that his speech would renounce them. To the contrary, his remarks were received as nonconfrontational, comforting, and lacking in a disruption of the long-standing social contract between blacks and whites (Washington, 1895).

Initially, Washington's speech was embraced by DuBois. But DuBois later became a harsh critic of Washington as he moved away from Washington's incrementalism and gradual pursuit of rights to full citizenship through his participation in the founding of the NAACP. In critique of Washington's position, DuBois (1903) offered that

> it has been claimed that the Negro can survive only through submission. Mr. Washington distinctly asks that black people give up, at least for the present, three things,
>
> First, political power,
> Second, insistence on civil rights,
> Third, higher education of Negro youth.
>
> This policy has been courageously and insistently advocated for over fifteen years. . . . As a result of this tender of the palm-branch, what has been the return? In these years there have occurred:
>
> 1. The disfranchisement of the Negro.
> 2. The legal creation of a distinct status of civil inferiority for the Negro.
> 3. The steady withdrawal of aid from institutions for the higher training of the Negro. (DuBois, 1903, pp. 41–42)

Looking back, the city of Atlanta had made a quick recovery in the years following the Civil War, earning for it the symbol of the phoenix in recognition of its legacy of rising from the ashes of devastation left by the Civil War. The city was named the new capitol of Georgia in 1868 and promoted as the "Gateway City to the New South." The country and Atlanta entered the 20th century with the segregation of the races remaining the "law of the land" as decreed by the 1896 Supreme Court decision. But race relations in Atlanta and the nation were to assume new dimensions with a growing sense of urgency for securing black rights following World War I and population and demographic shifts set in motion by the Great Migration.

The University and the country, as did the profession of social work, moved forward in the 20th century under the shadow of the legacy of slavery and the residual influences of two landmark Supreme Court rulings: the *Dred Scott* ruling that held blacks had no rights that whites where bound to affirm and the 1896 *Plessy v. Ferguson* ruling that relegated blacks to second-class citizenship in all areas of public life, including the soon-to-be-developed social welfare agencies that were developed under the reforms of the Progressive Era.

Paradoxically, America set about embarking on living out the ideal of the American Experiment anchored in the timeless premise of "we hold these rights to self-evident, that all men are created equal and endowed with the inalienable right of life, liberty and the pursuit of happiness." The nation embarked on this process blinded by the belief, that has been suggested in earlier discussions, may be explained by assumptions underlying cognitive dissonance theory that such a noble experiment in democracy could comfortably co-exist in a society in which the United States Constitution was framed to systematically deny African Americans the right to full citizenship and participation in the economic and social life of the country—a contradiction that set the stage for the need for a school of social work for Negro Social Workers in Atlanta, Georgia.

REFERENCES

Adams, M. W. (1930). *The history of Atlanta University, 1865–1929*. Atlanta: Atlanta University Press.

American Anthropological Association. (1998). Statement on race. https://www.americananthro.org/ConnectWithAAA/Content.aspx?ItemNumber=2583

Atlanta University Collection. Archives Division, Auburn Avenue Research Library on African American Culture and History, Atlanta-Fulton Public Library System. https://aspace-aafa.galileo.usg.edu/repositories/2/resources/79. Reports/Essays-by members of the American Missionary Association, 1869. Atlanta University collection. Auburn Avenue Research Library on African-American Culture and History. https://aspace-staging-aafa.galileo.usg.edu/repositories/2/archival_objects/36605. Accessed June 08, 2020.

Bacote, C. A. (1969). *The story of Atlanta University: A century of service, 1865–1965.* Princeton, NJ: Princeton University Press.

Benbow, M. (2010). Birth of a quotation: Woodrow Wilson and "like writing history with lightning." *Journal of the Gilded Age and Progressive Era, 9*(4), 509–533. http://www.jstor.org/stable/20799409

Boney, F. N. (2002). Joseph E. Brown (1821–1894). New Georgia Encyclopedia. http://georgiaencyclopedia.org

Born in Slavery: Slave Narratives from the Federal Writers' Project, 1936–1938. http://www.loc.gov/teachers/classroommaterials/connections/narratives-slavery/history.html

Catton, B. (2004). *The Civil War.* New York: Houghton Mifflin Company.

DeBoer, C. M. (2016). *His truth is marching on: African Americans who taught the freedmen for the American Missionary Association, 1861–1877.* New York: Routledge.

DuBois, W. E. B. (1899). *The Philadelphia Negro: A social study.* Philadelphia: University of Pennsylvania.

DuBois, W. E. B. (1903). *The souls of black folk.* Chicago: A. C. McClurg.

DuBois, W. E. B. (1941). Letter from W. E. B. DuBois to Alvin Jones, April 4, 1941. W. E. B. DuBois Papers (MS 312). Special Collections and University Archives, University of Massachusetts Amherst Libraries.

Harlan, L. R. (Ed.). (1974). *The Booker T. Washington papers, Vol. 3* (pp. 583–587). Urbana: University of Illinois Press.

Jones, A. (1941). Letter from Alvin H. Jones to W. E. B. DuBois, April 9, 1941. W. E. B. DuBois Papers (MS 312). Special Collections and University Archives, University of Massachusetts Amherst Libraries.

Library of Congress Digital Collections. (n.d.). *Born in Slavery: Slave Narratives from the Federal Writers' Project, 1936 to1938.* http://www.loc.gov/teachers/classroommaterials/connections/narratives-slavery/history.html

Richardson, J. M. (2009). *Christian Reconstruction: The American Missionary Association and Southern Blacks, 1861–1890.* Tuscaloosa: University of Alabama Press.

Rudwick, E. (1957). W. E. B. DuBois and the Atlanta University Studies on the Negro. *The Journal of Negro Education, 26*(4), 466–476. doi:10.2307/2293494

Sharfstein, D. J. (2011). *The invisible line: Three American families and the secret journey from black to white.* New York: Penguin Press.

Stampp, K. M. (1835). The Peculiar Institution: Slavery in the Ante-Bellum South (New York: Vintage, 1956). *See also Harold M. Hyman and William M. Wiecek, Equal Justice Under Law: Constitutional Development, 1875,* 13–14.

Strieby, D. D. (1886). *Forty years of missionary work—past and present (Vol. 40, No. 12).* New York: American Missionary Association.

Towns, G. (1942). The Sources of the Tradition of Atlanta University. *Phylon (1940–1956), 3*(2), 117–134. doi:10.2307/271517

Towns, G. (1948). Phylon Profile, XVI: Horace Bumstead, Atlanta University President (1888–1907). *Phylon (1940–1956), 9*(2), 109–114. doi:10.2307/2

University System of Georgia. (n.d.a). Dozier Named President of Savannah State University Atlanta—May 9, 2012. https://www.savannahstate.edu/News/2012/05/09/Dr-Cheryl-D-Dozier-named-president-of-Savannah-State-University

University System of Georgia. (n.d.b). Savannah State University President Dozier announces plans to retire as president Atlanta—January 4, 2019https://www.usg.edu/news/release/savannah_state_university_president_dozier_announces_plans_to_retire_as_pre

Washington, B. T. (1895). Washington delivers the 1895 Atlanta Compromise Speech Booker T. http://historymatters.gmu.edu/d/39/

Washington, B. T. (1901). *Up from slavery: An autobiography*. Garden City, NY: Doubleday.

FURTHER READING: ARCHIVAL DOCUMENTS

Administrative correspondence. (1885–1906). Horace Bumstead records, Series 3. Robert W. Woodruff Library of the Atlanta University Center, Inc. http://localhost:8081/repositories/2/archival_objects/68788

Atlanta University Bulletin. (1892–1894). Horace Bumstead records, Series 2. Robert W. Woodruff Library of the Atlanta University Center, Inc. http://localhost:8081/repositories/2/archival_objects/68785

Atlanta University Presidential Records. Frederick Ayer Records. Archives Research Center. Robert W. Woodruff Library at Atlanta University Center. http://localhost:8081/repositories/2/resources/86

Dr. Ayer appointment to Atlanta by the American Missionary Association (September 1, 1866). Frederick Ayer records, Robert W. Woodruff Library of the Atlanta University Center, Inc. http://localhost:8081/repositories/2/archival_objects/102773

John and Lugenia Hope Papers. (1888–1947). https://auctr.on.worldcat.org/oclc/38477184

Memorabilia. (1893–1906). Horace Bumstead records, Series 7. Robert W. Woodruff Library of the Atlanta University Center, Inc. http://localhost:8081/repositories/2/archival_objects/68822

CHAPTER 4

Legitimating the Need

The existence of black people in a predominantly unsympathetic hostile world is sufficient justification for specialized training for social work in the black community. For this
position the writer makes no apologies.

—Forrester B. Washington (1935)

As preface to a consideration of events of the early decades of the 20th century that influenced the environmental context and created the need for
a graduate school of social work for "colored" social workers, it is worthwhile
to reflect on the meaning of the "force" that W. E. B. DuBois referred to in
his characterization of blacks. It is a force that is, in fact, not only characteristic of the black experience but is also one that is universal and timeless and
runs deep in the souls of all people—and indeed underscores our common
humanity (Dubois, 1903).

It was this force that led to the settling of the original thirteen American
colonies, to the early settlers waging of a Revolutionary War to escape the
tyranny of a distant monarch, and to a Civil War in which Northerners and
Southerners viewed themselves as patriots while holding opposing views reasoned from the commonly held belief that they were endowed by their creator
with certain unalienable rights, that among these were "life, liberty, and the
pursuit of happiness." It is the force that led to the American Experiment so
defined by Alec de Tocqueville on his visit to the young nation as it was in the
process of defining itself as a democratic republic. Operating under the banner
of "Find a Way or Make One," it was undoubtedly this force that accounted for
the survival of the University in the face of substantial obstacles to become
one of the leading institutions of higher learning for blacks in the United
States of the 19th century.

Find a Way or Make One. Alma J. Carten, Oxford University Press (2021). © Oxford University Press.
DOI: 10.1093/oso/9780197518465.001.0001.

By the turn of the century, the University that had its beginnings in the ruins of the city of Atlanta amid the devastation left by the Civil War had evolved from a single classroom held in a discarded box car providing basic education to the children of freedmen to become an institution of higher education nationally known for its educational programs of excellence. It had successfully maintained financial solvency despite the withholding of fiscal appropriations by the Georgia state legislature because of the Board of Trustees' unwillingness to comply with state segregation laws prohibiting the co-education of the races. The Board had held firm to the commitment to provide liberal education to blacks in the face of conventional wisdom that the black race was of inferior intelligence. And, in spite of threats from powerful state officials to tax the school out of existence as punishment for its defiance, the Board successfully maintained the stability and continuing growth of the University.

Under the leadership of its first president, Edmond Asa Ware, the Board of Trustees had not wavered in its commitment to a diverse student enrollment, offering educational programs of the highest quality to mixed classes of black and white students and championing educational programs for blacks that provided access to both industrial and liberal education. This tradition had been carried forward by his successor, Dr. Horace Bumstead, who served as president of the University from 1888 to 1907. In order to do this, Dr. Bumstead, also a New Englander and Yale graduate, traveled extensively throughout the South and the North to solicit needed financial support from like-minded progressive individuals and philanthropic organizations. These efforts generated philanthropic support that included funds from the General Education Board, established by John D. Rockefeller in 1903 to grant support for education in the United States irrespective of race, sex, or creed, with an emphasis on the South and the education of blacks. Financial support was also received from the Peabody and Slater Funds that supported the cause of education for freed slaves and from a wealth of donations of various sizes from individuals who supported the cause of black education. The largest source of funds from an individual was a donation from a New York City merchant, William E. Dodge, whose obituary in the *New York Times* recognized the extensiveness of his work in "educating the colored people and the Indians" (*New York Times*, February 10, 1883). Dodge had made a number of visits to the University after shifting from the position of sending all blacks back to Liberia to believing that God had ordained white men to give generously to the cause of educating formerly enslaved blacks to assist them in becoming good citizens (Bacote, 1969, pp. 79–81). President Bumstead's successful fundraising efforts made it possible to reduce the University deficit and establish an endowment to begin ensuring its long-term financial stability (Bacote, 1969).

The University entered into the early decades of the 20th century under the presidency of Edward Twichell Ware (1907–1919), the son of Edmond Asa Ware. Edward oversaw the continuing financial solvency and stability of the University throughout the early decade of the century until illness forced him to submit his resignation in 1922. Dean Myron Winslow Adams was appointed by the Board as acting president in 1919 and was formally appointed president in 1922.

Noteworthy developments occurring during the term of Edward Twichell Ware included a cooperative arrangement made in 1912 among the University, Clark, Morehouse, Spelman, Morris Brown, and Gammon Theological Seminary to form the Atlanta Federation of Schools for the Improvement of Negro Country Life, of which Dr. Ware was appointed president. These schools came together to address problems impacting the welfare of blacks in both the urban and rural areas of Atlanta.

One of its first projects, undertaken in partnership with the Atlanta Juvenile Court system with funding from the Phelps-Stokes Fund, was the hiring of a black social worker to head an initiative to study crime among blacks in the city of Atlanta. Accordingly, with a research team comprised of Atlanta University faculty and Morehouse students, the initiative examined approximately 1,000 criminal cases.

Another collaborative arrangement under President Ware's presidency and made possible by funding support from the Phelps-Stokes Fund was a new course jointly offered by the University and Morehouse in business law and ethics at no tuition costs to students taking the course. During this period the University also began offering professional courses in education that led to the development of a Department of Education. This development led to subsequent brief consideration that the name of the University be changed to Atlanta University and Teacher Training (Bacote, 1969, pp. 157–158). All of these advances in academic programming were portents to bringing the Atlanta School of Social Work, then operating as an independent school, under the umbrella of the Atlanta University administrative structure.

John Hope became the first African American appointed president of the University serving over a term of 1929–1936. Serving over a transitional period, he was the president of both Morehouse and Atlanta University, overseeing the merger of the University, Spelman College and Morehouse College, that was designated as the Atlanta University Affiliation; and the process of transitioning the University from an undergraduate to a graduate school.

President Hope's ambitious long-term vision was set forth in a six-year plan designed to bring all of the colleges under one umbrella. This structure was to serve as a replication model of a center of higher education for blacks that allowed a sharing of resources in the interest of cost-saving and to avoid duplication of educational programs and that offered both undergraduate and graduate programs. This structure, over time, was to accommodate a graduate school in liberal arts and library sciences, a school of business administration, and a school of social work through an affiliation with the Atlanta School of Social Work. As a long-term goal, Hope envisioned as his "Six-Year Plan" that the University would have under its umbrella a research library; schools of law, medicine, dentistry, physical education, and theology; and an affiliation with the other Atlanta colleges (Bacote, 1969; p. 279; Woodson Archives, John Hope Collection).

Hope's vision of a school of social work was realized under the presidency of Rufus Early Clement, who had assumed the office of President of Atlanta University in 1937. Clement was the longest serving president of the University, holding the office from 1937 to 1957 and from 1966 to 1967. The affiliation of the Atlanta School of Social Work with Atlanta University began in September 1938 and was completed in September 1947, and the School became officially known as the Atlanta University School of Social Work (Adams, 1981, p. 12). With the affiliation, Atlanta University became the academic home of the nation's oldest social work program established for the education of blacks.

The 1912 catalog shows that Atlanta University had three divisions: the college and the normal school, each with a preparatory division. Enrollment that year was 403—40 college students, 62 normal students, 115 high school students in the college prep program, and 183 high school students in the normal program. At that time, half of the Atlanta University alumni were employed in teaching in schools throughout the South (Bacote, 1969; Woodson Archives: Atlanta University Collection). A welcoming message in the August 1915 edition of *Crisis* read

> The university is beautifully located in the City of Atlanta, Ga. The courses of study include High School. Normal School and College, with manual training and domestic science. Among the teachers are graduates of Yale. Harvard, Dartmouth and Wellesley. Forty-six years of successful work have been completed. Students come from all parts of the South. Graduates are almost universally successful. (Ware, 1915, p. 160)

From its beginning, the School had been grounded in the strong religious tradition of the American Mission Association. In keeping with the Mission's tradition of Christian service and its charge to send graduates out with a sense of purpose and duty in service to their own people, University life centered around the Association's dedication to providing a nonsectarian Christian education intended to instill in all students a deep sense of morality and duty to serve the black community.

Now functioning as a University comparable to other well-established universities of the period, Atlanta University boasted an infrastructure essential for sustaining university status. This included a reputation and pipeline for the recruitment of high-performing students, with the prerequisite secondary education to master the rigors of higher education; a committed and well-credential faculty; and a research arm for the generation of the state-of-the-art knowledge-building essential for advancing social reforms and progress in the interest of the African American community. And the extensive holdings of the Trevor Arnett Library now exceeded those of all other white or black institutions of higher learning in the South at the time. A program of student extracurricular activities was also firmly in place that included an athletic department, a debating team, and a musical choir that participated in regional competitions (Bacote, 1969).

Importantly, at this juncture of its history, the University also enjoyed the benefits of a highly engaged alumni that was strongly identified with its mission. Many of the alumni held positions in the professions in the North and South that otherwise would not have been available to them were it not for the education they had received at the University. Motivated by feelings of gratitude and a strong sense of service to their people, and now with the means to do so, the growing number of alumni were giving back in time and financial support to the University with contributions that were both generously and gladly given.

The closing years of the 19th century and early decades of the 20th century saw changing population and demographic trends in the nation and in the city of Atlanta that contributed to consequential systemic and cultural changes. These changes had implications for the continuing development of the University and were instrumental in creating societal conditions that laid the groundwork and need for a school that specialized in the education and training of social workers for practice in the black community.

At the turn of the century, despite its being promoted as the "Gateway to the New South", Atlanta was far from being a city noted for its racial progress. In describing the conditions of blacks in the city, Jacqueline Anne Rouse (1989), in her biography of Lugenia Burns Hope, quotes from Hope's notes on her perception of the status black Atlantans in which she states that by

> the turn of the century Atlanta was the most segregated city in Georgia. As early as 1890 Atlanta had instituted Jim Crow laws that separated the city into distinctive black and white areas. These discriminatory laws reinforce white supremacy by excluding blacks from public accommodations, by establishing residential ordinances that restricted the living patterns of Blacks and contributed directly to Atlanta's neglect of blighted areas, by exposing Black customers to shabby treatment when they entered downtown stores, and by excluding Blacks from political participation and denying them due process of law. (Rouse, p. 57; Lugenia Burns Hope Collection, Woodson Archives)

Practices of segregation and discrimination were legal in Atlanta, and violence was acceptable, if not expected, when undertaken in the interest of keeping blacks in their place and maintaining the status quo. Such was the case with the race riots that erupted in the city in 1906. The riot was fueled in part by the shifting ratio of the number of blacks to whites in the population that was creating a tipping point and disrupting the racial balances necessary for sustaining the equilibrium in black–white relations required for encapsulating blacks in a caste system from which there were no pathways of escape.

Atlanta's African American population was transitioning into a diverse mix of blacks comprised of those with little formal education migrating into the city from what had been rural plantations in the Old South. Upon their arrival they joined an elite class of professional and well-educated blacks who had benefitted from the concentration of institutions of higher learning for blacks in the city and for whom the city was already home. For whites, these population trends contributed to tensions because of fears among the working-class whites, mostly whites migrating from mountainous areas of the state, about black competition for new jobs created in the fast-developing manufacturing sector. These fears were combined with the ever-present fear among whites, irrespective of class or status, that the presence of an elite class of blacks comparable to that of whites posed a threat of the intermingling of the races. These tensions were further exacerbated by angst among whites that the quality of life enjoyed by an elite group of blacks exceeded that of some whites, thus increasing the possibility for the creation of an "uppity class" of blacks. Moreover, the greater intermingling of blacks who carried the bloodlines of their former enslavers with the so-called pure race of whites created a continuing blurring of skin color as a reliable criterion for assigning white privilege.

This seething racial acrimony was further inflamed by efforts of local politicians to disenfranchise blacks and unsubstantiated reporting in the white media that white women had been assaulted by black men. These circumstances of racial tensions had been building for some time and they set the stage for the eruption of the 1906 Atlanta race riots. The riots lasted from September 22 to September 24. When the riots ended, the estimated number of blacks who were killed was between 25 and 40, and numerous businesses had been destroyed (Dittmer, 1997; White, 1995).

The schools in the Atlanta Center did not escape the violence that raged throughout the city. As the violence continued to spread, the schools soon became the target of angry mobs of rampaging whites who threatened to burn down all Negro colleges. Targeting the Center was most likely because, for them, these schools were a symbolic representation of their combined worst fears about blacks achieving social equality and the debunking of myths and conventional wisdoms about the inherent superiority of the white race. At the same time, the University's brick buildings became a refuge for blacks who were fleeing their homes to escape the violence of enraged whites. Men sent their wives and children to seek refuge in the safety of the brick buildings of the University while they remained stationed in black neighborhoods, standing as armed guards to protect their homes and possessions.

Lugenia Burns Hope's notes and recollections of the events during the days of the riots record that the responsibility for protecting the campus fell to her husband, John Hope, who had been recently installed as president of Morehouse College (Rouse, 1989). President Hope, along with other male faculty members, were described as armed with the few guns and ammunition that blacks were able to obtain at the time, and they patrolled the campus in around-the-clock shifts. After martial law was declared, the group was joined by militia from other states who stood guard on Spelman's campus.

In the aftermath of the riots, there were concerns among the city's black and white leaders that the racial harmony that the city had been publicly known for would be replaced with a new sense of agency among blacks that in turn would lead to a more aggressive pursuit of black equality. An outcome of the violence resulted in the formation of a committee comprised of both blacks and whites with the goal to provide a means for cooperation between the two races (Burns, 2009; Godshalk, 2005; Rouse, 1989).

Acts of violence motivated by ethnic and racial differences have a long history in the United States. Race-based violence against blacks can be traced back to the brutality and terrorism that was necessary to maintain a servile black population to support the system of enslavement. The white backlash that accompanied emancipation saw an intensification of violence against blacks that escalated during Reconstruction with the advent of the Ku Klux Klan and their use of the most brutal forms of terrorism. Since the post-Reconstruction decades, it has been commonplace as well as predictable for race riots to flare up again and again in the 20th and the 21st centuries when the lingering effects of white supremacy are challenged in the continuing push for social and economic equality for black Americans. Furthermore, as was the case with the 1906 Atlanta riots, research findings indicate that when residential contact between blacks and whites increases, there is a significant increase in race riots. Consequently, the years during the Great Migration, which brought blacks and whites together in closer proximity, would see a significant rise in acts of violence against blacks in both the North and the South.

RED SUMMER OF 1919

A number of social forces can create tensions and racial acrimony that result in violence. In the summer of 1919, the most violent wave of anti-black riots and lynchings swept across the country. James Weldon Johnson, an 1894 graduate of Atlanta University and noted author of *Lift Every Voice and Sing*, which has become the Negro Anthem, was covering the riots from his post as field secretary for the NAACP. He coined the term "Red Summer" to describe these events and later attempted to organize a peaceful protest to the riots (see Erickson, 1960). As is in the case of most, the riots resulted from a complexity of causes. But, in the analysis of some historians, the riots of the Red Summer were different from those of past years in that blacks—including returning black veterans emboldened by the experiences in World War I—chose to fight back (Norvell & Tuttle, 1966; McWhirter, 2011). Moreover, an added new dimension of the 1919 riots as reported in a *New York Times* article asserted that glaring racial inequalities were leaving some segments of the black population susceptible to seduction by communist propaganda. The article also suggested that the war had created a "different Negro"; that is, one who was no longer willing to accept Booker T. Washington's brand of leadership, one who was becoming more militant and was now more influenced by DuBois's writings. In the Opinion column of the September 1919 edition of *Crisis*, DuBois encouraged blacks to "raise the terrible weapon of self-defense" (DuBois, 1919; Capeci & Knight, 1996). The *New York Times* article predicted that the nation had not seen the last of race riots if the country continued to equivocate in finding effective solutions to address the root causes of the race problem (*New York Times*, October 15, 1919).

The violence that erupts in black communities and is initiated by blacks, such as those occurring in urban areas after the assassination of Martin Luther King Jr. and the acquittal of the officers accused of the brutal beating of Rodney King, occur in the context of events that symbolize the entrenchment of white racism, a justice system seen as incapable of meting out justice that results in the fair treatment of blacks, and in protest to what is perceived to be egregiously flawed US institutions (Olzak, Shanahan, & McEneaney, 1996). Or, as Martin Luther King Jr. observed in a 1966 interview with American journalist Mike Wallace in discussing the reasons for the rising militancy among blacks with the advent of the Black Power movement, "riots are the language of the unheard" (King, 1966). Moreover, for blacks, it is the systems that are symbolic of societal injustices perpetrated by white society that are targets of the violence and destruction. With few exceptions, race riots in the United States have historically been instigated by whites with the specific intent to inflict physical harm on blacks. Furthermore, race riots are fueled by anti-black white backlash when advancements are made in the progress toward securing full equality and citizenship for blacks.

One of the earliest race riots occurred within the context of the Civil War. These were the infamous New York Draft Riots that occurred in July 1863 and that saw rampaging whites set on a path of violence against blacks in response to a new federal draft law requiring the involuntary enlistment of whites into the Union Army. The law fueled resentment among whites about the involuntary conscription to fight for the cause of the emancipation of black slaves—a cause they did not support and certainly not one for which they were willing to lay down their lives. The violence included the burning down of the Colored Orphan Asylum that had been established in New York City by two Quaker women to care for dependent black children. Were it not for the Orphanage, the children would have been abandoned to the streets since they were barred from care in orphanages established exclusively for the care of white children. Not only did the children survive the violence, but the agency itself continued to operate into the 20th century, and today is the parent agency of one of New York city's oldest child welfare agencies that continues to focus on the problems and needs of children of color (Billingsley & Giovannononi, 1972; Carten & Butler, 1998).

Nor was anti-black white backlash isolated to the South. The violence against blacks during the Civil Rights movement of the 1960s was present in both the North and the South. Moreover, as Martin Luther King Jr. observed, many were far more vitriolic in the North than they were in the South. For example, in taking the fight for black civil rights to the North in the 1960s, in what was one of King's first stops, as soon as he stepped from his car in Chicago on August 5, 1966, he was struck by a rock thrown from a mob of whites already waiting in angry anticipation of his arrival. In speaking to reporters later, King remarked "I have never seen, even in Mississippi and Alabama, mobs as hateful as I've seen here in Chicago" (Pearce, 2016).

The intensity of white bigotry accompanying the Civil Rights movement as it moved North is captured in the iconic photograph of a mob of angry whites surrounding 15-year-old Elizabeth Eckort, one of the nine students selected to integrate Central High in Little Rock, Arkansas, on September 4, 1957. What is an even more disturbing image is that of the face, distorted by anger, of Hazel Bryan, a white student who is the same age as Elizabeth. Hazel is at the head of the jeering crowd of adults hurling racial slurs at a lone black youngster who, unfortunately, because of a miscommunication was separated from the other students who had planned to walk together for that first day of School. Author David Margolick's (2011) biographical retelling of the back stories of the lives of the two women underscores what is now known from research on the lasting effects of trauma resulting from racism. Margolick recounts how the racial violence and resulting trauma affected Elizabeth Eckort at both the personal and community levels, while Hazel in adulthood emerged relatively unscathed from these events.

SUSTAINING A CONDUCIVE ENVIRONMENT FOR "RACE WORK"

At the time of the Atlanta race riots in 1906, Henry Hugh Proctor was pastor of the Congregational Church in Atlanta. He was a product of the historically black colleges and universities (HBCUs), having earned a BA degree at Fisk University. He later went on the earn a master of divinity degree from Yale University and, in 1904, was awarded an honorary doctoral degree from Clark University.

After the riots, in an effort to restore harmonious relationships between blacks and whites, Proctor, in collaboration with progressive white Atlantans, formed the Interracial Committee of Atlanta to quell the racial tensions that contributed to the riots. Believing that the riots were caused in part by the lack of recreational activities for blacks, he used the church as the base to promote establishing such amenities as a library, a kindergarten, an employment bureau, a gymnasium, a ladies' reading parlor, a music room, counseling services, and a model kitchen and sewing room for girls. He also helped open the first housing facility for young, employed colored women who had no other dwelling. In his autobiography *Between Black and White* (Proctor, 1925/1971), in keeping with the aspirational strivings of blacks, he was a proponent of self-help a means for the betterment of blacks as a race.

Although underreported, similar services were being developed for blacks in both the North and the South during this period. As was the case in schools developed for blacks during the period, many of these organizations were financed solely by blacks as well as by joint ventures between blacks and progressive whites and philanthropic organizations. The Black Church and women's clubs in the North and South were highly visible as sponsors of homes for the aged, kindergartens, day nurseries, and homes for lone young women who were fending for themselves in new urban environments. Many of these replicated models established by white charitable organizations and social reformers that excluded blacks (Carlton-LaNey, 2001).

Many of the reform efforts to improve the conditions of blacks were undertaken under the auspice of the Black Church, a historic center of black life during enslavement and into the present. The volume of activities undertaken under the auspice of the Black Church to establish normal schools, industrial schools, colleges, and universities led one historian to observe that never before had a wholly illiterate race been successful in reducing its illiteracy by half in a single generation (Billingsley, 1992; DuBois, 1909).

The work of individual pioneering African American social reformers undertaken from the tradition of self-help and mutuality as core values of social reform efforts by and for blacks are described by social work historian Iris Carlton-LaNey (1999, 2001). Carlton-LaNey, in observations about the fundamental values that guided social work practice at the beginning of the 20th century wrote that

> Progressive Era African American social workers' community practice was essentially "race work" to alleviate human suffering and concurrently organize and develop private organizations to change the system. The "race" men and

the "race" women who engaged in the emerging social work professions were among the "talented tenth," the educated elite of the African American community. (p. 311)

These observations are exemplified in the work of social reformers in the city of Atlanta, where black men and women interacted as equal partners in carrying out this "race work." Moreover, unlike white social reformers, who moved closer to the use of a medical model in what became for the profession of social work in the 20th century an ongoing quest for professional status, African American social reformers never saw a dichotomy between micro and macro practice. Current trends in the profession favoring micro-level interventions are the cause of angst within some ranks of the profession who believe that this approach has little effectiveness in solving systemic flaws in which contemporary social problems are rooted. Proponents of the efficacy of a dual approach for addressing contemporary social problems caution the profession about the possible long-term impact of veering off course from its founding mission to serve the poor and advocate for progressive reforms in unjust societal systems (Specht & Courtney, 1995).

Never losing sight of the priority of this mission, the pioneering social reformers working in the interests of the black community operated from the assumption that *cause and function* are inseparable and that the *personal is political*. Moreover, for those at the vanguard of reforms in Atlanta, being strategically located in a city that was a center for both black intellectualism and activism facilitated an environmental context that allowed for the seamless integration of activities of academia, social welfare organizations, and the black community. This was made possible under the guidance of a leadership committed to the common goal of the betterment of blacks, thus making possible the creation of a critical mass essential for meaningful change through collaborations and partnerships.

The cluster of schools of higher education for blacks in Atlanta were well placed to play a central role in advancing reform efforts for the betterment of blacks. The schools had become well established by the beginning of the 20th century and were contributing to the creation of a growing class of elite blacks. Throughout the beginning decades of the 20th century, operating in a context of legal segregation of the races where blacks were largely barred from admission to white institutions and having a near monopoly on the market, these institutions attracted the best minds in the black community.

Moreover, blacks themselves were especially attracted to these institutions because of their cause-driven missions and commitment to advancing the collective well-being of the black community. Consequently, for much of the later decades of the 19th and early decades of the 20th centuries, and resembling DuBois's vision of the "talented tenth," these colleges and universities attracted and graduated high-performing blacks to fill the ranks of the professions of medicine, law, education, religion, social work, and the sciences and humanities across the nation. Many of these individuals would claim a place in US history as well as international prominence—not only for advancing the cause of social justice that resulted in fundamental changes in American society, but also for making the quest for social justice for blacks a global cause as the country prepared to enter into World War I.

FIGHTING FOR DEMOCRACY AT HOME AND ABROAD

When the United States entered World War I, the contradictions of the American dilemma, as characterized by Swedish sociologist Gunnar Myrdal (1944) relative to the unequal treatment of blacks in a country founded on democratic principles, propelled America's "Negro Problem" onto the world stage. President Woodrow Wilson announced the declaration of war against Germany to Congress on April 2, 1917, with the words "the world must be made safe for democracy." Wilson, a Southerner, had conservative leanings on matters of race; he had segregated federal offices, and he had summarily dismissed from the Oval Office and chastised a delegation protesting the showing of the film *The Birth of a Nation* in the city of Boston. The delegation was led by Monroe Trotter, founder of the *Guardian* and a staunch advocate for black rights; they were dismissed by Wilson for the perceived "insolent" manner in which Wilson had been addressed by Trotter [Lunardini, 1979]. Considering his conservative leanings on matters of race, Wilson's framing of the war effort as one to secure the rights of American democracy on a global scale highlighted the hypocrisy of denying these basic rights of citizenship to African Americans at home. As a result, the country's entry into World War I had significant implications for the trajectory of the push for the economic, political, and social rights of black Americans and for race relations in the United States.

Blacks had served with distinction in the American military in virtually every military conflict in which the country had engaged since the American Revolution. This included the Civil War, in which blacks had fought for their own freedom under the command of white officers. In popular culture, the Academy Award–winning film *Glory* memorialized the incongruence of blacks laying down their lives in service to a country in which they were defined as *the other*, held in bondage, and, when freed, assigned to second-class citizenship.

Glory, a semi-documentary, was based in part on the personal letters of Colonel Robert Gould Shaw, who was from a Boston family of high prominence in the Abolitionist movement and commander of a Negro infantry. The film depicts the experience of the 54th Massachusetts Regiment Volunteer Infantry commanded by Shaw. This regiment is representative of the Negro infantry brigades that served in the Union Army during the Civil War, brigades authorized by

President Lincoln in the Emancipation Proclamation and commanded by white officers (Fishel, 966; Burchard, 1990). The film made aspects of the black experience real and accessible to a broad segment of the movie-going American public. It received a number of awards, including the best supporting actor award to Denzel Washington for his moving portrayal of Private Silas Trip. Washington's depiction captured the paradoxical nature and complexity of what DuBois characterized as the "double consciousness" of the psychological experience of blacks in America—of being in a society yet not a part of that society—and the need to define one's identity through the lens of oppressive white society. This is captured in Private Trip's blistering words about the realities of the black experience in America to a fellow black soldier: "Let me tell you something, boy. You can march like the white man; you can talk like him. You can sing his songs; you can even wear his suits. But, you ain't never gonna be nothing to him, than an ugly ass chimp . . . in a suit." Trip, a runaway slave, transforms from a state of self-deprecation born from internalized rage, to one of resistance and empowerment born from hope as he rose above the absurdities of the tenets of white supremacy to give his life to the cause of freedom.

Blacks may have been invested in fighting for their own freedom in the Civil War, but like most Americans, they were reluctant to support the country entering in a foreign war. And as a race they were divided about joining the ranks of a military that mirrored the segregation policies of American society. While some were reluctant to fight in a foreign war to promote in European countries the benefits of democracy that they did not enjoy in their own country, others saw this as an opportunity to advance the cause of black rights in the United States. DuBois was among those who supported black participation in the war effort, urging blacks to "Let us, while this war lasts, forget our special grievances and close our ranks shoulder to shoulder with our own white fellow citizens and the allied nations that are fighting for democracy" (Smith, 2008, pp. 239–240).

Although of short duration, Bacote (1969) wrote of the extensive contribution of Atlanta University to the war effort under the presidency of Edward Twitchell Ware, who was devoted to the cause of peace. These contributions were rendered in the form of support from individuals affiliated with the University, the use of its physical facilities and educational programs, and the use of the campus as a military post. When war was declared, a group of University students volunteered for service but were rejected because of their race. Later, following calls that officer training programs be set up in order for blacks to command black troops in a segregated military, on May 19, 1917, the federal government announced the creation of a training camp for 1,200 black officers in Des Moines, Iowa. Fifteen Atlanta University men were admitted to this program. Overall, of the substantial number of enlisted men participating in the war effort who had some affiliation with the University, twenty-seven were commissioned officers.

The University was also selected by the War Department Commission on Education and Special Training to instruct African American soldiers. This led to the establishment of the Army School for Mechanics and a Student Training Corp which was offered in collaboration with Morehouse College. Students who were enrolled in conservation and botany courses indirectly contributed to the war by planning "Victory Gardens"; this effort was supported by academic lecturers who encouraged community residents to plant their own gardens (Bacote, 1969, pp. 160–162).

Arguably, World War I did little to improve the lived experiences of African Americans in the United States. However, black soldiers returning from the war, who had risked their lives for the cause of democracy abroad and had experienced in European countries whites accepting them as equals, were less willing to be content with the denial of their basic rights at home. They were thus emboldened by their war experience to fight for equal rights in the United States. This created a changed mindset that motivated blacks to follow the lead of returning black veterans in fighting back against violent white back lash.

These were changes that also played a significant role as an impetus for the Great Migration spawned by the rise in industrialization and jobs that had been created to support the war effort. Although underreported in the literature, as suggested in publications authored by historians Lemann (1991) and Wilkerson (2011), the aftermath of World War I promoted one of the most consequential mass movements of people, that continues to have implications for the United States today. These changes were all a part of the continuing, unfolding chain of events that paved the way for the founding of the Atlanta School of Social Work.

ENVIRONMENTAL CONDITIONS DRIVING THE NEED FOR A BLACK SCHOOL OF SOCIAL WORK

The environmental conditions that produced a need for a school of social work for the training of "Negro" social workers occurred within the context of legal segregation, combined with the confluence of demographic sociopolitical trends occurring at the beginning of the era of the Great Migration. These societal changes were joined with the visionary leadership of black scholars and social reformers present in the city of Atlanta who were committed to the betterment of blacks at a time when race-based discrimination was an accepted way of life in the city and in American culture. Customs of racial discrimination were well-established as the explicit norm of life in the postbellum South. Moreover, the North was silently complicit in what had become practices of de facto and de jure policies of racial segregation. Resultantly, blacks, whether they lived in the North or the South, were excluded from being the beneficiaries of those reforms that were occurring during the Progressive Era that set the stage for the emergence of the nascent profession of social work.

In the years following the Civil War and Reconstruction, Atlanta quickly recovered from its near destruction following Sherman's firey March to the Sea. The economy was once again flourishing, and Atlanta was restored to being the most populous city in the state. Atlanta emerged with a renewed reputation as the center for manufacturing and transportation, a status that made it the "Gateway to the New South."

The economic growth and population shifts of Atlanta mirrored trends that were transforming the country as a whole. By the turn of the 20th century, the United States had surpassed the country it had waged a war against to secure its independence, and it was now a world power circulating goods manufactured in America to countries around the world. Atlanta was also undergoing major growth as it was also transforming from an agrarian to a manufacturing economy. The city was fast becoming known as a financial and transportation center, and it would soon rival the industrial centers of the Northeast.

Both the nation and the city of Atlanta were undergoing demographic shifts in population trends as the availability of manufacturing jobs sparked massive movements of immigrants from European countries and black migrants from the South to urban areas. Europeans were leaving their homelands to escape poverty and political and religious persecution. Blacks were migrating to Northern and Midwestern cities to escape the oppressive conditions of the segregated South, as well as from rural areas in the South to the newly industrialized Southern cities like Atlanta to escape the oppressive sharecropping system.

Operating together, capitalism and industrialism created unimaginable material gains and the creation of concentrated wealth for a class of businessmen that came to be called the "captains of industry," or, less favorably, as "robber barons." A laissez-faire capitalistic economy unfettered by government controls and regulations paved the way for the accumulation of personal wealth in the hands of a few and ignored the human and social costs of an overemphasis on material gains and personal wealth creation. Both European white immigrants and blacks migrating from the South were exploited and victimized by short-sighted business practices focused virtually exclusively on capital development while ignoring the human costs that would be borne by the masses of people.

White ethnic immigrants were easy prey for unscrupulous business practices during this period; their motivation to better their situations made them willing to work for little compensation under the most inhumane working conditions. Black migrants from the segregated South were also highly motivated to improve their circumstances through work, but their aspirations were all but ignored by the racism and discrimination that was undergirded by two landmark Supreme Court's decisions. The 1857 *Dred Scott* case (60 U.S. [19 How.] 393 [1857]) stipulated that no black individual, free or slave, could claim US citizenship, and the "separate but equal" doctrine established under the 1896 *Plessey v. Ferguson* (163 U.S. 537, 1896) Supreme Court decision covered virtually all areas of public life in the United States. These racial restrictions and segregationist policies would include the soon-to-be-developed social welfare agencies and social work education programs that emerged within the context of reforms spawned during the Progressive Era.

PUSH-PULL DYNAMICS OF IMMIGRATION TRENDS

The "push and pull" dynamic is a concept used by social scientists in immigration theory to explain the economic, political, and social factors associated with the movement and displacement of large populations of people from their countries of origins and the choices made for resettlement in the receiving country (Lee, 2009; Natter, 2018). The "push" factors that motivate people to leave their homelands are associated with extreme hardships such as economic instability and lack of employment, violence in its various forms, political disenfranchisement, and religious and other forms of personal persecution. Conversely, the "pull" factors for seeking refuge in the receiving country include the perception that here they will find the promise of a better life for their children and families, physical safety, and the personal freedoms denied them in their native countries.

It is this perception that has made the United States a historically popular country of resettlement for new arrivals from across the globe. Hope is ignited at the sight of the Statute of Liberty and the welcoming words of poet Emma Lazarus that are permanently inscribed on her pedestal "Give me your tired, your poor, your huddled masses yearning to breathe free." These welcoming words inspire the belief that opportunities promised by the American Dream are open to all, irrespective of race, religion, or creed.

The push-pull dynamics associated with the mass movement of people across national borders in search of a better life is universal and timeless. It is the reason the Founding Fathers sought refuge in the American colonies to escape the tyranny of the British monarchy. It is the reason we are today witnessing mostly people of color from the Northern Triangle—Honduras, Guatemala, and El Salvador—seeking protection in the United States as they flee from gang violence that targets women, children, and unaffiliated youth for extortion (Meyer & Pachico, 2018).

This dynamic also explains the mass migration of blacks from the South to the North during the Great Migration, during the years between 1916 and 1970 that saw millions of blacks leaving the rural South for northern cities.

The Great Migration is poignantly described by Pulitzer Prize–winning author Isabel Wilkerson in her book *The Warmth of Other Suns* (Wilkerson, 2010). Using verifiable historical data combined with engaging storytelling based on thousands of personal interviews, the author chronicles the lives of three individuals whose experiences are representative of the masses of blacks leaving the South for the North. All of those who left shared in common the belief that the promise of the American Dream could be realized through the new employment opportunities that were becoming available in developing industries and that they would find respite from the burden of the oppressive conditions of Jim Crowism in the South.

Life in the North provided some relief from the pervasive racism of the South. Despite the discrimination in employment, some black families were able to gain an economic foothold that paved the way for the emergence of a black middle class. But, for the most part, conditions in the North were not significantly different from those in the South. Moreover, while many blacks moved out, others had strong roots in the South and opted to remain. Moreover, those remaining may not have had the material resources or lifelines in the North provided by extended kin who had established a degree of economic stability in northern cities. According to reports, the number of blacks living in the South during these years outnumbered those living in the North. And despite the violence that came with the resurrection of the Ku Klux Klan and the repressive conditions of Jim Crowism and legal segregation the South remained the home for the largest share of blacks.

The outmigration of blacks from the South gradually unfolded in the aftermath of Reconstruction that saw the chipping away of black rights despite the promise of a "New South" where blacks would be afforded the rights of full citizenship. This was a promise unfulfilled in the post Reconstruction South, and there was little abatement of the oppressive conditions under which blacks lived in the realities of the New South.

The Black Codes effectively replaced the slave system, serving the dual purposes of ensuring a continuing supply of cheap labor and legitimating any form of violation of black civil rights by whites, including the taking of black lives for virtually any perceived transgression of the black/white social contract no matter how inconsequential. None of these egregious acts of lawlessness perpetrated by whites against blacks with impunity could find redress in the courts. The rule of law was flaunted with the stripping away of Constitutional rights of due process, equal protection under the law, and the right to the vote. Moreover, the tyranny and brutality of the Klan intensified to include public lynchings undertaken as occasions for recreation for whites in which the entire community took part including mothers with their children. And under the exploitive sharecropping system, persistent poverty was a guaranteed way of life for rural blacks.

Any one of these alone would have provided more than sufficient motivation to leave. Yet, despite the oppressive conditions that were a certainty of life, for complex reasons many chose to stay, and the postbellum South remained home to a large share of the black population. Yet despite the extensive social and economic need and hardships that were the companions of life in the South under the oppressive conditions of segregation laws and blatant racism and terrorism, blacks who chose to remain in the South and who needed help could not look to segregated white social agencies for a much needed assistance.

The largest share of blacks migrating from rural areas to Atlanta at the time were those who enjoyed the least benefits from their previous status of servitude. Moreover, many blacks in the postbellum rural South did not have the means or resources to join the Great Migration to escape the oppressive conditions there. Sharecropping and peonage, which replaced slavery with a free labor supply to support the postbellum economy, kept most rural blacks locked in a system that closely resembled enslavement. Indeed, some may well have been living in what had been the cabins of the slave quarters and were sharecropping on the very land that had been the plantations on which they had toiled under the system of enslavement.

Some blacks were fortunate enough to buy the land they were sharecropping and achieve economic dependence. For others, when the books were closed at the end of the harvesting season, after paying rent for the land and for supplies purchased from the landowners, most tenant farmers found themselves trapped in an inescapable cycle of debt and poverty. They were further disadvantaged by illiteracy and the Southern cultural code which ensured that the nefarious accounting practices of unscrupulous landowners were not challenged.

With this being the case, blacks migrating to Atlanta from rural areas were largely illiterate, with limited skills for work in the manufacturing industry centers that were developing in the city. Nor did life in rural farm communities provide experiences for migrants from rural regions of the state that equipped them to negotiate the complexities of life in urban Atlanta. Unsurprisingly, similar to urban areas in the North that were becoming densely populated by white ethnic immigrants that spawned the Settlement House movement, the neighborhoods where blacks settled were overcrowded and poorly serviced by the city. These neighborhoods became the city's slum areas, overburdened with crime, squalor, and breeding places of disease and other forms of urban decay that are the inevitable consequences and characteristic features of neglected city areas.

The worse slums in the city of Atlanta at the time were on the west side, between the Georgia Railroad and Atlanta University. These were areas of the city that were largely avoided by some middle-class blacks, many of whom were long-term residents of the city and were among the well-educated and elite class of blacks who had settled in the vicinity of the University.

These were some of the conditions and environmental forces that spawned the founding of the first school of social work for the training of "Negro" social workers in a city that was already the home of Spelman, Morehouse, Morris Brown, and Clark Colleges; Gammon Theological Seminary; and Atlanta University. The presence of these well-established institutions of higher learning for blacks and the leading academics and scholars who were affiliated with these institutions, most notably DuBois, made the city a center of black intellectualism.

Moreover, in response to the excessively brutal system of social, economic, and political oppression that blacks were living under in the segregated South, Atlanta also became a city of social activism. These oppressive conditions were the catalyst for the establishment of affiliate offices of national organizations that had emerged during the years of Progressive reforms to advocate for the rights of blacks. Among these were affiliate offices of the National Urban League (NUL), the NAACP, and branches of the Young Men's Christian Association (YMCA) and the Young Women's Christian Association (YWCA) (Adams, 1981). The NUL and the NAACP were established to serve the interests of blacks exclusively. The YMCA, since its founding in London, in 1844, advanced a historic inclusive agenda that opened its doors to all men, women, and children irrespective of race, creed, religion, or nationality and had formed Negro branches in Atlanta. The Neighborhood Union had been in operation since 1908, under the leadership of Lugenia Burns Hope, and had been providing community-based services that included healthcare and education campaigns, advocacy for school reforms, and creative arts and recreational activities for youth in under-served city neighborhoods.

These early activities of "race work" were undertaken by individuals imbued with a strong sense of altruism combined with a sense of racial pride and commitment to social and economic justice for blacks. Nonetheless, and unsurprisingly, their work and the organizations with which they were affiliated were underresourced and understaffed. And few if any of the personnel were professionally trained social workers. Nor were the social agencies that had emerged during the Progressive Era in the segregated South willing to open their doors to blacks despite the presence on any measure of the overwhelming need present in black communities.

ROOTS OF THE PROFESSION OF SOCIAL WORK

The Progressive Era, approximately the decades between 1890 and 1920, emerged from humanistic concerns for the unjust treatment of many populations as the country moved incrementally toward the aspirational goal of a more perfect union. With more being learned from the sciences and with leanings toward more humanitarian approaches, reform activities were carried out with the belief on the part of the pioneering social reformers of the period that major social problems were the by-products of rapid industrialization and urbanization and could be solved with the use of appropriate interventions.

By the mid to late 1800s, under the auspices of the Charity Organization Society (COS) and Settlement House movements, regarded as the roots of the profession of social work, organized social welfare responses emerged that combined personal social services, systematic social research, and legislative reforms. Together, the thrust of all of these activities sought to improve neighborhood living and working conditions with a scientific approach aimed at making charitable giving and organizations a more efficient and rational undertaking (Trattner, 1999).

The profession of social work and the soon to follow professional schools of social work emerged out of the social activism and social justice interests that were largely concerned with the plight of white, ethnic European immigrants during the Progressive Era. The new profession developed under the auspices of the COS and Settlement House movements, with their work in urban cities that were popular sites of resettlement for white ethnic European immigrants.

Concepts from social Darwinism formed the ideological underpinnings of the COS and resulted in practices informed by the harsh concept of "survival of the fittest" and the view that the solution to poverty rested with nature. Practices adopted by the COS also replicated scientific management approaches that had produced amazing results in productivity and efficiency in the manufacturing industries. The COS used the strategies of business management as a means for preventing fraud, improving service coordination, and avoiding service duplication in the rapidly emerging social service agencies in urban centers.

The direct service activities of the COS were carried out by volunteers known as "friendly visitors." Unlike the race men and women, who were equal partners in reform efforts, the visitors were the wives of prominent businessmen who assumed an administrative role in carrying out the work of the Societies. While their husbands carried out managerial tasks in the home offices, the women were dispersed to the field, where they were responsible for conducting social investigations and visits to the homes of the poor and tasked with collecting extensive information about all aspects of their personal lives. The hands-on direct service work conducted by the "friendly visitors" was more, if not exclusively, concerned with the moral uplift of the poor. This was achieved by the women's modeling for the poorer classes the lifestyles and values of the upper classes. These activities of the COS workers were focused on the personal behaviors of the poor and gave little attention to the environmental conditions within which they were living.

The Settlement House movement developed in the later decades of the 1800s and took an approach that differed from that of the Societies by focusing on the environmental conditions in which families were living. For example, departing from the ideology of the COS linking attribution theories of causation to the personal behaviors of the poor, theories of causation shaping the strategies of the Settlement House workers were based in the assumption that flawed political, economic, and social systems were responsible for social ills of the day and not the people themselves. Poverty and its social consequences were viewed as the by-products of social change and progress, and people were the victims and not the cause of what were inevitable societal forces and the unintended costs of societal progress and change. The Settlement workers emphasized human relationships and the mutuality and interdependence among all classes of people. The focus of their work was on reforming systems instead of changing individual behaviors and moral uplift, as modeled by the "friendly visitors" (Levin & Axinn, 1975; Trattner, 1999).

The ideological approaches informing what began as divergent views of the COS and Settlement House movements came together as social work's integrative ecological perspective. The integrative perspective formed the theoretical and conceptual underpinnings of social work education curriculum in the predominately white schools of social work as these were developing at the turn of the 20th century. With additional courses and curriculum content of relevance to the black community, this framework was also adopted as the foundation of the educational program developed at the Atlanta School of Social Work.

Together these perspectives continue to serve as the anchoring pillars of social work's person-in-the-environment, biopsychosocial framework which shapes both theory and practice and distinguishes the profession from the other helping disciplines. Acknowledging the historic challenges of achieving a balance between the micro and macro practice approaches, contemporary scholars' reviews of the history of social welfare underscore that neither approach is sufficient in itself as a stand-alone theoretical perspective for understanding people and the reasons for their success or lack of achieving satisfying and productive lives in an ever-changing societal context (Day & Schiele, 2012).

Despite having emerged in urban areas in response to the influx of European immigrants, and in keeping with legal mandates and cultural norms on matters of race, neither the COS or Settlement House movements were especially concerned about the plight of blacks who were migrating to urban cities in the North in search of employment opportunities. However, some of these early social reformers associated with the Settlement House movement joined the effort to support causes to improve conditions for blacks.

The literature reports that Jane Addams participated in the Niagara movement that brought together leading social reformers and scholars under the leadership of DuBois and led to the founding of the NAACP. The literature does not report an expansive involvement of the COS and Settlement House in advancing causes promoting the equitable treatment or full citizenship for black Americans, and the early settlements and social service agencies developed during the period were segregated. It may also be important to consider that reforms of the Progressive Era focused on social problems created by rapid industrialization, poverty, immigration, urbanization, and political corruption. The social activism of the period resulted in important legislation such as child labor laws, compulsory education, minimum wage laws, and reforms of corrupt political systems. However, it would be several decades later that racial equality for blacks became the target of social activism in which whites joined with blacks in the fight for black civil rights.

Jane Addams is the most well-known social reformer of the period. Addams's work at Hull House, in Chicago, is credited as laying the groundwork for the advocacy and social reform focus of the profession. Presidential historian Jon Meacham (2018) wrote of the close relationship between Addams and President Theodore Roosevelt that was based on their shared concern for advancing causes of social justice, which the president had undertaken under the banner of the new Progressive Party, also known as the "Bull Moose Party." Addams seconded Roosevelt's nomination at the new party's convention held in Chicago, in August 1912, asserting that

> A great party has pledged itself to the protection of children, to the care of the aged, to the relief of overworked girls, and to the safeguarding of burdened men. In thanking Addams, Roosevelt responded "I prize your action not only because of what you are and stand for, but for what it symbolizes for the new movement." (Meacham, 2018, p. 96)

The president later telegraphed Addams indicating his support of her interest in equal rights for women: "Our party stands for social and industrial justice and we have a right to expect that women and men will work within the party for the cause with the same high sincerity of purpose and with like efficiency" (Meacham, 2018, p. 96).

Roosevelt also sought the counsel of Booker T. Washington, who had risen to prominence as the recognized spokesperson for the black community and is frequently noted in the historical literature as the first black to have been invited to the White House by a sitting president. Factually, Frederick Douglass, a self-emancipated slave and the most eloquent spokesperson for the Abolitionist movement, was the first black man to have an audience with a sitting United States president at the White House. Douglass was invited to the White House by President Lincoln for a meeting to seek Douglass's counsel on the matter of slavery.

There was a significant difference between Douglass's invitation to the White House for a meeting with President Lincoln and Washington's visit to the White House with President Theodore Roosevelt, which was an invitation to *dine* at the White House. This was an invitation to *dine* at the White House. Washington's visit to the White House caused a good deal of uproar among whites in both the South and the North because such an invitation disregarded the timeless taboo against the social intermingling of the races. Nonetheless, Washington, because his status quo approach to the pursuit of black rights was more palatable to whites, continued to be the most influential spokesperson on matters of race during the period. His remained the voice that whites were most open to hearing.

RECOGNIZING THE NEED FOR TRAINING SCHOOLS FOR THE NEW PROFESSION

The emerging social welfare systems developing for whites during this era carried on the Poor Law tradition of categorizing those in need into the "worthy" and "unworthy" poor. They adhered to market-driven principles for legitimating need and capitalistic values for defining and understanding the causes of and solutions to poverty and unmet social need. This residual approach to social welfare policy and program development adopted in the United States did not serve the interests of anyone who was unfortunate enough to be the victim of social changes beyond their control, and for blacks the situation would be far worse.

The social activism of the Progressive Era and what was the nascent beginnings of the profession of social work also brought to light that good intentions alone were not enough to solve the complex social ills that were the by-product of rapid industrialization and the increasing maturation of capitalism. Therefore, as discussed earlier, largely resulting from the merging of ideologies and practice preferences developed under the auspices of the COS, which favored practice interventions focused on changing individual behaviors, and Settlement House workers, who favored interventions focused on the environment and the reform of unjust systems, schools of social work were established within the United States by the turn of the 20th century that incorporated this integrative approach.

The first of these training schools began as a summer session offered by the New York City COS in 1898, named the New York School of Philanthropy. The course offered on-the-job training to agency volunteer workers that resembled what is currently thought of as "coaching" or "shadowing," with novice or beginning workers receiving feedback on their work and opportunities to observe experienced professionals in action. In 1904, a full course of graduate study was offered under the New York School of Philanthropy. The school evolved from a free-standing social work program and was renamed Columbia University School of Social Work in 1963. Columbia University followed the tradition that had been established by the Atlanta School of Social Work when it relinquished its independent charter to become a part of Atlanta University and was renamed the Atlanta University School of Social Work. This move established the precedent of housing schools of social work within universities to draw upon the knowledge base of other academic disciplines and anchor social work education in the liberal arts perspective, which continues to be the foundation of professional social work curriculum today.

The professional schools in these early years developed under the auspices of the COS, which were located in the nation's urban centers. Their curriculum reflected the practice preferences and theoretical orientations of their founding members. Most of these schools were not immediately concerned with preparing social workers for agency practice that responded to the plight of blacks in the North or the South; this was the case even though blacks were overburdened by the increasing poverty and social ills spawned by dramatic societal changes that were reshaping the country and the Jim Crowism and de facto and de jure racism prevalent in both urban and rural areas during the period.

Dr. Kenneth Clark, the preeminent psychologist and first African American president of the American Psychological Association, conducted the famous "doll studies" with his wife, Dr. Mamie Clark, which provided the scientific evidence to support the landmark Supreme Court decision in the *Brown v. Board of Education* that struck down the separate but equal doctrine of the *Plessey v. Ferguson* decision. These studies provided evidence of a unanimous finding that "separate educational facilities are inherently unequal." Furthermore, their work and observations provide some insight for understanding the lack of concern for the plight of blacks, as Dr. Kenneth Clark remarked: "the iconic fact is that students, research workers and professionals in the behavioral sciences . . . are no more immune by virtue of their values and training to the disease and superstitions of American racism than is the average man" (Clark, 1997).

MARGINALIZATION OF BLACK SOCIAL WORK EDUCATION

Dr. Clark's words ring true when looking at the history of the development of social work education programs established in predominately white colleges and universities prior to the 1964 Civil Rights Act. Social work education in these institutions all but ignored the need for skilled practitioners to practice in the black community or the innovative approaches that were being implemented by African Americans to fill this gap.

For instance, a summary report of developments within accredited schools of social work for 1937 and 1938 made no mention of Atlanta University even though the School had been accredited since 1928 by the American Association of Schools of Social Work (AASSW), predecessor to the Council for Social Work Education (CSWE). Another example includes the Howard University social work program, although not accredited until 1940, however, courses in the social services had been offered by Howard University as early as 1914. And when the school became an autonomous division in 1935, it offered a course of study that conformed with the 1932 accreditation standards of the AASSW.

This summary report was concerned with accredited master's (MSW) programs; however, it is important to mention here that undergraduate courses in social work had been in place at Fisk University since 1911, having been established by George Edmond Hayes, a graduate of the New York School of Philanthropy and founder of the NUL. Neither did the survey give recognition to what at that time were prolific contributions that blacks were making to the field of social work education under various auspices.

More recently, there has been a greater willingness among social work scholars to address these glaring omissions and the failure of social work educators to challenge the existence of accredited social work education programs in racially segregated colleges and universities that were in place in the United States prior to the enactment of the 1964 Civil Rights Act, despite the stated historic concerns for social justice of these institutions (Kayser & Morrissey, 1998; Longres, 1972). The past decades have also seen an increase in the acceptance of research conducted by African Americans in mainstream professional journals. This research brings into the larger social work education community the significance of contributions of black scholars in the academy to social work education in the early years of the development of the profession and social work education.

One such example is research conducted by Gary and Gary (1994) focusing on Atlanta University and the Bishop Tuttle School. Using an exploratory historical method, the study yielded a wealth of information about the extensive contributions of African Americans to social work education in the early decades of the 20th century at the HBCUs. The investigation revealed that the Bishop Tuttle School played an important role in helping to professionalize social work training of blacks between 1900 and 1930, in designing curriculum to support competencies for addressing social conditions that affected blacks, and in introducing courses on the black experience and club work which had become a widely used intervention for community development and organization in black communities. These authors also recognized the contributions of pioneering scholars of the period, including those who played a central role in the development of educational programs that would ultimately become the hallmark of the Atlanta University School of Social Work.

It was this virtual ignoring of the problems and needs of the African American community by the profession and by developing schools of social work that provided the impetus for the launching of the Atlanta School of

Social Work. The School was spearheaded by a mix of leading black scholars affiliated with the institutions of higher learning for blacks in the city of Atlanta and social reformers associated with the new organizations that were established in the city to advocate for the rights of blacks, all of whom were committed to the betterment of the African American community. The anchoring principle for the development of the School's curriculum and course of academic study was fueled by the tradition of social reform established by DuBois over his academic career at Atlanta University and the progress achieved through obtaining objective data from the empirical research undertaken from an Afrocentric perspective. Furthermore, the founders, well-versed in national and international geopolitical affairs, knew that despite the aspirational hopes of blacks who had migrated to the northern and Midwestern states, conditions for blacks in these regions of the country were not significantly different from those in the South. Therefore, they envisioned that, over time, the School would produce a cohort of professional workers who would be dispersed throughout the nation, who themselves were closely identified with the black experience and armed with a professional education that prepared them to do the "race work" needed to advance the social justice and well-being concerns of the black community.

The groundwork for the design of the curriculum and educational program was influenced by the pioneering work of Lugenia Burns Hope's Neighborhood Union, a model of community-based action research. DuBois's *The Philadelphia Negro* published in 1899, was the first comprehensive ethnographic study of black Americans and replicated in DuBois's scholarship at Atlanta University. The study approaches of Hope and DuBois were undertaken from an Afrocentric perspective, and the work of both was based in the assumption that the problems faced by blacks were inextricably linked to the pervasive discrimination that shaped every segment of black life and their communities. The data- and value-driven approach that began with the work of these early pioneers served as the model for the approach taken to establish a training school to prepare a new class of professional workers to serve black communities. Franklin Frazier, who was the second director of the Atlanta School of Social Work also played a central role in influencing professional education for blacks (Frazier, 1928).

REFERENCES

Adams, F. V. (1981). *The reflections of Florence Victoria Adams*. Atlanta: Shannon Press, Ltd., in cooperation with the Atlanta University School of Social Work and the Alumni Association.

Bacote, C. A. (1969). *The story of Atlanta University: A century of service, 1865–1965*. Atlanta: Atlanta University Press.

Billingsley, A. (1992). *Climbing Jacob's ladder: The enduring legacies of African-American families*. Simon and Schuster.

Billingsley, A., & Giovannononi, J. M. (1972). *Children of the storm: Black children and American child welfare*. New York: Harcourt Brace.

Bulleting and catalog subscriptions (1886–1906). Horace Bumstead records, Series 2. Robert W. Woodruff Library of the Atlanta University Center, Inc. http://localhost:8081/repositories/2/archival_objects/68784

Burchard, P. (1990). *One gallant rush: Robert Gould Shaw and his brave black regiment*. New York: St. Martin's Press.

Burns, R. (2009). *Rage in the Gate City: The story of the 1906 Atlanta Race Riot* Athens: University of Georgia Press.

Capeci, D., & Knight, J. (1996). Reckoning with violence: W. E. B. Du Bois and the 1906 Atlanta Race Riot. *Journal of Southern History, 62*(4), 727–766. doi:10.2307/2211139

Carlton-LaNey, I. B. (Ed.). (2001). *African American leadership: An empowerment tradition in social welfare history* (pp. 99–110). Washington, DC: NASW Press.

Carlton-LaNey, I. (1999) African American pioneers' response to need. *Journal of Social Work, 44*(4), 311–321.

Carten, A. J., & Butler. (1998). Is it well with the child: A documentary history of an agency. Unpublished paper presented at the March 7, 1998, at 44th APM Council on Social Work Education, Orlando, Florida.

Clark, K. B. (1997). Kenneth Bancroft Clark papers, 2003. Manuscript/Mixed Material. Library of Congress. http://hdl.loc.gov/loc.mss/eadmss.s998002

The Crisis. (August 1915). https://www.marxists.org/history/usa/workers/civil-rights/crisis/0800-crisis-v10n04-w058.pdf

Day, P. J., & Schiele, J. H. (2012). *A new history of social welfare*. Englewood Cliffs, NJ: Prentice Hall.

Day, P. J., & Schiele, J. (2012). *A new history of social welfare*. London: Pearson Higher Education.

Dittmer, J. (1997). "Too busy to hate": Race, class, and politics in twentieth-century Atlanta. *Georgia Historical Quarterly, 81*(1), 103–117. http://www.jstor.org/stable/40583545

DuBois, W. E. B. (1899). *The Philadelphia Negro: A social study*. Philadelphia: University of Pennsylvania.

DuBois, W. E. B. (1903). *The souls of black folk*. Chicago: A. C. McClurg.

DuBois, W. E. B. (1909). Politics and industry. In *Address from the Proceedings of the National Negro Conference*.

DuBois, W. E. B. (1919). Opinion, W. E. B. DuBois. Let us reason together. *Crisis, 18*(5).

Erickson, A. J. (1960). Red Summer. In *Encyclopedia of African-American culture and history* (pp. 2293–2294). New York: Macmillan.

Fishel Jr, L. H. (1966). One Gallant Rush: Robert Gould Shaw and His Brave Black Regiment. *Civil War History, 12*(1), 80–81.

Frazier, E. F. (1928). Professional education for Negro social workers. *Hospital Social Service, 17*, 167–176.

Gary, R. B., & Gary, L. E. (1994). The history of social work education for black people 1900–1930. *Journal of Sociology & Social Welfare, 21*(1), article 7.

Godshalk, D. F. (2005). *Veiled visions: The 1906 Atlanta Race Riot and the reshaping of American race relations*. Chapel Hill: University of North Carolina Press.

John Hope Records, 1929–1936. By John Hope, Atlanta University. Office of the President. Archival Material 1929.

Kayser, J., & Morrissey, C. (1998). Historically significant memories in social work. Two perspectives on oral history research and the helping professions. *Reflections: Narratives of Professional Helping*, 4(4), 61–66.

King, M. L. (September, 27, 1966). 60 Minutes, Mike Wallace Interview. https://www. cbs.com/shows/60_minutes/video/55KnFpFwXmt4c7KPAhtQ80okA6ST_fXc/ mlk-a-riot-is-the-language-of-the-unheard/

Lee, C. (2009). Sociological theories of immigration: Pathways to integration for US immigrants. *Journal of Human Behavior in the Social Environment*, 19(6), 730–744. doi:10.1080/10911350902910906

Lemann, N. (2011). *The promised land: The great black migration and how it changed America*. New York: Vintage.

Levin, H., & Axinn, J. (1975). *Social welfare: A history of the American response to need*. New York: Dodd, Mead.

Longres, J. (1972). The impact of racism on social work education. *Journal of Education for Social Work*, 8(1), 31–41. doi:10.1080/00220612.1972.10671900

Lunardini, C. (1979). Standing firm: William Monroe Trotter's meetings with Woodrow Wilson, 1913–1914. *Journal of Negro History*, 64(3), 244–264. doi:10.2307/ 2717036

Margolick, D. (2011). *Elizabeth and Hazel. Two women of Little Rock*. New Haven, CT: Yale University Press.

McWhirter, C. (2011). *Red summer: The summer of 1919 and the awakening of Black America*. New York: Henry Holt and Company.

Meacham, J. (2018). *The soul of America: The battle for our better angels*. New York: Random House.

Meyer, M., & Pachico, E. (February 1, 2018. Commentary. Fact sheet: US immigration and Central American asylum seekers. https://www.wola.org/analysis/ fact-sheet-united-states-immigration-central-american-asylum-seekers/

Natter, K. (2018). Rethinking immigration policy theory beyond Western liberal democracies. *Comparative Migration Studies*, **6**(4). hhts://doi.org/10.1186/ s40878-018-0071-9

Myrdal, G. (1944). An American dilemma; the Negro problem and modern democracy (2 vols.).

New York Times. (February 10, 1883). A good-life work ended. The career of William E. Dodge suddenly closed.

New York Times. (October 5, 1919). For action on race riot peril, racial propaganda among Negros growing, and increase in mob violence set out in Senate brief for federal inquiry.

Norvell, S. B., & Tuttle, W. M. (1966). Views of a Negro during "the Red Summer" of 1919. *Journal of Negro History*, 51(3), 209–218.

Olzak, S., Shanahan, S., & McEneaney, E. (1996). Poverty, segregation, and race riots: 1960 to 1993. *American Sociological Review*, 61(4), 590–613. http://www. jstor.org/stable/2096395

Pearce, M. (2016). When Martin Luther King Jr. took his fight into the North, and saw a new level of hatred. Los Angeles Times, January 18, 2016.

Proctor, H. H. (1925/1971). *Between black and white*. Boston: Pilgrim Press. Reprint of 1925 edition. Freeport, NY: Black Heritage Library Collection Books.

Professional school developments 1937–38: A summary report of recent developments, new courses, faculty changes and registrations in accredited schools of social work. *The Compass*, 19(2), 19–30. https://www.jstor.org/stable/23705218

Rouse, J. A. (1989). *Lugenia Burns Hope, Black social reformer*. Athens: University of Georgia Press.

Rudwick, E. (1957). The National Negro Committee Conference of 1909. *The Phylon Quarterly, 18*(4), 413–419. doi:10.2307/273282

Smith, S. (2008). "The Crisis" in the Great War: W. E. B. DuBois and his perception of African-American participation in World War I. *The Historian, 70*(2), 239–262. http://www.jstor.org/stable/24454409

Specht, H., & Courtney, M. E. (1995). *Unfaithful angels: How social work has abandoned its mission*. New York: Free Press.

Trattner, W. I. (1999). *From poor law to welfare state: A history of social welfare in America*. New York: Simon and Schuster.

Ware, E. (1915). *Atlanta University. The Crisis, A Record of the Darker Races* (p. 160). New York: NAACP. https://www.marxists.org/history/usa/workers/civil-rights/crisis/0800-crisis-v10n04-w058.pdf

Washington, F. B. (1935). The need and education of Negro social workers. *Journal of Negro Education, 4*, 76–93.

White, W. F. (1995). *A man called White: The autobiography of Walter White*. Athens: University of Georgia Press.

Wilkerson, I. (2011). *The warmth of other suns: The epic story of America's Great Migration*. New York: Random House.

Wilson, W. (1917). Address delivered at Joint Session of the Two Houses of Congress, April 2, 1917; US 65th Congress, 1st Session, Senate Document 5.

CHAPTER 5

The Scientific Heritage

Social progress powered by science.
— American Academy of Social Work and Social Welfare, 2019

Although long accepted, if perhaps unevenly implemented in practice, as a profession enjoying community sanction and the public trust, social work is obligated to ensure that its practice interventions are based in the best available empirical evidence and produce outcomes that are the most desirable for target client populations. Moreover, with a code of ethics anchored in democratic principles, social workers are obligated to carry out these professional activities in ways that move American society toward the achievement of the aspirational goal of a more perfect union.

Yet, for much of its history, the profession has faced the worrisome challenge of meeting these professional imperatives at the same time that social workers have been increasingly finding more gratification from the use of micro level interventions and one-on-one direct service practice to change behaviors that are troublesome to the individual. Because some members of the profession see little use for research in their practice, claims have been made that professional preferences for micro-level intervention was having the effect of diminishing the emphasis on research and policy in the social work curriculum. Furthermore, taken together, these trends have raised concerns among the social work leadership about their implications for eroding social work's historic commitment to advocating systemic reforms in the pursuit of social justice for historically underrepresented populations and diminishing its credibility as a science-based profession.

The social work leadership has expressed a growing concern about these professional trends over the past several decades. For example, Gordon Hamilton, Associate Dean of the then New York School of Social Work at

Find a Way or Make One. Alma J. Carten, Oxford University Press (2021). © Oxford University Press.
DOI: 10.1093/oso/9780197518465.001.0001.

Columbia University, whose professional identification was that of case-worker, championed an approach that integrated policy, practice, and research. In a presentation at the 1952 National Conference on Social Work, she encouraged a broad perspective on practice anchored in the ethical use of science and set forth a compelling rationale for social caseworkers to assume an active role in the formulation of social policy (Hamilton, 1952). Hamilton was also sympathetic to the critique, voiced by social reformers of the decade, of caseworkers having "too passive of an attitude towards the reconstruction of the social order" (Hamilton, 1952, p. 9).

A January 1968 special edition of the *Journal of Social Work* paying tribute to Hamilton, entitled "Social Casework: Past, Present and Future," made similar observations. This special edition brought together a collection of papers in which the contributing authors presented various points of view on the efficacy of the casework method for solving the social problems brought to light during the turbulent years of the 1960s in which the special edition was published. In an article entitled the "Casework Predicament," Scott Briar wrote that the "very method that caseworkers had worked so hard and long to perfect, systematically excludes many of the people most in need of attention from caseworkers" (Briar, 1968., p. 6). In the same collection of articles, Aaron Rosenblatt reported the findings of a study examining social worker's valuing and use of research in their practice; he revealed that research was rated as "the least used or the least useful" in their various practice activities. For social work students, study findings indicated that research was the course that respondents reported as the "least helpful" in the social work curriculum (Rosenblatt, 1968, p. 56).

These observations are a sampling of the cautionary voices raising concerns about the implication of these professional trends for diminishing the credibility of social work as a knowledge-based profession informed by the best available empirical evidences from the sciences and for eroding the profession's historic concern for social justice.

THE 1915 FLEXNER SPEECH

The drift toward an overemphasis on direct practice had, in fact, been set in motion during the fledgling years of the profession, starting with the infamous Flexner Speech given at the Forty-Second Annual Session of the National Conference on Charities and Correction held in Baltimore, Maryland, in May 1915. An acknowledged expert on graduate professional education at the time, Abraham Flexner was invited to the Conference and asked to shape his remarks around answering the question "Is social work a profession?" In doing so, Flexner concluded that because social work claimed no knowledge base that was uniquely its own and functioned largely in an ancillary role with other professional disciplines, it was not a profession. The conclusions of the Flexner Speech sparked what would be an ongoing quest for professional status that has followed the profession into the 21st century (Flexner, 1915; Trattner, 1999).

Soon after the speech was given, Mary Richmond's classical book *Social Diagnosis* (Richmond, 1917) was published by the Russell Sage Foundation. With more than 500 pages, the carefully researched volume laid out a meticulously detailed process of the casework method of study, diagnosis, and treatment. The volume outlined what Richmond envisioned would establish a theoretical framework to inform the direct practice model that could be uniformly applied and used by caseworkers across all fields of practice, making modifications as required in drawing on the specialized knowledge needed for understanding the specific areas of client dysfunction. For example, the use of the casework method of study, diagnosis, and treatment would be used uniformly across practice areas, with the caseworker drawing on the specialized knowledge base of relevance to the practice setting or field of practice such as juvenile justice, child welfare, healthcare, mental health, and so forth. The volume was soon followed by Richmond's second publication *What Is Social Casework? An Introductory Description* (Richmond, 1922), thus making social casework up to that time the most clearly defined methodological approach to social work practice among all of what were the generally accepted social work methods of casework, group work, community organization, and administration (Social Welfare History Project, 2011).

MICRO AND MACRO PRACTICE: FINDING THE BALANCE

The profession was called upon to reexamine the nearly exclusive use of the casework method during the years of the Great Depression when it became clear that this method was far from sufficient in meeting the unprecedented suffering and destitution of the Depression years. And it did so again during the Civil Rights era, which called for a more activist approach and an inclusive theoretical framework for shaping the social work curriculum, one that moved away from the exclusive use of theories anchored in a Eurocentric worldview. Questions were also raised about the efficacy of the medical model that assumed the existence of individual pathology for client populations whose difficulties were rooted in flawed societal institutional structures. In light of the new knowledge generated during these periods from the examination of a significantly changed practice context, the cause of problems in social functioning of clients in need of social work services clearly could not be legitimately explained solely as the result of maladjustments in the psychological domain.

The culmination of increasing concerns about a drift away from shaping practice around the ecological perspective, person-in-the-social environment, and strengths perspective as the historic distinguishing feature of the profession influenced the undertaking of the Council of Social Work Education's 1960 Curriculum Study. The findings of the study were published in two volumes and called for social work education programs to achieve a greater balance in the teaching of micro- and macro-level content as well as an infusion of minority content into the curriculum with an emphasis on social justice for historically underrepresented groups (Boehm, 1959). Nonetheless, transforming from the professional title of caseworker, first to psychiatric social worker and, then, today, to clinical social worker—the latter often being used as synonymous with psychotherapist—micro level practice has remained a preferred intervention for a large share of practitioners. Moreover, drawing heavily on concepts from psychoanalytical theoretical frameworks, psychotherapeutic approaches are found to be the most challenging to quantify and measure (Fonagy, 2003). That being said, it does not to diminish the fact that the psychotherapies or talking therapies are helpful in some situations in relieving the psychological distress of some individuals.

THE SOCIAL WORK TWELVE GRAND CHALLENGES

Recent years have not seen an abatement in concerns among the professional leadership for a broader perspective on practice as well as the need for a greater emphasis on the central role of research for shaping an evidence-based approach to policy and practice anchored in science. The Social Work Grand Challenges is a national initiative of the Academy of Social Work and Social Research. Using the tag line "social progress powered by science," the initiative is designed to promote research as central to advancing the knowledge base of social work so that the profession can successfully meet the challenges it will confront in the 21st century. The initiative identifies twelve challenges concerned with solving the most pressing social problems of today and establishes a model for a coordinated national response for the profession to address these (American Academy of Social Work and Social Welfare, 2013; Padilla & Fong, 2016).

This national initiative came about as the culmination of several interrelated events occurring in the 1990s. These developments began in a 1991 initiative of the National Institute of Mental Health (NIMH) that brought to light the lack of empirical evidence to inform evidence-based practice and policy development for the profession. With funding support from the NIMH, concern for these issues subsequently led to the convening of a Task Force on Administrative Research Infrastructure Within Social Work Programs by the National Association of Deans and Directors (NADD). The purpose of the task force was to develop recommendations for administrative strategies and models and for social work programs to support federally funded research productivity and quality research career development. The April 1997 report of the task force identified administrative support and organizational arrangements that are currently being to use to build research infrastructures and support research development within social work education programs nationally (American Academy of Social Work and Social Welfare, 2014; Barth, Gilmore, Flynn, Fraser, & Brekke, 2014; Williams, 2015).

The work of the Dean's Task Force was undertaken under the auspice of the Institute for the Advancement of Social Work Research. The Society was founded in 1994 to support the advancement of social work research and the continued growth of the profession, and it currently collaborates with the CSWE, the Group for the Advancement of Doctoral Education in Social Work (GADE), and the St. Louis Group for Excellence in Social Work Research and Education to develop and promote social work research and scholarship in social work programs nationally.

THE PITTSBURGH SURVEY

The current efforts undertaken under the Grand Challenges are not the first time that science and research have been looked to as a means for adopting a more informed and planful approaches for understanding and developing evidence-based interventions for solving pressing social ills of the times. The Pittsburgh Survey is an example from social welfare history that used research as a tool for understanding the extent of poverty in the United States at the turn of the 20th century. Initiated in 1907, the Survey was undertaken under the direction of the New York City Charity Organization Society with the intent to study all aspects of the life of one industrial city (Pittsburgh, Pennsylvania) as extensively as possible, and it is considered the first major attempt to use research as a tool for understanding the causes of pervasive social problems in urban areas at the time (Trattner, 1999).

The findings of the team of researchers were published by the Russell Sage Foundation (1914) in six volumes between the years of 1909 and 1914. Of great significance is that these findings changed the prevailing moralistic view of the time which held that people impacted by poverty and social problems of urban life were the cause of their own suffering to a new understanding that poverty and related social problems are the inevitable consequences spawned by societal progress and change. Individual were, in fact, the victims of social problems accompanying these societal changes and not their cause.

The Survey produced extensive statistical data that documented the misery of urban life was contributed to by low wages, preventable diseases, industrial accidents, substandard housing, and lack of urban planning. The study findings validated the wisdom of using factual data to support systemic reforms, and the causal explanations of poverty and implications for its victims based on irrefutable factual information led Edward T. Devine, the Director of the New York City Charity Organization, to conclude that "Personal Depravity is as foreign to any sound theory of the hardships of our modern poor as witchcraft or demonic possession . . . these hardships are economic, social, transitional, measurable, and manageable" (Trattner, 1999, p. 183). Nonetheless, still considered "less than" and "the other" in a society anchored in doctrines of white supremacy, blacks did not benefit from these changed views about the causes of misfortune.

The Pittsburgh Survey paved the way for similar studies in other cities. The findings from these studies resulted in a shifting of the moralistic view that shaped the nation's begrudging responses to unmet need that had held sway in shaping welfare philosophy since the Colonial period under the country's Poor Law heritage that categorized the poor as "worthy" or "unworthy." Thinking shifted away from blaming people for their situation as a result of personal behaviors of indolence, intemperance, and immorality to a new understanding of the role of oppressive social systems as links in the causal chain producing social ills that had a disproportionate impact on marginalized groups.

This changing ideology underlying charitable work contributed to a more humanistic and scientific approach for solving what was now understood to be the social disservices that were the inevitable consequences of social progress and change that anyone could fall victim to through no fault of their own. This shift would ultimately lead to a changed social welfare philosophy that ushered in the American social welfare state and the safety net programs enacted under the landmark 1935 Social Security Act. Still functioning at the margin of American society, blacks, however, would continue to receive inequitable treatment in what was the most important and impactful legislation of the 20th century.

RESEARCH AND SOCIAL ACTIVISM IN THE BLACK COMMUNITY

The Pittsburgh Study was not concerned with illuminating the conditions under which blacks were living or finding solutions to the plight of blacks, and subsequent reforms brought about by the survey's findings were to the benefit of whites only. In Atlanta, the city in which the School of Social Work would be founded, the work of addressing the plight of blacks was addressed by the activities of scholars and social reformers that had been in process virtually since the end of the Civil War. W. E. B. DuBois and Eugenia Burns Hope both played a significant role in establishing the tradition of using empirical research and community activism as a means for advancing social progress and reforms in the pursuit of social justice and equality for the African American community.

THE PHILADELPHIA NEGRO

In 1897, DuBois was invited to the University of Pennsylvania for a temporary appointment to conduct a systematic investigation of social condition
in Philadelphia's Seventh Ward, which was densely populated by African
Americans. The data for the study were collected between 1896 and 1897
(DuBois, 1899). The DuBois study preceded the Pittsburgh Survey and was
the first sociological study conducted on an African American community. It
is considered the earliest example of sociology as a statistically based social
science (Lewis, 1995). An important feature of the DuBois study was that the
findings in the analysis and interpretation of the data were contextualized to
take into account the considerable environmental inequalities under which
blacks were functioning. When DuBois joined the faculty of Atlanta University
in 1897, his study became the model for conducting the Atlanta University
studies. Upon assuming leadership of the Atlanta University studies, DuBois
endeavored to bring a more scientific approach to the work than had his predecessor. His long-term goal was to bring together an interdisciplinary mix of
African American scholars to develop a systematic approach for examining
and disseminating research findings to a broad audience of social activists and
scholars that would work in the interest of the betterment of blacks.

THE NEIGHBORHOOD UNION

Lugenia Burns Hope was among the elite class of educated middle-class African
American women involved in the race work of the Progressive Era. She provided
the leadership in the establishment of the Neighborhood Union in Atlanta in
1908 that worked in tandem with the work being undertaken by DuBois in the
University (Rouse, 1984; Shivery & Smythe, 1942). The Neighborhood Union
pioneered the use of community-based participatory research and a public
health model for conducting community needs assessments that consider the
range of political, social, economic, and historical influences that contribute
to the creation and reinforcement of social problems impacting neighborhood
residents. Assuming a prevention stance, the public health model endeavors
to leverage the support of the community in problem-solving approaches that
prevent or mitigate their impact on community residents.

With DuBois and Hope paving the way, by the turn of the 20th century
African American intellectuals and social activists in Atlanta had laid the necessary groundwork to prepare a space for the launching of the first school
of social work in the South that was to have an emphasis on preparing black
social workers to serve the black community. The cluster of institutions of
higher learning for blacks that had been founded by missionary groups with
the support of the Freedmen's Bureau to educate the children of formerly

enslaved men and women were not only well established, but had also elevated their curricula above the grade and high school levels and were awarding fully accredited college degrees. And while each had been founded with distinct missions, they had developed collaborative relationships and affiliations that created greater access to higher education to an ever-growing number of African Americans. These affiliations now made it possible for enrollees to pursue study in a variety of academic disciplines at both the undergraduate and graduate levels now that the Board of Trustee's transitioning of Atlanta University to a graduate school.

The tradition of relying on the findings of research and community activism to advance social reforms to improve the conditions under which blacks lived had been enshrined in the academic culture of the University and the affiliated colleges owing to the pioneering scholarship of DuBois, who had joined the faculty of Atlanta University in 1897, and to the community organizing model introduced by Hope through the Neighborhood Union in 1908 (Ross, 1976; Rouse, 1989).

DuBois's ethnographic study of black life published by the University of Pennsylvania as *The Philadelphia Negro* (DuBois, 1899) was replicated by the founders of the School of Social Work as the model for undertaking a study process that would justify the need for the school and obtain information to guide academic policy decision-making and the design of the curriculum. Social work courses that had been offered through the Neighborhood Union and taught by Hope, agency-based social workers, and the faculty of Morehouse College would shape the design and organization of the curriculum of the new School.

DEMOGRAPHICS AND URBAN DECAY IN 19TH-CENTURY ATLANTA

Blacks migrating to the Atlanta from rural areas and in need of help from social agencies were largely illiterate, with limited skills for work in the manufacturing industries that were developing in Atlanta. Nor did life in rural farm communities provide experiences that equipped them to negotiate the complexities of life in urban Atlanta. Unsurprisingly, similar to urban areas in the North that were becoming densely populated by white ethnic immigrants and that spawned the Settlement House movement, the neighborhoods in which blacks migrating from rural areas of the state settled were overcrowded and poorly serviced by the city. Unsurprisingly, they soon became slums overburdened by crimes, squalor, unsanitary conditions and disease, and other forms of urban decay that are the inevitable consequences and characteristic features of neglected areas densely populated by marginalized groups.

The worst slums in Atlanta at the time were on the west side, between the Georgia Railroad and Atlanta University. These areas were typically avoided by middle-class blacks, many of whom were long-term residents of the city and among the well-educated and elite class of blacks who had settled in the vicinity of the University.

The pockets of slums densely populated by newly migrating blacks from the rural South were areas of concern to Hope and targets of the efforts of the Neighborhood Union, which was one of the central organizations joining with Atlanta University in the work of establishing a school of social work. The qualitative data collected by the hands-on work of the Neighborhood Union complemented the Atlanta University studies under DuBois's stewardship that emphasized the gathering and reporting of statistical quantitative data on conditions in black communities. Community organizing, now considered one of the primary methods of professional social work practice, was introduced by Hope who pioneered a model of participatory community-based applied research and use of the public health model.

Moreover, to use DuBois's metaphors of "the veil" and "dual consciousness," of living in two worlds for the cohort of men and women engaged in the race work of the period and who contributed to the founding of the school of social work there was never a false dichotomy between micro- and macro-level interventions, a dominating theme of mainstream social work professional discourse that influenced the development of social work programs in predominately white colleges and universities. Sharing the lived experience of their client populations as reflected in DuBois's view of "dual consciousnew" the work of the race men and women of the period was not obscured by this false dichotomy between micro and macro level interventions. They understood from the onset that cause and function were inseparable, and influenced by Dubois' emphasis on the scientific method, it was understand that preparing workers for practice in the black community required innovative educational programming anchored in credible scientific evidence designed to debunk myths of white hegemony, elevate the behaviors of a race of people who had long lived under the deplorable conditions of a system of enslavement, and promote systemic reforms to change doctrines of white supremacy deeply embedded in American laws and customs and instituted to sustain a four-century-old system of black enslavement.

Although both DuBois and Hope made noteworthy contributions in the 19th century to the nascent profession of social work and the tradition of using empirical research and community activism for advancing equality for blacks of that time, neither is sufficiently credited for their contributions in the mainstream social work literature. Moreover, it is likely not hyperbole to suggest that it is possible for graduates of accredited schools of social work to successfully complete degree requirements today without ever learning about the pioneering work and leadership of DuBois or Hope in the field.

This notwithstanding, a review of relevant historical literature of the context in which the School of Social Work emerged highlights that their work in their respective areas of scholarship, social activism, and community organizing laid the foundation that shaped the curriculum and academic programs of the School when it was established in 1920 as the Atlanta School of Social Work. Moreover, based on their association with pioneering white social activists of the period, including Jane Addams, although underreported in the literature, it is likely that their influence was felt in the social work programs that were developing in the predominately white schools of social work during this period.

The influence of the scholarship and activism of both DuBois and Hope continues to be reflected in contemporary theory development relevant to social work policy and practice with diverse client populations. Therefore, producing a documentary history of Clark Atlanta University Whitney M. Young Jr. School of Social Work could not be complete without a discussion of the indelible mark left by DuBois and Hope on the rich history of the School and the University. And, indeed, the field continues to benefit from their contributions as contemporary academics and activists, some perhaps even unknowingly, are influenced by their legacies.

REFERENCES

American Academy of Social Work and Social Welfare. (2013, November). *Introduction and Context for Grand Challenges for Social Work*. Grand Challenges for Social Work Initiative, Working Paper No. 1. Baltimore: Author.

American Academy of Social Work and Social Welfare. (2014). *Grand accomplishments in social work*. Grand Challenges for Social Work Initiative, Working Paper 2. Baltimore: Author.

Barth, R. P., Gilmore, G. C., Flynn, M. S., Fraser, M. W., & Brekke, J. S. (2014). The American Academy of Social Work and Social Welfare: History and Grand Challenges. *Research on Social Work Practice, 24*(4), 495–500. https://doi.org/10.1177/104973151452780

Boehm, W. (1959). *Curriculum study* (vols. 1–12). New York: Council on Social Work Education.

Briar, S. (1968). The casework predicament. *Social Work, 13*(1), 5–11.

DuBois, W. E. B. (1899). *The Philadelphia Negro: A social study*. Philadelphia: University of Pennsylvania.

Flexner, A. (1915). Is social work a profession? Social Welfare History Project. http://socialwelfare.library.vcu.edu/social-work/is-social-work-a-profession-1915/

Fonagy P. (2003). Psychoanalysis today. *World Psychiatry, 2*(2), 73–80.

Hamilton, G. (1952). The role of social casework in social policy. *Social Casework, 33*(8), 315–324. https://doi.org/10.1177/104438945203300801

Lewis, D. L. (1995). *W. E. B. Du Bois: Biography of a Race, 1868–1919*. New York: Henry Holt.

Padilla, Y. C., & Fong, R. (2016). Identifying grand challenges facing social work in the next decade: Maximizing social policy engagement. *Journal of Policy Practice, 15*(3), 133–144. doi:10.1080/15588742.2015.1013238

Richmond, M. E. (1917). *Social diagnosis.* New York: Russell Sage Foundation.

Richmond, M. E. (1922). *What is social casework? An introductory description.* New York: Russell Sage Foundation.

Rosenblatt, A. (1968). The practitioner's use and evaluation of research. *Social Work, 13*(12), 53–59.

Ross, E. (1976). Black heritage in social welfare: A case study of Atlanta. *Phylon (1960, 37*(4), 297–307. doi:10.2307/274495

Rouse, J. A. (1984). The legacy of community organizing: Lugenia Burns Hope and the Neighborhood Union. *Journal of Negro History, 69*(3/4), 114–133.

Rouse, J. A. (1989). *Lugenia Burns Hope, Black Southern Reformer.* Athens and London: The University of Georgia Press.

Russell Sage Foundation. (1914). The Pittsburgh District Civic Frontage, The Pittsburgh Survey. Findings in Six Volumes. Edited by Paul Underwood Kellogg. Philadelphia: Wm. F. Fell Co. https://www.russellsage.org/sites/default/files/Kellogg_The%20Pittsburgh%20District_0.pdf

Shivery, L., & Smythe, H. (1942). The Neighborhood Union: A survey of the beginnings of social welfare movements among Negroes in Atlanta. *Phylon (1940–1956), 3*(2), 149–162. doi:10.2307/271522

Social Welfare History Project. (2011). Mary Ellen Richmond (1861–1928): Social work pioneer, administrator, researcher and author. Social Welfare History Project. http://socialwelfare.library.vcu.edu/social-work/richmond-mary/

Social Casework: Past, Present, and Future. (1968). Social Work, *13*(1), 5. https://doi.org/10.1093/sw/13.1.5

Trattner, W. I. (1999). *From poor law to welfare state* (6th ed.). New York: The Free Press.

Williams, J. H. (2015, June). Unification, crafting imperatives, and defining a profession. *Social Work Research, 39*(2), 67–69. https://doi.org/10.1093/swr/svv008

CHAPTER 6

W. E. B. DuBois and Lugenia Burns Hope

It's not what you look at that matters, it's what you see.
— Henry David Thoreau, 1854

W. E. B. DuBois is without question the most influential black intellectual of the 20th century. And he is arguably the most outspoken and authentic moral leader on matters of race of his generation. Drawing generously upon scripture, his publications assumed a philosophical and poetic stance that framed the unequal treatment of blacks as a matter of morality. For DuBois, the use of the scientific method was the tool for solving "The Negro Problem." The consummate scholar and academician, DuBois held to the belief that the empirical evidence would be the best means for refuting empirically unfounded stereotypes about blacks and their inferiority as a race, building bridges between the races and paving the way for achieving equality and full citizenship for blacks (Dubois, 1906; 1910). An intellectual whose thinking was far in advance of his time, his political activism and scholarship has left a lasting imprint on Clark Atlanta University and the Whitney M. Young Jr. School of Social Work as well as on the thinking of contemporary black scholars and academics on matters of race.

DuBois prophetically wrote in *Souls of Black Folk* (1903), the book for which he is best known, "the problem of the 20th century is the problem of the color line—the relation of the darker to the lighter races of men in Africa and Asia and the islands of the sea" (p. 16). His concept of the "talented tenth" (DuBois, 1903) was borrowed from the writings of John Hope, his colleague and friend at Atlanta University, who himself was a notable intellectual of the period. Unlike that of his nemesis, Booker T. Washington, DuBois envisioned

Find a Way or Make One. Alma J. Carten, Oxford University Press (2021). © Oxford University Press.
DOI: 10.1093/oso/9780197518465.001.0001.

the destiny of blacks not as a subservient class of people forever denied full citizenship, but as educated in the classics and liberal arts and well informed to enjoy full equality and citizenship. Moreover, DuBois believed that, as a group, blacks would be especially well prepared to assume a leadership role based on their additional insights they would bring to solving problems on matters of race.

Dark Water: Voices from Within the Veil (DuBois, 1920) is a synthesis of much of DuBois's thinking, comprising his previously published works. The book opens with a postscript in which he speaks to what is a consistent theme of his writing: the paradoxical nature of the black experience and racism in American society.

> I have been in the world, but not of it. I have seen the human drama from a veiled corner, where all the outer tragedy and comedy have reproduced themselves in microcosm within. From this inner torment of souls, the human scene without has interpreted itself to me in unusual and even illuminating ways. For this reason, and this alone, I venture to write again on themes on which great souls have already said greater words, in the hope that I may strike here and there a half-tone, newer even if slighter, up from the heart of my problem and the problems of my people. (DuBois, 1920, p. vii)

Chapter one, "The Shadow Years," is presented in an autobiographical format in which DuBois described an idyllic childhood in his birthplace, Great Barrington, Massachusetts, "I come to the days of my childhood—they were very happy." There were only a small sprinkling of blacks in Great Barrington where DuBois was born.

> I was born by a golden river and in the shadow of two great hills, five years after the Emancipation Proclamation. The house was quaint, with clapboards running up and down, neatly trimmed, and there were five rooms, a tiny porch, a rosy front yard, and unbelievably delicious strawberries in the rear. (p. 3)

He concludes with a description of a complex multicultural family linage with the statement, "So with some circumstances having finally gotten myself born with a flood of new glow blood, a strain of French, a bit of doubt, but, thank God! No Anglo Saxon" (p. 5).

After his father's departure from the family, whom he characterized as "a poet, an adventurer, or a Beloved Vagabond," DuBois was reared by his mother with assistance from extended family members. When speaking about the great influence his mother had on him, he reflected that, in retrospect, he realized she "did not try to make me perfect. To her I was already perfect" (p. 11).

With Harvard as his goal, DuBois finished high school at age sixteen and went off to study at Fisk College. Upon graduation from Fisk, he attended Harvard University where he received a second bachelor's degree in 1890, his master's degree in 1891, and a PhD in 1895. He did postdoctoral study at the University of Berlin, in Germany, where he studied along with the internationally recognized scholar Max Weber. DuBois joined the faculty at Wilberforce College after returning from Germany in 1894. It was here that he was recruited by Dr. Horace Bumstead, the second president of Atlanta University, to join the faculty as professor of economics and history with a special assignment to develop a department of sociology.

Initially, DuBois was viewed by the Atlanta University students as a bit odd and unapproachable because of his formal manner and appearance, including a Van Dyke moustache, spats, and a gold-tipped cane. This was combined with his insistence on an exceptionally high standard of academic performance by students. A former student, recalling DuBois's distinguished appearance nearly a full century later, in an oral interview commented "I can still see him right now, coming across campus to his breakfast, with head high, his step quick, but dressed right, from the top of his head to the soles of his feet. He was immaculate!" (Dittmer, 1980, p. 26) Another former student, when reflecting on his experience with DuBois as his professor, commented on his use of the Socratic method of teaching to stimulate critical thinking. He recalled that "DuBois was a good listener, then he'd critique a question by asking questions. Ofttimes helping students to see the flaws in the question" (McFarlane, 2019). Thriving in the academic culture, DuBois participated enthusiastically in student and faculty social and academic events, often bringing nationally known individuals to speak at campus events. Soon after joining the faculty he became much sought after by students who had come to value his high standards of academic excellence, and they were eager to attend his classes and be mentored by him (Bacote, 1969; Branch, 1988; Dittmer, 1980).

In reflecting on his appointments at Atlanta University, DuBois wrote

My real-life work was done at Atlanta for thirteen years, from my twenty-ninth to my forty-second birthday. They were years of great spiritual upturning, of the making and unmaking of ideals, of hard work and hard play. Here I found myself. I lost most of my mannerisms. I grew more broadly human, made my closest and most holy friendships, and studied human beings. I became widely acquainted with the real condition of my people. I realized the terrific odds which faced them. At Wilberforce I was their captious critic. In Philadelphia I was their cold and scientific investigator, with microscope and probe. It took but a few years of Atlanta to bring me to hot and indignant defense. I saw the race-hatred of the whites as I had never dreamed of it before,—naked and unashamed! The faint discrimination of my hopes and intangible dislikes paled into nothing before this great, red monster of cruel oppression. I held back with more difficulty each day my mounting indignation against injustice and misrepresentation.

With all this came the strengthening and hardening of my own character. The billows of birth, love, and death swept over me. I saw life through all its paradox and contradiction of streaming eyes and mad merriment. I emerged into full manhood, with the ruins of some ideals about me, but with others planted above the stars; scarred and a bit grim, but hugging to my soul the divine gift of laughter and withal determined, even unto stubbornness, to fight the good fight. (Dubois, 1920, pp. 11–12)

DuBois did indeed fight the good fight. The processes of doing so led to an increasing radicalization in his thinking. Unfortunately, this also led to the loss of what had been his hopeful optimism about American democracy. In the later years of his career, DuBois also abandoned his optimism for and thinking about the "talented tenth." His vision had been that this would be a leadership class of exceptional black men educated largely at institutions of higher learning for blacks who were well-prepared and committed to solving the race problem. He abandoned this vision after repeatedly confronting the tenacious hold of racist ideology in American culture. With the loss of optimism about American democracy, he turned to socialism and the belief that change would come not under the leadership of the talented tenth, but by way of the masses of blacks who had the least and suffered the most (DuBois, 1935; 2000). This redefinition of previously held views led DuBois to join the Communist Party. He relinquished his American citizenship to become a citizen of the African country of Ghana. He died in Accra, Ghana, on August 27, 1963, on the eve of the historic civil rights march on Washington.

Influenced by W. E. B. DuBois and Lugenia Burns Hope, and going back to its first class of six students, in 1876, graduates of Atlanta University were becoming dispersed throughout the nation. By the turn of the century, these graduates held positions in academia as university presidents, deans, and professors. Correspondence from alumni kept the University current on events that were transforming the country nationally and in the South and the implications of these developments for the progress and betterment of African Americans. The information received from alumni served as an impetus for convening the Atlanta University Conference on the Negro Problem. The national feedback also led President Bumstead to conclude that there was a great need for a systematic and thorough investigation into the living conditions among the Negro population of cities (Chase, 1896, p. 5). Subsequently, Bumstead's proposal for an annual conference to examine the social, economic, and physical conditions of Black Americans was approved by the Board of Trustees.

The first of the Atlanta Conferences was held in 1896, under the direction of Trustee George G. Bradford, whose successor would be DuBois. Building on what he had learned from his Philadelphia study, DuBois endeavored to bring more scientific rigor to the study process than in the past. In describing his thoughts about an evolving program for Negro freedom, Dubois wrote

> This program at Atlanta, I sought to swing as if on a pivot to one of scientific investigation into social conditions, primarily for scientific ends: I put no special emphasis on specific reform effort, but increasing and widening emphasis on the collection of a basic body of fact concerning the social condition of American Negroes, endeavoring to reduce that condition to exact measurement whenever or wherever occasion permitted. As time passed, it happened that many uplift efforts were in fact based on our findings. (DuBois, 1944, p. 43, DuBois, 1948)

DuBois's vision was for the University to become a center for the study of problems impacting the black community (Lange, 1983). This would be achieved by facilitating an active collaboration with scholars throughout the South. Each year, the conference would address a specific issue and disseminate its findings throughout the country for wide practical use and, as DuBois wrote in the collection of documents that formed *What the Negro Wants* (1948), his intent was to "inspire our graduates in various communities to use the information we collect as a basis of concrete efforts in social betterment, and we can already point to some results of this policy."

In later years DuBois was to become a liability to the University. His outspokenness on matters of racism and the increasing radicalization of his thinking compromised the University's ability to solicit funding support from white philanthropic organizations. At the time, these organizations ascribed to a conservative ideology on race relations that was more in line with the incremental approach to black rights espoused by Booker T. Washington.

When DuBois retired from his appointment on June 30, 1944, as Professor and Chair of the Department of Sociology, he had served for two appointment periods within the University, from 1897 to 1910, and again from 1932 to 1944. On the occasion of his retirement, in acknowledgment of his unprecedented and distinguished service and unswerving commitment to the pursuit of equal rights for blacks in the United States and globally, the University conferred upon him the Honorary Degree of Doctor of Letters at the Sixty-Ninth Commencement on June 6, 1938. Furthermore, in recognition of his service to the University as a scholar and teacher, the Board of Trustees also conferred upon him the rank of Professor Emeritus and a lifetime pension with full benefits from the University annuity retirement plan that had been established by the Board in 1944. Today DuBois's contributions are commemorated by a life-size bronze portrait bust in the reference room of the Trevor Arnett Library (Bacote, 1969, pp. 373–374).

After leaving academia, DuBois's work for the ongoing push for full citizenship of African Americans was far from finished. He had left an indelible mark on the academic culture of the University. Moreover, his intellectualism and scholarship continue to influence contemporary African American scholars who are building on his thinking about the paradoxical nature of being black in America.

DuBois's insightful conceptualization of the paradoxical nature of the black experience in America is captured in part in his use of the concepts of the "veil" and "double consciousness." The metaphoric use of these concepts as he defined them, give a glimpse into the existential experiences of being African American *in* America but not *of* America on the psyche of blacks as individuals and as a collective community. His perspective on the paradox of race-based discrimination against blacks that was sanctioned in law and custom in a nation premised on democratic ideals continues to be of relevance in America in the 21st century. Whispers of his thinking are present in current social theory as carried forward in the scholarship of new generations of African American scholars who are contributing to knowledge-building for curriculum renewal in social work education programs.

We hear, for example, echoes of his thinking in the critical race theory, introduced by Derrick Bell, the highly acclaimed legal scholar and academic activist. Bell set forth a race-conscious theoretical framework to explain the implications of living in a racist society for blacks and the central role of the legal system in justifying and sustaining notions of white supremacy in the cultural landscape and institutional life of the country (Bell, 1992; Delgado & Stefancic, 1993).

Critical race theory is anchored in assumptions of the mega theoretical framework of critical theory (Cox & Hardwick, 2002) that attributes the inequality and oppression experienced by certain marginalized groups as inequalities that are rooted and sustained by societal institutional and structural flaws and not by the behaviors of individuals. Accordingly, critical race theory as conceptualized by Bell asks the fundamental question of what the American judicial system would look like if people of color were involved in meaningful decision-making positions. Concomitantly, he called for a critical appraisal of the "constitutional contradiction" inherent in a document prepared by framers of the concept of equality and freedom who themselves were in some manner complicit in the institution of slavery (Delgado & Stefancic, 2005).

Building on concepts and assumptions of critical race theory, Kimberly Crenshaw, founder of Columbia Law School's Center for Intersectionality and Social Policy Studies, introduced the concept of *intersectionality* as a subcomponent of black feminist theory. The concept of intersectionality calls for the consideration and critical examination of the interacting effects of gender, race, and class in contributing to the complexity of factors associated with the social problem of violence against women of color (Crenshaw, 1989). Intersectionality theory has since become a widely accepted framework in schools of social work nationally for teaching and understanding identity politics used by dominant power groups to justify the inequalities experienced at various systemic levels that create layers of social injustices and have a cumulative effect on populations who are categorized as "the other."

This shift in traditional paradigms on matters of race also found its way into the thinking of race-conscious social work educators. The activism of the civil rights years all but forced the social work education establishment to give more attention to the significance of race and culture in understanding human behavior, a concept that Forrester B. Washington had described earlier as the "existence of black people in a predominantly unsympathetic hostile world" (Washington, 1935).

The latter years of the 1960s saw the emergence of a new generation of African American academics and social scientists whose research was at the vanguard for informing culturally competent and race-conscious practice theories. Their scholarship introduced a new paradigm for conceptualizing the psyche of blacks, individually and collectively, that both shapes and is shaped by forces in the external environment. Moreover, their thought was instrumental in shifting theory building away from the use of words and language that defined the black experience in the pejorative and used negative depictions to a new lexicon that captured themes of empowerment, resilience, strengths, and adaptive and coping behaviors of African Americans (Billingsley, 1968; Chestang, 1972; Hill, 1972; Norton, 1978; Schiele, 1997; Solomon, 1976). The roots of these themes are evident in DuBois's writings about the paradoxes and tensions of being black in America, situations that simultaneously have the potential to result in personality fragmentation, but nonetheless do not erase an enduring sense of racial pride and optimism. These tensions are captured in the following quotes from the Postscript to *Dark Water: Voices from Within the Veil*:

> I have been in this world but not of it. I have seen the human drama from a veiled corner, where all the outer tragedy and comedy have reproduced themselves in microcosm within. Juxtaposed against "I believe in Pride of race and lineage and self. In pride of self so deep as to scorn injustice in other selves in pride of lineage so great as to despise no man's father. (DuBois, 1920, p.1)

DuBois's imprint may also be seen in the theoretical frameworks for faculty teaching of diversity and social justice content in accredited social work education programs. This is seen in a new emphasis on the development of more inclusive paradigms for teaching diversity and social justice content that draws on concepts from critical race theory and embraces intersectionality. This emphasis can facilitate a conceptual understanding on the part of students of the many forms of oppression and the cumulative effects of socially constructed stigmatizing conceptualizations of various attributes of human diversity and difference.

DUBOIS AND HOPE INTERACT WITH LEADING SETTLEMENT HOUSE ACTIVISTS

Throughout his tenure at Atlanta University, DuBois had also interacted with social reform icon Jane Addams and other women of the Settlement House movement (Deegan, 1988). Papers in the W. E. B. DuBois Collection at the University of Massachusetts hold a quantity of correspondence describing their work together with others on the founding of the NAACP and arranging Addams's visit to Atlanta University in 1908, following DuBois's invitation for her to participate in a conference on the Negro Family. Addams also authored an editorial in *Crisis,* and both Addams and DuBois were members of the Progressive Party (https://digital.janeaddams.ramapo.edu/collections/show/209).

Dorcas Bowles, Dean Emerita of the School of Social Work, and her colleagues (Bowles, Hopps, Clayton, & Brown, 2016) examined the relationship between DuBois and Addams, a relationship that the authors referred to as a "dance/partnership" because of its complex and layered nature. The authors conducted an analysis of the relationship within the context of the turbulent Progressive Era, as the nation transitioned from an agrarian to industrial urban society; the Great Migration; and the tenacity of Jim Crowism. In their analysis, the authors pose provocative "what-if" questions about the implications for the profession had the relationship between DuBois and Addams continued, given the commitment of both to social activism and evidence-based research as a tool for social reform. What impact, for example, would their coming together have had on the profession's increased favoring of the casework method and medical model and the diminishing of the centrality of research in maintaining social work's credibility as a science-based profession.

IMPERFECTIONS OF ICONIC LEADERS

Addams's influence in the field was without question the most consequential in shaping the profession of social work. Appropriately, reports of her contributions in the mainstream social work literature far exceed those of DuBois. Her influence is also felt in the work of Lugenia Burns Hope. In beginning her career as a social activist in Chicago, Hope was employed at Hull House, the Settlement House founded by Addams. Hope's experience at Hull House shaped her professional identity as a community organizer and activist, which she brought to her race work in Atlanta, Georgia. However, it is erroneous to assume that Hope's reform activities were a mere replication of those of the white Settlement House women of Hull House.

To the contrary, Hope's community activism in Atlanta was a continuation of a strong tradition of African American self-help and institution-building that began soon after the end of the Civil War. Moreover, her work was undertaken with a strong sense of racial pride, as was the case for the other race men and women of the period. This race work was undertaken with an authentic concern for democracy. The inclusiveness that characterized the work of the race men and women was absent from the white settlement workers whose interest was in elevating white ethnic European immigrants in the interest of democracy but gave little concern for advancing equality for blacks.

Hope had also experienced first-hand from her employment at Hull House that the welfare of blacks settling in Chicago, a popular city of resettlement for blacks migrating from the South, received little attention from the women of Hull House. One who did demonstrate interest in the plight of blacks was Mary White Ovington, who held an office on the Board of the NAACP and whose study *Half a Man: The Status of the Negro in New York* (Ovington, 1911/1969), received commendation from DuBois for its scientific rigor and acknowledgment of the environmental inequalities slowing the progress of blacks. Jane Addams had participated in the Niagra Movement that led to the founding of the NAACP and did not embrace conventional views about the innate or biological inferiority of blacks. However, although among the most outspoken progressives and liberals of the period, both Ovington and Addams looked to cultural determinants to explain racial disparities and the slowness of the social and economic progress of blacks in comparison to that of whites.

The research of Khalil Gibran Muhammad, Harvard Kennedy School scholar and historian and former executive of the New York City Public Library Schomburg Center for Research in Black Culture, calls attention to the fact that some progressive white liberals, even though rejecting biological determinism, did embrace cultural determinants for understanding the behavior of blacks. This is evidenced in the reform efforts of Ovington and Addams. Both refuted biological determinants of behavior, but both turned to culture determinants to account for the racial disparities in black and white progress observed during the period, as discussed by Muhammad (2010).

Ovington, for example, attributed the sexuality of black girls in New York City who were drawn into prostitution to a racial defect, explaining the historical cause of this to "Negroes themselves," owing to the impact of slavery on slowing the ability of black women to recognize the sanctity of home and the importance of feminine virtue. Addams concurred with Ovington's observations, remarking that, in consideration of their belated moral development, it was not surprising that some black girls were entering into a life of ill repute. Writing in a February 1911 editorial in the first issue of *Crisis*, Addams expressed the opinion that the problem of racial violence that was engulfing the country during the decade was not because of racism alone, but because large numbers of blacks had yet to be brought under social control (Muhammad, 2010, pp. 122–123).

There is a wealth of scholarly works as well as slave narratives and autobiographic accounts refuting these ill-informed stereotypical views held by Ovington and Addams about the impact of slavery on diminishing the morality of blacks and their ties to values supporting family, children, and community (Blasingame, 1975). Moreover, the information collected from the surveys conducted by the Neighborhood Union in Atlanta reveal that community residents abhorred the neighborhood conditions that spawned crime and houses of prostitution. These community residents worked side by side with Hope and her team to rid the neighborhood of these conditions (Ross, 1976; Rouse, 1989).

Other scholars have criticized Addams for what has been interpreted as racist attitudes that have been unintentionally expressed in her writings or public talks. For instance, Addams, at the request of her colleague Ida B. Wells, a central figure in anti-lynching work, had joined Wells in publicly speaking out against the lynchings of blacks (Hammington, 2005; Giddings, 2008). Mob lynching, even though beyond imagination in their heinousness and savagery, was commonly used following the Reconstruction era to terrorize blacks for any offense, no matter how inconsequential, that was perceived by whites to challenge white supremacy. This included the lynching of "uppity blacks" who did not know their place.

In speaking out against lynching in the article "Respect for the Law" (Addams, 1901), Addams's argument against lynching condemned mob violence in compromising the rule of law and disregard of due process. In making the argument, however, she assumed that blacks were guilty of the crimes, mostly that of rape, that whites had accused them of having committed. Soon after Addams's article was published, Wells (1901) wrote a rebuttal for the *Independent* entitled "Lynching and the Excuse for It." Although in agreement with the logic of Addams's argument, Wells's rebuttal focused on Addams's assumptions that blacks were guilty of the crimes of which they had been accused, which she saw as a reflection of Addams's acceptance of the myths and stereotypes of black men as "bestial" and "uncontrolled." Moreover, as reported in research conducted by the NAACP, the rape of white women by black men did not make up a significant number of the reasons for the lynching of blacks during the period—even when lynching was at an all-time high. White mobs would murder black men and women for such "crimes" as being too prosperous for a black, for talking back to whites, or the refusal to get out of the way for a white person to pass them on the sidewalk (White, 1948, p. 43).

Others have explained Addams's racial attitudes as being those of a woman of her times: she would by virtue of socialization into the dominant cultural norms be influenced by the prevailing racial views of the time that were based in the pseudo-science espoused in scientific racism. Whatever the case, there may well be lessons to be learned for the present from a closer scrutiny of Addams's racial attitudes and those of other professional icons.

Slavery and its legacy of Jim Crowism, segregation, and structural racism, as observed by Condoleezza Rice, former Secretary of State during the George W. Bush administration, are America's "birth defect" (Beavers, 2017). President Barack Obama, whose historical presidency elevated race to center stage in the national political discourse (Teasley & Ikard, 2010; Kennedy, 2011), refers to this legacy as a part of the nation's DNA (Chappell, 2015). Addams, who is revered by some as the accepted "Mother" of the profession, and other iconic figures whose influence continues to shape the socialization of new inductees into the profession and the mission of social work, are not immune from the psychological dissonance suggested in previous chapters that has allowed for racist notions of white supremacy to comfortably co-exist in a nation founded on democratic ideals and is mirrored in the core values of the profession. To avoid subjecting iconic figures who have played a central role in shaping these core values to the fullest of critical appraisal only contributes to sustaining the false narrative about American history on matters of race. The outcome will be to slow the nation's progress toward the aspirational goal of a more perfect nation. Neither is such avoidance in the best interests of the profession as it continues to grapple with issues of racism within its own ranks.

John Longres, Professor Emeritus at the University of Washington School of Social Work, has written extensively on matters of race and ethnicity and has been outspoken on challenges faced by the profession in promoting an antiracist agenda. In a paper originally presented at the Eighteenth Annual Program Meeting (APM) of the Council on Social Work Education (CSWE), Seattle, Washington, in January 1971, Longres wrote that social work education contributes to racism in three ways: through the selection procedure by which non-white student and faculty enter social work education, the educational process within schools of social work, and the socialization process within schools of social work (Longres, 1972).

Similar observations have been made in more recent publications. Bowles and Hopps (2014), for instance, speaking with the voices of women who were the "children" of race men and women of past years, conducted a historical review of the progress of the profession on matters of race. Their findings revealed, at best, a consistent pattern of social work's wavering in meeting the needs of vulnerable populations from the mid-20th century to the early years of the 21st century. A replicated content analysis of four major professional journals between 2005 and 2015 found a continuing pattern of failure of social work researchers to address institutional racism and the favoring of micro-level interventions when working with groups of color (Corley & Young, 2018).

The shortfalls of Jane Addams on matters of race were keenly felt by Lugenia Burns Hope. The absence of significant concern for improving the conditions under which blacks lived by the early Settlement House workers strengthened Hope's resolve to focus her activist work over her full career on the plight of blacks. In carrying out this commitment, Hope made significant and consequential contributions to the field. Yet the enormity of her contributions to the field are virtually absent from historical literature on the development of the profession of social work. The Archives in the Woodruff Research Center hold documents about her work in the Lugenia Burns Hope Collection, the Neighborhood Union Collection, and the John Hope and Lugenia Burns Hope Collection, and entries in the *New Georgia Encyclopedia* overview her life and accomplishments. Hope's biographer and historian, Jacqueline Anne Rouse, Professor of African American History and American Studies at Georgia State University, wrote the only published biography on Hope's work, entitled *Lugenia Burns Hope: Black Southern Reformer* (Rouse, 1989). Otherwise, there is a paucity of articles that record her substantial contributions that go far beyond the Neighborhood Union for which she is best known.

THE CONTRIBUTIONS OF LUGENIA BURNS HOPE

Lugenia Burns Hope was born into the comforts of a well-established middle-class family on February 19, 1871, in St. Louis, Missouri, to Louisa M. Bertha and Ferdinand Burns. With a father who was a successful carpenter and a mother who remained in the home to devote her full attention to child-rearing and household duties, Hope's early years were a childhood of privilege as the youngest of seven children. The family, as described by her biographer, was of mixed lineage of African American and European American ancestry, with deep roots in Mississippi (Rouse, 1989). The family fortune, however, shifted with the death of her father in 1880. His death influenced her mother's decision to move the family to Chicago to find better economic opportunities and for her daughter, Lugenia, who was about fifteen years old at the time, to have a better education.

The financial support of her older siblings made it possible for Lugenia to complete high school and allowed her mother to continue to remain at home to care for her. However, another reversal of family fortune occurred upon the loss of employment of an older sibling. This made it necessary for Lugenia to become the major wage earner for the family at the age of twenty-two—a responsibility that she was to carry from 1893 to 1897.

After working as a bookkeeper and then a dressmaker, Hope became involved in charitable work as the first black secretary of King's Daughters and with Hull House, where she had direct contact with a white immigrant client population (Rouse, 1989). It was during these early years that she developed a characteristic sense of independence and self-sufficiency. Based on her own lived experiences of both a life of privilege and a life among the working class, she gained insights into the plight of the poor and working classes.

Both of these organizations with which Hope was involved in her formative years as a social activist served a predominately white clientele. Therefore, the entirety of her work in Chicago was in white-dominated social work settings. Her skin coloring likely made her more acceptable to white social reformers, in keeping with white preferences favoring African Americans who were of mixed ancestry, as was the case with Hope. For Hope, these experiences illuminated the limited democratic vision of the Settlement House workers; she was exposed to the incongruence between practice implementation and the ideals of social work philosophies and the values of some progressive reformers. As a Christian with strong ties to the church, Hope was troubled by the hypocrisy of the Christian philosophy that was integral to the missions of white charitable organizations and which accepted the belief held by some white reformers that blacks were of an inferior culture. All were factors that strengthened her resolve to work with the African American community (Rouse, 1989).

Furthermore, as we learn from her biography, during her time at Hull House, Hope had first-hand exposure to the discrepancy between the equitable social work philosophies espoused and the scant attention given to the needs of African Americans. It was exposure to the failures and racism within white Christian reform movements—and later the complacency of white Christians in responding to racial violence—that solidified her commitment to working among the black poor and black working classes. This was her goal when she left Chicago to continue her reform work after her marriage to John Hope, first in Tennessee and later in Atlanta.

Lugenia was introduced to John Hope, who would become her husband and life partner in race work until his death in 1936, as a young adult when she was involved in charity work in Chicago. John Hope was of mixed racial origin and was born in Augusta, Georgia, on June 2, 1868. His parents were James Hope, who was Scottish, and Mary Frances Butts, who was a freewoman. The couple lived openly despite Georgia law at the time that prohibited interracial marriages (Davis, 1998). Like Lugenia, John Hope's world was one of privilege owing to both class and family lineage.

John and Lugenia met at the World Colombian Exposition held in Chicago in 1893 to commemorate Christopher Columbus's landing in the New World. Blacks were initially excluded from participation in the event, but, in response to outrage from the black community and with the intervention of Frederick

Douglass, to engage the black community, a segment of the Exposition was designated as "Negro Day." Lugenia attended the conference chaperoned by a prominent black physician and his wife. She met John Hope at the conference; at the time, he was a student of Theology at Brown University. After their meeting at the Exposition, the two began a correspondence that blossomed into a loving relationship and a long courtship that at times did not seem as if it would ever end in marriage (Rouse, 1989).

At the time of the couple's introduction, Lugenia had already become an independent, self-sufficient woman who was no stranger to the workplace: she was already an experienced social reformer and activist and had already determined that this would be her life's work. With an appealing personal appearance and a long list of suitors, John found Lugenia was not an easy conquest. She was also committed to remaining in Chicago to care for her aging mother. Therefore, securing a "yes" was by no means an easy task for John Hope, despite himself being much sought-after as a potential husband given his pedigree and educational achievements (Rouse, 1989).

Finally, with an understanding that the marital relationship would be one of equality and mutual respect, John reassured Lugenia that "we are to control our little realm mutually, neither of us to be the servant, yet both of us gladly serving each other in love and patience" (Rouse,1989, p. 23). After two years of an ardent long-distance courtship and poignant appeals, as described in correspondences from John to Lugenia, in an effort to win over her hand in marriage and the approval of her mother, John wrote to Lugenia "Tell her I shall promise to love you as your father loved her, and with God's help I shall never love you less" (Rouse, 1989, p. 22). The couple married on December 29, 1897, at Grace Presbyterian Church in Chicago: she was twenty-six and he was twenty-nine years of age.

Soon after their marriage, the Hopes left for Nashville, Tennessee, where John began his academic career as an instructor teaching in the classics at Roger Williams University, a liberal arts school that had been founded for the education of blacks soon after the Civil War. It was not too long after the couple had taken up residence in Nashville that John decided to take a position teaching in the classics at Atlanta Baptist College. The College had been founded in 1867, and it was renamed Morehouse College in 1913. The Hopes left for Atlanta in the fall of 1898, where they lived out the balance of their lives committed to race work for the betterment of African Americans.

It may be inferred from Lugenia's biography that the Hope's marital relationship was one of mutual love and respect. Yet it may also be speculated that it was not without the usual stressors of coupling combined with added demands of careers that took them both frequently away from home. During World War I, John spent time in Europe with American soldiers. And Lugenia, based on her success with the Neighborhood Union in Atlanta, was appointed

Special War Work Secretary for the YWCA's Council on war work. The appointment took her away from home to oversee training hostesses at Camp Upton, New York. She was also elected to serve on President Herbert Hoover's Colored Advisory Commission, and she worked with the American Red Cross after the Great Mississippi Flood of 1927.

Both Hopes had demanding schedules that involved local, national, and, for John, international events related to their race work. Both had the added burdened of coping with the pervasiveness of racism that shaped all aspects of black life during the period. Given their physical appearance, both of fair complexion and John with blue eyes, they may well have passed for white, as had some members of their families, if this had been their choosing. Despite the comforts of life that this choice would have given them and the escape from the hostile environment for blacks in the south it would have provided, the personal identities of both John and Lugenia were tied to their black heritage. Both were committed to devoting their lives to the betterment of the black community. Nonetheless, tensions can be inferred from correspondence in the John and Lugenia Hope Collection of the Robert Woodruff Library Archives.

John's letters, for instance, suggest that he may well have longed for a conventional Victorian Christian wife who was content with conforming to the expectations of societal ascribed gender roles in his urging his wife to slow down, that doing things was not "all of life" and encouraging her not to overextend herself in the interest of not losing her "poise and self-control" and to "store up some peace for the quiet years ahead" (Rouse, 1989, p. 37). On returning to the United States from a trip to Europe he lamented,

> My day is reaching to close. Eight days more and I shall be on the sea coming home, coming to you. How I dream of you all day long as I move about from place to place! Yet when I return you will be so busy that you will have no time to listen to me. Your work as mine takes me from you. You blame me, yet you are too busy for small talk. However, we have been a long time apart and you must be more with me. (p. 36)

Lugenia without question was a complex and energetic woman with an ability to astutely manage the responsibilities of her roles of mother, wife of a university president, and activist. We also learn from her biography that she was consumed with the need to fill every minute of every day with various social work activities. In the mind of her adult son, she was remembered as a "fighter" whose active life was a reflection of her determination to promote change (Rouse, 1989, p. 38), despite her husband's cautions about what he referred to as her "feverishness" and his encouragement not to "over-extend" herself and to exhibit more "self-control" (p. 37).

Her husband's appeals did not deter Lugenia from her zeal to make a difference. Her sense of urgency may have been a result of her sensitivity to what she believed to be the hypocrisy she experienced in the work of white reformers, from being enmeshed in the abject poverty and suffering of a community with which she shared a personal identification, and from living in close proximity to suffering, especially that of children. It may have also been related to loneliness from her husband's long absences or impatience with the unsubstantiated rumors of his infidelities, even though she outright rejected innuendos of unfaithfulness (Rouse, 1989).

The archival documents do raise some unanswered questions about their lives together as a married couple in which both partners were much sought after to contribute to the race work as speakers and consultants. Both were quite obviously highly invested in carrying out full careers as educators and social activists. Archival documents do not reveal the reason for John spending the last months of his life in MacVicar Hospital at Spelman College and not in the family residence, although this may be explained by the level of care he needed that could not be provided in the home. Nor do these documents explain reasons for Lugenia's decision to have her ashes dispersed over the campus of Morehouse campus and not being laid to rest next to the grave of her husband in the quadrangle of the Atlanta University campus as he had requested. Based on what is learned from archival documents, a qualitative narrative inquiry may well be a well-received scholarly undertaking that lends humanistic insights into the complexities of their relationship and the evolution of a marriage between two extraordinary people within the context of the history of the nation, when, despite being exceptionally gifted individuals, race-based discrimination was a dominating theme of their lives.

Despite what may have been personal or environmental stressors, and although Lugenia did not give up her life of independence and social activism that continued the tradition of black institution building, she gave proper attention to her role as the wife of a university president throughout her husband's tenure as president of Atlanta Baptist college (Morehouse) and Atlanta University. Their homes were opened to Morehouse students, and, when moving to the president's house after John's appointment to the presidency of Atlanta University, she prepared it to be a home as well as a guest house for out-of-state visitors and students. In her maternal role, she raised her children in a supportive atmosphere and brought them up to the realities of being black in a racist society, and she continued the tradition of black institution-building in her social activism (Rouse, 1989,)

Her son Edward reflected on the values she encouraged in her children and in Morehouse students. He remarks that

> Dignity and self-respect were fundamental aspects of her character. Money,
> while not to be ignored, was less important than a life of service to one's own

downtrodden people . . . the college students were taught that morality, dignity, and self-respect were more valuable than money or any earthly thing. (Rouse, 1989, p. 43)

Despite yearnings for a more conventional wife, as evidenced in some of his letters, her husband acknowledged her contribution to his success in his university presidencies of Morehouse College and Atlanta University.

I don't know how it would have been if I had never met you. I am absolutely sure that I should never have had the success that I have had or risen to positions that have come to me. I bow down to you, my dear little wife, in reverence and love for what you are to me—I am not changed or puffed . . . about anything that has come to me. I want you to share in all with me—the honor and the money. (p. 35)

BEGINNING RACE WORK IN THE CITY OF ATLANTA

Hope was motivated to continue her reform work outside of the home when the couple arrived in Atlanta. Her activism centered around improving the conditions of children, an issue to which she became even more committed after having her own children. DuBois had been at Atlanta University since 1897, directing the Atlanta Conferences on Negro Problems. Knowing of Hope's work in Chicago, he invited her to participate in a conference on the topic of the Negro Child.

One of her lectures was given under the title of "Family Life as a Determinate of Racial Attitudes of Children." The content of her talk spoke to the universality of the black experience, irrespective of time and place, and related to the need for black parents of all classes and status to teach their children about white racism. She cautioned that they must do this while, at the same time, avoiding encouraging in their children feelings of racial animosity toward whites.

Lugenia shared a personal narrative illustrative of this, one that is unique to black parenting, in teaching her son about respecting women regardless of their race or status. When the youngster responded in the way he had been taught and gave up his seat to a white woman, the woman's response to the gesture caused an unnecessary stir. In speaking about the incident, Hope reflected that had the woman simply ignored the child, the matter would have come to closure. Instead, she responded in a manner that the young child did not understand, thus posing a quandary for Hope, who reflected "I did not want to burden his young life because I knew it would have to come all too soon anyway. The Negro mother has to pray for patience and insight lest she forgets that above all her little ones must not become embittered" (Rouse, 1989, p. 33).

One of her first activities in Atlanta was Hope's affiliation with the Gate City Nursery and Free Kindergartens. The initiative came about from concern for what is referred today as "latch key" children, or the children of working mothers who were either left unattended and alone, locked in their homes or left to wander in the streets. Hope initially became aware of the virtual non-existence of recreational facilities for black children in Atlanta soon after the birth of the couple's first son. After bringing together a group of women and faculty wives, the group was successful in gaining the approval of the administration of Atlanta Baptist College to provide a part of the school's property for a playground. This initial work was the seed that later gave birth to the concept of the Neighborhood Union model of community organizing. The experience also played a role in Hope's joining with the work of the Gate City Nursery and Free Kindergarten initiative.

In addressing the greater need for childcare services for the vast majority of Atlanta's black children, she was influenced by the findings from past Atlanta University Conferences. The interest in childcare services came to fruition as a result of the Tenth Atlanta University Conference, held in 1905. The conference drew upon findings from studies of the past several years. An abstract from the Proceedings of a report on the matter stated that

> among the important questions of today is the need of day nurseries in cities and towns were children of parents who, by force of circumstances, or obliged to earn a living by working in service, may receive good and wholesome influences during the period of life when impressions are easily made and character readily molded either for the good or bad.

The activities of the Gate City Nursery and the panel of women who comprised the board was a part of the influences that would combine to shape formal social welfare programs for blacks in Atlanta and which led to the Neighborhood Union under the leadership of Lugenia Burns Hope.

THE LAUNCHING OF THE NEIGHBORHOOD UNION

According to archival documents (Ross, 1978; Rouse, 1984,1989), the possibly preventable death of a mother had she had connections with her neighbors and access to medical care and household help, was the impetus for Hope's conceptualization of the Neighborhood Union model of community organizing and needs assessment. The woman was a young mother of three who resided in the West End, a "colored" neighborhood in the vicinity of the University. The woman's husband and father of the young children was working to provide for the household, and he could not look after his wife. Nor did he have the money to obtain medical care for her or to pay for household help. Given the circumstances, without medical care or household help, the mother died isolated and alone.

Deeply troubled by the circumstances of this mother's death, and seeing this as an opportunity to make some much-needed improvements in the community infrastructure and blatant neglect from city officials, Hope convened a group of her friends, the wives of prominent black activists and intellectuals, and some working-class neighborhood women. Counting on their being able to leverage their influence as a group, the plan was to combine their financial resources and solicit the support of other women of Christian belief who were also mothers to launch an initiative and investigate the needs of their neighbors. The aim was to change the decrepit conditions that families faced in the West End.

The tragic death of this mother not only galvanized the community to join together; it also demonstrated Lugenia's gifted organizing and administrative skills. Shaped in part by segregation, the upper-, middle-, and poor and working-class African Americans in Atlanta often lived in close proximity to one another. The success of the model demonstrated the effectiveness of bringing together various classes of blacks to improve community conditions. The organization's inclusive leadership and membership structure was deliberately designed to diminish class barriers between black community residents who were living under the same oppressive community conditions irrespective of their class or social status.

The model was launched in Atlanta's West Side. The neighborhood was selected for the beginning of this community organizing experiment because it surrounded Atlanta University, and Spelman and Morehouse Colleges. Assuming a preventive approach to avoid the recurrence of a needless death of a mother whose situation was unknown to her neighbors, the decision was made in the first planning meeting that the organization would be structured so that every family in a neighborhood would be known. To accomplish this, the women were assigned a neighborhood in each district with the responsibility to conduct a house-to-house visit of every home. The data from these investigations were tabulated, aggregated, and analyzed. The initial investigations were conducted with the assistance of Morehouse students. The findings of these investigations revealed extensive unsanitary conditions, a lack of recreation, family disorganization, and delinquency. The neglect of city officials and their failure to provide basic services were reflected in streets that were in need of repair, insufficient street lightening, poor sewage, and other conditions of urban decay. Unsurprisingly, these neighborhood conditions made fertile grounds for crime, delinquency, and houses of prostitution to take root and thrive.

The final plan adopted by the Neighborhood Union was to divide the city into zones and districts. Eventually, every section of Atlanta would be studied and a house-to-house visit conducted to support a campaign to educate community residents on the practical knowledge of domestic science and elementary laws of good health. The work of the Neighborhood Union was based on a sense of Christian stewardship and morality, as reflected in its motto, a verse from the Bible: "Thy Neighbor as Thyself."

The charter of the Neighborhood Union, submitted in 1911 to the Georgia Fulton County Superior Court, identified Lugenia Hope as President, Dora G. Whitaker as vice president, and Maggie Williams as Secretary. The Charter specified that the organization was not an institution for financial gain or profit but purely of charitable and benevolent interests. Furthermore, the Charter stated that the organization would obtain revenues from donations and freewill offerings of its members and other persons interested in charitable work (Rouse, 1984, 1989). Ross (1978) presents a detailed and comprehensive overview and documents virtually every aspect of Neighborhood Union. This includes its constitution, organizational and governance structure, plan of organization, and organizational goals (Rouse, 1989, pp. 273–281).

The strategies adopted by the new organization, with some modifications, reflected Hope's past experiences in social activism. The primary goal of the Neighborhood Union was to "elevate the moral, social, and intellectual standards in each neighborhood" (Rouse, 1989, p. 98). The Neighborhood Union prioritized health in black neighborhoods, as seen in its offering classes in nursing, prenatal care, cleanliness, bathing infants, and the elderly. The work was undertaken in equal partnership with the membership, and leadership was encouraged among all classes of the neighborhood. Moreover, based on Hope's experiences in white-led service organizations and observations of the complacency of the white clergy in responding to violence against blacks during the 1906 race riots, the work was to be carried out as an authentic expression of Christian morality and teachings to address the inequitable treatment of blacks.

Hope had changed her church affiliation from the Presbyterian denomination to join the Baptist Church, which had a greater visibility in the South and that provided the added value of the National Baptist Convention, which had a strong national presence and commitment to activism. The Neighborhood Union provided a variety of services for black Atlantans to fill the gap left by the segregated white agencies. These services were child- and family-centered in nature and featured community health clinics staffed by volunteer physicians, dentists, and nurses, and neighborhood amenities such as art and recreational programs. The organization also petitioned the City Council and the Board of Health for infrastructure repair efforts to improve sanitation, sewage, health, housing, and streets.

As the organization became institutionalized in the city's social welfare infrastructure, it began to work cooperatively with the Atlanta Anti-Tuberculosis Association, the Red Cross, and the City Council. These organizations adopted its method of neighborhood investigations and data collection. The basis for evidence-based community planning was centered on extensive details from survey findings on the living conditions of families that included detailed information such as the size and condition of their yards, the presence of toilets and sinks, and the manner in which garbage was disposed. The organization continued to promote regular programming of family welfare, education, cultural meetings, and clubs.

By 1912, the organization and work of the Union had been implemented and tested and was so effective that eventually it was adopted by other cities and organizations. Beyond the local initiatives provided in Atlanta, the Neighborhood Union members also assisted in disaster relief around the South. At the national level, Hope received a personal telegram from then Secretary of Commerce Herbert Hoover asking her to contribute to relief efforts for 1927 Mississippi River flood that affected Mississippi, Kentucky, and Tennessee (Holly, 2012).

In response to changing community needs, the Neighborhood Union has modified its organizational structure three times since its founding to meet the changing needs of Atlanta residents. In 1908, it was designed to serve a single neighborhood: the West Side in the First Ward of Atlanta. In 1911, it was modified to include five sections of Atlanta: the First Ward, Fourth Ward, and South Atlanta, Pittsburg, and Vine City or Mechanicsville. The third modification came in 1915, when it was revised to include all neighborhoods of the city of Atlanta for use by the Anti-Tuberculosis Association, at which time the city was divided into sixteen zones (Shivery & Smythe, 1942; Ross, 1978; Rouse, 1984, 1989).

ORIGINS OF COMPREHENSIVE NEIGHBORHOOD-BASED SERVICES

With an emphasis on supporting family life and providing alternatives for community youth and emerging young adults, the women who were among Hope's cohort involved with developing social welfare programs and services were far more innovative, change-focused, and effective than they are given credit for in the mainstream social welfare literature. Acknowledging the paucity of historical literature that examines the contributions of the race women, Gordon (1991) conducted an extensive comparative analysis of literature with the intent to shed light on the similarities and differences of white and black women activists during the period of 1890–1945. The analysis concluded that the work of the black women resembled that of white Settlement House women and was focused primarily on replicating the work of the Black Church and joining with black club women to establish institutions for blacks from which they were excluded, such as orphanages and homes for the aged.

There are clear similarities in Hope's community organizing work with that of the white Settlement House workers carrying out reforms under the banner of "residence, research and reform." Similarities also exist with the Charity Organization Society (COS) "friendly visitors" use of home visitation and the collection of extensive information on the living conditions of the poor, work that ultimately led to scientific management in the administration of those social agencies emerging during the period. Yet there are distinctive existential differences between the underlying assumptions and values shaping the approach to social activism and the contributions of these two cohorts of exceptional women in advancing a formal US system of social welfare.

As did the white Settlement House workers, the race women lived in close proximity with those they served. They were neighbors under laws of racial segregation rather than neighbors of choice, as was the case with the women who lived under one roof in the white neighborhood-based Settlement Houses. Race women also had a close personal identification with community residents that came from a shared lived experience. Moreover, as their lives were constrained by both gender and racial discrimination, and they were advocating the equal rights of blacks and the betterment of the black community, they were fighting for their own equality and full citizenship and for an improved standard of living for their own families. Although the work of both cohorts of women was rooted in Christian morality, the work of the race women was anchored in a more authentic expression of Christian teachings based on their concerns for the equitable treatment of blacks. Moreover, seeing the welfare of blacks and whites as being inextricably linked, whites were not excluded from these efforts, while in the white-led organizations, blacks for the most part were excluded from participation.

The underlying assumptions of strategies implemented by the Neighborhood Union are also closely aligned with the concept of *maximum feasible community participation*. This concept was introduced as an essential strategy of President Lyndon B. Johnson's Great Society and in the Community Advisory Boards established under the 1964 Economic Opportunity Act. Introduced as a component of the War on Poverty community action programs, its effectiveness has been subjected to intense scrutiny by social scientists (Melish, 2014). Nevertheless, what was seen as a new paradigm for 20th-century social welfare harkened back to the Neighborhood Union model that embraced values integral to participatory democratic governance, citizen participation, engagement of community members in determining their needs and what would be most helpful in meeting these needs, and interest in the development of indigenous community leadership.

The principle of interracial collaboration was another strategy employed by the Neighborhood Union. The precedent was established by the founders of Atlanta University in their rejection of segregation of the races in its educational program despite a withdrawal of state funds. Within the same timeframe as the establishment of the Neighborhood Union, the Urban League was established in 1910, under the leadership of George Edmond Haynes, on this same principle. At the forefront, the Neighborhood Union developed in collaboration with the International Council of Women of the Darker Races and the Commission on Interracial Cooperation.

The Commission was an educational program offering courses on the history and accomplishments of blacks. They included contributions to the literature in 1913 for inclusion in all Atlanta schools, both black and white, private and public. The purpose was not to discourage any other literature or history but instead to get all children acquainted with the history of blacks. Encouraging the women to go slowly, Hope said "We feel that we can do this if we all pull together." She also encouraged the women to draw on the work of Carter G. Woodson, whom she referred to as "one of our strongest and best writers" (Rouse, 1989, p. 115). Such an educational program, which was likely the intent of the women, brought the contributions of Carter G. Woodson into general view. Despite his being a central figure in black history and an important American scholar, Woodson's work for the most part had been overlooked. In 1912, he became the first individual of slave parentage to earn a PhD in History; in 1915, he founded the Association for the Study of the Negro (now African American) Life and History, and he is credited with introducing Black History Month (Goggin, 1983).

The research conducted by Edyth Ross (1978), an Atlanta University School of Social Work professor, focused exclusively on welfare development in the black community between 1860 and 1930. Ross's study found that the work of black women reformers was much broader in scope than what Gordon (1991) identified. For example, beyond largely being limited to joining the efforts of the Black Church and club women of the period, Ross identified broader concerns that included establishing associations developed for the protection of black migrant women who were leaving the South during the years of the Great Migration to find employment in the homes of whites as domestics and in menial jobs in the formal labor force. These women were at risk for economic and sexual exploitation both as domestic workers in private white homes and in the workplace. Describing the scope of the interests and characteristics of black women involved in race work, Professor Ross wrote that

> Apart from the specific needs of unskilled migrant female labor, black women created, or continued, various organizations, collectively feeling the need to organize to deal with a broad range of welfare problems on a national scale. These women, for the most part of superior educational advantage, often educators or professional women themselves, worked assiduously in their local communities in the interest of promoting the social welfare of blacks. (Ross, 1978, p. 384–385)

Specifically referring to the work of Lugenia Hope in the Neighborhood Union in Atlanta, Ross indicates that the model has been replicated in many other cities. Hope is acknowledged as also having the added benefit of being a member of an exclusive sorority of women who were the wives of highly educated men, some of whom were the presidents of the growing number of historically black colleges and universities (HBCUs). These women were working hand in hand with their husbands in the interests of the betterment of the black community. Ross's entry identifies other

> outstanding women in education of prominence in national women's club work. Mary McLeod Bethune and Charlotte Hawkins Brown, both founders of educational institutions, assumed leadership in this generation over programs activated and previous generations by women such as Lucy Laney. In many cases, these women . . . were the wives of a professional man. . . . Many of these women had been classmates, educated in the colleges of the south; they tended to know each other socially as well as professionally. They organized the Greek Letters sororities and the National Council of Negro Women, and all the multiplicity of clubs which did social welfare work on local and state as well as national levels. (Ross, 1978, p. 385)

The work of the Neighborhood Union went far beyond the establishment of what is considered as being within the social welfare domain. Rouse (1984, 1989) highlights the multitude of programs undertaken that sought reforms across multiple sectors to address the pervasive and extensive unmet needs resulting from race-based inequities affecting the quality of life and family well-being in the black community. Included among these was exposing fraudulent business practices of white merchants to increase prices of food, revealing practices of leaving garbage uncovered to create unsanitary conditions in neighborhoods in support of exploitive businesses, and challenging city practices of dumping public waste in black neighborhoods.

The Neighborhood Union also conducted a comprehensive study of black public schools and petitioned the Board of Education to secure funds to address the multitude of physical and psychological hazards that undermined the education of black children. This occurred at a time when the system, with a seating capacity for 4,102 and an enrollment of 6,163, taught children in double sessions by the same teacher (Rouse, 1989, p. 74). The organization mounted campaigns and lobbied city government to hire black policemen in the black community. Other campaigns were undertaken to register voters and assist them in getting out to vote, educate the community about the role of the census, and lobby the city government for better police protection for black neighborhoods (Rouse, 1989, p. 129). The Institute on Social Work established at Morehouse in collaboration with Hope and the staff of the Neighborhood Union to teach the foundation of social work would be the blueprint for the curriculum developed at the Atlanta School of Social Work.

The Union celebrated its twenty-fifth anniversary in July 1933. The celebrations for the landmark event included a banquet and many accolades and testimonies honoring Hope for her leadership over her twenty-five years of service to Atlanta as a "friend of children" and "promoter of interracial goodwill." Mary McLeod Bethune spoke of her fearlessness in challenging and lobbying government in the interest of social injustice (Woodruff Archives).

Yet, based on what archival documents reveal about Hope's notable accomplishments, exceptional administrative and organizing skills, and her grit, sustaining the program was not without frustrations. At times, even to Hope, the challenges might have seemed insurmountable and felt like a thankless task. For example, we hear this expressed in her words,

> Did it ever occur to you how hard it is to get all of this work started—how many years it takes to get enough folks together to accomplish anything? Why? We have to work to get people together who have nothing in common and then get them sufficiently acquainted with one another to be able to work together. Then we see each other only once or twice a month and really there is very little accomplished. (Lugenia Hope, Memoranda. March 20, 1921, Neighborhood Union Collection)

Hope submitted her resignation from the Union on July 8, 1835, and she moved from Atlanta to New York City soon after the death of her husband in 1936. Apparently, leaving the campus was not without angst. Due to some conflicting feelings with the incoming administration, Hope left with the promise never to return: it was a promise she kept, only returning to the campus to participate in the laying of the headstone for her husband's grave (Rouse, 1989). She continued her life of activism after leaving Atlanta, becoming, in 1937, an assistant to Mary McLeod Bethune in her role as director of Negro Affairs for the National Youth Administration. Hope also continued to work for the NAACP periodically, and she participated in projects with DuBois; in failing health, she became less active in the latter years of her life, until her death in 1947.

LEGACIES OF DUBOIS AND HOPE

The contributions of DuBois and Hope have been the historic pillars and integral to the implicit and explicit curricula of the School of Social Work since its founding. Moreover, since the 1980s, the fundamental principles on which their work was based are reflected in the new directions of policy thrusts made by the Educational Policy and Accreditation Standards (EPAS) of the CSWE as increasing attention is being given to strengthening the teaching of diversity content in the social work education curriculum (Reichert, 1970). These interests are compiled in a collection of articles given at the Carl Scott Memorial over the period of 1988–1992 (Council on Social Work Education [CSWE], 1993).

Furthermore, as predominately white schools of social work have endeavored to continue to improve the integration and infusion of diversity content into their curricula, the imprint of DuBois's thinking has been felt in the scholarship of race-conscious academics for whom his thinking has served as the building blocks for critical race theory and for culturally competent and race-conscious approaches for shaping both social welfare policy and social work practice. These concepts have become increasingly favored by race-conscious faculty to support in their students critical thinking and in developing a conceptual understanding of the implications of all forms of oppression and socially constructed stigmatizing definitions of various aspect of human diversity and differences including race, gender, class, sexual orientation, and other personal identities (Holosko, Briggs, & Miller, 2018).

Vestiges of Hope's model of community organization and the engagement of impacted populations in the process of determining what their needs are and how these are best met is reflective of social work's core value of self-determination and are seen in the grassroots strategy shaping social activism at the vanguard of the Civil Rights movement of that emerged in the early decades of the 20th century (Frierson, 2019). One of many examples is Ella Baker, who began her career as a civil rights activist and student at Shaw University; Baker was a central figure in launching the Student Nonviolent Coordinating Committee, spawned by social activism of students in the HBCUs.

Pioneering organizations that developed at the vanguard of the 1960s Civil Rights movement are Mobilization for Youth, developed in the Lower East Side neighborhood in New York City, and the Metropolitan Applied Research Center, founded by Dr. Kenneth Clark, under the auspices of Harlem Youth Opportunities Unlimited (HARYOU) that planned anti-poverty activities in Harlem. Both of these organizations were structured around the model introduced by the Neighborhood Union of establishing partnerships between the community and activist-minded academics. The archival documents of Mobilization for Youth are housed in Columbia University Library Archives. Those of Dr. Kenneth Bancroft Clark and the Metropolitan Applied Research Center are housed at the Archives of the Library of Congress.

The contributions and legacy of Lugenia Burns Hope are memorialized in the Lugenia Burns Hope Center, established in 1994 by then community organizer Barack Obama to encourage leadership development, civic engagement, and community organizing in Bronxville, Chicago, the city in which Hope began her career in social activism (Frierson, 2019; Holly, 2012).

DuBois's contributions to the academic life of Atlanta University are enshrined in the bust of his likeness installed on the campus of Clark Atlanta University on July 18, 2015. *The Phylon: The Clark Atlanta University Review of Race and Culture* that DuBois founded at the University in 1940 continues publication as a semi-annual peer-reviewed journal. In keeping with DuBois's original vision, each issue addresses a specific topic of general interest to an interdisciplinary roster of faculty in the humanities and social sciences.

REFERENCES

Addams, J. (1901). Respect for law. *New York Independent, 53*(3), 8–20.

Bacote, C. A. (1969). *The story of Atlanta University: A century of service, 1865–1965.* Atlanta: Atlanta University Press.

Beavers, O. (2017). *Condoleezza Rice says America was born with a birth defect: slavery.* The Hill. https://thehill.com/homenews/news/332307-condoleezza-rice-says-america-was-born-with-a-birth-defect-slavery

Bell, D. (1992). *Faces at the bottom of the well: The permanence of racism.* New York: Basic Books.

Billingsley, A. (1968). *Black families in white America.* Englewood Cliffs, NJ: Prentice-Hall.

Blasingame, J. (1975). Using the testimony of ex-slaves: Approaches and problems. *Journal of Southern History, 41*(4), 473–492. doi:10.2307/2205559

Bowles, D. D., & Hopps, J. G. (2014). The profession's role in meeting its historical mission to serve vulnerable populations. *Advances in Social Work, 15*(1 Spring), 1–20.

Bowles, D. D., Hopps, J. G., Clayton. O. Jr., & Brown, S. L. (2016). Dance between Addams and DuBois: Collaboration and controversy in a consequential 20th century relationship. *Phylon (1960–), 53*(2 Winter), 34–53. http://www.jstor.org/stable/phylon1960.53.2.34

Branch, T. (1988). *Parting the waters: Martin Luther King and the Civil rights movement, 1954–63.* Macmillan.

Chappell, B. (2015). We are not cured: Obama discusses racism in America with Marc Maron. https://www.npr.org/sections/thetwo-way/2015/06/22/416476377/we-are-not-cured-obama-discusses-racism-in-america-with-marc-maron

Chase, T. N. (1896). *Mortality among Negroes in cities.* The Atlanta University Publications, no. 1. Atlanta: Atlanta University Press.

Chestang, L. (1972). *Character development in a hostile environment.* Chicago: University of Chicago Press.

Corley, N A., & Young, S. M. (2018). Is social work *still* racist? A content analysis of recent literature. *Social Work, 63*(4), 317–326. https://doi.org/10.1093/sw/swy042

Council on Social Work Education (CSWE). (1993). *Perspectives on equity and justice in social work.* In D. M. Pearson (Ed.), *The Carl A. Scott Memorial Lecture Series, 1988–1992.* Alexandria, VA: CSWE.

Cox, P., & Hardwick, L. (2002). Research and critical theory: Their contribution to social work education and practice. *Social Work Education, 21*(1), 35–47. doi:10.1080/02615470120107004

Crenshaw, K. (1989). Demarginalizing the intersection of race and sex: A black feminist critique of antidiscrimination doctrine, feminist theory and antiracist politics. *University of Chicago Legal Forum,1*, article 8. http://chicagounbound. uchicago.edu/uclf/vol1989/iss1/8

Davis, L. (1998). *A clashing of the soul: John Hope and the dilemma of African American leadership and black higher education in the early twentieth century*. Athens: University of Georgia Press.

Deegan, M. J. (1988). WEB DuBois and the women of Hull-House, 1895–1899. *American Sociologist, 19*(4), 301–311.

Delgado, R., & Stefancic, J. (Eds.). (2005). *The Derrick Bell Reader*. NYU Press. www. jstor.org/stable/j.ctt9qg47z

Dittmer, J. (1980). Interview with Mrs. H. S. Murphy, July 6, 1972, Atlanta. In *Black Georgia in the Progressive Era, 1900–1920*. Champaign: University of Illinois Press.

DuBois, W. E. B. (1903). *The souls of black folk*. Chicago: A. C. McClurg

DuBois, W. E. B. (1906). The economic future of the Negro. *Publications of the American Economic Association, 7*(1, 3rd series), 219–242. http://www.jstor.org/stable/ 2999974

DuBois, W. E. B. (1910 May). The economic aspects of race prejudice. *The Editorial Review, 2,* 488.

DuBois, W. E. B. (1920). *Dark water: Voices from within the veil*. New York: Harcourt, Brace.

DuBois, W. E. B. (1935). *Black Reconstruction in America, 1860–1818*. New York. Harcourt, Brace.

DuBois, W. E. B. (1944). My evolving program for Negro freedom. In R.W. Logan (Ed.), *What the Negro Wants* (pp. 31–70). Chapel Hill: University of North Carolina Press.

DuBois, W. E. B. (1948). What the Negro wants in 1948 [fragment], May 1948. W. E. B. DuBois Papers (MS 312). Special Collections and University Archives, University of Massachusetts Amherst Libraries.

DuBois, W. E. B. (2000). Close ranks, July 1918. In M. Marable & L. Mullings (Eds.), *Let nobody turn us around: Voices of resistance, reform, and renewal: An African American anthology* (pp. 242–243). New York: Rowman & Littlefield.

Frierson, J. C. (2019). Lugenia Burns Hope. *Journal of Health Care for the Poor and Underserved, 30*(2), xii–xvi.

Muhammad, K. G. (2010). The Condemnation of Blackness: Race. *Crime, and the making of modern urban America*. Harvard University Press.

Giddings, P. J. (2008). Ida: A sword among lions: Ida B. Wells and the campaign against lynching. New York: Harper Collins.

Goggin, J. (1983). Countering white racist scholarship: Carter G. Woodson and *The Journal of Negro History*. *Journal of Negro History, 68*(4 Fall), 355–375.

Gordon, L. (1991). Black and White Visions of Welfare: Women's Welfare Activism, 1890–1945. *The Journal of American History, 78*(2), 559–590. doi:10.2307/ 2079534

Hamington, M. (2005). Public pragmatism: Jane Addams and Ida B. Wells on lynching. *Journal of Speculative Philosophy, 19*(2), 167–174. http://www.jstor.org/stable/ 25670563

Hill, R. B. (1972). *The strengths of black families*. New York: Emerson Hall.

Holosko, M. J., Briggs, H. E., & Miller, K. M. (2018). Do black lives really matter—to social work? Introduction to the special edition. *Research on Social Work Practice, 28*(3), 272–274.

Kennedy, R. (2011). *The persistence of the color line: Racial politics and the Obama presidency*. New York: Vintage.

Lange, W. J. (1983). W. E. B. DuBois and the first scientific study of Afro-Americans. *Phylon (1960–)*, 44(2), 135–146.

Longres, J. (1972). The impact of racism on social work education. *Journal of Education for Social Work*, 8(1), 31–41. doi:10.1080/00220612.1972.10671900

McFarlaine, A. (2019). Personal communication February 18, 1919 Allen MacFarlane, on Carey Redrick, his father-in-law's remembering DuBois as his professor, New York University.

Melish, T. J. (2014). Maximum feasible participation of the poor: New governance, new accountability, and a 21st century war on the sources of poverty. *Yale Human Rights and Development Journal*, 13(1), 1–131.

Muhammad, K. G. (2010). *The condemnation of blackness: Race. crime, and the making of modern urban America*. Cambridge, MA: Harvard University Press.

Neighborhood Union collection. Robert W. Woodruff Library of the Atlanta University Center. http://localhost:8081/repositories/2/resources/8

Norton, D. G. (1978). *The dual perspective: Inclusion of ethnic minority content in social work education*. New York: Council on Social Work Education.

Ovington, M. W. (1911/1969). *Half a man: The status of the negro in New York. 1911*. New York: Hill.

Reichert, K. (1970). *Survey of non-discriminatory practices in accredited graduate schools of social work* (pp. 39–51). New York: Council on Social Work Education.

Ross, E. (1976). Black heritage in social welfare: A case study of Atlanta. *Phylon (1960)*, 37(4), 297–307. doi:10.2307/274495

Ross, E. (1978). Ross, E. L. (1978). *Black heritage in social welfare, 1860–1930*. Scarecrow Press.

Rouse, J. A. (1989). *Lugenia Burns Hope, Black Social Reformer*. Athens and London: The University of Georgia Press.

Rouse, J. A (1984). The legacy of community organizing: Lugenia Burns Hope and the Neighborhood Union. *Journal of Negro History*, 69(3/4), 114–133.

Schiele, J. H. (1997). An Afrocentric perspective on social welfare philosophy and policy. *Journal of Sociology & Social Welfare*, 24(2), article 3. https://scholarworks Hospital.wmich.edu/jssw/vol24/iss2/3

Shivery, L., & Smythe, H. (1942). The Neighborhood Union: A survey of the beginnings of social welfare movements among negroes in Atlanta. *Phylon (1940–1956)*, 3(2), 149–162. doi:10.2307/271522

Solomon, B. (1976). *Black empowerment*. New York: Columbia University Press.

Teasley, M., & Ikard, D. (2010). Barack Obama and the politics of race: The myth of post racism in America. *Journal of Black Studies*, 40(3), 411–425. http://www.jstor.org/stable/40648599

Thoreau, H. D. (2004). *Walden: 150th Anniversary Illustrated Edition of the American Classic*. Houghton Mifflin Harcourt.

Washington, F. B. (1935). The need and education of Negro social workers. *Journal of Negro Education*, 4, 76–93.

Wells, I. B. (1901). Lynching and the excuse for it. *The Independent*, 53(2737), 1133–1136.

White, W. F. (1948). *A man called White: The autobiography of Walter White*. Athens: University of Georgia Press.

FURTHER READING: ARCHIVAL DOCUMENTS

Charter. (1911). Neighborhood Union collection, Robert W. Woodruff Library of the Atlanta University Center. http://localhost:8081/repositories/2/archival_objects/12145

Constitution. (1908, 1925). Neighborhood Union collection, Robert W. Woodruff Library of the Atlanta University Center. http://localhost:8081/repositories/2/archival_objects/12147

Correspondence. Neighborhood Union collection. Robert W. Woodruff Library of the Atlanta University Center. http://localhost:8081/repositories/2/archival_objects/12112

DuBois, W. E. B. (n.d.). (William Edward Burghardt, 1868–1963). The Atlanta University studies of social conditions among Negroes, November 10, 1940. W. E. B. DuBois Papers (MS 312). Special Collections and University Archives, University of Massachusetts Amherst Libraries.

History. (1908–1933). Neighborhood Union collection. Robert W. Woodruff Library of the Atlanta University Center. http://localhost:8081/repositories/2/archival_objects/12141

Jane Addams Digital Collection. (n.d.) W. E. B. DuBois Papers. https://digital.janeaddams.ramapo.edu/collections/show/209

Memorabilia. (n.d.). Neighborhood Union collection, Robert W. Woodruff Library of the Atlanta University Center. http://localhost:8081/repositories/2/archival_objects/12120

Neighborhood Union Collection. A tribute of love and appreciation to Lugenia Hope, honoring her on the 25th anniversary of the founding of the Neighborhood Union. Box 7, folder 41. Archives Research Center, Atlanta University Center, Robert W. Woodruff Library.

Neighborhood Union Collection. Meeting Notes. Lesson III, Community organization, 1919, box 1, folder 18. Archives Research Center, Atlanta University Center, Robert W. Woodruff Library.

Neighborhood Union Collection. Newspaper article. Atlanta thanks college women for community service center, 1925, box 7, folder 26. Archives Research Center, Atlanta University Center, Robert W. Woodruff Library.

Neighborhood Union Collection. Photo. Neighborhood surrounding Atlanta University n. d., box 14, folder 15. Archives Research Center, Atlanta University Center, Robert W. Woodruff Library.

Neighborhood Union Collection. Speech. A survey of the opinions of a hundred heads of families respecting Washington park made jointly by the Neighborhood Union and Atlanta School of Social Work, 1924, box 7, folder 5, p. 2. Archives Research Center, Atlanta University Center, Robert W. Woodruff Library.

Neighborhood Union Collection. Speech. Address to the Committee of the House of Representatives of Georgia, 1915, box 1, folder 24. Archives Research Center, Atlanta University Center, Robert W. Woodruff Library.

Neighborhood Union Collection. Speech. Survey of colored public schools (1913–1914), 1914, box 7, folder 1. Archives Research Center, Atlanta University Center, Robert W. Woodruff Library.

Neighborhood Union Collection. Speech. The Cleveland meeting of the YWCA, 1920, box 14, folder 12. Archives Research Center, Atlanta University Center, Robert W. Woodruff Library.

Neighborhood Union Collection. Speech. We have but to look about us, 1908, box 1, folder 24. Archives Research Center, Atlanta University Center, Robert W. Woodruff Library.

Neighborhood Union Collection. Speeches and Lectures, ca 1908–1909 (n.d.). Robert W. Woodruff Library of the Atlanta University Center. http://localhost:8081/repositories/2/archival_objects/12133

Neighborhood Union Collection. YMCA War Council (1918–1919). Robert W. Woodruff Library of the Atlanta University Center. http://localhost:8081/repositories/2/archival_objects/12136

CHAPTER 7

The Launching

Many institutions have their initial organizations established by a single individual. Others grow out of a type of "milling process" in which a single individual plays the major role and other individuals play strong supporting roles. Many individuals contributed to the inception of training for Negroes in social work.

—Florence Victoria Adams (1981)

The 1920s was a decade of transitions that had rippling effects throughout the nation. The confluence of these trends was the final impetus for the launching of the Atlanta School of Social Work on October 14, 1920. Social work was also undergoing professional transformations by the 1920s and seeing a growing emphasis on professionalization and practice specializations. The Child Guidance Movement had been founded in the 1920s. The movement incorporated the preventive approach inspired by the autobiography of Clifford Beers, *A Mind That Found Itself* (Beers, 1908/2006), introduced by the Mental Hygiene Movement. The founding of Child Study Association of America, combined with lectures given by Sigmund Freud introducing psychoanalytic theory to America on his visit to Clark College in Worchester, Massachusetts in 1909, were also among the events that influenced the expanding theoretical framework shaping social work practice during the era. Moreover, the confluences of these developments were contributing factors to the profession's movement toward attaining the systematic body of knowledge that the 1915 Flexner speech asserted was lacking and essential for gaining professional status.

These developments strengthened the relationships between social work, psychology, and psychiatry; the use of the casework method of study, diagnosis, and treatment; and the medical model. Social workers, now referred to "psychiatric social workers," became valued members of interdisciplinary

Find a Way or Make One. Alma J. Carten, Oxford University Press (2021). © Oxford University Press.
DOI: 10.1093/oso/9780197518465.001.0001.

teams in mental health settings armed with a more in-depth understanding of the complexities of the personality and human growth and development across the life span. The stage was set for what was to become an enduring challenge to balance the profession's continuing favoring of anchoring theoretical frameworks for practice in psychiatry without diminishing its founding mission of championing the rights of the poor (Borenzweig, 1971). This ongoing challenge for the profession is examined in Porter Lee's classic *Social Work as Cause and Function* (Lee, 1937).

Now that the fledging profession was better able to claim ownership of a systematic body of knowledge that could be learned and taught to those seeking entry the new profession and armed with what had been learned from the Pittsburgh Survey and other studies examining the causes of poverty, it became apparent that the competencies and skills needed for a professional workforce were far beyond those of volunteer charity workers with good intentions and an altruistic spirit. To unravel and treat the complexity of causes associated with poverty would require a trained class of professional workers equipped with scientific knowledge to support skills and competencies for practice in a profession that was emerging as both science and art.

The rationale and need for a professional school of social work was advanced in papers presented by Anna Dawes on "The Need for Training Schools for a New Profession" and by Mary Richmond, who continued to hold considerable influence in the developing field, on "The Need for a Training School in Applied Philanthropy." In the same meticulous way that she had detailed the casework process in *Social Diagnosis*, Richmond's paper carefully laid out the details for establishing professional schools, including areas such as curriculum design, staffing, and costs (Trattner, 1999, p. 241). By the time of the launching of the Atlanta School of Social Work in 1920, schools of social work had been established in five of America's largest cities. Except for what is now the Chicago School of Social Administration, established in 1908, all had been established under the leadership of personnel of the Charity Organization Society (COS).

The nascent profession had not only founded schools of social work capable of transmitting to new inductees a systematic body of knowledge anchored in science, but professional organizations also were established to identify common needs and for the further socialization of its members into a common professional identity. Soon to follow was the establishment of professional journals that ensured wide dissemination of new knowledge. The name of National Conferences of Charities and Correction was changed in 1917 to the National Conference of Social Work. Pioneering journals such as *The Survey,* which had disseminated information about social service developments, were gradually replaced by new professional journals. *Social Casework, Child Welfare,* and the *Social Service Review* were all social work professional journals first published in the decade of the 1920s. These developments provided the means to disseminate new knowledge, cohesiveness, and esprit de corps among a professional membership, thus further solidifying social work's claims to professional status.

Professional associations also emerged that aligned with models of practice specializations. Included among these were the Association of Psychiatric Social Workers, the American Association of Medical Social Workers, and the American Association of Social Workers. These various specialized associations came together in 1955 under the umbrella of the National Association of Social Workers (NASW) that continues to be the largest social work professional organization in the United States (Trattner, 1999).

As the number of schools of social work continued to grow, it became apparent that some form of accrediting process would be needed. Spearheaded by Porter Lee, director of the then named New York School of Social Work, formerly known as the New York School of Philanthropy, and become the Columbia University School of Social Work in 1963, the heads of the seventeen existing schools of social work came together in 1920; this led to the establishment of the Association of Training Schools of Professional Social Work. After a complex evolutionary process and name changes from the National Association of Professional Schools of Social Work and then to the American Association of Schools of Social Work, the Council on Social Work Education (CSWE) was created in 1952. (NASW Foundation, 2004) Since its creation, the CSWE remains the accrediting and standard-setting body for all undergraduate and master's degree social work programs; it is charged to "to promote the development of sound programs of social work education in the United States, its territories and possessions, and Canada" (Kendall, 2002, p. 109).

Concurrent with this process of professionalization, policy developments occurring during the Progressive Era added new dimensions to theory informing social work practice by giving a new understanding of the importance of childhood in shaping the future adult (Child Guidance; Horn, 1989). These changes also affirmed the family as the primary societal institution essential for the socialization and well-being of children and an essential element of the foundation for ensuring the progressive development of American society. This was memorialized in a resolution of the first White House Conference of 1909, convened under the administration of President Theodore Roosevelt. The resolution acknowledged the irreplaceable role of the family in the assertion that no child should be deprived of a home life except for compelling reasons and never for the reason of poverty alone (Beck, 1973; DHEW, Children's Bureau, 1967; Pelton, 1987).

Acknowledging the family as an essential building block for the progressive development of society in theory and in the best of situations, this resolution might have served as an anchoring principle for all American social policy. Had this been the case, the country may well have avoided the fact that children under the age of eighteen are consistently the most impoverished population of Americans. This statistic has sadly been reported over the full course of US history, in stark opposition to its assertions of being a child- and family-centered society. Moreover, African American children are and have been throughout history disproportionately represented among the population of the nation's children who are poor.

The fate of the child, however, is tied to the fate of her parents. And with US social welfare policy still guided by a lingering "poor law" heritage, initial concerns about the transmission of "intergenerational pauperism" favored policies that came to be known as "rescue and punishment." This approach translated into removing children of the poor from their own homes and placing them in substitute living arrangements where it was believed it would be more likely for them to develop skills that promoted self-sufficiency and good citizenship. Correspondingly, the approach also served as a just punishment for parents who were viewed as complicit in their own poverty. These views were prominent at a time when mainstream thinking held being poor as equivalent to a criminal act.

These concerns for avoiding the pauperization of the population were later transformed into 21st-century concerns for the intergenerational transmission of what was defined as "welfare dependency." This perspective carried forth the tradition of rescue and punishment as the main professional response in the field of child welfare. Moreover, now intersecting with issues of class and race, this thinking accounts for the persistent disproportionate representation of poor children of color in the nation's foster care caseload (Everett, Chipungu, & Leashore, 2004).

The new awareness about the importance of childhood did not encourage a more sympathetic view of poor parents or concerns about the internal life of the family that compromised the well-being of children. More attention, however, was given to the risks in the external environment that imperiled child well-being. Child labor laws were in place by 1917, providing protections to minor children in the work environment, and, by 1911, all states had in place Mother's Pensions programs that provided income protection to children in lone-mother households (Axinn & Levin, 1982; Trattner, 1999). Also designated as "widows' pensions," these single-parent female-headed homes were considered to be among the worthy or deserving poor since the loss of income was due to the death of the father, the accepted major breadwinner for the family.

At the national level, the Child Welfare League of America had been founded in 1920 to serve as a means for advancing coordinated progressive policy developments for children, youth, and families (Lindenmeyer, 1997). Yet, in a nation still divided along racial lines and similar to mother's or widow's pensions programs with caseloads largely of white widows who were considered among the "deserving poor," in other emerging progressive social welfare programs African Americans were either excluded or not well counted among the beneficiaries. And despite the humanistic intents of these policy advancements, the institutional and cultural life of America continued to be rooted in assumptions of white supremacy—and deeply embedded in the customs and traditions of life in the South.

CONCURRENT CHANGES WITHIN THE UNIVERSITY

Atlanta University was also undergoing consequential transformations during the decades leading up to the founding of the Atlanta School of Social Work in 1920 as an independent institution of higher learning and the School's later academic affiliation with the University. Curriculum offerings of the University were becoming more liberalized and freed from the tradition of requiring all students to study the ancient languages. Modern languages were introduced; this gave students a choice of taking courses in French or German as opposed to Greek and Latin. Course offerings also were added that allowed students to learn about their own history. New courses were developed by Benjamin Brawley, a professor who introduced a course at Spelman and Morehouse that was required for all students in their junior year, entitled "Negro American History." At Atlanta University DuBois taught a sociology course for seniors entitled the "Social Condition of the Negro American" (Bacote, 1969; Dittmer, 1980, 1997).

Concomitantly, there was also a loosening of the strict behavioral codes for student conduct that were instituted under the American Missionary Association which required tightly regimented schedules of evening and morning prayers and additional meetings that emphasized Christian purity and duty. The music department, previously limited to courses and teaching in the classics (such as works by Chopin and Beethoven) and a sprinkling of traditional black spirituals, began to introduce new genres that were relevant to the black experience. Students also were enjoying the socialization experiences of Greek letter organizations that were in place by 1928.

Overall, the absolute authority assigned to the school administration, which was the general rule in black colleges founded by white missionary groups soon after the end of the Civil War, was being challenged. At the same time some began to question these institutions being under the virtual total control of whites. And while the sincerity of the teachers who had come to teach at the schools during the early years of their founding was seen as genuine, questions were raised about the ability of the new cohort of whites now teaching in the schools to understand the needs of black students. Moreover, claims were made that the racial biases of the faculty, or paternalism—whether conscious or unconscious—was communicating a "self-fulfilling prophecy" and promoting feelings of hopelessness and of being "less than" in their students (Bacote, 1969; Dittmer, 1980).

One response to these shifts in thinking and increased feelings of agency among blacks was Atlanta Baptist College's (Morehouse) appointment of John Hope as the first black president of the college. Later, Hope was appointed the first black president of Atlanta University. An outstanding and charismatic leader, Hope had not wavered in his commitment to the black cause since his student years. He was dedicated to race work at the time of his first teaching assignment at Roger Williams College; this was immediately prior to his accepting the teaching appointment at Atlanta Baptist College that brought him to the city of Atlanta. Ross (1978) cites from a 1947 publication of *Phylon*, authored by Will W. Alexander, a minister and participant in the Atlanta Interracial Commission, of his impression of John Hope. Alexander had first encountered Hope when he was a student at Gammon Seminary and Hope was at the time president of Morehouse College. In commenting on Hope's charismatic presence, Alexander observed "I was struck first with his light complexion and fair hair to one who was classed as colored. My greater interest was in his finely chiseled, intelligence face." He continued on to write that Hope would have stood out among any group of men, and that one might have the misimpression of him as possessing "austerity or aloofness" but "one could not doubt that here was an unusual person" (Ross, 1978, p. 374). Although not on the formal meeting agenda, Hope was noted to captivate the attention of the audience when he did speak. Hope was later elected president of the Interracial Commission, where the two men served together.

John Hope's namesake, Dr. John Hope Franklin, one of the nation's most accomplished historians, expressed a similar impression of John Hope. Dr. Franklin's publication *From Slavery to Freedom: A History of African-Americans,* is a seminal text on black history that enjoys a global distribution and is now in its ninth edition. The Foreword to *A Clashing of the Soul: John Hope and the Dilemma of African American Leadership and Black Higher Education in the Early Twentieth,* authored by Leroy Davis (1998), presents a scholarly examination of the complexities of Hope's personal and public lives. John Hope Franklin wrote the Forward to the Davis book, in which he comments on namesake's charismatic aura when meeting John Hope for the first time, when Franklin was a student at Fisk University and in Atlanta awaiting news of his acceptance from Harvard for graduate study. Reflecting on the encounter with Hope, Franklin wrote in the Forward

> I can say that this was not only an unforgettable moment, but one of the most exciting of my entire life. He did not have much time, but his generosity made it seem like an eternity especially since I was so excited that I was almost speechless. Placing his hands on each of my shoulders he said quietly but firmly, "so this is John Hope Franklin." (Davis, 1998, Franklin, p. x)

The context in which the University was changing was also affected by dramatic changes that were unfolding at the national level. At the turn of the century America had all but transitioned from an agrarian to an urban society. While more Americans were now living in cities, the South remained the home of the largest share of blacks. Industrialization and advances in manufacturing had made industrial education all but obsolete. With the exception of Hampton and Tuskegee, most of the institutions for blacks had reduced their focus on industrial education. Due to the cluster of schools in the Atlanta University Consortium, the city of Atlanta claimed the largest percentage of college-educated blacks in the state of Georgia. This was a situation that caused whites to bemoan that while they could easily find blacks conversant in foreign languages, it was nearly impossible for them to find good domestics or servants. They urged the schools to return to an emphasis on vocational programs of study. In this context, the status quo for the most part prevailed. Booker T. Washington continued to hold uncontested political power and the strong support of whites owing to his steadfast favoring of industrial education for blacks, which was essential to his incremental approach to their achieving economic equality.

The changing population trends experienced in the city of Atlanta included two new demographics. One of these were blacks who were a part of the Great Migration leaving farms for urban areas in the hopes of sharing in the new prosperity the country was experiencing. The other new demographic comprised whites migrating from mountainous regions of the state to Atlanta. In addition to their poverty, black and white migrants to the city shared in common a limited formal education, the hope of finding work in the new job market to improve their lot in life, and a mutual disdain for one another.

Blacks shared in the disdain of poor, uneducated whites held by the general population of whites from the middle and upper classes. This disdain was expressed in the derogatory term "poor white trash." And poor whites, no matter how little they had, including those living in abject poverty or who were "dirt poor," could claim an undisputed superiority to blacks irrespective of the class or status of the black individual. As DuBois observed in an oral history collection at Columbia University, despite their lower class standing, poor whites

> could follow the old aristocrats into the front entrance in railroad stations, and go with them to the best theaters and movies but in all places, he could sit above and apart from the "Nigger" class. He had a right to the title of Mister, he could sit in public parks, enter the public library where no Negro could enter, he grew to love those proofs of superiority. (Dittmer, 1980, p. 22; DuBois, 1963)

With blacks and whites living in closer proximity, the postwar years also saw an increase in tensions in the political, economic, and social climates influencing interracial relationships in Atlanta. The total segregation of the city of Atlanta in the1920s and the tensions between whites and blacks intensified when black veterans returned home from the war in Europe. This is described in the autobiography of Benjamin Mays, *Born to Rebel: An Autobiography* (Mays, 1971, 2011). Mays, who served as president of Morehouse College from 1940 to 1967, came to Atlanta to teach at Morehouse College in 1921. He devotes a full chapter in his autobiography to describing the state of Atlanta between 1921 and 1924. These interracial tensions were also occurring during the formative years of the School's development.

As he described, at the time of his arrival, the Klan was headquartered in Atlanta, and the city was the home of the Klan's Imperial Wizard. Since its rebirth at Stone Mountain, peaking in the early years of the decade of the 1920s, the Klan claimed a membership ranging from 2,500,000 to 4,000,000 throughout the United States. Many Klan members held elected offices in federal and state governments, and blacks were the primary target of acts of terrorism so horrific that they defy description. Recounting events of 1921 in Atlanta, Mays observed, "As I found to be the case throughout the South, segregation was god—the absolute—and was worshiped not only in secular life but in the 'House of God'" (Mays, 1971, 2011, p. 88).

LOSING HOPE IN THE PROMISES OF DEMOCRACY

Ironically, African American veterans who had willingly fought to make democracy safe for the world, and did so in a segregated military, upon their return home became the brunt of Klan terrorism. These acts of terrorism increased during the postwar years and included a dramatic increase in lynching. Lynching was a public, sadistic killing of blacks undertaken as community social events in which mothers with young children participated. These activities were carried out with a callous indifference to the fact that blacks had contributed to the war effort. Some had worked in defense plants that rolled out the machinery of war in record numbers, others had purchased war bonds that were needed to finance military operations. Still others had paid the ultimate cost of giving their lives to the cause of democracy.

Along with a growing sense of pessimism that blacks could never be treated equitably by whites, back-to-Africa movements emerged during the early decades of the 1920s, nationally and in the city of Atlanta. Jamaica-born Marcus Garvey is best known as the national leader of the Pan-Africanism movement under the banner of the Universal Negro Improvement Association (UNIA). The Association was headquartered in the Harlem community of

New York City from 1918 to 1927. Garvey envisioned the movement to be a vehicle for connecting blacks in the African diaspora across the globe and establishing black colonies and states in various locations around the world, primarily on the west coast of Africa and in Liberia. In Atlanta, a back-to-Africa movement was led by Bishop Henry McNeal Turner who was influential within the African Methodist Episcopal (AME) Church (Dittmer, 1980).

In his autobiography, Walter White reflects on his involvement with DuBois in efforts to launch the Pan-African Congress that would bring together blacks of African descent from across the diaspora and would be held in London, Paris, and Geneva in 1921 (White, 1948). Representing their organizational affiliations with the NAACP and the National Urban League (NUL), the two men traveled together to attend the first meeting of the Congress, which took place in London, England. Being the brainchild of DuBois and therefore anchored in DuBois's intellectual thought, the Pan-African Congress did not embrace the drama characteristic of the back-to-Africa movement under Marcus Garvey's flamboyant leadership style. Moreover, unlike Garvey's movement that barred whites and lighter skin blacks from participating in the movement, the Pan-African Congress welcomed all individuals who recognized the flaws of imperialism irrespective of their race, creed, or national origin. Adhering to policies of exclusion based on skin color being akin to those of white supremacy, Garvey's organizations were not supported by the NAACP or the NUL.

Neither the NAACP nor the NUL, the acknowledged premier organizations working on behalf of blacks, offered their public endorsement of Garvey's back-to-Africa movement. However, a letter from Jesse O. Thomas to DuBois indicates that these two premier organizations endeavored to work in tandem to pursue their differing but interrelated missions, possibly because DuBois was viewed as the go-to scholar on matters of Pan-Africanism. For example, soon after the founding of the school of social work, Jesse O. Thomas, from his position as Field Secretary of the NUL, wrote a letter to DuBois dated November 30, 1926. The correspondence is addressed to DuBois at 59 Fifth Avenue in New York City. Written on official NUL stationary, Thomas thanked DuBois in advance for any assistance he might offer in Thomas's charge to prepare an article on Garvey's back-to-African movement. The letter read "I shall be glad to have your candid reaction and whatever in fact this movement has had on the Negro as a group and thru Negroes on other groups" (Thomas, 1926).

DuBois's goal for the Pan-African Congress was to shed light on the world implications of America's race problem and its interrelatedness with the colonialism and imperialism practiced by other Western industrialized countries that contributed to the subjugation of colonized black and brown peoples in India, Africa, the West Indies, and other locations across the globe. The Congress also sought to improve the unconscionable health and educational conditions that were the plight of colonized people, who, as was the case for blacks in the United States, were systemically denied opportunities to share in the wealth their labor had created (White, 1948/1995).

Although White reflected on the extent to which his involvement with DuBois around the Pan-African Congress opened his eyes to the global implications of the race problem, it was not a cause to which he remained connected. And although DuBois remained committed to the ideology, the Pan-African Congress did not secure wide support in the United States. Nor did the largest share of blacks opt to return to Africa under the national leadership of Marcus Garvey. Neither did the movement take root in Atlanta under the leadership of Bishop Turner.

Marcus Garvey's political career ended after he was convicted of mail fraud, a federal offense, in connection with his businesses. After serving two years in an Atlanta federal prison, he was deported to Jamaica in 1927. Although a controversial figure whose greatest appeal is said to have been with the Anglophone Caribbean community, Garvey's influence on black thought on matters of self-reliance, economic independence, and nationalism was not without significant impact. A public park of the New York City Department of Parks and Recreation carries his name. Moreover, a more factual review of the mechanisms of the UNIA is now possible through an examination of Garvey's papers, now housed at the New York City Public Library Schomburg Center for Research in Black Culture. These papers were found in an abandoned building in Harlem in 1970 (Hunter, 1970). Although not granted, the most recent effort to obtain a posthumous presidential pardon was the appeal made by the Garvey Family, with the support of members of the civil rights leadership, to President Obama.

Back-to-Africa movements had a reach that exceeded what the black community was prepared to adopt at the time. However, together with the synergy of the Harlem Renaissance, the global problematizing of America's race problem spawned the growth of a new sense of black nationalism among black Americans that paired with the emboldened mindset of returning war veterans. Embracing the enduring trait of self-help ultimately led to a determination to develop institutions essential not only for survival but also for the progress of the black community in a hostile white society. The "New Negro" was now envisioning building autonomous institutions that were self-sustaining and black owned, controlled, governed, and patronized.

Combined, the pervasive attitudes of white supremacy that controlled all aspect of black life in Atlanta and the growing sense of economic and political agency among black Atlantans led to the emergence of a thriving business and professional class of blacks and a spirit of entrepreneurship in the city. This new outlook became the driving force behind what came to be known in Atlanta as "Sweet Auburn Avenue." Coined by John Westly Dobbs, the name promoted Auburn Avenue as the "richest Negro Street in the world" (Hatfield, 2018). In the face of these developments, at the Atlanta University Conference held in 1899, DuBois's urged blacks to develop business leagues and enter business in greater numbers. He asserted that "the growth of merchants among us would be a farsighted measure of self-defense and would make for wealth and mutual cooperation" (DuBois, 1989, p. 50).

"Sweet Auburn" Avenue had indeed become the home of one the largest concentrations of African American businesses in the United States. The changed mindset now linking traditions of self-help with nation building and the development of self-sustaining institutions by and for blacks created a new sense of self efficacy among black Atlantans in the postwar years and further fueled the dynamism of the environmental context in which the School was launched.

THE GOLDEN AGE OF THE BLACK EXPERIENCE

The postwar years saw Americans enjoying a new prosperity owing to the sale of wartime supplies to allied forces prior to entering the war and the following shift to a wartime economy upon entering the war in 1917. The United States saw a near doubling of its wealth between 1920 and the year of the fateful stock market crash of 1929. Together, this new prosperity and material benefits contributed to a national exuberance that replaced the war-weary and frugal atmosphere that engulfed the nation prior to the end of World War I. A new sense of euphoria in the national culture accompanied the ushering in of this new prosperity and consumerism of the 1920s, giving the decade the name the "Roaring Twenties."

The Roaring Twenties saw a virtual cultural revolution in America. The most common optic of the era is that of the "flapper." She is the bold depiction of a new generation of women who not only discarded the strict confines of the social and sexual norms of the Victorian era in both lifestyle and behavior but also flaunted it. In popular culture, the flapper as the depiction of the new woman is most frequently portrayed as a young, wealthy, fun-loving, appearance-conscious white female. However, black women were also counted among the new generation of liberated women enjoying new freedoms for women of the era. She had an especially high visibility in the "Jazz Age" occurring concurrent with the Roaring Twenties. Part of the Harlem Renaissance, the Jazz Age saw an introduction of a new genre of music and entertainment introduced by African Americans.

Spanning the years of 1917 to 1935, the Harlem Renaissance was a transformative phase of black life in America occurring over the decade of the twenties. Harlem became the mecca and the cultural center of black life in the country. Alain Locke, who became the first African American Rhodes Scholar in 1909, is considered the architect of the Harlem Renaissance and for what he envisioned as the "New Negro." James Weldon Johnson, now one of Atlanta University's most distinguished alumni for his civil rights activism, along with Zora Neal Houston and Langston Hughes, were among the new generation of black men and women who gained prominence in African American literature during the years of the Harlem Renaissance.

The locus of activities of the Harlem Renaissance took place in New York City's borough of Manhattan, in the black community of Harlem. However, a synergy was created that transcended Harlem. Although the locus of the movement consisted of black scholars, writers, and artists from across the country, others came to Harlem from across the African Diaspora that included the Caribbean and Paris. The convergence of these influences contributed to the transformation of African Americans into a people of increasing transatlantic political, social, and economic significance in what was defined as the "Golden Age" of the black experience (Mitchell, 2010).

AMENDMENTS TO THE CONSTITUTION

New legislation from the federal government was also contributing to the reshaping of the cultural landscape and growing democratization of the country. Landmark legislations of the decade were the 18th and 19th amendments to the US Constitution. The 18th Amendment prohibited the use of intoxicating liquors in the United States; it was enacted by Congress on October 18, 1919. The 19th Amendment, giving women the suffrage, was ratified by Congress on August 14, 1920. Both were consequential during the period in the ongoing push for racial equality and full citizenship for blacks. The 18th Amendment proved to be highly controversial and was seen as overreach on the part of the federal government in limiting individual freedom. Viewed as the most intrusive enactment of social control role by the state, the Amendment was subsequently repealed in 1933 by the 21st Amendment.

The race men and women of the period enjoyed high visibility during the decade of the 1920s. Their leadership created the political and social environments conducive for the enactment of progressive legislation of the period. However, their participation in the social activism of the Temperance and Woman Suffrage movements was tainted by the intractable racism that was prevalent throughout the nation and deeply entrenched in the culture of the South and in the state of Georgia.

The Temperance movement was one of international dimensions and of concern to blacks long before the Civil War. Linking temperance with the abolitionist movement when speaking at a temperance rally in Paisley, Scotland, in 1846, Fredrick Douglass recounted how slave owners used liquor as a tool of social control to suppress the desire of slaves to rebel or escape, asserting that "in order to make a man a slave, it is necessary to silence or drowned his mind" and "I am a temperance man, because I am an anti-slavery man" (Douglass, 1846, p. 291).

The largest share of blacks supported Prohibition. In addition to the moral imperatives that were central to white support of Prohibition, black activists embraced the logic advanced by Douglass that the use of alcohol undermined black progress as a race and reinforced white stereotypes of blacks. More nefarious reasons were adopted by whites operating on the assumption that blacks, who were stereotyped as characteristically docile, became a menace to whites when under the influence. Therefore, anti-Prohibition efforts were undertaken in the South to prevent access to liquor by blacks but not by whites—while at the same time requiring blacks to pay liquor taxes. Undeterred by the racism and their being excluded from white organizations supporting the Prohibition cause, blacks formed their own organizations to promote Prohibition and continued to have significant presence in the Temperance movement nationally (Walton & Taylor, 1971; Yacovone, 1988).

Black academics and social activists were also involved in the long and tedious struggle for woman suffrage, although the movement was tainted by good deal of contentiousness along racial lines. The influence of both Douglass and DuBois was felt in the Woman Suffrage movement: both men adopted a stance in support of universal suffrage as tensions arose from the conflation of issues of race and woman suffrage. These tensions included those that arose around the 15th Amendment that prohibited "denying a citizen the right to vote based on that citizen's race, color, or previous condition of servitude," thus making it possible for black men to have the vote while women, both black and white, remained disenfranchised.

Fearing that conflating the woman suffrage issue with race would result in the loss of support in the South, some white suffragettes resisted embracing the vote for black women (Buhle, Buhle, & Stanton, 1978). Nor could they support black men having the vote before women, which would be the case with the enactment of the 15th Amendment. With race yet again blurring the principle of equality, to build a logical rationale for their positions, the white female leadership drew upon assumptions of white supremacy and claims of the inferiority of blacks.

The willingness to tolerate racist appeals if it meant getting the vote was evident in the statements made by two of the most outstanding leaders in the fight for women's rights. It is perhaps useful to apply concepts from cognitive dissonance theory to illuminate the psychological dynamics that distorted the thinking of two iconic humanitarians and social activists for the rights of women when applying moral and ethical principles in securing equality for blacks. For example, contrary to equalitarian principles espoused by the feminist movement, Susan B. Anthony argued "If intelligence, justice, and morality are to have precedence in the government, let the question of woman be brought up first and that of the Negro last" (Pauley, 2000, p. 388).

Similarly, Elizabeth Cady Stanton, who along with Susan B. Anthony founded the American Equal Rights Association in 1866, said that she did not believe in "allowing ignorant Negroes and foreigners to make laws for her to obey" (Pauley, 2000, p. 388). Douglass expressed his deepest admiration of Anthony and Cady even as he chastised and expressed his deep sadness about the racism apparent in their public statements (Pauley, 2000, p. 366). DuBois, who had devoted a number of editions of *Crisis* to the topic of woman suffrage, always insightful and prophetic, in a 1911 editorial wrote, "the nemesis of every forward movement in the United States is the Negro question. Witness woman suffrage" (p. 243).

Unlike the factious discourse of some white suffragettes, black women were unequivocal in their lobbying for universal suffrage. Moreover, unlike white suffragettes who blamed their men for their inequitable treatment, for black women their quarrel was not with their men but with the systemic inequalities they experienced resulting from the intersection of race, class, and gender. Therefore, their concerns for the rights of women and feminist activities were not undertaken as a response to exploitation by black males. Moreover, while their men were not exonerated from gender-based bias, the social activism of the women was often undertaken in partnership with their husbands.

In Atlanta, Lugenia Burns Hope was among the black women with a strong presence in the Woman Suffrage movement (Rouse, 1984, 1989; Terborg-Penn, 1998). In her activism for woman suffrage, as was the case with Douglass and DuBois, Hope was committed to interracial collaboration and for the universal right to the vote. She did not shirk from pushing back against attempts on the part of white women to marginalize or exclude black women from full participation in reform efforts. When white women on the Atlanta Commission of Interracial Cooperation deleted from a preamble that was written by Hope to a document establishing a mechanism for the participation of black women in the Commission, Hope wrote a series of letters condemning the deletion and the rationale for it, that inferred the intellectual inferiority of black women.

> It is difficult for me to understand why my white sisters so strenuously object to this honest expression of a colored woman as put forth in the discarded preamble. After all, when we yield to public opinion and make ourselves say only what we think the public can stand, is there not a danger that we may find ourselves with our larger view conceding what those with the narrow view demand? (Rouse, 1989, p. 112)

Undeterred by the impenetrable wall that was the guardian of ideology underlying white supremacy and that excluded them from memberships in white women's organizations, reform-minded black women activists formed their own organizations. Hope, along with other black women, continued her activism in support of universal suffrage through the National Association of Colored Women that was formed in 1896.

Not only did the Harlem Renaissance awaken a new sense of cultural pride among African Americans during the postwar years, but black veterans returning from the war came with a new mindset based on their war experiences of being accepted by white Europeans as their social equals. But all was not entirely well with the nation in the decade of the 1920s as the country continued to aspire to achieve the goals of a more democratic society.

Still influenced by the crippling effects of doctrines of white supremacy, the climate of intolerance toward Germans that emerged during the war spilled over to "othered groups" in the United States at the same time as it intensified for blacks. With the growth of the Klan, there was a corresponding expansion of the umbrella of intolerance to include Jews, Catholics, and the foreign-born (Pegram, 2011). Restrictive immigration laws, such as the Johnson-Reed Act ratified by Congress in 1924, were passed that imposed quotas on immigrants based on their nationality. The Johnson-Reed Act, signed by President Calvin Coolidge, and an earlier act of 1917 required the use of literary tests and other restrictive requirements designed to bar groups of certain national origins deemed undesirable (US Department of State, Office of the Historian, Bureau of Public Affairs, n.d.; Imai, 2013).

By the time of the founding of the Atlanta School of Social Work, despite its purported image as the "Gateway to the New South," Atlanta was a city in which Jim Crowism was deeply entrenched in institutional structures and the cultural landscape of the city. Nearly, if not all public spaces were racially segregated. In some cases, this required black witnesses in court proceedings to be sworn in on Jim Crow Bibles (Dittmer, 1980, p. 21).

Racial segregation after the Civil War was not the same as what is seen in de jure or de facto patterns of racial segregation today. Blacks were always disadvantaged by race. However, patterns of racial segregation crept slowly into the lives of Atlantans, beginning with the emergence of Jim Crowism at the end of Reconstruction. Policies separating the races emerged in their most extreme forms following the Supreme Court 1896 ruling in *Plessey vs. Ferguson* (163 US 537). Considered a landmark decision of the Court, the law upheld the constitutionality of a Louisiana statute requiring railroad companies to provide "separate but equal" accommodations for white and black passengers and prohibiting whites and blacks from sitting in railroad cars that did not match with their race. Subsequently, the separate but equal doctrine became the law of the land, holding sway in the North and South until the 1954 ruling in *Brown v. Board of Education* struck down the separate but equal requirement in public schools. The 1964 Civil Rights Act ended segregation in all public places.

In the South, following the 1896 *Plessey v. Ferguson* ruling, signs for "colored" and "whites" appeared on all public facilities. Signs separating the races became common on public water faucets, entrances to public buildings, movie theaters, and all other places that determined where blacks could legally eat, drink, sit, work, or play, and even where they could be laid to rest in public cemeteries. The latter was the case in Atlanta, where the city-owned cemetery was divided by race until the City Council ended the practice in 1963.

However, like the peculiar system of slavery, according to the historical accounting of C. Vann Woodward, author of the book *The Strange Career of Jim Crow* (Woodward & McFeely, 2002), segregation in the South did not become commonly practiced until around the turn of the 20th century. In Atlanta soon after the ending of slavery, segregation of the races was more a reflection of class than it was of race, progressing from exclusion to legal segregation (Blasingame, 1973; Rabinowitz, 1976). Before the separate but equal doctrine, it was not unusual for blacks and whites to live together in the same neighborhoods. For example, black professionals and business owners could be found living in the same neighborhood as working-class low-income whites, and black domestic workers could be found living in homes behind those of their white employees. Moreover, blacks were far more interested in suitable housing than they were in living in integrated neighborhoods with whites at the time.

The new black arrivals to the city from rural areas, however, were characteristically tracked into decaying neighborhoods that were poorly served by the city despite the levying of residential taxes on their inhabitants. Law enforcement of black-on-black crime was virtually ignored by the police. The neglect that was the norm of city officials was combined with the entrenched poverty that resulted from blacks being barred from employment that paid a living wage but being charged higher rents for substandard housing. Unsurprisingly, neighborhoods densely populated by blacks became breeding grounds for crime, disease, and the urban social ills of the day. Race-based neglect on the part of city officials contributed to environmental conditions that far exceeded the capabilities of volunteers staffing the Neighborhood Union and developing agencies for blacks to effectively manage. The increasing numbers of rural blacks migrating to Atlanta who were in need of social services to support them in the transition from rural to urban living were barred from receiving help from segregated white agencies; this increased the strain on volunteer efforts to fill the gaps in services for blacks.

The growing hardship among blacks in underserved neighborhoods was the impetus for establishing the first Social Service Institute at Morehouse College. The Institute provided additional instruction for volunteer workers staffing the Neighborhood Union, which was the only source of help to blacks at the time. In September 1919, Gary Moore, Morehouse sociology professor, conducted the first Social Service Institute at the College, offering courses in community social services, home nursing, and child welfare. During the same time, the NUL opened its first field office in Georgia to advocate the rights of blacks and to push back against the continual erosion of black rights in the South. Jesse

O. Thomas was appointed director of the southeastern field office and subsequently came to play a central role in the founding of the School of Social Work.

THE CONTRIBUTIONS OF JESSE O. THOMAS

Historical documents most often credit Thomas for his contributions as one of the founders of the Atlanta School of Social Work in 1920. However, his autobiography, republished by his granddaughter Rosemary Braxton in 2015, illuminates his extensive efforts to improve the plight of blacks in a variety of venues in both the North and South until his retirement from public life. Thomas's legacy is honored at the Whitney M. Young Jr. School of Social Work, where his portrait is displayed in the corridor of deans in Thayer Hall, hanging among those of former directors, deans, and acting deans of the School near the dean's suite on the first floor of the building.

His legacy is also carried forward in the active professional lives of his two granddaughters, Rosemary Braxton and Nell Braxton Gibson. Both have kept at the center of their lives the promotion of social justice and equity that their grandfather had taught them. The scope of the work of Thomas's two granddaughters, along with that of other next-generation family members, is aptly stated by his granddaughter Nell Braxton Gibson, who participated in the early Civil Rights movement as a student at Spelman College, "Social Justice work has become somewhat of the family business" (Gibson, 2019, personal communication).

Jesse Thomas was one generation removed from slavery. He is counted among that generation of race men who were educated in a historically black university or college (HBCU) and who rose to national prominence in leadership positions in the ongoing fight to secure civil rights and citizenship for blacks. His grandparents were born into slavery, and his parents were among the southern blacks who were encapsulated in the sharecropping system. When Thomas experienced his family's loss of the land they had occupied for decades through the unscrupulous practices of the sharecropping system, he vowed that this would never be his fate. At a very young age he left his family home, determined to make his way to the Tuskegee Institute. While a student at Tuskegee, he became a favorite of Booker T. Washington, who recognized his great potential for leadership. Thomas attended the New York School of Philanthropy and, in 1919, was appointed the first director of the Southern Field Office of the NUL. At the time of Thomas's appointment, Eugene Kinckle Jones was Executive Director of the NUL. Jones had succeeded Dr. George Edmund Haynes, the founder and first executive director of the League, and was another of the principals who participated in the launching of the School.

Earning his degree at Virginia Union College, Eugene Kinkle Jones also is counted among the visionary men and women committed to the race work of the period who had earned their degrees at a HBCU. As the second director of the NUL, Jones led the organization through its formative years, achieving significant accomplishments until his retirement in 1941. Under his stewardship, the League's affiliate offices increased in numbers across the nation, and he was instrumental in removing barriers in employment for blacks and securing a place for their participation in labor unions (Armfield, 2011).

As Thomas wrote in his autobiography, at the time of the 1920 meeting of the National Social Work Conference held in New Orleans, Jones, unable to attend the conference, asked Thomas to speak in his place on the topic of the need f1or a training school for Negro social workers. Thomas, in his role as field director of the League's southern field office, was well acquainted with the great need for trained Negro social workers to serve blacks who were denied services in segregated white agencies. Speaking from the segregated area of the assembly hall in which the National Conference was held, the politically astute Thomas gave a compelling presentation on this need. His insistence on speaking from the space designated for blacks was especially effective in calling attention to the hypocrisy of holding the meeting of a National Conference on Social Work in a segregated facility (Thomas, 1967).

Thomas's presentation was successful in sparking the interest of both black and white participants of the Conference. Following the presentation, thirteen executive directors of Family Welfare Societies from across the southern region approached him about their interest in such a school. All were interested in taking a closer look at what would be the best location in the South for such a school, one that would ensure a close proximity to agencies serving blacks where field placements could be obtained. Each made a commitment to send at least one "colored" person to the school whose tuition would be paid for by their agency.

Florence Victoria Adams joined the faculty of the School in 1947 to develop course work in community organization, and she later served as acting dean after Whitney Young Jr. had stepped down from the deanship in 1961. Recounting the history of school from the year of its founding in 1920 through the 1970s, Adams observed that "many institutions have their initial organizations established by a single individual. Others grow out of a type of 'milling process' in which a single individual plays the major role and other individuals play strong supporting roles. Many individuals contributed to the inception of training for Negroes in social work" (Adams, 1981, p. 2).

Adams's reflections aptly describe the process of the founding of the School, considering the number of individuals and organizations that were instrumental in its launching. From a historical perspective, the foundations of the School had been laid immediately after the end of the Civil War, when representatives of the American Missionary Association arrived in Atlanta and found two former enslaved men setting up a school amid the chaos of a worn torn city: a first priority in the process of transitioning their people from enslavement to freedom.

Robert Cloutman Dexter, Executive Director of Atlanta Associated Charities, had accompanied Thomas to the New Orleans Conference and was also among those individuals who were instrumental in launching the School. Although dated June 1921, but likely authored earlier and before the National Conference, Dexter had outlined a rationale for the need for a training school for colored social workers in a paper on the "Negro in Social Work" published in the June 26, 1921 edition of *The Survey* (Dexter, 1921, p. 439; Ross, 1976).

Dexter described the added value of professionally trained "colored" social workers armed with the foundational knowledge of all social workers but combined with specialized knowledge about the problems of blacks. The delivery and teaching of this basic and specialized content would be further enhanced by their having a shared lived experience with the black community.

Dexter argued that his experience with white social workers practicing with black clients "convinces me that nine out of ten make either one or two mistakes—both fatal" (Ross, 1978, p. 439). One of these errors was for the white worker to insist that the "standards of family and social life which they consider those of normal white people" be applied to blacks; the other error was the belief that "because their clients are Negroes, they cannot be expected to have much in the way of standards." He argued that white workers using the first approach were content with "the dole" for blacks whether in the form of "relief or service." Those using the second approach, when carried to a "logical conclusion means that there is literally no constructive work done with colored people, and that the ideas of family and community life, economic and moral alike are uncultivated and unknown" (Ross, 1978, p. 439).

According to Dexter, "colored" social workers by virtue of sharing a lived experience and existential understanding of the systemic racism confronted by blacks, neither imposed on them standards which at the present were impossible for them to achieve, nor did they see blacks as "non-moral or unimprovable," and the knowledge the worker brought to understanding the black community was an "asset for problem solving" (Ross, 1978, p. 427).

After an exploratory process to further establish the need and location for the new school, it was decided that Atlanta would be best situated for a number of reasons. Previous research had identified and documented the presence of extensive need among blacks who were excluded from seeking help in racially segregated white agencies. There was a concentration of colleges in the city with well-established academic infrastructures that included Morehouse, with its experience of implementing the Social Service Institute, and a pool of faculty to draw upon for teaching. The city was also home to underresourced agencies that were already endeavoring to provide needed services to the black community despite insufficient resources and staffing. And finally, there was a cadre of individuals who leading the effort from academia, philanthropy, and social work organizations, both black and white, and who were willing to pool their organizational resources to support the establishment of such a school.

Mylan W. Adams, president of Atlanta University, although committed to the project, was at the time unable to commit the needed resources. John Hope, then president of Morehouse, stepped up to offer the volunteer services of Gary Moore, Morehouse Professor of Sociology, to serve a director, and the use of classroom space at Sales Hall on the Morehouse campus. These no-cost in-kind contributions made it possible to begin classes in the fall of 1920. Classes were taught by Morehouse faculty and personnel from local social agencies. Moore was the first director of the School. The course listings included economic social theory, medical social theory, medical social problems, community organization, statistics and record keeping, and an eight-hour weekly field work placement (Adams, 1981).

The announcement of the School's opening read

It is the object of the Atlanta school of social services to afford an opportunity for training in the principles and techniques of social work to colored young man and women. Trained Negro leadership and solving the social problems of the south is essential and it is to provide an opportunity for such training that this school is established. It is the outgrowth of a feeling which found expression in the national conference of social work at New Orleans of the tremendous need for college educated social workers.

Atlanta is the best opportunity of any city in the South for such a school. It has a large colored population, there is a splendid spirit of cooperation between the races, and there are several excellent schools and colleges. The various social agencies of Atlanta are in the forefront of the south and all of the leading organizations have developed strong colored departments. Including the Anti-tuberculosis Association, the juvenile court and the associated charities; the southern headquarters of the Urban League are in Atlanta, as well as one of the best organized branches. The classroom work will be at Morehouse College.

The school is fostered by a group of social workers and people interested in social work throughout the section and has a hardy backing and support of the educational institutions in Atlanta. The plan is to offer a one-year course in social theory and practice to qualified students beginning September 1920 and continuing through the academic year.

Beginning with a list of the faculty and their academic credentials, the statement goes on to present other pertinent information. The Faculty was listed as

Dr. John Hope,
President of Morehouse College

Gary W. E. Moore
Director of the School and
Professor of Sociology Morehouse College

Marion Pruitt, M. D.
Atlanta School of Medicine

Newdigate M. Owensby, MD
University of Maryland

Robert Cloutman Dexter,
Secretary Atlanta Associated Charities

Jesse O. Thomas,
Field Secretary Urban League for Southern States

Mrs. John Hope (Lugenia Burns Hope)
President Atlanta Neighborhood Union

Courses of study were listed:

Course I, Economics and Social Theory
  (a) First half year—Economic Theory
  (b) Second half year—Social theory
Course II, Medical Social Problems
  (a) First half year, Physiology and Health Problems; Sanitation, Public Health, Social aspects of Tuberculosis, Venereal Disease, etc.
  (b) Second half year, Psychology and Mental problems including study of Feeble-minded, Insanity and the elements of psychology as applied to work with individuals
Course III, Social Casework
  (a) The first half year will be confined mainly to the family and family case work.
  (b) The second half year deals with specialized case work, Child placing, Institutional work, Juvenile court, Adult Probation, and Industrial Case Work.
Course IV, Organization
  (a) Including Public City and Finance, Committee Organization, Social Programs, Recreation and Community Movements generally.
Course V, Statistics and Record Keeping
  (a) Elementary principles of statistics and their application.
  (b) Methods of collecting and presenting material and social surveys.
  (c) Principles of recordkeeping as applied to social case records. An original Investigation of some phase of Negro life in Atlanta

Course VI, Field Work

To be conducted under the auspices of the Anti-Tuberculosis Association, the Atlanta associated charities, and the Atlanta urban league. And addition there will be a course of 10 evening lectures by speaker is a note on the general subject of the field of social work, these courses these lectures will be open to the public but attended by students in the course is compulsory.

A section on "general information" included the following:

Admission:

Students must be at least 20 years of age and be graduates of high school or equivalent. They must present to the director satisfactory credentials of character and academic qualifications. The college opens September 28, 1920.

As the number of students to be enrolled during the coming year will be strictly limited, it is suggested that applications be made at the earliest possible moment to the director, Professor G. W. Moore.

Fees and Expenses:

The tuition fee for the use cost will be $25.00 payable in advance semi-annually. Students can secure board and lodging at reasonable rates.

Certificates:

A certificate will be given at the satisfactory completion of the year's course. During the first year all six courses will be required of each student for a certificate.

Positions for which this certificate should qualify would be district agents and executives and colored departments of Associated Charities and similar organizations; probation officers in juvenile court; attendance officers, recreation director's; Urban League secretaries and assistance; recreation directors, social service departments of churches, YMCAs, YWCAs, and welfare workers and industry.

Discipline:

The faculty reserves the right to ask any student to withdraw from the school who shows definite unfitness for social work.

All correspondences regarding the school should be addressed to:

Professor G. W. More

Morehouse College

West Fair St., Atlanta, GA

During its first years, the School was located on the campus of Morehouse College using space at Sales Hall; it later moved to downtown Atlanta in order to be closer to the students' field placement agency.

After its opening in 1920, the School's name was changed to the Atlanta School of Social Work, which likely accounts for discrepancies in the dates of the opening: the Atlanta School of Social Services opened on September 28,

1920, which is the beginning of the academic year, and the Atlanta School of Social Work was named on October 4, 1920.

The School opened with an enrollment of fourteen students, with Moore serving as Director until 1922. While on leave from his post as director to complete his PhD at Columbia University, Moore died in 1923. E. Franklin Frazier, who had been Moore's replacement at Morehouse, assumed the directorship of the School after Moore's death and served in the position until 1927 (Adams, 1981; Bacote, 1969). The School advanced in professionalization over the tenure of Frazier; under his directorship, it was incorporated and chartered on March 22, 1924, and moved to downtown Atlanta (Adams, 1981; Bacote, 1969; Ross, 1978).

During its founding and early years, there was a close alliance between the School and the NUL. The three directors who guided the School through the early years had all been League fellows at the New York School of Social Work. The Fellows program had been developed by George Edmond Haynes, himself a graduate of the New York School of Philanthropy, and co-founder of the NUL in 1911. The School of Social Work and the NUL were founded on shared principles of a commitment to interracial collaboration. They were concerned with assisting black migrants during the years of the Great Migration to adjust to life in new urban surroundings and to access social services and employment opportunities that would improve their living conditions. Linking policy, research, and practice, the approaches married academia with the social welfare community, working in partnership with a goal of supporting the progress of the black community in what would be a continuing struggle for equality and full citizenship.

In their beginning years, both the School and the League were dedicated to increasing the number of black professional social workers with skills for effective practice in black communities. George Edmund Haynes had begun this tradition with the establishment of a social science department at Fisk University that served as a collaborative model for recruiting black social workers and linking colleges with urban black communities. His strategy partnered League affiliates with black colleges and social welfare organizations. The colleges were encouraged to integrate instruction on economics and sociology in their curriculum and to supplement this with coursework on urban problems and organized methods of social services taught by Urban League staff who served as visiting lecturers to the schools. The fellowship program supported the recruitment and creation of a pipeline for identifying high-performing black students to offer them opportunities for study and practice experiences among their own people in cities (Weiss, 1974). The alliance between the School and the League resulted in the mutual and reciprocal reinforcement of a shared agenda that did not begin to wane until the decades of the 1970s.

REFERENCES

Adams, F. V. (July, 1981). *The reflections of Florence Victoria Adams*. Atlanta: Shannon Press, in cooperation with the Atlanta University School of Social Work and the Alumni Association.

Armfield, F. L. (2011). *Eugene Kinckle Jones: The National Urban League and Black Social Work, 1910–1940*. University of Illinois Press.

Axinn, J., & Levin, H. (1982). *Social welfare: A history of the American response to need* (2nd ed.). New York: Harper and Row.

Bacote, C. A. (1969). *The story of Atlanta University: A century of service, 1865–1965*. Atlanta: Atlanta University Press.

Beck, R. (1973). The White House conferences on children: An historical perspective. *Harvard Educational Review, 43*(4), 653–668.

Beers, C. W. (1908/2006). *The mind that found itself: A memoir of madness and recovery*. Online: Waking Lion Press.

Blasingame, J. (1973). Before the ghetto: The making of the black community in Savannah, Georgia, 1865–1880. *Journal of Social History, 6*(4), 463–488. http://www.jstor.org/stable/3786511

Borenzweig, H. (1971). Social work and psychoanalytic theory: A historical analysis. *Social Work, 16*(1), 7–16. https://doi.org/10.1093/sw/16.1.7

Braxton, R. (2015). Jesse O. Thomas (1885–1972). New Georgia Encyclopedia. http:georgiaencyclopedia.org

Buhle, P., Buhle, M. J., & Stanton, E. C. (1978). *The concise history of woman suffrage: Selections from the classic work of Stanton, Anthony, Gage, and Harper*. Champaign: University of Illinois Press.

Davis, L. (1998). *A clashing of the soul: John Hope and the dilemma of African American leadership and Black higher education in the early twentieth century*. Athens: University of Georgia Press.

Dexter, R. C. (1921). The negro in social work. *The Survey, 46*, 439–440.

Dittmer, J. (1980). *Black Georgia in the Progressive Era, 1900–1920*. Champaign: University of Illinois Press.

Dittmer, J. (1997). "Too Busy to Hate": Race, Class, and Politics in Twentieth-Century Atlanta. *The Georgia Historical Quarterly, 81*(1), 103–117. Retrieved from http://www.jstor.org/stable/40583545

DHEW, Children's Bureau. (1967). DHEW, Children's Bureau, 1967, Washington.; Pelton, 1987).

DuBois, W. E. B. (Ed.). (1899). *The Negro in business*. Publication 4. Atlanta: Atlanta University Publications.

Douglass, F. (1846). Temperance and anti-slavery: An address delivered in Paisley, Scotland on March 30, 1846. Renfrewshire Advertiser, April 11, 1846. In J. Blasingame et al. (Eds.), *The Frederick Douglass Papers: Series One—Speeches, Debates, and Interviews, Vol. I* (p. 205). New Haven, CT: Yale University Press.

Everett, J., Chipungu, S. S., & Leashore, B. R. (Eds.). (2004). *Child welfare revisited: An Africentric perspective*. Brunswick, NJ: Rutgers University Press.

Franklin, J. H. (1998). Foreword. In L. Davis, *A clashing of the soul: John Hope and the dilemma of African-American leadership and black higher education in the early 20th century* (p. x). Athens: University of Georgia Press.

Hatfield, E. A. (2018). Auburn Avenue (Sweet Auburn). New Georgia Encyclopedia. http:georgiaencyclopedia.org

Horn, M. (1989). *Before it's too late: The Child Guidance movement in the United States 1922–1945*. Philadelphia: Temple University Press.

Hunter, C. (1970). *Garvey's papers found in Harlem*, New York Times, May 8, 1970.

Imai, S. (2013). Immigration Act of 1924. Densho Encyclopedia. https://encyclopedia.densho.org/Immigration%20Act%20of%201924/

Kendall, K. (2002). Council on Social Work Education: Its antecedents and first twenty years. The Social Welfare History project. https://socialwelfare.library.vcu.edu/organizations/council-on-social-work-education/

NASW Foundation. (2004). Katherine A. Kendall (1910–2010): Social work pioneer, educator and first Educational Secretary of the Council of Social Work Education. *Social Welfare History Project*. Retrieved [6/10/2020] from http://socialwelfare.library.vcu.edu/people/kendall-katherine/

Lee, P. R. (1937). *Social work as cause and function: And other papers*. New York: New York School of Social Work.

Lindenmeyer, K. (1997). *A right to childhood: The US Children's Bureau and child welfare, 1912–46*. Champaign: University of Illinois Press.

Mays, B. E. (1971). *Born to rebel: An autobiography of Benjamin E. Mays*. New York: Charles Scribner's Sons.

Mays, B. E. (2011). *Born to rebel: An autobiography*. Athens: University of Georgia Press.

Mitchell, E. (2010). Black Renaissance: A brief history of the concept. *Amerikastudien/American Studies, 55*(4), 641–665. http://www.jstor.org/stable/41158720

Pauley, G. (2000). W. E. B. Du Bois on woman suffrage: A critical analysis of his crisis writings. *Journal of Black Studies, 30*(3), 383–410. http://www.jstor.org/stable/2645943

Pegram, T. (2011). *One hundred percent American: The rebirth and decline of the Ku Klux Klan in the 1920s* (pp. 10, 16, 20). Chicago: Ivan R. Dee.

Pelton, L. H. (1987). Not for poverty alone: Foster care population trends in the twentieth century. Journal of Sociology & Social Welfare, 14(2), article 4. https://scholarworks.wmich.edu/jssw/vol14/iss2/4

Rabinowitz, H. (1976). From exclusion to segregation: Southern race relations, 1865–1890. *Journal of American History, 63*(2), 325–350. doi:10.2307/1899640

Ross, E. (1976). Black heritage in social welfare: A case study of Atlanta. *Phylon (1960–), 37*(4), 297–307. doi:10.2307/274495

Ross, E. L. (1978). *Black heritage in social welfare, 1860–1930*. Scarecrow Press.

Rouse, J. (1984). The legacy of community organizing: Lugenia Burns Hope and the Neighborhood Union. *Journal of Negro History, 69*(3/4), 114–133.

Rouse, J. A. (1989). *Lugenia Burns Hope: Black southern reformer*. Athens: University of Georgia Press.

Terborg-Penn, R. (1998). *African American women in the struggle for the vote: 1850–1920*. Indianapolis: Indiana University Press.

Thomas, J. O. (1926). Letter from Jesse O. Thomas to W. E. B. Du Bois, November 30, 1926. W. E. B. Du Bois Papers (MS 312). Special Collections and University Archives, University of Massachusetts Amherst Libraries.

Thomas, J. O. (1967). *My story in black and white: The autobiography of Jesse O. Thomas*. New York: Exposition Press.

Trattner, W. I. (1999). *From poor law to welfare state: A history of social welfare in America*. New York: Simon and Schuster.

Walton, H., & Taylor, J. (1971). Blacks and the southern Prohibition movement. *Phylon (1960–), 32*(3), 247–259. doi:10.2307/273926

Weiss, N. J. (1974). *Whitney M. Young, Jr., and the struggle for civil rights*. Princeton, NJ: Princeton University Press.

White, W. F. (1995). *A man called White: The autobiography of Walter White*. Athens: University of Georgia Press. First published in 1948.

Woodward, C. V., & McFeely, W. S. (2002). *The strange career of Jim Crow*. New York: Oxford University Press.

Yacovone, D. (1988). The transformation of the black temperance movement, 1827–1854: An interpretation. *Journal of the Early Republic, 8*(3), 281–297. doi:10.2307/3123691

PART II

Moving the Legacy into the 20th Century

CHAPTER 8

Embracing the Black Experience

Education in the past has been too much inspiration and too little information.
—E. Franklin Frazier

The opening of the School in Atlanta occurred at a time when race relations had reached a troublesome nadir. All spaces in the city where blacks and whites interacted were racially segregated by both law and custom. Moreover, Georgia was among the southern states adopting a white-only primary following Reconstruction. As intended, this effectively disenfranchised blacks and made Georgia a one-party state in which the Democratic Party held uncontested political power. This would be the case until the southern democrats, led by South Carolina Democrat and devout segregationist, Strom Thurmond, began peeling away to join the ranks of the Republican Party in protest to the civil rights advancements for blacks made under the Truman administration (Sitkoff, 1971). Moreover, the dynamics of interracial relations became more complex in the city with increasing diversity within the black community. The city was becoming the home of a new demographic of migrating blacks from the rural areas of the state to Atlanta who influenced intraracial relations within the black community.

At the dawning of the new century, Atlanta was the home to more than 60,000 blacks, representing more than a doubling of the black population between 1890 and 1920. At the same time, the city was described as the most racially segregated city in the South. It was the first city in Georgia that had attempted to enact racial segregation by law, although without success (Dittmer, 1980, pp. 12–13; Rouse, 1989). The city's government officials had fought hard and successfully to maintain the doctrines of white supremacy as the social contract for defining white–black relationships in the city. The peculiar system of enslavement produced unequal results for blacks who were one

Find a Way or Make One. Alma J. Carten, Oxford University Press (2021). © Oxford University Press.
DOI: 10.1093/oso/9780197518465.001.0001.

or two generations removed from enslavement and seeking refuge in Atlanta to escape the blatant racism and exploitative sharecropping system in rural areas of the state.

Atlanta was not only segregated along racial lines: the black community itself was becoming characterized by class divisions that were defined by lineage, education, and skin color. Additionally, there were many pathways from enslavement to freedom, and the pathway taken had implications for the success of blacks in freedom.

Those who were self-purchased using their meager allowable earnings while in bondage, or purchased by a relative who earned enough in their own freedom to reconstitute their families that had been broken by the callousness of profit-driven plantation owners benefitted from having a head start on emancipation and the supports of a strong family structure with an established economic foothold in freedom. Those who escaped by way of personal courage, which was the pathway to freedom for iconic abolitionist orator Frederic Douglass, would succeed by the same grit or sheer luck that made their daring escapes possible and likely served them well in freedom. The 70,00 slaves led into freedom by the equally iconic and fearless Harriet Tubman through the network of safe houses of the Underground Railroad could draw upon the social capital and networks garnered over the process of their journey to freedom. Those who were manumitted by plantation owners because of a special bond or shared bloodline would continue to profit from the largess of their sponsors or the privileges that came with skin color.

The level of success and prestige of blacks in freedom was also influenced by their positions and status in the labor force in the system of enslavement. The community of people living under the system of enslavement was not without a hierarchy of class and status that served as the foundation of systemic inequalities passed on in the lives of blacks in freedom (Blassingame, 1975; Durant & Knottnerus, 1999; Harper, 1978). Frederick Douglass wrote of this hierarchy in his autobiography *My Bondage and My Freedom* (Douglass, 1855). Reflecting on the status of enslaved blacks on the plantation where he lived before his escape, Douglass wrote of a distinct system of class and status developed around the division of labor that shaped the lives of those enslaved by the social construction of their identities based on whether they labored in the main house or in the fields of the plantation owner. House servants were afforded an "aristocratic" type of status, while those who did back-breaking farm work were "lowly" field workers.

Based on the assumption that whiteness was a civilizing and bettering influence on blacks, concurrently, house servants were assigned all of the positive attributes associated with their privileged status largely derived from their close association with and mimicking of their white owners in terms of their use of language, behaviors, and their physical appearance based on a shared bloodline with their owners. Conversely, field slaves were assigned the least desirable attributes relative to behavior, physical appearance, and personal attributes.

Commenting on the hierarchical class structure that emerged in enslavement, W. E. B. DuBois observed that because house servants were brought into the closest contact with the culture of whites, a natural role of leadership would emerge among this class of blacks in emancipation. This was related to the fact that they had access to city and town life, were able to gain some amount of education, and were usually a blood relative of former owners. DuBois also envisioned that it would be this class of blacks who would assume leadership roles in the economic development of the black community in freedom (DuBois, 1906, p. 220).

These artificial distinctions were accepted and adhered to by blacks themselves. Experts on racial identity formation today, reasoning from a social learning theory framework for understanding the dynamics of racial identification, explain this as a process of internalized racism brought about by socialization experiences in a racist culture where blacks were assigned an inferior status. This resulted in the conscious or unconscious acceptance by blacks of the underlying assumptions of white supremacy.

Bacote (1969) wrote of the ways in which assigning privilege and status based on skin color was manifested in the culture of the University in a discussion of an organization for black males named the Owls. When initially established, the eligibility for membership was based on scholarship, but it later evolved into an elite group where membership was no longer based on scholarship but on light skin coloring and financial status (p. 243). The School was also sarcastically described by some blacks as "that half-white school" (Dittmer, 1980, p. 61).

Commenting on the differential treatment of blacks based on skin coloring in his autobiography, Walter White (1971/1995), an Atlanta University alumnus and well-known for passing for white when researching lynching as Field Secretary for the NAACP, acknowledged the more favorable treatment he received because of his lighter skin coloring. His father was employed as a postal worker and therefore the family enjoyed a comfortable lifestyle. White also observed that, depending on the context, skin color may well serve as a disadvantage. He described this as the case when he barely escaped with his life when the whites from whom he was obtaining information under the guise of being one of them learned he was black. White also wrote of how light skin coloring increased risk for a white family that was perceived as "uppity Negros," making their home a target of attack during the 1906 Atlanta riots from white mobs who reasoned that it was too good a home for blacks (White, 1971/1995).

Contemporary scholars have also weighed in on the implications of class and skin color for intragroup relations within the black community. For example, Maurice J. Hobson, Assistant Professor of African American studies and history at Georgia State University, sets forth as a central thesis of his political analysis undertaken from a historical perspective that class divisions between poor and working class blacks and the city's black elite have had a continuing influence on the progress of the black community in Atlanta well into the 21st century (Hobson, 2017). A study based on a nationally representative survey designed to examine the relationship of skin coloring to discrimination and health for African Americans found that skin color was a significant predictor of many forms of perceived discrimination from both blacks and whites and affected self-reported negative outcomes such as mental health, depression, and physical health (Monk, 2015).

Celebrity Oprah Winfrey has also examined the issue designated by the term "colorism" in one of her popular Master Classes. As reported in the *Washington Post,* a documentary has been produced on the issue (Anderson, 2015). The Association of Black Psychologists (2013; http://static.oprah.com/pdf/dark-girls.pdf) has published a professional statement entitled "On Dark Girls" that presents a historical overview of the origins of colorism and its implications for the mental health for females of color. In academia, faculty teaching from a race-conscious clinical perspective recognizes the importance of integrating this content, as it relates to internal dynamics within the black community, into class and field courses.

The term "colorism" was introduced by Alice Walker in her 1983 collection of essays, *In Search of my Mother's Gardens: Womanist Prose* (Walker, 2004). The collection is a compendium of essays written from a black feminist perspective, with black women engaged in cross-generational dialogue. One of themes expressed in the collection speaks to the commonalties of the experiences of black women that bind them together in positive ways despite their individual differences. One of these differences is skin color, as captured in the following excerpt, "Mama, why are we brown pink and yellow, and our cousins are white, beige and black. Answer: Well, you know the colored race is just like a flower garden with every color flower represented" (p. xi). Over time the term has taken on a more complicated and layered meaning, including that of intragroup racial discrimination based on the shades of an individual's skin color, or blacks' perceptions of their self-worth measured by gradations of skin color. It was these complexities and the effects on the psychological well-being of blacks reported by mental health professionals that, as discussed in the faculty focus group, were factors influencing a member of the School's full-time faculty to conceptualize and design an elective course around the social and psychological dynamics of skin color and its implications.

Attributes of ancestry, education, and color were all of significance in divisions in the socioeconomic groups of black Atlantans. Occupation was also a determinant of social standing and status. Black Atlantans who were in the upper social strata were typically of mixed ancestry. Included in this elite roster of blacks were members of the professions, businessmen, contractors, postal workers, and college teachers. This population of elites would grow along with the growth of an entrepreneurial class that emerged as "Sweet Auburn" Avenue (Dittmer, 1980).

Memberships in social clubs, lodges, fraternal groups, and churches were also of significance in determining the status of blacks. The Chautauqua Circle was founded in 1913 by a group of educated black women; this group was launched with a limited membership of fifteen as one of Atlanta's most elite clubs. The Chautauqua Circle was an outgrowth of the national Chautauqua movement, founded in 1874, in New York state to train Methodist Sunday school teachers during their summer vacations. Over time the movement expanded to provide educational and cultural experiences. Booker T. Washington was noted to be a frequent speaker at these events. With less formality, the Chautauqua Circle continues to be one of Atlanta's most highly respected black women's clubs (Riley, 2013). The Atlanta University Center, Robert W Woodruff Library holds the Chautauqua Circle Collection spanning the years between 1913 and 2010. The records in the Collection document the Circle's involvement in adult education and current social and economic issues and its assistance to local social welfare agencies (Atlanta University Center, Robert W. Woodruff Library, Chautauqua Club Collection).

The complex dynamics of what was accepted as the "Southern way of life" is deeply rooted in Georgia's racist traditions, going back to the colonial period. These dynamics were made even more complex by virtue of intragroup racial dynamics within the black community. These issues combined to make establishing a professional social work school within an environmental context that was incongruent with the democratic ideals on which the profession was based a daunting task.

This notwithstanding, the individuals spearheading the effort were unswerving in their fidelity to the principles and value underpinnings established by the founders of Atlanta University: interracial collaboration, the co-education of the races, maintaining standards of educational excellence, and instilling in students a commitment to using their education for the betterment of the black community.

With this as a beacon for guiding the work, the School's founders began the process of designing a social work training program for "Negro" social workers with an emphasis on practice in the black community. The black members of the group, most having themselves been educated at Atlanta University, were the embodiment of its founding traditions and values. Along with liberal white co-founders, the group set about accomplishing the task of establishing a school of social work in the South, further imbued with the tradition of selfless service that had been established by the School's first president, Dr. Edmond Asa Ware (Towns, 1942). President Ware also brought to the work an audacious vision that a university could be established for blacks at a time when the prevailing view advanced in pseudo-scientific theory of their innate intellectual inferiority as a race. His was indeed an audacious vision since at the time Atlanta was in shambles from Sherman's fiery onslaught and was a hostile environment that was far from coming to accept the loss of the southern cause that embraced the intractable belief of the inherent inferiority of the black race and built on a foundation of white supremacy.

This is not to suggest, however, that the pervasive racism in the city at the time was met by black Atlantans with feelings of complacency and hopelessness. Much to the contrary. The new sense of nation- and institution-building following post World War I years was further fueled by legal segregation and the Jim Crowism restricting black participation in the social and economic life of the city. Having no other option had added to the determination of blacks to act in their own best interest as they had always done in overcoming barriers of systemic inequities. It was these characteristics of the black community that led to an explosion of the thriving black business sector in which the School emerged.

SWEET AUBURN AVENUE

Spearheaded by Alonzo Herndon, a black business sector emerged in Atlanta to join the academic and activist organizations that had been established following Reconstruction. The son of a white plantation farmer who owned his Alonzo's mother, Herndon was born into enslavement. Many former slaves who acquired some amount of wealth after emancipation were able to do so by catering to whites in service positions that involved transferring the skills brought with them from the job hierarchy in the system of enslavement. This was Herndon's pathway to wealth. Entering with his family into freedom homeless and destitute, Herndon later became a successful black barber, catering to prominent white men in the early decades following emancipation. He parlayed his early business successes as an entrepreneur in the service sector into the formation of Atlanta Mutual Life that expanded into the states of Florida, Kansas, Kentucky, Missouri, Tennessee, and Texas (Henderson, 1977, 1990; Merritt, 2002).

Having no access to other forms of investments or savings, along with concerns for having a dignified burial or not burdening their loved ones with funeral costs, blacks have been historic consumers of life insurance policies. It was common during the period for insurance agents to have high visibility in black communities, selling policies door to door. Blacks eager to become insured but barred from opening accounts in white-operated banking establishments squirreled their meager savings away in safe places in their homes to ensure the timely payments of monthly premiums.

This attribute of the black community made it possible for Herndon to grow his insurance company and reinvest the profits back into the black community.

This strategy allowed him to amass a great personal fortune that made him one of the wealthiest black businessmen in the country. Moreover, with a strong sense of personal responsibility, he also used his wealth for the advancement of the black community. He participated in the founding meetings of the Negro Business League that was the brainchild of Booker T. Washington, and he was a member of the delegation of the Niagara movement under the leadership of DuBois which led to the founding of the NAACP. Herndon was also a generous supporter of Atlanta University, where his wife Adrienne Elizabeth McNeil was a professor, and he was among those providing financial support for the launching of the school of social work (Merritt, 2002).

Owing much to Herndon's business acumen and his commitment to the betterment of the black community, Sweet Auburn had indeed become the "richest black street in the world." By the 1920s, Auburn Avenue had become the commercial hub of black Atlanta and the center for business, social, and cultural institutions. It was home to leading black business firms including real estate, construction, newspapers, insurance companies, banks, and funeral homes. It was also the preferred site for the location of professional offices of African American physicians and dentists and for service-based and small businesses such as florists, grocery shops, and restaurants. With its churches, fraternal lodges, hotels, and establishments for entertainment, the "Avenue" offered all that was needed for the sustainment of a separate and well-serviced community of black Atlantans (Mason, 1997).

The legacy of black economic advancement is enshrined in Auburn Avenue being designated as a historical landmark in 1976. Auburn Avenue stands as a testimony to the self-help tradition of blacks and as a symbolic representation of what blacks have always done in response to forced racial segregation: they created a place of their own where they could eat, sit, play, and work where they pleased and have access to all of the amenities and luxuries they could afford.

Among the events occurring at the national level and having implications for the School's early development was the passing of the torch to a more proactive black leadership during the Great Depression, followed by Franklin D. Roosevelt's New Deal that redefined the role of the federal government in American social welfare. This redefinition and federalization of services brought social workers into public sector social services, created new opportunities of employment for black social workers, and, in turn, increased the School's student enrollment.

THE DEATH OF A CONTROVERSIAL ICON

The passing of Booker T. Washington, the accepted voice of black leadership by whites, was announced on the front page of the *New York Times* on Monday,

November 15, 1915. As reported in the National Park Service Bulletin (n.d.) upon learning of Washington's death, Theodore Roosevelt, said: "I am deeply shocked and grieved at the death of Dr. Washington. He was one of the distinguished citizens of the United States, a man who rendered greater service to his race than had ever been rendered by anyone else, and who, in so doing, also rendered great service to the whole country. I mourn his loss, and feel that one of the most useful citizens of our land has gone."

After being treated at St. Luke's Hospital in New York City for conditions related to hypertension, in keeping with Washington's wishes to be buried in the South where he was born, lived, and worked over his entire life, his body was accompanied by his third wife, his physician, and his secretary back to Tuskegee for burial. Ironically, the back-story of a man who had chosen the path of compromise and appeasement in his creation of an image of a New Negro who was acceptable to whites in death did not escape the scientific racism prevalent of the period, as reflected in the public announcement of his passing. As reported in the *New York Times* obituary, an attending physician had written in Washington's medical record that his death was due in part to "racial characteristics" (Harlan, 1983). There were also unfounded rumors circulating that his death was related to syphilis.

These overgeneralizations and the so-called scientific evidence of pseudoscience that were embraced by the medical profession portended the scandalous ethical violations of the US Office of Public Health in carrying out the infamous Tuskegee Syphilis Study, conducted to observe the progress of untreated syphilis in black males. Because the study has continuing implications for social work scholars and doctoral students conducting research that involves human subjects, it is worth elaborating upon here.

THE TUSKEGEE STUDY

At the time of the Tuskegee Study it was hypothesized that the epidemiology of syphilis was influenced by race. The study was conducted between 1934 and 1972 and carried out in partnership with Tuskegee Institute, the school Washington had founded and had served as its first principal. While individuals associated with Tuskegee gave their approval for the study and participated in its implementation, it is not known if they were told of the real purpose of the study or its methodology.

The study sample, comprised of black men who were illiterate sharecroppers, were told they were being treated for "bad blood." The term "bad blood" was typically interpreted by the men who were involved in the study and the black community in general to include a range of medical conditions. Although a significant portion of the men were infected with syphilis when the experimental study began, none was told their diagnosis. Nor did those infected with the disease receive treatment even when penicillin became available as an effective cure. The victims of this unregulated experimental study, one conducted with impunity and indifference to its human costs, included the men who died of syphilis, their wives whom they infected with the disease, and the children born with congenital syphilis from the disease being passed on from mother to child during childbirth.

The infamy of the Tuskegee experiment subsequently led to the 1978 Belmont Report and the establishment of the Office for Human Research Protections within the US Department of Health and Human Services. Today, these developments are codified under federal laws and regulations requiring the establishment of Institutional Review Boards(IRB). Sometimes referred to as Independent Ethical Review Boards, these committees are tasked with applying research ethics in the review of the methodologies of proposals for conducting biomedical research on human subjects. They have the authority to approve, reject, or monitor these studies to protect the rights and physical and psychological well-being of human subjects (USDHHS, Office of Research Protections   https://www.hhs.gov/ohrp/regulations-and-policy/belmont-report/index.html).

The Tuskegee study was shut down in 1972, following a public outcry when it was brought to light by the Associated Press. On May 16, 1997, President Bill Clinton formally apologized on behalf of the United States to victims of the experiment. Dr. David Satcher, whom Clinton had appointed US Surgeon General, was influential in Clinton's decision to make a public apology (Stolberg, 1997). Dr. Satcher, a 1963 Morehouse alumnus and founder and Senior Advisor of the Leadership Institute at the College, was among those in the audience, along with the survivors of the study. As personal reparation, following a 1973 class action lawsuit filed by the NAACP on behalf of the victims, the survivors of the study received a financial settlement and an agreement from the federal government to provide medical care to surviving study participants and their family members (Perkiss, 2008).

As a final footnote, research findings of factors influencing health-seeking behaviors and trust in healthcare providers highlight that is not hyperbolic to suggest that echoes of the Tuskegee study continue to generate anxiety among blacks irrespective of class or education whenever they or their loved ones are admitted for medical care in teaching hospitals today (Guinan,1993; Heller, 2015) or that the residual effects of the study influenced conspiracy theories at the height of the HIV/AIDS pandemic that disproportionately impacted black communities, with many charging the federal government as complicit in policies that deliberately infected black communities with the HIV virus (Bogart & Bird, 2003; Chandra et al., 2013; Nattrass, 2013).

A NEW SENSE OF BLACK AGENCY

With the new sense of agency and black nationalism spawned during the Golden Age of the "Negro" and the postwar years, the passing of Booker T. Washington opened the door for DuBois, along with the institutional support of the NAACP that he now headed, to become a more urgent and less conciliatory voice for the African American community. Under DuBois's leadership, the NAACP had grown rapidly from its initial founding in 1909 to a membership of 90,000 and 300 branches by 1919. The organization now embraced a more activist approach intended to make black Americans aware of their civil rights, push harder for the repeal of federal and state laws making racial segregation legal, and use the courts and legal action as tools for pursuing the right to vote and equality in access to education.

Walter White, an alumnus of Atlanta University, joined the staff of the NAACP in 1931, at the urging of university alumni James Weldon Johnson. White later gained national prominence serving as Executive Secretary of the organization until 1955. An added value that White brought to his work was his light complexion, blond hair, and blue eyes which gave him the cover he needed to pass for white and infiltrate the Klan. His surveillance and NAACP publications of his findings from these covert investigations of Klan activities, as discussed in his authobigrapy, brought to light for the general public the blatant murders of blacks and contributed to a decrease in the number of lynchings (White, 1971/1995).

SOCIAL WORKERS IN THE DEPRESSION

On the US economic scene, the widespread prosperity of the 1920s ended abruptly with the stock market crash in October 1929 that was followed by the Great Depression and an unprecedented period of hardship and suffering for the American people. Social worker Frances Perkins and Secretary of Labor on the Roosevelt Cabinet that crafted the landmark 1935 Social Security Act, in a 1962 speech recalled the especially devastating effects on American families.

> People were so alarmed that all through the rest of 1929, 1930, and 1931, the specter of unemployment—of starvation, of hunger, of the wandering boys, of the broken homes, of the families separated while somebody went out to look for work—stalked everywhere. The unpaid rent, the eviction notices, the furniture and bedding on the sidewalk, the old lady weeping over it, the children crying, the father out looking for a truck to move their belongings himself to his sister's flat or some relative's already overcrowded tenement, or just sitting there bewilderedly waiting for some charity officer to come and move him somewhere. I saw goods stay on the *sidewalk* in front of the same house with the same

children weeping on top of the blankets for 3 days before anybody came to relieve the situation! (Perkins, 1962)

Social work had again retreated into private-sector micro-practice before the nation began to feel the full brunt of the Depression; however, as the Depression deepened, social workers joined the ranks of the unemployed as a result of forced closings of charitable agencies and the drying up of funds from the state and private contributions. Concurrent with the loss of employment and deepening of the Depression was a growing disenchantment within the profession about the efficacy of micro-practice anchored in psychodynamic theory to solve the large-scale human suffering caused by the Depression. At least this was the case with a radical segment of the profession known as the Rank and Filers (Van Kleeck, 1934; Fisher, 1990).

The Rank and File movement emerged in New York City from the activism of a disenchanted group of young workers who were as concerned about their own economic plight as they were with that of the people they served. Influenced by the thinking of feminist activist and researcher Mary Van Kleeck (Selmi & Hunter, 2001), the movement turned its attention from function to cause and called for reforms that moved beyond those of the New Deal, which were viewed as failing to address the root causes of economic and income inequality in the country. Over time, the cause supported by this radical arm of the profession gradually subsided as emphasis shifted to expanding the benefits that had been put in place under the New Deal. Social work historians today suggest that this radical arm of the profession has received insufficient attention in the literature; they propose that this group represents one of the ongoing trends in the profession of reinventing itself with changing environmental and political contexts within which the profession continues to evolve. (Leighninger & Knickmeyer, 1976; Reisch & Andrews, 2014).

In the years leading up to the Depression, President Herbert Hoover held firm to the traditional conservative economic theory embraced by the Republican Party which purported that, absent artificial controls, the economic system would right itself through the natural forces of the market. Despite the rising panic, growing breadlines, and despair as the numbers of the unemployed continued to grow at an alarming rate, Hoover encouraged the American people to be patient in the belief that the economy would rally and the nation would again experience prosperity. Hoover did not waver from his "do nothing approach" as the country sank deeper into despair and hopelessness.

Nor was Hoover a friend of blacks. Walter White referred to him as "The man in the Lily-White House" (White, 1971/1995, p. 104), suggesting an association between the president and the Lily-White movement. This movement was introduced by a Texas Republican at the 1888 Republican Convention as an anti-black movement intended to appeal to white conservatives as a strategy for disenfranchising and rolling back gains made by African Americans during radical Reconstruction and rescinding the 13th Amendment (Mowry, 1940).

Lisio (2012) disputes the view of Hoover as a champion of anti-black causes and argues that the president in fact worked to promote racial progress within the Republican Party in the southern states. However, as White wrote in his autobiography, the president's lack of goodwill toward blacks came into public view with greater clarity when Hoover submitted to the Senate the name of Judge John J. Parker to consider for a lifetime appointment to the Supreme Court—a man who had openly supported policies for the disenfranchisement of blacks. Harkening back to the post-Reconstruction years in his support for the poll tax and literacy tests, Parker held the antiquated belief, as publicly stated in 1930, that "the participation of Negros in politics is a source of evil and danger and not desired by wise men of either race or by the Republican Party of North Carolina" (White, 1971/1995, p. 105).

To derail the Parker nomination, the NAACP mounted a national campaign with a well-coordinated effort from the national black press. This coordinated initiative, orchestrated by the NAACP under White's oversight, resulted in the withdrawal of the Parker nomination. Moreover, the success of the campaign established the NAACP as the premier organization for using the courts and the media as tools in the ongoing fight for the civil rights of blacks.

As was the case for most of the country, the state of Georgia and the city of Atlanta were hard hit by the Depression. The situation for blacks, especially for those in rural areas, was even worse. As the earnings of black farmers plummeted to virtually nothing, the outmigration to urban areas was again accelerated. At the same time, however, it was also slowed by news from the North that migrating blacks had not found refuge from racism in what they envisioned would be the "Promised Land." Instead, what they had found was that life in the North was no better than the one left behind. They were met with racism that was as pervasive as that from which they were fleeing. Moreover, it was now compounded by the anti-black white backlash accompanying the dire conditions of the Depression years.

As the Depression deepened, widespread unemployment and a paucity of jobs saw some cities calling for the firing of blacks to create jobs for unemployed whites (Brown, 1999; Sundstrom, 1992; Warde, 2016). In addition, policies of the federal housing authority prevented blacks from moving into white neighborhoods, and agricultural policies designed to maintain the stability of land-owning white farmers pushed out black farmers who were largely sharecroppers or tenant farmers (Brown, 1999; Trattner, 1999). Service jobs previously held by blacks were now coveted by whites. The prevailing view in these hard times was that no black should hold a job until every white was employed. In Atlanta, a group known as the Black Shirts modeled after the Nazism of Germany boldly paraded with racists signs discouraging the employment of black men so long as a white man was without a job.

As the country sank deeper into the Depression with no hope of relief from the Hoover White House, the demand for a response from the federal government led to the landslide election of Franklin Delano Roosevelt to the presidency in the 1932 election. In light of the unprecedented suffering faced by Americans, the then governor of New York, Roosevelt observed in his May 22, 1932 Commencement address given at Oglethorpe College University https://source.oglethorpe.edu/2012/05/22/remembering-fdrs-commencement-speech-at-oglethorpe/ that the country was "demanding bold persistent experimentation, it is common sense to take a method and try it. . . . If it fails admit it freely and try another. But above all else try something!".

ROOSEVELT AND THE NEW DEAL

Holding true to his campaign promise, upon entering office Roosevelt enacted a plethora of programs that gave life to his belief that economic security and liberty were synonymous. In his July 2, 1932, acceptance speech given at the Democratic Convention, he declared the "federal government has always had, and still has a continuing responsibility for the broader general welfare." He also set the nation on a new path in his promise to the American people in the same speech: "I pledge you, I pledge myself, to a new deal for the American people."

FDR's pronouncement that the American people had a right to expect their federal government to protect them from the want that came with the cyclical ups and downs of the economy was a fundamental reversal of the nation's "poor law" heritage that held people complicit in their own poverty and which was essential for safeguarding the core values of individualism and self-reliance as fundamental to capitalism. Progressive reforms undertaken by FDR's New Deal resulted in the virtual transformation of the economic and cultural landscape of the country. These fundamental reforms formally ushered in the American social welfare state with the enactment of the 1935 Social Security Act (SSA).

The 1935 law was lauded as a fundamental shift from the nation's Elizabethan "poor law" heritage that had shaped the American philosophy of social welfare since the Colonial period (Cohen, 1983). This shift changed the mindset of the quantification of need based on the perceived worthiness of the individual as well as the concept of "less eligibility," requiring that those supported by public funds were never to be supported at a level higher than that of the lowest paid worker (Katz, 1996; Jansson, 1993/2009; Trattner, 1999). No longer viewed as charity, the American social welfare state is anchored in the concept of equality, and benefits provided are based on entitlement and a right of citizenship. With the ushering in of the American social welfare state under the 1935 SSA, the US federal government allocated a portion of the country's gross national product to the financing of programs to provide for the social and economic security of citizens. Accordingly, since these were services that would be used by all people at some point over their life span, these services were to be paid for by the redistribution of income through the government's power of taxation.

The New Deal programs used a three-pronged approach of relief, recovery, and reform. Some direct relief came in the form of in-kind benefits of food, clothing, and fuel. The largest share of the benefits, and the most popular, came in the form of work relief through public works jobs that avoided the stigmatizing effects of a government dole. Programs directed toward recovery were aimed at preserving the country's free enterprise system and restoring the public's confidence in the financial system by putting in place policies that safeguarded the solvency of banks. Mortgage loans were provided to preserve private property and home ownership. Loans to farmers prevented farm foreclosures and ensured the continued production and distribution of the nation's food supply.

The alphabet soup of temporary programs touched every aspect of American life and culture. The Federal Emergency Relief Act (FERA) of 1933 established a system of federal relief to states to provide cash assistance to the needy throughout the country. The Public Works Administration (PWA) provided federal funds for job creation to relieve unemployment through large-scale construction projects. The Civil Works Administration (CWA) of 1933 had a similar goal of creating jobs, and it funded smaller projects designed to improve the nation's infrastructure. The CWA was also a popular program that was favored by both blacks and whites for its emphasis on work versus the dole, thus preserving a sense of self-worth. The Civilian Conservation Corps (CCC) was a highly popular New Deal program. Eligibility to the program was open to unemployed teenage males who were put to work on environmental and forest restoration projects throughout the country. The program had the added benefits of taking idle young men off the streets, where they were at risk of becoming troublemakers, and provided nutrition, medical care, and dental care to youths whose health had been severely neglected. Moreover, the requirement that they send a portion of their earnings home put money in the hands of their families and had the rippling effect of a continuing stimulation of spending needed to bolster the economy (Trattner, 1999).

The Federal Writer's Project was a component of the WPA that provided jobs for writers. Following patterns of discrimination that blemished all the New Deal Programs, blacks were initially excluded from participation in the Writer's Project. As these discriminatory practices were brought to light, Ralph Ellison, Zora Neale Hurston, and Richard Wright participated in the Project—all of whom went on to achieve national literary acclaim. The Metropolitan Museum of Art is the current home of a collection of works by African American Artists from the Federal Arts Projects (1929–1945) that depict the lives of African Americans during the Depression and New Deal and portray the history and contributions of blacks. Another enduring product of the WPA is the Slave Narrative Collection that is housed in the Library of Congress Digital Collection. Compiled in seventeen states during 1936–1938, the Collection is comprised of more than two thousand interviews with blacks living in freedom who tell in their own words the story of the country's shameful history of black enslavement.

Indisputably the most consequential social legislation that had far-ranging implications for the profession of social work was the enactment of the 1935 SSA. The signature legislation of the Roosevelt's New Deal, the act created the two-tier safety net program for Americans: the contributory social insurance programs that provided income support to the surviving dependents of workers in the event of their death or incapacitation and Social Security benefits for retired older Americans and means-tested public assistance programs for the poor.

SOCIAL WORK LEADERSHIP

Frances Perkins and Harry Hopkins, social workers from the Settlement House movement, were among President Roosevelt's closest advisers during his tenure as Governor of New York State. He brought both with him to the White House, and both played an essential role in the design and implementation of the New Deal and SSA (Abbott, 1941; Perkins, 1946). Perkins, as Secretary of Labor, the only female member of the president's cabinet, headed the Committee on Economic Security established by executive order of the president to be the architect of the SSA. The task of the committee was to study the problem of economic insecurity and make recommendations to Congress as the basis for legislation to provide a permanent plan of protection against threats to the economic security of Americans during times of unemployment, disability, illness, and old age. As head of FERA, Hopkins's directive that MSW-trained social workers be employed in each of the newly created public welfare offices was a game changer for the social work profession that also had significant implications for bringing professional social workers into public-sector social welfare.

The bill sent to Congress seeking the authorization of what was to become the SSA and cornerstone of the American social welfare state was highly controversial. Some believed that it pushed the country toward socialism and that the introduction of the social welfare state posed a threat of diminishing the workings of a capitalistic economic system. Roosevelt himself expressed disappointment that the act did not go far enough in its failure to include provisions for universal healthcare for Americans. The original act included Old Age Assistance, which was envisioned as a temporary program to provide immediate relief to the indigent elderly and would gradually disappear as more people were captured by the contributory social insurance programs or the retirement benefits to the elderly under Old Age Insurance. The Aid to Dependent Children (ADC) program, was a state-based program for children in needy families and included unemployment benefits, grants to states for maternal and child welfare and public health programs, and Aid to the Blind (Altmeyer, 1966; Cohen, 1960; Trattner, 1999).

The conditions under which blacks lived were improved by the New Deal's temporary programs and the permanent programs provided under the SSA, but these programs were not immune from the structural racism and discriminatory practices that were the accepted norm within American culture (Carten, 2016; Warde, 2016; Stoesz, 2016). Discriminatory practices contributed to a low participation of blacks in the work-related social insurance programs and resulted in their overrepresentation in programs that were considered the dole. The psychologically damaging effects of dependency on unencumbered cash benefits prompted FDR to say "We must quit this business of relief" was echoed by Forrester B. Washington, who headed the Negro Division of FERA and later was the director of the School of Social Work at Atlanta University.

Speaking from his post as Director of the Negro Division of the FERA about the backlash against blacks resulting from the panic created by the Depression and the harmful effects of long-term dependency on relief, Forrester B. Washington, in a presentation given at the sixty-first meeting of the National Conference on Social Work, held in Kansas City, on May 26, 1934 (Proceedings of the National Conference on Social Welfare, 1934, https://socialwelfare.library.vcu.edu/eras/great-depression/the-negro-and-relief-part-i/) spoke of the accumulation of inequities imposed on blacks to justify favorable treatment of whites.

> Many of the occupations had been held traditionally by Negroes, hence the employers had no factual basis for concluding that white labor would be more efficient than black in the particular trades in question. In fact, there were instances in which the white labor proved so unsatisfactory that the employers turned back to Negro labor. (Washington, 1934)

After speaking directly to the unequal treatment of blacks and outlining significant barriers confronting blacks in access to life-sustaining social welfare benefits, Washington stated in the speech that this was not only a southern problem, but that he had

> perhaps dwelt at too great a length upon conditions in the South. I have done so, however, only because the great mass of Negroes still resides in the South-and especially in the rural South. But I do not wish to give the impression that the

North is guiltless in disfranchising the Negro in industry and forcing the race to become in large numbers clients of the relief organizations.

In industrial and commercial centers throughout the North, the Negro has been (and is being) displaced by whites in jobs which he has held traditionally. If space permitted, I could insert a long list of occupations in northern cities in which pale faces have been substituted for black ones (Washington, 1934).

Washington also prophetically predicted in the speech what became a reality for urban blacks when, as argued by sociologist William Julius Wilson (1980; 1996), welfare replaces meaningful work. Making the following points in his Conference presentation Washington observed

First, there is the danger of making the Negro, as a race, a chronic dependent and forcing upon the Federal Emergency Relief Administration . . . and, second, there is the danger of developing racial friction through creating resentment on the part of the majority public against the presence of so many Negroes on the relief rolls. (Washington 1934)

Employment discrimination in the decades of the 1930s and 1940s led to the low participation of blacks in the favored work-related social insurance programs; this can be said to be the root of structural inequalities that have resulted in the persistent overrepresentation of African Americans on the public assistance rolls in the 20th and 21st centuries. During these decades, blacks typically worked in menial jobs. These jobs were not tied to the workforce, and blacks were typically paid in cash or "off the books." Therefore, they were not eligible for social insurance programs that required contributions from both employers and employees through payroll taxes. Nor did black families fare much better under the ADC program.

The ADC was an extension of the state-operated mothers' pension programs, where white widows were the primary beneficiaries. The criteria for eligibility and need were state-determined; therefore, blacks continued to be barred from full participation, especially in the South, which operated under strict adherence to the 1896 "separate but equal" Supreme Court decision. Southern blacks were also further disadvantaged by policies of states' rights, the most potent legacy of the Civil War, reserving certain political powers to the state versus the federal government. It was also envisioned by the framers that the ADC program would die a sort of natural death as more families were captured under the work related social insurance programs. This was not the case due to the racist roots of the program and continuing structural racism from which the country seemed unable to escape. Moreover, the residual effects of these inequities were carried forward when the program, under the Kennedy administration, was renamed the Aid to Families with Dependent

Children in the 1962 Public Welfare Amendments to the SSA, and again when it was replaced in 1996 by the Temporary Assistance to Needy Families program enacted under the Clinton administration.

Blacks were especially disappointed by Roosevelt's failure to support NAACP efforts for a federal anti-lynching bill. A communication dated March 19, 1936, to Walter White from Mrs. Roosevelt illustrated her disappointment that she could not sway the President to the side of the anti-lynching cause:

> My Dear Mr. White,
>
> Before I received your letter, I had been in to see the president . . . I told him it seemed rather terrible that one could not get anything done and I did not blame you in the least for feeling there was no interest in this very serious question. I asked him if there were any possibility of even one step taken, and he said the difficulty is that it is unconstitutional for the federal government to step into the lynching situation. The government has only been allowed to do anything about kidnapping because of its interstate aspects. The president feels that lynching is a question of educating and rallying good citizens and creating public opinion so that localities themselves will wipe it out. I am deeply troubled as it seems to be a terrible thing to stand by and let it continue and feel that one cannot speak out as to his feelings . . . I think your next step should be to speak to important people in the senate. (E. Roosevelt, 1936)

Despite these shortfalls and the reluctance of FDR to sign onto black causes for fear of losing the support of Southern democrats, the goodwill created by the Roosevelt administration, mainly through the efforts of First Lady Eleanor Roosevelt, motivated some blacks to shift their affiliation from the Republican Party of Lincoln to the Democratic Party. This good will toward the administration prompted Mary McLeod Bethune to observe that the Roosevelt era was the first time in their history that blacks could raise grievances with the expectation that their concerns would not be misinterpreted but heard with a sympathetic understanding (Brown, 1999).

Bethune was the only female member of FDR's Black Cabinet, which was a think-tank comprised of leading African American intellectuals and social activists who helped shape the New Deal programs (Brown, 1999; Weiss, 1983). Included among Bethune's numerous accomplishments are the Daytona Educational and Industrial Training School in 1904, a HBCU that is now named Bethune-Cookman University. As head of the Negro Division of the National Youth Administration, she was the highest ranking black woman in the Roosevelt administration. Sharing a close relationship with Lugenia Burns Hope, her influence would be felt in the shaping of the Atlanta School of Social Work.

During the period of the School's planning and at the time of its opening, training schools for the new profession of social work had already been developed in the latter part of the 19th century. By 1929, there were twenty-five graduate schools of social work in the nation, and most were located in the nation's urban centers. Many of the individuals who played a central role in the founding of the Atlanta School of Social Work in 1920 had been educated at the first of these schools, which had begun as a summer session offered by the New York City COS in 1898. This later evolved to offer a full course of study including an apprenticeship component as the New York School of Philanthropy. It continued to evolve from a free-standing social work program; it was renamed the New York School of Social Work and renamed again, in 1963, as the Columbia University School of Social Work. Columbia University followed the precedent established by Atlanta University of housing schools of social work within universities to draw upon the knowledge base of other academic disciplines and to anchor social work education in the liberal arts perspective, which continues to be the foundation of professional social work education.

The curriculum of the individual, predominately white, developing schools of social work reflected the practice preference and theoretical orientations of their founders. Therefore, these schools increasingly favored the use of the medical model as the conceptual anchor for the development of course offerings. The school that became the Atlanta School of Social Work, as conceptualized by the founders, was designed to include this general content essential for practice with members of the dominant white culture and infused additional specialized content viewed as essential for social work practice in the African American community.

Unlike schools of social work that had developed under the auspices of the COS, which emphasized the casework method, the School's curriculum from the onset included courses on research and community organization, as influenced by the legacy of DuBois and Hope, and commitment to the scientific method that continued to be emphasized under the directorships of E. Franklin Frazier and Forrester B. Washington. In the years leading up to the Depression, with mainstream social workers wedded to the medical model and psychiatric social work in private-sector mental health agencies, this gave graduates of the School an added advantage as it became clear that the large-scale hardships resulting from the failures of the mechanisms of the economic system could not be treated using intervention models formulated from psychodynamic theoretical frameworks.

Supported in large part by individual contributions, the School opened its doors in the fall of 1920 with an enrollment of fourteen students. The first classes were conducted in Sales Hall on the campus of Morehouse College. Courses were taught by faculty from the Consortium Schools, staff from

Atlanta social work agencies, and members of the Board of Directors. Later outgrowing these quarters, in 1923, the School was moved to "Sweet Auburn Avenue," moving first to Northeast 193 Auburn Avenue and later to 239 Auburn Avenue to occupy the top floor of the historic Herndon Building. The building had been constructed by Alonzo Herndon, who had risen to become one of Atlanta's wealthiest and most influential residents. As the School continued to grow, it was relocated again to Quarles Hall. In 1932, the building was physically moved from Chestnut Street and relocated to Southwest 247 Henry Street.

The three-story Quarles Building remained the home of the School of Social Work until 1995, when a fire destroyed 75% of the building (Jet, 1995). The building was renamed the Quarles-Washington Building to acknowledge the contributions of Rev. Frank Quarles, the legendary minister of Friendship Baptist Church, and Forrester B. Washington, director of the School from 1927 to 1954.

The fire and the destruction of the Quarles Building had a devastating, even traumatic impact on the School community. The building had stood as the symbolic representation of the legacy of the race men and women who had demonstrated that it was possible to aspire to the ideals of a more "perfect union," an aspiration they held on to even when faced with what seemed to be the insurmountable odds of developing a school of social work built on the premise of interracial collaboration in the segregated south at the turn of the 20th century.

Decades later, the emotions associated with the fire were palpable in the focus group conducted with members of the school's full-time faculty for the purposes of this book. The faculty members participating in the focus group were unanimous in their opinion that the presence of Dr. Richard Lyle had been invaluable in buffering the faculty against the full impact of both the physical and psychological losses accompanying the destruction of the building and its irreplaceable documents. He shepherded the school community through the traumatic period of the relocation of the School to the new site. Lyles also played a central role in overseeing efforts to salvage the documents and artifacts housed in the historic building. However, despite having contracted the services of a fire restoration company to salvage them, tragically most could not be saved or restored.

Lyle, a 1964 alumnus of the school, was among the last group of students to earn the master of social work degree as an Urban League Fellow, the program created by George Edmond Haynes as a pipeline for securing exceptional leaders for executive leadership in Urban League affiliates. He is also distinguished for his contributions to the School as its longest serving interim dean. As the University administration struggled to maintain financial solvency, Lyles is credited with providing stability for the School amid a troubling time of unsubstantiated allegations of questionable financial practices and disregard of the governance structures viewed as integral to the collegiality that distinguishes the culture of the academy. Lyle served as chair of the PhD program during the years when the School was defining the focus of its newly established program for a doctoral degree in social welfare, and he continues to hold a full-time faculty appointment teaching in the school's doctoral program.

A comprehensive renovation of the Thayer Building was completed to provide a new home for the Whitney M. Young Jr. School of Social Work. The renovated building provides space for offices, classrooms, and demonstration laboratories. The Building is the second oldest on the campus and has been designated a historical landmark.

THE DIRECTORSHIP OF E. FRANKLIN FRAZIER

After the untimely death of Gary Moore, E. Franklin Frazier, who had been Moore's replacement at Morehouse assumed the directorship of the School, serving a five-year term from 1922 to 1927 (Adams, 1981; Bacote, 1969; Ross, 1978). Similar to his contemporaries and others associated with the School's founding, Frazier had strong ties with the HBCUs. He was born into a middle-class family in Baltimore, Maryland, on September 24, 1894. He attended segregated public schools in Baltimore and, after graduation, enrolled in Howard University in Washington, DC. After graduating from Howard in 1916 he began a career in teaching at Tuskegee Institute. He later attended Clark University in Worcester, Massachusetts, earning his MA degree in 1920, writing on the topic of "New Currents of Thought Among the Colored People of America." Frazier continued his studies at the New York School of Social Work as an Urban League Fellow, the program founded by George Edmond Haynes to prepare a cohort of leaders to head the affiliate offices of the National Urban League. He later left the United States to study at the University of Copenhagen as a Fellow of the American Scandinavian Foundation. It was on his return from Copenhagen that he joined the faculty of Morehouse College, from which he was appointed director of the Atlanta School of Social Work.

The joint appointments with Morehouse College and Atlanta University allowed Frazier to marry his interests in sociology and social work. This was an orientation that influenced his conceptualization of the design of the academic program at Atlanta University that he carried with him to Howard University, where he played a central role in founding the social work program at Howard.

Howard University followed a historical path similar to that of Atlanta University, having been founded by missionaries in 1866, initially as a school for the training of ministers. The University is named for Oliver Otis Howard, the commissioner of the Freedmen's Bureau, who had used his influence to support Edmond Asa Ware's vision of a university for blacks in Atlanta, Georgia. The School of Social Work at Howard University was founded during the Depression years, when few of the schools of social work that had developed in predominately white universities accepted blacks, which was the case for all universities in Washington, DC. Along with Inabel Burns Lindsay, the first dean of the Howard School of Social Work and also an Urban League Fellow who studied at the New York School of Philanthropy, Frazier played a pivotal role in the School's founding and in the development of the core curriculum that placed an emphasis on service to the African American community. Like the social work program at Atlanta University, the social work program developed at Howard emphasized infusing the black perspective throughout its curricula.

Frazier played a central role in the development of the inaugural social work curricula in the social work programs of both Atlanta and Howard Universities. He also pioneered the bringing together of black sociological thought with black social work as both were being developed. Yet he is best known for his work as a sociologist, and his scholarship pertinent to social work has received scant attention in the literature.

An outspoken and controversial scholar and intellectual activist applying the tools and concepts drawn from modern sociological analytical theory, Frazier published extensively on problems encountered by Northern blacks (Edwards, 1968, 1974). A prolific author on the topic of race relations, his books *The Negro in the US*, *The Negro Family in the US*, and *Black Bourgeoisie* were published after Frazier had completed the PhD in sociology at the University of Chicago in 1931. Frazier's 1957 publication *Black Bourgeois* presented a controversial analysis of the trajectory of blacks from their origins in the poverty of the South to the achievement of middle-class status. Frazier asserts that this process resulted in a loss of this aspiring group's black historical roots and racial identity. Furthermore, according to his analysis, instead of securing the acceptance by whites that they coveted, the outcome for these aspiring blacks was an internalized sense of race-based self-hatred.

His PhD dissertation, *The Negro in the United States*, published as a book in 1939, was equally provocative albeit from a different perspective. Frazier's analysis was not optimistic and reported situations of family disintegration and dysfunction and of black youth moving from the poverty of the rural South only to fall victim to the social ills of the toxic environment of urban inner cities. This view portended Moynihan's description of the black family as a "tangle of pathology" in the publication, *The Negro Family: The Case for National Action*, sometimes referred to as the "Moynihan Report" (Moynihan, 1965). The Report was hotly disputed by black scholars, the most notable being Dr. Andrew Billingsley's *Black Families in white America* (1968) examination of the black family from a systems perspective. Billingsley's, objective scholarly analysis yielded a more positive view, and, in later publications focusing on strengths and durability, he defined the black family using adjectives like "strong," "adaptive," and "resilient" (Billingsley, 1992). Both Frazier and Billingsley describe various forms of family structures and the formation of black families that are of continuing relevance in the study and teaching of content on African American families in the 21st century.

The substantial body of Frazier's scholarship focused on the black church and the black family. He was highly critical of the black church and the emphasis of black ministers on emotions that, for Frazier, stressed "getting Negroes into heaven than in getting them out of the hell they lived in on earth" (Frazier, 1924, p. 252). As a social work educator and administrator, Frazier rejected the view that a favorable attitude and a desire to help on the part of the practitioner was sufficient for social work practice in the black community. Accordingly, he established high academic standards in the curriculum and equally high admission requirements for the acceptance of applicants (Frazier, 1923). Much like DuBois, whose intellectualism was anchored in sociological theory, Frazier placed considerable weight on the scientific method to support theory building to inform practice with demonstrated effectiveness for solving social problems affecting the black community.

Schiele (1999) is among the few social work scholars who have examined Frazier's contribution to social work theory building and its implication for social work practice in the 21st century. In a critical analysis of a substantive body of Frazier's scholarship, Schiele observed that it was during his tenure as director of the School that Frazier's conceptualization of social work theory expanded and crystallized. This allowed Frazier to make significant contributions for expanding the knowledge base of social work and made him among the first to integrate a "black perspective" into the knowledge base of the profession. Emerging from this analysis, Schiele suggests the following dominating themes that have continuing implications for the profession: the impact of enslavement on blacks and on the black family; a commitment to the application of the scientific method to identify, alleviate, and eliminate the social problems experienced by African Americans; the need for blacks to establish business cooperatives; and his scholarly critique of racism (Schiele, p. 110).

Platt and Chandler (1988) are also among contemporary authors calling attention to the low visibility of Frazier's publications and those of other black intellectuals in the 20th century social work literature. In regard to Frazier, they argue that his scholarship is of special relevance to the profession today since the country continues to grapple with the issues of race that troubled it in the early decades of the 20th century.

While other black intellectuals may have been reluctant to confront the potential risks of speaking forthrightly on matters of race, this was far from being the case with Frazier. His publications challenged the extant theory that advanced unfounded assumptions anchored in conventional wisdom and scientific racism that supported the status quo and a false narrative on matters of race. These flawed theories also found a place in the early development of social work education. For example, Edward Devine, founder of the New York School of Philanthropy, wrote in a 1920 article published in the *Survey* about the Klan "it is easy to laugh at the absurdities of the Klan, it's childish follies, it's illicit nomenclature, its fallacious conception of law and order. But it is not easily laughed out of existence—close at hand it is serious. It has a certain dignity of purpose" (Devine, 1922, pp. 10–11).

Frazier challenged the assumptions underlying scientific racism that influenced theory building in predominately white schools of social work. He refused to attend segregated social work meetings, remarking that he would not participate in meetings where blacks were treated as if they were unfit for human association. It was indeed Frazier's outspokenness on race matters and the controversy around the article "The Pathology of White Racism," published while he was the director of the School of Social Work that caused the greatest stir. Frazier's use of a psychodynamic formulation was akin to accepted concepts from the Freudian theory of projection and is now integrated into modern psychological thought in the concept of "splitting" and Festinger's theory of cognitive dissonance discussed in earlier chapters. Yet the article was met with considerable acrimony, as referenced by Platt and Challender (1988) in their article discussing the ongoing angst experienced by Frazier, a July 10, 1927, editorial in the *Atlanta Constitution* asserted that Frazier was "evidently more insane by reason of his anti-white complex than any southerner obsessed by his anti-negro repulsions" (p. 293) It would also be a factor in his resignation as Director of the Atlanta University School of Social Work.

Perhaps the wisdom and durability of Frazier's scholarship on race relations is that his formulations are anchored in an ecological perspective and a recognition of the significance of group exchanges as these evolve in social situations. In an article examining the underlying assumption of various causation theories for explaining racism, he concludes that further developments of a dynamic sociological theory of race relations may well call for a dismissal of prior theoretical formulations in favor of an ongoing re-examination of the constantly changing patterns of race relations in the United States (Frazier, 1947).

Following repercussions from the publication of the article in which Frazier defined white racism as equivalent to insanity, he left the directorship of the School. Frazier himself attributes his dismissal to a contentious relationship with an influential board member and the objections of some members of the board on his refusal to attend segregated meetings (Schiele, 1999). Adams (1981) wrote that his dismissal was related to his being overextended in carrying out his roles as a teacher, Principal Investigator (PI) of a number of research projects, and doctoral studies at the same time he was administering a school that was in the early stages of development.

Despite the shortness of his directorship, Frazier left a substantial legacy. This includes the School moving closer to greater professionalization. His commitment to the scientific method was reflected in an expanded curriculum that included new research course offerings (Adams, 1981). His efforts at professionalization of the School through the establishment of rigorous academic standards and admissions requirements were instrumental in it being accredited and, by 1927, being the leading voice for social work practice in the black community. His intellectual activism was influential during a time when the profession was aligning itself more closely with psychology (Brown, 2011).

After leaving the directorship of the School, Frazier went on to earn his PhD at the University of Chicago. He later was chair of the sociology department at Howard University and instrumental in founding the school of social work at that university, the country's second such school in an HBCU. He continued to conduct research, teach, and publish on topics of relevance to the African American community. While at Howard, he was appointed the first African American president of the American Sociological Association in 1948; his presidential address was entitled "Race Contacts and the Social Structure" (Frazier, 1949).

Frazier's successor was Forrester B. Washington, who held the position of Director of the School of Social Work from 1927 until his retirement in 1954. During Washington's tenure as director, the School was accredited by the Association of Schools of Social Work, on December 19, 1928. It began an affiliation with Atlanta University in 1938. It was officially named the Atlanta University School of Social Work. In 1947, the School gave up its charter as an autonomous school of social work to become an integral part of Atlanta University as one of its graduate schools. The relinquishing of the charter and affiliation with the University as one its graduate programs, gave the School the authority to award the MSW degree and shifted the financial responsibility of the School to the University (Ross, 1978, p. 444).

Of the three early directors of the school, all had been Urban League Fellows completing social work studies at the New York School of Social Work, thus continuing the tradition of the National Urban League's founder, George Edmond Haynes, of linking academia with practice in the interests of training a cohort of professional social workers uniquely prepared for practice in the African American community.

As the progress for securing full citizenship for blacks continued to push forward in the steady achievement of black rights, evolving events in the city of Atlanta were incrementally laying the foundation for the Civil Rights movement in the following decades of the 1950s and 1960s.

REFERENCES

Abbott, G. (1941). *From relief to social security: The development of the new public welfare services and their administration*. Chicago: University of Chicago Press.

Adams, F. V. (1981). *The reflections of Florence Victoria Adams*. Atlanta: Shannon Press, in cooperation with the Atlanta University School of Social Work and the Alumni Association.

Association of Black Psychologists, T. (2013). On Dark Girls. Retrieved from http://static.oprah.com/pdf/dark-girls.pdf

Altmeyer, A. J. (1966). *The formative years of social security*. Madison: University of Wisconsin Press.

Anderson, T. (2015). Q&A: 'Dark Girls' to 'Light Girls,' Bill Duke talks colorism in new film, January 18, 2015. https://www.latimes.com/entertainment/tv/showtracker/la-et-light-girls-bill-duke-20150117-story.html. Retrieved 6/11/19

Association of Black Association of Black Psychologists. (2013). Home page. http://www.abpsi.org/pdf/Dark_Girls_ABPsi_ARTICLE_JUNE_23_2013_Dr%20Grills.pdf.

Bacote, C. A. (1969). *The story of Atlanta University: A century of service, 1865–1965*. Atlanta: Atlanta University Press.

Billingsley, A. (1968). *Black families in white America*. Englewood Cliffs, NJ: Prentice Hall.

Billingsley, A. (1992). *Climbing Jacob's Ladder: The enduring legacy of African American families*. New York: Simon and Schuster.

Blassingame, J. (1975). Using the testimony of ex-slaves: Approaches and problems. *Journal of Southern History, 41*(4), 473–492. doi:10.2307/2205559

Bogart, L. M., & Bird, S. T. (2003). Exploring the relationship of conspiracy beliefs about HIV/AIDS to sexual behaviors and attitudes among African-American adults. *Journal of the National Medical Association, 95*(11), 1057.

Brown, A. (2011). Edward Franklin Frazier (September 24, 1894–May 17, 1962)—Advocate for social justice, administrator, author, and social work educator. Social Welfare History Project. http://socialwelfare.library.vcu.edu/social-work/frazier-edward-franklin/

Brown, M. K. (1999). *Race, money and the American social welfare state*. Ithaca, NY: Cornell University Press.

Carten, A. J. (2016). *Reflections on the American Social Welfare State: The Collected Papers of James R. Dumpson, PhD, 1930–1990*. Washington, DC: NASW Press.

Chandra L., Ford, S. P. Wallace, P. A., Newman, Sung-Jae, L., & William, E. C. (2013). Belief in AIDS-related conspiracy theories and mistrust in the government: Relationship with HIV testing among at-risk older adults. *Gerontologist, 53*(6), 973–984. https://doi.org/10.1093/geront/gns192

Chautauqua Circle Collection. (n.d.) Archives Research Center. Robert W. Woodruff Library at Atlanta University Center. http://localhost:8081/repositories/2/resources/25.

Chautauqua Circle Collection History, 1913–2011 (n.d.). Robert W. Woodruff Library of the Atlanta University Center. http://localhost:8081/repositories/2/archival_objects/126005

Cohen, W. J. (1960). *The first twenty-five years of the Social Security Act; 1935–1960.*

Cohen, W. J. (1960). *The first twenty-five years of the Social Security Act; 1935–1960.* In *Social work year book 1960* (pp. 49–62). New York: NASW.

Cohen, W. J. (1983). The advent of social security. In K. Louchein (Ed.), *The making of the New Deal: The insiders speak* (pp. 150–159). Cambridge, MA: Harvard University Press.

Devine, E. (1922). The Klan in Texas. *Survey, 48*, 10–11.

Dittmer, J. (1980). *Black Georgia in the Progressive Era, 1900–1920*. Champaign: University of Illinois Press.

Dittmer, J. (1997). "Too Busy to Hate": Race, Class, and Politics in Twentieth-Century Atlanta. *The Georgia Historical Quarterly, 81*(1), 103–117. Retrieved from http://www.jstor.org/stable/40583545

Douglass, F. (1855). *My bondage and freedom*. Online: CreateSpace.

DuBois, W. (1906). The economic future of the negro. *Publications of the American Economic Association, 7*(1), 3rd series, 219–242. http://www.jstor.org/stable/2999974

Durant, T. J., & Knottnerus, J. D. (Eds.). (1999). *Plantation society and race relations: The origins of inequality*. Westport, CT: Greenwood Publishing Group.

Edwards, G. F. (1968). *E. Franklin Frazier on race relations*. Chicago: University of Chicago Press.

Edwards, G. F. (1974). E. Franklin Frazier. In J. E. Blackwell & M. Janowitz (Ed.), *Black sociologists: Historical and contemporary perspectives* (pp. 85–117). Chicago: University of Chicago Press.

Frazier, E. F. (1923). Training colored social workers in the south. *Journal of Social Forces, 4*(May), 445–446.

Frazier, E. F. (1924). Social work in race relations. *The Crisis, 27*(6), 252–254.

Frazier, E. F. (1927). The pathology of race prejudice. *The Forum, 77*(6), 856–862.

Frazier, E. F. (1947). Sociological theory and race relations. *American Sociological Review, 12*(3), 265–271. http://www.jstor.org/stable/2086515

Fisher, J. (1990). The rank and file movement 1930–1936. *Journal of Progressive Human Services, 1*(1), 95–99.

Guinan, M. E. (1993). Black communities' belief in AIDS as genocide. A barrier to overcome for HIV prevention. *Annals of Epidemiology, 3*, 193–195. doi:10.1016/1047-2797(93)90136-R

Harlan, L. R. (1983). *Booker T. Washington: Volume 2: The Wizard of Tuskegee, 1901–1915*. New York: Oxford University Press.

Harper, C. (1978). House servants and field hands: Fragmentation in the antebellum slave community. *North Carolina Historical Review, 55*(1), 42–59. http://www.jstor.org/stable/23535381

Heller, J. (2015). Rumors and realities: Making sense of HIV/AIDS conspiracy narratives and contemporary legends. *American Journal of Public Health, 105*(1), e43–e50. doi:10.2105/AJPH.2014.302284

Henderson, A. B. (1977). Alonzo Herndon and black insurance in Atlanta, 1904–1915. *Atlanta Historical Bulletin, 21* (Spring).

Henderson, A. B. (1990). *Atlanta Life Insurance Company: Guardian of black economic dignity*. Tuscaloosa: University of Alabama Press.

Hobson, M. J. (2017). *The legend of the black mecca: Politics and class in the making of modern Atlanta*. Chapel Hill: University of North Carolina Press.

Jansson, B. S. (1993/2009). *The reluctant welfare state: American social welfare policies: Past, present, and future*. Belmont, CA: Brooks/Cole.

Jet Magazine. (1995). Three arson fires cause more than $1 million in damage to Clark Atlanta University buildings. April 10, 1995. Chicago: Johnson Publishing.

Katz, M. B. (1996). *In the shadow of the poorhouse: A social history of welfare in America.* New York: Basic Books.

Leighninger, L., & Knickmeyer, R. (1976). The rank and file movement: The relevance of radical social work traditions to modern social work practice. *Journal of Society and Social Welfare, 4,* 166.

Lisio, D. J. (2012). *Hoover, blacks, and lily-whites: A study of southern strategies.* Chapel Hill: University of North Carolina Press.

Mason, H. (1997). *Black Atlanta in the Roaring Twenties.* Dover, NH: Arcadia Publishing: Dover.

Merritt, C. (2002) *The Herndons: An Atlanta family.* Athens: University of Georgia Press.

Monk, E. P. (2015). The cost of color: Skin color, discrimination, and health among African-Americans. *American Journal of Sociology, 121* (2), 396–444. http://www.jstor.org/stable/10.1086/682162.

Mowry, G. (1940). The South and the Progressive Lily-White Party of 1912. *Journal of Southern History,* 6(2), 237–247. doi:10.2307/2191208

Moynihan, D. P. (1965). *The negro family: The case for national action.* Washington, DC: Office of Policy Planning and Research, US Department of Labor.

National Park Service Bulletin. (n.d.). Booker T. Washington Monumment. *The Death of Booker T. Washington* https://www.nps.gov/bowa/learn/historyculture/up-load/THE-FINAL-btwdeath-site-bulletin.pdf

National Commission for the Protection of Human Subjects of Biomedical and Behavioral Research. (1978). The Belmont Report. Washington, DC: Department of Health, Education and Welfare (DHEW), US Government Printing Office.

Nattrass, N. (2013). Understanding the origins and prevalence of AIDS conspiracy beliefs in the United States and South Africa. *Sociology of Health & Illness, 35*(1), 113–129.

Perkins, F. (1946). *The Roosevelt I knew.* New York: Viking Press.

Perkins, F. (1962). The roots of social security. Speech delivered at the Social Security Administration Headquarters, October 23, 1962, Baltimore, Maryland.

Perkins, F. (1962, October 23). *The roots of social security. Delivered at the Social Security Administration Headquarters.* Baltimore, MD.

Perkiss, A. (2008). Public accountability and the Tuskegee syphilis experiments: A restorative justice approach. *Journal of African American Law and Policy, 10* https://doi.org/10.15779/Z38VK6K]

Platt, T., & Chandler, S. (1988). Constant struggle: E. Franklin Frazier and black social work in the 1920s. *Social Work, 33*(4), 293–297. https://doi.org/10.1093/sw/33.4.293

Proceedings of the National Conference of Social Work. (1934). Proceedings of the Sixty-First Annual Session held in Kansas City, Missouri, May 20–26, 1934. [Formerly National Conference of Charities and Correction]. *JAMA, 104*(10), 858. doi:10.1001/jama.1935.02760100068031

Reisch, M., & Andrews, J. (2014). *The road not taken: A history of radical social work in the United States.* Routledge.

Riley, B. (2013). Ladies of the Club: The Chautauqua Circle notes a century of sisterhood, scholarship, and service. Atlanta, December 2, 2013.

Roosevelt, E. (1936, March 19). Correspondence to Walter White, executive director, NAACP, on anti-lynching bill. Records of the National Association for the Advancement of Colored People. Retrieved from http://www.loc.gov/teachers/classroommaterials/presentationsandactivities/presentations/timeline/depwwii/race/letter.html

Remembering Roosevelt's speech at Oglethrope University. https://source.oglethorpe.edu/2012/05/22/remembering-fdrs-commencement-speech-at-oglethorpe/

Ross, E. (1976). Black heritage in social welfare: A case study of Atlanta. *Phylon (1960-)*, 37(4), 297–307. doi:10.2307/274495

Ross, E. L. (1978). *Black heritage in social welfare, 1860–1930*. Scarecrow Press.

Schiele, J. H. (June 1999). *E. Franklin Frazier and the interfacing of black sociology and black social work*. Atlanta: Schiele Clark Atlanta University Press.

Selmi, P., & Hunter, R. (2001). Beyond the Rank and File Movement: Mary van Kleeck and social work radicalism in the great Depression, 1931–1942. *Journal of Sociology & Social Welfare*, 28(2), article 6. https://scholarworks.wmich.edu/jssw/vol28/iss2/6

Sitkoff, H. (1971). Harry Truman and the election of 1948: The coming of age of civil rights in American politics. *Journal of Southern History*, 37(4), 597–616. doi:10.2307/2206548

Stoesz, D. (2016). The excluded: An estimate of the consequences of denying Social Security to agricultural and domestic workers (CSD Working Paper No. 16-17). St. Louis, MO: Washington University, Center for Social Development.

Stolberg, S. G. (1997). Man in the news: 'America's Doctor' David Satcher. *New York Times*, September 13, 1997.

Sundstrom, W. A. (1992). Last hired, first fired? Unemployment and urban black workers during the Great Depression. *Journal of Economic History, 52*(2), 416–429.

Towns, G. (1942). The sources of the tradition of Atlanta University. *Phylon (1940-1956)*, 3(2), 117–134. doi:10.2307/271517

Trattner, W. I. (1999). *From poor law to welfare stateA history of social welfare in America*. New York: Simon and Schuster.

USDHHS, Office of Research Protections. https://www.hhs.gov/ohrp/regulations-and-policy/belmont-report/index.html.

Van Kleek, M. (1934). Our illusion regarding government. *Proceedings of the National Conference of Social Work, 61*, 473–485.

Walker, A. (2004). *In search of our mothers' gardens: Womanist prose*. New York: Houghton Mifflin Harcourt.

Warde, B. (2016). *Inequality in US social policy: An historic analysis*. New York: Routledge.

Washington, F. B. (1934). *The negro and relief*. A presentation given at the Sixty-First Meeting of the National Conference on Social Welfare. Kansas City, Missouri, May 20–26, 1934.

Weiss, N. J. (1983). *Farewell to the Party of Lincoln: Black Politics in the Age of FDR*. Princeton University Press.

Wilson, W. J. (1980). *The declining significance of race: Blacks and changing American institutions* (2nd ed.). Chicago: University of Chicago Press.

Wilson, W. J. (1987). *The truly disadvantaged: The inner city, the underclass, and public policy*. Chicago: University of Chicago Press.

Wilson, W. J. (2011). *When work disappears: The world of the new urban poor*. Vintage.

FURTHER READING

Library of Congress, Digital Collections. Born in Enslavement: Slave Narratives from the Federal Writers' Project, 1936–1938. Articles and Essays. An Introduction to the WPA Slave Narratives.

Series: Tuskegee Syphilis Study Administrative Records, 1929–1972 Record Group 442: Records of the Centers for Disease Control and Prevention, 1921–2006. https://www.archives.gov/atlanta/exhibits/item470-exh.html

CHAPTER 9

Curriculum Renewal in the Postwar Years

Those who are to do social work among Negroes need to know everything which is needed by those who work among whites and considerably more.
——Forrester B. Washington (1935)

While the New Deal programs of the Roosevelt administration brought some relief to the American people from the hardships of the Depression, it was the transition from a peacetime to a wartime economy that ended the Depression and brought new prosperity to the country. The state of Georgia benefited from the New Deal, but the full participation of blacks was limited in both the temporary recovery programs and the permanent benefits provided under the Social Security Act because of racially charged regional politics. Given the partisan contentiousness of Congress, it might well have been anticipated that any plan for policy reforms that came from northern liberals, who continued to be perceived as meddling in the traditional southern way of life, would be summarily rejected by powerful politicians in the South.

Roosevelt frequently visited Warm Springs, Georgia, for treatment of his polio. Having a home in Warm Springs he had built and named the "Little White House", Roosevelt had become a favorite son of some Georgians. These visits had also given him a new sensitivity to the plight of white and black sharecroppers and tenant farmers in rural Georgia, and these concerns were addressed in the provisions of the New Deal programs. But it was precisely because they helped poor whites and blacks that the programs of the New Deal were met with strong political opposition in the South.

Moreover, owners of large farm operations, resembling the plantations of the old south, were in strong opposition to New Deal reforms in farm policies

Find a Way or Make One. Alma J. Carten, Oxford University Press (2021). © Oxford University Press.
DOI: 10.1093/oso/9780197518465.001.0001.

because they lifted tenant and small farmers out of what resembled a system of serfdom. For the large farm owners, the New Deal reforms were not in their financial interest and diminished their iron control of the farm labor force ensured under the sharecropping system.

The political opposition to the New Deal programs in Georgia was led by Governor Eugene Talmage, an outspoken segregationist and white supremacist who was committed to the disenfranchisement of blacks and poor whites. Talmage publicly referred to blacks and Jews in derogatory racial terms, publicly boasted of having read Hitler's autobiography *Mein Kempt* more than once, and expressed his admiration of Hitler and Mussolini and his belief that there was a bit of a dictator in everyone (Anderson, 1975). For a full decade, over the course of two terms as the state commissioner of agriculture and three terms as governor of Georgia—although defeated by Ellis Arnall in 1942—Eugene Talmadge remained unchallenged in his pursuit of racist social, political, and economic agendas in the state.

Some progressive legislation was enacted under Arnall's governorship. Included among these was securing the right to vote for 18-year-olds, ending of the poll tax, abolishing chain gangs, and restoring the accreditation of the state university system that had been revoked because of Talmage's injection of racism into the system (Bailes, 1969). And while the 1946 Supreme Court ruling ended the white-only vote, Georgians were far from ready to give the vote to blacks. The determination to continue the disenfranchisement of blacks in the state was backed by Klan threats to punish any black showing up at the polls with an intention to vote, which successfully kept them away.

Eugene Talmadge reclaimed the governorship in 1946 but died before assuming office. After a controversial process (Elson, 1976; Cook, 1974) his son, Herman Talmadge, assumed the governorship and continued to implement policies in the spirit of his late father.

During the early years of the School, Atlanta was becoming more urbanized and described as cosmopolitan—but it was still dubbed by some as a "country city." Despite its adherence to a strict code of racial segregation, liberals saw the city as having the greatest potential for reuniting the South. When the School opened its doors in 1920, it was the only school of social work in the South. It was also the only school of social work in the country with courses and academic programs intentionally designed to support the education and training of a social work workforce prepared to promote the economic and social progress of African Americans. This remained the case until it was joined in this endeavor through the founding of the school of social work at Howard University in Washington, DC, during the years of the Great Depression.

At the national level, a number of events influenced the environmental context of the School over the early and middle years of its history. By the 1920s, no longer nascent, social work was becoming well established as a profession. Despite the marginalized status of training programs for blacks that had been developing in the United State since the turn of the 20th century (Gary & Gary, 1994; Peeples-Wilkins, 2006), owing to the activism of black intellectuals, the School had become the leading voice on social work in the black community.

Although of a contentious nature, more attention was being paid to the new paradigms in thinking on matters of race introduced by W. E. B. DuBois and E. Franklin Frazier. And DuBois, with the institutional support of the NAACP that he now led, had taken the fight for black rights to the courts.

Jane Addams had evolved in her thinking that had refocused her activism on the plight of immigrants to adopt a more global perspective. Her activism in the movement for world peace had earned Addams the distinction of being the second American woman to be awarded the Nobel Peace Prize. The prestigious award was given in acknowledgment of Addams's work in the Women's International League for Peace and Freedom. Addams founded the organization in 1919 and served as president for many years, working to sway powerful governments across the globe to disarm and pursue world peace.

There was a waning of Addams's influence as the sense of a common cause engendered by America's entry into the war in 1941 diminished reform efforts because of the general unwillingness to criticize the federal government in a time of war. That being said, in his January 6, 1941, State of the Union Address to Congress, in presenting the rationale for increasing the production of war materials to aid Britain, Roosevelt said to the American people, and indeed to the world, that the US was fighting for universal freedoms to which all people were entitled "the freedom of speech, the freedom of worship, the freedom from want, and the freedom from fear" (Borgwardt, 2005). Now enshrined in the "Four Freedoms Speech," these were rights that remained beyond the reach of black Americans. Therefore, the war years did not quiet, but instead propelled the struggle for black rights forward.

Harry Hopkins, continuing to play a significant role as advisor to the president, assisted Roosevelt in preparing the Four Freedoms Speech, which is counted as among the greatest of American presidential speeches and is a one of the documents in the Roosevelt Presidential Library (Crowell, 1955). The speech is also celebrated in the Four Freedoms Park, located in New York City on Roosevelt Island. The park was designed as a memorial to Roosevelt and to a speech that stands as a lasting symbol of America's promise.

The inspiring words of the Four Freedoms Speech, combined with the experience of blacks in the military, once again shed light on the hypocrisies of a country that engaged in military action in the pursuit of liberty and justice on foreign soils while at the same time of denying these rights to its own citizens at home. Thus, the US "Negro Problem" that had been brought into world view during World War I was once again rising to a level of international scrutiny.

In his classical publication *An American Dilemma: The Negro Problems and Modern Democracy* (1944), Gunnar Myrdal, a Swedish sociologist, echoed

DuBois's 1903 prediction in *The Souls of Black Folk* that the color line was the central problem of the United States in the 20th century. In his international travels, Supreme Court Associate Justice William O. Douglas reported being asked how the United States could tolerate the lynching of blacks—ironically, the postwar years had seen an increase in lynching and returning black veterans were the primary target.

Chief Justice Earl Warren, whose court made the landmark 1954 *Brown v. Board of Education* decision, in a talk given before the American Bar Association remarked that the American judicial system was on trial both at home and abroad regarding how it treats blacks in consideration of the spirit of the Constitution and the Bill of Rights (Carten, 2016). Moreover, American racism was not a matter that went unnoticed by the Soviet Union, and the hypocrisies of American democracy became a potent tool for Soviet propaganda.

There is speculation in the historical record (Pruitt, 2018) that the beginning of World War II and Hitler's rise to power was influenced by the harsh treatment of Germany under the terms of the Versailles Agreement crafted by the Allied powers, Britain, France, Italy, and Russia, at the end of World War I. The terms of the Treaty required Germany to give up or return territories and pay substantial financial reparations that resulted in the economic crippling of the country (Brezina, 2006). Moreover, it is speculated that Article 231 of the Treaty, known as the "War Guilt Clause" requiring Germany to accept blame for the war, set the stage for the rise of Nazism.

Being blamed for the war and the felt public shaming and humiliation engendered by the terms of the Treaty, left the German people susceptible to the rhetoric of a charismatic image maker who capitalized on an embittered peoples' feelings of unwarranted blame. The combined economic hardship resulting from the financial burden of having to pay for the extensive damage caused by the war and the country's increasing political instability were factors that created fertile ground for Hitler's rhetoric to take hold and flourish. The rhetoric advanced a form of right-wing populism, at the center of which was the Nazi ideology of a Nordic or Aryan people as a master race, and it found a scapegoat in the demonization of the Jewish people. Twenty years later, Adolph Hitler astutely capitalized on this German national malaise to ignite a global military conflict— staged in three theaters on the continents of Europe, Asia, Africa, and North America—and the mass killing of six million Jews.

Still in recovery from the Great Depression when World War II broke out, Americans were wedded to an agenda of isolation. Roosevelt supported the will of the American people and held to a policy of neutrality. At the same time, he recognized that the United States, as the world's foremost defender of democracy and guardian of the freedoms articulated in his Four Freedoms Speech, had a stake in the war as Nazi Germany and Fascist Italy under the dictatorships of Adolph Hitler and Benito Mussolini threatened democracies across the globe. As the war progressed, the militaries of the two dictators devastated Europe and all but depleted British finances in its waging a war against Germany.

Roosevelt devised the Lend-Lease program, officially known as An Act to Promote the Defense of the United States (Pub.L. 77–11, H.R. 1776, 55 Stat. 31), as a means of honoring the American people's stance on neutrality while at the same time making it possible to support the Allies without formally entering the war. Not requiring immediate repayment, the Lend-Lease program was explained, in the president's use of metaphor, as equivalent to lending a garden hose to a neighbor. The program was promoted as a good-natured gesture of helping one's neighbor, which was a concept Americans could easily identify with. The program is seen as an example of the president's political genius since it allowed him to achieve his goal of supporting the Allies in the war effort, but to do so in a way that enjoyed broad public support and avoided dividing the nation on the question of neutrality.

Harry Hopkins was again boosting the visibility of professional social work, now in international affairs. Hopkins had been an advisor to Roosevelt since his years as New York governor, and he was one of the three individuals who took on the formidable task of managing the Lend Lease program that was sending wartime supplies not only to Britain but to all the Allied forces. These supplies took the form of heavy military machinery, airplanes, tanks, trucks, ammunition, food, and other necessities. The Lend Lease program was the start of a shift from a peacetime to a wartime economy and a return to prosperity for the United States.

The United States entered the war on December 7, 1941, after the Japanese surprise attack on the US naval fleet at Pearl Harbor. Within hours after Roosevelt's address to the joint session of Congress declaring the December date as a "day that would live in infamy," Congress passed a declaration of war against Japan that Roosevelt immediately signed. The surprise Japanese attack resulted in the loss of thousands of unsuspecting military people and the near devastation of the American naval fleet at Pearl Harbor.

The unprovoked attack enraged the nation. Soon after the attack, and rationalized as a precaution against possible espionage by individuals sympathetic to the Japanese cause, President Roosevelt signed Executive Order 9066 (Roosevelt, 1942), which was to become a national badge of shame for the country. The Order authorized the forced relocation and incarceration in internment camps of hundreds of thousands of people of Japanese descent, most of whom were American citizens. The internment camps have become a regrettable policy adopted by the federal government and a historical lesson illustrating the destructive impact of the hysteria that arises during unusual times that can spiral into an intensification of racism and to the treatment with impunity the civil rights of innocent people who are perceived as "different" or demonized by being defined as the "the other."

This was in fact the findings of a bipartisan Commission on Wartime Relocation and Internment of Civilians established by the US Congress in 1980 and tasked to review the facts and circumstances of Roosevelt's Executive Order and make recommendations for remedies deemed appropriate. The Commission report, *Personal Justice Denied*, made no findings of disloyalty on the part of Japanese people. The report concluded, to the contrary, that a grave injustice had been done to the Japanese. The action taken by the government was described in the report as being motivated by "race prejudice, war hysteria and a failure of political leadership" (Kashima, 2011).

To compensate the Americans of Japanese descent who suffered the effects of the Executive Order, the report called for the US government to pay reparations to the internees and their heirs (Report of the Commission on the Wartime Relocation, 1983; Kashima, 2011). President Ronald Reagan apologized for the internment on behalf of the US government and signed into the law the Civil Liberties Act of 1988 (Pub.L. 100–383) authorizing the payment of reparations to Japanese people who had been interred in the camps and their heirs (Hatamiya, 1993).

World War II ended when President Harry Truman, who assumed the presidency upon Roosevelt's death on April 12, 1945, made a decision of unprecedented consequences to drop the atomic bomb—a weapon of mass destruction such as the world had never before known—on the Japanese cities of Hiroshima and Nagasaki (Rhodes, 1986). The bombings killed hundreds of thousands of people, most of whom were civilians. And many more were destined to die later resulting from radiation exposure. Following the event, the Japanese signed the documents of unconditional surrender aboard the *USS Missouri* on September 2, 1945, bringing an end to the war. It would also be the prelude to the Cold War.

World War II had taken the lives of an estimated 75–80 million people. Europe was left in shambles. The economies of Britain, Germany, and France had collapsed, major European cities had been all but destroyed, and the semblance of any Jewish life on the European continent had been virtually erased. Russia was soon to emerge as the second world power, and the Korean War that followed in six years introduced a Cold War that would last for another four decades.

The forerunner of the United Nations was the League of Nations, an organization conceived in similar circumstances during the first World War and established in 1919 under the Treaty of Versailles to encourage international cooperation, and maintain world peace. Having taken on the role of primary guardian of democracy, to contain the rise of communism and peaceable resolve future conflicts among nations, the US took the lead among the Allied Western countries in the restoration of the European countries that had been left in shambles.

The forerunner of the United Nations was the League of Nations, an organization conceived in similar circumstances during the first World War and established in 1919 under the Treaty of Versailles "to promote international cooperation and to achieve peace and security". Having taken on the role of primary guardian of democracy as an effort to contain the rise of communism, and prevent future global conflicts the United States took the lead among the Allied Western countries in the restoration of the European countries devastated by the war.

The 1948 Economy Recovery Act (Public Law 472, General Records of the US Government) was signed by President Truman on April 3, 1948. Also known as the "Marshall Plan," the policy is named for General George Marshall, who had led the Allied forces to victory in the war and later served as Secretary of State in the Truman administration. Marshall had conceptualized the plan to rehabilitate the collapsed economies of affected European countries as a means for preventing the spread of communism. The Marshall Plan called for a $15 billion expenditure over a four to five year period; it was seen as an investment in the restoration of war torn Europe to support the stability of democratic governments (Hogan, 1987). The investment paid off, and, by the early 1950s, the economies of the participating countries had been restored, the new markets restored economic stability in Europe, and the rippling effects of well-functioning economies abroad further boosted the prosperity being enjoyed in the United States that had begun with the production of war materials for Allied Forces before the United States had entered the war.

In the early years of the civil rights movement for blacks, Whitney M. Young Jr. later advocated for a replication of the Marshall Plan as the means for rehabilitating urban centers densely populated by African Americans (Weiss, 1989). Urban areas in the nation's major cities had been devastated by the migration of people and businesses to the suburbs, taking with them the tax base of these communities and leading to the inevitable erosion of essential community infrastructures. These trends were contributing factors to the entrenchment of poverty and joblessness and to a new demographic: the "new urban poor." It was this demographic that sociologist William Julius Wilson (1984, 2011) described as creating a permanent underclass of blacks concentrated in the nation's major cities who were troubled by social problems of crime, drug addiction, single female-headed families, out of wedlock births, and welfare dependency. These conditions set the stage for civil unrest that erupted in these neglected communities and the launching of the fight for black civil rights.

Another emerging new demographic of Americans were those who lived through the Depression and fought in World War II. This cohort of Americans are now collectively referred to as the "Greatest Generation," a term coined by American journalist and author Tom Brokaw (1998). With the country on the threshold of the Cold War, their uniqueness as a generation is memorialized in John F. Kennedy's iconic inaugural address given January 20, 1961 as the 44th President of the United States.

> Let the word go forth from this time and place, to friend and foe alike, that the torch has been passed to a new generation of Americans, born in this century, tempered by war, disciplined by a hard and bitter peace, proud of our ancient heritage, and unwilling to witness or permit the slow undoing of those human rights to which this nation has always been committed, and to which we are committed today at home and around the world. Let every nation know, whether it wishes us well or ill, that we shall pay any price, bear any burden, meet any hardship, support any friend, oppose any foe to assure the survival and the success of liberty.

The Greatest Generation are parents to the "Baby Boomers," a demographic of the postwar years that marks a dramatic increase in US birth rates. Born between 1946 and 1964, members of the Baby Boom generation are the beneficiaries of the affluence and rising quality of life of the postwar years resulting from the new prosperity created by the war effort and the hard work and sacrifice of their parents. Coming of age during a period of great social and political upheavals during the 1960s and 1970s, this generation played a significant role in the counterculture that resulted in dramatic changes in the cultural landscape of the nation.

As young adults, the Baby Boomers challenged the many forms of what for them were the hypocrisies of their parents' generation. This predisposition and collective angst accounts for their high visibility in human rights activism and protest movements against the Vietnam war of the 1960s and 1970s. They are also counted among the cohort of activist-oriented college students with significant participation in the Civil Rights movement of the 1960s.

The Civil Rights movement brought young activists together, black and white, from college campuses in the North and the South. They joined together as Freedom Riders traveling on interstate buses into the Deep South to challenge segregated bus terminals, in nonviolent sit-ins at lunch counters, and in the Mississippi Freedom Summer Project registering blacks to vote and establishing Freedom Schools and centers providing services and educating blacks about their rights. The work was undertaken on their part with an awareness that their lives were at risk when they challenged the white racism that was especially virulent in the Deep South. Nonetheless, with the full knowledge that they might be killed, they willingly put their lives on the line to fight for a cause—as captured in one of the freedom songs of the movement—with a determination not to be turned around. And some did pay the ultimate price.

Michael Schwerner, James Chaney, and Andrew Goodman were among the young people who were active in the community organizing efforts of Freedom Summer. They were murdered by members of the Klan, which a FBI investigation subsequently found was orchestrated by law enforcement officials. Their murders and the aftermath of the events following their murders are a significant part of the historical record of the Civil Rights movement. The three young men have come to symbolize the courage and sacrifice of young people who took part in the Civil Rights movement in the 1960s. In acknowledgment of their courage and sacrifice, they were posthumously awarded the Presidential Medal of Freedom by President Barack Obama in 2014.

As the School moved into its middle years there were a number of trends of significance and consequence in the ever-changing cultural landscape of the nation. The postwar years saw a questioning of white supremacy that mirrored Hitler's promotion of a master race and demonization of the Jewish people. The liberation of the concentration camps exposed the Holocaust and graphically illustrated the horrific outcome of racist ideology that progressively moves from the demagogic rhetoric of a single individual to governmental policy that is unchallenged by political loyalists.

The military experience, despite being racially segregated, resulted in many existential benefits for black Americans. Perhaps the most significant of which, whether at home or abroad, was the gratification that came from contributing to the defeat of Japanese militarism and the barbarism of the Nazi regime, thus taking part in saving Western civilization. African Americans were also able to take pride in the heroic actions of black serviceman such as the iconic Tuskegee Airmen, an elite group of African American bomber and fighter pilots who were led by Benjamin O. Davis Jr. during the war and conducted air combat in Italy, North Africa, and Germany. Their heroism is memorialized in the movie *Red Tails*. The film stars Cuba Gooding Jr. in the role of Commander Davis, who became the first African American General in the US Air Force. The surviving members of the Division were invited to preview the film at the Obama White House. Unlike the film *Birth of a Nation* previewed at the Wilson White House, *Red Tails* depicted a historically accurate narrative about the innate character of black males.

The benefits provided to veterans under the GI Bill made available bank loans for home mortgages, small business start-ups, and tuition for college education that provided a pathway to middle-class status and wealth creation for whites. These benefits were rendered ineffective for black veterans because of racial discrimination in bank lending practices and in housing (Roach, 1997; Boulton, 2007; Carten 2016). A beacon of hope, however, was provided by the historically black colleges and universities (HBCUs), which overextended themselves to ensure access to educational opportunities for black veterans barred from enrollment in white institutions of higher learning (Herbold, 1994).

At the policy level, A. Philip Randolph, founder of the first labor union for blacks, the Brotherhood of Sleeping Car Porters, threatened a 1941 March on Washington that encouraged Roosevelt to issue Executive Order 8802 (Roosevelt, 1941). The march was planned in the cause of jobs and to end discrimination in labor unions. Randolph called off the planned march with Roosevelt's signing of the executive order banning discrimination in defense industries. Still, the president continued to move cautiously in the pursuit of policies in the interest of black equality.

The Truman administration pursued these nondiscrimination policies more aggressively, implementing recommendations of the report of the Presidents Commission on Civil Rights entitled "To Secure these Rights." The Commission was established by Truman in 1946. It was tasked to examine civil rights and make recommendations for improvements. The findings of the Commission were the basis for Truman's issuance of executive orders for the desegregation of federal offices and the armed forces (President's Committee on Civil Rights, 1947). The postwar years also saw the enactment of the 1954 *Brown vs. Board of Education* Supreme Court decision, the most consequential civil rights legislation of the post war years. This groundbreaking law set the stage for the Civil Rights movement and civil rights legislation in the 1960s (Zietlow, 2004).

In the city of Atlanta, a number of individuals and organizations combined efforts to form a liberal movement seeking progressive changes in the city (Egerton, 1994). Among those who collaborated on this effort were Ralph McGill, the liberal publisher of the *Atlanta Constitution*; Mayor William Hartsfield; Governor Ellis Arnall; and the Southern Regional Conference that had been created in 1944 to replace the Commission on Interracial Cooperation. Leaders in higher education included Rufus Clement, the president of Atlanta University, and Morehouse President Benjamin Mays.

Paradoxically, concurrent with the hope for social change in the South, and with Atlanta taking the lead, violence against blacks took an upward climb. Acts of violence against returning veterans of color were increasing throughout the South, and law enforcement officials were the major perpetrators. The unprovoked violence against blacks was yet another illustration of the predictable white backlash that arise in response to continuing progress of blacks in achieving full citizenship. The white backlash of the postwar years was fueled by fears that returning black veterans, now armed and well trained from their service in the armed forces, could become a revolutionary force making it impossible to keep blacks in their place. Nonetheless, and in spite of the violent white back lash, returning Hispanic, black, and Native American veterans adopted the double V sign from Winston Churchill's "V for Victory," vowing to fight for their civil rights and victory over tyranny both abroad and at home (Alexander & Rucker, 2010).

In 1947, Georgia experienced the worst cases of violence against blacks of any southern state. Atlanta, described as the city "too busy to hate" and a model of racial progressiveness, was instead the city that Victoria Adams described as "solidly segregated in terms of eating places, streetcar transportation and to some degree the opportunities to try on certain pieces of clothing in the various department stores" (Adams, 1977).

On the world stage, World War II pushed the Allied Powers to examine their own policies of imperialism and colonization and ignited the quest for independence by colonized peoples across the globe whose labor and natural resources of their countries were being exploited. The NAACP, still the leading organization in the fight for black rights, was adopting a global perspective, with the growing conviction that the successful fight for black rights would need to be fought on a worldwide front.

In 1947, Walter White became involved in the political affairs of the Anglophone West Indies and the plight of the colonized native populations of these countries who were impoverished because profits from their agricultural labor were benefiting British absentee landlords (White, 1948/1971, p. 357). The organization had dispatched White and DuBois to the UN in 1945, to the Conference on International Organization to submit a proposal for the abolition of the colonial system abroad. DuBois followed up with the proposal in 1947, in a petition to the UN entitled "An Appeal to the World" (DuBois, 1946) linking the history of racism in the United States to the colonization of people of color across the globe.

Generously substantiated with facts, the 150-page petition outlined the egregious treatment of blacks in the United States from slavery to the postwar years. The petition was framed as being a matter of concern to the UN because of the organization's commitment to human rights and the rights of minorities. Beginning with the "peculiar institution" of slavery, the introduction to the petition described the roots of the paradoxical experience of the history of blacks in the country.

> It is all a strange and contradictory story. It could not be regarded as mainly either a theoretical problem on morals or a scientific problem of race. From either of these points of view, the rise of slavery in America is simply inexplicable. Looking at the facts frankly, slavery evidently was a matter of economics, a question of income and labor, rather than a problem of the right and wrong, or of the physical differences in men. Once slavery began to be the source of that income for men and nations, there followed a frantic search for moral and racial justification. Such excuses were found and men did not inquire too carefully into either their logic or their truth. (DuBois, 1946, pp. 1–2)

The School had weathered the Depression and war years under the directorship of Forrester B. Washington, who served in the position from 1924 until his retirement in 1954. During the years of Washington's leadership, the School experienced both gains and losses. Among the gains was that the School held a monopoly on social work education in the South, a position that it held until the social work program at the University of Georgia was established in 1964, as the second school of social work in the state.

Owing to its historic commitment to the co-education of the races the School reflected a degree of diversity in student enrollment and roster of full-time faculty despite state laws banning the co-education of the races. Prior to the opening of the program at the University of Georgia it was the only option for access to social work education for whites in the state. And when the School became affiliated with the University with the privilege of awarding the MSW degree, while whites were prevented from formally matriculating and therefore ineligible for being awarded the MSW degree white students taking courses at the School received a diploma in social work.

The School also benefitted from the new demand for social work jobs created by the beginning federalization of social welfare programs. The expanded access to social welfare benefits provided by the federal government, combined with Harry Hopkins's directive that new departments of social welfare in government-administered agencies must employ at least one full-time MSW-trained social worker, benefitted the School by stimulating interest in social work as an occupation and professional career. The new interest also affected the growth of the School; in fact, despite the decline in male enrollment with the advent of the war, overall enrollment in the School continued to increase during Washington's directorship. In 1924, the school had a reported seventeen full-time students enrolled in the program; that number increased to fifty-two full-time and forty-three part-time students by 1932. Graduates of the School could be found in several cities in the North and South during the austere years of the Depression, providing services to assist meet the needs of clients with a variety of presenting problems (Barrow, 2002).

The results of an MSW thesis study completed by Coleman (1947) reported findings that were reflective of the professional trends of the 1940s. The study also illustrated the steady and continuing impact of the School in contributing to a social work force dispersed throughout the country, well-prepared to serve a diversity of clients. For example, as reported in the narrative, more than half of the study respondents were employed in public-sector agencies serving both white and black clients. All were found to be working from accepted social work principles and practice techniques. Of the total number of respondents (N = 100) slightly more than half (n = 54) were employed in public agencies. The private agencies in which respondents were employed (n = 37) were described as offering a greater array of services to client caseloads that were of greater diversity than in the public-sector agencies.

In keeping with professional interest at the time, the largest share (n = 71) of the study respondents were caseworkers. Slightly less than half (n = 42) of the study sample were employed in agencies located in the southeastern region of the country. The states of Georgia and Alabama showed the highest concentration of graduates. In the eastern region of the country, Ohio ($n = 11$) and New York ($n = 10$) were the most popular choices for employment. Single women between the ages of twenty-two and twenty-six years were overwhelmingly ($n = 94$) represented among the study sample. And it should not be surprising that male graduates were earning salaries that were above those of female graduates despite similarities in qualifications and job responsibilities.

In the practice community, the postwar years also saw a retreat of social workers from the newly created public-sector jobs to practice as psychiatric social workers in family service agencies in the private sector. The resurgence of interest in micro-level practice in the field of mental health was supported by President Truman's signing of the 1946 National Mental Health Act that became law on July 3, 1946. The act established and provided funds for a National Institute of Mental Health (NIMH), thus making mental health needs a priority of the federal government (Trattner, 1999).

The need for mental health services was brought to light by the medical examinations conducted by the Selective Service to determine the fitness of draftees for service and that found many deficiencies in both physical and mental health. Although the untreated mental health needs were found early on, this became a more urgent reality when veterans suffering from the effects of traumatic wartime experiences also needed to re-establish healthy family relationships as a part of the process of readjustment to civilian life. The growing number of professional social workers seeking employment in private-sector mental health agencies to respond to these mental health needs left the field open for the School to build a growing expertise in the education and training of social work professionals who were skilled and committed to the delivery of broad-based services. Therefore, the School had the potential to bring an added value to the field that would be needed in the coming years as the nation turned its attention to the social ills confronted by the "invisible poor" as described by Michael Harrinton's 1962 classical research study *The Other America*.

THE DIRECTORSHIP OF FORRESTER WASHINGTON

Thus was the state of nation and the profession when Forrester Blanchard Washington was appointed to lead the School in the next chapter of its history. Washington was born in Salem, Massachusetts, in 1887; his family later moved to Boston where he attended public schools. After his high school graduation, he went on to earn his bachelor's degree from Tufts College in 1909. He earned graduate degrees from Harvard University in 1914 and Columbia University in 1917. Washington also studied at the New York School of Social

Work as a National Urban League (NUL) Fellow, making him the third director of the Atlanta University School of Social Work who was an Urban League fellow. Washington's appointment carried on George Edmond Hayes's vision of creating a cohort of social workers working in tandem with NUL affiliates across the country, thus creating a critical mass of professional workers for leadership in academia and social agencies unified by the theoretical and value underpinnings of an Afrocentric perspective.

Washington assumed the directorship of the School with a good deal of experience in the field of social welfare. He began his career as the first Executive Secretary of the Detroit Urban League in 1916. He led the organization when that city experienced rapid growth in its black population during the era of the Great Migration. He was an experienced researcher, having completed surveys in the cities of Detroit and Toledo, and research assignments in the states of Ohio and Pennsylvania before moving to Atlanta. These were all experiences that solidified his commitment to the use of science and the findings from empirical research as essential tools for understanding and informing problem-solving interventions. These experiences were translated into Washington's development of a strong research department at the School.

Washington also served for a short period on FDR's Black Cabinet and as the head of Negro Division of the Federal Emergency Relief Administration (FERA). As discussed, he was outspoken about the inequities experienced by blacks during the austere years of the Depression and the discrimination of the New Deal programs that prevented their full participation, and he cautioned against the negative psychological impact of an overreliance on public welfare programs by blacks.

The tradition of holding a White House Conference on Children every ten years had been established by the first conference held in 1909 and convened under the administration of Theodore Roosevelt. While director of the School of Social Work, Washington was appointed chair of the committee on minority children convened under the 1930 White House Conference, under the Hoover administration. Historical documents of the committee's findings highlighted the significant unmet needs of children of color. It concluded that the needs of Negro, Filipino, Indian, Mexican, and Puerto Rican children in most communities were found wanting.

Committed to the cause of social work education in service to the black community, Washington did not shy away from pointing out in his public talks and publications that blacks interacted within a "hostile environment." His predecessor, E. Franklin Frazier, chose to leave the city in the face of threats of violence toward himself and his family following the fallout from his publication establishing an equivalency between white racism and insanity; Washington, who was living with his family in Philadelphia at the time, took the opposite route. He left the North with the specific goal of joining the cause of educating black social workers in the South. He had been encouraging black social workers to take up practice in the South, and, after what he described as an epiphany, he decided to heed his own advice and devote his professional life to the education of social work for practice within the black community (Barrow, 2002).

Washington's temperament was such that he enjoyed more success than Frazier in navigating the oppressive Jim Crowism of the South and the paternalism or liberalism of well-intentioned whites who were associated with the University and the School. Now referred to as "microaggressions"—a term introduced by Harvard African American psychiatrist Chester Pierce in 1970—these paternalistic whites were much-needed benefactors who maintained the financial viability of the School. Barrow (2002, 2007), who conducted an analysis of primary and secondary data relevant to Washington's directorship of the School, wrote that, even when provoked, Washington was able to compartmentalize issues. This was a skill that enabled him to remain focused on conducting the business of the School and avoid being distracted by racially charged issues.

Similarly, Adams (1981), a member of the full-time faculty during Washington's full tenure as director, wrote of Washington's belief in good public relations and his ability to garner the support of individuals who may not have been of like mind on all of the issues, but were needed to contribute both their influence and material resources to the School during challenging periods and that he drew generously upon during the austere years of the Depression. The letterhead of the School displayed the names of both the Board of Trustees of the University and members of the School's Advisory board, including Mary McLeod Bethune and Walter Petit of the New York School of Social Work. From all reports, Washington was also adept at drawing on their support when needed to advance the School's mission.

Washington adopted a broader vision for the School, one that was captured in the 1999 Bulletin "*More Than a School: A Promotional Agency*" (Barrow, 2007; Intake, 1937). This was a part of his effort to promote the full professionalization of the School, which he endeavored to accomplish through several means. Included among these was the dissemination of a newsletter, contracting research studies that were conducted by the students and faculty, and bringing in well-known individuals from the social welfare community to give talks and conduct seminars. During the days of austerity to maintain fiscal viability of the School, Washington drew on his personal network of individuals who were connected to funding sources. For example, he customarily engaged with University Board of Trustees who were connected to the Rosenwald Foundations, local leaders of the Atlanta Community Chest, and the Georgia Tuberculosis Society (Adams, 1981).

Washington later modified efforts to promote the presence of the School and social work from a broader social welfare perspective when he came under criticism from the American Association of Schools of Social Work (AASSW), which at the time was the accrediting body of all schools of social work. Not only did the Association require Washington to narrow his vision for the School, but it ultimately led to the removal of courses that were specifically designed to provide knowledge, value, and skills essential for practice within the black community.

Unfortunately, Washington was not successful in staving off pressure from the AASSW despite the support of Atlanta University President Rufus Clement and influential members of the Board of Trustees. Resultantly, he had little choice but to narrow his vision for the School and forego the incorporation of special courses in the curriculum to support knowledge building of the black community and black experience. Under the threat of loss of accreditation and pressure from the AASSW, the special emphasis on African Americans in the curriculum offered under course titles such as Social Work Among Negroes in America, Industrial Problems of the Negro, Crime and the Negro, Conduct of Social Surveys in Negro Communities, and Recreation and the Negro, over time was reduced to a sole course entitled African Americans and Recreation.

The research department that Washington had so carefully constructed no longer existed, having been abandoned under similar pressure from the Association. Over the course of his tenure from 1927 to 1933, the mining of primary data conducted by Barrow (2002), owing to his commitment to the scientific method, revealed an enormous range of research studies conducted by the School for various organizations, including the City Welfare Office, Grady Hospital, and not-for-profit social welfare agencies. These studies were undertaken to address a variety of research questions, to develop an empirical basis for understanding the scope and dimensions of social problems affecting black communities, and for the development of interventions proved effective for improving outcomes for blacks.

The changing thrust of the curriculum and the erasing of key academic components, including what had been a highly productive research department undertaken in response to the accreditation process in the 1940s, lends credibility to what Associate Dean Lloyd Yabura claimed on the occasion of the School's fiftieth anniversary: "Thus began the genocidal process of white washing the curriculum in black schools" (Sanders, 1970, p. 31).

Washington's perspective on the education and training of black social workers is detailed in his article "The Need and Education of Negro Social Workers," published in the *Journal of Negro Education* (Washington, 1935). The generous use of quotes from the article are a reflection of the breadth and depth of his thinking on social work education. The article provides a comprehensive if not exhaustive explication of his perspective on social work education and practice with blacks. He wrote in the introduction that

The Negro people are the chief sufferers in the United States today from the unemployment crisis and they have benefited less from the Recovery Program than the white group. These facts do not need to be argued. They are obvious, at least to all Negroes, and plenty of data are available to others who need to be convinced. (p. 76)

To those who objected to his theses, he wrote,

The existence of the Negro group in a predominantly unsympathetic, hostile world is sufficient justification for specialized training for social work among Negroes. For this position, the writer makes no apologies. Most of the opponents of this position are suffering with an overburdened sense of inferiority. One factor which explains the opposition of certain Negro social workers is that they are confused in their own thinking. In spite of the fact that a number of them head Negro agencies which are claimed, according to their own statements, to be organized to relieve certain special problems from which Negroes as a group suffer, yet there is nothing especially unique about their services which distinguishes them from non-racial agencies except the color of their clients. Perhaps this also explains the futility and failure of many of their programs. (p. 89)

Washington expressed views on social work education that are currently echoed by contemporary social work educators who are concerned with the education of social workers for practice with blacks and other marginalized populations. These concerns have been advanced by an increased demand from social work students enrolled in the nation's predominantly white schools of social work that more attention be given to teaching content on equity and racial justice. This is exemplified in actions undertaken by students at the New York University Silver School of Social Work, as reported in the *Washington Post* that called for that school to improve its "deficient social-work education due to its lack of attention to racial justice" (Smith, 2019).

The value of specialized courses on matters of race essential to the social work core curriculum is no longer a contested minority viewpoint: it is a view that has gradually moved into the mainstream of social work education. Recent years have seen the introduction of a number of new initiatives as social work educators in predominately white schools of social work continue to grapple with the infusion or integration of diversity content into their curricula with focus on issues of racism (Roberts & Smith, 2002). These current interests mirror Washington's efforts to restore a black perspective in social work education during the decades of the 1940s and 1950s. In the 1935 article on the need for Negro social workers he wrote,

It is necessary to have specialized training to avoid the mistakes which have been made in the past in social work among Negroes; to protect the helpless Negro client from becoming the victim of futile experimentation and to avoid the waste of time and energy in the "trial and error" method. (Washington, 1935, p. 90)

Washington's position was that all social workers should be taught the core social work course content and that black as well as others social workers providing service to the black community should take specialized courses on practice in the black community.

MOVING INTO THE MAINSTREAM

Washington's views are seeing a resurgence as current social work educators and practitioners place an emphasis on the significance of race in the social work education curriculum and in agency practice. A number of schools of social work have adopted principles used by the Undoing Racism Model of the Peoples Institute for Survival and Beyond (Billings, 2016) as a means for addressing the root causes of the persistence of structural and racial inequities in institutional structures, from which schools of social work or health and human service systems are not immune (Mallon & McRoy, 2016; Tolliver & Burghardt, 2016).

The Smith College School of Social Work made a formal commitment to the Undoing Racism model and has emerged as an exemplar among the predominately white schools of social work in championing the inclusion of race-conscious content in the social work curriculum. Since 1995, the Smith College School has made a formal commitment to continuously learn and teach about and disrupt systems of privilege, inequality, and oppression that maintain white supremacy.

At the professional organizational level, the Council on Social Work Education (CSWE) introduced the Council on Racial, Ethnic, and Cultural Diversity as a component of its Commission for Diversity and Social and Economic Justice. The Commission is an institutionalization of various interest groups that emerged during the turbulence of the 1960s and that pushed the Council to examine its own commitment to the democratic values espoused by the profession. It is a permanent fixture of the Council's governance structure and tasked to expand the knowledge base and disseminate and encourage research about members of historically and emerging underrepresented groups. Similarly, the National Association of Social Workers (NASW) is focusing more sharply on issues of racial inequity in the convening of a think tank under the auspices of the Association's Policy Institute. The findings of the think tank are published in the report *Achieving Racial Equity: Calling the Social Work Profession to Action* (Social Work Policy Institute, 2014).

Washington also expressed his views on the more nuanced issues of race as presented in practice and that are of equal importance to worker readiness for practice in the black community. For example, commenting on transference in the cross-racial helping relationship he wrote that

> No matter what the white worker says or does, the Negro client will never come to the point of feeling absolutely certain of the white worker's attitude. There must be identification as between the client and worker for the latter to feel real security out of which there may develop real "transference." The white group has willed that such identification is not highly probable in this country. (Washington, 1935, p. 79)

Underscoring that social work is an optimistic profession, in addressing the importance of worker self-awareness and outlook, he wrote,

> Hence, the Negro social worker who has not become embittered, who has developed self-control, self-respect, and a wholesome philosophy of life and who has oriented himself or herself, has come nearer than anyone to solving the difficult problem of living in the complicated world of the Negro in the United States. This is a problem no white person has had to solve or could solve. Only a Negro social worker can impart the solution to a distressed Negro client. (Washington, 1935, pp. 79–80)

Moving beyond matters of race, Washington favored the teaching of a generalist curriculum versus specializations, a topic around which a lack of consensus still exists among social work educators today.

INTRODUCTION OF BLOCK FIELD PLACEMENT

One of Washington's most creative innovations at the School was the introduction of block placements in the field work curriculum. The major objective of the field practicum is to provide students with an agency practicum that allows for the application of knowledge, values, and skills in practice. The practicum continues to be the component of the social work curriculum in all CSWE-accredited schools that allows students to assume the professional role and integrate classroom theories with agency case practice.

The field practicum was introduced in the School's curriculum at the time of its inception, and it remains a requirement of the MSW program. Initially the School offered a practicum assignment to the first class of enrollees of eight hours each week; this was later extended from a quarterly basis to six months (Adams, 1981, p. 28). The practicum was and continues to be a requirement of the BSW degree when the School began to award the undergraduate degree in social work following its 1988 consolidation with Clark College.

For the MSW program, the practicum was originally designed to provide experience in a specific practice method of casework, group work, and community organization. The current practicum offered by the School allows for a broader choice to accommodate a range of student practice interests and provide opportunities that allow for the application of knowledge, values, and skills that support competencies consistent with the School's model of advanced direct social work practice in one of its two areas of specializations: mental health and children and families.

The concurrent field placement model, which was the model most commonly used by schools at the time of the School's opening, is designed so that students complete course work and field placements concurrently. The block placement model requires an intensive six-month, or full semester, off-site internship where the student is enmeshed in the professional role on a full-time basis. Over the period of the block placement at the agency, an on-site visit is conducted by a school-based faculty liaison. This was supplemented by students submitting periodic reports of assignments and their progress in achieving required learning objectives of the field curriculum.

When the block placement model was first introduced at the School, these placements were typically assigned to agencies in the North because social agencies in Atlanta and the South were racially segregated. Adams (1981) describes a number of incidents of cultural tensions because of differences in cultural norms between the North and South. Some of these are humorous, while others illustrate that racial prejudice and policies of discrimination in social work agencies common to the South were not unknown in northern agencies in which students were placed.

With foundation funding support, the Class and Field Institutes were introduced in the School's social work program in 1947. The Institute brought block placement field instructors to the School, at no expense to the participants, on an annual basis to interface with faculty and invited experts to address relevant topics of field education. Adams (1981) provides a detail listing of the topics and invited presenters of the Class and Field Institutes from 1947 to 1969. The topics of the early Class and Field Institutes reflect topics of concern to the CSWE and of relevance to social work education of the period. The Class and Field Institutes were discontinued in the early 1980s because of budgetary considerations.

The waning years of Washington's directorship saw a renewal of suspiciousness about the poor. The combined effects of racism and the country's residual tradition in the development of programs for the poor provide a lens for understanding the mindset that underlay coordinated attack against the poor that occurred in the 1950s. This attack was leveled against the Aid to Dependent Children (ADC) program and fueled by two trends that became characteristic of the caseload dynamics and demographics of the program's beneficiaries in the decades of the 1950s.

Concurrent with the increasing growth and cost of the ADC program was a dramatic change in caseload demographics. By the 1950s, the largest share of the caseload of the program that was originally designed to provide income protection to needy children in the homes of "deserving" white widows now comprised never-married women of color and their dependent children born out of wedlock.

Moreover, the constantly climbing caseload that was not showing a decline with the increasing quality of life and defeating the original vision of the architects of the ADC program, who believed that it would die a natural death as more families were captured by work-related social insurance programs.

To counter these trends, the country saw a flurry of punitive policies enacted to shrink the caseload by tightening eligibility to prevent new enrollments and throw families off the caseload who were believed to be defrauding the system. Restrictive policies included the use of residency requirements that barred eligibility to blacks migrating from the South and the new wave of Puerto Ricans migrating from the island in the 1950s. The "man in the house rule," designed to ferret out fathers believed to be living in the home, was introduced in New York City, and "suitable home" requirements, such as those adopted by Florida in the 1950s, allowed for closer scrutiny of parental behaviors that justified the closing of cases, the largest number of which were African American children who had been beneficiaries (Bell, 1965; Brown, 1999). As discussed by Carten (2016, among the media reporting the public's growing disenchantment with the program was the 1961 article in *Look* magazine entitled "Welfare: Has It Become a Scandal?" In southern states, discriminatory practices kept many African American children from receiving support through ADC programs, and, when money was provided, it was far less than that provided to white children. In Georgia, black children were underrepresented among beneficiaries of the program despite their overrepresentation among children in the state living in poverty. It was common for grants for white families to be in excess of those for black families (Soss et al., 2011). As the caseload continued to be disproportionately comprised of African American never-married mothers and their children, a clause was added in 1967 that was known as the "AFDC Freeze"; it placed mandatory limitations on federal reimbursement to states for children who were in need because of the absence of a parent due to desertion, illegitimacy, separation, or divorce.

What had become a coordinated national attack on the poor spawned and accelerated the growth of the National Welfare Rights Organization in the late 1960s. With the support of Martin Luther King Jr., the organization joined with CORE to become a part of leading organizations fighting for the civil rights of blacks. Founded by social activist and former chemistry professor Dr. James Wiley, the organization launched affiliate chapters across the country from its base in New York City. Wiley shared a close relationship with academic activists Richard Cloward and Frances Fox Piven, faculty of the Columbia University School of Social Work. Wiley adopted their strategy of flooding public welfare offices with new welfare applicants to force the replacement of public assistance grants with a program of guaranteed income for all people (Carten, 2016).

The book, *Regulating the Poor: Functions of Public Welfare* (Piven & Cloward, 2012) co-authored by the two Columbia University School of Social Work activists, has become a staple of required readings for a large share of schools of social work. Their central thesis is that the benefits of the welfare state and the purpose of antipoverty programs serve as instruments of social control to regulate the economic and political behavior of the poor; these program expand to restore social order during periods of civil unrest and are reduced to reinforce the work ethic when order is restored. The story of the welfare rights movement, in which poor women played a vital role, and the participation of social work academic activists in the movement must be told, but a full accounting of these important events is beyond the scope of this book.

BEGINNING OF THE CIVIL RIGHTS MOVEMENT

Up to this point in the School's history, a network of interrelated events and a confluence of trends influenced the environmental context that shaped the thrust of its educational programs and the success of its institutional sustainability. These same societal forces also paved the way for the Civil Rights movement. Beginning in the 1950s, these societal forces would converge in the decades of the 1960s to catapult the century-old struggle for black rights into the full view of the American public. The fight for black rights gained a new sense of urgency in the 1950s and 1960s with the murder of fourteen-year-old Emmitt Till, the arrest of Rosa Parks, and the advent of television that brought a new level of awareness to the country by bringing these events and the brutality and moral cost of white supremacy into the homes of ordinary Americans.

The Abduction and Murder of Emmett Till

The first event of the 1950s that played a critical role as a catalyst for the Civil Rights movement was the murder of Emmett Till, the circumstances of which unfolded over the summer of 1955. Slightly before celebrating his fourteenth birthday, Emmett, who lived with his mother on Chicago's south side, was visiting relatives in Money, Mississippi. On August 25, 1955, while making a purchase with his friends in a white-owned grocery store that catered to the black community, Emmett allegedly whistled at the wife of the store's owner. A few days later, the terrified youngster was kidnapped from the home of his uncle and aunt, Moses and Elizabeth Wright. He was dragged from his bed by a group of white men while his Uncle pleaded with the men to give the boy a whipping and let the matter end there. Determined to mete out what to them was an appropriate punishment for the teenager's egregious transgression of the code of behavior for blacks, the men took Emmett to a deserted place where he was severely beaten, shot, and his body thrown into the Tallahatchie River. When his mutilated body was discovered and returned to his family in Chicago, Emmitt's mother insisted on an open casket for the funeral services so that all could see the savagery of her son's murder.

The image of Emmett's remains in the open casket was published in *Jet* magazine, part of Johnson's Publications, an African American company with broad circulation in the black community. Jet reported the circumstances of Emmett's murder and the trial of the men accused of his murder and subsequently acquitted by a jury of all white men after sixty-seven minutes of deliberation. The trial and its outcome, by any measure a travesty of the American jurisprudence system, was subsequently picked up by the international press. The international coverage brought into world view America's indefensible treatment of African Americans that defied recompense in the judicial system.

The Defiance of Rosa Parks

The second event occurred in December 1955, in Montgomery, Alabama, with Rosa Parks' refusal to give up her seat to a white man in the "colored" section of a segregated city bus in Montgomery, Alabama. In keeping the "separate but equal" provision, the Montgomery City Code required blacks to be seated at the back of the bus, behind the line that separated black and white passengers. Bus drivers where given the authority to enforce the code, and, although not required by the code, some bus drivers had adopted the informal custom of moving the separating line back or requiring black passengers to give up their seats to whites when no seats were available in the white section. Following the code, blacks would routinely depart from the bus after entering the front of the bus to deposit their fare and reenter at the back of the bus to sit in the colored section.

Mrs. Parks was seated in the back of the bus on her way home after leaving her employment as a seamstress in a department store. When directed by the bus driver to give up her seat, as some other black passengers done when all of the seats in the white section were filled, Parks refused. The police were called and she was arrested and charged with violation of Chapter 6, Section 11 of the Montgomery City Code. She was taken to police headquarters, charged, photographed, fingerprinted, and later released on bail.

The records of her arrest can be retrieved from the National Archives. These documents record her age as forty-two, her "Nationality" as "negro", her "Occupations" as "alterations negro," and her "Complexion" as "Black." The report was filed on December 1, 1955, noting the place of occurrence "as in front of the Empire theater (on Montgomery Street)" and, with some alteration of the facts, the details of the event were described "we received a call upon arrival the bus operator said he had a colored female sitting in the white section of the bus, and would not move back (we May and Mixon) also saw her. The bus driver signed a warrant for her. Rosa parks, (c f) 634 Cleveland Court. Rosa Parks (cf) was charged with chapter 6 section 11 of the Montgomery city code." At trial she was found guilty, fined ten dollars in addition to four dollars for court costs.

Long before these events, Parks had been active in the Civil Rights movement. She participated in a mass meeting concerned with the murder of Emmet Till and later reflected that it was because of her thoughts about Emmett that she could not find it within herself to give up her seat (Houck & Grindy, 2008). At the time of her arrest, she was the secretary of the Montgomery Chapter of the NAACP. It was her association with the NAACP that led city activists and ministers to adopt the Montgomery Bus Boycott strategy, which ultimately led to the November 1956 Supreme Court ruling that segregation on public transportation was unconstitutional.

Rosa Parks continued her civil rights activism long after the central role she played in the Montgomery Bus Boycotts, and she wrote about these in her autobiography and memoirs (Parks & Haskins, 1992; Parks & Reed, 2000). She is memorialized in American culture as the "first lady of civil rights" and "the mother of the freedom movement." She was awarded the Congressional Medal of Honor in 1999.

The experiences of Rosa Parks and Emmett Till are a permanent part of the US historical record of the Civil Rights movement. The events surrounding their experiences speak to the forces of the human spirit when freedom is too long denied. Parks, reflecting on her defiance in refusing to give up her seat wrote "I was not tired physically. . . . No, the only tired I was, was tired of giving in." So was the spirit also expressed in the two words of Moses Wright, Emmet Till's uncle, as he stood up to point out in open court the white men who had murdered his nephew: "Thar he." He did so with the knowledge that his act of defiance of a black standing to openly accuse a white man made it necessary for him to flee his home and never again return to live in Mississippi.

The Advent of Television

The introduction of television as means for mass communication and reporting of the news to the American public was another factor that catapulted the Civil Rights movement onto the national and world stage. Television was among the many new amenities enjoyed by the American people during the years of the unfolding of the Civil Rights movement owing to the improved quality of life following the new postwar prosperity and an increase in leisure hours made possible by reforms in the work environment through organized labor. This new form of mass communication gave a new meaning to the press as the "Fourth Estate" of government. Television gave the media a greatly expanded reach, influencing public opinion and shaping policy developments on the pressing social issues of the day. National television news coverage of the Civil Rights movement brought the egregious treatment of blacks into the homes of virtually all Americans, making it all but impossible to ignore the brutality and moral costs of maintaining a system of white supremacy in the South.

By the 1960s, 90% of Americans owned televisions. Television coverage by the national media played a pivotal role in influencing the collective national conscience about the realities of race relations in the United States. Martin Luther King Jr., who emerged as the leader of the Civil Rights movement following the successful outcome of the Montgomery Bus Boycott, used television to advance the cause of the movement. After the brutality of the Selma march, King made it clear that television was added to his nonviolent strategy in the fight for black civil rights, vowing in an interview with the press that the Movement was not going away and the brutality of whites would no longer be obscured from public view, but now be visible to the entire nation under the glaring light of television (Madrigal, 2018). The optics of the new media of television included that of a fifteen-year-old girl in Little Rock being taunted by a mob of angry whites hurling racial slurs as the youngster tried to make her way to the first day of school; a teenage boy being held by police while mauled by attack dogs; the force of fire hoses turned on children and adults engaged in nonviolent demonstrations; the Bull Connor tank that symbolized the extent of police brutality in the South; and the historic March 7, 1965, march for voting rights in Selma, Alabama, a day known as "Bloody Sunday," where peaceful, nonviolent demonstrators were beaten so severely by state troopers on horseback armed with clubs and tear gas that a wounded, then twenty-five-year-old Congressman John Lewis believed it would surely be the day he would die.

Print media could not capture the horrific nature of this brutality in real time, but these events could now be transmitted across the nation and seen in living color on television in nightly news reports by all major networks. As events continued to unfold over the decade of the 1960s, television recorded the scope of the tenacity of white supremacy and the depths of the nation's potential for violence to preserve white privilege by any means necessary.

The country experienced a barrage of disturbing televised events that included the deployment of the National Guard in southern cities as elected state and city officials defiantly flaunted the rule of law in their refusal to comply with newly enacted civil rights legislation; the assassination of an American president and other national figures who stood on the side of the just treatment of all Americans; the Ku Klux Klan bombing of the 16th Street Baptist Church in Birmingham, Alabama, that took the lives of four young girls attending Sunday School class; and the riots that erupted in major US cities as the Civil Rights movement, initiated on Gandian principles of nonviolence, transitioned from passive engagement to militant protest.

Forrester B. Washington guided the School through the difficult years of the Great Depression and World War II. He completed his service to the School in 1954, at a time when the country was on the brink of what would be yet another transformative decade for the nation, the School, and the profession. In recognition of his substantial contributions to the University, Morehouse College awarded Washington the honorary degree of Doctor of Laws in 1943, for guiding the School from its infancy to a position of national prominence.

As reported in his *New York Times* obituary (August 27, 1963), after leaving the directorship of the School Washington had planned the development of the department of African studies for the New School for Social Research and traveled to Germany, Haiti, the British West Indies, the Virgin Islands, and other countries to study housing conditions. At the time of his death, he was a charter member of the NASW, and a member of the CSWE, the National Conference on Social Welfare, the Atlanta Community Chest, the Executive Committee of the Southern Regional Council of the Georgia Committee on Interracial Cooperation, and the American Committee of the International Congress of Social Workers (p. 31). When Washington stepped down from the directorship of the School of Social Work in 1954, his only disappointment was "being bothered," as Adams wrote, that he was never given the title of dean (Adams, 1981, p. 13).

Washington's successor was Whitney M. Young Jr., the first head of the School to hold the title of dean and for whom the School would be renamed in 2000. While Washington had reluctantly acquiesced to CSWE policies that began a gradual erosion of the School's Afrocentric perspective in the curriculum, Young, distinguished as a "power broker" skilled at negotiating the rights of blacks in the board rooms of the corporate sector, embraced these in the interest of leading the School into the 21st century. Committed to an agenda of racial integration, Young served in the deanship during a period that Adams (1981) described as a period in the history of the School when it became like any other school of social work.

Social work education was not immune from the effects of the chain of events that had catapulted the Civil Rights movement onto the national stage. The events occurring over the preceding decades were also pushing the profession to examine more closely its own policies that were anchored in a Eurocentric world view. Sparked by a small group of activist students enrolled in the Atlanta University Consortium Schools, the city of Atlanta became the locus of one of the most momentous movements in the nation's history.

REFERENCES

Adams, F. V. (1981). *The reflections of Florence Victoria Adams*. Atlanta: Shannon Press, in cooperation with the Atlanta University School of Social Work and the Alumni Association.

Alexander, L. M., & Rucker, W. C. (2010). *Encyclopedia of African American history*. Santa Barbara, CA: ABC-CLIO.

An Act to Promote the Defense of the United States (Pub. L. 77–11, H. R. 1776, 55 Stat. 31),

Anderson, W. (1975). *The wild man from Sugar Creek: The political career of Eugene Talmadge*. Baton Rouge: Louisiana State University Press.

Atlanta University School of Social Work. (1999). *More than a school—a promotional agency for social work*. Bulletin and announcements, 1949–1950.

Bailes, S. (1969). Eugene Talmadge and the Board of Regents controversy. *Georgia Historical Quarterly, 53*(4), 409–423. http://www.jstor.org/stable/40579012

Barrow, F. H. (2002). *The social welfare career and contributions of Forrester Blanchard Washington: A life course analysis*.

Barrow, F. H. (2007). More than a school: A promotional agency for social welfare: Forrester Blanchard Washington's leadership of the Atlanta University School of Social Work, 1927–1954. *Arete, 31*.

Bell, W. (1965). *Aid to dependent children*. New York: Columbia University Press.

Billings, D. (2016). Deconstructing white supremacy. In A. Carten, M. Pender Green, & A. Siskind (Eds.), *Strategies for deconstructing racism in the health and human services.* (pp. 91–100). New York: Oxford University Press.

Borgwardt, E. (2005). *A New Deal for the world: America's vision for human rights. Civil Liberties Act of 1988 (Pub. L. 100–383)* Cambridge, MA: Belknap Press.

Boulton, M. (2007). How the GI Bill failed African-American Vietnam War veterans. *Journal of Blacks in Higher Education, 58*(Winter), 57–61.

Brezina, C. (2006). *The Treaty of Versailles, 1919: A primary source examination of the treaty that ended World War I*. Primary Sources of American Treaties. New York: Rosen.

Brokaw, T. (1998). *The greatest generation*. New York: Random House.

Brown, M. K. (1999). *Race, money and the American social welfare state*. Ithaca, NY: Cornell University Press.

Carten, A. J. (2016). *Reflections on the American Social Welfare State: The Collected Papers of James R. Dumpson, PhD, 1930–1990.* Washington, DC: NASW Press.

Coleman, C. D. (1947). A study of jobs held by one-hundred graduates of Atlanta University School of Social Work from 1942 to 1946. Paper EP15605. ETD Collection for AUC Robert W. Woodruff Library, Atlanta.

Cook, J. F. (1974). The Eugene Talmadge–Walter Cocking controversy. *Phylon, 35*(June), 181–192.

Crowell, L. (1955). The building of the 'Four Freedoms' Speech. *Speech Monographs* 22(November), 266–283.

DuBois, W. E. B. (1946). Summary of an appeal to the World, ca. 1946. W. E. B. Du Bios Papers (MS 312). Special Collections and University Archives, University of Massachusetts Amherst Libraries.

Egerton, J. (1994). Days of hope and horror: Atlanta after World War II. *Georgia Historical Quarterly*, 78(2), 281–305. http://www.jstor.org/stable/40583033

Elson, C. M. (1976). The Georgia three-governor controversy of 1947. *Atlanta Historical Bulletin*, 20(Fall), 72–95.

Gary, R. B., & Gary, L. E. (1994). The history of social work education for black people 1900–1930. *Journal of Sociology & Social Welfare*, 21(1), article 7.

Harrington, M. (1966). *The Other America: Poverty in US*. Helicon.

Hatamiya, L. T. (1993). *Righting a wrong: Japanese Americans and the passage of the Civil Liberties Act of 1988*. Stanford, CA: Stanford University Press.

Herbold, H. (1994). Never a level playing field: Blacks and the GI Bill. *Journal of Blacks in Higher Education*, Winter, 104–110.

Hogan, M. J. (1987). *The Marshall Plan: America, Britain, and the reconstruction of Western Europe, 1947–1952*. Cambridge: Cambridge University Press.

Houck, D., & Grindy, M. (2008). *Emmett Till and the Mississippi Press* (p. x). Jackson: University Press of Mississippi.

Intake. (1937, June). Robert W. Woodruff Library of the Atlanta University Center, Archives and Special Collections, vertical file 3, pp. 1–16. Atlanta.

Kashima, T., & United States. Commission on Wartime Relocation and Internment of Civilians. (2011). *Personal justice denied: Report of the Commission on Wartime Relocation and Internment of Civilians*. Seattle: University of Washington Press. muse.jhu.edu/book/14017.

Madrigal, A. C. (2018). When the revolution was televised. *The Atlantic*, April 1. https://www.theatlantic.com/technology/archive/2018/04/televisions-civil-rights-revolution/554639/

Mallon, G. P., & McRoy, R. G. (2016). Children, youth and family serving systems. In A. Carten, M. Pender Green, & A. Siskind (Eds.), *Strategies for deconstructing racism in the health and human services* (pp. 143–168). New York: Oxford University Press.

Myrdal, G. (1944). *An American dilemma; the Negro problem and modern democracy* (2 vols.). Harper.

Parks, R., & Haskins, J. (1992). *Rosa Parks: My story*. New York: Dial Books.

Parks, R., & Reed, G. J. (2000). *Quiet strength: The faith, the hope, and the heart of a woman who changed a nation*. Grand Rapids, MI: Zondervan.

Peeples-Wilkins, W. (2006). Historical perspectives on social welfare in the Black community. *The Social Welfare History Project*. https://socialwelfare.library.vcu.edu/eras/great-depression/historical-perspectives-on-social-welfare-in-the-black-community-1886-1939/

Piven, F. F., & Cloward, R. (2012). *Regulating the poor: The functions of public welfare*. New York: Vintage.

President's Committee on Civil Rights. (1947). *To secure these rights: The report of the President's Committee on Civil Rights*. Washington: GPO.

Pruitt, S. (2018). How the Treaty of Versailles and German guilt led to World War II. https://www.history.com/news/treaty-of-versailles-world-war-ii-german-guilt-effects

Public Law 472 (The Marshall Plan, p. 1). General Records of the United States Government Record Group 11. National Archives and Records Administration.

Rhodes, R. (1986). *The making of the atomic bomb*. New York: Simon & Schuster.

Roach, R. (1997, August 21). From combat to campus: GI Bill gave a generation of African Americans an opportunity to pursue the American dream. *Black Issues in Higher Education*, 26–29.

Roberts, T. L., & Smith, L. A. (2002). The illusion of inclusion: An analysis of approaches to diversity within predominantly White schools of social work. *Journal of Teaching in Social Work*, 22(3–4), 189–211.

Roosevelt, F. D. (1941). Executive Order 8802—Prohibition of Discrimination in the Defense Industry, June 25.

Roosevelt, F. D. (1942). Executive Order 9066, February 19. US National Archives & Records Administration. https://www.archives.gov/historical-docs/todays-doc/?dod-date=625

Sanders, C. L. (1970). The legacy of Forrester B. Washington, Black Social Work Educator and Nation Builder Atlanta University School of Social Work. (November 12, 14, 1970). Proceedings of the 50th Anniversary.

Soss, J., Fording, R. C., & Schram, S. F. (2011). *Disciplining the poor: Neoliberal paternalism and the persistent power of race*. University of Chicago Press.

Smith, M. (2019). NYU social work school acknowledges 'institutional racism' after classroom episode. *The Washington Post*, February 24. https://www.washingtonpost.com/education/2019/02/22/nyu-social-work-school-acknowledges-institutional-racism-after-classroom-episode/

Social Work Policy Institute. (2014). *Achieving racial equity: Calling the social work profession to action*. Washington, DC: National Association of Social Workers.

Tolliver, W., & Burghardt, S. (2016). Education and training of a race-conscious workforce. In A. Carten, M. Pender Green, & A. Siskind (Eds.), *Strategies for deconstructing racism in the health and human services*. (pp. 33–50). New York: Oxford University Press.

Trattner, W. I. (1999). *From poor law to welfare state: A history of social welfare in America*. New York: Simon and Schuster.

Trattner, W. I. (1999). *From poor law to welfare state (6th ed.)*. New York: The Free Press.

Washington, F. (1935). The need and education of negro social workers. *Journal of Negro Education*, 4(1), 76–93. doi:10.2307/2292089.

Weiss, N. J. (1989). *Whitney M. Young, Jr., and the struggle for civil rights, Vol. 993*. Princeton, NJ: Princeton University Press.

White, W. F. (1995). *A man called White: The autobiography of Walter White*. University of Georgia Press.

Wilson, W. J. (1984). The black underclass. *Wilson Quarterly (1976-)*, 8(2), 88–99.

Wilson, W. J. (2011). *When work disappears: The world of the new urban poor*. New York: Vintage.

Zietlow, R. E. (2004). To secure these rights: Congress, courts and the 1964 Civil Rights Act. *Rutgers Law Review*, 57, 945.

ARCHIVES

Washington, Forrester B., Atlanta University, School of Social Work, 1948–1953 File—Box: 18, Folder: 59 The Atlanta Urban League papers document the.

Found in: Robert W. Woodruff Library of the Atlanta University Center, Inc. / Atlanta Urban League papers / President's Files / Grace Hamilton, 1942–1961, 1967 / Correspondence, 1942–1961, 1967

Washington, Forrester B., Director, Atlanta University, School of Social Work, 1947 File—Box: 240, Folder: 22

Atlanta School of Social Work - Washington, Forrester, 1930–1931
File—Box: 98, Folder: 7
The records of John Hope (1897–1953) Robert W. Woodruff Library of the Atlanta University Center, Inc. / John Hope records / Administrative and Institutional Files /
Atlanta School of Social Work - Washington, Forrester, 1931–1932
File—Box: 107, Folder: 15
Board Members. Gate City Day Nursery Association Collection, 1. Robert W. Woodruff Library of the Atlanta University Center, Inc. http://localhost:8081/repositories/2/archival_objects/140049 Accessed February 09, 2019.
Reid, Ira De A., 1945–1946. Rufus E. Clement records, Robert W. Woodruff Library of the Atlanta University Center, Inc. http://localhost:8081/repositories/2/archival_objects/71024 Accessed February 09, 2019.
Atlanta University School of Social Work
File—Box: 24, Folder: 23–26
The Scroll, 1920 January-March, November-December. Atlanta University printed and published materials, Robert W. Woodruff Library of the Atlanta University Center, Inc. http://localhost:8081/repositories/2/archival_objects/88427 Accessed February 09, 2019.
File—Box: 18, Folder: 59
Washington, Forrester B., Atlanta University, School of Social Work, 1948–1953. Atlanta Urban League papers, Robert W. Woodruff Library of the Atlanta University Center, Inc. http://localhost:8081/repositories/2/archival_objects/80863 Accessed February 09, 2019.
File—Box: 240, Folder: 22
Washington, Forrester B., Director, Atlanta University, School of Social Work, 1947. Atlanta Urban League papers, Robert W. Woodruff Library of the Atlanta University Center, Inc. http://localhost:8081/repositories/2/archival_objects/86566 Accessed February 09, 2019.
File—Box: 98, Folder: 7
Atlanta School of Social Work - Washington, Forrester, 1930–1931. John Hope records, Robert W. Woodruff Library of the Atlanta University Center, Inc. http://localhost:8081/repositories/2/archival_objects/62333 Accessed February 09, 2019.
File—Box: 107, Folder: 15
Atlanta School of Social Work - Washington, Forrester, 1931–1932. John Hope records, Robert W. Woodruff Library of the Atlanta University Center, Inc. http://localhost:8081/repositories/2/archival_objects/62582 Accessed February 09, 2019.
Frankie V. Adams Collection File—Box: 3, Folder: 28
Identifier: Series C. The Significance of Negro History Week, 1966 February 16. Frankie V. Adams collection, Series C. Robert W. Woodruff Library of the Atlanta University Center, Inc. http://localhost:8081/repositories/2/archival_objects/13743 Accessed February 09, 2019.
File—Box: 3, Folder: 32 Identifier: Series C Survival Education. Frankie V. Adams collection, Series C. Robert W. Woodruff Library of the Atlanta University Center, Inc. http://localhost:8081/repositories/2/archival_objects/13747 Accessed February 09, 2019.
File—Box: 3, Folder: 26 Identifier: Series Cracids, 1978 July. Frankie V. Adams collection, Series C. Robert W. Woodruff Library of the Atlanta University Center,

Inc. http://localhost:8081/repositories/2/archival_objects/13741 Accessed February 09, 2019.

Box: 3, Folder: 15 Identifier: Series C. Forrester B. Washington, 1963 December 9. Frankie V. Adams collection, Series C. Robert W. Woodruff Library of the Atlanta University Center, Inc. http://localhost:8081/repositories/2/archival_objects/13730 Accessed February 09, 2019.

Series—Box: 4 Identifier: Series E

Atlanta School of Social Work Scrapbook, 1931–1940. Frankie V. Adams collection, Series E. Robert W. Woodruff Library of the Atlanta University Center, Inc. http://localhost:8081/repositories/2/archival_objects/13760 Accessed February 09, 2019.

This scrapbook documents the Atlanta School of Social Work from 1931 to 1935. Adams collected memoranda, reports, and meeting minutes to show the development of the school and the programs with which she worked. Of special interest are the snapshots of the school's projects in field work. As a preservation measure, the scrapbook was disassembled and housed in folders.

Dates 1931–1940

Inventory of the White House Conference on Child Health and Protection records, Box/Folder 57:12,13,14).

National Archives. Page 1 Civil Case 1147 *Browder, et al* v. *Gayle, et al*; U. S. District Court for Middle District of Alabama, Northern (Montgomery) Division Record Group 21: Records of the District Court of the United States National Archives and Records Administration-Southeast Region, East Point, GA. National Archives Identifier 596074

Robert W. Woodruff Library of the Atlanta University Center, Archives and Special Collections, Atlanta University, Atlanta, GA.

CHAPTER 10

Reclaiming the Legacy

The unhealthy gap between what we preach in America and what we often practice creates
a moral dry rot that eats at the very foundation of our democratic ideals and values.
—Whitney M. Young (1964)

Along the Pedestrian Walk Way on the campus of Clark Atlanta University
a plaque erected by the Georgia Historical Society and the Georgia
Department of Economic Development reads,

> In February 1960, here at the site of Yates and Milton drugstore three students
> from Morehouse College—Lonnie King, Joseph Pierce and Julian Bond—
> began to rally students from Atlanta's other historically black institutions—
> Atlanta University, Clark College (now Clark Atlanta University), the
> Interdenominational Theological Center, Morris Brown College, and Spelman
> College—and launched the Atlanta student movement that helped to destroy
> Jim Crow in the American South. Following publication of an "Appeal for Human
> Rights," authored by Roslyn Pope, the students waged a nonviolent campaign
> that led to the desegregation of restaurants, movie theaters, parks and other
> federal, state, and local facilities. The first student sit-ins at 11 eating facilities
> in downtown Atlanta on March 15, 1960 led to the arrest of 77 students. Black
> and white leaders eventually negotiated a settlement that desegregated lunch
> counters in October 1961.

The curriculum of schools of social work offering a concentration in community organization as a practice method is anchored in the assumption
that change more often than not takes a bottom-up approach. The approach
seeks to bring together various stakeholders, individuals, small groups, and
formal and informal organizations at the community level in a process of

Find a Way or Make One. Alma J. Carten, Oxford University Press (2021). © Oxford University Press.
DOI: 10.1093/oso/9780197518465.001.0001.

social action that results in achieving mutually shared goals. This assumption was the conceptual anchor of the Neighborhood Union launched by Eugenia Burns Hope, who also participated in the design of the inaugural curriculum of the Atlanta School of Social Work that included courses on community organization and research. Her work pioneered a participatory planning process that engaged the black community in Atlanta neighborhoods, which were impacted by urban decay rooted in racial discrimination, in a process of self-determining their own needs and how these were best met. It was the skillful use of the community organizing strategy overseen by the then little known Barack Hussein Obama that won him the presidency in the 2008 elections—an outcome that left acclaimed American poet and civil rights activist Maya Angelou and millions of other American standing in awe of the election of an African American to the presidency of the United States, an event that none believed they would ever see in their lifetimes.

Looking back in history, the most frequently quoted words of Frederick Douglass were taken from his speech given August 3, 1857, before the beginning of the Civil War: "If there is no struggle, there is no progress," and "Power concedes nothing without a demand" (Black Past Remembered, 2007). And by the 1960s an aging W.E.B. Dubois had shifted from his belief that the "talented tenth" of exceptional blacks would be the force for change in the black community; to championing the organization of the masses of blacks, who carried a disproportionate share of the burden of the inequalities of an oppressive society, as the means for pursuing economic and social justice for themselves and ultimately for all oppressed and marginalized people (Holt, 1990).

It was this grassroots, bottoms-up approach undergirded by the principles of nonviolence and the community organizing method of planned change and reform that guided the strategy of the Civil Rights movement. And it was students and young people, black and white, from the North and the South, embracing the principles of nonviolent protest who were at the vanguard of the most tumultuous and transformative movement in American history. It was a movement that brought the nation closer than it had ever been before to achieving the aspirational goal of a "more perfect union." The Civil Rights movement was brought to full scale under the leadership of Dr. Martin Luther King Jr., Morehouse College's most famous alumnus, and Atlanta became the epicenter for the planning of the most transcendent movements of the nation's history.

STUDENT PROTESTS IN THE HBCUS

Dr. King is the unquestioned father of the Civil Rights movement and globally celebrated for his conceptualization of principles of nonviolence and passive engagement as the anchoring moral pillars of the movement. The extensive use of the lunch counter sit ins in the non-violent weaponry in the toolbox of engagement strategies was the brainchild of activist-minded students who were enrolled in the historically black colleges and universities (HBCUs).

The use of student sit-in as an engagement strategy occurred simultaneously with Dr. King's planning his departure from Montgomery, Alabama, to Atlanta where he would co-pastor Ebenezer Baptist Church with his father Martin Luther King, Sr., and continue planning the movement. The sit-ins were launched on February 1, 1960, in Greensboro, North Carolina, when four black male freshmen students from North Carolina A&T College—Ezell Blair Jr., Franklin McCain, Joseph McNeil, and David Richmond—staged the first lunch counter sit-in (Ray, 2015; Encyclopedia Britannica, 2015). And by some reports, in absence of a preplanned long-term follow-up strategy (Branch, 2007), the students went to the downtown Woolworth's and took seats at the whites-only lunch counter. They were not physically attacked by angry whites, an occurrence that became common in later lunch counter sit-ins, but they were admonished by some black Woolworth employees concerned that what they were doing would only make trouble for the black community. The Greensboro Four, as they came to be called, were not served that day, but sat quietly for the full day, promising upon leaving that they would return the following day at 10:00 AM.

As Taylor Branch described in *America in the King Years* (Branch, 2007), what emerged resembled an organic phenomenon as the Greensboro student action set into motion an unstoppable spontaneous chain of events that were felt across America. The news of what the Greensboro students called their "sit-down protest" as they took leave without having been served spread throughout the campus. By the following day the numbers of black and white student volunteering to join the four freshmen had grown to nearly one hundred. Now fortified by numbers, a plan was developed for the volunteers to occupy the lunch counter in round-the-clock shifts (Branch, 2007, pp. 270–271).

Following on the heels of the Greensboro sit-ins, sit-ins were launched in Nashville, Tennessee, under the leadership of James Lawson. Lawson was a veteran civil rights activist whom Dr. King referred to as the leading theorist and strategist of nonviolence in the world. A conscientious objector, in 1951 Lawson was sentenced to three years in federal prisons for refusing to enlist in the Korean War. With the intervention of the United Methodist Church, he was released to their Board of Missions after serving thirteen months and sent by the Board to teach in India. It was during his three years in India that Lawson studied and interacted with individuals who had a close association with the Gandhian philosophy of nonviolent protest, and he became convinced that principles of nonviolence could be applied in the United States.

With Dr. King's encouragement to come south and join the movement, Lawson moved to Nashville. He enrolled in the Divinity School at Vanderbilt University and began conducting workshops with community members,

Vanderbilt students, and students enrolled in four of Nashville's HBCUs: Fisk, American Baptist, Tennessee Agricultural and Industrial, and Tennessee State University. A young John Lewis, who was a student at Fisk, was among the students trained and mentored by Lawson and who later became a leader in the Civil Rights movement. Lawson later joined Ella Baker, also a veteran civil rights activist, in organizing the student leaders in the launching of the Student Nonviolent Coordinating Committee (SNCC). Lawson was subsequently expelled from the University because of his involvement in the Civil Rights movement. Decades later, the University redressed the decision of the executive board to expel Lawson by inviting him back to the School as a Distinguished University Professor. He is the first recipient of the University's distinguished alumni award, and, in 2007, the James R. Lawson Jr. Chair was established in his honor. Lawson donated a portion of his papers to Vanderbilt; these are housed in the Special Collections at the University Library.

The students enrolled in HBCUs in Greensboro and Nashville had modeled a protest strategy that energized a core group of students in the Atlanta University Consortium schools whose activism is memorialized by the plaque on the campus promenade. Continuing the momentum set in motion by the sit-ins in Greensboro and Nashville, Morehouse College students Lonnie King, Joseph Pierce, and Julian Bond were at the vanguard of the Atlanta student movement. They were later joined by students in the other Atlanta University Consortium Schools and by students enrolled in HBCUs across the South. John Mack and Johnny Parham were two students enrolled in the Atlanta University School of Social Work and were among the students mentored by Dean Whitney M. Young. While dean, Young continued his commitment to supporting and guiding the professional careers of students of high potential for leadership, and he assumed an active involvement in the activist student group in Atlanta.

In reflecting on the launching of the student movement in Atlanta, Johnny Parham described in his journal the anticipatory feelings among the student planners as they gathered together to embark on what they intuitively knew would be a historic event.

> [T]he sun had begun to cast a shadow over the campus quadrangle as six of us gathered, anxiously awaiting the arrival of, what we hoped would be hundreds of students. It was an early spring morning in Atlanta, and the air was filled with the smell of azaleas. The dogwood trees were in bloom with their familiar pink and white blossoms. Few of us noticed the beauty of the campus on that early morning of March 15, 1960. This was a culmination of intensive planning and strategizing that had practically consumed 15 students from the Atlanta University Center for more than three weeks. We were embarking upon Atlanta's first student led sit-in demonstrations against American apartheid as it was practiced in Atlanta, Georgia. (Parham, n.d.)

STUDENT DOCUMENT OF GRIEVANCES: "AN APPEAL FOR HUMAN RIGHTS"

The movement was propelled forward in Atlanta when students of the Consortium Schools outlined a statement of grievances in "An Appeal for Human Rights." The statement had been negotiated as an alternative approach agreed to by the Atlanta University administration that discouraged student leaders from using sit-ins as the first step in confronting racial segregation in the city.

"An Appeal for Human Rights" was published as a full-page ad in the March 9, 1960, Sunday edition of the Atlanta newspapers. The document had been drafted by Roslyn Pope, president of the Spelman leadership group, and signed by all of the student leaders from Clark, Morehouse, Morris Brown, and Spelman Colleges; Atlanta University; and the Interdenominational Theological Center. The statement boldly challenged the conventional thinking and image of Atlanta as a progressive city "too busy to hate" advanced by Mayor Hartsfield. The statement asserted that

> We want to state clearly and unequivocally that we cannot tolerate, in a nation professing democracy and among people professing Christianity, the discriminatory conditions under which the Negro is living today in Atlanta, Georgia— supposedly one of the most progressive cities in the South. (An Appeal for Human Rights, 1960; Dittmer, 1997)

With astute analytical precision the students' outlined critical areas of employment, housing, healthcare, voting rights and law enforcement that contributed to deep racial inequities that impacted race relations in the city and slowed the economic development and social progress of the African American community in Atlanta. The racial inequalities the students set forth in the 1960 Appeal have been found in subsequent research to have left an indelible mark and have had rippling effects on issues of racial equity over the full history of the city (Bayor, 1996).

In responding to the students, Mayor Hartfield, who had advanced the narrative of Atlanta as the city "too busy to hate," did nothing more than to thank the students for bringing these matters to the attention of the white community. Their appeal, however, was brought into wider public view when Spelman faculty Howard Zinn prepared an abbreviated version of the statement that was printed in *The Nation*.

Zinn's *A People's History of the United States* (Zinn & Damon, 1998) corrects the revisionist tradition of mainstream historians in distorting the factual experience of black and brown people in the United States. The publication is increasingly favored by social work faculty who are committed to teaching from a race-critical perspective. Zinn, an academic and intellectual activist, held a faculty appointment with Spelman College from 1954 until his termination by the Spelman president in 1963. The reasons for his termination are not clearly stated in the literature; however, his dismissal occurred at a time when he had become deeply involved in the Civil Rights movement and extended his support and encouragement to student activists at Spelman and other Consortium Schools (Duberman, 2012).

Soon after the publication of "An Appeal for Human Rights," a flood of sit-ins began across the city of Atlanta and the nation. On October 19, 1960, Dr. King and Morehouse student leader Lonnie King sat-in at the lunch room at Rich's Department Store in protest of the money of blacks being taken for the purchase of clothing and other items in the store while, at the same time, they were being denied service in the popular Magnolia Restaurant or to try on clothing they were purchasing. The two were promptly arrested along with dozens of others who were arrested at sit-ins in Rich's and at other locations across the city. The news of Dr. King's arrests created a fire storm of news reports across the country that led to the involvement of presidential candidate John F. Kennedy. With Kennedy's intervention King was released after a short two-day confinement in the Georgia prison system.

Despite the barriers imposed by the University administration and the black establishment in Atlanta, the student sit-ins continued unabated. Atlanta University President Rufus Clement, concerned about the image of the university and implications for fundraising, discouraged student activism, reminding students that their parents had sent them to college to get an education and not to be troublemakers or rabble-rousers.

The president's views were held by many of the prominent members of the black old guard and keepers of the tradition of status quo. This was a view that was also held by conservative members of the black community and faculty of the Consortium Schools. And although the social contract defining black and white relations that had created an elite and privileged class of black Atlantans to which they belonged and represented, there was another segment of the city's black community that continued to be disadvantaged by the inequities of what were now overlaid with class divisions.

Despite the objections of their elders, the students remained respectfully undeterred from their cause to achieve the equitable treatment of all black Atlantans. The Spelman students participated in the sit-ins wearing nylon stockings and white gloves, the customary attire for respectable southern black women of the day. Similarly, their male counterparts were appropriately attired in suits and neckties. None was swayed from their commitment to sit in nonviolent peaceable protest for the cause of civil rights for all black Atlantans.

Benjamin E. Mays, Morehouse College president, who from the start supported the students whom he referred to as "young warriors," wrote in his autobiography that when Morehouse students began to talk about the intolerable conditions in downtown Atlanta, he knew that the demonstrations were not far off (Mays, 2011, p. 287). Whitney Young, from his post as dean of the Atlanta University School of Social Work, also offered his informal and largely behind-the-scenes support to his social work students.

BEGINNINGS OF THE CIVIL RIGHTS MOVEMENT

The Civil Rights movement came to full scale under the leadership of the Reverend Dr. Martin Luther King Jr., who became the acknowledged moral leader of the country after his often quoted "I Have a Dream Speech." The speech was given before an audience of an estimated 250,000 at the historic August 28, 1963 March on Washington for Jobs and Freedom.

A. Phillip Randolph, and Bayard Rustin were the central planners of the event, which was undertaken in collaboration with the heads of the major civil rights organizations informally known as the "Big Six." The group included Dr. King, president of the Southern Christian Leadership; James Farmer, president of the Congress of Racial Equality; Roy Wilkins, president of the NAACP; Whitney Young, after he had moved on from the deanship to become the executive director of the National Urban League; and John Lewis, chairman of the SNCC. Dorothy Height, president of the National Council for Negro Women, was also present with the group. Dr. Height is distinguished as being the only woman included in major civil rights events with the Big Six, but her presence in the Big Six was diminished in media reporting.

James Farmer was the first to use the term "Big Six" when referring to the civil rights leadership as a collective. Farmer wrote in his autobiography, *Lay Bare the Heart* (Farmer, 1998), of the sexism and ageism of the period that predisposed the media—sometimes referring to the leadership as "the Big Four"—to diminish the presence of both Dr. Height and the young John Lewis when reporting on the leadership collective. Farmer speaks to this, describing Dr. Height as a "worthy successor of the legendary Mary McLeod Bethune" as president of the National Council of Negro Women. He writes of her as speaking "sparingly, but effectively and with conviction," and as "moving with grace and assurance as the spokeswoman" in what was a man's world in the early years of the movement (pp. 217–218).

There were many men and women who played a significant leadership role in the movement, but they stood in the shadow of the iconic presence of Dr. King, who was gifted with an unmatched eloquence in writing and speaking on behalf of the movement. Dr. King was awarded the Nobel Peace Prize for his leadership in the Civil Rights movement and his commitment to achieving social justice through nonviolence. In his memoir, *Stride Towards Freedom: The Montgomery Story* (1958), Dr. King describes the process of his becoming committed to the use of nonviolence and love as the foundation for shaping the Civil Rights movement.

DR. KING'S VISION OF THE BELOVED COMMUNITY

Dr. King was introduced to the concept of nonviolence and passive resistance as a student at Morehouse College when he read the American author and transcendentalist Henry David Thoreau's, essay on "Civil Disobedience," first published in 1849 (Thoreau, 1964). Thoreau, who was also an abolitionist, wrote that the individual, as a moral imperative, is not obligated to observe a law that requires her to be an agent of injustice to another. King's interest in nonviolence was further sparked after hearing a talk given by Dr. Mordechai Johnson, president of Howard University, after Johnson had returned from a recent trip to India where he had met Mahatma Gandhi. Johnson recounted in his talk Gandhi's successful use of nonviolence and the organization of the masses of the Indian people to gain the independence of India and freedom from oppressive British colonial rule.

These experiences influenced King's decision to apply Gandhian principles of nonviolence as the foundation of the Civil Rights movement. Moreover, he saw this as the pathway of achieving his vision of the "beloved global community"—an inclusive global community in which all people can share in the wealth of the earth, and no form of militarism, injustice, or inequality is tolerated by international standards of human decency (King, 1967).

Dr. King's concept of the Beloved Community was shaped by his definition of *agape love*, the highest form of love, which is unconditional and extends goodwill and benevolence to all humankind. For King, love and justice were linked; therefore, the movement would use the tools of both persuasion and coercion. The principles of King's philosophy of nonviolence and the path to the Beloved Community are described on the website of the King Center (https://thekingcenter.org/king-philosophy/).

HUMANISTIC VALUES AS PILLARS OF THE AUTONOMOUS SOCIAL WORK MODEL

Themes from King's principles of nonviolence and the Beloved Community are embedded in the School's educational philosophy. As the School of Social Work began to reconceptualize its curriculum at the time of the half-centennial of its founding, Dr. Kings definition of agape love became one of the pillars of the educational philosophy shaping the humanistic framework of the curriculum. The value orientation adopted incorporates the concept of love (agape), which is viewed as essential for collective human development. The concept of agape is noted as the first principle of the humanistic values perspective of the School's autonomous social work model, as described in the School's MSW Student Handbook (Clark Atlanta University, 2018–2019).

ATLANTA BECOMES THE EPICENTER OF THE MOVEMENT

As envisioned by progressive black and white Atlantans who believed the city would lead the struggle for black rights in the aftermath of World War II, Atlanta indeed became the "Cradle of the Civil Rights movement" in the 1960s. Atlanta is further distinguished as the birthplace of Martin Luther King and the home of the historic Ebenezer Baptist Church, founded by King's maternal grandfather, A. D. Williams. Dr. King and his father, Martin Luther King, Sr., served as senior ministers at Ebenezer Baptist Church. It is also the church where Dr. King's funeral services were held and attended by thousands who came from across the globe to pay homage to his life and legacy after he had been felled by an assassin's bullet in Memphis, Tennessee on April 4, 1963. King had taken a detour to Memphis to lend support to James Lawson who was organizing striking sanitation workers under the banner of "I am a man." After his assassination the city of Atlanta became the site of the Martin Luther King, Jr. Center for Nonviolent Social Change and the Martin Luther King, Jr. National Historic Site.

Atlanta is also where major planning for the Civil Rights movement took place as the movement began to take shape and materialize. The Southern Christian Leadership Conference (SCLC) was founded in Atlanta in 1957, tasked to develop a coordinated strategy for launching a nonviolent campaign across the South. The stated mission of the organization was "To save the soul of America." Many of these meetings were held at the Paschal Brother's Restaurant, another historic Atlanta site that became the unofficial headquarters of the movement during the early 1960s.

Power Breakfasts at the Paschal Brother's Restaurant

The restaurant was the site where Dr. King convened a diverse group of social activists from across the nation to plan the Poor Peoples March on Washington that he envisioned would bring together the poor of all ethnicities from across the nation. It was also where annual meetings of the School's Class and Field Institutes were held. The Class and Field Institutes were funded by the School and brought together faculty and field instructors from across the nation on an annual basis in an ongoing examination of evolving best approaches for integrating classroom theory into practice.

An untold number of early morning "power breakfasts" were held at the restaurant, attended by individuals who have since become iconic figures in the history of the Civil Rights movement. Among those who joined Dr. King in strategy planning sessions to organize sit-ins, marches, and voter registration campaigns, and where they came to seek refuge from the brutality of law enforcement and white mobs, were Andrew Young, John Lewis, Julian Bond, Maynard H. Jackson, Stokely Carmichael, and the Reverends Jesse Jackson and Ralph Abernathy. Stokely Carmichael later assumed leadership of the SNCC. Under Carmichael's leadership, the SNCC later broke with Dr. King's nonviolent philosophy to operate under an aggressive form of confrontation under the banner of "Black Power." The SNCC was thus taken far afield from the vision of pioneering civil rights activist Ella Baker, who had initially brought together in 1960, at Shaw University, students of the original sit-ins to form a locally based autonomous student-led organization.

In an article in the *Atlanta Journal* on the occasion of the death of the co-founder James V. Paschal, who established the restaurant with his brother Robert, Andrew Young was quoted as observing "I used to say that all the decisions in Atlanta were made between 6:30 and 8 in the morning, and they were made at Paschal's." He further observed that "Any politician in Atlanta who wanted to get elected needed the black vote, and the best place to get it was at Paschal's" (Brown, 2008). The restaurant has been moved to a new site with a more modern-day ambiance. The old building, located at 530 Martin Luther King Jr. Drive, is now a part of Clark Atlanta University that the University administration had expressed interest in restoring the building for use as a research center. Some would like to see it restored as a historic site of the planning of the Civil Rights movement (Saporta, 2018).

MOVING THE GRASSROOTS MODEL TO THE NATIONAL LEVEL

The events in set into motion by the HBCU students were unfolding within a context paralleling events driving what was quickly becoming a national Civil Rights movement. Ella Baker, a lesser known figure in the movement, was a principal player in these developments. It was under her tutelage that students formed the vanguard of establishing sit-ins as a template for a national strategy that led to the founding of the SNCC, headquartered in Atlanta.

Recognizing the potential of the grassroots, bottoms-up approach adopted by the students, Baker organized a meeting at Shaw University, her alma mater, to bring together the student leaders who organized 1960 sit-ins in Greensboro and Nashville. Always the consummate teacher, she believed that students were the hope of the future. She guided them into seeing the larger potential of their struggle, beyond that of having a hamburger or drink at a lunch counter, encouraging them to form their own independent organization based on nonviolent principles.

Baker was born in 1903, in Norfolk, Virginia, one generation removed from black enslavement. Baker's penchant for civil rights work was instilled in her by stories told by her grandmother of the injustices inflicted upon blacks during the years of enslavement. Her career as a civil rights activist began long before her involvement with the 1960 Civil Rights movement and spanned five decades, from 1930 until her death in 1986. Baker was educated at Shaw University in Raleigh, North Carolina, which is among the oldest of the HBCUs. After graduating as class valedictorian in 1927 she moved to New York City during the years of hardship of the Great Depression, where she was introduced to radical community organizing and political activism. She joined the staff of the NAACP in 1930, holding positions of field secretary and director of the affiliate offices in New York. In the early decades of the 1950s, she worked with Dr. King along with a small group of ministers who at the time were unschooled in the practical aspects of community organizing that became the strategy of the SCLC. (Ransby, 2003).

Baker played a central role at the front end of organizing the SCLC, although she never received a formal appointment to a position of leadership. She spoke to the reasons for her being overlooked in an oral history interview.

> I had no ambition to be (let's call it) executive director. If I had had any, I knew it was not to be. And why do I say that? Two reasons. One, I was a female. The other, I guess, a combination of female and non-minister, plus the kind of personality differences that existed between me and the Rev. Dr. King. I was not a person to be enamored of anyone. My philosophy was not one of nonviolence per se and I knew enough about organization (at least I thought I knew enough about organization) to be critical about some of the lack of procedures that obtained in SCLC. . . . Within the inner councils, whenever there was discussion, I did not try to force myself upon them recognizing the sensitivities that existed. Now, I did not hesitate to voice my opinion and sometimes it was the voicing of that opinion it was obvious that it was not a very comforting sort of presence that I presented.
>
> And I was dealing with ministers whose only sense of relationship to women in organization was that of the church. And the role of women in the southern church—and maybe all of the churches but certainly the southern churches— was that of doing the things that the minister said he wanted to have done. . . .
>
> No, and I wasn't a show plate. The average attitude toward the southern Baptist ministers at that stage, and maybe still, was as far as their own women were concerned were that they were nice to talk to about such things as how well they cooked, how beautiful they looked, and how well they carried out a

program that the minister had delegated them to carry out but not a person with independence and creative ideas of his own, but on whom they had to rely. They could not tolerate, and I can understand that they couldn't, and especially from a person like me because I was not the kind of person that made special effort to be ingratiating. I didn't try to insult but I did not hesitate to be positive about the things with which I agreed or disagreed. I might be quiet but if there was discussion and I was supposed to be able to participate, I participated at the level of my thinking. (Baker, 1974)

Andrew Young concurred with Baker's observations about her manner of self-presentation and her objective self-appraisal of being less than a compatible fit with the clergy leadership. He described her as "determined" and wrote that Baker's modeling of a role for women as one of independence and leadership had no tradition in the Baptist Church and was a source of dissatisfaction for everyone (Young, 1996, p. 147).

Committed to her roles of activist and mentor, Baker left the SCLC to more directly assist student civil rights activists in their organizing efforts. In April 1960 she organized a conference at Shaw University for the leaders of the student sit-ins and invited James Lawson to give the keynote address. The event led to the launching of the Student Non-Violent Coordinating Committee (SNCC). With the growing professionalization of the civil rights leadership, favoring the compelling authenticity of grassroots leaders, Baker also played a role in in the organization of the Mississippi Freedom Democratic Party. The Party had been formed in 1964 as an alternative to the all-white democratic Mississippi delegation that prohibited blacks from participating in state politics.

The Mississippi Freedom Party gave voice to Fanny Lou Hamer, one of the most iconic of the grassroots leaders. Despite harassment and physical brutality inflicted by law enforcement, Hamer spoke out fearlessly and passionately about the violence and intimidation experienced by blacks to prevent them from registering to vote. Her most often quoted remarks are "I am sick and tired of being sick and tired." And she is well-remembered for her impassioned nationally televised speech detailing the ordeal she endured when jailed for attempting to register to vote at the county courthouse in Indianola Mississippi. The speech was given at the 1964 Democratic Convention as an appeal for the seating of the Freedom Party. She ended by declaring to the nation and indeed to the world that if the party were not seated "I question America. Is this America, the land of the free and the home of the brave, where we have to sleep with our telephones off of the hooks because our lives be threatened daily, because we want to live as decent human beings, in America?" Hamer was posthumously inducted into the National Women's Hall of Fame in 1993.

Ella Baker, along with Bayard Rustin, played important roles in the movement and in the organization of the historic August 1968 Poor Peoples March on Washington. The contributions of Ruskin, openly Gay and a conscientious objector, similar to those of Ella Baker were obscured in a Movement characterized by a male dominated leadership at the helm of which were clergymen who were the embodiment of the moral teachings of the black church. John D'Emilio, in his biography *Lost Prophet: The Life and Times of Bayard Rustin* (2003), chronicles Rustin's life, at the center of which was his commitment to peace and equality.

The contributions of Ella Baker were elevated into the public view with the founding of the Ella Baker Center for Human Rights in September, 1996 based in Oakland, California. The Center was co-founded by Van Jones, news commentator, distinguished visiting fellow at Princeton University, and special advisor to the Obama Administration, to bring to light human rights abuses in the criminal justice system founded by Van Jones, news commentator, distinguished visiting fellow at Princeton University, and special advisor to the Obama administration. Based in Oakland, California, the mission of the Center is to bring to light human rights abuses in the criminal justice system.

LEGISLATIVE AND POLICY REFORMS SPAWNED BY THE MOVEMENT

Ultimately, the Civil Rights movement enjoyed the backing of the federal government with the enactment of the 1964 Civil Rights Act (Pub.L. 88–352, 78 Stat. 241). The law was signed into law by President Lyndon B. Johnson on July 2, 1964, and banned discrimination based on race, color, religion, sex, or national origin in all sectors of American life. The Act was followed by the 1965 Voting Rights Act that protected the rights of blacks to vote, as guaranteed by the 14th and 15th Amendments to the US Constitution. The Civil Rights movement moved forward with the support of the legislative branch of the federal government, now joined with the judiciary by way of the Supreme Court's landmark 1954 *Brown v. Board of Education* decision (*Brown v. Board of Education,* 347 U.S. 483 [1954]).

Howard University Law School graduate and first African American Associate Justice of the Supreme Court, Thurgood Marshall headed the NAACP legal team that litigated the 1951 class action lawsuit brought against the Topeka Kansas Board of Education. The lawsuit was undertaken on behalf of Oliver Brown, the named plaintiff, and twelve other black parents whose children were barred from attending the white school that was closer to their homes and were required by law to take a long bus ride to attend the segregated black school.

SIGNIFICANCE OF DRS. KENNETH AND MAMIE CLARK'S DOLL STUDIES

The *Brown v. Board of Education* case is one of the most consequential Supreme Court rulings of the 20th century in American history. Marshall argued the case using findings from a doll study conducted by psychologists Drs. Kenneth and Mamie Clark. The research design of the study was deceptively simple in light of the significance of the study findings in illuminating the magnitude of the impact of racism on the psyche of black children.

All of the children in the sample were black and, with the exception of one group, they all attended segregated schools. In conducting the study, the children were given two dolls, one white and one brown. They were asked to identify the dolls as being good or bad, the one they would like to have as a playmate, and the one who was most like them. Their responses revealed the psychological damage of racism on the formation of racial identity in children. For example, nearly all of the children identified the brown doll as most like them even as they simultaneously expressed preference for the white doll. The brown-skinned doll was seen as "bad" and the one they would not like to have as a playmate. Moreover, the study's area of inquiry evoked such intolerable levels of anxiety in some of the children that they became tearful or so agitated that they ran from the room when asked which of the dolls was most like them. Basing its ruling in part on the qualitative findings of the Clark study (Blakemore, 2018), in a unanimous decision the Court ruled that in public education "the doctrine of 'separate but equal' has no place. Separate educational facilities are inherently unequal."

Together, these historic events paved the way for striking down Supreme Court rulings in the 1856 Dred Scott case that said no black, slave or free, could ever obtain full rights of citizenship under the US Constitution, and the 1896 *Plessey v. Ferguson* decision establishing the "separate but equal doctrine" that legalized the separation of the races in all spaces in which blacks and whites came together. However, no timeframes or blueprints were given to indicate how these legislative and judicial reforms were to be implemented. And while *Brown v. Board of Education* outlawed segregation in public schools, the decision did not address issues related to teacher job protection. Moreover, the vagueness of the court directive that integration of public schools was to proceed "with all deliberate speed" afforded white supremacists sufficient time to mount a coordinated massive resistance. The decision of the courts outlawing the separation of the races in public spaces would not be easily implemented. Indeed, as anticipated, achieving the rights of black children to equal education would be far from an easy path, and, as predicted, the South and the state of Georgia mounted a strong opposition to the new law (Haney, 1978; Georgia Advisory Committee, 2007).

The Southern Manifesto was prepared by the US Congress in 1956, in opposition to the outlawing of segregation in public spaces. The document rebuked the court ruling declaring racial segregation as unconstitutional and an abuse of judicial power. The framers of the document pledged to use all legal means to bring about a reversal of the Supreme Court decision. The draft document was prepared by Republican State Senator from South Carolina, Strom Thurmond, and the final copy was written by Georgia State Senator Richard Russel. With few exceptions, the signatures included all of the members of Congress representing states comprising the Confederacy at the time of the Civil War (Badger, 1999).

Evoking the claim of *interposition*, a thinly veiled promotion of states' rights that had been explicitly found to have no constitutional legitimacy by the US Supreme Court, governors of the southern states of Georgia, Mississippi, South Carolina, and Virginia joined together in an agreement to block all efforts at racial integration. In Georgia the State Assembly voted to declare the 14th and 15th Amendments null and void in the state. Other actions undertaken in Georgia to subvert the implementation of desegregation laws included orders issued by the Board of Education requiring the termination of teachers who were members of the NAACP or who supported integration and the shutting down of any school district that integrated its public schools.

Policies of desegregation were met with strong opposition in both the North and the South. The North was not without its share of violence, as illustrated in Chicago, when Dr. King took the Civil Rights movement north in support of fair housing. In the North, desegregation was met with more covert forms of racism. The flight to the suburbs was accelerated and private schools were established whose admission policies were beyond the jurisdiction of the courts; this occurred along with other forms of de jure and de facto practices that were no less iniquitous despite their stated intent to protect the constitutional rights of whites.

Surfacing as it did historic concerns about miscegenation by bringing white and black children together in the classroom, in the South, school integration was met with vitriolic and blatant forms of defiance that were carried out under the leadership of elected governmental officials. This is seen in Alabama with Governor George Wallace's symbolic "stand in the school house door" to prevent the enrollment of two African Americans, James Hood and Vivian Malone, in the University of Alabama. And in his 1963 inaugural speech as governor of Alabama Wallace declared "segregation today, segregation tomorrow, segregation forever" (Culpepper, 1993).

In Georgia, Ernest Vandiver adopted the phrase "No, not one" as an expression of this opposition to school integration in his campaign for the governorship. (Roche, 1998) The tension-charged atmosphere in Georgia was reported as having been de-escalated by the intervention of a volunteer group of white housewives who championed a bill presented to the state legislature that allowed for the integration of some schools in the state (Martin, 2012). The plan had the support of Governor Vandiver, who had relented on his "No, not one," promise, thus sparing the state and the city of Atlanta the upheaval experienced by other geographic locations in the South. The integration of higher education in Georgia had long been under litigation by the NAACP. Victory was achieved in 1961, when the US District Court ordered the admission of Hamilton Holmes and Charlayne Hunter to the University of Georgia. Hunter-Gault, now an award-winning journalist and author, chronicles her experience in her autobiography *In My Place* (1993). The recalcitrant public officials in the South who stood in defiance of the rule of law they had vowed to uphold made it necessary for the federal government to call in the National Guard to escort black children past jeering crowds and to patrol the halls of public schools to ensure their safety. The optics of what is another shameful period of this country's history is captured in Norman Rockwell's portrait of six-year-old Ruby Bridges taking her historic walk on November 14, 1960, as the first child to integrate elementary schools in New Orleans. In the portrait, entitled *The Problem We All Live With*, the six-year old is being escorted by four federal marshal's past an angry mob of whites whose faces are not seen. By not portraying the faces of the four federal marshals or those of the crowd of angry whites, the painting captures the symbolism of the face being the mark of shame.

Rockwell's portrayal of six-year-old Ruby Bridges—books in hand, forward looking with a decisive stride—captures the concept of resilience in children. Few, if any, children of color will escape the blatant or insidious forms of racism they will invariably confront before reaching their majority. There is a growing body of knowledge from the empirical research that resilience, whether inborn or learned, can serve as a cloak of protection for children and prevent what otherwise could have an irreversible impact on their mental health that follows them into adulthood (Bryant-Davis & Ocampo, 2005; Miller & MacIntosh, 1999; Turner, 2014).

The painting is a permanent holding of the Norman Rockwell Museum. At the request of President Barack Obama and encouragement of Ruby Bridges, who is a member of the Museum Board of Directors and founder of the Ruby Bridges Foundation, the portrait went on loan to the White House from July to October, 2011, as part of an exhibit commemorating the 50th anniversary of the historic walk of a little six-year-old girl.

THE WORLD STAGE

As the Civil Rights movement was unfolding in the United States, other significant events were emerging on the world stage as the School moved toward the middle years of its history. Foremost among these was the beginning of the Cold War. Russia had emerged as the second world power at the end of World War II. While the two countries had fought as Allies during the war, the United States and Russia were now the central antagonists in the Cold War, representatives of the mutual mistrust and hostility between the free-market capitalist Western democracies and totalitarian communist states represented by the Soviet Union. The Cold War lasted into the early years of the 1990s, but the ideological war between communism and democracy continues into the present.

ANOTHER RED SCARE

The Communist threat in the post-World War II years or the "Red Scare" was a period that all but consumed national life in the United States between the years of 1950 and 1954. The term "red scare" captures the hysteria emanating from irrational fears about the internal threats by communist operatives who were purported to be carrying out subversive activities to bring down the American way of life. These fears were fueled by Wisconsin Republican Senator Joseph McCarthy. McCarthy began a crusade in the 1950s with a goal to ferret out what he alleged were communist agents hat he claimed had infiltrated the highest levels in the federal government, the state department and virtually all walks of life in American society operating under the guise of being ordinary loyal American Citizens.

McCarthy's unscrupulous and nefarious tactics, that included the misrepresentation and distortion of the facts, soon were brought to light under the closer scrutiny of Congress. More people began to view McCarthy's crusade against the threat of a communist takeover as "witch-hunting" and ultimately led to his censure by the US Congress. By the time his reign of terror had subsided, however, not only had the lives of innocent people been left in shambles, but questionable surveillance techniques had become institutionalized by the Federal Bureau of Investigation (FBI) under the administration of Edgar Hoover, who was the first and longest serving director of the agency.

It was subsequently revealed that Hoover used these same tactics to engage in covert monitoring of the activities of what he considered to be communist-inspired radical black activist organizations and their leadership. The Black Panther Party was one of these targeted organizations. The organization was initially founded in Oakland, California, by Huey P. Newton as the Black Panther Party for Self-Defense, with a mission to protect black neighborhoods from police brutality and to provide basic services to community residents that included health and nutrition programs such as its free breakfast programs for children. With the intensification of FBI surveillance as the organization moved more to the left, adopted a socialist political ideology, and supported the rights of citizens to carry guns as a means for self-protection, J. Edgar

Hoover declared that the Party was "the greatest threat to the internal security of the country" (Remnick, 2010, p. 308).

Dr. King and his close circle of advisors, viewed as no less of a radical threat than the Black Panther Party, were also the targets of FBI surveillance. The agency made generous use of questionable practices in an effort to discredit the morals of Dr. King and tie him and the movement to subversive communist activities (Gentry, 2001). Efforts were also made to taint the civil rights activism launched by the Atlanta University Consortium students by linking the student sit ins with the so called communist threat. In response to the publication of the student-prepared "An Appeal for Human Rights," Georgia Governor Ernest Vandiver is quoted as saying, "[t]hat statement was skillfully prepared. Obviously, it was not written by students. Regrettably, it had the same overtones which are usually found in anti-American propaganda pieces" ((Roche, 1998; WSB Television News Video Archive, University of Georgia, Athens).

THE SECOND RECONSTRUCTION

The Second Reconstruction refers to the era of reforms set into motion during the decades of the 1950s and 1960s and saw America endeavoring to redress the tenacious hold of white supremacy in American culture. Over the full course of the nation's history, flawed assumptions about the superiority of whites provided justification for the egregious violation of the constitutional and human rights of blacks. In challenging assumptions of white supremacy in which all American institutions were rooted, the struggle for black civil rights impacted virtually all segments of American society. However, these were decades awash with various causes of social justice and human rights.

Activists during the 1950s, 1960s, and into the decade of the 1970s pushed for the rights of many groups of historical concern to the profession of social work. National movements emerged advocating the rights of women, gays, and migrant farm workers. Concurrent with movements for human rights were the emergence of student movements for freedom of speech on university campuses in both the North and the South. The continuing escalation of the war in Vietnam gave rise to growing student protests against the war, and the Students for a Democratic Society arose as a major force in critiquing US foreign policies and involvement in the Cold War.

The continuing struggle for social reforms during the turbulent years of these decades saw the transformation of Dr. King's nonviolent approach to the militant and revolutionary stance captured in the slogan "Black Power." Eschewed by King and the establishment leadership of the movement, the phrase was introduced by SNCC president Stokely Carmichael and subsequently embraced by CORE and other newly forming militant and black nationalist groups that had joined the struggle for black rights (King Encyclopedia, 2006).

SOCIAL WORK EDUCATION

Social work education was not immune to the influences set into motion by reform movements engulfing American society at the time. Social work education became involved in a process of self-appraisal in a review of the Council on Social Work Education's (CSWE) Educational Policy and Accreditation Standards (EPAS). The process was undertaken amid claims from within the profession that there was an overemphasis on the Eurocentric world view as the standard setting perspective anchoring and undergirding the educational programming and curriculum of accredited undergraduate and graduate social work education programs.

The changes wrought by the Civil Rights movement, along with other events occurring during this era's constantly changing sociopolitical environment and cultural landscape, had significant implications for changes in US social welfare policy development, the profession of social work, social work education, and for the School.

The confluence of these societal changes again produced both challenges and opportunities that impacted the continuing institutional trajectory of the Atlanta University School of Social Work. Now under the deanship of Whitney M. Young Jr., the School was called upon to maintain its relevancy within the context of desegregation requiring predominately white schools of social work to admit blacks. Concurrent with desegregation were reforms in the CSWE accreditation standards requiring all schools of social work to adopt a more inclusive approach to curriculum development and to achieve a balance in micro and macro content in educational programming. Consequently, with these changes in CSWE educational policy standards, the School no longer held a monopoly on a curriculum area that had been the case since its founding. And, with desegregation, black institutions of higher learning no longer had exclusive access to the brightest and best of black minds. Thus began the draining of the black brain trust that had been established under the informal Black Cabinet of Franklin Delano Roosevelt's administration and that was a source for influencing public policy development in the interest of the black community.

LEGACIES OF THE ATLANTA UNIVERSITY
CONSORTIUM STUDENTS

The Atlanta University Consortium student leaders carried forth the HBCUs historic tradition of service in their future professional lives in the national Civil Rights movement, gaining prominence for their humanitarian work nationally and globally. Julian Bond was elected to the Georgia House of Representatives for four terms and for six terms in the Georgia State Senate; he was appointed Chair of the NAACP from 1998 to 2010.

Marion Wright Edelman, who was among the Spelman student activists, played a major role in the organization of Freedom Summer. As a young attorney and director of the NAACP Legal Defense Fund, after giving testimony before Congress about the extensiveness of poverty in the rural South that rivaled that of third world countries, she arranged a tour of the Mississippi Delta with a group of Senators so that they could see firsthand the depths of poverty and hunger in the region. She is credited with sensitizing Robert Kennedy, who was among the group, to the deplorable conditions under which the poor were living in the rural South; poverty became a center of Kennedy's platform when campaigning for the US presidency in 1968. Edelman is founder and CEO of the Children's Defense Fund and has received global acclaim for her advocacy on behalf of children and families. She is a recipient of the Medal of Freedom Award, received in 2000 from President Clinton, and is the recipient of the Albert Schweitzer Prize for Humanitarianism and the MacArthur "Genius" Award.

After completing a term of service in the military, Lonnie King returned to Atlanta to complete his studies at Morehouse and continued to play a central role as a social activist in the city. And as a doctoral candidate at the Georgia State University he was completing a dissertation study on the Civil Rights movement in Atlanta at the time of his passing. In the 1970s, as civil rights moved onto a new stage, he served as director of the Atlanta affiliate of the NAACP, playing a central role in the appointment of Alonzo Crim, who would be the first African American hired as superintendent of the city's Board of Education. On the occasion of his passing in March 2019, in giving his eulogy Atlanta Mayor Keisha Lance Bottoms said, "Lonnie left an indelible mark on the legacy of both Atlanta and the Civil Rights movement. His life was one of inspiration, one that was committed to the fight for tolerance, equality and fairness. Lonnie used his days to their fullest and will be sorely missed."

John Mack carried forth the tradition of social work activism inspired by Whitney Young, his mentor over the period of his enrollment in the Atlanta University School of Social Work. Mack served as the Executive Director of the Flint, Michigan, Urban League, and he was the longest serving Director of the Los Angeles Office of the National Urban League. In recognition of the magnitude of his service, which includes promoting community policing within Los Angeles black neighborhoods, on the occasion of his death in 2018 the flags in the city of Los Angeles flew at half-staff.

Johnny Parham, also mentored by Dean Young, moved to New York after graduation to continue a career in activism centered in the Harlem community, promoting civil rights in healthcare, and as director of the Brooklyn Branch of the New York Urban League. Along with Velma Banks, a 1958 alumnus of the school of social work, Parham is a founding member of the World Community of Social Workers that, for the past thirty years, has preserved Young's legacy in the

New York City social welfare and academic communities. With his MSW degree complemented by the Juris Doctorate (JD) degree, Parham continues to have a strong presence in advancing causes related to the HBCUs and is currently spearheading a funded initiative to grow executive leadership for the HBCUs.

Congressman John Lewis, a student at Fisk University at the time of the launching of the civil rights movement, has made the HBCU tradition of service in the interest of social justice the centerpiece of his iconic career. He has been elected for seventeen consecutive terms as the representative to Georgia's Fifth Congressional District. He was the youngest and now the only living member of the group who spoke at the 1963 March on Washington, and for decades has continued to be one of the most courageous and outspoken voices in the nation on matters of civil rights and social justice. His legacy to the history of the fight for black civil rights in the US is perhaps unmatched; these contributions have been affirmed by his being awarded the Pestilential Medal of Freedom in 2011 by President Barack Obama.

The historical accounts, including personal oral histories, of all of the core group of students, including Diane Nash, a Fisk student who played a central leadership role, and individuals who were at the vanguard of the Civil Rights movement in Atlanta and their continuing social activism in the cause for black civil rights are housed in the extensive archives of the Civil Rights Digital Library. The project is supported by a federal grant awarded to the University of Georgia.

REFERENCES

An Appeal for Human Rights. (1960, March 9). Atlanta Student Movement collection, Robert W. Woodruff Library of the Atlanta University Center. http://localhost:8081/repositories/2/archival_objects/22

Badger, T. (1999). Southerners who refused to sign the Southern Manifesto. *Historical Journal, 42*(2), 517–534. http://www.jstor.org/stable/3020998

Baker, E. (1974). Oral History Interview with Ella Baker, September 4, 1974. Interview G-0007. Southern Oral History Program Collection (4007) in the Southern Oral History Program Collection, Southern Historical Collection, Wilson Library, University of North Carolina at Chapel Hill.

Bayor, R. H. (1996). *Race and the shaping of twentieth-century Atlanta.* Chapel Hill: University of North Carolina Press.

Black Past Remembered. (2007, January 25). Frederick Douglass, "if there is no struggle, there is no progress." https://www.blackpast.org/african-american-history/1857-frederick-douglass-if-there-no-struggle-there-no-progress/

Blakemore, E. (August 31, 2018). How Dolls Helped Win Brown v. Board of Education. *Deceptively simple doll tests helped convince the Supreme Court to strike down school segregation.* https://www.history.com/news/brown-v-board-of-education-doll-experiment

Branch, T. (2007). *Parting the waters: America in the King years 1954–63.* New York: Simon and Schuster.

Brown, R. (2008). Remembering a soul food legend who nurtured civil rights leaders. *Atlanta Journal*, December 5.

Bryant-Davis, T., & Ocampo, C. (2005). The trauma of racism: Implications for counseling, research, and education. *Counseling Psychologist, 33*(4), 574–578.

Clark Atlanta University Whitney M. Young. Jr. School of Social Work. (2018–2019). MSW Student Handbook. http://www.cau.edu/school-of-social-work/Programs/2018-2019-MSW-Handbook.pdf

Culpepper, C. E. (1993). *The schoolhouse door: Segregation's last stand at the University of Alabama*. New York: Oxford University Press.

D'Emilio, J. (2003). *Lost prophet: The life and times of Bayard Rustin*. New York: Simon and Schuster.

Dittmer, J. (1997). "Too Busy to Hate": Race, Class, and Politics in Twentieth-Century Atlanta.

Duberman, M. (2012). *Howard Zinn: A life on the left*. New York: New Press.

Encyclopedia Britannica. (2015). Greensboro sit-in. February 12, 2015. https://www.britannica.com/event/Greensboro-sit-in

Farmer, J. (1998). *Lay bare the heart: An autobiography of the Civil Rights movement*. Fort Worth: Texas Christian University Press.

Frazier, E. F. (1960). Problems and needs of negro children and youth resulting from family disorganization. *Journal of Negro Education* (Summer). 276–277.

Fried, A. (1997). *McCarthyism: The great American Red Scare: A documentary history*. New York: Oxford University Press.

Gentry, C. (2001). *J. Edgar Hoover: The man and the secrets*. New York: WW Norton.

Georgia Advisory Committee to the United States Commission on Civil Rights. (2007). 35 Public School Districts Have Unitary Status 74 Districts Remain Under Court Jurisdiction, December, 2007.

Haney, J. (1978). The effects of the Brown Decision on black educators. *Journal of Negro Education, 47*(1), 88–95. doi:10.2307/2967104

Holt, T. (1990). The political uses of alienation: W. E. B. Du Bois on politics, race, and culture, 1903–1940. *American Quarterly, 42*(2), 301–323. doi:10.2307/2713019

Hunter-Gault, C. (1993). *In my place*. New York: Vintage.

King Encyclopedia. (2006). Stokely Carmichael. The Martin Luther King, Jr. Research and Education Institute. Stanford, CA: Stanford University Press.

King, M. L. (1958). *Stride toward freedom: The Montgomery story*. London: Souvenir Press.

King, M. L. (1967). *Where do we go from here: Chaos or community?* Boston: Beacon Press.

Martin, J. (2012). How housewives and the "Atlanta Nine" integrated Georgia's public schools. CNN, October 19, 2012. https://www.cnn.com/2012/10/19/us/how-housewives-and-the-atlanta-nine-integrated-georgias-public-schools/index.html

Mays, B. E. (2011). *Born to rebel: An autobiography*. Athens: University of Georgia Press.

Miller, D. B., & MacIntosh, R. (1999). Promoting resilience in urban African American adolescents: Racial socialization and identity as protective factors. *Social Work Research, 23*(3), 159–169. https://doi.org/10.1093/swr/23.3.159

Parham, J. (n.d.). Journal, Reflections on Atlanta University Consortium sit-ins.

Ransby, B. (2003). *Ella Baker and the black freedom movement: A radical democratic vision*. Chapel Hill: University of North Carolina Press.

Ray, M. (2015). Greensboro sit-ins. United States History Encyclopedia Britannica. https://www.britannica.com/event/Greensboro-sit-in

Remnick, D. (2010). *The bridge: The life and rise of Barack Obama*. New York: Pan Macmillan.

Roche, J. (1998). *Restructured resistance: The Sibley Commission and the politics of deseg-regation in Georgia*. University of Georgia Press.

Saporta, M. (2018). Clark Atlanta's president wants university to be economic engine for Westside. *Atlanta Business Chronicle*, October 1Sidel9.

Thoreau, H. D. (1964). *Essay on civil disobedience*. Salem, MA: Pyramid Books.

Turner, E. A. (2014). Racism in America: Helping your child be resilient: Tips for parents on tackling racism and discrimination. *Psychology Today*. https://www.psychologytoday.com/ca/blog/the-race-good-health/201411/racism-in-america-helping-your-child-be-resilient

WSB-TV (1962, July 30). News film clip of Georgia governor Ernest Vandiver speaking to reporters about the Civil Rights movement in Albany, Georgia, from a press conference in Atlanta, Georgia.

WSB-TV. News film collection, reel 0946, 51:01/59:48, Walter J. Brown Media Archives and Peabody Awards Collection, The University of Georgia Libraries, Athens, Georgia, as presented in the Digital Library of Georgia.

Young, A. (1964). *An easy burden: The Civil Rights movement and the transformation of America*. New York: HarperCollins.

Zinn, H., & Damon, M. (1998). *A people's history of the United States*. New York: New Press.

CHAPTER 11

Shifting Ideology in US Social Welfare Philosophy

We are confronted primarily with a moral issue. . . . It is as old as the scriptures and is as clear as the American Constitution.

—John F. Kennedy, 1962

In the 1950s, preceding the Civil Rights movement, Americans were enjoying a higher quality of life owing to the benefits introduced by the 1935 Social Security Act that were incrementally expanded during the postwar years. The expansion of benefits under the introduction of the American social welfare state had contributed to a rising in the quality of life for many Americans but not for all. Racial discrimination remained the nation's albatross. Discrimination and exclusionary practices continued to exclude blacks from full participation in these programs and contributed to the poverty rates for blacks remaining persistently high. Influenced in part by discrimination and systemic barriers, blacks were among the segment of Americans who had become entrapped in a cycle of intergenerational poverty despite America's growing affluence.

The Affluent Society (Galbraith, 1958) and *The Other America* (Harrington, 1962) illuminated the growing wealth gap and inequality in America. Both books influenced the theoretical and value framework for the social welfare reforms initiated under the Kennedy administration and carried out under the Johnson administration. The progressive reforms of the Great Society were subsequently reshaped with the advent of a new conservative ideology during the decades of the 1970s and 1980s. This growing conservatism was influenced by Charles Murray's book (1985) that questioned the efficacy of the War on Poverty programs and called for their dismantlement.

Find a Way or Make One. Alma J. Carten, Oxford University Press (2021). © Oxford University Press.
DOI: 10.1093/oso/9780197518465.001.0001.

The profession, social work education, and the School continued to respond to unfolding events during the waning years of the Civil Rights movement. The National Association of Black Social Workers (NABSW) was launched in protest to what was viewed as the exclusionary practices of the National Conference on Social Welfare. The Council on Social Work Education (CSWE), in response to protests from its membership, began to institute reforms to increase the participation of previously underrepresented groups in its governance structure. The new sense of academic agency brought to the School by a new cohort of faculty was the catalyst for the School to embark on a process of revisioning its educational philosophy.

THE PARADOX OF POVERTY IN THE MIDST OF PLENTY

In his book, *The Affluent Society*, Harvard economist John Kenneth Galbraith (1958) called attention to the flaws of a nation consumed with materialism and wealth creation at the expense of the welfare of the general public. The titled of his book was interpreted by some to mean that poverty had been eradicated in America. To the contrary, for Gailbraith the belief of an affluent America was "conventional wisdom," a term that he coined; that is defined as commonly held knowledge accepted to be true, but factually this may not be the case. Gailbraith argued in the book, that there was indeed an unprecedented affluence in the nation, but that wealth was concentrated in the private sector, and stood in sharp contrast to conditions of extreme poverty becoming characteristic in the growing masses of Americans. Gailbraith he questioned the morality of a nation consumed with materialism and wealth creation while ignoring the cost of these indulgences in the corporate sector to the general population.

Michael Harrington's study, *The Other America: Poverty in the United States* (1962), put a human face on the statistics of the poor brought to light in Galbraith's earlier publication.

> Here are the migrant farm workers, the aged, the minorities and all of others who live in the economic underworld of American life. The poor get sick more than anyone else in the society. That is because they live in slums, jammed together under unhygienic conditions; they have inadequate diets, and cannot get decent medical care. When they become sick, they are sick longer than any other group in the society. Because they are sick more often and longer than anyone else, they lose wages and work, and find it difficult to hold a steady job. And because of this, they cannot pay for good housing, for a nutritious diet, for doctors. At any given point in the circle, particularly when there is a major illness, their prospect is to move to an even lower level and to begin the cycle, round and round, toward even more suffering. (p. 15)

Since its publication in 1962, *The Other America* has become a classic and is a required reading by the largest share of schools of social work. Harrington's research identified pockets of poverty among segments of Americans he referred to as the "invisible poor." It was a population of Americans who were hidden from the view of mainstream American in isolated rural, urban, and mountainous geographical areas of the nation and enmeshed in an intergenerational cycle of unrelenting, debilitating poverty.

Harrington's findings in large measure provided the theoretical framework for the progressive social welfare policy advancements in the 1960s under the Johnson administration's War on Poverty. The populations identified by Harrington as among the those Americans defined as the "invisible poor" included blacks in northern urban areas that had been blighted by the effects of trends accompanying white flight to the suburbs, southern blacks living under the harsh conditions of poverty exacerbated by blatant white racism, mountain whites isolated in areas of Appalachia, West Virginia, and Kentucky impoverished by the effects of environmental exploitation that depleted natural resources that were economic base of these regions, Native Americans disadvantaged by the effects of policies of "manifest destiny" in the settlement of the country that resulted in their near extinction as a people, Mexican Americans and Chicanos who were overrepresented among migrant and seasonal workers whose labor had been exploited in the farming industry, and new Puerto Rican immigrants who were discriminated against because of class, ethnic, and linguistic differences.

THEORIES OF CAUSATION

Galbraith's identified two forms of poverty in his examination of theories of attrition and causation models. One was *case poverty* that he explained as caused by some characteristic unique to the individual, such as mental illness, physical disability, or addiction. *Insular poverty*, on the other hand, affected large groups of people who were entrapped in situations where everyone is poor and isolated from mainstream society. In the case of insular poverty, a cycle of self-perpetuating poverty is created when people are living under undesirable conditions such as poor schools, limited access to healthcare, and deplorable environmental conditions that operate together to keep people locked in a cycle of poverty exacerbated by behavioral maladaptations emanating from their efforts to cope with what are in fact intolerable situations.

Galbraith's descriptions of the effects of insular poverty were the underlying assumptions of the controversial culture of poverty theories that emerged during these years and that were initially introduced by anthropologist Oscar Lewis. In what would become classical research field studies on Latino families, *La Vida* (Lewis, 1966, 1998) examined the lives of Puerto

Rican families living in the slums of San Juan and the Bronx in New York. *The Children of Sanchez*, published earlier in 1961, used personal narratives to bring the reader into the interior life of a Mexican family living in the slums of Mexico City (Lewis, 1961). For Lewis, the culture of poverty referred to a process that normalized behaviors and belief systems that are significantly different from mainstream society that are passed down from generation to generation.

THE MOYNIHAN REPORT, WELL-INTENDED OR VICTIM BLAMING

Daniel Patrick Moynihan is among the nation's best known and longest serving public servants. His career of service includes an academic appointment at Harvard, four terms as a US senator from New York, and advisor to the republican and democrat administrations of John Kennedy, Lyndon Johnson, Richard Nixon, and Gerald Ford.

Moynihan's book, *The Black Family: A Cause for National Action* (1965), was released while he was the Assistant Secretary of Labor under the Johnson administration. The theme of a culture of poverty was integral to Moynihan's formulations relevant to the black family. The title of chapter four "Tangle of Pathology," which examined the implications of family structure and adult gender roles for the economic progress of the African American community, set off a firestorm of claims that the report smacked of "blaming the victim."

The phrase "blaming the victim" was initially used by sociologist William Ryan in the his classic book first published in 1976 of the same name to refute ideology used to justify racism and social injustice against blacks. (Ryan, 2010). Ryan's theory of blaming the victim holds that people are held complicit or felt to be the cause of their misfortune because of their own personal behaviors. But this fails to take into account the larger societal conditions that are beyond their control and that are the root cause of their misfortune. These assumptions about success and lack of success are embedded in an American culture of individualism and self-reliance, the value underpinnings of capitalism. They also serve as the foundation of the "American Dream," that happiness and economic success is possible to everyone who is motivated to work hard and sacrifice.

Although more conventional wisdom than scientific fact, these beliefs have played a central role in shaping the residual approach to social welfare policy development in the United States. The residual approach is a reflection of the nation's poor law heritage that quantifies need based on the perceived worthiness of the individual. Moynihan's use of the pejorative phrase "tangle of pathology" led to a fire storm of criticism from civil rights activists and black scholars. Not only did the phrase pathologize the black family, but it linked racial stereotypes with existing stereotypical thinking that the poor were not motivated or well tied to the work ethic. Thus, his work added to the conundrum of the nation's ambivalent social welfare state and suspiciousness about the poor (Katz, 1989, 1996; Axinn & Levin, 1997; Jansson, 1993) and that was now further inflamed with the introduction of race into the political discourse.

Moreover, Moynihan's short-sightedness or insensitivity to the power of language and words on matters of race in his use of the phrase also diminished attention that might have been given to an objective appraisal of the report (Acs, Braswell, et al., 2013). Citing E. Franklin Frazier's earlier study, *Problems and Needs of Negro Children and Youth Resulting from Family Disorganization* (1960), that itself was not without controversy, the report called for a much-needed national effort to address the historical inequities experienced by blacks in concluding

> The policy of the United States is to bring the Negro American to full and equal sharing in the responsibilities and rewards of citizenship. To this end, the programs of the Federal government bearing on this objective shall be designed to have the effect, directly or indirectly, of enhancing the stability and resources of the Negro American family. (Moynihan, 1965)

The controversies ignited by the report were worsened by Moynihan's 1970 memorandum when an advisor to President Richard Nixon recommending that the administration adopt a policy of "benign neglect" on matters related to the African American communities and the problem of racism (Acs, Braswell, et al., 2013). Yet again, Moynihan's message may have been misunderstood, as he said had been the case with the 1965 study. Nonetheless, "benign neglect" as interpreted by public officials gave the thumbs up to begin cutting funds to programs in urban areas that on any measure continued to be sorely needed. This began the process of replacing the liberalism of the Johnson administration that had spawned the expansion of programs for the poor under the Great Society with a new conservatism introduced under the Nixon administration and continued under the policies of New Federalism of the Reagan administration. This introduction of a new conservatism began chipping away at the programs introduced under the New Deal and expanded under the Great Society and had the greatest impact on African American families.

SOCIAL WELFARE REFORMS UNDER THE KENNEDY AND JOHNSON ADMINISTRATIONS

At the height of the violence of the white backlash accompanying the continuing unfolding of the Civil Rights movement, and in an effort to quell the violence, President Kennedy spoke to from the Oval Office on July 11, 1963.

The president's televised speech was given against the backdrop of elected officials acting in defiance of the rule of law and public schools that were being patrolled by the National Guard. With the moral authority invested in the office of the presidency, Kennedy elevated the issue of race in America to a matter of morality, saying

> We are confronted primarily with a moral issue. . . . It is as old as the scriptures and is as clear as the American Constitution. . . . One hundred years of delay have passed since President Lincoln freed the slaves, yet their heirs . . . are not fully free. They are not yet freed from the bonds of injustice. . . . This Nation will not be fully free until all its citizens are free. (Kennedy, 1962)

Shaped by a life of wealth and privilege, Kennedy had been sensitized to the pervasiveness of poverty in the United States as he campaigned for the presidency. This new awareness influenced his introduction of progressive reforms expanding the social welfare state to meet the needs of a significantly changed America since the Great Depression. He introduced the 1962 Public Welfare Amendments to the Social Security Act, stating

> at the time the Social Security Act established our present basic framework for public aid, the major cause of poverty was unemployment and economic depression. Today, in a year of relative prosperity and high employment, we are more concerned about the poverty that persists in the midst of abundance. (Kennedy, 1962)

Embracing themes of social justice, equality, and the eradication of poverty, social welfare reforms enacted under the Kennedy administration began with the 1962 Public Welfare Amendments. As has commonly been the case, the Aid to Dependent Children (ADC) program was the central target of reform efforts. Under the 1962 reforms, the program was renamed Aid to Families with Dependent Children (AFDC), reflecting an enhanced benefit structure that included cash allowances to children and their caretakers, along with supportive services to their families. In introducing the reforms Kennedy said

> This measure embodies [a] new approach—stressing services in addition to support, rehabilitation instead of relief, and training for useful work instead of prolonged dependency. Our objective is to prevent or reduce dependency to encourage self-care and self- support—to maintain family life where it is adequate and to restore it where it is deficient. (Kennedy, 1962)

Social work was afforded higher visibility in what was to be Kennedy's new service approach. The reforms provided new funds for the training of social workers. The training was designed to prepared MSW social workers to carry out both functions of eligibility determination and to conduct comprehensive biopsychosocial assessments to decide what services were to be turned on for the client. The reforms also provided grants for the training of MSW social workers that increased access to social work education and brought more professionally trained social workers into the public sector.

President Kennedy was assassinated in Dallas, Texas, on November 21, 1963. Kennedy's assassination left his vision for a more just society to be carried out under the administration of Lyndon B. Johnson. The murder of the young and charismatic president, who symbolized a new era in America, numbed the country, but his assassination also brought a new cohesiveness among Americans. This cohesiveness as a nation created a political climate that made for an expansion of social welfare programs nearly comparable to those enacted under President Roosevelt's New Deal. Moreover, while the reforms of the New Deal addressed the inequalities resulting from the natural forces of an unregulated free enterprise market economy, the programs of the Johnson administration's Great Society targeted segments of the American population that Harrington identified as the "invisible poor," that had been left out because of societally imposed institutional and structural barriers that restricted their access to the opportunities of the American Dream.

THE WAR ON POVERTY AND THE GREAT SOCIETY

The programs instituted under Johnson's Great Society were nearly as expansive as those initiated under FDR's New Deal. A primary intent of the Great Society was to strike a blow against the pervasive racism in the country that had impeded black progress; the initiative was also designed to improve the lives of other Americans identified as among the invisible poor. The mix of Great Society programs drew on many theories for understanding the causes of poverty and effective strategies for solving these problems. Not only were these programs designed to treat the symptoms of poverty impacting people, but also to eradicate and prevent poverty in American society (Johnson, 1966).

These were years of a good deal of optimism in the field of social welfare about the possibility of using social policies, undergirded by statistical data, as tools for planned change to reduce inequalities in American life. Social workers from academia and the practice community played a central role in crafting the War on Poverty programs. The profession is credited with the introduction of *program evaluation* as research methodology that was advanced during the period of the Great Society as a viable study approach for determining which program strategies achieved the most desirable outcomes for targeted client groups.

The Great Society programs were designed to address both insular and case poverty, as defined by Galbraith. As such, the programs' strategies were a reflection of social works ecological perspective that recognized the interactive effects of people with their environments.

To address the structural and institutional barriers and protect the rights of all American citizens Congress passed the Civil Rights Act of 1964 on July 12, 1964, outlawing discrimination in public accommodations and in programs receiving federal funding. The 1964 Act was followed by the 1965 Voting Rights Act that strengthened the 15th Amendment by prohibiting states from using any form of test or other device to bar American citizens from their right to vote based on race, creed, or English proficiency.

In his January 8, 1964, State of the Union address to the nation President Johnson introduced an unconditional "War on Poverty" pledging that

> This administration today here and now declares an unconditional war on poverty in America. I urge this Congress and all Americans to join me in that effort.... Poverty is a national problem, requiring improved national organization and support. But this attack, to be effective, must also be organized at the State and local level. For the war against poverty will not be won here in Washington. It must be won in the field, in every private home, in every public office, from the courthouse to the White House. (Johnson, 1964)

Following the State of the Union address, President Johnson gave the commencement address on June 4, 1965, at Howard University. Further elaborating the themes of his State of the Union address, the speech outlined the complex network of issues needing to be addressed in the ongoing effort to achieve a more perfect union that embraced the aspirations of those for whom the American Dream was beyond their reach because of systemic barriers. The president announced his plan to convene a White House conference of scholars; experts; outstanding men and women, black and white; and officials from all levels of the federal government under the theme of "To fulfill these rights" that was an expression of the moral and value underpinnings of the thrust of the reforms.

> The objectives of the initiative were to help the American Negro fulfill the rights which, after the longtime of injustice, he is finally about to secure. To move beyond opportunity to achievement. To shatter forever not only the barriers of law and public practice, but the walls which bound the condition of many by the color of his skin. To dissolve, as best we can, the antique enmities of the heart which diminish the holder, divide the great democracy, and do wrong—great wrong—to the children of God. And I pledge you tonight that this will be a chief goal of my administration, and of my program this year, and in the years to come. And I hope, and I pray, and I believe, it will be a part of the program of all Americans. (Johnson, 1965)

The Great Society initiative was carried out as a 13-point program. The Economic Opportunity Act of 1964 (P.L. 88-452), also known as the "Anti-Poverty Bill," created a separate federal agency that was headed by Sargent Shriver and operated under the philosophical stance expressed by President Johnson in his speech introducing the act and was echoed in the preamble of the legislation.

> The United States can achieve its full economic and social potential only if every individual has the opportunity to contribute to the full extent of his capabilities and to participate in the works of society . . . the policy of the United States is to eliminate the paradox of poverty in the midst of plenty. . . . by opening up opportunities for education, training, work and to live in decency and dignity. (Johnson, 1964, p. 508)

The Great Society programs replicated many programs of the New Deal and touched virtually every segment of American life. Volunteers in Service to America (VISTA), modeled after the Peace Corps that sent individuals abroad to work on service projects, provided young activist students with opportunities for domestic service. The VISTA program sent youth to work on poverty projects that targeted rural Mississippi, Appalachia, and urban inner-city neighborhoods to prepare inner-city youths for workforce participation. The Upward Bound and work study programs legislated under the Higher Education Act of 1965 continue to make college enrollment within the reach of low-income high school students. Project Head Start provided early childhood educational experiences to preschool-aged children. Although Head Start has become less of an early childhood program and more a childcare program with the increasing emphasis in welfare reforms on work requirements for mothers of young children, and although underfunded, it has been one of the most popular antipoverty programs.

After Johnson's election in 1964, he continued to pass landmark social legislation. These included Medicare that provided universal healthcare coverage to the elderly and Medicaid, a means-tested program that provided healthcare coverage for the poor, as well as the Food Stamp Act of 1964, also means-tested and now named the Supplemental Nutrition Assistance Program (SNAP). With modified eligibility criteria and recent cutbacks under the current White House administration, the program had been the largest federal program providing nutrition benefits to needy families and to households with an elderly member. The Model Cities program gave city officials in the nation's blighted urban areas funds to experiment with demonstration programs in housing and urban renewal. Additional federal funds were also allocated to schools in low income community districts and for medical research, legal service, and beautification projects (Trattner, 1999). What became a controversial concept of *maximum feasible participation,* a pillar of the Community Action Programs, replicated Eugenia Burns Hope's Neighborhood Union model and brought community residents into the decision-making process of determining their needs and how these were best met.

The impetus of the War of Poverty programs slowed as urban riots continued despite reform efforts and as the Vietnam war diverted attention away from social welfare reforms. Ronald Reagan, in an offhanded remark to reporters after his election to the presidency, is quoted as saying "a war had been waged against poverty and poverty won." Reagan's remarks reflected the position of the conservative right that the antipoverty programs were ill-conceived and had fallen far short of meeting the proposed grandiose goals of the initiative. Moreover, the programs were accused of having contributed to the perpetuation of intergenerational poverty and welfare dependency.

With the shift in the underlying philosophy of US social welfare policy advanced under the Nixon and Reagan administrations, as Michael Harrington's study *The Other America*, had shaped the liberal ideology and values of the Great Society that saw a great expansion in programs for the poor, Charles Murray's 1984 *Losing Ground; American Social Policy 1950–1980*, shaped the conservative ideology of the new conservatism introduced in the 1970s that argued for the abolishment of these programs. The central thesis of Murray's position on social welfare programs for the poor was that these programs did more harm than good because they contributed to a diminished sense of personal responsibility and incentivized and reinforced bad behaviors.

Murray's later co-authored publication, *The Bell Curve: Intelligence and Class Structure in American Life* (Murray & Herrnstein, 1994), further inflamed the racial discourse and the poverty debate in the country. The book linked intelligence with race and was a reiteration of the thinly veiled racist assumptions of Losing Ground; and hypothesized a correlation between social problem causation and cognitive ability. The policy implications of the conclusions drawn from the findings of both of these controversial studies discouraged investing public dollars in social programs designed to prevent or mitigate the effects of poverty on low income communities since these programs could not compensate for genetic determinants, and were therefore doomed to fail. Since their publication, the findings of both studies have been discredited because of their questionable research methodologies. Upon a close appraisal, they seem to be but a resurfacing of empirically untested assumptions underlying theories of 19th century Social Darwinism and scientific racism.

The conservative ideology and policies of New Federalism embraced by the Nixon and Reagan administrations was the beginning of the dismantlement of social welfare programs for the poor that concluded with the 1996 Personal Responsibility and Work Opportunity Reconciliation Act (PRWORA) enacted under the Clinton Administration.

LAUNCHING THE NATIONAL ASSOCIATION OF BLACK SOCIAL WORKERS

Neither the profession nor social work education were immune from the dramatic changes in the country being driven by the effects of the continuing unfolding of the Civil Rights movement and the growing conservative mood of the country. The National Association of Social Workers (NASW) saw the peeling away of social workers representing historically underrepresented ethnic and racial groups to form separate organizations in protest of the slowness of mainstream professional organizations to modify their operational procedures and policies to be more in line with the new emphasis on inclusion.

Dr. James R. Dumpson, who was appointed to the deanship of the Fordham University Graduate School of Social Work in 1967 making him the first African American appointed dean of a predominately white school of social work, recalled the founding of the NABSW in an unpublished oral history interview. He reflected on the circumstances leading to the organization's founding. According to his recollections the seed was planted when he, along with other black social workers, walked out of the National Conference on Social Welfare. "We went across the street to a church. It must have been Chicago. I don't remember the city. We went across the street and formed the Association of Black Social Workers" (Stafford, n.d., James R. Dumpson Private Collection, Carten, 2016).

Cenie Williams, a 1968 graduate of the New York University Silver School of Social Work, was among the group that Dumpson recalled had staged the walk-out from the Conference and subsequently was among the founders and first president of NABSW. Williams, who had concentrated in community organization in the social work program, in a relatively short period of time during his term as president, affiliate chapters were established in cities across the country and in the US Virgin Islands. He was honored in October 2010 with a Distinguished Alumni Award by the Silver School of Social Work. In citing his accomplishments, the award read,

> the first elected president of the National Association of Black Social Workers (NABSW). He served as president from 1970 to 1974 and as executive director from 1974 to 1982. He organized over 80 NABSW chapters in the United States with affiliates in South Africa, the Caribbean, and Canada. He developed many community programs that brought positive changes in the New York Community, and built the New York City Chapter into the organization's largest chapter. (November 30, 2010)

Atlanta University School of Social Work alumni Morris F. X. Jeff is a past president of the NABSW. Jeff is distinguished as being among the first scholars to published on black-on-black crime, and commended for his efforts to bring a social work perspective to the New Orleans Department of Public Welfare over his tenure as commissioner of the agency. Jeff is a recipient of Atlanta University School of Social Work's distinguished alumni award. He is credited with introducing the term "*Harambee*," translated from Swahili as "pulling together" or "we all pull together" into the NABSW's professional value framework and service philosophy.

This phrase, suggesting cooperative effort among blacks, had been adopted by Jomo Kenyatta, the president of Kenya as a motto of his country's commitment to working together to build a new nation when the country achieved independence in 1963. The term is currently institutionalized in the closing ceremony of the NABSW annual conference to honor Jeff's legacy and as an embodiment of the commitment of social workers of African descent to work together to make human service systems and professional social work practice relevant to the needs of the African American community. The Association continues to be the largest professional organization for black social workers and now has affiliates in African countries.

The formation of special-interest ethnic professional associations and organizations and the increased enrollment of activist-oriented students who had participated in the human rights movements and who saw the social work degree as a means for acquiring the professional skills needed for community organizing and social activism were among the confluence of trends driving changes in social work education during these years.

REFORMS IN SOCIAL WORK EDUCATION

The conundrums facing social welfare of the decades indicated that there was indeed a need to rethink the principles shaping US social policy as well as the implication of race for the formulation of American social welfare policys (Jencks, 1992). Moreover, the push for equity and inclusion during the waning years of the 1960s called for changes and innovations that required the virtual reshaping of the profession and social work education. The CSWE Curriculum Policy Study was an early effort to examine the social work curriculum in response to changes wrought by the Civil Rights movement. The Curriculum Policy Study was undertaken in 1955 and chaired by Dr. Werner W. Boehm. Boehm was at the front end of the process of reviewing existing CSWE educational policies. The findings from the thirteen volumes of the study brought a resurfacing of the historic theme of "cause and function," that was now joined with concerns related to an appropriate integration of diversity content in the social work curriculum. Editorial notes of the publication stated,

Frequent allusion is made in the current literature to the need for the field to develop a framework that includes social science as well as behavioral theory. There is general agreement that the solution is not to be found by discarding the present psychological base in favor of new socio-cultural insights, or by merely adding one set of concepts to the other. Rather the task is that of building theory through a process of integration and careful testing. (Family Service Association of America, 1960, p. 6)

Boehm suggested that the process of integration would not be easily achieved. His prediction that it would likely be a process that would never be completed and would require ongoing collaboration between schools and agencies rings true as the profession and social work continue an ongoing cycle of reinventing themselves to remain relevant in an ever-changing environment.

INCLUSION OF THE BACCALAUREATE DEGREE

In the early years, the exclusive concern of the Council's Commission on Accreditation was the accreditation of MSW programs, the acknowledged degree for preparation for professional social work practice. Doctoral-level (PhD) social work programs have never been within the purview of the Council's Commission on Accreditation. Within a new climate of inclusiveness, as described in an oral history interview with James R. Dumpson, who was CSWE president at the time—a position that he held simultaneously with the deanship of Fordham University Graduate School of Social Services—it was only after considerable debate that the deans of the schools of social work and the leadership of the NASW arrived at a consensus that recognized practitioners with the baccalaureate degree as the entry level for professional social work practice (Mullen, 1991; Carten, 2016, p. 137).

CSWE accreditation standards were subsequently revised to include standards of performance for social work programs awarding the bachelor of science degree in social work (BSW), and, in 1974, the Council for Higher Education Accreditation (CHEA) authorized CSWE to accredit baccalaureate social work programs. The School began awarding the Bachelor of Science (BS) degree in social work that had been previously awarded at Clark College before the 1988 consolidation and that brought the awarding of graduate and undergraduate degrees under the newly created Clark Atlanta University.

FOCUS ON RACISM AND INCLUSION

The CSWE began a concentrated effort to confronting issues of racism and the absence of inclusiveness in its own organization in the latter years of the

1960s. This attention was occurring against the backdrop of the turbulence of the Civil Rights movement that saw an increase in riots in urban areas, more urgent confrontational actions from the minority membership, and the publication of the report of the Kerner Commission. The Commission was convened by President Lyndon Johnson to examine the cause of riots that were erupting in inner-city black communities across the country. The dire findings of the report concluded that the cause of the rioting was white racism and that the nation was "moving toward two societies, one black, one white— separate and unequal." If left unremedied, according to the report's findings, the country faced a "system of 'apartheid'" in its major cities. (United States Advisory Committee on Civil Disorders, 1968).

An examination of the Council's efforts to combat racism and sexism in its own ranks was conducted by Trolander (1997). In keeping with the 1964 Civil Rights Act, the CSWE Board had issued a policy in 1965 explicitly banning racial segregation or discrimination in practices of hiring, assignment, promotion, or other conditions for staff employment. And in response to the growing discontent among the membership, it had conducted an informal survey on race relations and reported the results of the survey in its March 1968 newsletter (Trolander, 1997). Following the survey, the Black Student Caucus submitted an urgent list of demands to the House of Delegates prefaced with the claim that "the CSWE, in structure, is a subtle form of white racism" (p. 117). The student demands called for the strategic development of a recruitment plan targeting black students and the historically black colleges and universities (HBCUs), an increase in the presence of black faculty in schools of social work, and revisions in the admissions requirements and curriculum content to reflect the black experience.

Dr. James R. Dumpson, who had been tapped as the first African American appointed dean of a social work program in a predominatel white university, was also the elected president of the CSWE. Holding these two positions simultaneously afforded Dumpson considerable influence in shaping CSWE accreditation and governance policies, and in turn social work practice. The James R. Dumpson Collection containing documents of his substantial contributions to social welfare and social work education are housed in the Archival Holdings of the Fordham University Walsh Library on the Rosehill campus (Carten, 2016).

As president of the CSWE, Dumpson played a role in negotiating the process of acknowledging the baccalaureate degree as the entry level of professional education, and he served in many capacities to shepherd the organization through these turbulent years. Included among these are chairs of the Commission on Minority Groups, the Ad Hoc Committee on By-Law Revisions, and elected president and vice president of the Board (CSWE, 1972, p. 1). His term as president was during a period when the Council was facing the effects of new demands on social work education that accompanied the

Civil Rights movement. In reflecting on these experiences in a 1991 oral history interview with Mullen he observed,

> I remember during my tenure as president, how I helped to reform, or reconstitute the House of Delegate that in the hope would be more representative of the total field of social work education. I remember we brought in students as members to define special population groups that we now refer to as quotas. But we had to have so many minorities, women, men, and divided the ethnic minority groups into Black, Latino, Asian and Native American. We talked about proportional representation of graduate and undergraduate deans and faculty having proportional representation in the House of Delegates. We enriched social work education as to diversity input. . . . We included such interest groups as the Gay and Lesbian Faculty—and to the horror of some faculty and administrators in those days who wanted to know what in the world were we doing. Today in 1991 nobody would think about sexual orientation, or ethnic content, or the right to have it infused into the curriculum. (Carten, 2016, p. 137–138)

Dumpson worked in close collaboration with Carl Scott in managing the changes occurring during these years. Scott had been brought on to the CSWE staff in 1968 as a senior consultant on minority groups with the initial charge to take on assignments related to the recruitment and retention of minority social work students and to increase the numbers and effectiveness of minority faculty in schools of social work (Pearson, 2013; Trolander, 1997).

CSWE MINORITY FELLOWSHIP PROGRAM

The Minority Fellowship Program (MFP) was established by the federal government in 1973 with the recognition that there was a dearth of minority mental health professionals in a system in which the largest percentage of service consumers were members of minority groups. Moreover, absent the minority perspective, interventions and educational programs were formulated from the deficit model, based on an assumption of psychopathology that contributed to the persistence of deep racial disparities in service outcomes. At the same time, there was little interest among the leadership of behavioral health educational programs in the integration of culturally competent content into these programs.

Funding for the MFP was initially provided under the US Department of Health and Human Services (USDHHS), National Institute of Mental Health (NIMH). With the creation of the Substance Abuse and Mental Health Services Administration (SAMHSA) as a new division of the USDHHS, the program is currently jointly funded by the NIMH and SAMHSA. The program is part of a national effort to build a competent behavioral health workforce across all disciplines to carry out research-based interventions that improve outcomes for diverse consumer groups (SAMHSA, 1981). Since its establishment it has awarded sustained grants to professional associations with a view toward increasing the number, capacity, and leadership presence of minority individuals with doctoral degrees in mental health and substance use disorder services, research, training, policy development, and program administration.

The MFP grantee behavioral health professional associations include the American Psychiatric Association, the American Psychological Association, the American Nurses Association, the American Association of Marriage and Family Therapy Counselors, the National Board for Certified Counselors and Affiliates, and the CSWE. These awards have provided supports to Fellows that have made it possible for them to obtain doctoral degrees, engage in post-doctoral research, pursue careers in academia and clinical settings, and attain prominence in their chosen fields. Initially established to support doctoral-level professional education, the program was expanded in 2014 under the Obama administration to provide fellowships to master-level behavioral health professionals.

LEADERSHIP OF CARL SCOTT AND E. ARACELIS FRANCIS

Carl A. Scott and Dr. E. Aracelis Francis were central to the institutionalization of the CSWE MFP. Serving as the founder and director of the program from 1974 to 1986, Carl Scott created and administered both the research and clinical service components of the MFP initiatives at the CSWE. Dr. Francis was his successor and served more than twenty years (1986–2007) in the position of Executive Director of the Council's MFP. Her presence was an asset to the program in assisting Fellows to manage common challenges that students of color face in adjusting to predominantly white institutions. She was described as akin to a "den mother" for hundreds of minority social work doctoral students nationwide who stayed in the program and completed their degrees owing in large part to her seemingly around the clock availability, reassuring manner, and problem-solving wisdom.

The MFP continues to play an essential role in preparing minority group members for leadership positions in practice, research, teaching, and policy advancement in public and private organizations serving underrepresented and underserved populations. Since its inception in 1974, CSWE's MFP has provided support to slightly more than 600 social work Fellows with funding from both SAMHSA and NIMH. Over this period, the program has produced a national network of alumni who continue to collaborate and support one another in career advancement, publications, research, and conference presentations. The CSWE maintains communication with alumni of the program through the Alumni listserv, networking opportunities at CSWE's Annual Program Meeting.

In tribute to the enormity of Carl Scott's contribution to CSWE, including launching the MFP, on the occasion of his 1986 passing, the Council established the Carl A. Scott Memorial Fund. Since 1988, the Fund has sponsored the Carl A. Scott Memorial Lecture at the CSWE Annual Program Meetings. *Perspectives on Equity and Social Justice: The Carl A. Scott Lecture Series 1988–1992* is a compendium of lectures, edited by Dr. Dorothy Pearson, by scholars on matters that are an exemplification of Scott's work and the Council's mandate to promote social justice. The selection process for identifying the individual to give the annual Scott Lecture is competitive and now undertaken under the Council's Commission for Diversity and Social and Economic Justice.

The various interest groups that were spawned at CSWE during the civil rights era are now under the Council's Commission for Diversity and Social and Economic Justice. This Commission is one of Commissions comprising the CSWE governance structure. It is charged by the CSWE Board of Directors with promoting in social work education inclusion, equity, social and economic justice, and the integration of knowledge of how the multiple aspects of human diversity intersect. The Commission for Diversity and Social and Economic Justice serves as the umbrella for the Council on Disability and Persons with Disabilities; Council on Racial, Ethnic, and Cultural Diversity; Council on the Role and Status of Women in Social Work Education; and the Council on Sexual Orientation and Gender Expression.

THE ATLANTA UNIVERSITY SCHOOL OF SOCIAL WORK POST DESEGREGATION

Whitney M. Young Jr. was appointed to head the School as dean after Forrester B. Washington's retirement by Atlanta University President Dr. Rufus Clements; Young served in the deanship from 1954 to 1961. Young's deanship was book-ended by the ending of racial segregation in education following the 1954 *Brown v. Board of Education* decision and the early years of the Civil Rights movement.

The 1954 decision made it possible for the School to legally enroll and award the MSW degree to whites and provided the option for blacks to enroll in predominately white schools of social work. Desegregated had an impact on student enrollment. However, as Adams (1981) wrote, Young's captivating personality and gift for connecting to individuals from all walks of life combined with a more aggressive approach to outreach and recruitment plan. Adams wrote of her participation in these enhanced recruitment efforts undertaken by Dean Young by way of her conducting interviews with potential students in Atlanta and in her visits to universities in other geographical regions. According to Adams, although there was some decline, due to these increased outreach efforts, student enrollment was maintained at a sufficient level. Moreover, black students opting to enroll in predominately white schools to take advantage of the scholarship awards offered by these schools indicated that it was not because they had anything against the Atlanta University School of Social Work, but simply because they wanted to "get away from home" (Adams, 1981, p. 18).

Young entered the deanship strongly identified with the profession of social work. He had altered his original choice for a career in medicine upon discovering while completing his tour of duty in a segregated military his substantive mediating and negotiating skills and his natural attributes for engaging individuals who were of different minds on controversial issues. This led him to enroll in the School of Social Work at the University of Minnesota, where he earned his MSW degree in 1947. The topic of his master's thesis was the history of the St. Paul, Minnesota, Urban League. These early experiences were what for Young's would be a long-term relationship with the National Urban League. His association with the League began with his first employment as a professional social worker at the St. Paul affiliate, after which he served as Director of the affiliate Urban League office in Omaha, Nebraska. The latter being the position from which he was appointed to the deanship of the Atlanta University School of Social Work, and he resigned the deanship to head the National Urban League.

The affiliate offices of the League served as field placement sites for students completing block placements that had been established under Washington's directorship of the School. Therefore, in addition to establishing long-lasting mentorships with talented students, Young's early professional experiences in the League affiliate offices provided him with critical insights into the challenges of bridging the link between classroom theory and providing real-time practice experiences for students in their agency internships. All of which served him well in the deanship. When he entered the deanship, the culture of the academy and the social work program at Atlanta University were not strange to him.

Young did, indeed, make notable contributions to restoring the reputation of the School, which had been declining over the last years of Washington's directorship. However, these were to be far overshadowed by his achievements as a civil rights activist at the national level after leaving the deanship to become Executive Director of the National Urban League. These accomplishments are discussed in Chapter 13, which is devoted exclusively to his life and legacy as a social worker and civil rights activist.

With Young's departure, Florence Victoria Adams was appointed acting dean of the School. A graduate of the New York School of Social Work, which became the Columbia University School of Social Work, Adams had been brought to the School in 1931, with a specific assignment of developing the group work and community organization curriculum sequences. Although these were curriculum areas of emphasis in the early years of the School's founding, over time they experienced a diminishing popularity among students as new federal grants became available for mental health scholarship awards. These awards, established under the Truman administration with the establishments of the NIMH, strengthened student interest in psychiatric social work.

Moreover, the School faced additional challenges because the city of Atlanta had yet to live up to its public image of being a progressive city on matters of race relations. Racial discrimination had a continuing impact on the environmental context of the School that influenced both the viability of the School and the quality of social work practice and service delivery in the black community. Adams observed in an interview, for example, that the School's graduates were leaving the South because of racial barriers, salary differentials, and the scarcity of job openings, combined with very limited opportunity for promotion. She observed that, of 124 graduates over a four-year period, only seven had remained to work in Atlanta. Of this number, three were employed by the state or by Fulton County, major providers of public social services of which blacks were the primary consumers. Most went north to find employment, which was said to be true in other fields as well. A 1962 employment survey concluded that most graduates of the Atlanta University Center schools had to leave Atlanta if they were to find positions on par with their qualifications (Bayor, 1996, p. 114).

Viewing her appointment as acting dean as one of "place holder" until the search committee identified a permanent appointment to the deanship, Adams described her tenure as acting dean as a status quo position, and she made few changes to programs that had been put in place by Whitney Young. In preparing to step down from the position, Adams penned a letter to Dr. Rufus Clements, Atlanta University president, identifying a number of concerning issues as the School prepared for a new deanship.

Prefacing the substance content of the letter, dated August 9, 1961 and housed in the Florence V. Adams collection in the Woodruff Archives, Adams wrote

> before I get into "hot water" with you, I want to thank you for the excellent support you have given me and my efforts to serve as the dean of the school of social work for this year. A number of things did go awry and in my opinion many of these were the results of accumulated circumstances and/or grievances. (Woodruff Archives, Adams Collection)

Adams continued her correspondence to thank the president for accomplishments on the matter of faculty salaries despite a shortfall in gains from student tuitions. And while the school was receiving grant awards to substantially aid in the recruitment of students for casework, they faced continuing challenges in obtaining scholarship funds for group work and community organization students. The letter described a number of challenges related to declining student enrollment that resulted in budgetary issues of consequential significance for a private, school dependent in part on student tuition, a situation further exacerbated at that time by delinquencies in tuition payments. Despite these challenges, Adam's communication indicated that the faculty remained diligent in their efforts to maintain standards of excellence in the quality of the educational programs despite a declining readiness of students to take on the rigors of graduate-level study in a professional program, the overextended faculty workloads, and the deterioration of the quality of the work environment due to shortfalls in funding needed for the upkeep and maintenance of the building.

As Adams prepared to step down from the position of acting dean, the position would be filled by Dr. William S. Jackson. Dr. Jackson earned a diploma from Atlanta University, a PhD from New York University, and an honorary degree from West Virginia State College. He brought to the School expertise in community organization and a continuing commitment to George Edmond Haynes's vision of the role of the Urban League in growing leadership to serve black communities. At the time of his retirement from the deanship, the School was beginning to experience the impact of desegregation.

The challenges that social work educators faced in the aftermath of desegregation were addressed by Dean Jackson in a study undertaken to gain insights into the implication of Title VI of the 1964 Civil Rights Acts for schools of social work. The results of the study, "The Civil Rights Act of 1964: Implications for Social Work Education in the South," were given at the January 27, 1966, CSWE Fourteenth Annual Program Meeting and published in the 1966 *Journal of Social Work Education.*

Data for the Jackson study were compiled from surveys sent to three groups—schools, social agencies, and NASW chapters—to obtain information about admission policies and practices, integration of student body, integration of faculty, and integration in field placements. Surveys were sent to a fifteen-state region, including approximately 55% of the black population in the Deep South, Southwestern, and border states. Social agencies were asked about integration of their staff and boards of directors, client caseloads, and the criteria used for determining client eligibility for agency services. And NASW chapters were asked specifically about the extent of integration in their membership and problems which interfered with integration. All were asked if they had signed the statement of compliance and what changes had been made in policies and practices.

Based on the survey findings, Jackson identified the following critical issues to address: the removal of barriers in admission requirements that prevented blacks from having equal access to opportunities in social work education, the recruitment and appointment of qualified blacks, the expansion of availability of integrated field instruction placements, and the securing of a more dynamic leadership from social work educators. The survey findings also revealed an unevenness in attention among the respondents given to the implementation of the Act, a finding leading Jackson to draw upon a quote from Whitney Young: "You can't talk about democracy and justice and human dignity in a school where there are no Negroes or only White Anglo-Saxon American Protestants" (Jackson, 1966, p. 45).

As the only school of social work in the state until the establishment of the social work program at the University of Georgia in 1964, enrollment at the School since its founding had included a small number of whites. However, the racial climate in Atlanta and in the country was not such that it would encourage whites to attend in large numbers a predominately black school of social work. And the Supreme Court doctrine of "separate but equal," which justified racial segregation, had prevented whites from matriculating in the School or for the School to award graduate social work degrees. Whites had continued to advocate for a school of social work that allowed them to matriculate and be eligible to receive full credits for courses taken and to be awarded the MSW degree.

A second School of Social Work was opened at the University of Georgia in Athens, and it became fully accredited by the CSWE in the spring of 1966. Harkening back to the early years when the Atlanta University faculty had given generously of their time to participate in what was to become Savannah State University and to preserve its policy on the co-education of the races, the faulty of the Atlanta University School of Social Work participated in setting up the School at the University of Georgia. And it was this sharing of their expertise that was essential to the University of Georgia School of Social Work successfully meeting CSWE accreditation requirements (Adams, 1981).

When the school of social work was founded at the University of Georgia in 1964, and reflecting past policies of the Georgia State Department of Education that did not recognize higher education in the liberal arts for blacks, some touted it as the first school of social work in Georgia. Since that time, the School in its publications has recognized the Whitney M. Young Jr. as the first school of social work established in the state and itself as the first public state-funded school of social work in the state.

With a main campus in Athens, Georgia, the Graduate Social Work program at the University of Georgia has been steadfast in its commitment to the values of the profession, reflected in the diversity of its faculty and student enrollment and educational programs. The social work program has received continuous reaffirmation since its founding in 1964, and currently awards the social work degree at the undergraduate, master's, and doctoral levels under its stated mission to prepare "culturally responsive practitioners and scholars to be leaders in addressing social problems and promoting social justice, locally and globally, through teaching, research, and service."

Dr. June Gary Hopps is the current occupant of the Thomas M. "Jim" Parham Professorship of Family and Children Studies at the Graduate School of Social Work at the University of Georgia. The chair was established in 2001 to honor the contributions of Parham to social policy and work on behalf of children and families in governmental appointments at the state level, and at the federal level with the Carter administration in the 1970s. As occupant of the chair, Dr. Hopps, serves the School as an authority in the area of public policy as it relates to families and children.

Dr. Hopps is also a distinguished alumnus of the Atlanta University School of Social Work, and an embodiment of the values embraced by the HBCUs. She earned the undergraduate degree at Spelman College, and, in keeping with the mission of the Atlanta University School of Social Work, she has devoted her professional career to the advancement of social justice causes in the interest of the African American community, for which she has received national recognition. She is the recipient of the NASW Pioneer Award and the Significant Lifetime Achievement in Social Work Education in 2017, which is the highest award given by the CSWE for exemplary contributions in social work education as a scholar, teacher, and administrator. In her October 27, 2017 CSWE acceptance speech entitled: *From Social Apartheid to Social Justice: Social Work's Journey (or Struggle)* given at CSWE Annual Program Meeting in Dallas, Texas, her remarks were a reflection of the priorities of the founders of the Atlanta School of Social Work, and as was her custom Dr. Hopps focused on the most critical issues facing the profession and social work education as she observed:

> [T]he profession should develop a broader curriculum which would include content on economic structure and process. This would help prepare professionals for understanding the angst stemming from groups who feel alienated and the emergence of new political movements. Social workers deal with the impact of inequality, but we do not address prevention. Instead of advocating equal and exact justice; we merely speak of macro-injustices and call for economic justice, environmental justice, and social justice. Then we structure the curriculum around micro-interventions which locate structural problems within the individual, family and small groups. What a contradiction. By not giving more attention to macro content, do we inadvertently suggest our own powerlessness? (Hopps, 2017)

As Dean Jackson prepared to step down from the deanship of the Atlanta University School of Social Work in May 1968, the School, the state of Georgia, and the city of Atlanta were yet again moving into a new era of change. As

Adams wrote, the social work students during Dr. Jackson's deanship were becoming more demanding in their activism for black equality.

> [L]uckily the students' ideas of relevancy, identity a Black Power did not cause them to destroy the image of the School. They used their ideas with a degree of sanity, for many of their concerns were focused on curriculum content and administrative matters of the School. (Adams, 1981, p. 24)

This conservative disposition of the student body would be replaced by a more activist orientation as the School prepared to enter into the decades of the 1970s. This was influenced by the confluence of trends occurring in state and city politics and the faculty's recommitment to the legacy of Forrester B. Washington.

The School's mid-centennial year in 1971 was viewed as a symbolic crossing over as the fiftieth anniversary occurred simultaneously with the accidental drowning death of Whitney M. Young in Lagos, Nigeria, and with the School's recommitment to the legacy of Forrester B. Washington and an emphasis on a black perspective in social work education. Atlanta was also moving closer to achieving its image of a progressive city on race relations with the election of Maynard Jackson as Atlanta's first African American mayor. Jackson served for two consecutive terms (1974–1978 and 1978–1982) and was elected for a third term in 1990. Jackson's mayoralty ushered in an era of liberalism and progressive policy development that was responsive to the aspirations of blacks, His terms as mayor began to chip away at the racism that had characterized the city.

At the state level, Lester Maddox served as Governor of Georgia from 1967 to 1971. At least for a period, he would be the last staunch segregationist elected to the Georgia governorship. Presenting himself as a caricature of a responsible elected official, Maddox demonstrated to the nation the absurdities of white supremacy in his efforts to bar blacks from being served at his white-only Pickwick Restaurant. The restaurant specialized in fried chicken and Maddox's handing out of ax handles to be used by whites against blacks seeking to be served in the white-only restaurant (dubbed "Maddox drum sticks") became an optic of wide media coverage.

Maddox was succeeded as governor by Jimmy Carter, who brought a new civility to Georgia politics, stating in his gubernatorial inauguration speech on January 12, 1971, "the time of racial discrimination is over. . . . No poor, rural, weak, or black person should ever have to bear the additional burden of being deprived of the opportunity for an education, a job, or simple justice." The statement also paved the way for a new recognition of the contributions that the HBCUs brought to higher education in the United States.

With Dean Jackson's resignation from the deanship, an interim committee was appointed to provide administrative oversight to the School until a new dean could be appointed. The three-member committee was comprised of senior faculty members Professors Genevieve T. Hill, Edyth Ross, and Lloyd Yabura. Professor Hill was subsequently appointed to the deanship, serving in the position from 1968 to 1979.

REFERENCES

Acs, G., Braswell, K., Sorensen, E., & Turner, M. A. (2013, June). The Moynihan Report revisited. Washington, DC: The Urban Institute. http://www.urban.org/UploadedPDF/412839-The-Moynihan-Report-Revisited.pdf

Adams, F. V. (1981). *The reflections of Florence Victoria Adams.* Atlanta: Shannon Press, in collaboration with the Atlanta University School of Social Work and the Alumni Association.

Axinn, J., & Levin, H. (1997). *Social welfare: A history of the American response to need* (4th ed.). White Plains, NY: Longman.

Bayor, R. H. (1996). *Race and the shaping of twentieth-century Atlanta.* Chapel Hill: University of North Carolina Press.

Carten, A. J. (2016). Reflections on the American social welfare state. In *The collected papers of James R. Dumpson, PhD, 1930–1990.* Washington, DC: NASW Press.

Council on Social Work Education. (1972, September–October). [Untitled item.] Social Work Education Reporter, p. 1.

Council on Social Work Education. Commission for Diversity and Social and Economic Justice. Charge from the Board of Directors. https://www.cswe.org/About-CSWE/Governance/Commissions-and-Councils/Commission-for-Diversity-and-Social-and-Economic-J#:~:text=The%20Commission%20for%20Diversity%20and,aspects%20of%20human%20diversity%20intersect.

Family Service Association of America. (1960, January). *Social casework. Appraisals of the curriculum study.* Editorial Notes, XLI (1), 5–6. Albany, NY: Author.

Frazier, E. F. (1990). Problems and needs of negro children and youth resulting from family disorganization. *Journal of Negro Education,* Summer, 276–277.

Galbraith, J. K. (1958). *The affluent society.* Boston: Houghton Mifflin.

Harrington, M. (1997). *The other America.* New York: Simon and Schuster.

Hopps, J. G. (2017). Address delivered by June Gary Hopps, recipient of the 2017 Significant Lifetime Achievement in Social Work Education Award, Council on Social Work Education Annual Public Meeting at Dallas, Texas, Sunday, October 22, 2017.

Jackson, W. S. (1966). The civil rights of 1964: Implications for social work education. *Social Work Education Reporter,* 14(3), 23–29.

Jansson, B. (2009). *The reluctant welfare state: American social welfare policies: Past, present, and future.* Belmont, CA: Brooks/Cole.

Jansson, B. S. (1993). *The reluctant welfare state: A history of American social welfare policies* (2nd ed.). Pacific Grove, CA: Brooks/Cole.

Jencks, C. (1992). *Rethinking social policy.* Cambridge, MA: Harvard University Press.

Johnson, L. B. (1964, August 20). Remarks upon signing the Economic Opportunity Act. http://www.presidency.ucsb.edu/ws/?pid=26452

Johnson, L. B. (1965, June 4). Commencement address at Howard University: "To fulfill these rights." http://www.lbjlib.utexas.edu/johnson/archives.hom/speeches.hom/650604.asp

Johnson, L. B. (1966). *Public papers of the presidents of the United States: Lyndon B. Johnson, 1965* (vol. 2, entry 301, pp. 635–640). Washington, DC: Government Printing Office.

Katz, M. (1989). *The undeserving poor: From the war on poverty to the war on welfare.* New York: Pantheon Books.

Katz, M. B. (1996). *In the shadow of the poorhouse: A social history of welfare in America.* New York: Basic Books.

Kennedy, J. F. (1962, July 26). Statement by the president upon approving the Public Welfare Amendments Bill. http://www.presidency.ucsb.edu/ws/?pid=8788

Lewis, O. (1961). *The children of Sanchez: Autobiography of a Mexican family.* New York: Vintage Books, Random House.

Lewis, O. (1966). *La Vida: A Puerto Rican family in the culture of poverty, San Juan and New York.* New York: Random House.

Lewis, O. (January 1998). The culture of poverty. *Society, 35*(2), 7.

Moynihan, D., P. (1965). *The Negro family: The case for national action.* Washington, DC: US Department of Labor, Office of Policy Planning and Research.

Mullen, E. J. (1991, October 11). Fordham University Oral history project. Interview of James R. Dumpson. Transcript, No. 100.

Murray, C. (1985). *Losing ground: American social policy, 1950–1980.* New York: Basic Books.

Murray, C., & Herrnstein, R. J. (1994). *The bell curve: Intelligence and class structure in American life.* New York: Free Press.

New York University Silver School of Social Work. Distinguished Alumni Awards, November 30. 2010. https://socialwork.nyu.edu/news/2010/silver-school-honorsdistinguishedandrecentalumni.html.

Pearson, D. M. (2013). Scott, Carl A. In *Encyclopedia of Social Work.* Oxford University Press.

Substance Abuse an d Mental Health Services Administration. The Minority Fellowship Program. https://www.samhsa.gov/minority-fellowship-program

Ryan, W. (2010). *Blaming the victim.* New York: Vintage.

Stafford, W. (n.d.). Interview with James R. Dumpson. Dumpson private collection.

Trattner, W. I. (1999). *From poor law to welfare state: A history of social welfare in America* (5th ed.). New York: The Free Press.

Trolander, J. A. (1997). Fighting racism and sexism: The Council on Social Work Education. *Social Service Review, 71*(1), 110–134. https://www.jstor.org/stable/30012609

United States. National Advisory Commission on Civil Disorders, Kerner, O., & Wicker, T. (1968). *Report of the National Advisory Commission on Civil Disorders: Special Introduction by Tom Wicker of The New York Times [chairman, Otto Kerner].* Bantam Books.

PART III

At the Midpoint and Looking Beyond

CHAPTER 12

Crossing Over

No! No! No! his black professional colleagues cried, there is no such thing as black social work! We should treat people as people, after all we are all human beings.
—Lloyd Yabura (1970)

The School approached its mid-centennial a in 1970 at a time when the country and the profession were seeing a waning of the social justice concerns that had fueled the struggle for civil right in the preceding decades of the 1950s and 1960s. By the 1970s, a new conservativism was emerging in American that soon replaced the liberalism that had propelled the Civil Rights movement forward and led to the enactment of progressive reforms under the Great Society.

Within the profession, the new conservatism accelerated the movement of social workers from agency-based practice and the public sector to independent practice. Among black social workers, the new conservatism was the impetus for the coming together of social work educators, practitioners, activists, and scholars motivated by the desire to advance a strategic approach for shaping professional education, policy, and practice in the African American community.

At the School, the faculty embarked upon a process of curriculum renewal that reconnected the School to its founding mission as a black school of social work. The Black Task Force, supported by the Council on Social Work Education (CSWE), brought together the social work faculties from Howard and Atlanta Universities, and other schools, to identify relevant content on the black experience for integration into the social work education curriculum. As a result of community organizing efforts, the National Association of Black Social Workers (NABSW) became the umbrella membership organization for African American social workers and a means for disseminating information

Find a Way or Make One. Alma J. Carten, Oxford University Press (2021). © Oxford University Press.
DOI: 10.1093/oso/9780197518465.001.0001.

about practice pertinent to the black community through the convening of an annual conference. And on the East and West Coasts, a new cadre of scholars and black thought leaders was emerging in academia who were advancing an Afrocentric and black perspective in their scholarship and teaching. A select group of social work faculty were at the vanguard of advancing the black and Afrocentric perspectives by writing and teaching in schools of social work. Among these were Barbara Solomon, who introduced empowerment theory for practice in the black community (Solomon, 1976), and Leon Chestang, whose Occasional Paper published by the University of Chicago, *Character Formation in a Hostile Environment,* discussed the various adaptations made by African American in an effort to accommodate the paradoxes of being black in American society (Chestang, 1972). Dorothy Norton's formulation of the dual perspective gave insight into the implications for minority group functioning in nurturing and sustaining communities (Norton, 1979), as did Elaine Pinderhughes's early work on teaching empathy in cross-cultural practice (Pinderhughes, 1979).

THE SYMBOLIC CROSSING OVER OF THE SCHOOL AT THE MID-CENTENNIAL

Due in part to a process of attrition, at the time of the School's mid-centennial the stewardship of the School was being passed to a new generation of scholars and black thought leaders. Influenced by social and ideological movements of the preceding decades, the new professoriate brought to the School a sense of academic agency that resulted in a recommitment to the founding mission of the School and to the legacy of Forrester B. Washington. The autonomous social work practice model was introduced by the faculty on the occasion of the School's mid-centenarian October 1970. The rationale for the re-envisioning of the curriculum at this juncture of the School's history is detailed in the Excerpt from the proceedings of the 50th anniversary entitled *Revisiting the Legacy of Forrester B. Washington, Educator and Nation Builder* (Sanders, 1970).

In keeping with Forrester B. Washington's call for social workers to assume an active role of advocacy to influence social welfare policy and practice with African Americans, this re-envisioning was a reaffirmation of Washington's urgings. No longer complacent, the new faculty cohort was not content with maintaining the status quo in the interest of ensuring the School's survival under the threat of loss of accreditation. In preparing to step down as acting dean, Florence Victoria Adams commented on the process that had over time eroded the School's influence in shaping social work education in the black community and the intent to reclaim this stature with a renewed commitment to its founding mission.

[D]uring the period from 1950 to 1960, the Atlanta University School of Social Work became a prototype of every other school of social work, a consequence of the school's response to pressures from accrediting and funding sources. Today, the Atlanta University School of Social Work has gone full cycle and is reaffirming its historical mandate with a more pluralistic orientation. It clearly articulates its commitment to provide quality education to people of all ethnic heritages who wish to help oppressed people and to engage in the humanization of an oppressive social order and the elimination of racism. (Adams, 1981, pp. 27–28)

In describing the conceptual underpinnings of the curriculum of the autonomous social work model that the faculty was now adopting, Adams wrote that

the educational framework evolves around the successful integration in the curriculum of (1) humanistic values; (2) the meaning and significance of the black experience in human service delivery; (3) dialectical and dialogical engagement and transactional relationships which respect cultural integrity; (4) a problem-solving methodology consistent with the needs of individuals, families, groups, organizations and communities; (5) an understanding of people as biopsychosocial and spiritual beings; (6) social welfare policy development and analysis; (7) use of the scientific method to test prevailing theoretical constructs, analyze presenting problems, assess existing social service models and move towards development of concepts and techniques with humane applications; and (8) practice experiences which afford students the opportunity to test out the theory, develop functional skills of intervention and become humane social service practitioners. (Adams, 1981, pp. 27–28)

Associate Dean Lloyd Yabura, who is acknowledged by some as being the brain child of the autonomous social work model, encouraged the incorporation of strategies of the Neighborhood Union model pioneered by Lugenia Burns Hope into the model. Hope's work preceded the founding of the School and introduced community organizing, needs assessment, and community engagement specifically designed to target underserved black neighborhoods, as discussed in Chapter 6. The faculty's embrace of the values and strategies of the autonomous practice model therefore may well be considered a reaffirmation of the intent of the School's founders. The environmental conditions that created the need for a training school for "colored" social workers when the school was founded in 1920 had improved, but the persistence of these inequalities at the time of the mid-centennial was evidence of the continuing relevance of a curriculum design emphasizing competencies for practice in the black community in the 20th century.

CONCEPTUAL UNDERPINNINGS

The conceptual underpinnings of the autonomous practice model adopted by the faculty were in keeping with Washington's expressed favoring of the generic approach. Practice models favoring the generalist approach had been an evolving process of knowledge building for the profession over the decades of the 1950s and 1960s. The advancing of the generalist model by the faculty at this time was occurring when social work students and faculty were calling for more inclusive theoretical frameworks for informing practice, and questioning the deficit approach embedded in the casework method that dominated the field and relied heavily on psychodynamic theory for assessing problem causation and planning treatment interventions.

The autonomous social work model was anchored in the broader theoretical framework provided by General Systems Theory (GST), introduced by Australian biologist Karl Ludwig von Bertalanffy in the early decades of the 20th century. GST may be viewed as a mega theory that explains the reciprocity of interactions between natural and man-made systems. Similar to Critical Theory, it may be applied to many fields of study. Such was the case for Russian-born American psychologist Urie Bronfenbrenner, who applied the conceptual underpinnings of GST to human systems. His formulation of ecological systems theory emphasized the interactive effects of the multiple systems within which children grow and develop and explain their behaviors. Borrowing from the physical sciences, the ecological model places emphasis on the adaptive capacities of the human organism that contribute to strengths and resilience.

With CSWE's adoption of a competency-based curriculum in 2008, Bronfenbrenner's conceptualization of ecological system theory as applied to human systems is reflected in Competency 2: Engage Diversity and Difference in Practice and operationalized as the ability to "apply and communicate understanding of the importance of diversity and difference in shaping life experiences in practice at the micro, mezzo, and macro levels" (Council on Social Work Education [CSWE], 2015). This competency serves as an anchoring principle of the School's autonomous social work model and Afrocentric perspective that together continue to shape the design of the School's curriculum in both explicit educational programming, and the implicit or symbolic representation of the values of the autonomous model in the School's culture. Accordingly, social work practitioners adopting the approach advanced by the School's autonomous practice model use strategies that give equal attention to individual behaviors and to the unjust societal systems that impede people in their quest for self-actualization.

The reconceptualization of the School's curriculum in the 1970s to assume a more activist stance was happening within the context of demographic changes occurring in the city of Atlanta. By the 1970s, African Americans had become the majority demographic in the city, and they used the power of the vote to elect Maynard Holbrook Jackson Jr., in 1973, as Atlanta's first African American mayor. Jackson served as vice mayor under Mayor Sam Massell. He then served two consecutive terms as mayor between 1974 and 1982, and he was elected to serve a third term as mayor from 1990 to 1994. Over his terms in office, black Atlantans were given a voice in the political process, and the city was moving closer to the realization of its image as representative of a progressive New South.

Mayor Jackson had strong roots in the black community in Atlanta and in the city's historically black colleges and universities (HBCUs). A graduate of Morehouse College, his maternal grandfather John Wesley Dobbs had coined the name "Sweet Auburn Avenue," that described Auburn Avenue as "the richest Negro street in the world." Dobb's daughter, and Jackson's mother, Irene Dobbs Jackson, was a graduate and later professor at Spelman College; her civil rights activism in the city resulted in her being the first African American to receive a library card from the main branch of the Atlanta Public Library (Rice, 2019).

Jackson's father, Rev. Dr. Maynard Holbrook Jackson Sr., also a "Morehouse Man," carried forth the tradition established by his father of combining politics with the ministry in earning a divinity degree at the Garrett School of Divinity and carrying out missionary work in Africa in his early career. In later years he was a civil rights activist and pastor of the New Hope Baptist Church in Dallas, Texas, prior to his move to Atlanta, where he pastored Atlanta's historic Friendship Baptist Church (Christensen, 2011).

Maynard Holbrook Jackson Jr. carried on the family tradition in his political career in Atlanta. Weathering the long-standing, below the surface ire related to the disingenuousness of marketing Atlanta as the city "too busy to hate," as mayor of Atlanta Jackson put in place policies that were responsive to the aspirations of black Atlantans. He introduced the Neighborhood Planning Unit system that created a more equitable approach for Atlanta residents to influence decisions made by city officials that influenced the quality of life in their neighborhoods. Committed to giving blacks a voice in city planning, he stood in opposition to public works projects that disregarded the significance of the meaning of neighborhood for community residents. He promoted policies of affirmative action that removed barriers to economic opportunities for blacks and opened up union memberships from which they had previously been barred.

Included among Mayor Jackson's accomplishments were reforms in law enforcement that addressed historic concerns about police brutality and the insensitivity of Atlanta's overwhelmingly white police department to the needs of the black community (Rice, 2019). Jackson's tenure as mayor coincided with the years of the tragic murders of black children occurring over the years of 1979–1981. The case, which remains highly controversial a near half-century later, involved the abduction and murder of approximately twenty-eight African American children, most of whom were males and residents in inner-city neighborhoods (Headley, 1998).

Perhaps the most notable of Jackson's accomplishments are the roles he played in the building of a new terminal at the Hartsfield Atlanta International Airport and securing Atlanta as the city to host the 1996 Summer Olympics. In acknowledgment of his significant contributions to the project, the name of the airport was changed in 2003 to the Hartsfield-Jackson Atlanta International Airport after his death.

Along with Andrew Young, the heir apparent to the Martin Luther King Jr. legacy and Jackson's successor over his four-year gap period as mayor, Jackson promoted Atlanta as the best choice for hosting the 1996 Summer Olympics. In presenting the case to the International Olympic Committee, Young and Jackson argued that, in addition to being known for its racial harmony, as the home of Martin Luther King Jr., the city was an embodiment of King's vision of the "Beloved Community" and international cooperation and therefore a model for the diversity of races and ethnic groups that would be attending and participating in the Games. Their arguments prevailed. Winning the Committee vote with a wide margin over the sentimental favorite of Athens, Greece, Atlanta became the third American city to host the Summer Games (Reid, 1990).

The Games commenced with President Bill Clinton's announcement: "I declare open the Games of Atlanta, celebrating the XXVI Olympiad of the modern era." The president's declaration was followed by a pageantry of activities that included the singing of the US National Anthem and Gladys Knight's rendition of "Georgia on My Mind," the official song of the state of Georgia.

A memorable image of the events was that of Mohammed Ali lighting the cauldron in the opening ceremonies. Ali arguably is unmatched as an iconic figure in the history of American sports for his athletic ability and for his championing of civil rights. A tearful President Clinton was among the thousands of observers across the world who looked on as Ali, who had become a global symbol of civil rights, now unsteadied by the symptoms of Parkinson's disease, was the last link in relay of athletes who had carried the Olympic torch through forty-three states and over 15,000 miles, to its final destination of the Olympic stadium.

In later years, the accounting is mixed on the economic legacy of the Games to the city of Atlanta. There is, however, consensus that the Centennial

Olympic Park in downtown Atlanta transformed what had been an area of urban decay into an area where children now run and play (Newman, 2018).

Mayor Jackson's policy of the active engagement of the black community dovetailed with the School's recommitment to the Forrester B. Washington's ideals of a black school enmeshed in community engagement and activism on the behalf of the black community. These interests created new opportunities for student learning assignments related to social justice and activism undertaken with the guidance and mentoring of faculty. The students were no longer conservatively complacent, as described by Adams (1981) as they were under the deanship of William Jackson, and as a student body content with focusing on the internal mechanisms of the School involving issues of curriculum development and educational programs.

ALUMNI REFLECTIONS ON COMMUNITY ACTIVISM AT THE SCHOOL IN THE 1970S

Dr. Ruby Gourdine and Richard Morton, alumni of the class of 1973–1975 who were enrolled in the School during the period of its introduction of the autonomous social work practice model, described a culture of social activism led by a dynamic faculty that had a lasting and significant impact on shaping their professional social work identities. In personal communications with the writer, both described a sense of purpose and service to the black community instilled in them as students that has remained with them over the full course of their professional careers.

Richard Morton described and clarified the origins of the School's autonomous social work practice model.

> I must indicate that it was during the 1970s that AUSSW launched the Autonomous Social Work Practice Model—undergirded by humanistic values from an Afrocentric perspective. No, it was not at Howard University under the leadership of neither Dr. Douglas Glasgow, Dr. Joan Wallace or Dr. Jay C. Chunn. Yes, it was the brainchild of Lloyd Yabura under the guidance and sanctions of Dean Genevieve Hill. Truly, those were some remarkable years of being challenged by such Professors as Howard Standback, Ricardo Millett, Althea Truiett, Naomi T. Ward and Edyth Ross—just to name a few!
>
> I am truly indebted to these authentic social work pioneers who not only expected, but demanded the best from their students. To each one of these social work pioneers and change agents I say "thanks!" (Morton, 2019)

Dr. Ruby Gourdine, who is currently a member of the full-time faculty at the Howard University School of Social Work, was equally exuberant in reflecting on her student experiences during the early years of the shift to the autonomous practice model. Over her full professional career, as she recounted, the black perspective has remained at the center of her scholarship and of her various roles as educator, clinician, administrator, consultant, and researcher. In recalling her student experiences in the social work program, she reflected on the impact of Professor Edyth Ross, whose presence and enthusiasm created a classroom climate described by Dr. Gourdine as "captivating."

Professor Ross was among the team of faculty who were breathing new life into the restructured curriculum and the integration of the theoretical and value underpinnings of the autonomous social work model into classroom course work and the agency practicum. Professor Ross taught in the social policy curriculum sequence and, as Dr. Gourdine observed,

> She convinced students to get involved in Maynard Jackson's run as the first African American mayor of Atlanta. I passed out literature and followed his accounts in the newspapers and we followed it in class. I was able to attend his victory party and most of the African American civil rights leaders and politicians were there. It was so amazing! I got to see Jesse Jackson, Julian Bond, his father, and others. (Gourdine, 2019)

In reflecting on her experiences with Professor Mamie Darlington, who was among the new cohort of faculty engaged in implementing the new model of autonomous social work practice and who served as interim dean of the School from 1987 to 1989, she said "I just loved her commitment to students and civil rights. I remember as a part of my assignment we had to attend a school board meeting and at that time Benjamin Mayes was chair. It was such an invigorating experience for me" (Gourdine, 2019).

SHIFTING NATIONAL PRIORITIES

In the national arena, by the 1970s, attention had shifted from the War on Poverty to the Vietnam war. As protests against the war escalated, a beleaguered President Johnson announced that he would not seek or accept the nomination of the Democratic Party to run for re-election in the 1968 presidential elections.

As the 1970s approached, the Civil Rights movement had progressed from nonviolent engagement to militant confrontation. Moreover, the riots in inner-city areas persisted despite the substantial social welfare expenditures of the Great Society programs. Corresponding with these increasing federal expenditures, was the continually rising welfare rolls that the general public erroneously believed were responsible for increases in taxes and the rise in the national debt. These simultaneously occurring events left Americans longing for some respite—and it was this sense of national malaise and longing for a return to normalcy that was the context of the 1968 presidential election.

THE 1968 PRESIDENTIAL ELECTIONS

The 1968 presidential election campaign was undertaken at a time when the country was eager for a return to normalcy. The American people had been numbed by the assassinations of Martin Luther King Jr. and Robert Kennedy and were growing increasingly weary of the widespread riots in the nation's cities despite the investment of funds in the War on Poverty programs. Protests in the interests of civil rights were shifting to protests against US involvement in the Vietnam war. Both Martin Luther King Jr. and Bobby Kennedy had joined the growing widespread protests against the Vietnam war. King had given his controversial April 4, 1967, speech at Riverside Church "Beyond Viet Nam" raising the war to the level of a matter of morality (King, 1967). And, democratic candidate, Robert Kennedy entered the 1968 race for the presidency on a campaign platform promise to lead the country out of the war while pursuing an honorable peace.

When campaigning for the presidency as a republican, Richard Nixon capitalized on the mood of the country in coining the term the "silent majority." He described this as the majority of Americans who were not speaking out but whose aspirations were being pushed aside by loud and disruptive voices who demanded much but contributed little to national life. Nixon's presidential campaign was carried out under the platform motto of "the silent majority" combined with a campaign promise to restore "law and order" in the nation.

In the Deep South, traditions of racism and white supremacy continued to hold sway at the time of the 1968 presidential elections. George Wallace had entered the race for the presidency as a third-party candidate under a platform banner of "Stand up for America." The motto carried an implicit, covert, and coded theme of racism that had been Wallace's explicit racist message as governor of Alabama as he stood by the school house door in defiance of federal desegregation laws with the promise to supporters of his intent to ensure "segregation today, segregation tomorrow, segregation forever."

Running against Democrat Herbert Humphrey and Republican Richard Nixon, Wallace's raucous campaign rallies were orchestrated to manipulate his supporters by simultaneously raising their fears about the loss of privilege guaranteed by the doctrines of white supremacy that he then attempted to abate by promising that, as president, he would repeal the 1965 Voting Rights Act and push back the civil rights legislation of the previous decades that he claimed had pitted race against race and class against class.

In Georgia, the racially divisive and segregationist political agenda was carried forward by Lester Maddox, a staunch segregationist who served as Georgia governor from 1967 to 1971. Maddox was succeeded by Jimmy Carter, who held the office of the governor from 1971 to 1975. Carter attempted to bring a new civility into the racial dialogue in the state.

In 1971, Carter appeared on the cover of *Time* magazine, touted as the face of the "New South" (Nordheimer, 1971). However, the New South promoted by Henry W. Grady, democratic political leader, industrialist, managing editor of the *Atlanta Constitution,* and white supremacist, in the early decades following the Civil War had yet to materialize. Moreover, despite his significant achievements, Grady's promotion of the New South that encouraged collaboration with the North to promote industrial growth in the South failed to address the disenfranchisement, exploitation, and violence against blacks that continued to be prevalent in the region (Grem, 2018).

STUDENT PROTESTS AGAINST THE VIETNAM WAR

Nixon won the 1968 presidency. He began his presidency at a time when inner-city riots and demonstrations against the war reached their peak with the escalation of the bombings in Vietnam. When he entered office, college campuses across the country were engulfed in student protests against the US involvement in the war. It became necessary to call in the National Guard to restore order and control the ever-growing student demonstrations and boycotts that were engulfing college campuses across the country in protest to the escalation of the bombings.

Staying true to his campaign promise of law and order, President Nixon called in the Ohio National Guard to restore order when student protests were mounting in violence on the campus of Kent State University in Kent, Ohio. What has come to be known as the Kent State Massacre of May 4, 1970, is another symbol of the pathos of the period. In the chaos of the rioting, some of the National Guardsmen were reported as having turned their guns on the protesters, as they were caught in a mob of protesting students. The spraying of bullets in the encounter resulted in the deaths of four students. The tragic event is memorialized in John Filo's Pulitzer Prize-winning photograph of a young woman kneeling over the body of one of the dead students.

Although less publicized, ten days later, on May 11, 1970, police officers shot and killed two black students at Mississippi's Jackson State College, now Jackson State University (Spofford, 1988). The student protests on the Jackson State campus were likely more of a protest against the entrenchment of racism in the state, and the racial inequities in funding to HBCUs that contributed to the poorly kept conditions of the school's facilities than against the escalation of the war.

As was likely the case for the largest share of the HBCUs in the southern region of the country at the time when racist policies ensured an inequitable distribution of resources among black and white institutions of higher learning, Jackson State was underresourced, and this undermined the quality of student education and the quality of campus life. As one Jackson State student explained to members of the President's Commission on Campus Unrest established to investigate the causes of the student protests on campuses across the country,

> like some people say the Viet Nam issue . . . but I don't think that is true, when you go to class every day and in overcrowded classrooms and it is hot and sweaty in there, you just get fed up with it, and you know you should have had more classrooms and your classrooms should have been cool and you are sitting in a 100-degree classroom and that night it's the same thing and you ain't got nothin' to do. You just got to do something, and it is just one thing led to another. (Lesher, 1971)

No criminal or civil cases were ever brought against the city and state police who were responsible for the killing and injury of Jackson State students. The National Guardsman involved in the Kent state shootings who were indicted by the Grand Jury on felony or misdemeanor charges were all acquitted. A civil suit brought by the parents of the Kent State students resulted in a settlement for all of the students who were killed or wounded. The students, or their families, who were the victims of the Jackson State police shootings have never received any form of compensation (Simpson, 1990).

SOCIAL WELFARE AND THE NIXON ADMINISTRATION

When Richard Nixon settled into the Oval Office, he set into motion policies of a new conservativism that began chipping away at the safety net programs enacted under the Social Security Act of 1935 and expanded under the liberalism of the Great Society programs. Nixon's election was the beginning of a new conservatism that replaced the liberalism that had prevailed in the United States since the presidency of Franklin Delano Roosevelt, thus effectively returning the country to a philosophy of social welfare closely aligned with its poor law heritage.

Nixon introduced the New Federalism that embraced themes of the conservative philosophy of social welfare of self-help, self-reliance, individualism, privatization, and the devolution of certain activities of the federal government involving social services back to the states. Also included in his rolling back of liberal programs of the previous decades was his opposition to busing to achieve racial integration in the nation's schools. In his public address to the nation on March 17, 1972, he outlined his plan, which was to be submitted to Congress, that busing be stopped (New York Times, 1972). The full implementation of Nixon's conservative agenda would be left for Ronald Reagan, his Republican successor to the White House to carry out.

For both Nixon and Reagan, the generous programs that had been enacted under the New Deal and expanded under the Great Society were a wasteful spending of government dollars on programs that supported what for them were "welfare chiselers" and "welfare queens." Again, national ire was focused on the Aid to Families with Dependent Children (AFDC) program and a resurfacing of Moynihan's argument that the female-headed family is responsible for the growth of a black underclass in America (Moynihan, 1965).

By the 1970s, the AFDC caseload was no longer comprised of mothers who were the deserving white widows and for whom the program was initially designed, but was instead disproportionately comprised of never-married black women and their children. These changes in the demographics of the AFCD caseload were the context for the inclusion of a clause in the 1967 public welfare amendments that mandated limitations on federal reimbursement to states for children who were in need because of the absence of a parent due to desertion, illegitimacy, separation, or divorce.

Furthermore, along with changing population demographics, a rising national debt that was attributed to the rise in the welfare rolls and costs to the American taxpayer further inflamed the poverty debate. The debate became more toxic with the introduction of the narrative of the single parent female headed household and the absent father being responsible for the disproportionate impact of social problems on the African American community and for the growth of a "black underclass."

Dr. Sara McLanahan is the William S. Tod Professor of Sociology and Public Affairs at Princeton University, where she directs the Bendheim-Thoman Center for Research on Child Wellbeing (CRCW) and the Education Research Section, and recipient of the Distinguished Scholar Award from the American Sociological Association Family Section.

McLanahan has been most prolific in conducting research to impact policy that affects the well-being of children. Her 1985 study is one of the few research projects undertaken to examine the role of family structure in the reproduction of poverty. Using longitudinal data from the Michigan Panel Study of Income Dynamics, the study examined a number of hypothesis to establish a relationship of statistical significance between family structure and the reproduction of poverty. Study findings were mixed and inconclusive on the hypotheses examined. However, study findings contradicted the assumption that any family structure that deviated from the traditional two-parent nuclear family implies pathology and inappropriate socialization of children (McLanahan, 1985, p. 898).

Despite the rollbacks in programs developed under the Great Society and the stigmatizing narrative about those who looked to government programs for help, there were a number of progressive social welfare policy developments at the federal level during the Nixon administration. Nixon was a strong advocate for healthcare reform to ensure access to basic healthcare to all American families. Perhaps the most consequential of his social welfare initiatives were indexing Social Security retirement benefits to the cost of living, expanding the Food Stamp program, and the 1972 enactment of the Supplementary Security Income (SSI) program that provided enhanced financial assistance to low-income aged, blind, and disabled individuals. The 1975 Earned Income Tax Credit (EITC) provided a refundable tax credit to low- and modest-income working families. The Comprehensive Employment Training Act (CETA) of 1973 was established to provide job training and placement for adults who had experienced long-term unemployment and job training for youths.

Although never garnering enough support by Congress to be enacted into law, by far the most ambitious initiative undertaken in the Nixon administration's efforts to reform public welfare was the proposal for a Family Assistance Plan (FAP). The plan called for a guaranteed minimum income for families of a certain income level as a replacement to the AFDC program. The enactment of the Title XX Amendment to the Social Security Act also had major implications for the profession, with the consolidation of funding for personal social services that continues to be the funding stream for programs in which social workers have high visibility (Stern & Axinn, 2018; Trattner, 1999).

The amendments to the Social Security Act calling for the separation of income assistance from services reversed the tradition established by Harry Hopkins that mandated the presence of MSW trained social workers in the newly established departments of public welfare. The 1962 Public Welfare Amendments of the Kennedy administration also called for a social work presence in both eligibility determination and client needs assessment. Separation of services impacted all of the cash assistance programs, including AFDC, SSI, and general assistance, the city- and state-funded means-tested cash assistance program. The policy change was met with mixed reviews by the social work leadership who were concerned about the implications of the change for the quality of care to clients (Dowling & Dumpson, 1980; Piliavin & Gross, 1977).

Policy choices inevitably have both unintended and intended consequences, which was the case with separation of services. Separation on the one hand respected the client's right to self-determination and dispelled conventional thinking that the presence of financial need was an indication of personal or behavioral dysfunction. At the same time, giving decision-making to eligibility technicians trained in a single function resulted in the diminishing of the professional perspective in decision making at the point of entry into the service continuum, the point at which the choices made about which services to turn on will be a determining factor in client outcomes. Furthermore, the policy change was yet another link contributing to the diminishing presence of social workers in the public sector and on the front line in providing services to clients with the highest levels of need.

THE NIXON IMPEACHMENT AND RESIGNATION

Ironically, Nixon, who secured the oval office with a campaign promise to restore law and order, was the second president in American history to be impeached for the flagrant disregard of the rule of law in his efforts to cover up the Watergate debacle. His impeding impeachment led to his resignation from the office of the presidency on August 9, 1974. The scandal led to jail terms for high-ranking members of his cabinet who were found complicit in the flagrant disregard of the rule of law and the oath to carry out their duties as set forth in the US Constitution.

Spiro Agnew, Nixon's vice president, had resigned a year earlier in the face of evidence of political corruption that included allegations of bribery while occupying the office of the vice presidency. Agnew's resignation created a domino effect that led to the subsequent indictment and conviction of virtually all of the key players in Nixon's "law and order" administration.

THE ONE TERM PRESIDENCIES OF GERALD FORD AND JIMMY CARTER

With Nixon's resignation, Vice President Gerald Ford assumed the office of the presidency. Ford's first official act as president was to give a full and unconditional pardon to Richard Nixon for any crimes he may have committed against the United States. In defending his pardon of Nixon, Ford said that his intent was to put the nation on a path of healing and avoid what would have no doubt been a long and disconcerting trial.

Ford served one four-year term as president, from August 9, 1974, to January 20, 1977. He secured the nomination at the 1976 National Republican Convention but was defeated in the general election by the Democratic Party nominee and former Governor of Georgia, Jimmy Carter. President Carter was the first Georgian elected to the office of the presidency, and he served in the office from January 20, 1977, to January 20, 1981. He entered office with a strong commitment to pursue a civil rights agenda. As previously discussed, Carter introduced a plan for the federal government to provide enhanced supports to black institutions of higher learning that led to the launching of the White House initiative on HBCUs. The initiative has received continuing support from the White House under changing administrations.

Of special interest to social workers is the enactment of the 1980 Adoptions Assistance and Child Welfare Reform Act (PL 92-276) that was signed into law by President Carter on June 17, 1980. The law is considered a landmark legislation in the field of child welfare in its requirement that "reasonable efforts" were made to prevent the removal of children from their own homes and the reunification of families in those cases in which removal was required to ensure the safety of the child. The legislation reversed the nation's century long history of "rescue and punishment" that resulted in the unnecessary removal of children from their birth families and had an especially egregious impact on African American children and their families.

SOCIAL WELFARE UNDER THE REAGAN ADMINISTRATION

The new conservatism initiated under the Nixon administration was brought full circle under the policies of New Federalism of the Regan administration. In his first inaugural address to the nation on January 20, 1981, in speaking to the economic and social ills facing the nation, Regan stated his belief that "government is not the solution to our problem; government is the problem." Indeed, this was a belief that was to have a dramatic impact on the reshaping of governmental social welfare policy that had held sway since the New Deal.

The new conservatism embraced by the Reagan administration was anchored in the concept of American exceptionalism and informed by core values of the Republican Party favoring limited governmental interference in the affairs of the states or in the lives of citizens, personal responsibility, and traditional values as the moral foundation of American society. These core values of Republican conservatism served as guiding principles for reshaping the nation's fiscal and social policies over the years of the Regan administration.

The administration's conservative fiscal policies were popularized under the term "Reaganomics." Premised in the assumption that a "rising tide lifts all boats," Reaganomics provided the rationale for the adoption of regressive taxation policies that took a larger portion of income from low income earners, on the premise that the upward distribution of income was the best way to ensure a robust and stable economy. Taxation policies benefitting the wealthiest Americans were a significant departure from Keynesian economic theory that a strong economy required government controls and the downward redistribution of income through progressive taxation policies that protect those at the lowest rungs of the economic ladder and who are at higher risk for the loss of salaried employment that accompanies the cyclical ups and downs of the market.

On matters related to the social welfare state, in Reagan's view social spending only contributed to the problems of poverty by diminishing the significance of the work ethic that was essential to a capitalistic economy. Joining with Nixon in the demonization of the poor in his use of the derogatory term "welfare chiselers," Reagan advanced a narrative of the "Welfare Queen" as representative of what he claimed were the thousands of individuals on the nation's welfare rolls who were defrauding the government out of hundreds of thousands of dollars. With its emphasis on personal responsibility, policies of the New Federalism focused on dismantling the social welfare state with the devolution of responsibility for social welfare programs to the states. Funding for social services expenditures was capped under the Title XX Social Services Block Grant (SSBG), and local social service districts were given the discretion to customize their service plans to meet the needs of their individual jurisdictions.

In keeping with Reagan's belief that the federal government was not the solution but the cause of the problems associated with the nation's social welfare system, policies of devolution empowered states to administer their social welfare programs absent federal oversight—and this included doing away with them all together. Policies of devolution all but ignored the principle set forth in the US Constitution that the federal government alone has the imminence of power to protect the general welfare and promote the common good. Absent the protection of the federal government, poor blacks in the Deep South were potentially vulnerable to the capriciousness of southern state officials, where racism continued to play a central role in policies of eligibility determination and for establishing standard of need that had implications for the adequacy of social welfare benefits. And in poorer states with low per capita income, poor residents would be at potential risk of inequitable treatment when public officials faced difficult allocative decisions about use of funds during austere economic periods.

The Regan administration favored traditional values over the empirical evidence from science. For example, in the face of rising rates of teenage pregnancy, concurrent with climbing numbers of adolescents infected with the HIV virus, federal funds were allocated to exclusively support abstinence programs. First Lady Nancy Reagan spearheaded the "Just Say No" initiative as the approach adopted by the administration as the solution to the rise in chemical addictions among American youth, an approach contrary to the disease model long adopted by the allied health professions for the diagnosis and treatment of addictions. And despite data reported by the Center for Disease Control (CDC) forecasting the seriousness of the looming threat of the AIDS crisis, the moralistic orientation of the administration and its definition of the epidemic as a problem of the gay community prevented the mounting of a timely and appropriate response to a crisis that, in the end, would assume a trajectory that impacted growing segments of the populations who could not be blamed for their diagnosis.

The response of the federal government to the AIDS crisis would shift, with the lessening of public stigmatization associated with the disease, when Ryan White, a teenager infected with AIDS after receiving a blood transfusion for the treatment of hemophilia. Ryan's story put a human face on the impact of the epidemic, and, as a result of his courageous social activism, Congress enacted the Ryan White Comprehensive AIDS Resources Emergency Act (CARE) in 1990. The legislation has been reauthorized five times since it was enacted, in 1996, 2000, 2006, 2009, and 2013.

The legislation is now named the Ryan White HIV/AIDS Program and administered by the Health Resources and Services Administration's (HRSA). The Program is the largest federal program focused specifically on providing HIV care and treatment services to low-income people living with HIV who are uninsured or underserved. The program is included under the Affordable Care Act (ACA), the signature legislation of the Obama administration, and provisions under the ACA remain a critical component of the nation's response to HIV (Health Resources and Services Administration, 2019).

Reagan continued to cut funding for programs for the poor, including child care, school lunch and other nutrition programs, subsidized housing, energy assistance, family planning, mental health and substance abuse treatment, legal aid, and job training (Trattner, 1999). What the government does or does not do has both a quantitative and qualitative impact on the lives of people. And the dramatic slashing of programs under the Reagan administration saw rising poverty rates in already impoverished communities and the advent of new and different kinds of social problems. Urban cities like Atlanta, densely populated by blacks, were especially hard hit by the crack cocaine epidemic that brought with it the advent of substance abuse among women in their childbearing years and took a devastating toll on the lives of infants and children. Moreover, huge tax cuts to the wealthiest Americans combined with cuts in social welfare expenditure to support defense spending saw a rise in what was to become intolerable gaps in income among the American people and the largest federal deficit in the nation's history.

The 1988 Family Support Act Pub.L. 100–485 was the signature public assistance reform legislation of the Reagan administration. The act was signed into law by the president in October 1988. The major provision was the Job Opportunities and Basic Skills Training Program that required single parents receiving public assistance and whose children were over the age of three to work, the strengthening of child support enforcement requiring noncustodial parents to contribute to the financial support of their children, and the continuation of transitional benefits. The transitional benefits were offered to counter what had been determined to be disincentives for leaving welfare. These benefits extended eligibility to Medicaid after leaving welfare and provided funds to support the costs of child care, transportation, and other expenses that enabled recipients to work or participate in job training programs (Trattner, 1999).

THEORETICAL UNDERPINNINGS OF THE NEW CONSERVATISM

Social welfare historian Michael Katz's book, *The Undeserving Poor: From the War on Poverty to the War on Welfare* (1989), traces the change in ideology underlying the American social welfare state that shifted policy discourse and debate from a war on poverty in the 1960s to a war on welfare in the 1980s. In the 1960s, Michael Harrington's *The Other America* (1962) focused national attention on structural inequalities that provided the value underpinnings for the liberal reforms of the War on Poverty. In the decades of the 1980s, social welfare reforms of the Reagan administration were guided by the theories of conservative political scientist Charles Murray, as presented in his book, *Losing Ground: American Social Policy, 1950–1980* (1984).

As discussed in Chapter 11, a central thesis of Murray's work in both of his controversial books, *Losing Ground* and the *Bell Curve* (1994), was that the means-tested programs for the poor encouraged dependency, undermined self-sufficiency, and directed government funds away from more deserving groups. Moreover, for Murray, government programs only perpetuated these problems, and therefore all programs for the poor should be abolished because they encouraged bad behaviors, the most notable of which were sexual promiscuity and out-of-wedlock births.

It is worth emphasizing again here, that for many scholars in the field, both books were based on questionable research methodologies and were an echo of empirically untested assumptions underlying theories of 19th-century Social Darwinism and the belief that, in leaving the poor to fend for themselves, the process of natural selection would solve the problem of poverty.

The virtual abandonment of the safety net philosophy that had guided American social welfare policy since the New Deal and resultant cuts in government funding of social welfare programs that led to the continued shrinking of the social welfare delivery systems also had implications for the profession of social work.

SOCIAL WORK AND THE NEW CONSERVATISM

The profession of social work was also experiencing a watershed moment during the 1970s. As the School of Social Work was adopting a more socially activist stance, the profession was once again leaning away from its founding mission of service to the poor and marginalized populations and moving to a growing interest in independent practice with privileged populations who were seen as more amenable to "talk therapies" and who had the financial means to pay for services on a fee for service basis (Alexander, 1972; Specht & Courtney, 1995). The new conservatism and privatization instituted under the Reagan administration allowed for the contracting out of social services previously provided by governmental agencies to private-sector, not for profits and provided increased incentives for social workers to move into independent practice in much greater numbers.

By the 1970s, what had been an enduring theme of the profession since the 1915 Flexner speech of a continued favoring of micro-level practice by a growing segment of the profession was acknowledge in policy with the advent of state regulation of professional practice. The beginning of state licensure laws regulating the practice of the profession made social workers eligible to qualify for membership on insurance panels and receive third-party payments for their services. Combined with cuts in social welfare expenditures that led to the elimination of some programs and a shrinking of social services and loss of social service jobs, policies of privatization under the Reagan administration and the advent of licensure accelerated the movement of social workers out of agency-based practice. The new title for what had been the "psychiatric social worker" engaged in the primary method of social casework in private sector mental health and family service agencies was that of "clinician," engaged in psychotherapy or other psychoanalytic-based therapeutic approaches carried out in independent practice.

STATE REGULATION AND LICENSURE

The National Association of Social Workers (NASW) Delegate Assembly had approved a resolution to pursue licensing of social work practice in each state. And, as more states were adopting policies regulating the profession, concurrent with the rise in the number of social workers in private practice, the American Association of State Social Work Boards (AASSWB) was founded in 1979 to develop uniform national credentialing examinations for social work licensing and certification. In 1999, the name of the Association was changed to the Association of Social Work Boards (ASWB). Since its founding, the ASWB has provided support to state regulatory boards in carrying out their primary function, which is to protect the interest of consumers. Although these are not uniform across the country, today all fifty states and the District of Columbia have statutes that are governed under the ASWB. These statutes establish policies relative to title protection, or who is entitled to use the title of social worker, the scope of practice of each level of licensure, examining boards, continuing education requirements to maintain practice currency, and disciplinary procedures for policy infractions.

SOCIAL WORK LICENSURE IN GEORGIA

Georgia offers a two-tier structure for social work licensure: the licensed master of social work (LMSW) and the licensed clinical social worker (LCSW). While graduates of accredited CSWE undergraduate social work programs (BSW) may practice under the supervision of a licensed social worker, the Georgia state licensing structure does not license practice at the BSW level.

The Georgia Composite Board of Professional Counselors, Social Workers, and Marriage and Family Therapists was created by the Georgia General Assembly in 1984, to oversee licensure policies for the behavioral health professions in the state. The Board is comprised of ten members appointed by the Governor and includes three professional counselors, three social workers, three marriage and family therapists, and one consumer member. The Composite Board is the legal entity for regulating the practice of these professional disciplines and for the enforcement of the state's licensure laws in the state. And, as in the case of all state entities overseeing the regulation of the profession, the primary objective is to ensure a minimal level of competency for professionals holding a license in a specific discipline to ensure the protection of the interests and welfare of clients seeking services from these professional disciplines (see https://sos.ga.gov/index.php/licensing/plb/43).

THE SIGNIFICANCE OF A MINORITY PRESENCE
IN MENTAL HEALTH

At the time of the research conducted for this book, none of the members of the Georgia Composite Board was a professional of color. The absence of a minority presence on the Board is worthy of attention here because of what has been learned from science about the importance of a minority perspective in mental health policy and service development (Neighbors, Jackson, et al., 1989: Hu et al., 1991; Neighbor, Bashshur, et al., 1992; Snowden, 2001; Carten, 2006). This is especially important to address given the population demographics in the state of Georgia and the implications for equity in access to and availability of mental health services to all state residents.

According to US Census reports, with a population of approximately ten million, Georgia is the most populous state in the nation. Georgia is also among those southern states that have remained home to the largest share of American blacks. And while many blacks reside in the rural regions of the state, the city of Atlanta is the second largest black metro area in the country, with a reported black population of 54% in 2010 (World Population Review, 2019). Moreover, as reported by the Substance Abuse and Mental Health Administration (SAMHSA), nearly 4% of adults in Georgia suffer from serious mental health problems (SAMHSA, 2017). And reports from the Office of Minority Mental Health indicate that African Americans, like other ethnic and racial minority groups, experience more psychological distress and suffer the worse outcomes, while simultaneously having the least access to quality mental health services.

Mental Health: Culture, Race, and Ethnicity: A Supplement to Mental Health: A Report of the Surgeon General (USDHHS, 1999; 2001) is considered a landmark publication in the field of mental health. The extensive research conducted to prepare the report identified the pervasiveness of racial disparities and barriers in access to mental health services for ethnic and racial minority groups. The report was published at the time of the appointment of Dr. David Satcher as US Surgeon General. Dr. Satcher is currently on the faculty at the Morehouse College of Medicine, and he is Founder and Senior Advisor to the Satcher Health Leadership Institute at the Medical College. As Surgeon General, Dr. Satcher spearheaded a national effort to raise public awareness about the stigma associated with mental illness that was the most significant barrier to access to treatment and to draw attention to approaches that had the potential to eliminate racial and ethnic disparities in mental health outcomes.

The report findings identified striking racial disparities relative to access, utilization, availability, quality of care, and treatment outcomes. A primary finding of the report was that pervasive racism at all levels of the mental health system slowed theory development essential for a knowledge base to inform race-conscious practice with ethnic and racial minority groups. In its conclusions, the report underscored that in a system in which state, county, and local communities carry primary responsibility for the organization, administration, and delivery of these services, the leadership and those who control the organization of local programs are in a position to influence the level of resources that federal and local governments invest in these services—making a minority presence on gate-keeping administrative structures of critical importance. This priority is missing in the composition of the current membership Georgia Composite Board.

Social work licensure has not been without controversy because of concerns about potential bias influencing service access and availability, and the quality of care for ethnic and racial minorities. The leadership of the NABSW and the New York City and state chapters were in opposition to the state regulation of the profession for these reasons. Based on an analysis of a segment of the New York state database, the association leadership argued that there is inherent cultural bias in the licensure exam and in the long term, these structural inequities would diminish the presence of social workers of color in a system where a racially and ethnically diverse workforce was essential (Carten, 2006; 2016).

The literature is virtually silent on the impact of state regulation on agency-based practice in the public and not-for-profit sectors serving predominately clients of color. However, the NABSW's claims may have some merit, if indirectly, in the literature reporting that with the new economic opportunities that came with privatization of the human services, social workers in independent private practice serving well-insured middle- and upper-income clientele have been the greatest beneficiaries of state regulation of the profession and licensure (Daley & McLane, 1985; Land, 1987).

Ever mindful of the potential influence of structural inequities, the ASWB has subjected every test item in credentialing exams to a rigorous statistical analysis to rule out gender and racial bias and to delete those items where a racial or gender bias is found to be present by a group of social work experts. It reports that results over several years have shown that ASWB exams are statistically free from race and gender bias (ASWB, 2018).

ASWB PATH TO LICENSURE

The Path to Licensure Program is an initiative of the ASWB designed to bridge social work education and state regulation together in the classroom in an effort to strengthen student and faculty knowledge of professional regulation and its important connection to public protection and social work values and ethics. The program is likely responsive to the growing number of students enrolling in schools of social work motivated by their interest in pursuing a career in independent, private practice as a psychotherapist. This growing national trend among prospective students seeking enrollment in social work program raises yet another dilemma for social work educators. For example, a national survey of the perceptions of MSW social work faculty on the relationship between licensing examinations and social work education found disparate views among students and faculty. Students, on the one hand, perceived the licensure exam as important to the profession and significant to their future. Faculty, on the other hand, only gave attention to the examination in the advisement process (Cherry, Rothman, & Skolnik, 1989).

It is likely that the professional trends favoring private practice will continue to be a central force driving professional policy and practice in social work and the behavioral health professions. In schools of social work, student interest in the inclusion of licensure in the curriculum content, combined with the ASWB weighing in by way of the Path to Licensure program with its stated purpose to "bring the worlds of education and regulation together in the classroom" (ASWB, 2018), will likely build a stronger case for faculties in social work education programs to accommodate these interests in the design of curriculum content. Such a development raises the possibility of further straining an already overcrowded curriculum in which two years seems too short a time to teach the basics for beginning professional practice while ensuring a sufficient integration of the liberal arts perspective as the foundation for supporting critical thinking in a field of increasing complexity if schools are to produce graduates capable of serving as stewards of the core values of the profession.

With the increasing phenomena of state regulation of the profession, social workers are well reminded of the centrality of concerns of social justice to the mission of the profession. Licensure protects consumers and elevates the importance of the profession to the position of authority that it deserves—much desirable goals. In today's political climate and ever shrinking benefits and services provided under the American social welfare state, licensure, as a privilege granted by the state—that is not without partisan political interests—and regulates who can and cannot deliver services and, in doing so, controls consumer access to services known to be critical to their overall well-being, the issues of social justice are especially salient and must be of equal concern to the profession.

NASW PROFESSIONAL CREDENTIALS

The NASW offers several advanced professional credentials and specialty certifications to members who have achieved a high level of professional proficiency. These include the Academy of Certified Social Workers, the Qualified Clinical Social Worker, and the Diplomate in Clinical Social Work. According to the NASW Credentialing Center, the Academy of Certified Social Workers, established in 1960, remains the most widely recognized and respected professional social work credential (credentialing@naswdc.org).

The NASW professional credential differs from the social work license issued by the state in that the state credential is authorized for use only in the state jurisdiction in which it is issued. The NASW credential/specialty certification signifies that the holder has met the highest national standards developed in the social work profession, in addition to having experience and supervision working with certain populations. All holders of NASW credentials and specialty certifications are members in good standing in the NASW and have agreed to adhere to the *NASW Code of Ethics* and NASW Standards for Continuing Professional Education, as well as standards for best social work practice.

THE NEW LEADERSHIP OF DEAN GENEVIEVE HILL AND
THE NEW PROFESSORIATE

Activities marking this benchmark date in the School's history, as the profession began favoring practice specialization, were incorporated in the theme of "Crossing Over." The theme was symbolic of the School's reaching the midpoint of its history, at a time when the faculty was considering fundamental changes in the curriculum that would place renewed emphasis on its founding mission. With the stepping down of Dr. William Jackson from the deanship in May 1968, the School was overseen by an interim committee of senior faculty that included Genevieve T. Hill, Edyth L. Ross, and Lloyd Yabura. Genevieve Hill was subsequently appointed to the deanship and held the position from 1968 to 1979.

Dean Hill earned her MSW degree at Smith College, the first school of social work to offer a training program for psychiatric social workers, and she completed postgraduate training at the nation's most prestigious psychiatric institutes. With her expertise in the areas of counseling and teaching rather than administration, she accepted the appointment with some reluctance. Adams in her book reflecting on the history of the School (Adams, 1981) wrote that despite the absence of a background in administration, Dean Hill's appointment to the deanship was favored by the university administration at that time because of her decades-long history with the School, which supported her familiarity with its problems and needs, and her democratic leadership style that promoted cohesiveness among the faculty. Moreover, her professional portfolio which indicated membership on the boards of an extensive number of the country's most prestigious national professional organizations was an indication of her prominence and status in the field.

Hill's deanship was during a period of the School's history when it moved into a new phase under the leadership of a professoriate comprised of a younger generation of scholars who endeavored to recapture its image as a "black" school of social work and who were committed to a macro approach for solving the stubborn persistence of social problems troubling the black community. Dean Hill served as chair of the CSWE Black Task Force that led to the continuing refinement of the School's conceptualization of the autonomous social work practice model undergirded by humanistic values and the Afrocentric perspective.

CSWE BLACK TASK FORCE

The School of Social Work introduced a model for autonomous social work practice that had emerged from the work of a federally funded project undertaken in collaboration with the CSWE, faculties from the two predominately black schools of social work at Howard and Atlanta Universities, other schools of social work, and experts in the fields of the black family and black child development.

The Black Task Force was an outgrowth of the experiences of the CSWE's Commission on Minority Groups that had focused on five identified minority groups: African Americans, Asian Americans, Chicanos, Native Americans, and Puerto Ricans. The work of the Commission on Minority Groups led to the recognition that while there were common concerns shared by the target minority groups, there were also issues that were unique to each of the five groups requiring individual attention. This recognition led to the Council's sponsorship of a workshop in June 1970, entitled "The Problems and Needs of the Black Community: Issues, Development, Perceptions, and Implications for Social Work Practice. The group identified two areas of major concern: (1) the need to identify curriculum content on black Americans and (2) the development of programs to increase the number and enhance the utilization of black social work educators in graduate schools of social work and undergraduate programs of social welfare.

Two meetings of the Task Force—one held on the campus of Atlanta University and one on the campus of Howard University, the home of the two most well-known "black" schools of social work at the time—were chaired by Genevieve Hill, dean of the Atlanta University School of Social Work and staffed by Dr. E. Aracelis Francis, CSWE project associate. During these meetings, the Task Force hammered out a beginning identification of relevant black content for integration into the social work education curriculum. The central concern of the work as recorded in the Task Force Report was

> that all those engaged in social work have a basic understanding of the history, lifestyles, survival mechanisms, and behavior of blacks that is an outgrowth of their particular experience as actors and reactors in an oppressive system. . . . Therefore, the focus was on how schools should move from token courses on black content to their inclusion in the core curriculum. (Francis, 1973, p. v)

The Task Force provided a context for the development of a perspective that influenced the shaping of the core curricula of the social work programs at both Atlanta University and Howard University. The work produced by the Task Force was also intended to provide guidelines for the inclusion of a black perspective in the core content of the predominately white schools of social work.

The process of change toward the incorporation of race-conscious content in educational programming undertaken by the two predominately black schools of social work differed in that the student activism at Howard University had spawned a change process that would impact the entire university relative to how it would define itself as a black university. The outcome of the process as envisioned by the Howard University faculty participants would be an agreed upon definition of the black perspective that would be adopted by all of the divisions and professional schools within the entire university. While the Atlanta University faculty participants, in contrast, the focus was only on the School of Social Work. The process of curriculum renewal was to be guided by the perspective that had emerged from the vision of the cohort of faculty that had conceptualized the autonomous social work model and the Afrocentric perspective.

THE BLACK PERSPECTIVE SPEARHEADED AT HOWARD UNIVERSITY

A study conducted by Howard University School of Social Work faculty, Drs. Ruby Gourdine and Anne Brown, examined the change process at Howard University resulting from the social activism of the civil rights years. This change process is described in detail in their book *Howard University School of Social Work in the 1970s, Social Action, Advocacy and Agents of Change.* (Gourdine & Brown, 2016) The book focused on the decade of the 1970s that was selected by Gourdine and Brown as being the bridge decade connecting the early history of institution building at the School of Social Work, under the leadership of the School's first dean, Inabel Burns Lindsay with the changes that came with the struggle for social justice in the 1960s. The significant contributions of Inabel Burns Lindsay to the development of the School in its earliest years are examined by the current dean of the School, Dr. Sandra Crewe and her Howard faculty colleagues in their article: *Inabel Burns Lindsay: A social worker, educator, and administrator uncompromising in the pursuit of social justice for all* (Crewe, et. al., 2008).

The decade of the 1970s saw the conceptualization at Howard University of what was designated as the *black perspective*, and it was envisioned that this perspective would undergird both the academic culture of the University and guide the process of curriculum renewal at the School of Social Work. The black perspective began to take shape at the Howard University School of Social Work under the deanship of Dr. Douglas Glasgow, who articulated it as a basis for mobilizing people.

> It indicates direction, and in bodies of philosophical view of life, provides a framework for interpreting events, and speaks to the issues of black people's continuity. In essence, it is an ethnocentric view that points the way for blacks to analyze conditions and determine the actions most appropriate from their own unique vantage point . . . it represents a positive ethnocentric emphasis that guides black people's striving for mobility. (Gourdine & Brown, 2016, p. 75)

A detailed overview of the black perspective and the six guiding anchoring principles that were developed during the study period of the Gourdine and Brown book continues to shape University life at Howard; and the explicit and implicit curriculum at the School of Social Work is presented in "Appendix 2: The Black Perspective: Our Guiding Philosophy" (Gourdine & Brown, 2016).

CURRICULUM RENEWAL AT THE ATLANTA UNIVERSITY SCHOOL OF SOCIAL WORK

At the School of Social Work at Atlanta University, as outlined by Adams (1981), the work produced by the Black Task Force contributed to the following guidelines for the reconceptualization of the curriculum:

1. A revised educational philosophical consisting of an autonomous social work practice, multimethod problem-solving skills, humanistic values, and the Afrocentric perspective as a universal framework for understanding oppressed people and the forces which influence their social functioning
2. An organized curriculum supporting two concentrations: clinical practice and policy, planning, and administration, and substantive areas specialization choices of Comprehensive Health, Family and Child Advocacy, and Institutional Development
3. A practicum sequential plan to be initiated in a first-semester Skills Laboratory under faculty direction; a second semester, six-month concurrent placement, and a second-year, six-month block placement, the latter to be focused increasingly in the Southeast, to reflect the School's commitment to influence human service delivery in its own geographic region
4. An expansion of the School's educational models to include the regular-day, two-year full-time program; an accelerated program (eleven months); a three-year part-time program; an off-campus degree program; and an international human services degree program
5. Continuing education training for personnel of the Georgia Department of Human Services, geared to understanding poverty and multicultural understanding (pp. 25–26).

At the time that the Atlanta University School of Social Work was in the process of re-envisioning its curriculum, the social work practice literature was seeing the emergence of a theoretical framework anchored in the systems perspective that supported a sharper explication of the generalist practice model. For example, in the 1970s, the Pincus and Minahan textbook, *Social Work Practice: Model and Method* (1973) became widely used among social work educators who were advancing an integrated approach to practice. While the casework method, which dominated the field, embraced the medical disease model that locates problems within the individual and takes attention away from the environment, an integrated perspective considers problems of the environment and the reciprocal transactional interactions between the individual and the multiple systems in their environments. Social workers adopting this model practice across a range of practice settings and are not confined to a singular role, but are prepared to move seamlessly between multiple interrelated and interchangeable roles that may include those of broker, educator, advocate, and therapist, each of which is selectively drawn upon as dictated by the situation of the client and the ongoing dynamic assessment conducted by the worker.

The integrated generalist model of social work practice was further articulated by Columbia University Professors Alex Gitterman and Carol Germain in the 1980 publication *The Life Model of Social Work Practice.* Using ecology as a metaphor for broad-based practice, these authors asserted that

> [f]or social work, ecology appears to be a more appropriate metaphor than the older, medical disease metaphor that arose out of the linear world view because social work has been more committed to both helping people and to promoting more humane environments. . . . The ecological perspective provides an adaptive, evolutionary view of human beings in constant interchange with all elements of their environments. Human beings change their physical and social environments and are changed by them through a process of continuous reciprocal adaptation. (Gitterman & Germain, 1980, p. 5)

THE ATLANTA UNIVERSITY AUTONOMOUS SOCIAL MODEL APPLIED IN PRACTICE

Owing to the scholarship and research of the faculty at the Atlanta University School of Social Work that was contributing to an expanded knowledge base for advancing a race-conscious approach to practice, the School at this time was also beginning to influence social work practice with blacks in the state of Georgia.

One example of this is found in the review of the School's on-site archival documents. Professor Jualynne Dodson—who was among the School's new professoriate who were conceptualizing a race-critical approach to practice—developed a training model for the application of an Afrocentric perspective into a model for child welfare practice in Georgia. The model was based on findings from a federally funded three-year research study undertaken by the faculty, entitled "Black Stylization and Implications for Social Welfare." The findings from the study served as the empirical basis for the design of a model child welfare training program that was implemented in Georgia with the leadership of Dr. Dodson, and published as *An Afrocentric Educational*

Manual: Toward a Non-deficit Perspective in Services to Families and Children (Dodson, 1983).

At the time of its implementation, the demographic composition of the Georgia public assistance caseload for the AFDC program was consistently becoming overwhelmingly comprised of minorities, according to statistical data presented in the Foreword to the Manual. Growing from 197,835 in 1970, with minorities comprising 78% of the caseload, by 1980, the population of minority recipients enrolled in the program comprised 82% of the caseload. Moreover, despite the overwhelming representation of minorities on the caseload, the racial composition of the staff was largely white (Johnson, 1983).

An assessment of the service delivery system in the state found what was described as a "deficiency" in the Department's understanding of the cultural dimensions of service delivery. The training program addressed this need. Dodson spoke to the purpose and need for the program in the Introduction to the Manual.

> Human service professionals are particularly charged with the role of providing social services to families and children in a way that recognizes and builds on their cultural strength. Unfortunately, however, social service professionals have not been active leaders and this regard.
>
> To employ cultural strengths requires both an analytical approach to culture as a human phenomenon and specific factual clarity about the cultural behaviors of clients. A knowledge of specific culture behaviors is the information base for determining which policies, strategies and skills support the cultural integrity of clients. Without this knowledge, the human service professions are destined to perpetuate this the existing deficit-oriented treatment an intervention approach to family and children services.
>
> This manual is one step towards solving this problem by bringing knowledge of the cultural behaviors of Afro-Americans to social service providers. The development of this manual had its roots in research begun several years ago with a project on the unique cultural behaviors of Afro- American children in Atlanta, Georgia. (Dodson, 1983, p. 3)

In commenting on the outcome of the program in the Foreword to the published document, Dr. Patricia Johnson, Director of the Georgia Department of Human Resources, wrote that while Dr. Dodson's workshop focused on African American culture and behaviors, the conceptual underpinnings of the model were felt to be appropriate for use with other cultural groups. Dr. Johnson also summarized the gains of the workshop with an authenticity that was admirable given the difficult nature of its content. She summarized the following as gains experienced by the trainees and trainers participating in the program:

--Staff members experienced the painful realization that they did not truly understand the psychological and/or social dynamic operative with the group to which they had been providing a range of services over various periods of time;

--Participation in the program forced trainees to examine longstanding personal values and attitudes towards minority clients. This self-examination involved white workers as well as the limited number of minority staff. Interactions with the training process brought to the forefront entrenched feelings of "low status" clients dealing with the "higher status" agency and its representatives; and

--For administration of the agency and those responsible for the content and the provision of training, the cultural workshops provided a framework for feedback relative to needed changes in program as change occurred with individual staff and in social work practice as a whole. (Johnson, 1983, Foreword)

The training program provides documentation of the School's fulfillment of the goal of providing continuing education and staff development programs for the Georgia Department of Human Resources. The extent of the distribution of the Dodson Training Manual could not be ascertained from the documents found among the School's on-site archives. However, the Manual was published by the University of Tennessee School of Social Work, Office of Continuing Education, under the auspices of the National Child Welfare Training Center. Therefore, it is plausible that the manual was disseminated among public-sector child- and family-serving agencies in the southern region of the country.

Archival documents on this period of the School's history, such as self-study reports or minutes of faculty meetings or those of the standing committees of the School, were not found among those reviewed in the School's on-site archives. Such documents could lend insights into the process of the faculty's conceptualization of the philosophical underpinnings of the autonomous social work model. At this juncture of the School's history, based on what can be plausibly inferred, the faculty at the time was embarking on a path that aspired to develop a theory for practice within the black community that would bridge the philosophical underpinnings of the educational programs of the early years of the school with new knowledge generated by the social activism of the Civil Rights movement, woven together by the School's unique brand of Afrocentric perspective and autonomous social work model of practice.

The Dodson Manual, along with Yabura's essay in the *Excerpt from the Proceedings of the 50th Anniversary of the Atlana University School of Social Work* (Sanders, 1970) are evidence of faculty efforts, at the midpoint of the School's history, to impact social work practice in the black community in Atlanta, and perhaps throughout the South. Faculty efforts were devoted to restoring the founders' emphasis on partnerships between academia and the practice community and linking research undertaken from the Afrocentric perspective that dispelled the conventional wisdom of the hegemony of white supremacy that continued to dominate the southern way of life in the state and in Atlanta.

The new cohort of faculty under the leadership of Dean Hill ambitiously set upon a radical path in striving to develop a theory for social work practice in the black community by drawing on lessons learned from the past. While progress had been made in achieving social justice for blacks, in large measure blacks continued to interact within the "hostile environment" that was the context of Foresster B. Washington's directorship of the School at the same time that race-critical courses had been gradually purged from the curriculum as a prerequisite for the School's maintaining its accreditation.

Speaking with the voice of radical change, Yabura articulated a new thrust for the School.

> We find AUSSW in the 1970s returning full circle to the mandate of the founders of our school. This mandate involves survival, restoration and redemption— three constant, recurring themes of the black experience. Having been forced to travel this full circle, we find ourselves once again having to "put it together." No more being forced to travel that circle to accredit our educational programs in the eyes of Europeans. . . . Now we have come full circle again to do what predecessors like Jesse Thomas, Forrester B. Washington, Frankie Adams, Whitney Young, and William S. Jackson knew in their efforts to be true—namely it is our collective mandate as a faculty, as a school, to work in the interest of African restoration, redemption, and survival. (Sanders, 1970, pp. 31–32)

Moreover, what emerged as educational strategies synthesized in the autonomous social work model prepared social workers for practice in a "hostile environment" while building on the new knowledge available from a growing body of empirical evidence that challenged the scientific racism that had shaped social work practice and service delivery in the black community for much of the 20th century.

The re-envisioning of the School's educational programs also drew on sociological theory that reflected the influence of W. E. B. Dubois and E. Franklin Frazier, thus strengthening the liberal arts perspective and a grounding of the curriculum in the broader framework of systems theory. Also harkening back to Washington's vision of being "More than a school—a promotional agency for social welfare" (Atlanta School of Social Work Bulletin, 1930–1931), the faculty endeavored to design course content that gave students the intellectual tools for understanding the political dimensions of the profession and of social policies as having the potential for creating the kind of society that made it possible for all individuals to reach their full potential.

THE UNIVERSAL APPLICABILITY OF THE
AFROCENTRIC PERSPECTIVE

The Afrocentric perspective as developed by the faculty in the 1970s was seen as having a universal applicability within the broader conceptualization of pluralism as captured in Martin Luther King's vision of the "beloved community," one shaped by agape love. Anchored in King's discipline of theology, agape was the highest form of love, embracing transformative powers and the path to building community, equity, and justice. This is the form of love adopted by the faculty who pioneered the autonomous social work model as the first pillar of the School's conceptualization of humanistic values. The humanistic value framework continues to shape the current educational philosophy and policies of the School as presented in the Student Handbooks.

Dr. Gourdine, who studied under faculty who were at the vanguard of re-envisioning the School's curriculum and the autonomous social work practice model, recalled that, when a student, C. Wright Mills book *The Power Elite* (1956/1981) was required reading in her course with Dr. Dodson. Dr. Gourdine continues to use the book in the social work courses she now teaches at Howard. Mills, a Columbia University professor, was a prolific writer, and his publications were a sharp critique of the power differentials in all American institutional structures. His intellectual legacy continues to be felt in schools of social work through faculty teaching from a critical perspective, as is the case with Dr. Gourdine, for whom Mills's publications have become staple reading for her students.

Mills introduced concepts that are widely used in the professional social work lexicon and that are drawn from his classical works, *The Power Elite* (Mills, 1956/1981) and *The Sociological Imagination* (Mills, 1959/2000). These concepts, such as "personal troubles and public issues" and "the personal is political," provide a broader lens through which to examine societal inequalities across all institutional structures and encourage critical thinking among students about the power differentials in American society that have implications for the manner in which they carry out practice with marginalized client populations, as well as for understanding the social control functions of the profession of social work.

NABSW EMERGES AS THE UMBRELLA PROFESSIONAL
MEMBERSHIP ORGANIZATION FOR BLACKS

By the decade of the 1970s, the NABSW had established chapter affiliates in major cities and was well on the way to becoming the acknowledged collective voice of the black social work professional community. The Association had convened its second annual conference in Washington, DC, in February 1970.

The conference was indeed well on the way to becoming the premier meeting place of black thought leaders for theory and policy development for social work practice in the black community and for practitioners who were the front-line workers in agency-based practice. The conference was reminiscent of the Atlanta University Studies conceived by Dubois as a means for bringing together black scholars from across the country to develop a systematic approach for conducting research that brought to light and found solutions to social problems impacting the black community.

The annual conference of the NABSW brought together stakeholders from academia, the practice community, government policy-makers and administrators, and the private and public sectors to focus on issues of relevance to African Americans. It differed, however, from the "talented tenth" model advanced by Dubois in not excluding members of the lay community from participation. The academic professional credential was not a requirement for membership in the Association or for the submission of articles for publication in *Black Caucus*, a journal developed under the auspices of the New York City chapter of the NABSW.

An article published in the May 1970 edition of *Social Casework* entitled "Implications of White Racism for Social Work Practice" (Shannon, 1970) was an indication of the growing willingness of mainstream professional social work journals to accept articles authored by blacks on topics of social work practice in the black community. In large measure, however, African American scholars continued to face challenges in preparing manuscripts written from the black perspective that met the editorial requirements of mainstream white publications.

Black Caucus was launched under the leadership of Cenie J. Williams, then executive director of the New York City chapter of the NABSW, as an inseparable part of the work of the Association. The journal was published semiannually by the Association's New York City chapter; its aim was to provide a creative library and journalistic outlet for its members and others involved with the black community on issues of significance to the field of social work and social services. According to the editorial commentary, it was to serve as an organ for positive change and enlightenment for professionals and laymen who were interested in social welfare. Articles accepted for publication included those submitted by social workers, psychologists, psychiatrists, and nonprofessional workers in allied fields, as well as from literature and the arts. The diversity of thought as stated by the editorial board gave insight into the social conditions, needs, or aspirations of members of the black community.

The editors also emphasized that that the journal did not seek to "please or placate but to educate." And, in that regard, it would not shy away from the consideration of provocative articles or those that challenged conventional wisdom in a reconceptualization of the definition of social problems impacting the black community, which the editors saw as the pathway to meaningful change (The Editors, *Black Caucus*, Editorial Statement, 1970). The journal experienced a setback with the death of Dr. Lloyd DeLaney, a psychologist and professor at Queens College and civil rights social activist who was among the journal's editors (New York Times, November 9, 1969).

NABSW POLICY STATEMENTS

Neither did the NABSW shrink from adopting policy positions that challenged mainstream thinking on matters related to social welfare policy's impact on the black community. One of the most controversial position statements of the Association was the September 1972 position statement on the trans-racial adoption of African American children. The introduction to the position statement read:

> The National Association of Black Social Workers has taken a vehement stand against the placement of black children in white homes for any reason. We affirm the inviolable position of black children in Black families where they belong physically, psychologically and culturally in order that they receive the total sense of themselves and develop a sound projection of their future. (NABSW, 1972)

The position statement rejected the notion that black families were not motivated to adopt black children and called upon agencies to develop alternative programs designed specifically for the recruitment of black adoptive families and the revision of racist policies that had successfully barred blacks from being considered suitable candidates as adoptive families.

The statement was interpreted by many child welfare professionals, both black and white, as the Association's advancing a position contrary to established best adoption and child welfare practice that called for the least restrictive setting for children in need of out of home care. It was assailed by some as an example of reverse racism that was not in the best interest of dependent black children. Nonetheless, the Association held firm to a policy position that has not been amended since the statement was released in September 1972. Retrospectively, although met with sharp criticism when it was published in 1972, the values explicit and implicit in the Association's position statement have been supported in findings from empirical research and are now embraced as best child welfare practice and codified in child welfare law.

In research, *Children of the Storm: Black Children and American Child Welfare*, authored by Andrew Billingsley and Jeanne M. Giovannoni, was the first empirical study that brought to light the historical discrimination experienced by black children in the nation's child welfare system (Billingsley & Giovannoni, 1972). Since that time there has been a preponderance of research studies documenting the unequal treatment of black children at virtually every point in child welfare decision-making (Courtney et al., 1996; Everett, Chipungu, & Leashore, 1991). The findings from these studies paved the way for legislative reforms based in a new understanding of the significance of culture and race in the planning of health and human services for diverse populations.

Cultural competency, or the recognition of the significance of race, ethnicity, and culture in the delivery of health and human services, and race-conscious policies that specifically target the historical inequities impacting African Americans are now firmly established in the field of child welfare. These contemporary priorities are reflected in the implicit values embedded throughout the NABSW position statement validating the cultural strengths and traditions of black families and encouraging policies and practices that acknowledge these traditions.

One example from the practice of a cultural and race-conscious program that builds on the strengths and values of the black community is the "One Church One Child Program." The program was initially implemented in Chicago, under the leadership of the city's clergy with a mission to find one family in every African American church to adopt one child. The program is now being successfully replicated in state and local social service jurisdictions nationally.

The success of the program can be attributed in part to its incorporating the findings of what is now a classical research study, *The Strengths of Black Families* (Hill, 1972), conducted by Robert Hill, then Research Director of the National Urban League. Hill challenged the "tangle of pathology" view of black families presented in the 1965 Moynihan Report. Following the path established by Dr. Andrew Billingsley's classic publication *Black Families in White America* (1968), in which he draws on historical data to effectively argue from a systems perspective that the achievements of blacks have been exceptional and enormous within the context of the pervasive systemic and institutional barriers they have had to surmount in American society. Subsequent published research conducted by Dr. Billingsley on the African American family and community has continually deconstructed the myths, misconceptions, and conventional wisdoms that have contributed to the perpetuation of a false narrative about the behavior of black Americans (Billingsley, 1992).

Hill's study contributed to the continued building of an empirically informed knowledge base about the black community first established by Billingsley. The study, which has become a staple on the reading lists of many faculty teaching in social work and other behavoiral health professional programs, identified cultural strengths characteristic of black families derived from an analysis of US Census data. Included among these are the adaptations necessary for survival and advancement in a hostile environment; a high achievement orientation, a strong work ethic, strong family and kinship bonds, a flexibility and adaptability of family roles, and a strong religious orientation. Findings from

Hill's study, although published nearly four decades ago, are of continuing relevance and have contributed to the new emphasis on culture and race that is emerging as essential in the medical and behavioral health professions.

IMPLICATIONS FOR CHILD WELFARE POLICY AND PRACTICE

With the new emphasis on cultural competency, the positive attributes of black families identified by Hill are also reflected in progressive child welfare legislative developments of the past decades that have increasingly favored strategies that kept families together and recognized the importance of extended kinship relationships in preserving family ties for black children. This new emphasis began with a fact-finding process that led to the Supreme Court decision rendered in *Miller v. Youakim* (44 U.S. 125, 99 S. Ct. 957 [1979]). The fact-finding process revealed a historic preference for the placement of children with kin and led to the subsequent Supreme Court ruling that removed distinctions between foster care payment rates for relative and non-relative caretakers. The Adoptions Assistance and Child Welfare Reform Act (P.L. 96-272), enacted under the Carter administration, as discussed is considered a landmark child welfare reform legislation in the validation of the rights and needs of children for permanent, stable attachments and continuity of family relationships, and it acknowledged the importance of kin. And while provisions around the termination of parental rights contributed to contentiousness among child welfare professionals, the early permanency intents of the Act were further strengthened by the 1997 Adoptions and Safe Families Act (PL105-89).

21ST CENTURY POLICY ADVANCEMENTS FOR CHILDREN AND FAMILIES

The Fostering Connections to Success and Increasing Adoptions Act (P.L. 110-351) was signed into law by President George W. Bush on October 7, 2008. The law corrects past practices that have been especially harmful to African American and Native American children. The expanded provisions and services to kinship caretakers are especially significant to African American children, who comprise the largest segment of children placed in the homes of relatives. The kinship guardianship provision in the law allows for legal guardianship of the child by a relative without terminating the parental rights of birth parents. This was not a possibility under prior child welfare reforms that required the termination of the rights of the birth parents in order for kin to assume guardianship, which contributed to the reluctance of a relative, often a grandparent, to assume formal guardianship of the child that required severing the parent–child relationship.

The Family First Prevention Services Act is the most recent legislation signed into law under the current administration on February 8, 2018, and this legislation continues to prioritize keeping families together. However, despite three decades of progressive reform legislation, the problems of the nation's troublesome child welfare system are far from solved. Similar to the crack cocaine epidemic of the 1980s that saw dramatic increases in the nation's foster care caseload, with the greatest increase in urban black communities, the increase in foster care between 2012 and 2016 is attributed to the opioid epidemic that is having as equally a devastating impact on rural white communities.

According to the Adoption and Foster Care Analysis and Reporting System (AFCARS), the federal agency that collects case-level data on state and tribal agencies providing Title IV-E services on all children who are in foster care and those who have been adopted with Title IV-E involvement, after a steady increase, the nation's foster care caseload is began to show some decline, falling from 441,000 at the end of fiscal year (FY) 2017 to approximately 437,300 at the end of FY 2018. There was a corresponding decrease in the number of children entering care in FY 2018, falling from 270,000 in FY 2017 to 263,000 in FY 2018 (Children's Bureau, Report #25, November, 8, 2018).

CHILD AND FAMILY WELL-BEING IN RURAL GEORGIA

Georgia is among the six states, including Alaska, Minnesota, Indiana, Montana, and New Hampshire, where the foster care caseload has more than doubled. Illustrating the devastating link between parental substance abuse and child well-being, Georgia's Division of Family and Children Services, the state agency responsible for overseeing foster care services, reported that of the 12,872 children who are in foster care in the state, substance abuse was a factor in 40% of the cases where children were removed from their homes. Moreover, the agency has had to roll back kinship care policy requiring that kin be considered as the first choice for placement of children in court ordered out of home placement of a child because of challenges in identifying relatives who themselves were not impacted by the devastating effects of the disease of chemical addictions.

Georgia is also among the states comprising the Greater Appalachia Region, follows the chain of the Appalachian Mountains from southern New York to northern Mississippi. The Region includes all of West Virginia and parts of Georgia, Alabama, Kentucky, Maryland, Mississippi, New York, North Carolina, Ohio, Pennsylvania, South Carolina, Tennessee, and Virginia.

Nearly half of the region is rural, contrasting with the largest of share of the nation's population that is urban.

J. D. Vance, in his memoirs of growing up in the region, *Hillbilly Elegy: A Memoir of a Family and Culture in Crisis* (Vance, 2016), offers a compelling sociological analysis woven together with the author's personal experiences. He poignantly described the devastating impact on a population of Americans that began with the loss of employment accompanying the gradual decline in the region's position as the manufacturing center of the country. Predictably, the interrelated effects of these transformative changes in the economic system led to an unconscionable rise in poverty rates and the creation of a community malaise that paved the way for rural white communities in the region to be riddled by drug addiction and the virtual collapse of institutional and social structures essential for supporting family and community stability.

These systemic changes impacting white rural Americans paralleled the trajectory of events occurring in urban black communities with the introduction of illegal drugs and the advent of crack cocaine. Children being raised by grandparents and relatives became common in biological families troubled by chemical addictions and problems of domestic violence, mental illness, homelessness, child abuse, and neglect that were the inevitable consequences of the crack cocaine epidemic of the 1980s and the first wave of the opioid crisis that began in the 1990s. Although the crack cocaine and opioid crises impacted individuals, families, and communities across the nation, the social consequences of these epidemics have had an especially devastating impact on urban black communities and rural white communities already suffering the effects of rising poverty rates that accompanied the loss of jobs in the manufacturing sector.

In response to the urgency and pervasiveness of substance abuse and opioid addiction, the US Surgeon General's Office has adopted an evidence-based public health approach that draws on the best available evidence from science and recognizes the interacting effects of the physical and psychosocial environments. Jerome Adams assumed the office of the Surgeon General on September 5, 2017, to become the 20th Surgeon General of the United States. As Surgeon General, Adams has shared his personal story about the impact of the disease on his own family and has been outspoken about his brother's struggle with the disease, a course that involved addiction and incarceration. The Office of the Surgeon General is tasked with providing the nation with the best available scientific evidence available about how to improve health and reduce the risk of illness and injury. The Office collaborated with SAMHSA to create the publication *Facing Addiction in America: The Surgeon General's Report on Alcohol, Drugs, and Health* (USDHHS, 2018). The publication provides a comprehensive overview and is an extensively referenced document on the crisis that is useful for behavioral health professionals and the general public.

FAMILY AND CHILD WELL-BEING IN URBAN ATLANTA

A report from the Annie E. Casey Foundation examined the implications of the intersection of poverty with race, place, and child and family well-being in the city of Atlanta in an examination of city's Neighborhood Planning Unit (NPU) system. The NPU system was established in 1974, under the mayoralty of Maynard Jackson, and divides the city into twenty-five NPUs, which are citizen advisory councils that make recommendations to the Mayor and City Council on zoning, land use, and other planning issues (Annie E. Casey Foundation, 1970/2015).

The report presents glaring differences in the conditions in which children lived in the city of Atlanta, based on race. As described in the report, the east-west Interstate 20 (I-20) is the dividing line that separates the well-resourced wealthy, majority-white communities in the northern section of the city from the majority-black communities in the south. African Americans were found to comprise approximately 80% of the population in the poorest NPUs, and a scant 20% of black children lived in communities with low poverty rates as compared to 94% of white children who lived in communities with low poverty rates.

The report underscores the reality of the intersection of poverty, race, and place with high-poverty areas concentrated in the predominantly black NPUs. Study findings indicate that more than 40% of families in neighborhoods with the highest percentage of black residents live below the federal poverty level for a family of four. Despite an urban renewal program, poverty in these neighborhoods has persisted, rooted in the city's history of racial segregation that continues to impact the access of blacks to community resources that are essential for supporting child well-being, including employment opportunities, affordable housing, access to child care, and well-functioning public school system (Annie E. Casey, 2015).

INITIATIVES OF THE SCHOOL OF SOCIAL WORK TARGETING CHILD AND FAMILY WELL-BEING

Space has been given to a discussion of mental health and child and family well-being because they are the fields of practice that are the focus of the School's two areas of concentration. As showcased on its website, the School is currently engaged in addressing the inequities highlighted in the findings of the Annie E. Casey study with programs undertaken by the Center for Children and Families. The Center is currently engaged in initiatives that target the city's West End and Vine City. Both are among the neighborhoods identified in the Casey Foundation report as having the highest percentage of black residents and the highest child poverty rates.

As reported in the *Proceedings* of the School's 90th Anniversary, the faculty established a Families and Children Research Center and reestablished the certification in school social work under the deanship of Dr. Vimala Pillari (Clark Atlanta University Celebrates, 2010). In its current reiteration as the Center for Children and Families (CCF) under the leadership of Dr. Eyitayo Onifade, the current director, it is envisioned that, with continued capacity-building, the Center will provide a structure for the faculty to carry out initiatives and funded research studies that address pressing social problems that compromise child and family well-being in underresourced and high-need black communities in the city. As described on the School's website, the activities of the Center are shaped by its mission

> [t]o improve the health and well-being of African-American children and families. CCF is guided by the Afrocentric perspective in providing direct practice, training, research, and policy commentaries to practitioners and stakeholders related to health, mental health, and community practice. (Clark Atlanta University Whitney M. Young School of Social Work, Center for Children and Families)

Looking back in time, the target communities for the current work of the Center were the same communities that were the focus on the work of the Neighborhood Union founded under the leadership of Eugenia Burns Hope. As discussed in Chapter 5, emerging from a concern about child and family well-being, Hope introduced the Neighborhood Union model that pioneered the practice of dividing the city into districts and zones as a manageable means for conducting community needs assessments to develop program and services to fill the gap left by policies of racial segregation that barred blacks from being served by white agencies at a time when services for black children were virtually nonexistent.

A BRIEF WORD ABOUT DOCTORAL SOCIAL WORK EDUCATION

Finally, a consequential and significant outcome of the synergy of the 1970s that was promoting changes in social work theory and practice within the black community was also the impetus that led to the development of doctoral level social work programs at the nation's two best known HBCUs-- Howard and Atlanta Universities. As the two Schools engaged in the re-examination of an educational philosophy shaping curriculum that emphasized education for practice in the black community, questions were concurrently raised around the need for a program of study beyond the master's degree to prepare a cohort of scholars to conduct research, publish, and teach in HBCU social work programs, who were also committed to the infusion and integration of a black perspective in the social work curriculum.

Practically, the doctoral program was also needed to address the shortage of doctoral level credentialed black professionals in the field of social welfare generally. The limited number of minority scholars whose lived experiences enhanced their ability to conduct research to improve services in minority communities coincided with concerns of the CSWE that led to the establishment of the Minority Fellowship Programs.

At the time when the schools were considering the need to establish doctoral degree programs, doctoral level education in social work was experiencing considerable growth. Kurzman (2015) in a review of the evolution of doctoral level social work programs reported that since the first doctoral programs were established at Bryn Mawr College and the University of Chicago in 1920, there were more than eighty recognized doctoral social work programs in the United States and Canada. Between 1965 and 1975, the years in which the social work faculties at Howard and Atlanta Universities were considering establishing doctoral programs, twenty new social work doctoral programs had been established (Kurzman, 2015).

Doctoral social work programs are not accredited by the CSWE. The Council and the NASW still consider the MSW to be the terminal degree for social work. The Group for the Advancement of Doctoral Education in Social Work (GADE), although not an accrediting body, the Group was founded in 1970 to promote excellence in doctoral education in social work through networking, information sharing and advocacy. It also disseminates guidelines to promote excellence in social work education programs awarding both the PhD and DSW degrees. (http://www.gadephd.org/)

Although not within the scope of concern of this volume, doctoral social work programs have their own unique histories, have themselves gone through a number of transformations, and currently face their own unique challenges (Anastas & Kuerbis, 2009; Kurzman, 2015). Some of these are related to the profession's historic identity problems and newer challenges related to social work's status as a profession or a science. Moreover, the return of the DSW has surfaced new debates within the profession related to what, if any, area of the social work curriculum can be claimed as the exclusive knowledge domain of either and which of the two degrees is of greater value, the PhD, which is aligned with science, or the DSW, aligned with practice.

The decision to establish a doctoral program in social work at Howard University School of Social Work emerged while the University was continuing to strengthen its position as a research university. This process was facilitated by a Ford Foundation grant to explore options for a research center to support doctoral programs within the University. The planning for the doctoral program was completed under the deanship of Jay Chunn and approved by the board of directors for implementation in April 1976. In announcing the program, the Board of Trustees asserted that the program would be the first Doctor of Social Work program offered in a predominantly black university "anywhere in the world" and that it was among only thirty such programs offered in the United States at the time. The program initially began as a DSW degree and shifted to the PhD in 1997, under the deanship of Dr. Richard England. Dr. Dorothy Pearson was appointed associated dean and served as the first chair of Howard's doctor of social work program (Gourdine & Brown, 2016, pp. 56–57).

The social work doctoral degree was established at Atlanta University in 1983, thus becoming the second doctoral program established in an HBCU. The program was founded during the tenure of Clarence Coleman, who served as dean from 1979 to 1984. In keeping with George Edmond Hayes's vision of partnering schools of social work with affiliate offices of the National Urban League to grow a leadership with competencies to serve the black community, the program, as conceived by Dean Coleman, was to continue the tradition of serving as a pipeline for preparing leadership for Urban League affiliates.

Today the tradition of conducting research established by DuBois in the Atlanta University Studies and Lugenia Burns Hope's community-based action research is carried forward in the objective of the School's doctoral program. A primary objective of the program is to increase the number of African American and other historically underrepresented groups preparing for careers in teaching, research, social policy analysis, human service management, and organizational development. According to information published in the program's Student Handbook, since introduced in 1983 as one of the School's degree-bearing programs, more than one hundred graduates are in positions of leadership in academia, policy-making governmental agencies, and private sector social work agencies (Clark Atlanta University Whitney M. Young, Jr. School of Social Work, PhD Program).

Based on information obtained from alumni participants in the focus group, a growing number of the School's PhD graduates are engaged in entrepreneurial private practices providing services to underserved populations in the city of Atlanta under contractual agreements with city and state governmental agencies.

As the School recommitted itself to the vision of its founders on the occasion of its mid-centenniain October 1970, it also learned of the tragic accidental drowning death of Dean Whitney M. Young on March 11, 1971, in Lagos, Nigeria. On behalf of the faculty, Dean Genevieve Hill wrote In Memoriam in the Excerpt of the 50th Anniversary Proceedings about former Dean Young:

> While these proceedings embrace the theme of "Crossing Over," which represents the midway and turning point for Atlanta University School of Social Work this theme has also become symbolic of Whitney's "Crossing Over." He represented

the quintessence of all traits, skills and knowledge that social work education promotes. He was able to bridge the disparity between social work theory and social action, for him "to think it was to do it." . . . Whitney was deeply involved in changing racist and oppressive conditions. He fought fiercely for all people's human dignity. The world has lost a warrior!

Whitney's far reaching impact on much of the world was thunderous. He died at his post, pursuing equality, justice, and unity for all black people. His last remarks to us in November indicated that he was marching for victory and unity. (Hill, 1970, p. iv)

As the School moved into the decades of the 1980s and '90s and closer to its Centennial year, it did so with a new branding that reconnected it to its founding mission and armed with the legacies of the iconic leadership of E. Franklin Frazier, Forrester B. Washington, and now Whitney M. Young, Jr.

REFERENCES

Adams, F. V. (1981). *The reflections of Florence Victoria Adams*. Atlanta: Shannon Press, in collaboration with the Atlanta University School of Social Work and the Alumni Association.

Alexander, L. (1972). Social work's Freudian deluge: Myth or reality? *Social Service Review, 46*(4), 517–538. http://www.jstor.org.proxy.library.nyu.edu/stable/30020732

Anastas, J. W., & Kuerbis, A. N. (2009). Doctoral education in social work: What we know and what we need to know. *Social Work, 54*(1), 71–81.

Annie E. Casey Foundation. (1970/2015). *Changing the odds: The Race for results in Atlanta*. New York: Association of Black Social Workers Journal. Black Caucus.

Association of Black Social Workers. (1970). Black Caucus, Editorial Statement. New York, New York, 2008 Madison Avenue.

Association of Social Work Boards (ASWB). (2018). Path to Licensure. https://www.aswb.org/educators/path/

Billingsley, A. (1968). *Black families in white America*. Englewood Cliffs, NJ: Prentice-Hall.

Billingsley, A. (1992). *Climbing Jacob's ladder: The enduring legacies of African-American families*. Simon and Schuster.

Billingsley, A., & Giovannoni, Jeanne, M. (1972). *Children of the storm: Black children and American child welfare*. New York: Harcourt, Brace, Jovanovich.

Carten, A. J. (2016). *Reflections on the American social welfare state: The collected papers of James R. Dumpson, PhD, 1930–1990*. Washington, DC: NASW Press.

Carten, A. J. (2006). African Americans and mental health. In J. Rosenfeld & S. Rosenfeld (Eds.), *Community mental health: Direction for the 21st century* (p. 125). New York: Routledge.

Cherry, A., Rothman, B., & Skolnik, L. (1989). Licensure as a dilemma for social work education: Findings of a national study. *Journal of Social Work Education, 25*(3), 268–275. http://www.jstor.org.proxy.library.nyu.edu/stable/23042600

Chestang, L. W. (1972). *Character development in a hostile environment*. Chicago: University of Chicago Press.

Children's Bureau, An Office of the Administration for Children and Families. AFCARS Report #5 Published November 8,2018. https://www.acf.hhs.gov/cb/resource/afcars-report-25

Christensen, N. (2011, March 31). *Maynard Jackson Sr. (1894–1953)*. https://www.blackpast.org/african-american-history/jackson-reverend-maynard-sr-1898-1953/

Clark Atlanta University Celebrates. (2010). Sustaining our roots, building our future. The Whitney M. Young, Jr. School of Social Work, 90th Anniversary, October 8–9, 2010.

Clark Atlanta University Whitney M. Young, Jr. School of Social Work, PhD Program. https://www.cau.edu/school-of-social-work/graduate-programs/phd-program/index.html

Clark Atlanta University Whitney M. Young, Jr. School of Social Work, Center for Children and Families. https://www.cau.edu/school-of-social-work/center-children-families.html

Courtney, M., Barth, R. P., Berrick, J. D., Brooks, D., Needell, B., & Park, L. (1996). Race and child welfare services: Past research and future directions. *Child Welfare, 75*(2), 99–137.

Crewe, S. E., Brown, A. W., & Gourdine, R. M. (2008). Inabel Burns Lindsay: A social worker, educator, and administrator uncompromising in the pursuit of social justice for all. *Affilia, 23*(4), 363–377. https://doi.org/10.1177/0886109908323974

Daley, W., & McLane, S. P. (1985). Mandated benefits for a new provider class: LICSW's. *Clinical Social Work Journal, 13*(4), 367–376. https://apps.who.int/iris/bitstream/handle/10665/112828/9789241506809_eng.pdf;jsessionid=E100E20661A12652786D042BE9775DBC?sequence=1

Dodson, J. E. (1983). *An Afrocentric educational manual: Toward a non-deficit perspective in services to children and families.* The Atlanta University School of Social Work. Child Welfare Center Training Program, University of Michigan School of Social Work. University of Tennessee School of Social Work Office of Continuing Education. Found in onsite archives, CAU Whitney M. Young, Jr. School of Social Work.

Dowling, M., & Dumpson, J. R. (1980). Separating income maintenance and social services: Can we assure accountability? *Journal of Socio-Economic Studies, 5*(1), 39–52.

Everett, J., Chipungu, S. S., & Leashore, B. R. (1991). *Child welfare: An Africentric perspective.* Brunswick, NJ: Rutgers University Press.

Francis, E. A. (Ed). (1973). *Council on Social Work Education Black Task Force Report: Suggested guidelines for the integration of black content into the social work curriculum.* New York: CSWE.

Gitterman, A., & Germain, C. B. (1980). *The life model of social work practice.* New York: Columbia University Press.

Gourdine, R. M., & Brown, A. W. (2016). *Howard University School of Social Work in the 1970s: Social action, advocacy, and agents of change.* Baltimore, MD: Black Classic Press.

Gourdine, R. M. (2019). Personal communications, and documents shared as School of student experiences over her period of enrollment in the 1970s. (September, 22, 2020; November 6, 11,12, 20, 2019).

Grem, D. (2018). Henry W. Grady (1850–1889). New Georgia Encyclopedia. http://georgiaencyclopedia.org

Harrington, M. (1962). *The other America: Poverty in the United States.* New York: Penguin Books.

Headley, B. D. (1998). *The Atlanta youth murders and the politics of race.* Carbondale: Southern Illinois University Press.

Health Resources and Services Administration (HRSA). Ryan White HIV/AIDS legislation. https://hab.hrsa.gov/about-ryan-white-hivaids-program/ryan-white-hivaids-program-legislation

Hill, G. (1970). In memoriam to Whitney M. Young Jr. (1921–1971). In C. L. Sanders (Ed.), *Proceedings 50th Anniversary at the Atlanta University School of Social Work,* November 12–14, 1970.

Hill, R. B. (1972). *The strengths of black families.* New York: Emerson Hall.

Hu, T., Snowden, L. R., Jerrell, J. M., & Nguyen. T. D. (1991). Ethnic populations in public mental health: Service choices and level of use. *American Journal of Public Health, 18*(11), 1429–1434.

Johnson, L. P. (1983). Foreword. In J. E. Dodson (Ed.), *An Afrocentric educational manual: Toward a non-deficit perspective in services to children and families.*

Katz, M. (1989*). The undeserving poor: From the war on poverty to the war on welfare.* New York: Random House.

King, M. L. (1967). *Beyond Viet Nam.* Stanford, The Martin Luther King, Jr. Research and Education Institute. Martin Luther King, Jr. Political and Social Views Nonviolence Viet Namese Conflict, 1961–1975.

Kurzman, P. A. (2015). The Evolution of Doctoral Social Work Education. *Journal of Teaching in Social Work, 35*(1–2), 1–13. doi:10.1080/08841233.2015.1007832

Land, H. (1987). The effects of licensure on student motivation and career choice. *Social Work, 32*(1), 75–77. http://www.jstor.org/stable/23713620

Lesher, S. (1971). *Jackson State: A year after.* New York Times Archives. https://www.nytimes.com/1971/03/21/archives/article-23-no-title-jackson-state-a-year-after-we-resent-everyone.html

McLanahan, S. (1985). Family structure and the reproduction of poverty. *American Journal of Sociology, 90*(4), 873–901.

Miller v. Youakim, 440 US 125 (1979).

Mills, C. W. (1956/1981). *The power elite.* New York: Oxford University Press.

Mills, C. W. (2000). *The sociological imagination.* Oxford University Press.

Morton, R. Personal communications, September 10, 19, 2019.

Moynihan, D., P. (1965). *The Negro family: The case for national action.* Washington, DC: US Department of Labor, Office of Policy Planning and Research.

Murray, C. (1984). *Losing ground: American social policy, 1950–1980.* New York: Basic Books.

Murray, C., & Herrnstein, R. J. (1994). *The bell curve: Intelligence and class structure in American life.* New York: Free Press.

National Association of Black Social Workers (NABSW). (1972). Position Statements. Trans-racial adoption position statement. https://cdn.ymaws.com/www.nabsw.org/resource/collection/E1582D77-E4CD-4104-996A-D42D08F9CA7D/NABSW_Trans-Racial_Adoption

Neighbors, H. W., Bashshur, R., Price, R., Selilg, S., Donabedian, A., & Shannon. G. (1992). Ethnic minority mental health service delivery: A review of the literature. *Research in Community and Mental Health, 7*(1), 55–71.

Neighbors, H. W., Jackson, J. S., Campbell, L., Williams, D. (1989). The influence of racial factors on psychiatric diagnosis: A review and suggestions for research. *Community Mental Health Journal, 25*(4), 301–311.

New York Times. (1972). Transcript of Nixon's statement on school busing. March 17, 1972. https://www.nytimes.com/1972/03/17/archives/transcript-of-nixons-statement-on-school-busing.html

Newman, H. K. (2018). Olympic Games in 1996. New Georgia Encyclopedia. http://georgiaencyclopedia.org

New York Times. (November 9, 1969). DR. LLOYD DELANY OF SEEK PROGRAM; Psychologist, Who Led Fight for Integration, Dies at 46. https://www.nytimes.com/1969/11/09/archives/dr-lloyd-delany-of-seek-program-psychologist-who-led-fight-for.html

Pincus, A., & Minahan, A. (1973). *Social work practice: Model and method.* Itasca, IL: FE Peacock Publishers.

Pinderhughes, E. B. (1979). Teaching empathy in cross-cultural social work. *Social Work,* 24(4), 312–316.

Reid, T. R. (1990). Atlanta is awarded '96 Summer Olympics. September 19, 1990. *Washington Post.*

Rice, B. R. (2019). Maynard Jackson (1938–2003). New Georgia Encyclopedia. http://georgiaencyclopedia.org

Sanders, C. L. (Ed.). (1970). The legacy of Forrester B. Washington, black social work educator and nation builder. In C. L. Sanders (Ed.), *Proceedings 50th Anniversary at the Atlanta University School of Social Work,* November 12–14, 1970.

Shannon, B. E. (1970). Implications of white racism for social work practice. *Social Casework,* 51(5), 270–276.

Simpson, W. (1990). Review: Lynch Street: The May 1970 Slayings at Jackson State College. *Journal of Southern History,* 56(1), 159–160. doi:10.2307/2210708

Snowden, L. R. (2001). Barriers to effective mental health services for African Americans. *Mental Health Services Research,* 3(4), 181–187.

Social Security Act, P. L. 74-271 (1935).

Bryant-Solomon, B. (1976). *Black empowerment. Social Work in Oppressed Communities.* New York, NY: Columbia University Press.

Specht, H., & Courtney, M. E. (1995). *Unfaithful angels: How social work has abandoned its mission.* New York: The Free Press.

Spofford, T. (1988). *Lynch Street: The May 1970 slayings at Jackson state college.* Kent, OH: Kent State Press.

Stern, M. J., & Axinn, J. (2018). *Social welfare: The history of American response to need* (9th ed.). London: Pearson.

Substance Abuse and Mental Health Services Administration (SAMHSA). (2017). *Behavioral health barometer: Georgia, Volume 4: Indicators as measured through the 2015 National Survey on Drug Use and Health, the National Survey of Substance Abuse Treatment Services, and the Uniform Reporting System.* HHS Publication No. SMA–17–Baro–16–States–GA. Rockville, MD: Substance Abuse and Mental Health Services Administration.

THE TRIPARTITE MISSION OF THE ACADEMY

Trattner, W. I. (1999). *From poor law to welfare state* (6th ed.). New York: The Free Press.

US Department of Health and Human Services (USDHHS). (1999). *Mental health: A report to the Surgeon General.* Rockville, MD: Author.

US Department of Health and Human Services (USDHHS). (2001). *Mental Health: Culture, race, and ethnicity: A supplement to Mental Health: A Report of the Surgeon General.* Office of the Surgeon General (US); Center for Mental Health Services (US); National Institute of Mental Health (US). Rockville, MD: Substance Abuse and Mental Health Services Administration.

US Department of Health and Human Services (USDHHS), Office of the Surgeon General. (2018). *Facing addiction in America: The Surgeon General's spotlight on opioids*. Washington, DC: HHS.

Vance, J. D. (2016). *Hillbilly elegy: A memoir of a family and culture in crisis*. London: William Collins.

Voting Rights Act, 42 U.S.C. § 1973 (1965).

World Population Review. (2019). Atlanta Population. (2019-10-29). http://worldpopulationreview.com/us-cities/atlanta/)

Yabura, L. (1970). The legacy of Forrester B. Washington, black social work educator and nation builder. In C. L. Sanders (Ed.), *Proceedings 50th Anniversary at the Atlanta University School of Social Work*, November 12–14, 1970.

CHAPTER 13
Enduring Legacy of Whitney M. Young Jr.

The World Has Lost a Warrior!

—Genevieve Hill (1971)

Whitney Moore Young, Jr. was appointed dean of the School of Social Work in 1954. He retired from the deanship in 1961 to become the executive director of the National Urban League (NUL). Over his deanship, Young had maintained the School's financial viability and its image of academic excellence. He had accomplished this during a challenging period spanning the early years of desegregation that posed new challenges to the School as it was now called upon to compete with the well-resourced social work programs in the predominately white universities. Moreover, with desegregation, the School no longer had a monopoly on attracting the best and brightest minds of the African American community.

In the face of these challenges, Young did indeed make notable contributions to restoring the reputation of the School, which had been declining over the last years of Washington's directorship owing to changes that came with desegregation. His accomplishments in academia, however, were to be far overshadowed by his achievements as a civil rights activist at the national and international levels. Few would disagree that Young's contributions as a civil rights leader far exceeded those to academia and social work education. On the other hand, most would agree that it was his social work skills, understanding of human behavior, and respect for differences that facilitated his ability to bridge the divide between disempowered black communities and the power elite of white America. As Dennis C. Dickerson wrote in his 1998 biography *Militant Mediator: Whitney M. Young, Jr.*, these attributes were the

Find a Way or Make One. Alma J. Carten, Oxford University Press (2021). © Oxford University Press.
DOI: 10.1093/oso/9780197518465.001.0001.

foundation for Young's unique ability to blend interracial mediation with direct protest that catapulted him onto the international stage as a civil rights leader in the struggle for human rights after stepping down from the deanship of the Atlanta University School of Social Work.

Young's appointment to the deanship provided an opportunity for him to nurture and expand his interests in civil rights in the city of Atlanta, an interest that he soon took to the global stage. The next chapter of his career as leader in the Civil Rights movement was solidified when he left academia to head the NUL in 1961. His growing presence on the international stage is illustrated by his 1966 participation in an initiative sponsored by *Time* magazine that sent a group of influential US businessmen to Eastern Europe tasked with fostering communications between American business leaders and individuals who yielded political and economic power in other parts of the world. Young was the only member of the group who was not a CEO of a Fortune 500 Company (Weiss, 1989). At the time of his accidental death, he was on a similar mission in Lagos, Nigeria, as a participant in a conference sponsored by the Ford Foundation to increase understanding between Africans and Americans (Charlton, 1971; Weiss, 1989).

A LIFE INTERRUPTED

Young's rise to the status of a civil rights leader of international prominence is reflected in the national, indeed, the world response to the news of his accidental downing while swimming at a beach near Lagos, Nigeria, on March 11, 1971. His untimely death at the age of forty-nine shocked the nation and the world. In an unprecedented presidential action, Richard Nixon ordered an Air Force plane to Nigeria to bring Young's remains home.

At the Young home in New Rochelle, New York, as described by Young's biographer Nancy Weiss (1989), the news of her husband's death was met with disbelief and denial by his wife Margaret, who was still mourning the death of her father. Lauren, the younger of the couple's two daughters, a high school student, was stymied by being picked up from school, not knowing that she was being driven home to prevent her learning on her car radio of her father's death while driving herself home, as was her custom. Marcia, the Young's eldest daughter, was living in Dakar, a country in West Africa, with her husband, Robert Boles, who was completing a Guggenheim Fellowship, and the couple's ten-month-old son Mark. In a personal interview in which she always affectionately referred to Young as "daddy" in discussing the events surrounding her father's death, Marcia recalled the offer made by King Hassan II of Morocco to send his plane to Dakar to pick up her family in order for her to accompany her father's remains back to the United States. But in the end it was arranged for the Air Force plane dispatched by President Nixon to stop in Dakar to fetch the family. Marcia and Young's oldest sister Arnita Boswell spent most of the trip beside Young's flag-draped coffin. The two women, along with an entourage of civil rights and business leaders who were among the attendees at the Lagos conference, were on board as the plane, piloted by General Daniel "Chappie" James Jr., the highest ranking black man in the Air Force, left Lagos and landed at New York's LaGuardia Airport, where it was met by Mayor John Lindsay and a group of dignitaries.

The last rites of the civil rights leader, were in keeping with the American custom of grandeur in honoring the greatest and most revered of the nation's fallen heroes. Services were held for Young at three stops along the route to his final resting place, where he was buried next to his mother in the family plot in the Greenwood cemetery in Lexington, Kentucky. At the Lagos service before Young's remains left Nigeria, a young Reverend Jessie Jackson gave the principal eulogy for attendees of the conference that had been convened on Afro-American Affairs. Expressing his deep admiration, Jackson referred to Young as the "father figure of the Civil Rights movement" and ended the service with the group holding hands and singing the civil rights anthem "We Shall Overcome."

In New York City, Young lay in state in the majesty of the historic Riverside Church overlooking the Hudson River, where thousands came to pay their respects and view his remains. As always, the NUL symbol of equality button (=) was in the lapel of Young's suit. Included among his honorary pallbearers were former President Lyndon B. Johnson; Roy Wilkins, executive director of the NAACP; Henry Ford, II; playwright Amiri Baraka; McGeorge Bundy, president of the Ford Foundation; Ramsey Clark, former US Attorney General; Dr. George Wiley, director of the National Welfare Rights Organization; and Vernon Jordan, who later succeeded Young as executive of the NUL (Johnson, 1971a; Weiss, 1989).

Among the thousands of individuals in the procession of mourners were members of the US Congress, government officials, dignitaries, civil rights leaders, and Urban League board members and staff. A large share of the mourners were ordinary Americans from all walks of life, some of whom were simply among the curious who did not know Young and others whose lives had been personally impacted by his unswerving and relentless pursuit of social justice for all Americans. In leaving New York City, the cortege drove through Harlem, where it was met with an outpouring of people who came to pay their respects. On the final stage of his journey, Young's return to Lexington, Kentucky, the cortege was met with a similar outpouring of people.

President Richard Nixon and First Lady Patricia Nixon led a White House delegation of twenty-four Washington officials who were present for the brief grave-side services held at Greenwood Cemetery on March 17, 1971. Whitney Moore Young Sr., Young's father, whom he had referred to as his most significant role model for living a purpose-driven life, was among the Young family mourners led by Young's widow Margaret and his two daughters Marcia and Lauren. Supreme Court Justice Thurgood Marshall was among the officials present as President Nixon gave the eulogy that was broadcast live on radio and television (Johnson, 1971b).

Nixon and Young were of significantly different minds on matters of policy that impacted the black community. With little support from blacks, Nixon's motivation to give the eulogy at Young's service was undoubtedly to gain political capital within the black community. Nonetheless, his eulogy reflected a genuine understanding of Young's character, as reflected in the following excerpts from the president's eulogy that began with . . .

> Mrs. Young, friends of Whitney Young:
>
> It is customary on such an occasion for the one who has the honor to deliver the eulogy to say that we are gathered here to pay our last respects to the deceased. I do not say that today. I say, rather, that today a grateful Nation will pay its respect to Whitney Young by continuing the work for which he dedicated his entire life.

Young's genius, as the president remarked was his knowing

> how to accomplish what other people were merely for. He was a very complex man, and he understood the complexities of the society in which he lived and the goals which he sought to achieve. He was not a patient man, but he understood the uses of patience.
>
> And he was not a moderate man in terms of his goals, but he knew the uses of moderation in achieving those goals.
>
> All of us who have heard him speak recognize him as one of the most eloquent speakers of our time, and, yet, Whitney Young will be remembered as a doer, not a talker.
>
> What monument do we build to him? He leaves his own monument, not one, but thousands, thousands of men and women in his own race who have a chance, an equal chance, that they otherwise might never have had except for what he did; and thousands of others not of his own race who have an understanding in their hearts which they would not have had except for what he taught. (Nixon, March 17, 1971)

As a lingering remnant of Kentucky's segregated past, Greenwood Cemetery, Young's final resting place, had separate sections for blacks and whites. At the time of Young's death legal segregation in the United States had been outlawed. And while a few blacks had been buried in the white section, no applications had been made by whites for burial on the side of the cemetery designated for blacks (Weiss, 1989).

These informal practices reflected the indelible mark of racism on American society that Young had devoted his entire life attempting to eradicate. The nation had made progress on race relations, with Young having made significant contributions to that progress. However, the hope he had expressed in one of his public speeches to see the end of the need for the Urban League over his lifetime had yet to be realized. His life, that had begun in Kentucky, had been brought full circle as he returned to his final resting place, but the work of achieving a more perfect union was far from done.

THE EARLY YEARS

The life of Whitney Moore Jr. began on July 31, 1921, in Lincoln Ridge, Kentucky. He was born into the protected environment of campus life at the Lincoln Institute, a boarding school for blacks founded by whites who adopted Booker T. Washington's incrementalistic approach and emphasis on vocational education for blacks. At the same time of the founding and fledging years of a school for the training of "colored" social workers amid the pervasive racism in the state of Georgia and city of Atlanta. Young was spending his early childhood and youth growing up on a campus that sheltered him and his two older sisters, Arnita and Eleanor, from the full impact of racism that was present in the surrounding village of Lincoln Ridge and the state of Kentucky.

Considered one of the border states along with Delaware, Maryland, and Missouri, that by mid-Civil War, included West Virginia, the economy in the early history of Kentucky was built around the cultivation of tobacco. And while the state's economy was dependent on an enslaved and servile labor force, the system of enslavement was not as integral to the economy as was the case in Georgia and other states in the Deep South. Moreover, with abolitionists being a majority in the state when the Civil War erupted, Kentucky sided with the North and remained in the Union. This ambiguous history on matters of race was reflected in the societal environment in which Young spent his childhood and young adult years. The ambiguity of the larger environment no doubt influenced Young's ability to maintain a persona that was nonthreatening as he interacted with whites while he simultaneously and forcefully pushed for the civil rights of blacks.

Although racism was not as pervasive in Kentucky as it was in the Deep South, as was the case in all of the other southern states, signs for "colored" and "whites" separated the races in all public places. Young felt the psychological impact of the insidious nature of white racism at the young age of five, a critical developmental stage for children in the formation of a positive sense of self and racial identity.

Young's first encounter with white racism involved an experience in which he was angrily questioned by an usher after innocently wandering into the lobby of the segregated theater. He was subsequently rescued by his parents, hurried out, and taken up to sit it the balcony, called the "crow's nest," which was the section of the theater reserved for blacks. Although confusing and hurtful for a five-year-old, Young later observed that the experience and the manner in which his parents had intervened he understood later to be lessons for all black children to learn that are critical life survival skills of "not talking back" and "staying in your place." For Young, these lessons of deference taught by his parents and necessary for his survival were tempered by the companion messages of pragmatism that his father taught to his son and to all of the students at Lincoln Ridge, "to accept the unpleasant and cope with it instead of running away from it" (Weiss, 1989, p. 10), and those role-modeled by his mother of open defiance to the Jim Crowism that defined black and white relations in the environment in which he grew up.

Secured by a strong attachment to both of his parents, molded in Young a sense of self-efficacy that enabled him to transverse the very different worlds of black and white life to become a successful and self-actualized adult. Maslow's hierarchy of human needs and Kohlberg's theory of the stages of moral development are commonly used by faculty teaching the human behavior in the social environment curriculum sequence in social work programs. Concepts from these theoretical frameworks are useful for understanding Young's high levels of achievement despite the racism of his environment and how, as an adult, he could achieve a level of moral development that motivated him to devote his life to securing the greater social good of equity and justice for all members of American society and eventually for the world community.

FAMILY LIFE

Young was the only son of parents Whitney M. Young Sr. and Laura Ray Young. Together they served as a buffer between Young and his sisters Eleanor and Arnita and the racism in the village of Lincoln Ridge that lay beyond the protective confines of campus life. Both of Young's parents were themselves exceptional individuals who guided their children through the hypocrisy of the white world with the expectation that much was expected of them in contributing to the betterment of the black community.

Young's father had progressed up the career ladder at Lincoln Institute, a historically black college initially founded and run by whites, from janitor to teacher and to principal. The elder Young is credited with saving the School with what he called a "Faith Plan" to keep it open when the white Trustees made the decision to close the School at a time of declining student enrolment and concurrent financial downturn. The Plan involved the elder Young's aggressive outreach and solicitation of donations to restore the financial viability of the School. Young's aptly named Faith Plan in the end benefitted from the fortuitous death of a benefactor who bequeathed a $10,000 gift to the School, the amount needed to pay off debts and remain open.

During the administrative watch of the senior Young, the school transitioned from the exclusive focus on industrial education embraced by Booker T. Washington. While under the control of the white Board of Trustees, the School was tethered to a curriculum that offered only industrial education that would keep blacks encapsulated in psychological and material servitude. Young, when principal of the School, devised a strategy for pushing back against the Trustee's policy of providing only industrial education that at the same time did not alienate whites and pose the risk of losing their much needed funding support.

To offset potential conflict with the board, Young's orchestrated what in essence was a "shadow curriculum" in which, during the times of the on-site visits of Trustees, the students were dutifully engaged in classrooms or in the fields learning domestic or agriculture skills or those essential to employment in the vocations or as domestic servants. After the departure of the Trustees the student resumed their usual studies in the classics and liberal arts. With desegregation following the 1954 Supreme Court decision in *Brown v. Board of Education*, the senior Young faced similar challenges in maintain the financial viability of the School as his son faced as dean of the Atlanta University School of Social Work.

The elder Young's own background modeled a valuing of education, a value that was instilled in his children. He had earned the bachelor's degree in education by taking evening course at the Louisville Municipal College for Negroes, and in 1944 was awarded the MA degree from Fisk University. An outstanding and prominent educator in his own right, in 1955, the elder Young was awarded the honorary Doctor of Education degree by Monrovia College, a missionary school in Liberia run by the African Methodist Episcopal Church. (Dickerson, 1998; see also Lincoln Foundation http://lincolnfdn.org/dr-whitney-m-young-sr/).

Young's mother, similar to Lugenia Burns Hope who served as matron at Morehouse, functioned in the role of matriarch of campus life and oversaw the discipline and rearing of the Young children. She opened the family home to students and faculty at Lincoln Institute, to whom she became known as "Mother dear." Unlike her husband, Laura Ray Young's background was one of privilege that instilled in her a sense of entitlement and self-efficacy. After beginning campus life with her husband amid the restrictions of segregation, she did not tolerate being called by her first name, ignored signs designating areas as "colored" or "white," and refused to follow the custom that forbid blacks from trying on articles of clothing before purchasing them. Despite—or perhaps because of—her manner of personal deportment combined with her status as matriarch of campus life at Lincoln Institute she was well respected by both blacks and whites, and this respect earned her the appointment as postmistress for the community.

INFLUENCED BY NATURE AND NURTURE

As described by his biographers, Young's personality and character were shaped by the pragmatism taught by his father of using creative strategies to overcome barriers and imbued with the defiance and humanitarianism role-modeled by his mother (Dickerson, 1998; Weiss, 1989). Together these parental influences molded a formidable character within the context of virulent racism of the larger environment. Whether by nurture, nature, or the interacting effects of both, Young's personal attributes and moral grounding would serve him well and distinguish him in the roles of "power broker" and "militant mediator" in both the corporate sector and the Civil Rights movement.

Campus life at the Lincoln Institute allowed the Young children to enjoy privileges that were shared by their peers, who were the children of faculty members both black and white. They were also exposed to the members of the "black elite" and to iconic figures such as W. E. B. Dubois and Mary McLeod Bethune who were frequent visitors to the campus. Their playmates were the children of privilege whose parents were members of the faculty or among the black elite of the times.

The 444-acre campus served as a private playground for the Young children and their friends, making it possible for them to avoid the potentially psychologically crippling effects of segregation, with signs of "colored" and "white" that stood as silent reinforces of messages of "less than" that shaped all aspects of black life and was implanted in the impressionable psyche of children from the earliest years of their lives. The Young children and their friends mingled with students enrolled at Lincoln Institute, and they were part of many campus activities, including commencement exercises and extracurricular social and religious events.

Theses existential benefits enjoyed by Young, his siblings, and friends are replicated on the campuses of historically black colleges and universities (HBCUs) today, providing environments where young adults are afforded the blanket of protection that supports positive self and racial identities that will serve them well in the American culture that continues to grapple with undoing the insidious effects of structural and institutional racism.

After completing primary education in the neighboring segregated elementary school, Young enrolled in the high School at Lincoln Institute at the age of twelve, at a time when the country was feeling the full effects of the Depression in 1933. At the time of Young's enrollment, the School was run by whites who were wedded to Washington's accommodationist philosophy introduced in his Atlanta Compromise speech. And by the time of his graduation in 1937, Young's father was the principal and the School was transforming in terms of its educational philosophy. The faculty was now all black and a changed culture began to predominate that resembled that of an extended family in which faculty established strong mentoring relationships with their students. Similar to Atlanta University in the early and middle years of its history, the environment at Lincoln was highly structured and regulated. There were numerous rules and regulations that included what today are considered socially constructed gender roles, and required times that set aside for study and religious observation. Over time these rules became less restrictive as they gradually became co-mingled with the informal forms of extracurricular activities developed by the students themselves (Weiss, 1989).

Young stood out at Lincoln in athletics, scholarship, extracurricular activities, and social life. He graduated in 1937 as the class valedictorian at the age of fifteen. These accomplishments were met with some consternation by his father who worried that his young age and selection as class valedictorian would raise suspicions that his son had benefitted from his father being the School principal. However, according to the prevailing view of the faculty, this was not the case, and the honors were indeed merited by Young's outstanding performance and engaging personal attributes (Weiss, 1989).

KENTUCKY STATE COLLEGE

Young continued his academic studies in 1941, as a student at Kentucky State College for Negroes. It was a familiar and comfortable academic setting, being very similar to the academic culture of Lincoln Institute. Young had enrolled in Kentucky State with the intention of earning the bachelor of science degree with a view toward attending medical school at either Meharry Medical College or Howard University after graduation.

Young's plans to pursue a career in medicine at either Howard or Meharry were not surprising. Both institutions were part of the professional programs opened in the HBCUs to provide access to medical education for blacks in an era of racial segregation. The medical school at Howard University was founded in 1868, soon after the end of the Civil War, and continues to carry on its founding mission with an emphasis on preparing students to provide healthcare in medically underserved communities. Meharry Medical College was founded as the Medical Department of the Central Tennessee College in 1876. With Howard University located in Washington, DC, Meharry is distinguished as being the first medical school established for blacks in the South. Both programs are distinguished by being the only two black medical programs favorably reviewed by the Flexner Report (Flexner, 1910).

THE FLEXNER REPORT AND CLOSING OF BLACK
MEDICAL SCHOOLS

An accepted expert on graduate school education, Abraham Flexner, who had decreed that social work was not a profession in the infamous Flexner Speech given at the 1915 Social Welfare conference, had also been obtained by the Carnegie Foundation to examine medical education in the United States and Canada. The Report made sweeping recommendations for medical schools to establish higher standards for admission and graduation and called for the closing or merging of what Flexner concluded was an excessive number of medical programs at the time. Howard and Meharry were the only two programs to survive the recommendations made in the Flexner Report that resulted in the closing of all of the approximate fourteen medical programs that had been established in the HBCUs.

That being said, and not to diminish the achievement of the medical schools at Howard and Meharry, the medical profession was not immune from the empirically flawed assumptions of the pseudoscience of scientific racism that justified racism and the classification of blacks as an inferior race. The recommendations set forth in the Flexner Report were tainted by the racist ideology of the period, which the author of the Report embraced, and disproportionately impacted the medical programs established in HBCUs.

Dr. Louis Wade Sullivan, founder of the Medical School at Morehouse College and Secretary of the US Department of Health and Human Services (1989–1993) is distinguished as a healthcare policy expert and advocate for quality minority healthcare. Dr. Sullivan, in a co-authored article examining the continuing effects of the Flexner Report, argues that the recommendations of the report adversely affected black medical schools in ways that have continuing implications for the development of a diverse representation of medical professionals for the allied health professions and the availability of healthcare in underserved communities. According to the authors, the racism embedded in the recommendations of the report resulted in a dramatic reduction in the number of predominantly black medical schools and the revision in admission standards that put medical education beyond the reach of blacks for decades. Furthermore, it set forth a limited vision of black physicians in the American healthcare system that resulted in the marginalization of black medical schools and their graduates (Sullivan & Mittman, 2010).

FINDING A LIFE PARTNER

According to his biographer Young's performance as an undergraduate student at Kentucky State was not outstanding—that is, until he met Margaret Buckner, who was to become his life partner until his death in

1971. Margaret had also been born in Kentucky. However, her parents, both of whom were teachers in the state's segregated school system, moved the family to Aurora, Illinois, where Margaret grew up. She earned a bachelor's degree in English and French from Kentucky State College for Negroes, where the couple met and later married after a campus courtship. After their marriage in 1944, she earned her master's degree in educational psychology at the University of Minnesota while Young was in military service. Margaret joined the faculty at Spelman college, teaching educational psychology, during Young's tenure as dean of the Atlanta University School of Social Work. She assumed a less public life, concentrating of raising the couple's two daughters, Marcia and Lauren, after the family had taken up residence in New Rochelle, New York, upon Young's appointment as director of the NUL, headquartered in New York City.

After her husband's death Margaret was involved in an active public life that in part was devoted to carrying on his legacy in the fight for human rights. She traveled to Nigeria alone in 1974. Two years later, she accompanied President Jimmy Carter on a state visit to the country. Also active in the affairs of the United Nations, she was a member of the 1974 US Delegation to the General Assembly embarked to Yugoslavia where she presented a paper on "The Promotion and Protection of Human Rights of National, Ethnic and Other Minorities." And, in 1978–1979, she was a participant on a UN panel considering the US relations with China.

Through her personal interest in journalism and writing, she advanced her unique perspective as an author of children's books and publications such as "A Negro Mother Speaks of Her Challenging Role in a Changing World" for *Parents' Magazine* (1964) and the public affairs pamphlet "How to Bring Up Your Child Without Prejudice" (1965). These documents and others are found in the Margaret B. Young papers in the Young Collection at Columbia University (Columbia University Libraries, Margaret B. Young 1921–2010 bulk 1965–2000).

With a partnership dedicated to the fight for human rights, the couple sacrificed much that they might have enjoyed in their personal marital relationship. This is poignantly illustrated in Young's last letter to his wife. He had written the letter on the same day of his tragic death in Lagos. The letter, however, did not reach his wife until she returned to their home after his funeral services in Lexington, Kentucky.

Dearest Margaret,

The only negative thing so far about this trip is your not being here with me and the heat. The latter I can adjust to, the former I cannot. I really look forward more and more to our visits together to these kinds of new different places and people. I hope you are making gains in recovery from the terrible strain and ordeal of your father's passing. I worry so much about you. I have done some thinking and am going to try much harder to be more considerate. This I know I can and must do, no one deserves it more than you. My travel I can't help but so much, but maybe you can go more with me. I love you dearly. (Weiss, 1989, p. 229)

Young's last correspondence to his wife has echoes of John Hope's letter written to his wife Lugenia Burns Hope as he was returning from a European trip conducting the "race work" of the time, indicating that the work had taken a toll on their personal relationship. However, the Young's daughter Marcia Cantarella, when interviewed, similar to the recollections of Jesse O. Thomas's granddaughter Nell Braxton Gibson, observed that her parents' work had spawned new generations for whom the pursuit of social justice had become "the family business."

A FAMILY HERITAGE OF CARING

Marcia, for example, reported a long list of notable accomplishments by relatives whose careers reflect a concern for social justice. Among this listing in the immediate family include Similar to Marcia, Young's sister Eleanor, is well-published in the field of higher education, holds a doctorate in education had earned the highest academic degree offered in the academy; and Eleanor was the first African American dean at the University of Louisville. The Youngs' youngest daughter, Lauren Young Casteel, was inducted into the Colorado Women's Hall of Fame in 2014 for her advocacy and social justice work.

Young's sister Arnita, a graduate of Atlanta University School of Social Work where her brother held the post of dean, held a faculty appointment at the University of Chicago. Arnita's daughter, Young's niece, Bonnie Boswell, is a graduate of Harvard University and the Massachusetts Institute of Technology (MIT) and an award-winning journalist. She is the producer of the film *The Powerbroker: Whitney Young's Fight for Civil Rights,* a documentary that brings into wider public view Young's contributions in the Civil Rights movement. The film was viewed at the Obama White House soon after its completion and introduced by First Lady Michelle Obama. The film has been copyrighted by the National Association of Social Workers (NASW) as *The Whitney M. Young Leadership Teaching Guide*. The project was made possible by grant support from the Rockefeller and Carnegie Foundations and developed as a means for cultivating skills for social work students to carry out Young's philosophy of equality and social justice. The guide is currently widely used nationally by schools of social work as a tool for teaching leadership skills and to enhance content in the policy sequence.

Influenced by his experiences in a segregated military led Young to a change of mind about pursuing a career in medicine. He was drafted into the military after the United States entered World War II following the Japanese attack on Pearl Harbor. While in the military Young completed an electrical engineering program at MIT, and, as customary, he was assigned to an all-black regiment overseen by a white officer. The military brought black and white soldiers closely together in shared spaces; for most, this was a new and sometimes uncomfortable experience. It was these situations that brought to light Young's exceptional interpersonal skills and ability to mediate the racial tensions that emerged between black and white soldiers that set him on a different career path.

After his discharge from the military he enrolled in the social work program at Minnesota University, earning his MSW degree in 1947. He completed block placement at the Minneapolis affiliate office of the NUL writing his master's thesis on the history of the St. Paul Urban League. His student experiences of completing field placements in League affiliate offices began what would be a long-time professional association with the Urban League, starting with his first job after graduation as the industrial relations secretary at the St. Paul Urban League and later as the director of the Omaha Urban League.

While executive secretary of the Omaha Urban League affiliate office, Young began an association with Atlanta University School of Social Work when the organization became a block placement site for social work students. During the time, he was also teaching social work courses at the University of Nebraska and Creighton University. Over the course of the League affiliation with the social work program at Atlanta University, Young developed long-lasting mentoring relationships with talented students as well as critical insights into the challenges of bridging the link between classroom theory and providing real-time practice experiences for students in their field placements. All of this served him well when he accepted the offer of the deanship at the School, since the culture of the academy and the social work program at Atlanta University were not strangers to him. Young also entered the deanship advantaged by the relationship between the Clement and Young families. Young was a protégé of President Clement, a mentorship that grew from the professional relationship between the elder Young and President Clement based on their being prominent black educators of the period.

Because of her concerns about the potential psychological impact on their daughters, Margaret was ambivalent about the move to Atlanta and living in an environment of racial discrimination and segregation that was the accepted way of southern life. Young, however, accustomed to negotiating the discrimination prevalent in the south, was undeterred. He saw the move as both a challenge and an opportunity: a challenge to restore the School of

Social Work to its early level of national prominence while at the same time an opportunity to advance his interest in working on the cause of black civil rights in a city that had yet to live up to its image as the "gateway to the New South" (Weiss, 1989). In contemplating the appointment, Young mused "I was challenged by this opportunity to salvage and once again make this one of the leading schools of social work run by black people, in a black University, for black students" (Weiss, 1989, p. 58). The appointment package also included the added caveat of Young's being distinguished as the first head of the School to be appointed to the position with the title of dean.

ACADEMIA AND THE DEANSHIP

Young began his appointment as dean in 1954, succeeding Forrester B. Washington. As dean, he moved decisively to institute changes to improve the image of the School and restore its financial viability. His efforts at faculty recruitment resulted in an increase in the number of full-time faculty who were more racially and gender diverse. The curriculum was strengthened with his support of faculty development initiatives that encouraged and made possible their attendance at regional and national professional meetings. And his acuity in obtaining federal grants and his amazing fundraising skills secured funds to support student scholarships and new programs in social work fields of practice that were becoming increasingly popular, including psychiatric social work and medical social work.

Young's charisma and growing reputation on the campus and in the city of Atlanta was a central factor in recruiting exceptional students to the School of Social Work. Johnny Parham was among those who came to the School because they wished to study with Young and learn about his activist approach to social work. Parham was initially exposed to Young during his freshman year as a student at Morehouse College. Morehouse students were required to attend the regularly held Chapel services where students were exposed to what Parham described as "extraordinary speakers." Young was presented at one of these meetings as "the dynamic young dean of the School of Social Work." As Parham recalled, although he did not find Young's speech to be "memorial," he was deeply impressed by Young's formidable presence. It was this initial exposure, along with Young's growing prominence on campus, that influenced Parham's decision to pursue a career in social work and enroll in the Atlanta University School of Social Work after his graduation from Morehouse College. It was to be for Parham a decision well-made, as he observed.

> Upon enrolling in the School of Social Work, it became immediately apparent that Dean Young took a special interest in his students. He sought to learn

our fields of interests in order to assure that the field work placements would prepare us for productive careers. During my second year, I became actively involved in the student sit-ins that ushered in the 1960 Civil Rights movement. Whitney became an unofficial advisor to the AUC students who waged an all-out attack on racial segregation in Atlanta. Given the prominent role played by students of the AU School of Social Work, Whitney made certain that leaders in the field of social work were aware of the potential involvement of social work students. (Parham, 2019)

Counted among Young's talented protégés, Parham continued a mentoring relationship with Young after his graduation, when he had embarked on a professional career in New York City and Young had taken up the reins of leadership at the NUL office in Manhattan. At Young's invitation, Parham participated with him in leading a workshop at the National Conference of Social Welfare, convened in Atlantic City, on the value of applying principles from community organization to address racial segregation. Once again commenting on Young's presence, that was now moving onto the national stage, Parham wrote:

During that experience I developed a full appreciation of the depth of his prominence that extended beyond academia. Wherever he moved about during that four-day conference, there was no doubt as to whom leadership rested within the field. . . . In 1960 leadership of America's social welfare organizations was totally controlled by a majority of White males with a sprinkling of White women. Not only was Whitney poised to lead a national organization, he was highly regarded in the field of social work education. (Parham, 2019)

As his protégé Parham continued to undertake projects with Young under the auspices of the NUL. Their association continued into the beginning years of the Civil Rights movement, when progressive thinking social work students and faculty were calling for a greater integration of diversity content and challenging the Eurocentric world view as a requirement for undergirding the curriculum of accredited social work programs and practice in social work agencies. He successfully worked with Young in implementing a program designed to replicate the model initially conceptualized by League co-founder George Edmond Hayes of establishing partnerships between schools of social work and affiliate offices of the League to serve as a pipeline for growing a leadership committed to careers in service to the black community. The project, as described by Parham, involved the identification of a racially diverse group of high-performing social work students from across the nation enrolled in the social work programs at both HBCUs and predominately white universities. The students were trained to form an Urban Peace Corp and dispersed to high-need, underserved urban neighborhoods, tasked to study community conditions and provide services to meet the needs of residents (Parham, 2019).

CIVIL RIGHTS ACTIVISM

While carrying out his duties as dean of the School of Social Work, as was the case with his work with Urban League in Minnesota of engaging with the larger community, Young became involved in the Atlanta community outside of campus life and stepped in to fill the vacuum in leadership on matters of civil rights. Still a segregated city, Young assumed the deanship of the Atlanta University School of Social Work as the Civil Rights movement was beginning to gain momentum in Atlanta. The brutal murder of Emmitt Till and the defiance of Rosa Park had set into motion the Civil Rights movement and spawned new organizations like the Southern Christian Leadership Conference, the Council on Racial Equality, and the Student Nonviolent Coordinating Committee. These organizations joined the older organizations of the NAACP, the NUL, and the Brotherhood of Sleeping Car Porters to form what became known as "The Big Six." Their coming together was a strategic leveraging of the combined influence of these premier civil rights organizations into a singular power bloc. Young became a member of the group when he was later selected to head the NUL.

Along with academic leadership as dean, Young also became engaged with the social activism emerging in Atlanta that was undertaken to deconstruct the myth of the city as the gateway to the "New South." He was among the leadership of the Greater Atlanta Council for Human Rights that played a central role in the integration of the Atlanta public library, and he was among the group of young black professional and business men who came together to organize a group they named the Atlanta Committee for Cooperative Action (ACCA). The group was envisioned to be a think tank whose membership spoke in a voice different from conservative old guard black leadership in the city that had not spoken out against the status quo.

In keeping with Young's academic orientation of using data-driven approaches for advocating policy change and reform, after a year of research and data collection, the group produced a document entitled "A Second Look: The Negro Citizen in Atlanta." The document exposed the hypocrisy of the myth of Atlanta as the "New South" and the city "too busy to hate" by documenting the pervasive inequalities experienced by black Atlantans in virtually all areas of the city, including employment, education, housing, healthcare, and law enforcement.

"A Second Look" was widely circulated. At the national level, coverage of the document by the *New York Times* promoted it as a plan for political action, and the *Atlanta Constitution* predicted that the document was the beginning of blacks confronting racial segregation in public places in the city. The publication was also embraced by the students in the Atlanta University Consortium Schools who formed the core of the leadership that drew on data from "A Second Look" to produce "An Appeal for Human Rights." Moreover, it was this student-prepared document that signaled the entrance of students in the Atlanta Consortium schools into the national student movement in civil rights. Young was among the handful of faculty who encouraged the students to assume an activist stance that included social work students John Mack and Johnny Parham.

The national prominence afforded to Young as a result of his activism in Atlanta while holding the deanship and his keynote speech given at the NUL 1959 annual conference, with its theme of "The Role of the Urban League in the Current American Scene" (Weiss, 1989, p. 73), increased his visibility among influential members of the League's national board of trustees. He had also received national recognition as the 1959 recipient of the Florina Lasker Award, given for his outstanding professional leadership in public service and civil rights. Florina Laker (1884–1949), for whom the award is named, was a social activist and member of a prominent philanthropic Jewish family whose social activism included her work as secretary of the New York Labor Standards Committee and the American Civil Liberties Union, and her authorship of *The Care and Treatment of the Jewish Blind in the City of New York* (Gunther, 1960). The Lasker Award was one that Young shared with his social work colleague Gordon Hamilton. Hamilton was the 1957 recipient of the Award in recognition of her "superior achievement as a practitioner, educator, scholar, thinker and leader in the profession of social work" (Sicherman & Green, 2012). These achievements and his growing national recognition as a civil rights leader led Young to the next chapter of his professional career when, after a highly competitive search process, he was selected executive director of the NUL in 1961, a position he held until his death in 1971.

A BRIEF HISTORY OF THE NUL

The Urban League was among the activist organizations formed within the context of the Great Migration, which saw the outpouring of six million blacks from the rural South to urban areas, and the Progressive Era, a period of humanitarian reforms to solve the social problems accompanying rapid industrialization and the maturation of capitalism occurring over the decades between 1890 and 1920. Not only were blacks victimized by the unscrupulous practices of the captains of industry of the period, but they also suffered the effects of blatant racism that had become deeply entrenched in American society since the end of Reconstruction. Moreover, the new migrants were ill-prepared for life in complex urban environments.

The Urban League developed to serve the interest of blacks whose plight was not of immediate concern to white activists of the period. The reform efforts of the white social activists of the Progressive Era targeted white ethnic immigrants from western European countries. The activism of the League targeted black migrants who were a part of the Great Migration of blacks seeking refuge from the oppressive condition of the South and hoping to find opportunities for employment created by the rapid industrialization occurring in urban areas in the northern and midwestern regions of the country.

The Urban League developed from the merging of the interests of three New York City-based organizations: the National League for the Protection of Colored Women, the Committee for Improving the Industrial Conditions for Negroes in New York, and the Committee on Urban Conditions Among Negroes in New York. The three committees came together in 1910 to form a single organization, initially called the National League on Urban Conditions and later the NUL.

While a number of individuals participated in the work of founding the organization, George Edmond Haynes and William Henry Baldwin Jr. are generally credited with giving shape to the major thrust of the organization (Weiss, 1974). Haynes, who was the first graduate of the New York School of Philanthropy and first African American to receive a PhD from Columbia University, became the first executive director of the League. With training in social service work, Haynes supported the professionalization of social services and the use of scholarly research as the basis for progressive policy development in the interest of obtaining full equality and citizenship for blacks.

Baldwin, the League co-founder, was a successful white businessman who had given up his career in business to become president of the Boston Young Men's Christian Association (YMCA). With Baldwin being a strong advocate of Booker T. Washington's favoring of industrial education as the best way to improve the situation of blacks, the two men differed in their beliefs about the underlying philosophy of the mission of the League. Both, however, were strong proponents of interracial collaboration as the best approach for solving the problems of blacks, and they shared the belief that the prospects of the future of the two races were inextricably bound together (Weiss, 1974).

The early work of the League was carried out by black and white representatives from the business, professional, and religious communities. Key players comprised an interdisciplinary mix of doctors, lawyers, social workers, educators, and newspaper editors. These collaborative partnerships opened employment opportunities and created new social services that had not been accessible to blacks from white organizations. Modeling the work of the Neighborhood Union, the activities of the League included scientific investigations that studied health, housing, sanitation, and employment conditions in black communities. The results of this process of information gathering and analysis formed the basis for advocating broad-based system reforms to improve living conditions, meet basic material needs, and establish adequate recreational facilities. Direct counseling services were provided to support appropriate behaviors in sanitation, health, hygiene, and homemaking to recent migrants arriving from rural areas and who were unfamiliar with urban life.

THE LASTING LEGACY OF THE LEAGUE

A lasting contribution of the League under the leadership of Hayes was the development of professional training schools for blacks dedicated to increasing the number of black professional workers with prerequisite skills for effective social work practice in the black community. He established a social science department at Fisk University, developed as a collaborative model and strategy that partnered League affiliate offices with black colleges and social welfare agencies. Colleges were encouraged to integrate courses in economics and sociology into their curricula, supplemented with instruction on migration, urban problems, and organized methods of social services. This enhanced coursework was taught by League staff appointed as adjunct or visiting faculty.

The strategy of linking schools of social work with League affiliate offices was carried forth by Eugene Kinckle Jones, who assumed the directorship after Haynes stepped down, and served as director of the League from 1917 to 1941. Jones continued to grow the organization and the tradition of linking League affiliates with schools of social work, and he played a central role in launching the Atlanta School of Social Work. Lester Granger was head of the National Urban League from 1941 to 1961 and was Young's predecessor and mentor. Granger continued to push for black civil rights under the Eisenhower administration and established a beginning relationship between the National Urban League and the Southern Christian Leadership Conference.

Never veering from its historic mission and core principles of interracial collaboration and the use of research as a tool for advancing blacks rights and social reform, the League has shifted its mission to respond to changing environmental contexts during the tenures of the presidents and CEOs of the National Urban League in the post-civil rights years: Vernon Jordan (1972–1981), John Jacobs (1982–1994), Hugh Price (1994–2002), and Milton Little, who served as interim president in 2003 until the time of the appointment of the Mark Morial in 2003 who is the current President and CEO.

In 1980, Vernon Jordan introduced the practice of publishing "The State of Black America." The Report produces a scholarly critical analysis of the status and progress of blacks on racial equality in America across indicators of economics, employment, education, health, housing, criminal justice, and civic participation. Now in its 49th edition, the Report is considered the foremost publication providing race critical statistical reporting and analysis on the living conditions and progress of black Americans based on well-being indicators of quality of life and material resources.

The Report also is widely used among schools of social work as a supplementary textbook for teaching diversity content across all core curriculum sequences. The 2019 Report, published under the administration of Mark Morial, who is a frequent national spokesman on the Report and implications for black America and the nation, made concerning findings about efforts to suppress the voting rights of African Americans and Russian interference in American elections. Speaking to efforts to suppress the black vote, Morial stated in the 2019 Report that "The right of African Americans to vote—our right to participate in the civic processes of this nation—quite simply is under attack." (Morial, 2019, p. 5)

YOUNG'S LEADERSHIP AT THE NUL

As Young was gaining national visibility, few were surprised that he was soon on a career trajectory that would take him beyond the Atlanta and the world of academia. As Genevieve Hill commented, "we knew he had to go. . . . He had done his growing here and left a legacy, and it was time for him. We regretted it, terribly. We were saddened but we knew for him, it was time" (Weiss, 1989, pp. 76–77).

With Atlanta University President Rufus Clement's approval of a sabbatical, Young began a year-long fellowship at Harvard University. This was a thinking time that allowed him to interact with thought leaders in the social sciences in the academy and prepared him for what would be a transition from the world of academia in the South to that of the not-for-profit social service sector in the North as the Civil Rights movement was also transitioning into a full scale national movement.

In the largest share of the literature on his career accomplishments, Young is credited with elevating the organization and expanding the mission of the NUL from that of a conservative social work agency to its being counted among the nation's premier civil rights organizations. The University announced Young's departure from the deanship in the spring of 1960. With the completion of his year long sabbatical, Young assumed the position of executive director of the League in 1961 and settled into the national offices located at East 48th Street in Midtown Manhattan.

Young carried with him a strong social work professional identity and social work perspective to the executive office of the League. And, by virtue of his earlier experiences with League affiliates in Nebraska and Minnesota, he was knowledgeable about the differing and complementary roles of volunteer policy-making boards and the salaried executive and professional staff tasked with implementing board policies.

This understanding served him well as he assumed the office of executive in an organization in which, although wedded to a model of interracial collaboration, prominent, wealthy white members of the board held considerable influence and power as stewards of the organization's mission that drives the thrust of policy development and program implementation. As the executive, who serves at the pleasure of the board, Young moved cautiously in setting the organization on a new course. Focusing his attention on working collaboratively with prominent white members of the board, a first priority focused on putting in place structural changes to secure the organization's financial viability, increase staff service giving capacity in the affiliate offices, and improve its national image.

Owing to his fundraising abilities, combined with the influence of well-connected members of the Board of Trustees, the League was on firm financial footing with a substantial increase in foundation funding within the first year of Young's appointment (Weiss, 1989). However, with the escalation in the civil rights protest, Young and the Board were soon faced with the need to adopt a political position that preserved the conservative tradition of the League that at the same time was aligned with the activism and urgency of the cause advanced by the Civil Rights movement. Young issued a statement to this effect soon after taking up the leadership that cautiously addressed the politics of the issue.

> Racial problems in America are manifested in many ways and at many levels, and therefore a multiplicity of techniques and approaches are required to successfully cope with them. No single organization can profess to have a monopoly in this field or to have all the answers as to methodology.
>
> The Urban League movement is committed to the use of such methods as research, conference, public education and community organization. However, it has no quarrel with other efforts under responsible leadership using legally acceptable methods and seeking the same ultimate goal of a free, democratic and healthy society as does the Urban League. (Weiss, 1989, p. 101)

As the Civil Rights movement began to gain national support, Young shifted his thinking and began to use his substantial persuasive skills to move the Board of Trustees to assume a more activist stance on matters of black civil rights. In doing so, he nonetheless preserved the uniqueness of the League as a professional organization whose priorities and policy positions continued to be anchored in science and whose activities were carried out by a professional staff.

For example, in an oral history interview recorded in the Robert Penn Warren Civil Rights Oral History Project, (https://kentuckyoralhistory.org/ark:/16417/xt7vq814qz03) in identifying the difference between League and other civil rights organizations of the day, he observed that the Civil Rights movement required a variety of activities from organizations working toward achieving the same goals.

Accordingly, Young described the role of the League as that of supplementing and complementing the work of other civil rights organizations by undertaking activities that gave meaning to slogans of "equal opportunity" or "freedom now" since first class citizenship, as he expressed in the oral history interview, also required blacks to have the material resources and qualifications to take advantage of the new opportunities that came with the breakdown of racial barriers. Young differentiated the League from other civil rights organizations in describing the League as the

> social engineers, the strategists, we are the planners, we are the people who work at the level of policy making and policy implementation. We are the professional arm working with the highest echelon of the corporate community, the highest echelons of the governmental community—both at the federal, state and local level—the highest echelons of the labor movement. We do the research we are the professional arm. Unlike the other organizations we are the professional organization . . . at present we have 525 full-time staff; 350 these are professional people with their master's degrees or over, working full time in some 65 communities around the country where 85% of the urban Negro population live. (Young, 1964)

At the time of the interview, Young noted that there were thirteen League affiliates in the South and fifty-two in the North, all of which were located in urban areas, and the League's Constitution required that the ethnic composition of their staffs and Boards of Trustee mirrored the demographics of the communities in which they were located.

As the League adopted a more activist stance, Young was counted among the leaders of the "Big Six" civil rights organizations that planned the March on Washington where Martin Luther King gave his memorable and often quoted "I Have a Dream" speech. Young was among the other speakers, and was introduce by A. Philip Randolph as the "brilliant executive director of the NUL, and one of the leaders of the civil rights movement." Young began his remarks emphasizing that while the civil rights organizations used different methods, they were united as never before around the goal of achieving first-class citizenship for all Americans.

Absent the statistical numbers, Young's remarks, supported by his excellent and eloquent public speaking skills, painted a graphic image of the glaring racial disparities the undermined black lives from the cradle to the grave. He ended his remarks by conveying a sense of urgency in what had been an unending struggle for black rights since the end of Reconstruction.

[T]he hour is late. The gap is widening. The rumble of the drums of discontent resounding throughout this land are heard in all parts of the world. The missions which we send there to keep the world safe for democracy are shallow symbols unless with them goes a living testament that this country practices at home the doctrine which it seeks to promote abroad. How serious our national leaders are will be measured not by words but by the speed and sincerity with which they pass necessary legislation, with which they admit to the tragic injustice that has been done our country and it's Negro citizens by historic discrimination and rejection, and until they take intensive remedial steps to correct the damage in order to give true meaning to the words equal opportunities. This is the real significance of our march today, August 28, 1963. Our march is a march for America. It is a march just begun. (March on Washington for Jobs and Freedom, 1963)

Over the course of his tenure as executive director of the NUL, Young never participated in a nonviolent demonstration, nor was he ever arrested for refusing to obey what was deemed to be an unjust law, a badge of honor and central strategy of the Civil Rights movement. He did, however, become distinguished for "speaking truth to power," in never shying away from pointing out the discrepancies between word and deed of what the nation and the profession professed to stand for. This predisposition was reflected in a paper Young presented at the mid-centennial meeting of the Family Service Association of America in Miami beach, Florida, on November 17–21, 1967, and published in the April 1968 edition of *Social Casework* entitled "Tell It Like It Is" (Young, 1968a). In calling attention to what social agencies and social workers could do to remain true to the profession's mission Young wrote

Leadership is needed if this nation is to make justice a reality. And social agencies have both a formal commitment to assume that leadership and the know-how about people to make it effective. Social workers know what alienation and rejection mean and about both the psychological and physiological impact of poverty.

The Community Chest is still, for the most part, dominated by the establishment, which includes the labor unions. And the social work profession allowed itself to be bypassed in the planning of urban renewal and even initially in the antipoverty program. Now, today, we must and can speak up. We do not need to be quiet. We have won our spurs as professional social workers and we do not need to continue to try to be little psychiatrists. There is great status in the offing for social engineers and social reformers, for people who know the answers to some of the vexing problems of the city—and most of those problems are human. (Young, 1968a, p. 209)

He was equally outspoken in calling out discrepancies between words and deeds on matters of equal rights. For example, in what is lauded as a landmark presentation given at the 1968 Convention of the American Institute of Architect (AIA) was laced with blunt criticism of the hypocrisy of its policy on racial inclusion. Young was invited to give the keynote address at the 1968 Convention at a time when there had been what was seen as an egregious misuse of federal funds that were intended to revitalize devastated urban communities for the poor but to the contrary, had resulted in disrupting entire neighborhoods and displacing community residents. The AIA was not among the voices that had spoken out against this injustice, and Young was invited by American Institute of Architect (AIA) President Robert Durham to the give the keynote speech as a means for addressing the discontent swirling around the circumstances of these occurrences.

Standing before an audience that was virtually absent of minority representation, Young began his remarks by observing

I will not apologize for being presumptuous, as the Governor did. However, if I seem to repeat things you have heard before, I do not apologize, any more than I think a physician would apologize for giving inoculations. Sometimes we have to give repeated vaccinations, and we continue to do so until we observe that it has taken effect.

One need only take a casual look at this audience to see that we have a long way to go in this field of integration of the architects. I almost feel like Mr. Stanley looking for Dr. Livingston—in reverse—in Africa. I think I did see one and wanted to rush up and say: Dr. Livingston, I presume! (Young, 1968b, p. 1)

Young's speech has had a lasting impact on the AIA. The speech motivated the AIA to review its policies from a social justice and race-critical perspective, and, since the time the speech was given, the AIA has passed resolutions, modified its code of ethics, and sponsored a number of programs in an effort to create a more inclusive, diverse, and equitable profession. To accomplish this, since 1972, the AIA has given an award in Young's name to distinguish an individual architect or architectural organization whose projects are an embodiment of social responsibility and actively address a relevant issue related to affordable housing, inclusiveness, or universal access (Zeiger, 2018).

As president of the NASW, Young was equally as vocal in calling the profession of social work to task for its gradual veering away from its fundamental mission as stated in the preamble of the NASW code of ethics.

> The primary mission of the social work profession is to enhance human well-being and help meet the basic human needs of all people, with particular attention to the needs and empowerment of people who are vulnerable, oppressed, and living in poverty. A historic and defining feature of social work is the profession's focus on individual well-being in a social context and the well-being of society. Fundamental to social work is attention to the environmental forces that create, contribute to, and address problems in living (NASW.org.)

Young was elected president by the membership of the NASW, the world's largest association for professional social workers. He served as president from 1969 to 1971 while he was the executive director of the NUL. Young's presidency of NASW coincided with the waning years of the Civil Rights movement and the resurgence of "victim blaming" narratives that accused the poor as being complicit in their own misfortune. This changed environment saw the profession retreating yet again from "cause to function." This was also a time of the beginning dismantling of the safety net programs for the poor that had been integral to social welfare programs since the enactment of the 1935 Social Security Act, a regression that began under President Nixon's introduction of a conservative agenda under policies of New Federalism.

With the continuing diminishing of a social work presence in reform activities, Young constantly urged social workers not to become complacent or to abandon the profession's historic mission to serve the poor and other marginalized populations. In an address given at the 1967 meeting of the National Conference on Social Welfare, he encouraged the profession to pursue the new opportunities for promoting social justice causes for blacks created by policy reforms instituted under the Johnson administration.

The 94th meeting of the National Conference on Social Welfare met in Dallas, Texas, on May, 1, 1967. The theme of the conference was "Humanizing Our Cities," and Young was among the keynote speakers. Greetings to the Conference were brought by President Lyndon B. Johnson. In his opening remarks, Johnson observed that the newly established cabinet position on Urban and Housing Development combined with the Model Cities program, which was a part of the Great Society and had legislated coordinated social program development and urban renewal projects to address the root causes of urban poverty, were all causes for optimism. This optimism was reflected in Johnson's remarks that challenged the profession to assume leadership in eradicating the paradox of poverty in a nation of great wealth, a cause that now had the full support of the White House.

> In my state of the Union message I stressed that the War on Poverty will not be won in Washington but it must be won in the field, and every private home, and every public office, from the courthouse to the White House. You, the social workers of America are the nation's front line troops; you are already in the field; you have met the enemy face-to-face, not once, but many times, with the odds heavily against you.
>
> Today, in view of the response to my call for action, the odds are at last in your favor. You will find citizens from many walks of life fighting shoulder to shoulder with you, supporting the programs you have long advocated.
>
> The success of your national conference this year, devoted as it is to the theme of "social welfare's responsibility to communities and change" is important, not only to you and to the people you serve, but to each and every American. May your work this week speed the day when the United States stands before the world as the first nation in all history to free all of its people from the age-old enemy of want. (Johnson, 1967, p. xi, Proceedings of the National Conference on Social Welfare, 1967, p. xi)

Johnson had appointed Robert Weaver Secretary of the newly established Department of Housing and Urban Development, making Weaver the first African American to be appointed to a US cabinet level position. Weaver, a Harvard graduate with a PhD degree in economics, had an extensive portfolio as a public servant, and in academia, that extended back to the early years of his career when he was a member of FDR's "Black Cabinet." Weaver was among the major speakers at the Conference. Supporting the Conference theme of "Humanizing our Cities", in his presentation that was entitled "Government in Urban Development," Weaver spoke of the importance of incorporating the "physical with the social side" in urban renewal programs.

Also emphasizing the incorporation of the physical and social, and embracing social work's ecological perspective, the title of Young's remarks was "Social Welfare's Responsibility in Urban Affairs." In delivering his remarks, he spoke candidly about the need for social workers to be involved in politics and large scale systemic reform efforts and the need to exhibit a "crusading zeal and political sophistication."

As a member, and later as president of the National Association of Social Workers, Young also spoke candidly, and at times with harsh criticism about the profession's retreat from large scale social justice reforms. In his presidential address given at the 1967 National Conference on Social Welfare, he chastised the profession, remarking that "Social work was born in an atmosphere of righteous indignation . . . somewhere along the line the 'urge to become professional' had overcome this initial crusading impulse." And he criticized the profession for being overly interested in becoming respected professionals, which he asserted resulted in making a "fetish of method- ology, and a virtue of neutrality and objectivity." His remarks also offered sharp criticism in the assertion that too many social workers "looked down their noses" at the poor and avoided confronting issues of race and religion. Young also spoke with optimism as he challenged the profession to return to its heritage and founding mission of social justice and service to the poor and marginalized populations: "We must plan to spark change and the seeds of indignation in the mind of every citizen suffering from want. We must be the catalyst of change, not the maintainers of the status quo" (Trattner, 1999, pp. 311–312; Weiss, 1989, p. 207).

These were continuing themes in Young's messages to the membership over the terms of his office as NASW president. In his 1969 address to the NASW Delegate Assembly he stated that,

> We, as a country have blazed unimagined trails technologically and industrially. We have not yet begun to pioneer in those things that are human and social. . . . I think that social work is uniquely equipped to play a major role in this social and human renaissance of our society, which will, if successful, lead to its sur- vival, and if it is unsuccessful, will lead to its justifiable death. (NASW News, May 1969)

As his term was drawing to an end, and at a time when many of the gains in human rights were being rolled back under a changed social welfare philos- ophy spurred by the new conservativism of the Nixon administration, again using NASW News as a platform Young asserted

> The crisis in health and welfare services in our nation today highlights for NASW what many of us have been stressing for a long time: inherent in the responsi- bility for leadership in social welfare is responsibility for professional action. They are not disparate aspects of social work but merely two faces of the same coin to be spent on more and better services for the people who need our help. It is out of our belief in this broad definition of responsibility for social welfare that NASW is taking leadership in the efforts to reorder our nation's priorities and future direction, and is calling on social workers everywhere to do the same (https://www.nasw-pa.org/page/192)

Mitchell I. Ginsberg, emeritus professor and dean of Columbia's School of Social Work, and James R. Dumpson, the first African American dean of the Fordham University Graduate School of Social Services, are distinguished by professional careers in which they have made substantial contributions in academia, social work professional associations, and public service. Both men were leaders in academia, the Council on Social Work Education, and the NASW, and both had been appointed to the position of commissioner of the New York City Department of Public Welfare. They were among the outspoken social work leaders who joined Young in encouraging the profession to assume a more visible stance in social and political activism. Nonetheless, with Young's passing along with the rise of a conservative social welfare ideology, the following decades saw a continued diminishing of a social work presence and voice at the national level on matters of social welfare and concerns for social and economic justice for the poor.

ADVISOR TO PRESIDENTS

Young's moderate approach to addressing racial inequalities, combined with his ability to speak candidly about emotionally charged racial issues without evoking defensiveness in whites, were attributes that had given him access to the power elite of the corporate world, also served as his pathway to the White House and advisor to US presidents. Young served as advisor to three American presidents: John F. Kennedy, Lyndon B. Johnson, and Richard M. Nixon. His relationship with Kennedy was constrained by Kennedy' s reluctance, in the interest of political expediency, to assume a clear position on civil rights for fear of placing his re-election at risk by alienating the southern white Democrats. While he was invited to the Nixon White House, neither Young or the other civil rights leaders were in sync with the Nixon administration because of the president's conservative stance on social welfare and his promoting the pejorative narrative of "welfare chiselers" about those who looked to government programs for help.

Young shared the closest relationship with President Johnson because of his authentic commitment to a civil rights agenda. Upon entering office, Johnson had thrown the full force of the office of the president behind the continuing struggle for civil rights, and he moved decisively to pass the civil rights legislation that had been introduced to Congress by Kennedy prior to his assassination. Moreover, the two men were of like mind in developing a grand strategy for eradicating poverty in America, that were set forth in what Young had conceptualized as a "Domestic Marshall Plan," and the Johnson administration's vision of the Great Society.

THE DOMESTIC MARSHALL PLAN

Young had begun conceptualizing the Domestic Marshall Plan over the period of his sabbatical at Harvard, between his stepping down from the deanship and his selection to head the NUL. The Plan was modeled after the Marshall Plan, officially known as the European Recovery Program that was signed into law by President Harry Truman on April 3, 1948. The Marshall Plan authorized the United States to invested billions of dollars to rebuild the Western European economies devastated by World War II. Similar to the Marshall Plan, which was undertaken to restore the economies of these countries to reduce the risk of their coming under communist influence, the replication of a Domestic Marshall Plan in urban America, as conceived by Young, was to rebuild devastated urban communities to prevent the further alienation of blacks that was reflected in the growing militancy of the Civil Rights movement.

Young's Plan called for the investment of $145 billion over a ten-year period to rebuild and prevent the further decay of neglected US urban communities. The NUL was to lead the ten-point plan, envisioned as a decade-long multilevel intervention targeting employment, education, health, and welfare services. The initiative was based in the concept of compensation and special treatment, as Young expressed at the 1961 Annual Conference of the League.

> I contend over many protests, that the Negro for over 300 years has been given the special consideration of exclusion, he must now be given by society special treatment, through services and opportunities, that will ensure his inclusion as a citizen able to compete equally with all others. (Weiss, 1989, p. 150)

The League later issued a policy statement in 1963 calling for a special effort

> which may appear to be in conflict with the principle of equal treatment for all, [but] is required to overcome the damaging effects of generations of deprivation and denial and to make it possible for the majority of American Negros to reach the point at which they can compete on a basis of equality and the nation's increasing the complex and fast moving industrial economy. (Weiss, 1989, p. 152)

Although Young's Domestic Marshall Plan was never implemented as an initiative of the League, there is some reporting in the literature that aspects of the initiative were incorporated into the Great Society programs of the Johnson administration.

At the time of Young's accidental death at the age of forty-nine, he was entering into what is defined as midlife by experts on transitions of the human life cycle. Characteristic of the life stage, as reported by his biographer, Young was in a life course trajectory where he was re-examining the directions that his future professional career would take. As he had outgrown his role as dean of the School of Social Work, he was finding less gratification in his role as

League executive that, during his tenure as executive, had become the nation's leading civil rights organization (Weiss, 1989). Ironically, the persona that had enabled Young to move with ease between the power elite of white America and disempowered black communities had, with the growing militancy and shift from tactics of engagement to those of revolution to achieve black rights, resulted in Young's being labeled as overly subservient and submissive to the interests the white establishment.

THE LEGACY

Young's was indeed a professional life interrupted by his untimely death. Counted among his achievements was the authorship of two books: *To Be Equal* (1964) and *Beyond Racism* (1970/1969). Both are written almost as a soliloquy, spoken in a singular voice endeavoring to lead the reader to a moral higher ground, to join him in a quest for a civil and just society in which it was possible for every individual to achieve full self-actualization. He had received numerous awards including the Medal of Freedom, awarded by the Johnson administration, which is the highest award given to an American citizen. He had appeared on the cover of the August 11, 1967, edition of *Time* magazine. The US Postal Services has honored him with a postal stamp as a part of its Black Heritage Series. (Peebles-Wilkins, 2013).

Young's name is memorialized on many public edifices across the nation. In academia and in the profession, his legacy has been preserved through the naming of the school of social work at Clark Atlanta University for him in 2000. A teaching guide has been prepared by NASW to accompany the documentary film of his life, *The Power Broker: Leadership Lessons from Whitney M. Young Jr.*, and the NASW sponsors the Whitney M. Young Dorothy Height Reinvestment Act. In New York City, the World Community of Social Workers, founded by a group of members of the National Association of Black Social Workers and alumni of the school of social work at Clark Atlanta University, convene an annual meeting to bring his message to new generations of social workers.

In a 1979 speech given at a memorial service for Young entitled "What of Equal Opportunity Now?" James R. Dumpson underscored that the work to which Young had devoted his life was far from being completed/

> As 1979 begins, it is apparent that the most serious problems confronting Black America are its intolerably high levels of unemployment, especially among young blacks; the threat of the recession; the continuing assaults on the principles of affirmative action; and the creeping malignant growth of a "new negativism" that calls for a weak, passive government and indifference to the plight

of the poor. . . . The challenge is to repair the damage caused by historic neglect so that this nation can be what it has the potential to become but never has been—a truly open, pluralistic, integrated society. (Carten, 2015, p 131)

The decades of the 1980s and 1990s, and into the new millennium would see a continued dismantlement of the American social welfare state and an abandonment on the part of the federal government of the safety net philosophy. Consequential events having a transformative impact on the country included the 1996 Personal Responsibility and Work Reconciliation and Opportunity Act (PRWORA) of the Clinton administration that indeed "changed welfare as we know it." The September 11, 2001, terrorists attacks thrust the nation into a state of constant vigilance to ward off future terrorist attacks. And the 2008 election of Barack Obama as the first African American president created a euphoric psychological effect that, for many Americans, signaled what was hoped to be the nation's entering into a post-racial society.

The School of Social Work, now a part of the Clark Atlanta University administrative structure, had joined professional trends favoring micro practice and adopted a sole concentration in advanced clinical practice. It faced, as did all schools of social work, new challenges in the 21st century. Included among these were meeting the demands of an increasingly competitive environment in academia, increased accountability demands on the profession to anchor theory and practice in science, and the rise of a conservative right that attacked the foundation bedrock principles of the profession.

The state of Georgia, along with other Southern states, had been incrementally moving from being Democratic to staunchly Republican since South Carolina Senator Strum Thurman and Georgia Senator Richard Russel crafted the Southern Manifesto vowing to "by all legal means necessary" strike down the Supreme Court ruling outlawing segregation. The image of Atlanta, often referred to as the "black mecca of the South" is juxtaposed against it being the city with the worse income inequality in the United States and poverty rates for black children that are higher than in any other American city.

REFERENCES

Brigham, T. M. (1970). *Beyond Racism: Building an Open Society, Whitney M. Young, JR.* New York, McGraw-Hill Book Company, 1969.

Carten, A. J. (2015). *Reflections on the American social welfare state: The collected papers of James R. Dumpson, PhD, 1930–1990.* Washington, DC: NASW Press.

Charlton, L. (1971). Drowning given as cause of Whitney Young's death. *New York Times,* April 13, 1971.

Columbia University Libraries Archives Collection. Margaret B. Young papers, 1921–2010, bulk 1965–2000.

Dickerson, D. C. (1998). *Militant mediator: Whitney M. Young Jr.* Lexington: University of Kentucky Press.

Flexner, A. (1910). *Medical education in the United States and Canada*. New York: Carnegie Foundation for the Advancement of Teaching.

Gunther, J. (1960). *Taken at the flood: The story of Albert D. Lasker*. New York: Harper.

Hill, G. (March 16, 1971). In Memoriam, To: Whitney M. Young, Jr. (1921–1971). In The Legacy of Forrester B. Washington, Black Social Work Educator and Nation Builder, pp. iv–v, Excerpts from the Proceedings of the 50th Anniversary of the Atlanta University School of Social Work. November 12–14, 1970. Atlanta, Georgia.

Johnson, T. A. (1971b). Nixon leads mourners at Young Funeral. *New York Times*, March 18, 1971.

Johnson, T. A. (1971a). Thousands here pay tribute to Whitney Young Jr. *New York Times*, March 16, 1971.

March on Washington for Jobs and Freedom. (1963). Part 7 of 17, August, 28, 1963. Boston, MA: WGBH Media Library & Archives. http://openvault.wgbh.org/catalog/A_FDC80454052747988DEA7F89F4D23B9F

Morial, M. H. (2019). National Urban League. (2019). State of Black American, Getting 2 Equal: United Not Divided. https://nul.org/news/read-2019-state-black-america-report https://nul.org/news/read-2019-state-black-america-report

Nixon, R. (March 17, 1971). Eulogy Delivered for Whitney M. Young, Jr. Burial Services in Lexington, Kentucky. https://www.presidency.ucsb.edu/documents/eulogy-delivered-burial-services-for-whitney-m-young-jr-lexington-kentucky

Parham, J. E. (December 6, 2019). *Whitney M. Young, Jr.* Unpublished statement prepared by the author on his recollections of his relationship with Young.

Peebles-Wilkins, W. (2013). Young, Whitney Moore, Jr. In *Encyclopedia of social work*. https://socialwelfare.library.vcu.edu/eras/young-whitney-m-jr/

Proceedings of the National Conference on Social Welfare. (1967). https://quod.lib.umich.edu/n/ncosw/ACH8650.1967.001?view=toc

Sicherman, B., & Green, C. H. (2012). *Notable American women: The modern period: A biographical dictionary*. Cambridge, MA: Belknap Press.

Sullivan, L. W., & Mittman, I. S. (2010). The state of diversity in the health professions a century after Flexner. *Academic Medicine, 85*(2), 246–253.

Trattner, W. I. (1999). *From poor law to welfare state (6th ed.)*. New York: The Free Press.

Weiss, N. J. (1974). *The National Urban League, 1910–1940*. New York: Oxford University Press.

Weiss, N. J. (1989). Whitney M. *Young, Jr., and the struggle for civil rights*. Princeton University Press: N.J.

Young, W. (1964, April 13). Interview by R. P. Warren. *Robert Penn Warren Civil Rights Oral History Project*. Lexington: Louie B. Nunn Center for Oral History, University of Kentucky Libraries. https://kentuckyoralhistory.org/ark:/16417/xt7vq814qz03

Young, W. M. (1968a). Tell it like it is. *Social Casework, 49*(4), 207–212.

Young, W. M. (1968b). American Institute of Architect. Full Remarks of Whitney M. Young Jr. AIA Annual Convention in Portland, Oregon June 1968.

Young, W. M. (1964). *To be equal*. New York: McGraw-Hill.

Young Jr, W. M. (1970). Beyond Racism?. *J Nat Assn Wom Deans Counselors*.

Zeiger, M. (May, 8. 2018). Remembering Whitney M. Young Jr.'s Landmark Speech. Architect. https://www.architectmagazine.com/practice/remembering-whitney-m-young-jrs-landmark-speech_o

CHAPTER 14

Entering into the Millennium and Beyond

A system of education is not one thing, nor does it have a single definite object, nor is it a mere matter of schools. Education is that whole system of human training within and without the school schoolhouse walls, which molds and develops men.

—DuBois (1903)

The decades of the 1980s, 1990re-s, and into the 21st century saw technological, demographic, and environmental changes in the United States that were as transformational as those wrought by the Industrial Revolution and the Great Migration. These changes had a continuing effect on the reshaping of US social welfare policy, the profession, social work education, and, in turn, the continuing trajectory of the School.

The School moved forward in a sociopolitical and cultural context that had become increasingly conservative and even punitive in its approach to social welfare policy and programs for the poor. For the profession, the passing of Whitney M. Young Jr. resulted in the loss of a prominent social work voice and presence at the national level influencing US social welfare policy in the interest of the black community has yet to be reclaimed. And, based on the document review, the recommitment to Forrester B. Washington's vision of a "black school" on the occasion of the School's 1970 mid-centennial had not been sustained in the following decades, as envisioned by the new and activist-oriented professoriate that had conceptualized the autonomous social work practice model. Nonetheless, the Afrocentric perspective and the autonomous social work model as conceived during the process of curriculum renewal undertaken by the faculty under the deanship of Genevieve Hill continued as it does today to be the stated anchors of the School's educational philosophy.

Find a Way or Make One. Alma J. Carten, Oxford University Press (2021). © Oxford University Press.
DOI: 10.1093/oso/9780197518465.001.0001.

The presidency of Ronald Reagan began on January 20, 1981. Never a friend of social welfare programs for the poor, at the beginning of his presidency Reagan offhandedly remarked to reporters that a "war had been waged against poverty and poverty won." Analysis of the impact of the Great Society programs on reducing poverty were mixed. Critics and political opponents claimed that the programs did more harm than good and did nothing more than coddle the poor. Moreover, the programs were accused of contributing to the entrenchment of intergenerational dependency and seen as an irresponsible use of public tax dollars since there was little evidence of their effectiveness. Advocates favoring the programs, on the other hand, commended them for being well-conceived but underfunded and not of sufficient duration to reverse the effects of the nation's residual approach to social welfare that had shaped US policy over the full history of the country until the enactment of the 1935 Social Security Act. While poverty had not been eradicated, as President Lyndon Johnson had envisioned, the nation's poverty rate had been cut almost in half, falling from its peak of 26% in 1967 to 13% in 1980.

The effectiveness of the Great Society programs continues to be debated today. Elements contributing to the decline in the poverty rates during the period, most experts agree, could be attributed to the interrelated effects of all of the anti-poverty programs—including Medicaid, food stamps, and Head Start—combined with the increase in the minimum wage, a strong economy, and the availability of jobs in the manufacturing sector. Moreover, despite the controversies, the data reveal that children and minorities fared far better during the years of the War on Poverty than they ever had up to that time.

Findings from recent studies conducted by the Pew Research Center and the Center on Budget and Policy and Priorities have shown some decline in the current US poverty rates owing to an improved economy (Shapiro & Trisi, 2017). The United States, however, continues to have higher child poverty rates than any of the other advanced economy countries. And while poverty rates have decline over the past forty years for African American and Hispanic children, they currently comprise nearly two-thirds of the children in poverty (Wilson & Schieder, 2018).

Child poverty rates for Georgia and the city of Atlanta are especially bleak. Kids Count is a publication of the Annie E. Casey Foundation that compiles statistical data for use as a tool for public officials and child advocates to advance policies that help children. According to data reported in the 2019 Kids Count Data Book, Georgia is among the nation's ten worst states in the care of its children. Data compiled by the Foundation indicate that 33% of children in rural regions of the state and 21% of those in urban areas live in poverty. And, according to findings reported in the 2015 study published by the Foundation, "Changing the Odds, Racing for Results in Atlanta," black children in Atlanta are poorer than black children in any other American city (Annie E. Casey Foundation, 2015).

THE POOR WILL ALWAYS BE WITH US

With cutbacks in social spending and continued chipping away at programs of the Great Society under the Nixon and Reagan administrations, the declining poverty rates that were seen in the aftermath of the Great Society were not sustained in the following decades. Michael Harrington's 1963 publication, *The Other America,* had jarred the nation's moral conscience and paved the way for the War on Poverty programs. Harrington's 1984 publication, *The New American Poverty*, which he said was not intended to be a sequel to the now classic original study, began with the following foreboding message:

> The poor are still there.
>
> Two decades after the President of the United States declared an "unconditional" war on poverty, poverty does not simply continue to exist; worse, we must deal with structures of misery, with a new poverty much more tenacious than the old. (Harrington, 1984, p. 1)

According to Harrington, the old poor, comprised of whites in Appalachia and blacks in urban inner-city areas, had not gone away; their situation had only worsened within what was a new context. Among the new groups of poor identified by Harrington were the blue-collar unionized workers who had lost their jobs because of the shutdown of US plants, and a developing working class comprised of immigrants from Latin American countries, the Caribbean, and Southeast Asia. A segment of the immigrant poor, as described by Harrington, were the undocumented, who were working in sweatshops across the nation, and terrified of being sent back to their native homelands by US Immigration Services. Among those who were documented were ethnic minorities who worked in low-skill, low-wage jobs. In discussing the causes of changes contributing to the new poor and the worsening conditions of the old poor, Harrington wrote

> They are many, but they include the broadening of poverty; the popular disillusionment with the social welfare policy developed in the United States from the time of Franklin Roosevelt through the administration of Lyndon Johnson; the internationalization of the economy and forces of production; and the complex technological revolution rapidly transforming work patterns throughout the world. "The new poverty" will be a policy issue of the first order for the rest of the decade, and probably for the rest of the century. Though some may accuse

me of being wildly optimistic, I am willing to hazard that this second term of the Reagan presidency marks the beginning of the end of the conservative era in American politics. I believe that we are on the eve of a new period of social change. I say this because I am absolutely convinced that Ronald Reagan has not solved any of the fundamental problems of the American economy. (Harrington, 1984, p. 1)

THE ASCENDANCY OF A NEW CONSERVATISM

Harrington was overly optimistic in his prediction that the conservative era would wane with Reagan's leaving the presidency. Moreover, Reagan's tightening of the welfare to work requirements of the 1988 Family Support Act did not result in a decline in the welfare rolls. And by the decade of the 1990s, the effects of dramatic cuts in social welfare programs under policies of the New Federalism had taken a toll of an increase in social problems of homelessness, substance abuse, crime, child abuse and neglect, and HIV/AIDS—all of a magnitude and scale at which the profession of social work had little prior experience.

Contrary to Harrington's prediction, conservatism did not decline in the post Reagan era but in fact accelerated. The 1994 midterm elections saw a takeover of the House of Representatives by the Republican Party and the advent of the ultra-right conservative Tea Party Movement, bringing an end to the near forty-year control of the US House of Representatives by the Democrats. The 1994 elections occurred at the mid-point of the presidency of Bill Clinton and is referred to as the "Republican Revolution." The Republican-controlled Congress acted swiftly to put in place reforms that reflected the values of traditional conservative ideology. Included among these reforms was the In Defense of Marriage Act that defined marriage as a union between one man and one woman and gave states the right to refused to recognize same-sex unions acknowledge by law in other state jurisdictions. The 1996 Personal Responsibility and Work Opportunity Reconciliation Act (PRWORA) (P.L. 104-193) was a dramatic overhaul of welfare that ended long-standing angst about the nation's public assistance programs that had historically targeted the Aid to Dependent Children program and marked the final dismantlement of the nation's safety net programs.

The ultra-right conservative Tea Party Movement gained power in the Republican Party soon after the 2008 election of Barack Obama to the US presidency. Embracing an ethos of American exceptionalism and populism emphasizing personal responsibility, the limited role of government, and reduced social spending, the movement became a major force in US politics. Those supporting the movement were especially concerned about the shifting demographics in the US because of the fear of whites losing their place as the numerical majority. This concern was symbolized in the intensification of white backlash following Obama's election as the nation's first African American president. Obama's election intensified concerns of the new ultra-right conservative ideology that changing demographic trends would lead to the erosion of white Anglo-Saxon Protestant norms that had historically dominated American culture, society, and the country's political leadership.

ENDING WELFARE AS WE KNOW IT

After the sweeping win in the 1994 midterm election, within the first 500 days the new Republican-controlled Congress crafted the Contract with America that was soon followed by the 1996 Personal Responsibility and Work Opportunity Reconciliation bill (PRWORA). The new law, also known as the Welfare Reform Bill, was signed by President Clinton on August 22, 1996.

The Personal Responsibility Act was among the list of eight proposed reforms included in the Contract with America that was the blueprint for the 1996 Welfare Reform Bill. Other proposals in the Contract included provisions that restricted eligibility of teenage mothers to public assistance and denied increases in cash payments to mothers giving birth to additional children while receiving welfare in an effort to discourage out of wedlock births and encourage two-parent family formation; a lifetime limit of five years to benefits paid by the federal government as a means for reducing welfare expenditures; and the reinforcement of the work ethic by requiring recipients to begin working within two years of receiving benefits.

The objectives of the proposed Family Reinforcement Act, which was among the proposals included in the Contract with America, sought to reinforce the central role of the family in American life and parental responsibility for care of dependent children by requiring a stricter enforcement of child support payments from noncustodial parents and the establishment of paternity at the time of the child's birth.

The bill addressed long-standing criticism of an old system said to give insufficient flexibility to states, discouraged work and responsible fatherhood, and contributed to the rising rates of out-of-wedlock births, but did little to reduce child poverty. The Aid to Families with Dependent Children, previously an entitlement program that provided an uncapped source of funds for eligible families based on need, was abolished and replaced with the Temporary Assistance for Needy Families (TANF), which required parents to work as a condition of receiving benefits. Funds for the federal categorical programs were consolidated into one block grant, and states were given the largest share of the responsibility for designing and implementing their own public assistance programs.

The bill set off a firestorm of controversy. It was seen by liberals as the final destruction of what was already a fragile safety net, with restrictive eligibility requirements that denied access to assistance to those who needed it most and a benefit structure so meager that it did more psychological harm than provide a pathway out of poverty through meaningful work at a living wage.

With the Clinton administration preoccupied with designing a policy for universal healthcare, a first priority of the administration, the bill sent to Congress by the Republican-dominated Congress trumped the welfare reform plan being crafted by President Clinton's Working Group on Welfare Reform, Family Support, and Independence co-chaired by David Ellwood, a leading scholar on poverty and welfare. The Republican bill was twice vetoed by President Clinton and sent back to Congress for revisions. The third time he signed the bill, amid dire predictions that it would push the poor deeper into poverty and do irreparable harm to the nation's poor children.

Today, not only have welfare programs for the poor since the enactment of the 1996 law all but disappeared in most states, but cash assistance programs for the poor are virtually nonexistent. Moreover, the poor have become all but invisible in today's political discourse. This discourse gives attention to the growing income inequality in the United States and the concentration of wealth in the top percentile of the population. However, there is seldom a use of the word "poverty" in this discourse in spite of the reality that 15% or 42.6 million of the total population of Americans live in poverty.

Discussions about poverty in America are also constrained by problems in defining and measuring poverty. Poverty may be defined and measured in either relative or absolute terms. *Relative poverty* is measured within the context of income inequality and the quality of life and the disparities of wealth between income groups within a given society. The United States continues to measure poverty in *absolute terms*, using the 1960 model designed by Mollie Orshansky, a civil servant employed as a researcher and analyst by the Social Security Administration. In devising the threshold, she used the Agriculture Department's least expensive recommended food plan for subsistence that was varied according to family size. Orhansky's formulation was officially adopted by the federal government in 1969. Although not without controversy, her formulation has been used since then, with adjustments for inflation, to establish the official federal poverty line.

The Violent Crime Control and Law Enforcement Act of 1994 (H.R. 3355, Pub.L. 103–322) was another highly controversial bill of the Clinton administration. Enacted with strong bipartisan support, the bill was signed into law by the president on September 13, 1994. It was enacted at a time of dramatic increase in the rates of violent crimes and murders in inner-city areas that corresponded with the introduction of crack cocaine into communities already made vulnerable by rising poverty rates following cuts in service programs for the poor. The law contained the "three strikes" provision mandating life imprisonment without the possibility of parole for individuals, including children, convicted a third time for certain crimes and felonies of a violent nature. Changes in sentencing laws combined with increased funding for new prisons came together in "a perfect storm" to create the new social problem of mass incarceration. The devastating impact of the law on black communities and the racial disparities in prison population that arose in the wake of its implementation formed the context for the advocacy efforts of legal scholars like Michele Alexander, author of *The New Jim Crow* (2011), and Bryan Stevenson, author of *Just Mercy* (2014). Twenty years later, Clinton acknowledged before an audience at the annual meeting of the NAACP that the bill made the "problem worse" and "I want to admit it" (Baker, 2015).

Although all but forgotten, the President's Commission on Race Relations was created in 1997 by Executive Order 13050 to address race relations in the United States. The initiative was designed to bring Americans together in conversations about race. The initiative was chaired by the preeminent African American historian Dr. John Hope Franklin with the official title of "One America in the 21st Century: The President's Initiative on Race" (https://clintonwhitehouse4.archives.gov/media/pdf/PIR.pdf).

A NEW PATH FOR THE SCHOOL

The growth of ultra-right conservatism in the nation, the abandonment of the safety net philosophy by the federal government, and the entrenchment of social problems were all consequential events shaping the continuing trajectory of the School in the decades leading into the new Millennium. The 1988 consolidation of Atlanta University with Clark College brought the two institutions together under one administrative structure. The consolidation involved a study process undertaken by members of the Boards of the two institutions. The joint committee convened to study various options, including the consolidation, submitted its report entitled "Charting a Bold New Future" and recommended the consolidation of the two institutions. The recommendation was accepted by both Boards, creating on June 24, 1988, a new institution designated as Clark Atlanta University (CAU).

The consolidation created a new corporate structure that would govern the affairs of both institutions under one board of trustees and one university president. The consolidation was overseen by President Thomas W. Cole, Jr., who served as president of both Atlanta University and Clark College over the transitional period of 1988–1989 and later as the first president of the consolidated CAU from 1988 to 2002. Dr. Cole was awarded an honorary degree for his service to the university during the installation ceremonies of Dr. George T. French Jr., who was appointed by the Board of Trustees in July 2019 as the fifth president of CAU.

The School of Social Work prepared for reaffirmation in 1999 under the new CAU consolidated administrative and governance structure, in which the largest share of the School's administrative functions was transferred to the university central administration. With the 1988 consolidation that brought the BSW program housed at Clark College and the 1983 addition of the PhD program, the School now awarded the social work degree at all levels of the BSW, MSW, and PhD as it prepared for the 1999 CSWE reaffirmation process.

As the School approached the Millennium, similar to Florence V. Adams's observation of the program in the 1950s and 1960s prior to the School's recommitment to the vision of Forrester B. Washington, it was once again becoming like every other school of social work, but still emphasizing an Afrocentric perspective in its curriculum. At this juncture of the School's history, the shift from the generalist approach to the advanced clinical concentration may likely have been influenced as much by the reaffirmation requirements of the Council on Social Work Education (CSWE) as by professional trends favoring micro practice (Schilling, Morrish, & Liu, 2008).

The 1999 self-study documents submitted to CSWE in preparation for reaffirmation and based on course titles suggested that the School may have been in the process of moving toward a specialization in clinical practice (Clark Atlanta University School of Social Work, 1999). A 2003 Internal Review prepared by Dean Bowles that had been approved by the faculty in 2002 indicated the MSW specialization was advanced clinical practice. The conditions established for reaffirmation described in the 1999 Site Team Report reaffirming the program indicated that the School continued to face challenges related to its unique identity as a social work program in a historically black college and university (HBCU).

For example, the site team report dated October 20, 1999, to university President Dr. Thomas W. Cole Jr. from the Chair of the Commission on Accreditation site indicated that the Commission had voted to reaffirm the combined social work degree programs, the BSW and MSW, for the full eight-year cycle ending June 2006 (Baskind, 1999, p. 1). With changes in the Educational Policy and Accreditation Standards (EPAS) policies on diversity and inclusion that held all social work programs to a high standard of nondiscrimination and human diversity, one of the conditions of the School's reaffirmation was related to concerns about the lack of diversity among the students and faculty, as indicated in the Report.

> The commission found in reviewing the combined program's self-study and site visit report that it serves primarily an African American student population and that the full time and part time faculty are African American. This finding is of serious concern to the commission since it is not clear how the program meets the requirements of the standard cited above related to diversity as this is defined by color, ethnicity, national origin and race. In the program's response

to the site report it was reported that there were several new student recruitment efforts being planned. Please report on these efforts. This response also indicated that a plan has been adopted to recruit and hire faculty who are not African Americans. Please present this plan and results realized since it was put in place. (Baskin, 1999, pp. 2–3)

THE MILLENNIUM AND BEYOND

The emphasis and priorities of the School are reflected in the various themes expressed in continuing acknowledgment of benchmark dates in its history. The School celebrated its 75th Diamond Jubilee Anniversary on October 6–8, 1995, under the interim deanship of Dr. Richard Lyle. The theme of the three-day conference was "Accepting the Challenge Set by the Diamond and Forging Ahead." The theme of the workshops, "Trends and Developments from the Field," was in keeping with the tradition of the School and constructed to connect theory with practice, class, and field. The workshops were conducted by faculty and addressed central issues facing the profession and the black community at the time under the following titles: "Strategies for the Prevention of Alcohol Abuse and Violence Among African American Families," "Approaches for Developing a Private Practice," "Creative Strategies for Self and Community Empowerment," and "The Personal Responsibility Act of 1995: Implications for African Americans."

The School celebrated its 80th anniversary in October 2000 under the deanship of Dr. Dorcas Bowles and the presidency of Thomas W. Cole Jr. The 80th anniversary celebration was undertaken over a two-day period, October 27–28, 2000, under the theme of "Eighty Years of Legacy, Heritage, and Success: Investing in Our Future." It was on the occasion of the celebration that the School was renamed the Whitney M. Young Jr. School of Social Work (Clark Atlanta University School of Social Work, 2000).

Dean Bowles was well known for her scholarship and prolific contributions to the social work literature, and as a administrator in higher education. She is a graduate of Tuskegee University, a HBCU that is now a historical landmark. She has a long history of service to the University and to the School that includes interim provost and vice president for academic affairs at CAU, and she has served as dean of the School of Social Work on three different occasions. Prior to her administrative appointments at CAU, she served as acting dean of the School of Social Work at Smith College, and dean of the School of Social Work at the University of Texas at Arlington.

The renaming of the School when Dr. Bowles held the deanship suggested that, the growing interest in micro-level practice, would not detract from the established tradition of advocacy and social reform of its founders and as modeled by the career of Whitney M. Young, Jr. This tradition was affirmed in President Thomas W. Cole Jr's quoting Young in his congratulatory letter to Dean Bowles commending the naming of the School in Young's honor, in writing

> Young summed up his life worked in the quote:
> "I am not anxious to be the loudest voice or the most popular. But I would like to think that at a crucial moment I was an effective voice of the voiceless and effective hope of the hopeless."
> At the 80th anniversary celebration of the school of social work for Whitney M. Young Jr. who served as dean from 1954 to 1960 it is most befitting that the school be named in his honor. (Cole, October 28, 2000)

In the School's *Internal Academic Programs' Review*, adopted by the faculty on May 22, 2002 (Clark Atlanta University Whitney M. Young Jr. School of Social Work, 2003), indicated that the School had joined professional trends favoring micro practice with the adoption of a sole concentration in advanced clinical social work practice. The Report also indicated that, as required by EPAS the School was anchored in the University's tripartite mission of research, teaching, and service that for CAU was carried out in the tradition established by the HBCUs.

The School's mission as defined in the document affirmed its "commitment to the search in finding solutions to problems of poverty, social, economic and environmental injustices, sexism, racism and other forms of oppression in society, while preserving the heritage of the African Diaspora." This mission as described in the Report was operationalized through the educational goals of its three degree-bearing programs in social work: the BSW program that prepared students for entry-level generalist professional practice, the MSW to educate students for excellence in advanced clinical practice, and the PhD program to produce competent leaders in the field of social work who will work to affect positive social change (Clark Atlanta University Whitney M. Young Jr. School of Social Work, 2003).

The School celebrated its 85th anniversary on October, 7–9, 2005, under the deanship of Dr. Rufus Sylvester Lynch, who served as dean from 2004 to 2007. Embracing the founding mission of the School, the theme of the 85th celebration was "Examining Issues of Racial Disparities After Forty Years of Integration: Implications for the Social Work Profession." The celebration was undertaken as a three-day national conference that examined key areas of racial disparities and their implications for the focus of social workers. In inviting human service professionals from across the country to join in the discussion, In his remarks in the program brochure Dean Lynch stated

The story of Atlanta University School of social work, now the Whitney M. Young. Jr. School of Social Work, is important in helping to raise the public consciousness of how this institution developed a unique training perspective that acknowledge the need for change in the social, economic and political structures affecting African Americans. Although more than a quarter of a century has passed and great strides have been made, America and the Diaspora continue to have limited strategies for meeting the disparities in employment, education, health, housing and political representation that affect African-Americans and other people of color. That's why I encourage you to be a part of the solution to formulate a 21st century plan, at this landmark junction, our 85th anniversary. (Lynch, 2005, p. 2)

Borrowing on the vision of Forrester B. Washington, the first priority of the Seven-Point Plan developed by Dean Lynch and outlined in a Memorabilia Booklet entitled *CAU Whitney M. Young Jr. School of Social Work, "More than a School—A Promotional Agency for Social Welfare"* was intended to

Capitalize on the legacy of Whitney M. Young Junior, by forming a National Board of Advisors dedicated to rebuilding the infrastructure for the school, identifying a suitable resource, and documenting the contributions that Whitney made to social and economic justice both nationally and internationally. (Clark Atlanta University Whitney M. Young Jr. School of Social Work, n.d., p. 28)

The School moved forward within a context of persistent poverty in the United States that continued to have a disproportionate impact on blacks. In September 2011, the US Census Bureau reported that more than 46 million Americans—approximately one in six—were living below the official poverty line, as defined in 2010 as an annual income of $22,314 for a family of four. The report revealed that some groups were especially hard hit by the growth in poverty. For example, the poverty rate for blacks was 27%, and 26% for Hispanics. The data from the report of poverty rates were especially alarming for residents in the Rust Belt cities that had been the industrial heartland of America. These included Reading, Pennsylvania, with a poverty rate of 41.3% followed by Flint, Michigan, at 41.2%. Thirty-five percent of all American children were being raised in poverty.

Conventional thinking holds that the face of poverty is best portrayed in the decay of urban inner-city areas densely populated by blacks. However, the harshness of poverty is experienced more severely in rural areas of the South. Georgia is among the ten states with the highest poverty rates in the US, along with Mississippi, Louisiana, Kentucky, West Virginia, Arkansas, Alabama, New Mexico, Arizona, and Oklahoma.

Poverty was especially severe in Georgia, with blacks being disproportion-ately impacted as the School looked toward its 90th anniversary. Not only was it a time when poverty rates had risen to unconscionable levels, but the era also saw an increasing racial polarization of Americans that was being fueled by a rising conservatism that had taken on racial overtones.

The School celebrated its 90th year on October 8–9, 2010, during deanship of Dr. Vimala Pillari, who served as dean from 2008 to 2015. The theme of the 90th anniversary was "Sustaining Our Roots, Building Our Future" (Clark Atlanta University, 2010). The dean's statement in the 90th anniversary bro-chure announced the School's establishment of a Families and Children's Research Center and the reestablishment of a certification for school social work (Pillari, p. 6).

The dire state of populations of historic concern to the founders of the School and to the profession was acknowledged in the statement of Dr. Carlton E. Brown, who served as president of CAU from 2008 to 2015. Speaking to the mission of the School at the time of its founding and at the time of its 90th anniversary his message read

> Lest we forget, from its very conception it stood as a defiant symbol of hope and pride against the daunting shadow on the American nadir, when racism, segregation, lynching and rampant disenfranchisement stained the fabric of our "more perfect union."
>
> The mission and purpose of the School then, as now, guided hundreds of scholars to build, fortify, and empower a people, a community and a nation through research, scholarly discourse, diligent field service and impactful, evoc-ative instruction. Our alumni reflect the sterling record of service and the high standard of intellect that has over the past nine decades become a hallmark of the Whitney M. Young, Jr. School of Social Work.
>
> Today, our students face myriad challenges and, while technology, glob-alism and socio-economic influences have changed the dynamics of modern social work, challenges to the health, welfare and freedom of families, and communities, particularly those in communities of color, persist. Therefore, our mission is as pertinent today as it was in 1920. Without a doubt, the need for dedicated, well educated professionals to successfully execute it is more impor-tant than ever before. It is in this light and with this call to service—that we persevere. (Brown, 2010, p. 4)

The historic centennial year of the School is being celebrated under the cur-rent dean, Dr. Jenny L. Jones, an alumna of the School's doctoral program, who was appointed to the deanship in 2016. The Centennial Celebration began with a kickoff event at the 2019 CSWE APM, where Dean Jones presented a paper on the contributions of HBCU social work programs to social work education. The celebration was planned to include a year-long schedule of events that would conclude in October 2020. The activities of the School's Centennial were undertaken under the theme of "Looking Back Moving Forward." The School's Centennial took place concurrently with the installation of Dr. George T. French Jr. as the fifth president of CAU. President French was appointed by the Board on June 21, 2019; his administration moved forward under the banner of "Facing the Rising Sun Together," adapted from the phrase, "Facing the rising sun of our new day begun. Let us march on 'til victory is won," from the poem written by University alumni James Weldon Johnson that has become the Negro National Anthem.

THE STATE OF SOCIAL WORK EDUCATION

With the dawning of the Millennium, the profession and social work educators, as they as they had always done, redefined themselves in an ongoing effort to maintain a reasonable balance between the professional interest of social work practitioners and educators and the public purposes of the missions of their professional associations. The CSWE continued to move forward in solidifying the advances made in response to social movements of the 1960s and 1970s. Policy changes were now in place that resulted in a more inclusive governance structure, and the Commission on Accreditation (COA) EPAS required the integration of diversity content into the curriculum of all social work programs awarding the BSW and MSW degree.

As discussed in Chapter 12, other accomplishment that addressed issues of inclusion and equity included the leadership of Carl Scott, who guided the early work of the Council on diversity, served as consultant to the Council's five Minority Task Force Groups, and secured funding for the CSWE Minority Fellowship Program (MFP) that provided doctoral fellowship awards to support the development of minority behavioral health professionals. The social work deans and the leadership of the National Association of Social Workers (NASW) had come to an agreement that accepted the baccalaureate degree as the entry level of professional social work practice, thus opening the door for CSWE accreditation of BSW social work programs.

In speaking to the comprehensive changes enacted by the CSWE Delegate Assembly under his term as president of the Council, Dr. James R. Dumpson, who was the first African American elected to the position, commented on the progress made over his presidency in an oral history interview.

> I became president of Council, Ed, at a time when social work education was in turmoil . . . particularly on the issue of graduate and undergraduate education for the profession. NASW, if you remember—was pushing for recognition of a baccalaureate level of social work education as the first professional degree of

social work practice. The deans and faculties of the graduate schools were saying there was no way this could happen. After NASW formerly took this position, the CSWE was called upon because of its function in accreditation and social work education policy to be the leader in bringing together these two opposing views. (Mullen, 1991)

Dumpson continued in the same interview to comment on accomplishments that resulted in a more inclusive CSWE governance structure for blacks and other historically underrepresented groups of concern to the profession

I remember during my tenure as president, how I helped to reform, or reconstitute the House of Delegates that in the hope would be more representative of the total field of social work education. I remember we brought in students as members to define special population groups that we now refer to as quotas. But we have to have so many minority women, men, and divided the ethnic minority groups into Black, Latino, Asian and Native American. We talked about proportional representation of graduate and undergraduate deans and faculty having proportional representation in the House of Delegates. We enriched social work education as to diversity input. . . . We included such interest groups as the Gay and Lesbian Faculty—and to the horror of some faculty and administrators in those days who wanted to know what in the world were we doing. Today in 1991 nobody would think about sexual orientation, or ethnic content, or the right to have it infused into the curriculum. (Mullen, 1991)

Despite these notable accomplishments, sustainable change on these matters proved elusive. The subsequent decades would see an erosion of what were notable accomplishments within the ever-changing context of the profession and social work education.

During this period, there was substantial increase in the number of CSWE-accredited BSW, MSW and joint MSW-BSW programs, and in the number of PhD programs. BSW programs increased from 150 to 404; the number of MSW programs from 79 to 139; and social work doctoral programs increased from 29 to 67. Concurrent with the rising number of CSWE-accredited social work programs was a continuing diminishing of minority enrollment in these programs. For example, in 1969, 21.6% of full-time MSW students were minorities (Council on Social Work Education [CSWE], 1969); by 1975, this had decreased to 21% and, by 1985, to 17.1% (CSWE, 1976, 1986; Schilling, Morrish, & Liu, 2008).

Dumpson called attention to the diminishing presence of students of color in social work programs across the nation, and he also joined the chorus of concerned voices about the profession's drifting away from its founding mission. He voiced these concerns in his Keynote Address for the Carl Scott

Memorial Lecture given at the 1993 CSWE APM. Drawing on data from a Columbia University Study, he said that

> According to the Minority Leadership publication, between 1974 and 1991 the percentage of social work master's degrees earned by minorities fell from 21.6% to 16.7%. While the number of master's degrees awarded to Asian American and Mexican American students increased, the percentage of degrees awarded these two groups respectively decreased by 16.2% and 4.1% respectively. The picture for African Americans is a particularly bleak one. . . . According to the report the number of degrees awarded to African Americans actually declined by 21.6%. If knowledge of the magnitude of this decline does not constitute grounds for a call for action, then the question is what it takes for us to respond. (Dumpson, 1993, pp. 12–13)

This diminishing presence in minority enrollment maybe attributed to shortfalls in schools giving attention to strategies of both recruitment and retention. This is reflected in qualitative findings of the study that Dumpson referred to in the keynote address at the 1993 APM, in which some students of color reported feeling as if they were uninvited guests in classrooms of little diversity and a lack of enthusiasm for course content that gave scant attention to social action, advocacy, community organization, and other large-scale interventions that were, for them, more effective for solving the problems of their communities of identification.

Dumpson's remarks in the Keynote Address also expressed his concerns about what was occurring at a time when black communities were disproportionately impacted by what had become intractable social problems.

> Throughout the history of the profession, there seems to have been a fluctuating imbalance between interests in social reform and advocacy and professionalization and specialization. The preference to pursue social work solely as a for-profit private enterprise has paralleled the growth of a conservative social welfare ideology within and outside the profession. I concur with Courtney and Spechin their 1994 book *Unfaithful Angels: How Social Work Has Abandoned its Mission* that if continued, these trends can leave a tremendous gap in services traditionally provided by social workers. Moreover, poor, minority clients will be among those who suffer the most from the lack of availability of services. (Dumpson, 1993)

THE STATE OF PROFESSIONAL MEMBERSHIP ASSOCIATIONS

The Delegate Assembly of the NASW continued to make policy changes and revise the Code of Ethics to keep pace with changes in the practice environment and to strengthen nondiscrimination policies and ethical imperatives.

Recognizing the growing interest among social workers in private practice, the NASW Delegate Assembly issued a 1964 position statement asserting that "The National Association of Social Workers recognizes private practice as a legitimate area of social work, but it affirms that practice in socially sponsored organizational structures must remain the primary avenue of implementation of the goals of the profession." On matters of racial inclusion, the first revision in the original 1960 Code of Ethics occurred in 1967, when an ethical principle was added to address nondiscrimination. The 2008 revision incorporated sexual orientation, gender identity, and immigration status into the existing nondiscrimination standards. Also during the early decades of the 21st century, addressing structural racism was established as a national priority of the NASW, as reported in a 2007 publication of the Association entitled *Institutional Racism and the Social Work Profession: A Call to Action* (National Association of Social Workers [NASW], 2007).

The National Association of Black Social Workers (NABSW) was also changing within the context of the evolving times. By the 1990s, the influence of the radicalism of the Black Power movement of the 1960s, which Joyce M. Bell, author of *The Black Power Movement and American Social Work* (Bell, 2014), argued had a significant influence on shaping black professional associations, was becoming less of an issue because mainstream professional associations had made good faith efforts to amend policies that integrated the demands for more inclusiveness. Moreover, frontline black social workers entering into the profession between the latter years of the 1960s and the 1990s were interested in helping the poor and achieving social justice for blacks. However, they were more inclined to pursue these professional interests through micro-level practices to change the behaviors of individuals than they were to use macro-level interventions or advocacy aimed at broad-based system change and reforms. And while the membership of the NABSW had increased significantly, concurrent with this increase in membership, black frontline workers were also joining mainstream membership associations or opting for dual membership with these associations and NABSW, as certification and licensure were fast becoming requirements for employment in both agency-based and independent social work practice.

These were also decades that saw a generational divide between black social workers. The older generation, often Baby Boomers, were less inclined to sign on to the nationalist or separatist orientation that some of the younger generation of black social workers, who had come of age during the Civil Rights movement, evidenced a greater willingness to embrace. Florence V. Adams, for example, is said to have declined an invitation to have a scholarship established in her name, presumably exclusively for blacks, nor was she said to be inclined to favor the feminist movement in the profession, explaining that she supported mixed gender and racial professional organizations (Bell, 2014).

Whatever their professional bias, black social workers were united in the support of black mothers who were recipients of public welfare and who were being scapegoated as the public discourse on public welfare assumed a more victim-blaming stance, along with Reagan's promotion of the narrative of the "welfare queen." Emboldened by a new sense of agency generated by the human rights movements of the civil rights years, welfare recipients were shedding the stigma and shame of the welfare mentality and replacing it with a new sense of entitlement. This new sense of agency galvanized the poor to organize under the leadership of Dr. George Wiley to form the National Welfare Rights Organization (NWPO). A professor of chemistry at Syracuse University, Wiley had abandoned a career in academia to form the NWRO in 1966. The Organization was the umbrella for organizing thousands of public assistant recipients across the country to demand social justice and fair treatment by bureaucratic public welfare departments overseeing public assistance programs for the poor. The National Welfare Rights Movement is an important component of US social welfare history, but, as noted earlier, is beyond the scope of this manuscript. The public papers of Wiley's work in civil rights and welfare reform are found in a number of repositories including those held by the Library of Congress.

GEORGIA AND THE CITY OF ATLANTA

Georgia, along with other Southern states, had been steadily exiting the Democratic Party since South Carolina Senator Strom Thurman and Georgia Senator Richard Russel led the crafting of the 1956 Southern Manifesto that vowed to use all legal means necessary to strike down the 1954 Supreme Court ruling outlawing segregation in public schools. The document had the unanimous support of Georgia legislators. The signatories to the Manifesto included Georgia's two state senators, and all of the Georgia members in the House of Representatives. As a Red state in the Deep South, Georgia has been strongly rooted in the conservative ideology of the republican party, at least since the exodus set by the in motion by the Southern Manifesto. The cross migration from left leaning states will likely have political implications for the state as it continues to grapple with the remnants from its white supremacist past.

What for many is seen as a far-right conservative ideology has been carried forward under the leadership of an incumbent president under the banner to "Make America Great Again." With features of populism, the movement tended to appeal to conservative whites who felt abandoned by their government. Feelings of anger provoked by this sense of abandonment have made some receptive to the incumbent president's use of rhetoric that communicates coded messages of white supremacy. These developments have contributed to the creation of a political climate that raises concerns about the threat of a "new normal" that many feared would threatened to return the country back to a racist past of intolerance.

The violence generated under what is emerging as this "new normal" has also fueled the rise in white nationalist groups and hate crimes under the banner of white supremacy. This was the context in which the Charleston Church Massacre on June 17, 2015, occurred, in which nine parishioners of the Emanuel African Methodist Episcopal Church were murdered by a self-proclaimed white supremacist. The tragic Church Massacre underscored for many Americans the dangers of allowing the unchecked growth of racist ideology in a nation premised on democratic ideals.

These developments and the rise in hate groups were a catalyst for bringing the attention of the nation to focus on Civil War Confederate monuments throughout the South that commemorated the Southern "Lost Cause" and individuals past and the 20th century revered for their support of white supremacy. This subsequently led to a national movement to remove confederate symbols from official public locations. This was far from being an easy task. Indeed, considerable controversy was engendered among groups of differing minds about individuals representing the southern cause in fighting the Civil War. In the minds of some, these individuals were traitors and racists; while others held them up as icons and heroes (Joyner, 2015).

Controversies initially arose in Georgia fueled by a pro-white, pro-confederation rally organized in April 2016 at the Stone Mountain Park outside of Atlanta. This was the site of the rebirth of the Ku Klux Klan a near century ago, soon after the release of D. W. Griffith's film *The Birth of a Nation*. The white power "Rock Stone Mountain" rally was attended by Klansmen and white nationalist groups under the banner of "Save Our Monuments." The monument of concern was the images of Confederate Robert E. Lee, Stonewall Jackson, and Jefferson Davis that were carved into the face of the mountain. Thus far, the Atlanta chapter of the NAACP and the Southern Christian Leadership Conference (SCLC) have been unsuccessful in demands for the removal of the 90-by-900-foot bas-relief sculpture. The Atlanta City Council passed a resolution for an alternative plan to amend the carving to include other historical figures, such as the Rev. Martin Luther King Jr. or President Jimmy Carter.

As attention shifted to confederate symbols in public places in the capitol of the state, Georgia was found to have a preponderance of Confederate-era symbols but only a handful depicting the black experience in the Civil War and its aftermath. These monuments also pay homage to men who played a role in the illegal removal of the Cherokee from their ancestral lands, which were turned over to white settlers for the cultivation of cotton, and to a long list of 20th-century segregationists who were steadfast in their determination to prevent African Americans from obtaining full citizenship and social equality.

John H. Gordon, a Confederate general under the command of Robert E. Lee, holds a prominent place on the capitol grounds, sitting astride his horse in full dress uniform. After the war, he served as a Georgia state senator and governor of the state. Gordon is also known for heading the Georgia Ku Klux Klan, which he referred to as "peaceable and law-abiding citizens," and he championed the enslavement of blacks as being "morally, socially and politically right." Also counted among the 20th-century figures commemorated at the state capitol are Richard Russell and Eugene Tallmadge, whose portraits hang inside the capitol and whose statutes stand outside on the capitol grounds.

Russell is well known for his enormous influence in the US Congress with colleagues across the aisle and as advisor to Republican and Democratic presidents. Socialized in the culture of the Old South and southern way of life, he was never in support of racial integration and is equally well known for his opposition to federal civil rights legislation. Eugene Talmadge, branded "the wild man from Sugar Creek," was more outspoken and flagrant as a staunch segregationist in serving three terms as governor of the state. He boasted an admiration for dictators, fired a professor who supported integration and resulted in the University of Georgia losing its accreditation, and he led the state's attack on FDR's New Deal programs that would have improved the lives of small farmers. Nonetheless, he remained a favored son, an appeal that led *Time* Magazine to observe "that few men had appealed so successfully to ignorance and bigotry" (https://www.todayingeorgiahistory.org/content/eugene-talmadge). What has turned out to be an highly emotionally charged controversy about who stays and who leaves continues to unfold.

Stacey Abrams in recent years has emerged as a rising star in Georgia state government. An African American and Yale Law School graduate, she has ties to the HBCUs as a graduate of Spelman College, where her interests in activism and politics began. Abrams is a veteran of Georgia politics, having served eleven years in the Georgia House of Representatives. In 2018, Abrams became the Democratic nominee for Governor of Georgia, becoming the first black woman to become the gubernatorial nominee for a major party in the United States. Since losing that election, she has consistently raised claims that the election was unfairly conducted and launched the organization Fair Fight to ensure that the vote of every citizen in the state of Georgia is counted.

If Georgia is staunchly Republication and Red, the city of Atlanta stands in sharp contrast in being staunchly Democratic and Blue. Atlanta is the state capital and largest city in Georgia, and it is the ninth most populous city in the United States. Blacks comprise 51.4% of the population and, as such, are the largest demographic in city. Blacks are followed by whites, who comprise 41.3% of the city's population; Asians at 3.7%; and Hispanics of any race at 4.7%. With blacks as the majority demographic, the city has had an unbroken roster of Democratic black mayors since 1973, with the election of Maynard Jackson who was the first African American mayor of Atlanta.

The current mayor of Atlanta is Keisha Lance Bottoms, who was elected in 2017 to become Atlanta's 50th mayor. A native of Atlanta, she is also a product of the HBCUs, having earned her undergraduate degree from Florida A&M University in Tallahassee; she later earned a law degree at Georgia State University. As mayor, Bottoms has been a strong advocate and supporter of social work causes. For example, she established the city's first Office of Equity, Diversity, and Inclusion, and she appointed a coordinator for LGBTQ Affairs. She signed on to President Obama's My Brother's Keeper initiative, launched by the Obama administration, that uses a mentoring model to address the persistent barriers to opportunities faced by young people of color that prevent them from reaching their full potential. With the program in Atlanta having a long list of young people waiting for mentors, Mayor Bottoms partnered with Big Brothers Big Sisters of Metro Atlanta to find mentors for youth who were waiting to be matched to mentors. In response to the widely contested policy of the current White House administration's Immigration and Customs Enforcement (ICE) policy of separating immigrant children from their parents, she signed a mayoral executive order that Atlanta will no longer accept children whose parents are detained by ICE absent reassurance that the current administration's policies of breaking families apart at all points entry are rescinded. While the current law prohibits Atlanta from being a Sanctuary City, Mayor Bottoms was clear in her expectation for Atlanta to convey an image of a safe and welcoming city. The Mayor's Office of Equity, Diversity, and Inclusion is carried out under the visionary goal of creating "One Atlanta" (Umontuen, 2018).

The vision of One Atlanta is an ambitious one. But it does provide an opportunity to address the historical and paradoxical nature of the black experience in America that is graphically portrayed in the experiences of Atlanta's black communities. The concentration of institutions of higher learning for blacks in the city founded soon after the Civil War was a central force that made the city a historic home for an elite class of blacks. These were men and women privileged by education, heritage, and the unintended benefits of legal segregation that spawned "Sweet Auburn Avenue" and the growth of a black professionals and business class of black Atlantans who held a virtual business monopoly on meeting the service and material needs of blacks. The existential benefits enjoyed by this class of blacks, privileged by the "peculiar institution of slavery," are examined in Chapter 8. W. E. B. Dubois commented on the implications of this hierarchy of blacks in freedom in observing that house servants, by virtue of having been brought into closer contact with white culture, enjoyed access to life outside of the plantations and often shard a bloodline with plantation owners. They were envisioned as the class of blacks who would assume leadership roles in the economic development of the black community in freedom (DuBois, 1906, p. 220).

Beginning in the late 1990s, Atlanta's established black "old elite," for whom the city had been home for generations, were joined by an influx of young well-educated professional black Millennials following a reverse migration trend in which blacks were returning to the South. In the push-pull dynamics of immigration, unlike the Great Migration occurring between 1917 and 1970, for this recent second migration, the South has become the receiver versus sender of blacks seeking an improved quality of life. A study completed by the Brookings Institute found that the South has become a regional magnet for attracting a well-educated, privileged class of black Millennials (Brookings Institute, 2004; Frey, 2004). Texas, Georgia, and Florida were states to which black Millennials were moving in the greatest numbers, and Atlanta was by far the most popular city of resettlement in the 1990s.

The concentration of this new demographic of blacks in Atlanta led *Ebony* magazine in 1970 to coin the term "Black Mecca" to characterize a cohort of blacks who enjoyed lives of status and privilege. This is juxtaposed against data that show the city as having the worse income inequality in the United States and the worst poverty rates for black children—understandably since the fate of children is tied to that of their parents. In Atlanta, being poor is equivalent to being black and a near certainty of living in DeKalb or Fulton Counties. Race continues to shape the city. Ironically, poverty is concentrated in the surrounding areas as when the School was founded. A number of social scientists have conducted research in an effort to explain the paradoxical nature of black experience in Atlanta. These studies have found that race-based political decision-making and white racism have been contributing factors to the entrenched patterns of residential racial segregation, the rise of an elite and privileged class of blacks, and the persistence of a black underclass (Bayor, 1996; Hobson, 2017; Massey & Denton, 1993; Pomerantz, 1996).

THE UNITED STATES IN THE 21ST CENTURY

America began the early decades of the 21st century under the weight of changing demographic and population trends, the globalization of the economy, environmental changes, the threat of financial crisis that portended the second Great Depression, and the enactment of welfare reforms that signaled the country's final abandonment of the safety net philosophy. Without question the most catastrophic event of the new millennium was the September 11, 2001, terrorists attacks that changed the face of American society. The election of Barack Hussein Obama as the nation's first African American president was a transformational event in that it was optimistically, if prematurely, envisioned as an indication of the country entering into a post-racial era.

The September 11 attacks, also referred to as 9/11, involved the high jacking of American airplanes by militants associated with the extremist group al-Qaeda. Two of the planes targeted the World Trade Center in New York City's Financial District and destroyed the Twin Towers in the World Trade Center. A second plane caused considerable destruction to the Pentagon in Washington, DC. A third plane en route to the US Capitol was brought down by the passengers and crashed in Pennsylvania. The event thrust the country into a post-terrorist era of constant vigilance to prevent future attacks. Unfortunately, the fear of future terrorist attacks influenced a rise among Americans in support of anti-Muslim policies and a backlash against Muslim communities. For the profession, the attacks raised awareness of the implications of trauma on mental health and, in doing so, increased the visibility of social workers as the professional discipline with well-established expertise in the field of trauma-informed care, and led to the introduction of new courses offerings on trauma in school of social work programs.

Barack Obama had campaigned for the presidency on an agenda of inclusion, hope, and change under a banner of "Yes We Can." The nation met the presidential hopeful when he was Illinois State Senator and gave the Keynote Address at the 2004 Democratic National Convention, where he asserted

Well, I say to them tonight, there is not a liberal America and a conservative America—there is the United States of America. There is not a black America and a white America and Latino America and Asian America—there's the United States of America. (Obama, 2004, https://www.pbs.org/newshour/show/barack-obamas-keynote-address-at-the-2004-democratic-national-convention)

And on November 4, 2008, in speaking to the jubilant crowd at the Chicago rally after the announcement was made that he had been successful in his historic bid for the US presidency, again with hope and optimism, he stated

If there is anyone out there who still doubts that America is a place where all things are possible, who still wonders if the dream of our founders is alive in our time, who still questions the power of our democracy, tonight is your answer. (Obama, 2008, https://www.nytimes.com/2012/11/07/us/politics/transcript-of-president-obamas-election-night-speech.html)

The signature social welfare legislation of the Obama administration was the enactment of the Patient Protection and Affordable Care Act (ACA) that was signed into law by the president on March 23, 2010. This was an accomplishment that had been beyond the reach of virtually every presidential administration beginning with FDR's unsuccessful attempt for such a plan to be a part of the Social Security Act. The American Recovery and Reinvestment Act signed by President Obama in February 2009 was also a consequential policy of the Obama presidency that warded off what economists predicted would be another Great Depression. The law also contained provisions that restored antipoverty benefits that helped children and blacks who were inevitability hurt most in times of economic down turns. The In Defense of Marriage Act was repealed under the Obama administration, as was the Don't Ask Don't Tell policy of the Clinton administration that encouraged homosexual individuals to conceal their sexual orientation in order to serve in the US military. The Violence Against Women Act, originally crafted by Obama's Vice President Joe Biden in 1994, with bipartisan support of Congress, was reauthorized under the Obama administration.

The School of Social Work entered the 21st century confronting challenges faced by all such schools in the continued unfolding of social forces that had implications for the profession and social work education. Social workers in the academy faces the continuing challenge of balancing its dual identity as an academic discipline based in science that meets university expectations for research and publications and as a profession whose activities in the academy are guided by a professional code of ethics (Wheeler & Gibbons, 1992; Austin, 1997). In the 21st century, the profession is entering into the Digital Age, with schools offering course online and some schools making it possible to earn the MSW totally online. This is a development not without controversy. For some social work educators, web-based education diluted the quality of education and training in a value-based profession with emphasis on the importance of human relationships, important facets that were lost in the impersonality of web-based educational programs. Others saw this as a means for making access to social work education available to a larger pool of candidates and to increase income that could be used to innovate, grow and improve the quality of the educational programs of the schools.

Globalization is also a trend influencing the profession, advancing social workers' interest in social justice and poverty as these concerns presented themselves on the world stage. These international interest have incentivized schools to establish off-site programs in other countries and to increase the ethnic and racial diversity in student enrollment by including students from non-Western cultures. This is also a time in which schools of social work are experiencing growing protests among a progressive-minded student body demanding a more inclusive academic environment and for academic course work that prepares them for roles in solving pressing national and world social problems such as environment and climate change, world poverty and inequality, immigration, and the increases in violence related to intolerance in its many forms. Social work students are also well represented in the Me Too and Black Lives Matter movements. Both are international activist movements that arose as grassroots efforts to bring to light the pervasiveness of sexual violence against women and violence against blacks.

As President Obama's eight-year term ended in January 2017, the notion that his presidency signaled America's entry into an era of post-racist society had been rebuked by social work scholars and those in other academic disciplines who reminded us that the work is far from done (Dawson & Bobo, 2009; Dyson, 2016; Kennedy, 2011). The aftermath of the Obama administration witnessed the beginning of an era of incivility in political discourse described as more vitriolic than at any other time in the nation's history. Moreover, the US political climate of today resembles that seen in the country during the years of the School's founding. The difference at this juncture of the history of the nation and the School is that intolerance is no longer simply a black–white binary, but is also directed toward new groups of black and brown people and non-Christian religious groups.

REFERENCES

Allen, R. (2017). Racism is everywhere, so why not move South? *New York Times*, July 8, 2017.

Alexander, M. (2011). *The new Jim Crow: Mass incarceration in the age of colorblindness*. The New Press.

Annie E. Casey Foundation. (1970/2015). *Changing the odds: The Race for results in Atlanta*. New York: Association of Black Social Workers Journal. Black Caucus.

Austin, D. (1997). The institutional development of social work education: The first 100 years—and beyond. *Journal of Social Work Education*, *33*(3), 599–612. www.jstor.org/stable/23043092

Baker, P. (2015). Bill Clinton concedes his crime law jailed too many for too long. *New York Times*, July 15, 2015.

Baskind, F. R. (1999). Chair, Commission on Accreditation, October 20, 1999, Cover letter to Dr. Thomas W. Cole, Jr., President Clar Atlanta University reporting findings of the October 1999 meeting of the Commission on Accreditation for reaffirmation of the combined degree program in social work at Clark Atlanta University. Found in on-site documents at the WMYJSSW.

Brown, C. E. (2010). CAU President remarks, in Clark Atlanta University Celebrates Sustaining our Roots Building our Future. The Whitney M. Young, Jr. School of Social Work 90th Anniversary, October 8–9, 2010.

Dawson, M. C., & Bobo, L. B. (2009). One year later and the myth of a post-racial society. *Du Bois Review: Social Science Research on Race*, *6*(2), 247–249.

Bayor, R. H. (1996). *Race and the shaping of twentieth-century Atlanta*. Chapel Hill: University of North Carolina Press.

Bell, J. M. (2014). *The Black power movement and American social work*. Ithaca, NY: Columbia University Press.

Brookings Institute Center on Urban and Metropolitan Policy. (2004). *Moving beyond sprawl: The challenge for metropolitan Atlanta*. Living Cities Census Series. Washington, DC: Brookings Institute.

Clark Atlanta University. (1999). Copy of the commission letter requesting interim report, October 20, 1999.

Clark Atlanta University. (2010). *Clark Atlanta University celebrates. Sustaining our roots, building our future.* The Whitney M. Young Jr. School of Social Work 90th Anniversary. October 8–9, 2010. Atlanta: Author.

Clark Atlanta University School of Social Work (2000). 80th Anniversary. *Eighty years of heritage, and success: Investing in the future (1920–2000).* October, 27–28, 2000. Atlanta: Author.

Clark Atlanta University School of Social Work. (1999). Self-Study, BSW/MSW Programs. Volume III, Supplementary Materials. Submitted to the Council on Social Work Education, Commission of Accreditation for Reaffirmation of Accreditation. Atlanta: Author.

Clark Atlanta University Whitney M. Young Jr. School of Social Work. (2017). Dr. Jenny Jones, Dean. *Find a Way or Make One.* Annual Report AY 2017–18. Atlanta: Author.

Clark Atlanta University Whitney M. Young Jr. School of Social Work. (2003). *Internal academic programs' review, BSW program, MSW program, PhD program.* January 31, 2003. Submitted by Dorcas Bowles, Dean, to Dr. Winifred Harris, Provost & Vice President for Academic Affairs.

Clark Atlanta University Whitney M. Young Jr. School of Social Work. (n.d.) *More than a school—A promotional agency for social welfare.* Dr. Rufus Sylvester Lynch, Dean. Memorabilia Booklet. Atlanta: Author.

Cole, W. T. Jr. (October 28, 2000). Office of the President, Clark Atlanta University. Whitney M. Young, Jr. (1921–1971). In Clark Atlanta University School of Social Work. 80th Anniversary: Eighty Years of Legacy, Heritage and Success: Investing in the Future (1920–2000). Atlanta, Georgia.

Council on Social Work Education (CSWE). (1969). *Statistics on social work education.* New York: Author.

Council on Social Work Education (CSWE). (1976). *Statistics on social work education in the United States: 1975.* New York: Author.

Council on Social Work Education (CSWE). (1986). *Statistics on social work education in the United States: 1985.* Washington, DC: Author.

Dubois, W. E. B. (1906). The economic future of the Negro. *Publications of the American Economic Association,* 7(1), 219–242.

Dumpson, J. R. (1993, March 1). Achieving diversity: Taking stock and looking forward. Presented as the Carl R. Scott Memorial Lecture at the Council on Social Work Education, Annual Program Meeting, New York.

Dyson, M. E. (2016). *The Black presidency: Barack Obama and the politics of race in America.* New York: Houghton Mifflin Harcourt.

Dyson, M. E. (2016). *The Black presidency: Barack Obama and the politics of race in America.* New York: Houghton Mifflin Harcourt.

Frey, W. H. (2004). *The new great migration: Black Americans' return to the South, 1965-2000.* Washington, DC: Brookings Institute, Center on Urban and Metropolitan Policy.

Harrington, M. (1984). The new American poverty. *Black Law Journal,* 9, 199.

Harrington, M. (1985). The new American poverty. *National Black Law Journal,* 9(2).

Harrington, M. (1966). *The Other America: Poverty in US.* Helicon.

Hobson, M. J. (2017). *The legend of the black Mecca: Politics and class in the making of modern Atlanta.* Chapel Hill: University of North Carolina Press.

Joyner, C. (2015). Statues, portraits offensive to many, sacred to others. *The Atlanta Journal-Constitution*, September 5, 2015

Kennedy, R. (2011). *The persistence of the color line: Racial politics and the Obama presidency*. New York: Vintage.

Luckey, I. (1995). Douglas S. Massey and Nancy A. Denton: *American Apartheid: Segregation and the making of the underclass* (book review). *Social Service Review, 69*(4), 733.

Lynch, R. S. (October 7–9, 2005). "Examining issues of racial disparities after 40 years of integration: Implications for social work practice." Whitney M. Young, Jr. School of Social Work, Clark Atlanta University. 85th Anniversary Celebration and National Conference. Atlanta, Georgia.

Massey, D. S., & Denton, N. A. (1993). *American apartheid: Segregation and the making of the underclass*. Cambridge, MA: Harvard University Press.

Mullen, E. J. (1991, October 11). Fordham University Oral history project. Interview of James R. Dumpson. Transcript, No. 100.

National Association of Social Workers. (2000). *Code of ethics of the National Association of Social Workers*. Washington, DC: Author.

National Association of Social Workers. (2007). *Institutional Racism and the Social Work Profession: A Call to Action* (National Association of Social Workers President's Initiative Weaving the Fabrics of Diversity. https://www.socialworkers.org/LinkClick.aspx?fileticket=SWK1aR53FAk%3D&portalid=0

Obama, B. H. (2004). Kenote Address at the DNC National Convention. https://www.pbs.org/newshour/show/barack-obamas-keynote-address-at-the-2004-democratic-national-convention

Obama, B. H. (November 7, 2012). Transcript of President Obama's Election Night Speech. https://www.nytimes.com/2012/11/07/us/politics/transcript-of-president-obamas-ele

Patten, E., & Krogstad, J. M. (2015). Black child poverty rate holds steady, even as other groups see declines. Pew Research Center. https://www.pewresearch.org/fact-tank/2015/07/14/black-child-poverty-rate-holds-steady-even-as-other-groups-see-declines/

Pomerantz, G. M. (1996). *Where Peachtree meets Sweet Auburn: The saga of two families and the making of Atlanta*. New York: Scribner.

Pillari, V. (2010). Dean's remarks, in Clark Atlanta University Celebrates Sustaining our Roots Building our Future. The Whitney M. Young, Jr. School of Social Work 90th Anniversary, October 8–9, 2010.

Schilling, R., Morrish, J., & Liu, G. (2008). Demographic trends in social work over a quarter-century in an increasingly female profession. *Social Work, 53*(2), 103–114.

Shapiro, I., & Trisi, D. (2017). *Child poverty falls to record low: Comprehensive measure shows stronger government policies account for long-term improvement*. Washington, DC: Center on Budget and Policy Priorities.

Stevenson, B. (2014). *Just Mercy: A Story of Justice and Redemption*. New York: Spiegel & Grau.

Tice, K. (1990). Gender and social work education: Directions for the 1990s. *Journal of Social Work Education, 26*(2), 134–144. www.jstor.org/stable/23043133

Umontuen, I. (2018). Mayor Keisha Lance Bottoms announces executive action stopping Atlanta from accepting ICE detainees. Voice News Network. https://www.theatlantavoice.com/articles/mayor-bottoms-announces-executive-action-stopping-city-of-atlanta-fro

Wheeler, B., & Gibbons, W. (1992). Social work in academia: Learning from the past and acting on the present. *Journal of Social Work Education, 28*(3), 300–311. www.jstor.org/stable/23042927

Whitney, M. Young, Jr. School of Social Work, Clark Atlanta &University. 85th Anniversary Celebration and National Conference, October 7–9, 2005. Atlanta, Georgia.

Wilson, V., & Schieder, J. (June 8, 2018). *Economic Policy Institute.* The rise in child poverty reveals racial inequality more than a failed war on poverty. https://www.epi.org/publication/the-rise-in-child-poverty-reveals-racial-inequality-more-than-a-failed-war-on-poverty/

CHAPTER 15

Moving Forward into the 21st Century

The good we secure for ourselves is precarious and uncertain until it is secured for all of us and incorporated into our common life.
—Jane Addams (1892)

Reflecting the paradoxical nature of the black experience in the United States, the Whitney M. Young Jr. School of Social Work celebrates this landmark year at a time when the political climate in the United States resembles that of the country at the time of its founding a full century ago. In the city of Atlanta to address the unmet need in black neighborhoods at the time, although progress has been made in securing social justice and civil rights for blacks, African Americans are disproportionately represented among the city's poor. And some black Atlantans are encapsulated in the city's most impoverished, underserved, racially segregated neighborhoods. With the resurgence of the many forms of intolerance, inequalities, and incivility seen in today's political discourse, perhaps there are lessons to be learned from the histories of the University and the School.

FACING THE RISING SUN TOGETHER

Evolving through many stages from its founding as the Atlanta School of Social Work, to the Atlanta University School of Social Work, and to the Whitney M. Young Jr. School of Social Work, today the official name of the School is Clark Atlanta University Whitney M. Young Jr. School of Social Work. The School celebrates its centennial concurrent with the beginning of the administration of Dr. George T. French, Jr. who was appointed to lead the University

Find a Way or Make One. Alma J. Carten, Oxford University Press (2021). © Oxford University Press.
DOI: 10.1093/oso/9780197518465.001.0001.

by the Board of Trustees on June 19, 2019, making him the fifth president of Clark Atlanta University (CAU).

Moving forward, President French will be at the helm of a University that is thriving and growing, as described in the CAU 2018–2019 Annual Report. The Report, entitled "Cultivating Lifted Lives," provides a comprehensive overview of a University dedicated to the pursuit of excellence in carrying out the tripartite mission of research, teaching, and service (Clark Atlanta University, 2019).

The University and the School of Social Work have been amazingly resilient in managing the effects of historic obstacles confronting historically black colleges and universities (HBCUs). (Harris, 2019) Both have been able to sustain institutional viability despite the historic government underfunding of HBCUs, the effects of which have been felt more sharply by the private HBCUs. In the "Message from the Board of Trustees," Gregory B. Morrison, Board Chair, spoke of the successes of the University over the 2018–2019 academic year.

> CAU's accomplishments in 2018 include a record-setting year that positions us to do even greater things in the future. This 2019 Annual Report illustrates our current financial strength, the start of new academic programs, and the current search for a new President. During this transition, we are pleased to maintain stability at the top with Lucille Maugé serving as our Interim President. President Maugé is not new to CAU. Over the past 13 years, she has served as Chief Compliance Officer, Chief Financial Officer, and, most recently, Executive Vice President. Her business and financial acumen, coupled with her superb management skills, are an asset to CAU.
>
> In the spirit of "cultivating lifted voices" the Board of Trustees overwhelmingly supports President Maugé's four priorities for the University as we move forward. They are the Student Experience, the Center for Cancer Research and Therapeutic Development, Scholarships, and Cyber Security. (Morrison, 2019, p. 2)

As described in the 2018–2019 Annual Report, the University is "a comprehensive, private, urban, coeducational institution of higher education with a predominantly African-American heritage. It offers undergraduate, graduate and professional degrees, as well as certificate programs, to students of diverse racial, ethnic and socioeconomic backgrounds." The University is classified by the Carnegie Classification of Institutions of Higher Education as a Research 2 University of "high research activity." *US News and World Report* ranks it as thirteenth when using the methodology described in Chapter 2, in which HBCUs are compared only with one another and those currently listed as a part of the US Department of Education's HBCU registry. The undergraduate enrollment of the University is slightly less than 4,000, and undergraduate tuition and fees for the 2019–20 academic year are $23,672 and slightly higher for the professional schools. The largest percentage of students are African American, with a growing number of international students.

The University's academic programs are carried out under four divisions of the School of Arts and Sciences, and three professional schools: Business, Education, and Social Work. With four departments of Communication Arts, the Humanities, the Natural Sciences and Mathematics, and the Social Sciences, the School of the Arts and Sciences is the largest academic division of the University. It is also the School that offers the liberal arts course of study that includes knowledge in the humanities and social behavioral and biological sciences that are the historic knowledge base for the liberal arts perspective of professional social work education (Reid & Peebles-Wilkins, 1991).

The University has long put behind it the financial and enrollment emergency faced by the Trustees and reported in a *New York Times* article and in the Report of the American Association of University Professors (AAUP). The crisis events centered around the University Board of Trustees's termination of the appointments of fifty-five full-time tenured faculty members, with no advanced notice and four weeks of unconditional severance salary (American Association of University Professors, 2011; Dewan, 2009). Apparently these actions of the Trustees were taken in an effort to increase the cash flow into the University budget to avert a looming financial crisis. These decisions, however, were challenged for failing to comply with university governance policies established by the American Association of University Professors (AAUP). The findings of the AAUP team that conducted an investigation of the events are reported in the 2011 Bulletin of the AAUP: *Academic Freedom and Tenure: Clark Atlanta University* (https://www.aaup.org/issue/2011-bulletin). In an interview aired on the University radio station, President French enthusiastically described a University that is now strong and thriving. According to French, with an endowment of 100 million dollars, an operating budget of 110 million dollars, CAU is the best positioned university in the US—black or white! (Maynard, 2/7/2020).

The service-driven mission of the University has made it a highly favorable academic home for the School of Social Work. Today, the social work degree bearing programs offered by the School can be especially attractive to a new generation of students of a variety of ethnic and racial backgrounds interested in a career in social work because they want to make a difference in a world that, over the course of their lifetimes, has become increasingly unjust and unequal. The School is also accommodating to the interest of progressive-minded students for opportunities to interact with other students who look like them and with faculty with whom they share a lived experienced that facilitates the establishment of strong mentoring relationships that are carried over and serve them well in their professional lives after graduation and exposure to curriculum and academic programs that reflect a positive view of their communities of identification (Harris, 2019).

The School of Social Work is a beneficiary of the institutional stability of its parent institution, and it begins this landmark date in its history, similar to the University, building, on a track record of success. The current dean, Dr. Jenny L. Jones, was appointed to the deanship in 2015. She spoke about her aspirations and vision for the School in an interview on the University's radio station, aired November 27, 2017 (Maynard, 2017). The dean spoke to the long history and legacy of the School with alumni who are practicing throughout the nation and abroad. The BSW program was described as preparing graduates for entry-level generalist practice, the MSW program has a specialization in advanced clinical practice, graduates of the program, after meeting state prerequisites, are well prepared to sit for the LCSW credentialing examination, and the PhD program prepares seasoned social workers to be leaders in a variety of organizational settings.

The School's website lists among its accomplishments that of being among "the best 100 schools of social work" in the *US News and World Report*, and is ranked at 96 among the 262 social work programs based on the peer-review methodology used by the *Report,* as described in Chapter 2. With an enrollment that hovers around two hundred, and a full-time faculty of eighteen, the School is able to maintain a faculty-to-student ratio that supports the meaningful engagement of students outside of formal classroom settings and is conducive for establishing authentic faculty–student mentoring relationships in the values-based social work professional program. The School is also distinguished among three schools of social work located in Atlanta by its sole concentration in advanced clinical practice, with an emphasis on the Afrocentric perspective in its curriculum. And it is the only school of social work in the Georgia HBCUs awarding the social work degree at all three levels: BSW, MSW, and PhD.

The Afrocentric perspective continues to serve as the philosophical underpinnings of the curriculum. The current faculty have high visibility in advancing the educational philosophy of the School in presentations at professional conferences nationally, regionally, and locally. The following statement is an excerpt from the presentation of faculty members at the 2019 annual conference of the National Association of Black Social Workers:

> The Afrocentric Perspective from its inception, focused on ways in which African culture and African heritage affect the worldview, values and behavior of people, and takes into account the African origins of African Americans in America and the diaspora; and America's response to their quest for social and economic justice and equality.
>
> While much has changed for the better, there are still societal factors that contribute to social and economic justice concerns both nationally and

internationally. These oppressive systems and policies continue to hinder individuals and groups from realizing their fullest potential as human beings, in contemporary times.

It is within this context that the Afrocentric Perspective continues to be relevant and provide reinforcement for continual sensitivities to the need for filtering all social, economic and political phenomena through this decontaminating culturally grounded social work practice model. (Wright, Jones, & White, 2019)

As illustrated in the School's 2017-2018 Annual Reort "Find a Way or Make One," faculty, through their research and publications, are also contributing to advancing and disseminating knowledge to the wider social work education community. The scholarship of individual faculty also illustrate the applicability of and ways in which an Afrocentric perspective may be integrated into the core courses of baccalaureate and graduate social work programs (King, 2019).

The successes enjoyed by the University and the School of Social Work stand in sharp contrast to the well-being of a segment of the black community in Atlanta. The entrenchment of pockets of poverty severely compromises the well-being of children and families in the surrounding neighborhoods in which the University and School are geographically located. Since its inception the well-being of children and families has been a central concern of the School. Indeed, it was concern for children that led Luvenia Burns Hope, along with students from Morehouse, to conduct research that informed the strategies adopted by the Neighborhood Union designed to improve health and well-being outcomes of children and families.

The extensive need and the entrenched social problems plaguing some Atlanta black neighborhoods for generations is replicated in urban black communities across the nation. Combined with current societal and professional trends, these conditions create opportunities for the School to recapture its place as the leading voice on social work practice in the black community, a voice established by African American thought leaders and scholars during the early and middle years of the school's history—E. Franklin Frazier, Forrester B. Washington, Whitney M. Young Jr.—and carried forward in the 1970s by a new professoriate that conceptualized the Afrocentric perspective and the autonomous social work practice model.

ADVANCING THE TRADITION OF EXCELLENCE IN SERVICE TO THE BLACK COMMUNITY

As discussed in Chapter 12, the landmark study, *Mental Health: Culture, Race, and Ethnicity: A Supplement to Mental Health: A Report of the Surgeon General* (USDHHS, 2001) brought to light the pervasive racial disparities and barriers in access to mental health services for ethnic and racial minority groups. Since the time of this report there has been a significant growth in the research examining the detrimental impact of racism on the equitable access to resources provided by the mental health system. African Americans were found to receive a poorer quality of care, lacked access to culturally competent services, even as they headed the list of Americans who are living under conditions of poverty that significantly increase the level of psychological distress. Today, there is a growing interest in examining the ink link between racism, trauma and psychological disorders that have implication for the mental health of children and youth.

The American Pediatric Association recently issued a statement on the impact of racism on children that begins in the womb (Trent, Dooley, & Dougé, 2019). The rise in suicide rates among black youth has been especially alarming. As reported in a study conducted by Dr. Michael Lindsey, the Connie Silver Professor and Chair of the McSilver Institute for Policy and Research and his colleagues, black male children aged 5–12 are committing suicide at rates higher than any other racial group. Suicide rates for African American teens have also increased dramatically (Lindsey, Sheftall, Xiao, & Joe, 2019).

The School's specialization in advanced clinical social work practice, with concentrations in mental health and children and families, places it in an especially opportune position to conduct research and develop educational programs from an Afrocentric perspective to address the extensively documented gap in access and availability of race-conscious mental health services to blacks; and the more recent research interest in examing the implications of racism for the mental health of children and youth.

KNOWLEDGE BUILDING FOR THE PROFESSION

The School has much to offer to the Social Work Grand Challenges, discussed in Chapter 5, a national initiative of the American Academy of Social Work and Social Research. The initiative is a call to action for social workers across the country to work together in solving the nation's most challenging problems using the tag line of "social progress powered by science." The assertion that "Social Is Fundamental" and the use of the African proverb "If you want to travel fast, go alone. But if you want to travel far, go together," adopts what has been a been a historic value of the HBCU tradition, as well as a reflection of the humanistic values adopted by the School of Social Work during the period when the Afrocentric perspective and autonomous social work practice model were introduced.

In elaborating the ninth of the Grand Challenges to "End racial injustice," the focus of which is to prepare the profession to address structural racism and its impact on ourselves and our clients, a statement retrieved from the Grand Challenge website asserts:

> As of 2013, there is not a single profession in the US that requires its professionals to demonstrate an understanding of structural racism, nor has a single profession or association established an official base of competencies to address race and racism. https://grandchallengesforsocialwork.org/grand-challenges-for-social-work/prepare-the-profession-to-address-structural-racism-and-its-impact-on-ourselves-and-our-clients/

This statement fails to acknowledge that developing a theory for social work practice in the black community and preparing a cohort of workers with the knowledge and skills to understand and address structural racism has been a historic concern of the School virtually since its founding. This was reflected in the first course offerings, when the School opened its doors in 1920. This content was further refined under the directorships of E. Franklin Frazier and Forrester B. Washington during the early decades of the school's history. The work was further advanced by the Black Task Force, chaired by Dean Genevieve Hill, and undertaken with the sponsorship of the Council on Social Work Education (CSWE) and federal funding. The Task Force Group brought the faculties of social work together from Atlanta and Howard Universities, and other schools, to craft the Afrocentric perspective associated with the program at Atlanta University, and the black perspective of the social work program at Howard—and these continue to inform the curricula of both schools.

CURRICULUM RENEWAL FOR THE 21ST CENTURY

In the upcoming 2022 CSWE reaffirmation and self-study process, the faculty will engage in what has been a customary process since its first accreditation in 1928, making it the first accredited school of social work in the South. The reaffirmation process allows the faculty to engage with the School's various stakeholder groups in a comprehensive review of all aspects of the program through the lens of its mission. These interests were initially carried forward as an interracial collaboration between the progressive social welfare leaders of the period. In the middle years of the School's history, this interest was carried forward under the directorships of E. Franklin Frazier and Forrester B. Washington. And in the civil rights and post-civil rights eras, it moved forward under the deanships of Whitney Young and Genevieve Hill. Moreover, looking back over the School's history and the history of social work and social work education, progressive curriculum renewal and reforms in CSWE and National Association of Social Workers (NASW) policies occurred at times when the hypocrisy of the nation's professed democratic goals and its treatment of blacks and other marginalized populations was exposed or when these values were under large-scale attack. At this time in its history, when the United States faces an uncertain future in retaining its position as the leading world democracy, there could be no better time for the School to reclaim its position as one of the leading and most respected voices for providing state-of-the-art education programs to support empirically based best social work practice in the black community.

THE ONGOING QUEST FOR A MORE PERFECT UNION

Ta-Nehisi Coates, Pulitzer Prize-winning African American scholar and graduate of Howard University, one the nation's most prestigious HBCUs, observed that "By erecting a slave society, America created the economic foundation for its great experiment in democracy" (Coates, 2014). The legacy of black enslavement has moved to the center of the nation's political discourse.

Today, US political discourse in many ways resembles that present when the University was founded in the ruins of Atlanta following the devastation left by the Civil War. It was a time when the country faced the gargantuan task of integrating four million newly freed men, women, and children into a society when neither the North nor the South had come close to reckoning with the regional issues that divided the country, at the center of which was redressing the shame of black enslavement.

Professor Louis Gates is the Alphonse Fletcher University Professor and Director of the Hutchins Center for African and African American Research. He is the preeminent American historian and scholar on the African American experience. Among his many accomplishments is the creation of the Emmy Award-winning six-part PBS documentary, *The African Americans: Many Rivers to Cross*. In his most recent publication, *Stony the Road: Reconstruction, White Supremacy, and the Rise of Jim Crow* (Gates, 2019), Professor Gates suggests that the fundamental questions that an examination of the period of Reconstruction forces the nation to consider are: Who is entitled to citizenship? Who should have the right to vote? What is the government's responsibility in dealing with terrorism? And, what is the relationship between political and economic democracy? (Gates, 2019, p. 6). On matters of race, although no longer a black–white binary, but still pertinent to the new demographic of black and brown peoples, these are questions that have yet to be answered; today, they have come to the fore, sometimes painfully so, in the racial divisiveness of the nation.

The introduction of HR 40 in the House of Representatives on January 1, 2019, put the question of four centuries of black enslavement squarely before the US Congress, and indeed before the American public. The bill calls for the establishment of a Commission to Study and Develop Reparation Proposals for African Americans, tasked to examine slavery and discrimination in the American colonies and the United States from 1619 to the present and to recommend appropriate remedies. Among other requirements, the commission will identify (1) the role of federal and state governments in supporting the institution of slavery, (2) forms of discrimination in the public and private sectors against freed slaves and their descendants, and (3) lingering negative effects of slavery on living African Americans and society Parenthetically, these all seem to be relevant topics for social work doctoral dissertation studies.

Since the civil rights era, social work and social work education have made ongoing efforts to bring the profession closer in line with those ideals that are the anchoring moral pillars of the profession. In an ongoing commitment to achieving this goal, eradication of racism has been established as a national priority for the 21st century. With the topic of reparations on the political agenda of the country, the deteriorating state of race relations in the United States has opened authentic conversations about race. Partly as reparation for the denial of education and in recognition of their substantial contributions to higher education, these developments have given increased visibility to the HBCUs and prompted calls for extensive new federal funding to compensate for years of government underfunding to support their important contributions to American higher education. These are all new developments that may well be cause for optimism as the nation continues its ongoing quest for a more perfect union.

HONORING THE FOUNDERS

At the time of this writing, the culminating event of the year-long activities planned by the Centennial Committee was to take place in October 2020. This coincides with the initial opening of the School on October 4, 1920, with an enrollment of fourteen students. The names of the members of that first class, which began a one-hundred-year journey for the School, were not uncovered in documents reviewed for the completion of this book. We do know from the available archival documents that they were taught by an extraordinary roster of professors.

Elders hold a position of respect and honor in African American culture. Valued for their wisdom and knowledge, they are the unifying force between the past and the future, teachers of the moral values of peace, justice, and interpersonal relationships of cooperation, harmony, and humility. It is fitting to end this book in the African tradition of paying homage to those who have passed away with a symbolic pouring of the libations in gratitude to the students and their teachers who laid the foundation for the School whose mission is as relevant today as it was at the time of the School's founding: Jesse

O. Thomas, Lugenia Burns Hope, Dr. John Hope, Gary W. E. Moore, Marion Pruitt, Newdigate M. Owensby, and Robert Cloutman Dexter.

Amani na Maarifa! Peace and Knowledge!

REFERENCES

Addams, J. (1892). The Subjective Necessity for Social Settlements, https://wwnorton.com/college/history/archive/reader/trial/directory/1890_1914/22_ch24_05.htm

American Association of University Professors. (2011). Academic freedom and tenure: Clark Atlanta University. https://www.aaup.org/report/academic-freedom-and-tenure-clark-atlanta-university

Clark Atlanta University. (2019). Annual Report 2018–2019. *Cultivating Lifted Lives.* https://www.cau.edu/presidents/Annual-Report.FINAL.-VERSION.8.29.19_REV-2-Final.pdf

Clark Atlanta University Whitney M. Young Jr. School of Social Work. (2018). Annual Report 2017–2018. *Find a Way or Make One.*

Coates, T. N. (2014). The case for reparations. *The Atlantic, 313*(5), 54–71.

Dawson, M. C., & Bobo, L. B. (2009). One year later and the myth of a post-racial society. *Du Bois Review: Social Science Research on Race, 6*(2), 247–249.

Dewan, S. (2009). Economy hits hard on black campuses. *New York Times,* February 18, 2009.

Dyson, M. E. (2016). *The Black presidency: Barack Obama and the politics of race in America.* New York: Houghton Mifflin Harcourt.

Gates, Jr., H. L. (2019). *Stony the road: Reconstruction, White supremacy, and the rise of Jim Crow.* New York: Penguin Press.

Grand Challenges. Prepare the Profession to Address Structural Racism and Its Impact on Ourselves and Our Clients. https://grandchallengesforsocialwork.org/grand-challenges-for-social-work/prepare-the-profession-to-address-structural-racism-and-its-impact-on-ourselves-and-our-clients/

Harris, A. (2019). Why America needs its HBCU. *The Atlantic,* May 16, 2019.

King, I. R. (2019). Diaspora model: Teaching the Afrocentric perspective to social work students. *Urban Social Work, 3*(S1), S70–S85.

Lindsey, M. A., Sheftall, H., Xiao, Y., & Joe, S. (2019). Trends of suicidal behaviors among high school students in the United States. *Pediatrics, 144.* doi:10.1542/peds.2019-1187

Maynard, R. (2017). Interview with Whitney M. Young, Jr. School of Social Work Dean Dr. Jenny L. Jones on CAU Now-Lifting Every Voice on WCLK. November 27, 2017. https://www.wclk.com/post/cau-now-lifting-every-voice-features-school-social-work-dean-dr-jenny-l-jones

Maynard, R. (2020). Interviews with Dr. George T. French Jr., CAU President WCLK. February 7, 2020.

Morrison, G. B. (2019). Message from the Board of Trustees, In Lifting Cultivated Lives, 2018–2019. Clark Atlanta University, Annual Report. https://www.cau.edu/presidents/Annual-Report.FINAL.-VERSION.8.29.19_REV-2-Final.pdf

Reid, P., & Peebles-Wilkins, W. (1991). Social work and the liberal arts: Renewing the commitment. *Journal of Social Work Education, 27*(2), 208–219. www.jstor.org/stable/23043159

Trent, M., Dooley, D. G., & Dougé, J. (2019). The impact of racism on child and adolescent health. *Pediatrics*, *144*(2), e20191765.

US Department of Health & Human Services. (2001). Mental health: Culture, race and ethnicity: A supplement to the report of the Surgeon General.

Wright, D., Jones, K., & White, G. (2019). *The Afrocentric perspective in social work practice: "The CAU way."* Professional Development Workshop, NABSW 51st Annual National Conference. April 26, 2019, Atlanta, Georgia.

A CLOSING MESSAGE FROM THE DEAN

This book, *Find a Way or Make One*, highlights the historical context of a school of social work founded 100 years ago by black folks for blacks. This important contribution to the social work literature details the development of the school through its accomplishments, challenges, and changes over the past 100 years. Moreover, the book's contribution to social work education as it relates to historically black universities and colleges (HBCUs) is to be lauded. And while the School has gone through many periods of change and growth, our commitment to excellence is unwavering. The contributions of our committed faculty, brilliance of our students, and wisdom and support of alumni and friends of the Whitney M. Young, Jr. School of Social Work supports the pedagogical ethos for which we are known at the bachelor, master, and doctoral programmatic levels.

As we enter our 100th year, there is much upon which we proudly reflect, particularly during a time when issues regarding disparity and inequality among African Americans continue to persist. We have remained steadfast in ensuring that the Afrocentric perspective is integrated into our curriculums, which reinforces the ideology and principles around the development of the School. In keeping with the historic mission of cooperation versus competition, the development of school resources advancing Afrocentric perspective competence in the classroom, on campus, and in the field have been well received.

The school prepares social work professionals to create multifaceted systems to reduce the inequities that marginalized families face daily. Most recently, the School relaunched the Center for Children and Families. The relaunching of the Center is timely, given the persistent societal issues that families are faced with in providing for their children's basic needs. The mission of the Center is to improve the health and well-being of African American children and families. The Center's mission is aligned with my vision for the School, which is "innovation matters."

Our conference participation, guest lectures, and faculty publications contribute to our prominence and reputation, as well as to the reputation of Clark

Atlanta University. As the School moves forward, I see a new decade on the horizon that will strengthen the School through strategic collaborations in areas such as continuing education, financial capability and asset building, data science, increased partnerships in field education, and the plan for an Endowed Chair. As we stand together in the elevation of "making a way or finding one," we recognize that the preservation of who we are, what we stand for, and respect for history was at the forefront 100 years ago and continues to guide us as we prepare social work scholars to lift up marginalized populations.

—Dean Jenny L. Jones
April 7, 2020

APPENDIX A

The Historical Context

THE ANTEBELLUM PLANTATION ERA

1619 Enslaved Africans arrive in the New World marking the beginning of two and a half centuries of black enslavement in North America and the start of an economic engine fueling the economy in Georgia and the Confederate States.

1730 English settlers arrive in the 1730s, led by James Oglethorpe, and found Georgia as the thirteenth original Colony. Slavery was prohibited in the colony by British law and moral code, but, owing to an agricultural economy based on "King Cotton" and a compliant free labor force, the ban was lifted in 1749. By the time of the American Revolution there were an estimated 18,000 enslaved persons in Georgia.

1775 The American Revolutionary War (1775–1783) saw the fledging thirteen colonies revolt against their British absentee landlord, and, with the assistance of France, they won independence from Great Britain, giving birth to the United States of America.

1780–1804 This began the decades that saw the outlawing of enslavement in the Northern states, beginning with An Act for the Gradual Abolition of Slavery enacted by Pennsylvania in 1780, which prohibited the importation of slaves into the state. The law decreed that all children born in the state were free, no matter their condition or race.

1785 Georgia becomes the first state to charter a state-supported school on January 27, establishing the University of Georgia as one of the oldest universities in the United States. The state would later use the state allocation as a means for undermining the steadfast commitment of the Board of Trustees of Atlanta University to interracial education and to offering education for blacks in the classics and liberal arts.

1787 The US Constitution becomes the supreme law of the land on September 17, with the Preamble stating "We the People of the United States, in Order to form a more perfect Union, establish Justice, insure domestic Tranquility, provide for the common defense, promote the general Welfare. . . ."

The first Constitutional Convention is held in Philadelphia, Pennsylvania, from May 14 to September 27, to correct flaws in the Articles of Confederation. Philadelphia served as the capital while the permanent president's home was being built by black slaves and indentured servants in Washington, DC. This was for political expediency since, apart from John Adams, the first twelve presidential occupants owned slaves that they brought with them to the White House; thus, began the psychological dissonance and constitutional contradiction that justified the unequal treatment of blacks in law and custom.

1788 Georgia becomes the fourth state of the United States of America.

1792 The cornerstone for the White House is laid on October 13, and, over the next years, a construction team comprised of both enslaved built the Aquia Creek sandstone structure.

1807–1808 Ending of the Atlantic Slave Trade.

The Act Prohibiting Importation of Slaves and terminating the Atlantic slave trade is enacted March 2: effective as of 1808, by federal decree, no new slaves were to be deported into the United States. The law had been promoted by Thomas Jefferson in his 1806 State of the Union Address. Georgia, along with other Southern states, ignored the federal law and began the inhumane practice of slave breeding, forcing coerced sexual relationships on enslaved females to increase the stock of an enslaved labor force without incurring cost.

1830 This year marks the beginning of the abolitionist movement as a more organized, radical, and immediate effort to end slavery.

The Indian Removal Act is signed into law by President Andrew Jackson on May 28, authorizing the president to grant unsettled lands west of the Mississippi in exchange for Indian lands within existing state borders.

1838 This year begins the forcible removal of the Cherokee Nation from ancestral lands that they occupied and cultivated for centuries and the transfer of these fertile lands to white settlers to farm cotton, the main staple of the Southern economy. Cherokees were moved from Alabama, Georgia, North Carolina, and Tennessee. Approximately 4,000 Cherokees died on this forced march, known as the "Trail of Tears."

1845 The abolitionist movement gains momentum with the 1845 publication of *Narrative of the Life of Frederick Douglass (1818–1895)* and *My Bondage and My Freedom*, published in 1855. By the time of the Civil War, Douglass is the leading voice of the abolitionist movement in the United States and abroad.

1846 The American Missionary Association (AMA) is founded on September 3, 1846, in Albany, New York, with a mission to abolish slavery, educate blacks, promote racial equality, and spread Christian values. More than 500 schools were established by the AMA in the decades following the Civil War; these enrolled students of all races. Interest later expanded to creating colleges and universities for blacks in the South, the impetus for the establishment of Atlanta University.

1849 Thoreau's *Civil Disobedience* is published, a book influential in shaping Martin Luther King Jr.'s., conceptualization of the moral justification of the civil disobedience strategy adopted by the civil rights movement.

1857 The Supreme Court's March 6 ruling in the Dred Scott case establishes in law that blacks had no rights that whites were bound to acknowledge and no black, free or slave, could claim US citizenship.

1858 Abraham Lincoln delivers his "House Divided" speech when accepting the Illinois Republican nomination for the Senate, marking his entrance into national politics; the speech asserted that government could not stand in a nation that was half free and half slave.

1860 Abraham Lincoln is elected the sixteenth president of the United States on November 6, over a deeply divided Democratic Party, becoming the first Republican to win the presidency. Having freed the slaves, the Republican Party became the party for African Americans until the shifting of black loyalty to the Democratic Party under the administration of Franklin D. Roosevelt in the 1930s.

The Southern Manifesto, aiming to unite the Southern slaveholding states through secession, is circulated on December 13, with thirty signatures, including Georgia.

1861 On January 19, Georgia becomes the fifth state to secede from the Union.

1861 The Civil War begins on April 12, with the Confederates attack on Union soldiers at Fort Sumter, South Carolina.

1863 The Emancipation Proclamation is issued as an executive order by President Lincoln on January 1; it applies to blacks in the slaveholding rebellious states.

1864 The Burning of Atlanta by General Sherman's infamous March to the Sea leaves Atlanta in ruins and totally devastates the Confederate Army, signaling the beginning of the end of the war.

1865 The Civil War officially ends on April 9, with the surrender of Robert E. Lee to Ulysses S. Grant at Appomattox Courthouse on April 9, 1865.

The Thirteenth Amendment to the US Constitution abolishes slavery and involuntary servitude, except as punishment for a crime. It was passed by the Senate on April 8, 1864, and by the House on January 31, 1865. The amendment was ratified by the required number of states on December 6, 1865.

President Lincoln is shot and killed on April 14 by Confederate sympathizer John Wilkes Booth and dies the following morning. Lincoln's Vice President Andrew Johnson assumes the presidency.

THE POST-BELLUM ERA

1865 Reconstruction begins in the spring under the presidency of Andrew Johnson. Johnson's favoring of state's rights left landowning whites free to construct their own policies, and slavery was all but replaced by the Black Codes that controlled all aspects of black life and labor.

The Ku Klux Klan is formed by Confederate veterans in Tennessee as a secret society to deter progressive federal policies during Reconstruction that promoted black rights.

The Freedmen's Bureau, formally known as the Bureau of Refugees, Freedmen, and Abandoned Lands, is established by Congress on March 3 to help freedmen and poor whites in the aftermath of the Civil War. Oliver Otis Howard, a Union General, was appointed Commissioner in May.

1867 As Commissioner, Howard, establishes Howard University in Washington, DC, which is named for him; he serves as Howard's president from 1869 to 1874.

Frederick Ayer is the first missionary sent by the American Missionary Association to Atlanta to begin the work of setting up the first classes for the children of freed slaves in the ruins of the Civil War. The Storrs School was the seed for Atlanta University, which became the academic home of the School of Social Work

Edmund Asa Ware is sent by the Association to join Ayer as the workload grew. Under Ware's leadership, on October 16, 1867, the state legislature grants a charter for the School for a life of twenty years under the name and title of the "Trustees of the Atlanta University"; the motto chosen for the University seal was "I will find a way or make one."

1867 Atlanta Baptist College is founded to educate freedmen to become ministers and teachers and is renamed Morehouse College in 1913.

1868 The capital of Georgia is moved from Milledgeville to Atlanta and coined the "Gateway City to the New South."

1872 Much criticized by Southerners, the Freedmen's Bureau is dismantled by Congress in the summer of 1872. By this time, serving as the first federal relief agency, it had fed millions, built hospitals, provided healthcare, negotiated labor contracts with freedmen, legalized their marriages, and assisted them to locate lost relatives. In partnership with the American Missionary Association and other charities, it had established hundreds of schools for blacks including Atlanta, Howard, Fisk, and Hampton.

1881 Tuskegee Institute is founded by Booker T. Washington (1856–1915) who becomes its first principal; the Institute is to provide industrial education exclusively. Washington's is the leading black voice on race relations in the United States until his death.

1888 Horace Bumstead is appointed President of Atlanta University following the death of Edmond Ware; he serves as president from 1888 to 1907. With the Board holding firm to providing liberal and classic education for blacks, the state appropriation was withdrawn on his watch, thus requiring a stepping up of fundraising efforts to keep the University open.

Under requirements of the 1862 Morrill Act, the Georgia state legislature withdraws the $8,000 appropriation to Atlanta University due to the Board of Trustee's refusal to comply with state policies that ban the co-education of the races and allow only rudimentary education for blacks. The fracture led to what is now Savannah State University; School of Social Work alumni Dr. Cheryl Dozier served as president from 2011 to 2019.

THE PROGRESSIVE ERA 1890–1920

1877–1880 The Charity Organization Society (COS) and the Settlement House movements, considered the roots of modern social work, emerge from concerns for the plight of white ethnic European immigrants seeking refuge in the United States. The moralistic model endorsed by the COS, which endeavored to change individual behaviors, and that of the Settlement House, which targeted change of systemic injustices, came together to form the profession's integrative person in the social environment model.

1874 The Chautauqua Circle is formed by well-educated black women in Atlanta and works to effect change for poor and working women; it promoted education, community involvement, and racial pride.

1885 Booker T. Washington delivers his controversial "Atlanta Compromise" speech at the Atlanta Cotton States and International Exposition, asserting that "in all things that are purely social, we can be as separate as the fingers, yet one as the hand in all things essential to mutual progress."

1893 John Hope and Lugenia Burns meet at the Chicago World Columbia Exposition; they married in 1897. The couple moved to Atlanta in 1898 to begin a life-long spousal partnership in service to the black community, common to the race men and women of the period.

1894 James Weldon Johnson completes studies at Atlanta University and begins a long and distinguished career, becoming the University's most distinguished alumni.

1897 W. E. B. Dubois is appointed to the Atlanta University faculty by President Horace Bumstead and is tasked to teach history and economics and establish a sociology department. DuBois holds two faculty appointments at the University, first in 1897–1910, and again in 1932–1944. While at the University, DuBois wrote his best-known works, *The Souls of Black Folk, Dusk of Dawn*, and *Black Reconstruction*; established *Phylon*, a journal for the dissemination of scholarly works on the African American experience; and pioneered science as the engine for driving social change and progress for the black community with the establishment of the Atlanta University Studies.

1896 The US Supreme Court landmark decision in *Plessy v. Ferguson* upholds the constitutionality of laws enforcing racial segregation in public facilities, thus establishing the "separate but equal" principle that stands until struck down by the 1954 *Brown v. Board of Education* decision under the Warren Court.

1898 The New York School of Philanthropy is established under the auspices of the New York City COS as an outgrowth of summer classes training COS "friendly visitors"; it is renamed the Columbia University School of Social Work in 1963.

1899 *The Philadelphia Negro*, authored by W. E. B. DuBois and commissioned by the University of Pennsylvania, is the first sociological case study of a black community in the United States and one of the earliest examples of sociology as a statistically based social science. The study preceded the Pittsburgh Survey (1907–1908), a sociological study of the city of Pittsburgh, Pennsylvania, funded by the Russell Sage Foundation.

THE TWENTIETH CENTURY

1901 Booker T. Washington's invitation by Theodore Roosevelt to dine at the White House with the First Family on October 16 promotes national outrage from whites because of the taboo against social encounters between the two races.

1903 DuBois publishes *The Souls of Black Folk*, in which he challenges Booker T. Washington's incrementalistic approach to securing economic and social equality for blacks.

1904 The Daytona Educational and Industrial Training School for Negro Girls is founded by Mary McLeod Bethune (1875–1955). The only female black member of FDR's Negro Cabinet, she founded the National Council for Negro Women in 1935 and is one of the most influential black female social activists of her generation.

1906 John Hope (1868–1936) becomes the first black President of Morehouse College, then Atlanta University in 1920, serving as president of both institutions during the formation of the Atlanta Affiliation.

Atlanta race riots erupt as white backlash in response to blacks and whites living in close proximity and with the advancement of black rights; tensions were exacerbated by inflammatory media reports that black males were assaulting white women.

1907 Edward Twichell Ware (1869–1885), the son of Edmond Asa Ware, the first president of the University, assumes the presidency of the University, serving until illness forced him to resign in 1922. Dean Myron Winslow Adams was appointed acting president in 1919, and formally appointed president in 1922.

1908 Motivated by the preventable death of a young African American mother who died alone and isolated because the family could not afford child care or medical care, Lugenia Burns Hope establishes the Neighborhood Union with a mission to conduct community surveys of the status of every home in Atlanta's black neighborhoods to prevent future such tragedies.

1909 The first White House Conference on the Care of Dependent Children is convened under the administration of Theodore Roosevelt. The Conference acknowledges the irreplaceable role of the family in the lives of children and establishes the principle that no child should be deprived of a home for the reason of poverty alone.

The Niagara movement (1905–1910) is organized by black intellectuals led by DuBois, in which Jane Addams participated. It led to the founding of the National Association for the Advancement of Colored People and publication of the magazine *The Crisis* edited by DuBois.

1910 The National League for the Protection of Colored Women, the Committee for Improving the Industrial Conditions for Negroes in New York, and the Committee on Urban Conditions Among Negroes in New York merge to form a single organization initially named the National League on Urban Conditions and later the National Urban League (NUL).

The Flexner Report on medical education in the United States and Canada, authored by Abraham Flexner, is published under the auspices of the Carnegie Foundation. The Report resulted in the closing of all medical schools that had developed in historically black colleges and universities (HBCUs) except for the Howard University Medical School in Washington, DC, and Meharry Medical College in Nashville, Tennessee.

1911 State-operated Mothers Pension Programs, the forerunner of the federal Aid to Dependent Children (ADC) program, provides cash assistance to mother-only homes; it largely enrolled white widows considered deserving or worthy of receiving aid.

1915 The D. W. Griffith film *Birth of a Nation* is viewed at the White House at the invitation of President Woodrow Wilson amid widespread black protest.

The positive response to the film spawned the resurgence of the Ku Klux Klan at Stone Mountain, in Dekalb County outside of Atlanta, Georgia.

Abraham Flexner's speech "Is Social Work a Profession?" at the National Conference on Charities and Correction held in Baltimore, Maryland, May 12–19, begins the profession's ongoing quest for professional status and a gradual favoring of the medical model and the psychotherapies.

1916 Beginning of the Great Migration; during the years between 1916 and 1970 millions of blacks left the South for northern cities, and blacks in the rural areas of Georgia moved to Atlanta to escape the oppressive sharecropping system.

1917 Mary Richmond's (1861–1928) *Social Diagnosis* is published by the Russell Sage Foundation.

The Harlem Renaissance begins; Alain LeRoy Locke (1885–1945), the first African American Rhodes scholar, envisioned the New Negro and was championed as the "Father of the Harlem Renaissance."

1919 Marcus Garvey (1887–1940) founds the Universal Negro Improvement Association (UNIA), headquartered in Harlem, as a black nationalist movement encouraging a back-to-Africa movement for blacks in the Diaspora.

Red Summer occurs during the late winter, spring, and summer, and terrorist attacks across the United States by anti-black white supremacist result in the deaths of hundreds of blacks; emboldened by the war experience, black veterans chose to fight back.

Eugene Kinkle Jones (1885–1954) succeeds George Edmond Haynes to become the second director of the NUL and continues the tradition of partnering with HBCUs as a pipeline for growing leadership for League affiliates.

1919 Jesse O. Thomas (1885–1972) is appointed first director of the NUL's Southern Field Office for the Southern Region of the United States in Atlanta, Georgia.

1920 Standing in for Eugene Kincle Jones, Jesse O. Thomas delivers his speech on the need for a training school for Negro social workers from the segregated section of the auditorium where the 1920 National Conference of Social Work in New Orleans was held.

The Atlanta School of Social Work holds its first classes on October 4, 1920, with an enrollment of fourteen students; Gary Moore, Morehouse professor, was appointed the School's first director and served until his death in 1921 while on academic leave completing PhD studies at Columbia University.

1922 E. Franklin Frazier (1994–1962), who had been Moore's replacement at Morehouse, assumes the directorship of the School after Moore's death, serving in the position until 1927. Combative and a strong proponent of black social work, he is credited with the professionalization of the curriculum; under his directorship the School was incorporated and chartered on March 22, 1924.

Frazier's controversial 1927 publication while director of the School, *The Pathology of Racial Prejudice,* drawing an equivalency between white racism and insanity, is said to be among the reasons for his resignation from the directorship of the School.

1927 Forrester B. Washington (1887–1963) becomes the third director of the Atlanta School of Social Work, serving until his retirement in 1954. Equally committed to black social work, Washington authored *The Need and Education of Negro Social Workers.* During his tenure, the School was renamed the Atlanta University School of Social Work when it gave up its independent charter and became a part of the University. The course content related to blacks and the research department developed over Washington's tenure were purged from the curriculum by the American Association of Schools of Social Work so that the School could maintain its accreditation status.

1928 The Atlanta School of Social Work is accredited by the American Association of Schools of Social Work, the forerunner of the Council on Social Work Education (CSWE).

1929 John Hope is the first African American to serve as president of Atlanta University (1929–1936). Serving over a transitional period, President Hope was the president of both Morehouse and Atlanta University and oversaw the coming together of the University, Spelman College, and Morehouse College that was designated as the Atlanta University Affiliation; he also oversaw the process of transitioning the University from an undergraduate to a graduate school. President Hope's ambitious long-term vision was set forth in a six-year plan designed to bring all the Schools together as the Atlanta University Center Consortium, the largest contiguous consortium of African Americans in higher education in the United States. The consortium structure allows for students to cross-register at the other institutions in order to attain a broader collegiate experience. They also share the Robert W. Woodruff Library.

Porter R. Lee serves as editor of the *Milford Conference Report* in 1929, overseeing the report "Social Case Work, Generic and Specific"; his classic publication, *Social Work Cause and Function*, articulated the ongoing tension in the profession of advocacy for broad-based societal change reform or micro-level interventions.

1930 White House Conference on Children takes place under President Herbert Hoover on Child Health and Protection; Forrester B. Washington chairs a subcommittee on Minority Children that brings to light the plight of black, Puerto Rican, and Mexican children.

1931 Florence Victoria Adams is recruited to join the faculty by Forrester B. Washington to develop a community organization sequence. She authored *The Reflections of Florence Victoria Adams,* which is a history of the Atlanta University School of Social Work from its beginning in 1920 to 1979. It was published after her death on August 29, 1979, and copyrighted in 1981. The book contains the names of graduates of the School from 1928 to 1979.

1932 Franklin D. Roosevelt is elected President; the New Deal and 1935 Social Security Act signal the birth of the American Social Welfare State. Forester B. Washington, from his post as Director of the Negro Division of the FERA, speaks out against the racism that prevented the full participation of blacks in these programs. Georgia's governor Eugene Talmage was a major opponent of the New Deal program that threatened the oppressive sharecropping system.

1934 The Tuskegee Study is initiated by the US Department of Public Health. The ethical abuses of the study, which was not shut down until 1972, were of enormous magnitude and believed to continue to be factor in African Americans' distrust of the healthcare system. These ethical violations led to the protective policies related to human subject research instituted by the US Department of Health and Human Services.

1935 The School of Social Work at Howard University becomes an autonomous division with the University. With the leadership of E. Franklin Frazier, and Inabel Burns Lindsay, the School's first dean, becomes the second school of social work in a HBCU.

1938 The Atlanta School of Social Work becomes affiliated with Atlanta University.

1941 FDR's "Four Freedoms Speech" once again illuminates the hypocrisy of the treatment of blacks and brings this issue to the forefront of the national discourse. A. Philip Randolph called off the planned March on Washington when FDR issued an executive order prohibiting discrimination in employment in the defense industry.

1947 The Atlanta School of Social Work gives up its independent charter to become known as the Atlanta University School of Social Work.

1952 The CSWE is founded.

1954 Whitney Young Jr. (1921–1971) is the first head of the School appointed to the title of dean; he serves until his resignation in 1961 to head the NUL.

The landmark *Brown v. Board of Education* Supreme Court decision strikes down the "separate but equal doctrine," sparking a coordinated effort by southern elected official to resist desegregation, beginning with the 1956 Southern Manifesto led by Georgia officials to undertake all legal means necessary to reverse the decision of the Court.

1955 The August 1955 abduction and murder of fourteen-year-old Emmitt Till (1941–1955) in Money Mississippi, and Rosa Parks' (1913–2005) refusal to give up her seat on a public bus to a white passenger on December 1, 1955, in Montgomery, Alabama, ignite the launch of the Civil Rights movement.

The CSWE Curriculum Policy Study undertaken in 1955 and chaired by Dr. Werner W. Boehm is at the forefront of the process of review of the CSWE Educational Policy and Accreditation Standards (EPAS). The findings from the thirteen volumes of the study resurfaced the historic theme of "Cause and Function," now joined with concerns related to the lack of diversity content in the social work curriculum.

1960 The first student sit-ins begin on February 1, 1960, in Greensboro, North Carolina, when four black male freshmen students enrolled in the HBCU North Carolina A&T College stage the first lunch counter sit-in that began an unstoppable national movement.

1960 Students of the six HBCU colleges within Atlanta University Center write and sign "An Appeal for Human Rights," published as a full-page ad in the March 9, 1960, Sunday edition of the Atlanta newspapers, challenging racial segregation in public and private facilities in Atlanta.

1961 Whitney M. Young, Jr. resigns the deanship to head the NUL in New York City, and his family takes up residence in New Rochelle, New York.

Florence Victoria Adams becomes acting dean of the School, serving from 1961 to 1968.

1962 The Public Welfare Amendments to the Social Security Act are enacted under the Kennedy administration and expand services and benefits offered under the ADC program, which is renamed Aid to Families with Dependent Children (AFDC). The Reforms increase social work presence in public welfare.

Michael Harrington's study *The Other America, Poverty in the United States* (1962), puts a human face on the statistics of the poor, introducing the term "the invisible poor" to describe pockets of poverty populated by urban blacks and Appalachian whites.

1963 The Civil Rights movement comes to full scale under the leadership of the Reverend Dr. Martin Luther King after his iconic "I Have a Dream" speech, given at the August 28, 1963, March on Washington for Jobs and Freedom. Whitney Young, as head of the NUL, was among the "Big Six" Civil Rights Leaders speaking at the March.

Atlanta becomes the epicenter of the Civil Rights movement; the Paschal Brother's Restaurant is the place of "power breakfasts," where civil rights leaders met to plan strategies for the movement.

At the height of the violence of the white backlash accompanying the continuing unfolding of the civil rights movement, President Kennedy speaks from the Oval Office on June 11, 1963, saying to the nation that civil rights are a moral issue.

President Kennedy is assassinated in Dallas, Texas, on November 21, 1963.

1965 The Great Society initiative is launched under the Johnson administration as a thirteen-point program that declares an "unconditional war on poverty." The Economic Opportunity Act of 1964, is also known as the "Anti-Poverty Bill."

1967 Publication of Jesse O. Thomas' autobiography, *My Story in Black and White*, details the circumstances surrounding the 1920 founding of the Atlanta School of Social Work.

1968 Martin Luther King, Jr. is assassinated on April 4; his funeral services bring hundreds of ordinary Americans and dignitaries from across the globe to the city of Atlanta.

The National Association of Black Social Workers (NABSW) is launched when a group of black social workers walks out in protest at the 1968 National Conference on Social Welfare.

Dr. William S. Jackson steps down from the deanship in 1968 as the HBCUs begin to feel the effects of desegregation. He presented the findings of his research study that examined the impact of desegregation on schools of social work in the south at the at the January 27, 1966, CSWE 14th Annual Program Meeting in presenting, and later published in the 1966 *Journal of Social Work Education* as "The Civil Rights Act of 1964: Implications for Social Work Education in the South."

An interim committee comprised of Edyth Ross, Lloyd Yabura, and Genevieve Hill is appointed to lead the School, until Genevieve T. Hill assumes the deanship; she served from 1968 to 1979.

1970 *The Black Caucus* is published under the leadership of Cenie J. Williams, then executive director of the of the National Association of Black Social Workers (NABSW). The journal was published semi-annually by the Association's New York City chapter. The journal aimed to provide a creative journalistic outlet for its members and others involved with the black community on issues of significance to the field of social work and social services.

The School celebrates its mid-centennial in October 1970 and recommits itself to its identity as a black school of social work, as detailed in the published proceedings of the 50th anniversary entitled "Revisiting the Legacy of Forrester B. Washington, Educator and Nation Builder." Under the leadership of Dean Genevieve and Associate Dean Lloyd Yabura, the faculty adopted the Autonomous Social Work Practice Model anchored in the Afrocentric perspective and humanistic values embracing Martin Luther King's concept of the Beloved Community and agape love.

The Civil Rights movement shifts to the war in Vietnam as student protests erupt across the nation's college campuses. As the violence escalates, on May 4, 1970, four unarmed college students are shot and killed by Ohio National Guardsmen at Kent State University.

Two black students at Mississippi's Jackson State College, now named Jackson State University, are killed by police officers on May 11.

1971 The accidental drowning death of Whitney M. Young, Jr. occurs on March 11, 1971, in Lagos, Nigeria. A US Air Force plane is dispatched by President Nixon to bring his remains home; he lay in state in Riverside Church before being taken home for burial at the family plot in Lexington, Kentucky, where Nixon gave the eulogy.

1973 The Report of the CSWE Black Task Force is published. The work of the task force had been undertaken with federal funding; it was chaired by Dean Genevieve Hill and staffed by Dr. E. Aracelis Francis and was an outgrowth of the experiences of the CSWE Commission on Minority Groups. Over the course of two onsite meetings, faculties from the social work programs at Howard College and Atlanta University conceptualized and defined the Afrocentric and Black perspectives.

With demographic population shifts in Atlanta, blacks use the power of the vote to elect Maynard Holbrook Jackson Jr. (1938–2003) as the first black mayor of Atlanta. Atlanta University students are assigned by faculty to community organizing projects that encourage political activism.

The Minority Fellowship program is established by the federal government in 1973. Carl Scott obtains the participation of CSWE to advance minority education in doctoral-level education.

1978 Atlanta University School of Social Work faculty Edyth Ross publishes *Black Heritage in Social Welfare,* a comprehensive documentation of the contributions of blacks to social welfare from 1860 to 1930.

1979 Clarence Coleman is appointed dean, serving in the position until 1984. An alumnus of the School, the topic of his thesis was "A Study of Jobs Held by One-Hundred Graduates of Atlanta University School of Social Work from 1942 to 1946." The PhD program was instituted, as envisioned by George Edmond Hayes, to serve as a pipeline for leadership development to staff NUL affiliates.

The National Association of Social Workers (NASW) Delegate Assembly approves a resolution to pursue licensing of social work practice in each state. The American Association of State Social Work Boards (AASSWB) is founded to develop uniform national credentialing examinations for social work licensing and certification. In 1999, the name of the Association was changed to its current name of Association of Social Work Boards (ABSW).

The United States sees the beginning of the ascendancy of conservative social welfare philosophy and a gradual chipping away of the safety net programs and dismantling of the American social welfare state under policies of New Federalism. As poverty escalated under service cuts, black communities in Atlanta and across the nation experienced a rise in new and different kinds of social problems.

1984 Dr. Creigs C. Beverly serves as Dean of the Atlanta University School of Social Work until 1986. A 1965 graduate of the School and a 1984 Fulbright Scholar, he came to the School to teach in the social welfare policy curriculum and later served as an associate dean responsible for the coordination of all curriculum areas.

1987 Mamie Darlington is appointed interim Dean of the School until 1989. A Spelman College graduate, she had taught for twenty years at the School before her two-year appointment as interim dean. She held a BA in psychology from Spelman College, a MSW from Atlanta University, and a PhD in educational administration and supervision from Georgia State University.

1988 On June 24, the Boards of Trustees of Atlanta University, a graduate school, and Clark College, a liberal arts undergraduate school, make the decision to consolidate the two institutions under the same administrative and governance structure, and the School becomes the Clark Atlanta University School of Social Work.

Dr. Thomas Cole, Jr., chair of the transition, served as president of both Clark College and Atlanta University (CAU) over the transition process and was appointed as the first president of CAU, serving from 1988 through 2002.

With the consolidation and the movement of the BSW program from Clark College to Atlanta University, the School began awarding the BSW, MSW, and PhD social work degrees.

1989 Lou Beasley, PhD, serves as dean of the Atlanta University School of Social Work through 1994; she earned her MSW from the University of Tennessee and her doctoral degree in social welfare from the University of Denver. She is best known for her scholarship and practice focused on children and families.

1994 Richard Lyle, 1964 alumni of the School, is appointed interim dean, serving though 1998.

1994 The highly controversial Violent Crime Control and Law Enforcement Act is signed into law by President Bill Clinton that, in retrospect, is viewed as a central driver of the mass incarceration that had a devastating impact on black communities nationally.

1995 Quarles Washington Hall is destroyed by fire on March 18, resulting in the loss of irreplaceable documents in the School's historical archives.

1996 The Personal Responsibility and Work Reconciliation Bill is signed into law by President Clinton on August 22, resulting in fundamental reforms in programs for the nation's poor by stressing work in exchange for temporary assistance.

1998 Dorcas Bowles, EdD, is named Dean of the Clark Atlanta University School of Social Work through 2003. During her tenure, the School was renamed the Whitney M. Young Jr. School of Social Work.

The Advisory Board of President Clinton's initiative on race, chaired by Dr. John Hope Franklin, publishes its report in September, entitled *One America in the 21st Century, Forging a New Future.*

THE 21ST CENTURY

2000 Clark Atlanta University School of Social Work is renamed the Whitney M. Young Jr. School of Social Work.

2003 An internal review prepared by Dean Bowles indicates that the faculty had approved advanced clinical practice as the area of concentration for the MSW program.

2004 Rufus Sylvester Lynch, PhD, is appointed Dean of the Whitney M. Young Jr. School of Social Work; he developed a seven-point plan for moving the School forward.

2007 Walter Broadnax, PhD, serves as the second CAU president from August 1, 2002, through July 31, 2007.

2008 Carlton E. Brown, EdD, is appointed third CAU president, serving from August 1, 2008, through June 30, 2015.

Barack Hussein Obama is elected 44th president of the United States, and the first African American to serve in the office. First elected in 2008, he won a second term in 2012.

Vimala Pillari, PhD, is appointed dean of the Whitney M. Young Jr. School of Social Work, serving through 2015; she earned her doctorate in social welfare at Columbia University and taught at the University of Madras in Tamil Nadu, India. Under her deanship, the Center for Children and Families (CCF) was founded and the certificate program in school social work reestablished.

2010 The Patient Protection and Affordable Care Act (ACA), the signature legislation of the Obama Administration, is enacted by the 111th US Congress and signed into law by President Barack Obama on March 23.

2013 *Clark Atlanta University, Charting a Bold New Future,* authored by Dr. Thomas Cole, is published; it covers twenty-five years of the history of the University and the work of individuals who participated in the 1988 consolidation of Atlanta University with Clark College.

The Social Work Grand Challenges is instituted as a national initiative of the Academy of Social Work and Social Research, running under the tag line "social progress powered by science."

2015 The investiture of Ronald A. Johnson, PhD, the fourth President of Clark Atlanta University, is held on July 1 with a theme of "Lifting Every Voice."

Jenny L. Jones, PhD, is appointed dean of the Whitney M. Young Jr. School of Social Work, effective July 25. A graduate of Valdosta State University in Georgia, she earned an MSW from California State University and a doctoral social work degree from the Whitney M. Young Jr. School Social Work; a child welfare expert, she reinvested the School's Children and Family Center.

2019 George T. French, Jr., PhD, is appointed by the Board of Trustees on June 19, 2019, as the fifth president of Clark Atlanta University. The new administration adopts the theme "Facing the Rising Sun Together."

2020 The CAU Whitney M. Young, Jr. School of Social Worker enters its centennial year on a track record of success and is prepared for CSWE reaffirmation, scheduled for 2022.

APPENDIX B
Past Presidents

ATLANTA UNIVERSITY

1869–1885: Edmund A. Ware
1885–1886: Thomas S. Chase (Acting)
1886–1887: Horace Bumstead (Acting)
1887–1888: Cyrus W. Vance (Acting)
1888–1907: Horace Bumstead
1907–1922: Edward T. Ware
1922–1923: Myron W. Adams (Acting)
1923–1929: Myron W. Adams
1929–1936: John Hope
1936–1937: Florence M. Read (Acting)
1937–1967: Rufus E. Clement
1968–1969: Thomas D. Jarrett (Acting)
1969–1977: Thomas D. Jarrett
1977–1983: Cleveland L. Dennard
1983–1984: Kofi B. Bota (Acting)
1984–1987: Luther S. Williams
1987–1988: Dorcas D. Bowles (Acting)
1988–1989: Thomas W. Cole, Jr.

CLARK COLLEGE

1869–1870: D. W. Hammond
1870–1871: Uriah Cleary
1871–1872: I. Marcy
1876–1877: J. B. Martin
1877–1881: R. E. Bisbee
1881–1890: E. D. Thayer

1890–1893: William H. Hickman
1893–1896: David C. John
1896–1897: Wilbur P. Thirkfield (Acting)
1897–1903: Charles M. Melden
1903–1910: William H. Crogman
1910–1912: G. E. Idleman
1912–1915: William W. Foster
1915–1923: Harry A. King
1923–1924: John W. Simmons
1924–1940: Matthew S. Davage
1940–1941: James P. Brawley (Acting)
1941–1965: James P. Brawley
1965–1976: Vivian H. Henderson
1976–1977: Charles Knight (Acting)
1977–1987: Elias Blake, Jr.
1987–1988: Winifred Harris (Acting)
1988–1989: Thomas W. Cole, Jr.

CLARK ATLANTA UNIVERSITY

1988–2002: Thomas W. Cole, Jr.
2002–2008: Walter D. Broadnax
2008–2015: Carlton E. Brown
2015–2018: Ronald A. Johnson
2018–2019: Lucille H. Maugé

From https://www.cau.edu/presidents/past–presidents.html

Directors and Deans

ATLANTA SCHOOL OF SOCIAL WORK DIRECTORS

1920–1921: Gary W. Moore
1922–1926: E. Franklin Frazier
1927–1954: Forrester B. Washington

ATLANTA UNIVERSITY SCHOOL OF SOCIAL WORK DEANS

1954–1961: Whitney M. Young Jr.
1961–1961: Florence Victoria Adams*
1961–1968: William S. Jackson
1968–1979: Genevieve T. Hill
1979–1984: Clarence D. Coleman
1984–1986: Creigs C. Beverly

CLARK ATLANTA UNIVERSITY SCHOOL OF SOCIAL WORK

1987–1989: Mamie Darlington *
1989–1994: Lou Beasley
1994–1998: Richard Lyle *

CLARK ATLANTA UNIVERSITY WHITNEY M. YOUNG JR. SCHOOL OF SOCIAL WORK

1998–2003: Dorcas Bowles
2004–2007: Rufus Sylvester Lynch
2008–2015: Vimala Pillari

2015–Present: Jenny L. Jones
*Interim, Acting Deans
Florence Victoria Adams: 1960–1961
Janice S. Vaughn: 1984 (Summer)
Mamie R. Darlington: 1987–1989
Richard Lyle, PhD: 1994–1998, 2003–2004, 2007

APPENDIX D

Acronyms

AASWSW	American Academy of Social Work and Social Welfare
AAUP	American Association of University Professors
ABSW	Association of Social Work Boards (formerly AASWSW)
ACA	Patient Protection and Affordable Care Act
ADC	Aid to Dependent Children
AFDC	Aid to Families with Dependent Children
AMA	American Missionary Association
BSW	Bachelor of Science in Social Work
CAU	Clark Atlanta University
CETA	Comprehensive Employment Training Act of 1973
CSWE	Council on Social Work Education
CWRA	Child Welfare Reform Act
EITC	Earned Income Tax Credit
FAP	Family Assistance Plan
GADE	Group for the Advancement of Doctoral Education in Social Work
GST	General Systems Theory
HBCU	Historically Black Colleges and Universities
HRSA	Health Resources and Services Administration
LCSW	Licensed Clinical Social Worker
LMSW	Licensed Master of Social Work
MFP	Minority Fellowship Program
MIS	Minority-Serving Institutions
MSW	Master of Social Work
NAACP	National Association for the Advancement of Colored People
NABSW	National Association of Black Social Workers
NADD	National Association of Deans and Directors
NASW	National Association of Social Workers
NCES	The National Center for Education Statistics
NIH	National Institute of Health
NUL	National Urban League

NWRO	National Welfare Rights Organization
PWU	Predominately White Universities
SAMHSA	Substance Abuse and Mental Health Administration
SSBG	Social Services Block Grant
SSI	Supplementary Security Income
SSWR	Society for Social Work and Research

INDEX

For the benefit of digital users, indexed terms that span two pages (e.g., 52–53) may, on occasion, appear on only one of those pages.

"Bull Moose Party" (Progressive Party), 86
Bumstead, Horace, 53, 57–58, 66, 107
Bundy, McGeorge, 324
Burns, Ferdinand, 116
Burns, Louisa M. Bertha, 116
Bury My Heart at Wounded Knee (Brown and Brown), 27
Bush, George W., 310–11

Cantarella, Marcia, 323–24, 333
"captains of industry" ("robber barons"), 79
CARE (Ryan White Comprehensive AIDS Resources Emergency) Act of 1990, 291
Carl A. Scott Memorial Fund, 264
Carlton-LaNey, Iris, 74–75
Carmichael, Stokely, 234, 242
Carnegie Classification system, 20–21
carpetbaggers, 46
Carten, A., 214
Carter, Jimmy, 16–17, 270, 284, 288–89
case poverty, 250
casework method of social work, 96
Casteel, Lauren Young, 333
CAU. *See* Clark Atlanta University
CCC (Civilian Conservation Corps), 178
CDT (cognitive dissonance theory), 30
Center for Children and Families (CCF), 314
CETA (Comprehensive Employment Training Act) of 1973, 287, 413
Chandler, S., 187
Chaney, James, 202
Charity Organization Society. *See* COS
Charleston Church Massacre, 371
Chautauqua Circle, 169
CHEA (Council for Higher Education Accreditation), 18, 260
Cherokee nation, 27
Chestang, Leon, 275–76
Chicago School of Social Administration, 137
child and family well-being
    Adoption and Foster Care Analysis and Reporting System, 311
    Adoptions Assistance and Child Welfare Reform Act, 310
    Atlanta University's initiatives targeting, 313–14

Family First Prevention Services Act of 2018, 311
Fostering Connections to Success and Increasing Adoptions Act of 2008, 310–11
in rural Georgia, 311–12
in urban Atlanta, 313
Child Guidance Movement, 136
Children of Sanchez, The (Lewis), 250–51
Children of the Storm study (Billingsley and Giovannoni), 308–9
Children's Defense Fund, 244
Child Study Association of America, 136
Child Welfare League of America, 139–40
Churchill, Winston, 203
"city on a hill" concept, 27–29
Civilian Conservation Corps (CCC), 178
Civil Liberties Act of 1988, 199
Civil Rights Act of 1964, 237, 255
Civil Rights movement, 215–20. *See also names of specific activists*
    Atlanta as epicenter of, 233
    "Big Six" leadership, 231, 337, 343
    Brown v. Board of Education, 5–6, 150, 197, 203, 238
    doll studies, 238
    Emmett Till, 215–16
    Freedom Riders, 201
    Freedom Schools, 201
    legislative and policy reforms as result of, 237
    March on Washington for Jobs and Freedom, 231
    Martin Luther King, Jr., 231–32
        Beloved Community concept, 232, 280, 306
        "I Have a Dream" speech, 231
        Nobel Peace Prize, 231–32
        part of the "Big Six," 231
        principle of nonviolence, 232
    Mississippi Freedom Summer Project, 201–2
    overview, 215
    Paschal Brother's Restaurant, 233–34, 403
    Red Scare and, 241–42
    Rosa Parks, 216–17
    "Second Reconstruction," 242
    sit-ins, 225, 227, 230–31